Second Edition

PASSPORT

An Introduction to the Travel and Tourism Industry

David W. Howell, CTC

Associate Professor
Institute of Travel, Hotel, and Restaurant Administration
Niagara University, New York

South-Western Publishing Co.

MW01223408

Copyright © 1993
by SOUTH-WESTERN PUBLISHING CO.
Cincinnati, Ohio

ISBN: 0-538-70617-1

1 2 3 4 5 6 7 8 9 0 DH 1 0 9 8 7 6 5 4 3 2
Printed in the United States of America

Managing Editor:	Betty B. Schechter
Editorial Production Manager:	Linda R. Allen
Production Editor:	Martha G. Conway
Associate Director/Design:	Darren Wright
Production Artist:	Steven E. McMahon
Cover Photographer:	Michael Melford ©/ The Image Bank

Howell, David W., CTC.
    Passport: an introduction to the travel and tourism
industry/David W. Howell.—2nd ed.
    p.   cm.
    Includes bibliographical references and index.
    ISBN 0-538-70617-1
    1. Travel agents—Vocational guidance. 2. Tourist
trade-Vocational guidance. I. Title.
G155.A1H68 1992
338.4'791068—dc20   91-32472
                                                       CIP

PREFACE

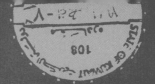

The second edition of *Passport: An Introduction to the Travel and Tourism Industry* builds on the success of the first edition. The entire text has been updated to reflect changes in the travel and tourism industry. These changes include the introduction of new systems of automation, current environmental issues of concern to travel professionals, and a recognition of the worldwide political changes that will have a tremendous impact on the industry. Every chapter in the second edition of *Passport* includes new features on personalities and companies that have contributed to the phenomenal success of the travel industry. Many new charts, graphs, and tables have also been added to illustrate key points in the text.

The travel and tourism industry is one of the largest and most dynamic industries in the United States today. For many years it was the "poor relation" among industries, receiving little attention from government and barely recognized in educational institutions. But now federal, state, and local governments are waking up to the fact that this is a major industry that can generate millions of dollars in revenue. At the same time, educational institutions are expanding their programs to include courses in travel and tourism. This is a response both to the increased demand for travel industry professionals and to the need for specialized training for travel professionals.

If you are planning to be a travel professional, you need to know much more than the travel agent of 25 years ago. While the world has not become any larger, the number of people who travel around it certainly has. And the choices available to today's travelers are more varied than ever before. Modern transportation makes it possible for people to go virtually anywhere in the world. And the ever-expanding hospitality industry offers them places to stay when they get there.

With so many places for travelers to go, and so many ways of getting there, travel professionals need to know their way around countless schedules and directories. Fortunately, you are entering this industry at a time when most of the tasks once done by hand have been automated. Whether you plan to work in a travel agency, in an airline office, in a hotel, or in one of the many other businesses that make up the travel and tourism industry, you will almost certainly have a computer to help you in your work. Without computers, the speed and efficiency that people expect from today's travel professionals would be impossible.

Passport: An Introduction to the Travel and Tourism Industry gives students planning a career in travel an overview of the industry today. The book is designed to help you understand the roles played by the various components of the travel and tourism industry, and to help you decide which of many different careers would best suit you.

CONTENT AND ORGANIZATION

Passport is divided into five parts and fifteen chapters. Part One introduces you to the travel industry as a whole. You will learn about the history of travel and discover the reasons for the growth of travel in the past few decades. The role of government both as regulator and promoter of travel and tourism is discussed. You will also become acquainted with today's travelers. There are three main types of travelers—vacation and leisure, business and professional, and travelers visiting friends and relatives—and each type has different motivations, needs, and expectations. Finally, Part One introduces you to the various channels of distribution in the travel industry, and to the role of automation in selling and distributing travel products.

Part Two focuses on transportation and accommodations. Three chapters explore three different kinds of transportation—airlines, ground transportation, and maritime transportation. The history of each kind of transportation is explained briefly, but the emphasis is on exploring the role and significance of each transportation mode today. The effects of deregulation of the airline industry are described in depth, and the importance of the car rental industry is discussed. A component of the travel industry that has been experiencing major growth is the cruise industry. You will learn of the efforts being made to expand upon that growth. In the final chapter of Part Two, you will learn about the hospitality industry—hotels, motels, and resorts. This industry, too, has experienced dramatic growth. You'll discover what hotels are doing to attract more business and how the typical hotel is organized.

Tourism systems and services are the subject of Part Three. You'll discover what goes into developing a destination for tourism, from providing fresh water and food to building new ports, airports, and hotels. The many different kinds of destinations for tourists are described in detail. These include national parks and forests, theme parks, museums, sports facilities, and shopping malls. Finally, Part Three discusses tours and charters—packages arranged by travel professionals that include a number of different components such as transportation, accommodations, and sightseeing. You'll learn how these packages are created and how they are sold.

Part Four is concerned with business travel—an important source of revenue for the travel industry. You'll learn what the airlines and hotel industry have been doing to attract and keep business travelers. You'll also read about the role of the business travel department. Business travel often involves going to meetings and conventions. The many different kinds of meetings are described and the variety of locations for them are discussed. The final part of Part Four looks at incentive travel—travel offered to corporate employees as a reward for a job well done.

The many different distributors of travel and tourism products are the focus of Part Five. The operations of travel agencies are described in detail and the trend toward specialization within the travel agency industry is discussed. You'll learn how a travel agent sets up a new business and what skills will be looked for in new employees. You'll also discover what goes into promoting and selling a travel product—from advertising in newspapers and on television to producing travel videos to conducting public relations campaigns. The final chapter of the book looks into the future of travel and tourism. It predicts trends that are likely to change the way travel products are sold and promoted and suggests ways that travel professionals can prepare for the changes ahead.

Most of the chapters in *Passport* conclude with a section that focuses on the career opportunities in the area under discussion. You'll be truly amazed at the vast range of jobs offered by the travel and tourism industry. Whether you prefer to work on your own or with others, indoors or outdoors, at home or on the road, there's sure to be a career to suit your tastes and abilities.

LEARNING AIDS

To help you understand what you are reading, a number of learning aids are provided:

Objectives. Each chapter begins with a list of the objectives. These will help you focus on the main points of the chapter and see the sequence of topics to be covered.

Glossary Terms. Every industry has its own language and the travel and tourism industry is no exception. As you work through this book, you will learn many new words and terms. This task has been made easier for you by highlighting in a bold type within the text words and terms that may be unfamiliar to you and by defining them in context. The travel industry also uses many ab-

breviations and acronyms. These are spelled out for you the first time they are used in any chapter; thereafter the abbreviated forms are used.

Check Your Product Knowledge. To help you check that you have understood what you have just read, review questions are included at the end of each major chapter section. Make sure you can answer the questions at the end of each section before you move on to the next section.

Summary. To help you review content and locate quickly the main ideas in a chapter, a summary is provided, in list format, at the end of each chapter.

Key Terms. Another learning aid is the list of key terms that appears at the end of each chapter. These are the terms that appear in bold type in that chapter. The lists provide an at-a-glance reminder of the chapter content. You may want to look through the list when you complete the chapter and look up any words that you cannot define, either in the chapter itself or in the glossary of terms that appears at the end of the book.

What Do You Think? This end-of-chapter list of discussion questions and critical thinking questions helps you look beyond what you have read in the chapter. The questions challenge you to think about what is happening in the travel and tourism industry and to formulate your own opinions about industry trends.

Dealing with Product and Dealing with People. The end-of-chapter materials conclude with two case studies or activities that challenge you to deal with a hypothetical situation involving a travel product or customer. The purpose of these activities is to help you become familiar with the kind of day-to-day situations that travel professionals encounter.

Special Features. In addition to the text learning aids, each chapter includes three special features designed to entertain as well as instruct. One "Profile" feature in each chapter focuses on the life and achievements of an individual selected for his or her contribution to travel and tourism. Among the individuals you will read about are Henry Ford and Thomas Cook. Another "Profile" feature focuses on important and successful companies in the travel world. You'll find out how American Express got started, and how Club Med has grown and evolved over the years. The third kind of feature, called "A Day in the Life of . . . ," explores the daily routines of people who work in the travel and tourism industry. Among those who describe their jobs are a flight attendant, a ship's purser, and a travel agent.

Worksheets. At the end of each chapter, four worksheets are provided. The worksheets are designed to reinforce what you have learned in the chapter. Some worksheets require you to conduct independent research into travel and tourism facilities in the region where you live. Others challenge you to think beyond what you have been reading by asking you to solve hypothetical problems. And others ask you to locate and use the sources of information that travel professionals use daily. Your instructor will assign the worksheets. Some of them may be used as a basis for classroom discussion. Others may be used as mini-tests and graded by your instructor.

Instructor's Resource Manual. An Instructor's Resource Manual is available to accompany this text. This comprehensive manual contains chapter overviews, lecture outlines, answers to "Check Your Product Knowl-

edge" questions, discussion guidelines for end-of-chapter pedagogy, lists of suggested resources, transparency masters, and chapter tests.

Acknowledgements

The author wishes to thank Marianne Ansbro, CTC, of Tompkins Cortland Community College; Daren Bloomquist of El Paso Community College; Jeanie Harris, CTC, of Long Beach City College; and Leslie Huerta of Lincoln School of Commerce for reviewing the manuscript and offering valuable suggestions for improvement.

CONTENTS

PART 1

WELCOME ABOARD

"For my part, I travel not to go anywhere, but I go. I travel for travel's sake. The great affair is to go."
—*Robert Louis Stevenson*

Objectives

When you have completed this chapter, you should be able to:

■ List five factors in the growth of the travel industry.
■ Explain the travel industry's impact on economics and culture.
■ Describe the travel industry in terms of direct and indirect employment.
■ Name areas of knowledge important to the travel professional.
■ Explain travel as an industry, with seven components that provide products and services enabling people to travel.

■ Tell how the travel industry functions in the marketplace.
■ List ways the government promotes and regulates the travel industry.
■ Discuss how geography influences the travel industry.
■ List questions about destinations that travel professionals should be able to answer.

Welcome aboard! With this traditional greeting, passengers on airplanes and cruise ships begin journeys to new destinations. This phrase also welcomes you—a future travel professional—to the travel industry. You have chosen an exciting career.

The travel industry is big business. It spans the globe and provides employment and revenue in almost every nation. Furthermore, the travel industry is a dynamic business. According to some sources, it is the largest and the fastest growing industry in the world. Figure 1-1 shows how world tourism has grown in the past three decades. In the United States, the travel industry is the third-largest retail or service industry, ranking just behind automobile dealerships and food stores in terms of business receipts.

THE GROWTH OF TRAVEL

If you're like most Americans, you've probably traveled to many places during your lifetime. Perhaps you spent a summer touring Europe or backpacking in the Colorado Rockies. You might have scrapbooks filled with photos and souvenirs of trips to Washington, D.C., San Francisco, or Montreal. Maybe you're saving money for a cruise to the Bahamas.

The United States is a nation of travelers. Every year millions of Americans take business trips and vacation trips. (A *trip* is usually defined as travel to a place 25 miles or more from home, excluding commutes to and from work.)

The world is traveling to America, too. More than 39 million international travelers came to the United States in 1990, most of them from Canada, Mexico, Great Britain, and Japan.

Reasons for the Growth of Travel

The modern travel industry began in the late 1950s and early 1960s. Many companies that are now giants in the industry trace their origins to those days. In 1958, about 1 million Americans traveled outside the United States; by 1970, this number had grown to 5.5 million.

There are several reasons for the growth of the travel industry during the fifties and sixties. A relatively peaceful political climate promoted travel. Stronger economies in the industrialized nations meant that people had more money to spend on travel. The introduction of passenger jet service made traveling faster, less expensive, and more comfortable. Television documentaries on subjects such as the wildlife of Africa, the

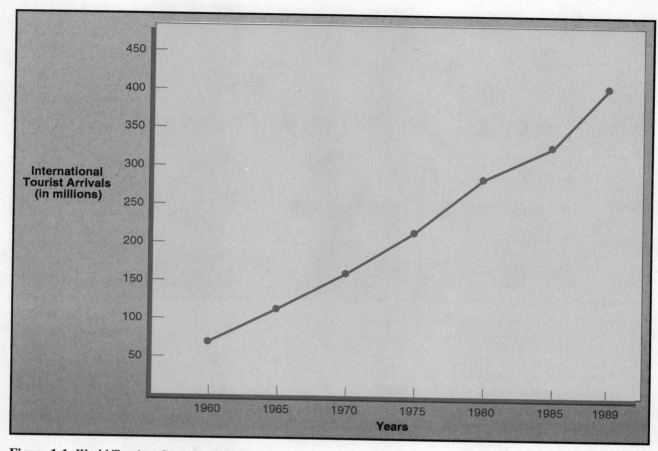

Figure 1-1 *World Tourism Growth, 1960–1989*
Source: World Tourism Organization, Travel Industry World Yearbook

mountains of Nepal, and the dancers of Bali stimulated viewers to visit faraway peoples and lands.

Since 1970, the number of people traveling has grown even more. In the United States, increased ownership of automobiles and improved highways have enabled more people, especially families, to travel. With more women earning salaries in the labor market, family budgets for travel have expanded. Longer paid vacations from work have given people more time to travel. The increase in the number of senior citizens has also been a boon to the travel industry. Retired from jobs and freed from mortgage payments, many older Americans have the time and money to travel in any season. Finally, the operations of American businesses throughout the nation and the world—requiring on-site visits and face-to-face communication—have done much to promote travel.

The Impact of the Growth of Travel

The growth of the travel industry has had a tremendous influence on the economies of the United States and other nations. Worldwide spending for travel in 1988 was

an amazing $2.1 trillion. Nations have recognized the potential of travel for improving relations among cultures. Because of the economic and cultural importance of the travel industry, governments around the world are attaching more and more importance to tourism development and promotional planning. Canada, Australia, New Zealand, France, and Greece are just a few of the countries that have created government departments specifically to oversee their tourism industries.

Economic Impact. The travel and tourism industry has become a major contributor to the economy of the United States. First, the industry provides employment for millions of people. According to one estimate, about 6 million people hold jobs directly related to travel, and millions more hold jobs indirectly related to travel. These numbers translate into billions of dollars in salaries and wages. Travel industry employees in turn pour this money back into the economy when they pay taxes or make purchases and investments.

Second, the travel and tourism industry provides profits for hundreds of businesses and corporations. These include airlines and cruise lines; railroad, motorcoach, and car rental companies; hotels, motels, and

Illus. 1-1 *The travel industry is now one of the world's largest industries.*
Source: Monkmeyer Press Photo Service/Arlene Collins

restaurants; amusement and theme parks; shops, museums, and theaters; and intermediaries—travel agents, wholesalers, and tour operators. Americans spent $542 billion on domestic travel in 1988 (see Table 1-1). In the same year, foreign visitors to the United States spent approximately $37 billion. Taxes paid on travel products and services also generate billions of dollars in revenue for federal, state, and local governments.

Categories	Expenditures (in billions)	Percent of U.S. Total
Public Transportation	$72	13%
Personal Transportation	200	37
Lodging	54	10
Food	75	14
Entertainment and Recreation	28	5
Purchases	113	21
	$542	100%
Foreign Visitor Spending	$37	
Grand Total	$579	

Table 1-1 Tourism Expenditures in the United States, 1988
Source: Travel Industry World Yearbook, 1990, produced by Child and Waters, Inc., New York

In some cases, the travel and tourism industry has helped revive economically depressed areas. For example, in the United States, waterfront restorations featuring shops, restaurants, and entertainment complexes are attracting tourists to the downtown areas of some major cities. Baltimore's Harborplace development, which includes the National Aquarium, is a fine example of successful restoration.

Cultural Impact. "Understanding through travel is a passport to peace" was the slogan of the European Travel Commission in the 1950s. Through travel, people of different cultures get to know each other, and this knowledge increases the possibility of peaceful coexistence among nations. The Helsinki Accords, signed by 35 nations in 1975, acknowledged the contribution of international travel to the development of mutual understanding. In 1985, the United States and the Soviet Union agreed to expand programs fostering greater travel and people-to-people contact between the two nations. This was the only formal agreement signed at the Geneva summit meeting. In the late 1980s, the United States and the Soviet Union agreed to greatly expand air service between the two nations.

In a large country such as the United States, with its many cultural groups, travel can also ease tensions and promote understanding.

Travel Growth and Employment

As the travel and tourism industry grows, it generates new jobs. Between 1978 and 1988, there was a 22 percent increase in total employment in the United States.

Figure 1-2 shows employment trends in four sectors of the travel and tourism industry. At the same time, travel industry employment increased an astonishing 49 percent. Domestic travel, in fact, has been growing so rapidly that there have been shortages of workers in the hospitality industry, in travel agencies, and in the airline industry.

Direct Employment. The travel industry offers an unusually broad range of employment opportunities. Some workers, such as cruise directors, flight attendants, travel agents, and hotel desk clerks, interact with travelers on a daily basis. Others, such as hotel managers, accountants, and housekeepers, are behind the scenes working to ensure the comfort and safety of travelers. Jobs range from those requiring a high level of skill and intensive training to those requiring little skill and virtually no training. The following list indicates some of the employment areas in the travel industry:

■ Managerial (hotel manager, historic sites supervisor, museum director).

■ Technical (air traffic controller, safety inspector, motorcoach dispatcher).
■ Marketing and sales (salesperson in a gift shop, travel agent, airline reservations sales agent).
■ Clerical (motel desk clerk, clerk-typist in a state tourism department).
■ Food and beverage preparation and service (chef, bartender, server).
■ Cleaning service (hotel housekeeper, room cleaner, aircraft cleaner).
■ Personal service (flight attendant, bellstaff, social director at a resort).
■ Mechanical (airplane mechanic, automobile mechanic, general maintenance worker).
■ Transportation (airplane pilot, ship captain, bus driver).

The travel and tourism industry provides hundreds of thousands of job opportunities from coast to coast and border to border in the United States. In fact, the travel and tourism industry is ranked among the top three em-

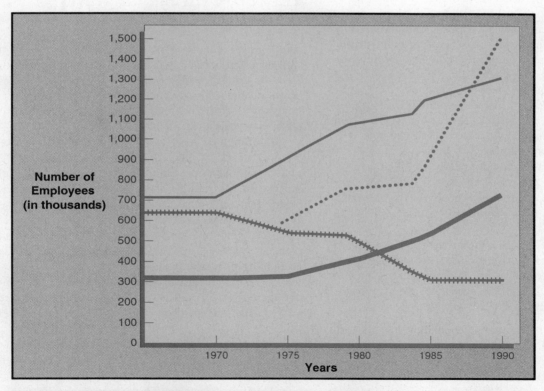

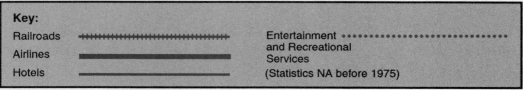

Figure 1-2 Growth of Employment in Travel and Tourism
Source: U.S. Bureau of Labor Statistics

Illus. 1-2 *The travel and tourism industry offers many opportunities for women and minorities.*
Source: Left: Photo Courtesy Marriott Hotels.; Right: Courtesy of Delta Air Lines, Inc.

ployers in all but 13 states. It is the largest employer in 13 states, the second largest employer in 15 states, and the third largest employer in 9 states. And unlike many other industries, the travel industry offers a high degree of flexibility; there is no need to go where the jobs are because they are everywhere. So if you want a job in the travel industry, you can probably find one.

The travel industry has long provided employment for women and minorities. More than 4.5 million women, nearly 1 million blacks, and almost 800,000 Hispanic Americans are employed by the travel industry. In addition, the industry provides nearly 4 million jobs for youths between the ages of 16 and 24. Many of these jobs are part-time or seasonal. These jobs enable young people to earn money for education and explore possible future careers.

Another benefit of working in the travel industry is the possibility of free or reduced-rate travel. Many components of the travel industry, including airlines, car rental companies, cruise lines, travel agencies, and tour operator companies, offer pass privileges to their employees.

Indirect Employment. Many people have jobs that are indirectly related to the travel industry. These people supply support services for workers who deal directly with the public. Writers and editors for travel publications, researchers for marketing firms, and managers of contract laundry services for hotels are just a few of the many employees in support services.

In addition, certain kinds of organizations assist the travel industry in several vital areas. Some plan and finance new attractions. Others train new personnel. Instructors in vocational training institutions, real estate developers, and bankers are some of the employees in travel-related organizations.

Travel Growth and the Travel Professional

As the travel industry grows, it will continue to recruit well-educated and highly motivated men and women for careers as travel professionals. These professionals include travel agents, hotel and restaurant managers, airline pilots, recreation directors, tour operators, and owners of motorcoach companies.

You might be seeking a career in the travel industry because of its glamorous image — exotic destinations, luxurious cruise ships, high-flying jets, beautiful scenery, ancient castles and cathedrals. The travel industry does, of course, have this attractive side. But it is also a business, and, if you are going to be a successful travel professional, you must understand and practice the basics of business. These basics include accounting, financial management, personnel administration, communications, and marketing and sales. Understanding the relationship of government to the travel business is also necessary for a successful travel career.

As a travel professional, you must have a sincere desire to help other people. Throughout this book you will find references to the motivations, needs, and expectations (MNEs) of travelers. These three forces shape people's travel plans. Successful travel professionals make a point of understanding the MNEs of the people they serve.

Finally, as a travel professional, you will need to be creative and flexible in keeping up with an industry that is constantly growing and changing. For those who are prepared to make the effort, the travel industry offers many exciting and rewarding opportunities.

Check Your Product Knowledge

1. What are five reasons for the growth of the travel industry in the last 35 years?
2. How has the growth of travel influenced the United States economy?
3. How is direct employment in the travel industry different from indirect employment?
4. What are some areas of knowledge with which the travel professional should be acquainted?

TRAVEL AS AN INDUSTRY

During the 1960s, analysts began to view travel as an industry, rather than as a miscellaneous collection of transportation companies. An *industry* is a group of businesses or corporations that produce a product or service for a profit. With the billions of dollars in income it generates, travel can certainly be categorized as an industry.

The Seven Components of the Travel Industry

The travel industry comprises thousands of companies that produce products and services for travelers. These companies range in size from small businesses to multinational corporations. The roadside hamburger stand is just as much a part of the industry as is a major airline. (And to a hungry traveler, the hamburger stand may be even more important.) The combined efforts of all these travel and tourism companies enable people to travel from one location to another. The companies can be organized into seven groups, or components, according to their function (see Figure 1-3). Three components provide the most basic service—transportation. These are the components that get people where they're going and get them from place to place once they arrive:

- Air transportation and services.
- Maritime transportation and services.
- Ground transportation and services.

Two components care for and entertain travelers:

- The hospitality industry.
- The tourism industry.

Two components provide the means for distributing the products and services of the other components to travelers:

- Wholesale companies.
- The travel mart.

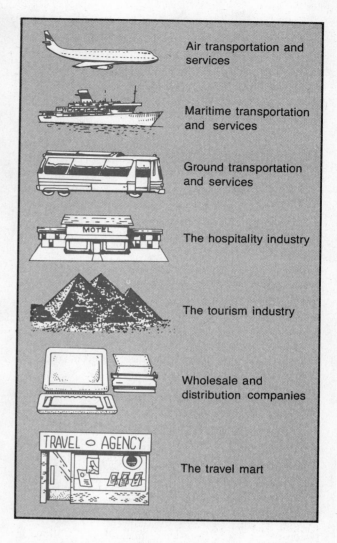

Figure 1-3   The Seven Components of the Travel Industry

Since the companies are grouped by function, and not by size, both an international airline with a fleet of 200 airplanes and a one-airplane air taxi company would be in the first component. Each provides air transportation for travelers. Likewise, since the high-rise hotel and the roadside motel both provide traveler accommodations, they are in the hospitality component—despite the differences in size and scope of operations.

Air Transportation and Services. Airplanes are very important to the travel industry. The air transportation component includes scheduled air carriers, supplemental air carriers, air taxi operators, and aerial sightseeing and excursion companies.

Scheduled air carriers are airline companies, such as United Airlines and Northwest Airlines, that provide service on a regular basis. The business traveler who needs to get from Dallas to Phoenix is likely to book a flight on an airline that makes regularly scheduled flights. With approximately 250 companies, scheduled air carriers comprise the largest segment of the air transportation component. Some airlines fly long-distance international and domestic routes, while others confine their services to a particular region. In 1988, United States scheduled airlines transported more than 450 million passengers.

Supplemental air carriers, or charter companies, provide air travel for groups at net rates that can be lower than regular fares on scheduled airlines. (The rates depend on the number of passengers, length of trip, and destination.) An organization like the Sons of Norway might *charter*, or hire, an airplane to take its members on a vacation trip to Oslo. The planes used by supplemental air carriers are often the same size as those used by scheduled air carriers.

Air taxi companies also provide transportation on a charter or contract basis. As the name implies, they function in much the same way as taxicabs do. Using smaller airplanes, air taxi companies fly passengers or supplies to destinations that may not be accessible to scheduled air carriers. For example, business travelers may use an air taxi company to fly to two or three different corporate locations within the same day.

Maritime Transportation and Services. Sailing is one of the oldest forms of transportation. *Maritime*, or oceangoing, transportation includes passenger shiplines, cruise lines, and passenger freighters. This component also includes companies that ferry passengers and cars across lakes, rivers, or channels, as well as companies that provide harbor sightseeing cruises and riverboat excursions.

Passenger shiplines, which carry passengers between major ports, flourished in the decade following World War II. However, with the introduction of transatlantic jet service in the late 1950s, passenger liners began to disappear. Today, several ships, including the *Queen Elizabeth II* and *Vistafjord* (Cunard Lines) and the *Royal Princess* (Princess Cruise Lines), still offer passenger service between Western Europe and North America.

Many passenger shiplines survived by changing into cruise lines. Rather than focusing primarily on transportation, cruise lines provide a total travel experience. These floating hotels may offer swimming, sunbathing, dancing, gambling, sumptuous dining, nightclub entertainment, and first-run movies. They dock at ports like San Juan and St. Thomas for shopping and sightseeing. Cruises have become very popular for vacations. About 200 cruise ships worldwide offer vacations to such destinations as the Mexican Riviera, the islands of the Caribbean, and the Greek islands.

Passenger freighters are cargo ships with some first-class cabins aboard. Passengers can travel anywhere in the world the freighter goes. Because their ports of call can change as business dictates, freighters have more flexible itineraries than do cruise ships. For

many travelers, that element of surprise adds excitement to the trip.

Ground Transportation and Services. *Ground transportation* (or surface transportation) is so basic that it is almost taken for granted. The various forms of ground transportation are, however, the underpinnings of the entire travel industry. Bus companies, car rental companies, passenger railroad companies, and taxicab and limousine companies are included in this component. While buses and trains used in mass transit systems primarily transport workers to their jobs, they also transport visitors to museums, zoos, theaters, and sporting events in metropolitan areas.

The *motorcoach*, or bus, industry provides transportation between cities. Greyhound and Trailways Lines, the largest intercity motorcoach company in the United States, operates 3,900 buses. Buses have also become popular for escorted one-day trips and for longer vacation trips. Many people, especially senior citizens, enjoy seeing the countryside as they travel, but they would rather leave the driving to someone else. Gray Lines, the world's largest excursion bus company, offers about 1,500 sightseeing excursions each year.

Car rental companies, such as Hertz, Avis, and National Car Rental, provide important, on-demand transportation for travelers who fly or take the train to their destinations and who then want to drive to their hotel or meeting place. In certain destinations, such as Florida and California, car rentals provide transportation for vacation and leisure travelers who are visiting several different regions or cities. In 1960, there were 112,000 rental cars, which generated $216 million; in 1989, there were more than 1.5 million cars, which generated $8 billion. This tremendous growth is directly linked to the increase in the number of people, especially business travelers, journeying by air.

The passenger railroad, vital to the transportation network of Europe, is far less in demand in the United States, where it was dealt a serious blow by the introduction of passenger jet service and by the increased use of buses and automobiles. By 1970, railroads accounted for only 7 percent of domestic passenger miles. Since 1971, however, the government has been trying to revive railroad transportation through the work of Amtrak. This semi-public railroad corporation covers some 24,000 route miles in 528 cities in 44 states. After receiving millions of dollars in subsidies and after coping with many difficulties, Amtrak appears to be making advances.

Another type of ground transportation is the limousine. Hotels use limousines to transport guests to and from airports. Restaurants and tourist attractions have also begun to offer limousine service. Some limousines are large, luxury automobiles; others are vans. *Limousine and Chauffeur* magazine estimated there were 7,000 limousine companies in the United States in 1990.

PROFILE
America West Airlines

America West Airlines, based in Tempe, Arizona, is one of the few success stories to have resulted from the deregulation of the airline industry in 1978. The new airline had a dramatic beginning. In 1981, its founder, Edward R. Beauvais, took out a second mortgage on his home to raise money to get the airline started. Within two years, Beauvais had raised enough money to acquire three airplanes and hire 280 employees. As of early 1991, America West had 14,000 employees and 104 planes.

Before 1978, the airline industry was closely regulated by the government and it was virtually impossible for a new airline to compete with established lines. After 1978, airlines were allowed to open new routes and set their own fares. Many newcomers—such as Midway, Air Florida, and People Express—started up quickly and began to muscle in on the larger carriers. America West, which didn't come along until 1983, was one of the last of the new airlines to be established after deregulation.

Most of the new small airlines lasted only a few years before they were either acquired by larger competitors or went out of business. America West had one major advantage over the other upstarts: Beauvais was an experienced airline consultant who was able to see where other airlines had gone wrong and could avoid making the same mistakes.

Beauvais recognized from the beginning that in order for America West to survive, it needed to become the dominant airline at one or more hub airports. He concentrated on developing America West hubs first at Phoenix, then at Las Vegas. By the early 1990s, America West was flying more than 190 daily flights out of Phoenix's Sky Harbor International Airport and more than 140 daily flights out of Las Vegas's McCarren International Airport.

America West has grown so rapidly that by 1991 it had become the ninth-largest airline in the United States, with about $1 billion a year in revenues. Still it hasn't been all smooth sailing for America West. In 1987, after doubling in size and adding routes to New York City and Baltimore, Maryland, the airline suffered $45 million in losses. Beauvais responded to the crisis by cutting back routes and solidifying the airline's business plan. America West recovered immediately and began a more modest expansion.

One of the factors that has made America West so successful is its emphasis on people—both employees and customers. Its employees have a large stake in the company. Employees are required to purchase stock equivalent to 20 percent of their first year salaries, making the employees part-owners of the airline. In addition, the company distributes 15 percent of its profits each year among its employees. As part-owners, the employees have a strong incentive to provide good service to their customers. This commitment to quality is evidenced by America West's excellent on-time performance record.

The company also provides a very generous benefits package to its employees. Benefits include 24-hour child care facilities and an on-site medical clinic at the Phoenix airport. America West even offers an employee assistance program to help employees deal with psychological and financial problems.

In 1989, America West flew more than 13 million people to 58 destinations in the United States and Canada.

Photo Source: America West Airlines

9

The Hospitality Industry. Travelers who don't stay with friends and relatives usually depend on the hospitality industry. The various branches of this component shelter, feed, and entertain travelers. The component includes accommodations (overnight lodging), resorts and casinos, restaurants and clubs, and convention centers and other meeting places.

The hospitality industry has a long history. In ancient times when people began to venture from their homes, they needed shelter on their journeys. The shelter may have been a roadside inn. Today in this country, there are 44,000 establishments that provide shelter, ranging in size from small roadside motels to huge 3,000-room resort hotels. With almost 3 million rooms, the United States leads the world in travel accommodations.

Most hotels and motels are individually owned, but usually as part of a chain. Holiday Inn is the largest chain in the world.

Major hotels are no longer just places to stay overnight. With beautifully designed interiors, a variety of restaurants and bars, and many recreational facilities (saunas, swimming pools, fitness centers, tennis courts), hotels are being marketed as places to spend weekend vacations. Some hotels also rely heavily on convention business and provide meeting rooms and exhibition areas.

The Tourism Industry. Niagara Falls, the Pyramids of Egypt, and the World Series, in spite of their obvious differences, are alike in that they are all major tourist attractions. The tourism component of the travel industry is concerned with attractions and events that draw travelers to an area.

Attractions may be natural or constructed. Every year, thousands of tourists enjoy the beauty of Yellowstone National Park, the Rocky Mountains, and other natural or scenic attractions. Constructed tourist attractions include historic buildings, museums, theme parks, shopping malls, and recreational facilities (golf courses, tennis courts, marinas). Events such as professional games, parades, fairs, plays, and festivals attract tourists who like to get caught up in the action. Such events range in size and scope from the Olympics, Mardi Gras, and the Super Bowl to small-town fairs and rodeos. The main difference between attractions and events is that attractions are usually permanent while events are usually temporary, with planned time duration.

Wholesale Companies. Wholesale companies buy the products of the first five components. Because they buy in large quantities, they receive discounts. Wholesalers make a profit by marking up the price of the products and then selling them through retail travel agencies.

There are three main types of wholesale operations in the travel industry. Charter operators buy airplane seats, hotel rooms, car rentals, or other travel products and sell them to tour operators or to the public. Tour operators assemble transportation, lodging, and sightseeing packages for various groups of travelers; they usually provide the group with an escort or guide. Inbound oper-

Illus. 1-3 *Tourist attractions, both natural and constructed, draw travelers to an area.*
Source: Left: Rich Tourangeau-National Park Service; Right: © A. Carey/THE IMAGE WORKS

ators are specialized types of tour operators providing travel packages for foreign visitors to the United States. In the early 1990s, there were more than 2,000 tour operator companies in the United States.

The Travel Mart. The word *mart*, short for marketplace, refers to the many outlets through which people can obtain travel information, make reservations, and pay for trips. This component includes retail travel agencies, business travel departments, scheduled airline ticket offices, and travel clubs.

In a retail travel agency, travel agents deal with all kinds of clients—the young couple going on a honeymoon cruise, the retired couple planning a round-the-world trip, the college student going to Europe for the first time. Travel agents help excited travelers plan their trips, make reservations, and obtain tickets.

Retail travel agencies, which can be operated independently or as part of a chain, are located in department stores, shopping malls, or suburban and downtown business districts. Some agencies specialize in a specific type of travel: business or pleasure, domestic or international, individual or group. As travel has increased, so has the number of travel agencies. Today, there are more than 37,000 travel agencies in the United States.

Some corporations have their own business travel departments (BTDs). BTDs handle the travel arrangements of employees traveling for business purposes. Workers in a BTD carry out work similar to that done by travel agents. The main difference is that the customers are company employees only, and most travel arrangements are for business purposes.

Travelers can also purchase travel products through a travel club. Travel clubs specialize in selling unsold travel products, such as a cabin on a cruise ship or an airline ticket to Europe, at discounted prices. To take advantage of these travel bargains, travel club members pay an annual fee and must have flexible schedules so that they can leave for a trip on short notice.

On military bases and other government installations, military personnel and certain civilians can use the services of scheduled airline ticket offices (doing business as SATO, Inc.). SATOs will be discussed in greater detail in Chapter 13. All travelers can make purchases at airline, bus, and railroad ticket counters; in this way, travelers are purchasing travel products directly from the producers.

Interrelationship of Components

Although the components of the travel industry operate independently and frequently compete with each other, they are really part of an overall system. Travelers use more than one component when they travel. For this reason, what affects one component can affect others. The permanent closing of a tourist attraction, such as a ski re-

sort, reduces business for the transportation components that brought skiers to the area and for the hospitality businesses that housed and fed them. Likewise, the expansion of a particular component increases business for other components. When the airlines expanded international travel in the early 1960s, American hotel chains also expanded overseas. Holiday Inn now has hotels in more than 50 countries, including Poland and Yugoslavia. Both Ramada and Sheraton are scheduled to open hotels in Moscow.

The travel industry has recognized this interrelationship by putting various components together and selling them as a *package*. A package might be an *intermodal package*—one that includes more than one form of transportation. For example, the price of a Caribbean cruise usually includes airfare to and from the point of departure. Or a package might include a day of sightseeing by chartered bus, with lunch at a popular restaurant. Such packages have made travel more convenient and less expensive for many people.

The following case study illustrates the interrelationship between the components of the travel industry:

After seeing a newspaper ad for a package tour, Karen Carlson, a single accountant from the Midwest, decided to go to Cancun, Mexico. For $799, she received round-trip airfare, ground transportation to and from the airport, and hotel accommodations for seven nights at the El Dorado Hotel. Getaway Vacations, a local travel agency, made the arrangements.

On Friday morning, Ms. Carlson departed on Sky World Airlines. On the plane, she was served a complimentary breakfast and beverage. To get the passengers in the mood for Mexico, the flight attendants taught them some simple phrases in Spanish.

After arriving in Cancun, Ms. Carlson settled into her hotel room and then made a reservation for the 9 P.M. show at the El Grande Hotel. A coworker had told her not to miss the show, with its authentic Mexican music and dancing.

Ms. Carlson was very pleased with her accommodations that week. She ate breakfast at her hotel and dinner at the El Rancho Hotel. Since all the pools and beaches had lunch counters, she didn't have to go too far from the water to get a sandwich.

After three days of swimming and sunning herself, Ms. Carlson decided to do something different. She arranged to go sightseeing on Tuesday. She opted for a tour of the ancient Mayan ruins at Chichén Itzá. A motorcoach picked up Ms. Carlson and the rest of the tour group at the hotel. As she boarded the bus, Ms. Carlson paid the tour guide $35 for the tour. (The full tour price was $50, but Ms. Carlson had a discount coupon for $15 provided as part of her package price.) At noon, the tour bus stopped at a restaurant. The people on the tour ate lunch and browsed in a souvenir shop located next to the restaurant.

Thomas Cook

Thomas Cook, founder of the world's first travel agency and entrepreneur extraordinaire, was born in England in 1808. Cook quit school at the age of ten and worked at a series of jobs, including gardening, fruit selling, and bookselling. In 1828, at the age of 20, he became a Baptist missionary and an ardent supporter of the temperance movement. It was his interest in the cause of temperance that began his career in travel.

One day, in the early summer of 1841, Cook was on his way to a temperance meeting in Leicester. At the time he was working for a Baptist publisher in Loughborough, about ten miles away. An idea occurred to him: Why not arrange for a special train between Loughborough and Leicester for those who planned to attend the upcoming quarterly temperance meeting in Leicester? Cook approached the Midland Counties Railway company with his idea. The company agreed, and Cook advertised the arrangement. On July 5, the historic excursion took place—historic because it was the first publicly advertised excursion train to run in England.

Conditions were a bit rough. The 570 travelers were crammed into nine "tubs"—seatless third-class carriages open to the elements. Already, however, Cook's planning skills were evident. He had negotiated a specially reduced fare of one shilling per person for the trip. He also arranged for a picnic lunch to be served before the afternoon procession, and at the end of the line he set out tea for 1,000 people. Despite the primitive conditions of the ride, the trip was a reasonable success. By 1844, the railway had agreed to run the excursion regularly if Cook would guarantee the passengers. And he did, having by now left the ministry to start his own travel agency.

In the next several years, Cook organized other temperance-related tours. They were especially popular with people of limited income, who had never before had the opportunity to travel. As his agency grew, it began to serve all kinds of travelers, no longer limiting itself to the cause of temperance.

Cook's excursions did not venture outside the British Isles until he conducted excursions from Leicester to the French port of Calais for the Paris Exposition of 1855, a kind of world's fair. Foreseeing the business possibilities in European travel, the next year he organized "A Great Circular Tour of the Continent." Cook led the tour himself but, because he knew no foreign languages, also employed an interpreter. The tour left from Harwich, England, and moved through Belgium, Germany, and France, finally ending back at the English port of Southampton. So many travelers signed up for the tour that a repeat tour had to be scheduled six weeks later to take care of the overflow.

It took a few years for Cook's agency to institute regular service to Europe. Cook personally conducted another tour to Switzerland in July 1864, the same year his son, John Mason Cook, joined him in his firm (which became Thomas Cook & Son). John Mason Cook specialized in promoting the company's American tours. He did much to make Thomas Cook & Son a worldwide travel agency.

Extremely energetic and a top organizer, Thomas Cook used his group purchasing power to gain concessions from railroad companies and hotels. His agency was soon so dominant that he was able to impose on many hotels his system of accommodation cards. These were somewhat like coupons. They entitled Cook's clients to reduced rates on rooms in hotels throughout the world. Cook was not, however, without his critics. One writer compared his group tours to cattle drives. Yet business thrived. Thomas Cook died in 1892, and his business passed to his son. Today there are Thomas Cook & Son branches all over the world.

Cook's enterprising spirit changed the face of travel. He was responsible for the coining of a new phrase, the "Cook's tour," which means a whirlwind tour that lightly touches down in many places. In a larger sense, Cook was important because of the pioneering role he played in the area of organized mass travel. Thanks to Thomas Cook, the age of the grand tour gave way to the age of tourism.

In the afternoon, the tour guide led the group through the ruins, describing the sights and providing interesting information about the Mayan people. Ms. Carlson found the trip fascinating.

On Thursday, Ms. Carlson took a boat ride to Isla Mujeres, a small island. There, she and the others on the boat trip went snorkeling and ate a picnic lunch.

The next morning, thoroughly satisfied with her trip, Karen Carlson boarded Sky World for the flight home. Many travel professionals working for air, ground, and maritime transportation services; the hospitality and tourism industries; and the travel mart had helped her have a wonderful time.

Travel as a Product and as a Service

Industries generate either products or services. The garment industry manufactures suits, dresses, shirts, blouses, and other items of clothing. These are products. The health care industry, on the other hand, provides services, such as diagnosing illness, relieving pain and discomfort, and setting broken bones.

Some authorities say the travel industry provides products, while others say it provides services. Actually, the travel industry provides both products and services.

Travel as a Product. Almost all products are *tangible*, that is, they can be seen and touched. They have weight and occupy space. Televisions, furniture, clothes, and appliances are all tangible.

The travel industry produces a few tangible products such as food and beverages. However, most of its products are *intangible*, that is, they cannot be seen or touched. Intangible travel products include a flight on an airplane, a stay in a hotel room, a ride on a bus, relaxation on a warm beach, a reunion with family members, fun at a nightclub, a view of the ocean, and much more. None of these things can be weighed or measured or stored in a room. Unlike an old car or washing machine, travel products cannot be junked. They exist as experiences, which yield to memories.

Travel as a Service. A service industry is distinguished by three characteristics. First, its employees perform actions that benefit or serve customers. Second, its employees are professionals. They are expected to perform their duties with a high level of expertise and to be able to give their customers information and counsel. Third, a special attitude or relationship exists between the employee performing the service and the customer receiving it. These three characteristics definitely describe the travel industry.

At the local full-service gas station, the attendant fills your car's fuel tank, cleans the windshield and checks the oil. All these actions benefit or serve you, the

driver. In much the same ways, members of the travel industry provide travelers with benefits. They help to plan trips, transport passengers to their destinations, arrange a place to stay, and much more.

Travel professionals are like other professionals. Just as an attorney gives you legal advice and an accountant offers you financial guidance, the travel professional is able to provide the travel products and services most suitable to your needs.

Doctor-patient, attorney-client, and teacher-student are familiar professional relationships. Each relationship assumes a certain attitude and way of behaving on the part of the people involved. In the travel industry, the relationship is host-guest, with the travel professional as the host and the traveler as the guest. This relationship assumes that the host will focus attention on the needs and welfare of the guest and strive to make his or her travel experience cheerful and fulfilling. Maintaining this relationship is very important if travel professionals expect customers to return.

Check Your Product Knowledge

1. Why is travel called an industry?
2. What criterion is used to assign a particular travel company to a component?
3. How are wholesale companies and the travel mart different from the other components?
4. In what ways does the travel industry provide products?
5. In what ways is travel a service industry?

THE TRAVEL INDUSTRY IN THE MARKETPLACE

When the word *marketplace* is mentioned, you might imagine a town square filled with flower carts, vegetable stands, and crafts. You can almost hear the noisy merchants selling their goods and see the crowds clamoring to get a better look.

A marketplace, however, can be anywhere buyers and sellers meet to exchange goods and services for money—a high-priced boutique, a Salvation Army outlet, a grocery store, a gas station. In the travel industry, the marketplace may be an office in a travel agency. The sellers are wholesale distributors and retail companies; they sell products and services supplied by air transportation, maritime transportation, and ground transportation companies and by the hospitality and tourism industries. The buyers are the travelers.

The Free Enterprise System

The United States government owns the Florida Everglades, Devil's Tower in Wyoming, and Abraham Lincoln's Kentucky birthplace, as well as many other parks, monuments, and historic attractions. In addition, federal, state, and local government funds are used to operate mass transit systems, airports, docks, harbors, and highways.

However, these examples of government ownership of travel enterprises really illustrate the exception. In fact, 90 percent of the travel and tourism businesses in the United States are privately owned and operated. This is in contrast to many countries, where the majority of travel enterprises are owned and operated by the government.

The travel and tourism industry in the United States functions within the *free enterprise system*. In a free enterprise system, privately owned businesses are allowed to compete with each other in the marketplace with a minimum of government interference. Owners are free to make as much money for themselves as they can.

As part of the free enterprise system, the United States travel and tourism industry is a business like any other business. To stay in business, it must produce good products and services, sell them at a fair price, and earn a profit. The ability to make a profit provides an incentive for owners of travel companies to put forth their best efforts. Many economists believe that the free enterprise system is more efficient than a government-controlled system, better suited to change, and more conducive to growth.

The 4 Ps of Marketing

Marketing refers to getting travel products and services to the consumer. To make a sale, travel professionals must coordinate the 4 Ps of marketing:

- Product.
- Price.
- Place.
- Promotion.

A travel agent probably wouldn't have much success trying to sell a disco-till-dawn singles' cruise to an elderly couple. The successful travel professional knows how to bring the right product or service to the right place at the right time and at the right price.

Product. This category includes all products and services produced by the components of the travel industry. Products range from a bus ride across town to an ocean cruise around the world. If you think about the seats available on just one bus, you realize that there are hundreds of millions of travel products and services available for sale at any given time and that these can be sold over and over.

Price. This category is the cost of the product or service to the consumer. The price is based on the supplier's expenses in producing the product and the distributor's expenses in marketing it. With the growth of travel and increased competition for the travel dollar, the price of travel products today is quite reasonable. Open your newspaper to the travel ads, and you will be amazed at how far you can go for just $200.

Place. This category refers to any marketplace where buyer and seller are brought together: retail travel agency, business travel department, travel club, scheduled airline ticket office, ticket counter. Sellers set up their marketplaces in locations that are convenient to the majority of buyers. With increased competition in the marketplace, sellers are looking for new places to distribute products and services. Already, along with bread and milk, you can purchase bus tickets and airline tickets at some supermarkets.

Promotion. This category refers to the ways sellers create consumer interest. To inform consumers that various products and services are available, sellers advertise on television and radio and in newspapers and magazines. They might also offer special deals, such as two airline tickets for the price of one, to create even more excitement. Giving away trips for two as prizes on television game shows has become a popular form of promotion.

Promotion includes the very important area of marketing research. Researchers interview travelers at airports and resorts, conduct surveys aboard buses and airplanes, and leave questionnaires in hotel and motel rooms. Through this research, they attempt to determine consumer preferences, buying behavior, trip-planning behavior, and customer satisfaction. The information is used to improve existing travel products and services and to plan new ones.

Check Your Product Knowledge

1. In the travel industry, where is the marketplace? Who are the buyers? Who are the sellers? What do they exchange?
2. How is the travel marketplace in the United States different from the travel marketplace in many other countries?
3. What are the 4 Ps of marketing? Why are they important?

GOVERNMENT AND THE TRAVEL INDUSTRY

Although travel enterprises in the United States operate within the free enterprise system, they are not allowed to do absolutely anything they want. Local, state, and federal governments promote and regulate many travel enterprises, regardless of their size or location. Knowing how the government affects the travel and tourism industry is an important part of your product knowledge.

Government and Promotion

Recognizing the economic benefits of the travel and tourism industry, the government promotes travel and tourism by providing facilities, publicity, and concessions and incentives.

Facilities. The government raises and budgets tax dollars for building, maintaining, and operating facilities that enable people to travel. State and local governments supply most of the funds for roads, airports, and river and harbor facilities, while the federal government finances all air-traffic control operations. Local and state governments also issue bonds (borrow money) or levy special taxes to pay for a facility, such as a convention center or stadium, that will bring visitors to the area.

Parks, monuments, historic sites, recreational areas, and scenic trails and waterways all comprise another type of facility provided for by the government. The federal government alone has set aside 80 million acres of land for public recreation and enjoyment.

Publicity. If you live in Michigan, you might have seen a television ad inviting you to visit Wyoming. Or, if you live in Colorado, you might have seen an ad extolling the wonders of Tennessee. By calling a special toll-free number, you could order a travel packet containing more tourist information.

This is an example of how the government advertises attractions and events to stimulate travel and tourism. As they look for ways to replace jobs lost in manufacturing and agriculture, state governments in particular are increasing the size of their tourism offices and granting them larger budgets for promotion. In 1980, state governments spent less than $90 million for promotion. By 1989, this figure had almost quadrupled to over $340 million.

Concessions and Incentives. Federal, state, and local governments help the travel and tourism industry to grow by giving it concessions and incentives. To attract a travel company to an area, the government might reduce or waive payment of taxes for a certain time. This allows the company to use more of its financial resources in getting started. The government might also aid a travel com-

Illus. 1-4 *The government promotes travel and tourism through advertising, allocating funds for tourism offices, and offering concessions and incentives to the travel industry.*

pany by granting it a contract that gives government business to the company. The domestic airline industry in this country developed as a result of federal government contracts to deliver airmail. Finally, the government aids the travel and tourism industry by giving travelers incentives to spend more money. Tax-free shopping at international airports is an example of this form of government support.

Government Regulation

To ensure public safety and to maintain an orderly system, the government regulates the travel industry. The government does this by requiring licenses and certificates, imposing rules and regulations, levying taxes and fees, and controlling international travel.

Licenses and Certificates. To drive a car legally in the United States, you must pass a written examination and a road test. This process is overseen by state governments, which also administer tests and issue licenses to all bus drivers, chauffeurs, and many other vehicular operators. A license indicates that the person has completed the necessary training and possesses the skills to operate the vehicle safely. Airline pilots and railroad engineers must also be tested and licensed. Their licenses are issued by the federal government.

Just as you must obtain a license for your car, all vehicles used in the travel industry must be registered with the government. Vehicles used for public transportation are also subject to periodic safety inspections, and transportation companies must be certified in order to do business.

Another type of licensing applies to the hospitality industry. Local governments issue food and liquor licenses to restaurants and bars. These licenses enable the government to control the number, location, and hours of such establishments in a community. To remain in operation, bars and restaurants must also conform to government safety and health standards. For instance, food must be stored at proper temperatures, and employees must wash their hands before handling food. To ensure customers' safety in case of a fire, bars and restaurants must have the proper number of exits specified by government guidelines.

Rules and Regulations. To prevent monopolistic practices and unfair prices, the government requires transportation companies to keep a list of their *tariffs* (schedule of rates) on public file; approves or disapproves of fares, routes, and hours of operation; and allows or disallows mergers of companies. Since 1978, however, the federal government has largely ceased regulation of the airlines. This resulted from arguments that airlines, if deregulated, could improve their services. The Interstate Commerce Commission continues to regulate railroads and bus lines.

As with any other business, the government monitors working conditions in the travel industry and enforces the minimum wage.

Taxes and Fees. If you've ever driven the interstate highway across northern Illinois, Indiana, and Ohio, you know that having an ample supply of quarters, dimes, and nickels will speed your journey along. Road tolls are one means the government uses to raise money. The government also levies taxes and fees for the use of other facilities; these include airport landing and user fees, and port and harbor charges. The revenue from sales taxes on travel products—such as restaurant meals or a stay in a hotel room—also goes to the government. Although taxes and fees are primarily a way of raising revenue, they can discourage companies and travelers if charges are too high.

International Travel. The federal government encourages foreign travelers to visit the United States. Some visitors, however, are definitely not welcome! These include cocaine smugglers, political subversives, and people with certain infectious diseases. By issuing visas and other documents, the government controls who may enter the country and under what conditions.

Through customs inspections and border checks, the government attempts to control what products travelers bring into the country. Illegal drugs, explosives, and insect-infested fruit, for example, are dangerous to the health and welfare of United States citizens and are not allowed.

Of course, before any travel can occur between the United States and another country, the two nations must have extended diplomatic recognition to each other. They must also have negotiated agreements on commerce, navigation, visa issuance, and consular and air transport rights.

Check Your Product Knowledge

1. Why does the government get involved in the travel industry?
2. In what three ways does the government promote travel?
3. In what four ways does the government regulate travel?

GEOGRAPHY AND THE TRAVEL INDUSTRY

As a travel professional, you should know geography. This does not mean that you must be able to plot the latitude and longitude of individual cities or memorize every country's chief exports and imports. Instead, you must know enough geography to give a traveler an idea of what to expect at his or her destination, and to make recommendations for travel there. Furthermore, you need to understand how geography influences the total travel industry.

Destination Geography

Many travel professionals deal in destinations, or places. Most travelers are not familiar with the destinations they have chosen. As a result, travel professionals must be able to answer questions regarding three aspects of the destination's geography: locational, cultural, and physical.

Locational. Locational geography refers to travelers' most basic question about their destination: Where is it? A travel agent must be able to locate the place on a map and show the client its position in relation to other cities, regions, or countries.

The next question is: How do I get there? The travel agent must be able to plan an *itinerary*, or route, for the

A Receptive Operator

I own a tour business, but my business differs from other tour operators in two important ways. First, I don't sell tours to the general public; I sell to other tour operators, bus companies, and travel agents. Second, I specialize in one particular geographic area, the New England area. The terms *receptive operator, reception services,* and *destination manager* all refer to people like me who specialize in serving travelers in one small geographic vicinity.

I am one of about 160 receptive operators in the United States. We are a very recent but growing addition to the travel industry. We are a sort of wholesaler or subcontractor of tours. Let's assume that you own a tour business called All-Star Tours. You have a group of retired people who want to tour New England during the fall when the leaves change color. However, your regular tour packages do not include any tours of New England.

You could either turn down the group or hire a tour company like mine to conduct the tour. If you hire my company, my tour director will meet your busload of tourists at the start of the tour and conduct it for you. The tour director will welcome your guests "on behalf of All-Star Tours." Your clients will never know that they are actually being served by my company.

There are several advantages to using receptive operators. The major advantage is that because I specialize in one particular geographic area, I am able to provide the highest quality tours of that area. I know all of the hotels, restaurants, and tourist attractions there. My tour guides are the most knowledgeable about the history and development of the region. I give local hotels and restaurants a lot of business; they, in turn, give me superb service and special discount rates that I can pass on to my customers and they can pass on to theirs.

Another advantage is that I can be much more flexible than regular tour operators. I can custom tailor my tours to meet the needs and interests of the group. Because of this ability, I am often called upon to provide tours for foreign visitors to the United States. I recently tailored a tour for a group of German bankers and another for a group of Japanese industrialists. I employ only about eight full-time workers, but my payroll includes several part-time tour directors who speak German, French, Japanese, Spanish, and other languages.

My full-time employees spend their day arranging tours, negotiating with hotels and restaurants, writing brochures, seeking out new attractions and routes, and so on. I spend the bulk of my day in sales activities. I may be on the phone all day calling bus companies, travel agents, and tour operators. I want as many of these companies as possible to be aware of my agency's services so that when they need me, they know where to find me.

I also spend a lot of time at travel industry conferences and trade shows. For example, I attend the World Travel Market trade show in London each year. I run a booth at the show where I can meet British travel agents and tour operators and familiarize them with my services.

I wasn't always a receptive operator. I started out as a tour escort. Then I had my own tour company for a while. You really need experience as a tour operator before trying to specialize in receptive services. In addition, you need as much experience as you can get in running a small business. You have to know how to estimate profits and expenses and how to manage people and perform the necessary paperwork to run a business. And, of course, you must know how to organize and conduct tours.

Running a receptive services business is a very risky venture. It is usually seasonal, which means that it makes money only a few months of each year, but it must employ workers and spend money year-round. Despite these drawbacks, I enjoy being a receptive operator very much because I like being able to serve people and I like being my own boss. I am very proud of my geographic region and gain a great deal of satisfaction showing it to visitors. I also love to travel myself so I know what other travelers want and expect from a well-run tour.

Photo Source: Judith Pszenica

Illus. 1-5 *The travel professional must possess in-depth knowledge of geographic areas, including locational, cultural, and physical geography.*

journey. Along with this the travel agent must know how accessible a particular destination is. Some travelers will only choose direct flights to well-traveled places, while others will find adventure in journeying to remote areas.

Once arrived at a destination, a traveler will expect other travel professionals to answer more specific questions. For example, a business traveler will want to know the location of factories, office buildings, and convention centers, and directions for how to get to each.

Cultural. Cultural geography refers to the political, historical, social, artistic, and religious characteristics of travel destinations. Travelers will ask questions such as: What should I see and do? Will I be able to communicate with the people? What kind of food can I expect? How much money will I need? Is it safe to drink the water?

Travel professionals use their knowledge to inform travelers about local customs and prepare travelers for various differences. If travel agents suspect that a destination will cause severe culture shock, they may suggest an alternate place to go. For example, they may discourage people who would be upset by crowds or by poverty from visiting certain cities in Asia.

Physical. Physical geography involves climate and terrain. Travelers will ask: What is the weather like? What

kind of clothes should I bring along? Travel professionals should be able to inform travelers about the average temperature and rainfall of their destination. They should also advise travelers about any conditions that will seem unusual. For example, people who go to the Scandinavian countries (the "Land of the Midnight Sun") in the summertime should be aware that there will be almost 24 hours of daylight every day. Windows in hotel rooms are equipped with blackout curtains to prevent sunlight from disturbing sleep at night.

System Geography

In addition to knowing about specific destinations, travel professionals need a broad view of the influence of geography on travel. All travel components operate within a geographic system, or area. Each system has its own climate, terrain, and political and cultural divisions that determine the level of tourist activity and the kinds of travel enterprises needed. As travelers move from geographic system to geographic system, the kinds and types of components needed may change.

Physical. Climate is a major influence on travel. Warmer climates tend to draw more travelers than do colder ones.

In the United States, the warm states of Florida, California, and Texas account for more than one-quarter of the nation's tourism receipts. In Europe, vacationers flock to the sunny Mediterranean.

Seasonal variations affect transportation and accommodation rates. Rates are generally lower in the off-season. Travel professionals should know what an area is like during the off-season as well as during the on-season. Some travelers may prefer to take advantage of less crowded conditions and lower rates in the off-season.

Terrain, too, is a major influence on travel. Some fortunate areas have a marvelous natural attraction that stimulates tourism; people flock to Arizona, for instance, to see the Grand Canyon. Travel enterprises in a mountainous area will take advantage of the terrain by building ski resorts. An area with many lakes will build a resort industry offering visitors opportunities to swim, water ski, and fish.

The terrain determines how accessible an area is. Few people vacation in the Amazon River basin because the dense jungle makes travel difficult. Terrain also determines what transportation is necessary to get to an area. Travel professionals should know if a large body of water lies between the originating point and the point of destination of an overland journey. If so, they may need to schedule transportation on a ferry.

Cultural. Geographic areas have political boundaries — city, state, country. Governments influence how open or how closed an area is to travel and what restrictions are placed on travelers. Travel industries in Western Europe, for instance, are more highly developed than are those in Eastern Europe because, until very recently, the governments of the East European nations restricted travel. Travel to the Persian Gulf area was severely restricted in the early 1990s when war broke out. The governments of many nations advised their citizens to stay away from the area.

Travel professionals need to inform clients about the requirements for passing from one political jurisdiction to another. For international travel, this means helping clients obtain passports, visas, or other travel permits; informing them about necessary vaccinations; and explaining customs regulations. Travel professionals should be able to explain how to exchange currency. People who are traveling between states in this country may also require certain information, such as differences in traffic laws.

Locational. The location of a geographic area influences travel and the type of travel components. Remote, undeveloped locations may have a standard of living different from what a traveler is used to. Items commonplace to the traveler — such as toothpaste, toilet paper, or ketchup — may be unavailable or very expensive. Travel professionals need to prepare travelers for these differences.

Countries with small geographic areas, high standards of living, and high population density generate the most international travel. The countries of Western Europe — where travelers can cross several international boundaries in a short amount of time — are the best example. The United States and Canada, with their high standards of living, do not generate as much international travel because of their large size and more isolated location. Australia and New Zealand provide good examples of how geographic isolation can hamper international tourism, although this is now changing.

Learning About Destinations and Systems

Learning about geography is an ongoing process. The travel professional must keep up to date because destinations and systems are constantly changing. For example, if hotel workers in Honolulu are on strike, creating chaos in the hospitality industry, a travel professional would probably suggest that clients postpone a vacation trip to Hawaii. A political disturbance, a natural disaster, an outbreak of cholera, or an unfavorable shift in the currency exchange rate might be other factors that would temporarily discourage travelers from going to a particular destination.

A travel professional should also know when a destination is likely to be saturated—that is, when there are too many people for the area to handle comfortably. In the summertime, London is extremely crowded with tourists. The number of tour buses visiting the changing of the guard at Buckingham Palace each day must now be rationed. British tourism officials are promoting visits to the quaint hamlets outside London instead.

If a destination has become polluted, travel professionals should know so that they can advise clients. Some travelers will be very upset to see how acid rain is destroying beautiful buildings and works of art in many European cities. They might be dismayed by the litter in many national parks in the United States.

A travel professional can keep up with destinations and systems in several ways. One way is through visits. Travel professionals can take familiarization trips (*FAM trips*) to inspect hotels and restaurants, sample attractions, and experience the local culture. FAM trips are sponsored by airlines, resorts, and other travel and tourism suppliers to showcase established vacation spots and to help develop new destinations. They enable travel professionals to determine whether these areas meet their clients' vacation needs. Travel professionals can also learn about destinations on personal vacation trips. Or they can learn from the travel experiences of other professionals or clients who have recently returned from trips.

It is impossible, however, for travel professionals to obtain firsthand accounts of every destination. Another way to find out about destinations is through written sources:

- Atlases.
- Brochures published by government tourist offices (GTOs), tour operators, or suppliers.
- Guidebooks.
- Trade publications.
- Travel magazines.
- Travel sections of newspapers.

A third way to learn about destinations is through membership in professional organizations such as the American Society of Travel Agents (ASTA). The meetings and publications of such organizations keep members informed of the latest trends and developments in the travel industry.

Check Your Product Knowledge

1. Why is a knowledge of geography important for the travel professional?
2. What are three ways the travel professional can learn more about destinations and systems?
3. What topics relevant to the travel industry does geography include?

Summary

- The travel industry has grown tremendously in the last 35 years. It is the third-largest retail or service industry in the United States in terms of sales.
- A calm political climate throughout most of the world, improvements in transportation, a rise in personal income, and an increase in leisure time have all stimulated the growth of travel.
- The travel industry offers a variety of job opportunities requiring a range of skills, training, and experience.
- Travel professionals must possess a knowledge of business, psychology, and geography. They must be able to adapt to a dynamic industry and understand the consumer's motivations, needs, and expectations.
- Travel is an industry because it is composed of companies that work as a profit-making system to provide travelers with products and services.
- Travel companies can be grouped by function into seven components. Three components furnish transportation, two provide accommodations and entertainment, and two distribute travel products and services.
- Travel products are mainly intangible. They include a ride on a train, a visit to a national park, a stay in a hotel.
- Travel services provide benefits to travelers. They are performed by professionals within a host-guest relationship.
- The travel industry in the United States functions within the free enterprise system in which privately owned businesses compete with a minimum of government interference.
- To be successful in the marketplace, the travel professional must bring the right product or service to the right marketplace at the right time and at the right price. The travel professional must also promote the product and determine whether it satisfies the consumer.
- Recognizing the travel industry's potential to generate jobs, the government promotes travel by providing facilities, publicity, and concessions and incentives.
- The government regulates travel by requiring licenses and certificates, imposing rules and regulations, levying taxes and fees, and controlling international travel. Government regulation seeks to protect the health, safety, and welfare of citizens.
- The climate, terrain, location, and politics of a geographic area affect the level and type of travel activity.
- The travel professional must be able to give travelers a clear picture of any destination. Knowing locational, cultural, and physical geography enables travel professionals to do this.

Key Terms

trip
industry
charter
maritime
ground transportation
motorcoach
mart
package
intermodal package
tangible
intangible
free enterprise system
tariff
itinerary
FAM trip

What Do You Think?

1. Do you think the travel and tourism industry will continue to grow? Why or why not?
2. Which of the seven components of the travel industry do you think will experience the most growth? Why?
3. Should the federal government spend more money or less money on travel and tourism? Give reasons for your answer.
4. Why, do you think, are accurate travel statistics hard to find?
5. What are some of the main attractions of a career in travel and tourism?

Dealing with Product

Welcome to "Yourtown." At the end of each chapter, you will be asked to do some problem solving involving both the travel product and the people who buy and use this product. Quite often, you will be asked to refer to "Yourtown," meaning either your hometown or, if you are studying on campus, the city or town nearest your place of study.

Let's begin by examining travel and intangible products. Why do we consider travel to be an intangible product? What types of intangible products (outside of the travel industry) are available in Yourtown? Are these intangible products similar to or different from travel products?

Next, think of the various components of the travel industry that you were introduced to in this chapter. Once again, using Yourtown as a reference point, list as many examples as you can of each of these components and the products that each one offers to the travelers of Yourtown.

Dealing with People

All travelers have their own set of motivations, needs, and expectations (MNEs). However, these MNEs are situational—they will vary depending on the type of traveler and the type of travel. Put yourself to the test in the following brief self-study. The motivations for each trip are given. What do you think your expectations would be if you were traveling from Yourtown to:

1. Paris and Rome for a two-week vacation.
2. Toronto for a wedding.
3. Atlanta for a sales meeting.
4. New Orleans for the Super Bowl.
5. Chicago for a job interview.
6. Seattle for a cruise.

Use your imagination. Are you the same person in each of these scenarios? What does this exercise tell you about the statement that "the travel professional must possess a knowledge of business, psychology, and geography"?

WORKSHEET 1-1   TRAVEL AND THE ECONOMY

The travel industry has a huge impact on the economy of the United States. The table below shows the amount of money taken in by selected components of the travel industry in recent years. Study the table and then answer the questions that follow.

BUSINESS RECEIPTS OF TRAVEL INDUSTRY COMPONENTS, 1975 TO 1988

Receipts (in millions of dollars)					
Year	Air Transportation	Ground Transportation	Hospitality	Tourism	TOTAL
1975	10,301	1,409	64,069	18,760	94,539
1980	23,405	2,081	116,890	29,409	171,785
1982	25,488	2,283	137,342	34,661	199,774
1984	31,437	2,551	158,489	39,484	231,961
1986	33,846	2,466	181,189	45,532	263,033
1988	41,654	2,467	211,812	53,922	309,855

Source: U.S. Travel Data Center, Washington, D.C. The 1988–89 Economic Review of Travel in America

1. What were the total United States industry receipts in 1988?

2. What was the overall pattern of travel receipts from 1975 to 1988?

3. Which component nearly tripled its receipts between 1975 and 1988?

4. What happened to air transportation receipts between 1975 and 1988?

5. Which component showed the lowest total receipts between 1975 and 1988?

Construct a table or graph to show the growth of tourism in Yourtown. The information could be in terms of number of visitors, amount of revenue generated by local travel components, or number of people employed locally by the travel industry. Contact Yourtown's chamber of commerce for appropriate data.

WORKSHEET 1-2   DESTINATION GEOGRAPHY

First, choose a travel destination—the more exotic and unfamiliar to you the better. Then do research on this destination so that you can draw up a geographic profile that would be useful to a tourist.

LOCAL GEOGRAPHY

1. Name of destination

2. Location of destination

3. How to get there

CULTURAL GEOGRAPHY

4. Language(s) spoken

5. General health conditions

6. Type of food

7. Type of clothing worn

8. Currency used and exchange rate in dollars

9. Cost of living

10. Availability of basic items

11. Unusual conditions or customs

PHYSICAL GEOGRAPHY

12. Climate, in winter and summer

13. On-season and off-season

14. Clothing needed

15. Terrain

16. Local transportation

WORKSHEET 1-3   TRAVEL AS AN INDUSTRY

The seven components of the travel industry are:

- Air transportation and services.
- Maritime transportation and services.
- Ground transportation and services.
- The hospitality industry.
- The tourism industry.
- Wholesale companies.
- The travel mart.

Look over the four trips described below. For each one, list the components of the travel industry that would be involved. Explain how each of the components would be used.

1. The Cipriani family of Omaha, Nebraska, is planning to visit the Grand Canyon this summer. They are going to travel by car and they plan to camp out.

   _____

   _____

   _____

   _____

   _____

   _____

   _____

2. Peter Macy of Pittsburgh wants to take a Caribbean cruise that includes visits to several islands.

   _____

   _____

   _____

   _____

   _____

   _____

   _____

3. Sylvia Schumacher of Minneapolis plans to attend a company sales meeting this fall in Hilton Head, South Carolina. She will travel with several other people from the company.

   _____

   _____

   _____

   _____

   _____

   _____

   _____

4. The Kleins, a retired couple living in Orlando, Florida, would like to visit London on one of the package tours that includes hotel, sightseeing, and theater tickets.

   _____

   _____

   _____

   _____

   _____

   _____

   _____

WORKSHEET 1-4   4 Ps OF MARKETING

In Chapter 1 you learned about the 4 Ps of marketing—product, price, place, and promotion. Study the ad below and then answer the questions about the 4 Ps.

1. **Product**

    What are the tangible benefits of the product?

    _____

    _____

    What might be some of the intangible benefits of the product?

    _____

    _____

    _____

2. **Price**

    What is the cost of the product?

    _____

    _____

3. **Place**

    Where can buyer and seller meet to transact business?

    _____

    _____

4. **Promotion**

    What has the seller done to create consumer interest in the product?

    _____

    _____

    _____

    _____

GREAT ESCAPE WEEKEND

Friday, Saturday or Sunday
at the all new Zenith

$**49** plus tax
per night
standard room

$54 Hillcrest Room $59 Lakecrest Room
1–4 persons per room

- Complimentary continental breakfast
- Complimentary drink coupon
- Indoor pool, whirlpool & sauna
- Cable TV, free parking

Limited rooms available at these prices

Ask about our Ski Package–$59

1-800-555-5555

Zenith Hotel
1500 N. Main St.
Allentown, NY 14526

The ad on this page promotes a product of the hospitality component of the travel industry. Look through the travel section of the newspaper and find ads for the products of the other components. Identify the 4 Ps of marketing in each ad.

CHAPTER 2 ▲ THE TRAVELERS

"The world is a great book, of which they who never stir from home read only a page."

—St. Augustine of Hippo

Objectives

When you have completed this chapter, you should be able to:

- Explain how the concept of travel has changed through the ages.
- Describe the three main groups of travelers and their motivations, needs, and expectations (MNEs).
- Explain why people travel for pleasure in terms of both Stanley Plog's theory on personality types and Abraham Maslow's theory on need satisfaction.
- Explain why the travel industry classifies travelers into groups, or segments, and how it obtains information about each segment.

- List some of the reasons people who live in this country might choose to travel within the United States.
- Discuss the special issues of international travel, such as documentation, customs regulations, common health problems, and foreign currency.
- Define inbound tourism and describe the MNEs of travelers who come to the United States.

Passengers on Flight 723 from Seattle/Tacoma are deplaning at Gate 11 on the Gold Concourse. Glancing at her watch, a business executive hurries down the ramp. She is followed by a group of Japanese tourists who are loaded down with cameras and flight bags. Next comes a young family—the mother is carrying an infant, while the father is trying to hang on to a rambunctious two year old. Also among the passengers are a newly married couple returning from a cruise to Alaska and an elderly woman whose granddaughter attends the University of Washington. When most of the passengers have deplaned, a flight attendant comes down the ramp guiding a young man in a wheelchair.

These are modern-day travelers. As a travel professional, you must get to know these people in order to serve their needs. You must know who they are, why they travel, and where they go.

A BRIEF HISTORY OF TRAVEL

Throughout history, there have been travelers. The Old Testament describes the journey of the Israelites from Egypt to the Promised Land. The walls of a temple in Luxor, Egypt, chronicle the pleasure cruise of Queen Hatshepsut to the ancient land of Punt (now Somalia). History books give accounts of famous travelers, such as the Vikings, Marco Polo, and Christopher Columbus. Fossil remains of *Homo erectus* have been found in Western Europe, Africa, and China—revealing that even prehistoric people were travelers.

Requirements for Travel

In the time of the Roman Empire, a wealthy citizen could travel quite easily. The Roman government had built a magnificent network of roads. Fresh relays of horses were available every five or six miles. A single system of currency throughout the empire facilitated payments for food and lodging. Most important, the *Pax Romana*, or Roman peace, guaranteed travelers a high degree of safety.

In order for travel to flourish, there must be an efficient transportation system and an atmosphere of peace and political stability. Travel—especially travel for pleasure—also requires economic prosperity and leisure time. When the Roman Empire declined, so did travel. The wealthy class disappeared, roads deteriorated, and the countryside was overrun by hoodlums.

In the Dark Ages that followed (approximately A.D. 500 to A.D. 1450), travel became what it has generally been throughout most of history—dangerous and difficult. In fact, the word travel, which originated during this time, comes from a root word meaning "heavy labor." Peasants rarely left their villages. When merchants and clergy had to travel, they journeyed by foot or by crude ox-drawn carts over rough terrain.

It was not until the period of the Industrial Revolution, which began in the mid-1700s in Europe, that travel started to be more common. Then, a series of advances in transportation—the development of the stagecoach, then the steamboat, and finally the railroad—made travel easier in North America as well as in Europe. In addition to technological changes, social changes contributed to the growth of travel. A middle class, with money and leisure time, was developing. Wishing to escape occasionally from bleak city life, these people retreated to seaside resorts for recreation.

In the twentieth century, the development of automobiles and motorcoaches created a demand for better roads, and people were soon driving all over the United States and Canada. With the first transatlantic jet passenger plane flight in the late 1950s, fast, comfortable, and economical international travel became possible.

In the last 35 years, the volume of travel has increased tremendously. Partly the result of improvements in transportation, this increase is also attributable to economic prosperity and social changes. Whereas only wealthy people journeyed for pleasure in the past, today people from most economic classes in industrialized societies have money to spend on travel. And with more women in the work force, families have an additional source of income for travel. Paid annual vacations and holidays give people more leisure time to devote to travel. People are better educated today. In general, the more education a person receives, the more likely he or she is to travel. People are also living longer. Retired from the work force with their homes paid for, many senior citizens can take trips any time of the year. For most Americans, travel has become a normal expectation associated with the good life.

Reasons for Travel

Throughout history, most travel was undertaken because of necessity—not for pleasure. People traveled to satisfy basic needs for survival. They searched for food and shelter or fled from enemies. Many people traveled in search of a better life. Perhaps they were looking for gold, silver, and other treasures that would make them rich. Or they scouted for fertile farmland to which they could move their families.

This is not to say that no one ever traveled just for the fun of it. Even in ancient times, some pleasure travel occurred. During a typical season, 700,000 tourists would crowd into Ephesus, a city in Asia Minor, where they were entertained by acrobats, animal acts, jugglers, and magicians. Wealthy Romans made excursions to Greece to take in the Olympic Games, theatrical productions, and festivals.

Of course, some people were motivated to travel just out of curiosity. They wanted to know what lay beyond the horizon or around the bend in the road. Perhaps sailors joined the crews of the *Nina*, *Pinta*, and *Santa Maria* in 1492 because they wanted to find out what would happen when the ships reached the edge of the world.

There have been other motivations for travel as well. During the Middle Ages, people went on pilgrimages to holy cities and shrines. They did so to pay homage to a saint or to fulfill a vow. Some pilgrims dressed in sackcloth and walked barefoot as a sign of penance. The passport originated in 1388 when King Richard II required English pilgrims to obtain and carry permits before they could travel to France. The Crusades (1095-1291), in which Christians attempted to wrest control of the Holy Land from the Muslims, were the most ambitious religious journeys of all.

Travel for the purpose of conducting trade—in other words, business travel—has been going on for centuries. Traders from Phoenicia, a civilization that existed from 1100 B.C. to 332 B.C., sailed from port to port in the Mediterranean world. Early travel in China and India was based on trade.

Notions about cures for ailments of the body have also influenced travel. To relieve his rheumatism, the Roman emperor Caracalla (A.D. 188-217) journeyed to mineral springs located north of Rome. Juan Ponce de León, a Spanish explorer, discovered Florida in 1513 while searching for the fountain of youth. In the 1800s, it was fashionable for members of European high society to visit various German spas (different spas claimed effectiveness for different maladies). These people sipped mineral water all day and then entertained themselves with banquets, dancing, and gambling all night.

Destinations of historic and cultural significance have attracted travelers through the ages. This reason for travel originated with the grand tour in the seventh century. As part of their education, youth of the British aristocracy undertook an extended tour of Europe. Accompanied by tutors and servants, the young gentlemen visited cathedrals, castles, and galleries, especially those of France and Italy. They learned to speak several languages and were introduced to Europe's aristocracy. The grand tour usually took three years.

Check Your Product Knowledge

1. How is the modern concept of travel different from that of the Middle Ages?
2. In order for travel to occur on a wide scale, what conditions are necessary?
3. What have been some reasons for travel throughout history?

WHO TRAVELS TODAY?

In the past, wealthy travelers had similar expectations of travel. For example, in the 1920s, anyone who was anybody took the grand tour of Europe. It was fairly easy for hotel managers, captains of cruise ships, and other travel professionals to anticipate the needs of these travelers and to serve them satisfactorily.

Today's travelers are not so similar in nature; they form a larger and more diverse group of people. However, as a travel professional, you can begin to know today's travelers and their motivations, needs, and expectations (MNEs) by dividing travelers into three general categories: the vacation and leisure traveler; the business and professional traveler; and the traveler visiting friends and relatives. Figure 2-1 shows the percentage of trips taken in each of these categories. Later, you will learn more about the individual differences within these three categories.

The Vacation and Leisure Traveler

The family taking a two-week vacation to Disney World. The college student spending the summer exploring Europe. The retired couple taking a one-week cruise to Bermuda. These people represent the vacation and leisure traveler. Rather than lying in a hammock in the backyard, they use their leisure time to travel.

Discretionary Travel. Vacation and leisure travel is often called *discretionary travel*. The word *discretion* refers to the ability to make a choice, judgment, or decision. (You may have heard someone say, "Use your own discretion," when you've had a decision to make.) Vacation and leisure travelers take trips because they want to—travel is voluntary for them. They choose whether to stay home, drive to the mountains, or fly to the Caribbean.

Likewise, the money that vacation and leisure travelers spend is called discretionary income. Discretionary income is the money that's left over after the necessities of life—shelter, food, clothing—have been purchased. People choose how they want to spend their discretionary income. While some choose to spend it on travel, others may choose to spend it on boats or second homes. Since there is much competition from many industries for consumers' discretionary income, the components of the travel industry work together to persuade consumers to spend their money on travel.

The Pleasure Seekers. In general, vacation and leisure travelers seek pleasure and relaxation. However, since what gives pleasure varies from individual to individual, one person's idea of the perfect vacation is another person's idea of a total waste of time and money. Some travelers enjoy exploring ancient ruins, while others prefer sunbathing by the ocean. More will be said about specific motivations for pleasure travel later in this chapter.

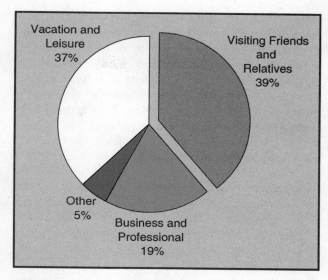

Figure 2-1 Why People Travel
Source: U.S. Travel Data Center

Another feature of vacation and leisure travel is that the pleasure comes not only during the trip but also before and after. Planning the itinerary, shopping for clothes to take along, and researching the destination can be as enjoyable as the trip itself. Once back home, putting together a scrapbook about the trip or talking about it to friends and relatives sustains the pleasure.

Purchasing Travel Products and Services. When they purchase travel products and services, vacation and leisure travelers are essentially buying an experience they hope will be pleasurable. To satisfy their needs, vacation and leisure travelers will select products and services from several of the travel components. They will certainly select products from the tourism component,

Illus. 2-1 *Vacation travelers travel because they want to.*
Source: Ulrike Welsch/Photoedit

such as tickets to a theme park or a concert. They will probably purchase hospitality products and services, although some vacationers travel by recreational vehicle and camp along the way. Depending on the size of the group, the type of trip, the distance of destination, and the time involved, vacation travelers may or may not choose air transportation. For example, even though air transportation is sometimes less expensive, families who want to visit many sites en route to their destination will find it more convenient to travel by automobile.

Vacation and leisure travelers have time to shop around for the product that best suits their needs. Often they wait for a bargain to appear before they decide on a definite trip. Their schedules are usually flexible so that they can take advantage of the travel restrictions that accompany discounted airfares. Vacation and leisure travelers are likely to purchase a package of travel products, including transportation, accommodations, and sightseeing.

The Business and Professional Traveler

A sales representative who sells pharmaceutical products to physicians and pharmacists throughout Pennsylvania, Ohio, and West Virginia. An efficiency expert who inspects operations at a company's branch locations. A lobbyist for a midwestern farmers' co-op who must attend congressional hearings in Washington, D.C. These people represent business travelers.

Business travel is *nondiscretionary travel*. Business travelers usually do not have a choice about whether or not they want to travel—nor do they usually decide where they want to travel. Travel is part of their job description. They must travel to get their job done.

A variation of business travel is professional travel. Professional travelers attend conventions and seminars related to their jobs. These meetings usually provide participants with information and skills to help them perform their jobs better. For example, a physician might attend a medical convention to obtain the latest information on the treatment of allergies. A sales representative might attend a seminar on how to improve selling skills.

Professional travel is also nondiscretionary in the sense that travelers do not decide the date or location of the convention or seminar. On the other hand, it is discretionary in that attendance at conventions and seminars is often optional. Some professional travelers are also business travelers, and vice versa. For example, a salesperson who often travels for business may also attend an annual sales convention.

Time is very important for business and professional travelers. They must arrive at meetings on time. They must get their work done on time. Since every minute away from their home office costs money, they can't afford to waste time on delays and errors.

Illus. 2-2 *For business travelers, travel is part of a day's work.*
Source: Compaq Computer Corporation

When they purchase travel products and services, business and professional travelers are essentially buying time. Products that furnish convenience of location, speed, and efficiency provide them with time. Business and professional travelers generally purchase air transportation to and from their destination, a rental car for on-demand local transportation, and accommodations in a major hotel near their meeting site.

The schedules of business and professional travelers are less flexible than those of vacation and leisure travelers. Often, because they can't plan their trips far in advance, they can't take advantage of discount airfares and other bargains. To obtain speed, efficiency, and convenience, business and professional travelers must often pay higher prices for travel products and services. Chapters 11 and 12 describe the MNEs of this group of travelers in more detail.

The Traveler Visiting Friends and Relatives

The father who takes his children to Michigan every summer to visit their grandparents. Alumni who attend their college's reunion. The son and daughter who return home because their father is ill. These people represent the traveler visiting friends and relatives.

Travelers visiting friends and relatives, often referred to as VFR, form the largest group of travelers.

Conrad Hilton

When Conrad Hilton was a child, his father ran a $1-a-night rooming house for traveling salesmen who were passing through San Antonio, New Mexico. Conrad was the second of eight children. As a boy, it was his job to meet late-night trains and guide travelers to the Hiltons' large adobe house where five rooms were kept for guests. From this small beginning, Conrad Hilton built one of the greatest hotel empires of all time.

Hilton was born in San Antonio in 1887, the son of a Norwegian immigrant. He attended Saint Michael's College in Santa Fe, New Mexico. After graduation, he managed his father's general store and traveled around New Mexico selling groceries to miners and trappers in exchange for gold dust and pelts. During World War I, Hilton served as a second lieutenant in the U.S. Army. After the war in 1919, he went to Cisco, Texas, intending to spend $5,000 to buy a bank. When the bank deal fell through, Hilton purchased the 40-room Mobley Hotel instead.

The Mobley was the beginning of Hilton's hotel empire. Using profits from the Mobley, Hilton began buying and building other hotels in Texas. By the 1930s, when the Great Depression hit, Conrad Hilton owned eight hotels. At a time when most other hotel owners went into bankruptcy, Hilton managed to keep five of his hotels. After the Depression ended, Hilton ventured out of Texas and started buying some of the most famous and most luxurious hotels in the United States. Among his purchases were the Waldorf-Astoria and Plaza hotels in New York City, the Stevens and Palmer House hotels in Chicago, the Sir Francis Drake Hotel in San Francisco, and the Mayflower Hotel in Washington, D.C.

Hilton renamed the Stevens Hotel in Chicago the Conrad Hilton. Usually, however, he did little to change the identity or character of the hotels he purchased. He believed that when he purchased a hotel, he was purchasing not just the building but the hotel's history and traditions as well.

In 1946, Hilton formed the Hilton Hotel Corporation and named himself as president. As a corporate manager, Hilton had his own distinct style. He rarely got involved in the day-to-day details of hotel operations. Instead he liked to surround himself with competent executives who took care of the details for him. Under Hilton's loose rein, the corporation continued to grow throughout the 1940s and 1950s. In 1949, Hilton opened the Caribe Hilton, a 300-room hotel in San Juan, Puerto Rico. With the Caribe, Conrad Hilton began to branch out into international hotels. His Hilton International company built or operated hotels in Mexico, Turkey, Spain, and several other countries.

By 1965, Hilton owned or operated 61 hotels in 19 countries and employed 400,000 people. The corporation was estimated to have been worth more than $500 million, and Hilton's personal wealth amounted to more than $150 million. In 1967, Hilton sold Hilton International to TWA. Hilton has been described as a charming, courteous man with enormous energy, able to dance all night and work all day with little or no sleep. He continued to work full time until just a few days before his death in 1979 at the age of 91. After his death, his son Barron took over the hotel chain.

Barron Hilton has continued to expand the Hilton empire. In the 1970s, Barron purchased two hotel-casinos in Las Vegas, Nevada, and a third in Reno, Nevada. Hilton's three Nevada casinos have been very profitable. In 1987, they accounted for about half of the hotel chain's revenues.

Barron Hilton has also revived the Hilton company's international operations. Unable to use the Hilton name outside of the United States (because of the sale of Hilton International), Barron Hilton started a new chain named the Conrad International Hotels. The new international chain has hotels in Queensland, Australia; Monte Carlo; Cancun, Mexico; and the island of Saint Martin in the French West Indies. Barron Hilton plans to enlarge the Conrad International chain to 20 hotels within the next few years. Today, the Hilton Corporation, which owns or operates more than 275 hotels, is one of the largest hotel chains in the world.

VFR travel may be discretionary or nondiscretionary, depending on the reasons for the trip. If a traveler must go out of town because of an emergency, such as an illness or a death in the family, then the travel is nondiscretionary. On the other hand, if a traveler wants to visit high school friends or spend some time with family members simply to enjoy their company, then the travel is discretionary.

Travelers who visit friends and relatives for pleasure are like leisure travelers in their purchase of travel products. Travelers who visit friends and relatives because of an emergency are more like business travelers, with an added element of stress. In either case, they are likely to purchase only transportation, and perhaps some tourism products. The friends and relatives usually supply the accommodations (a spare bedroom or the living-room sofa) and meals.

Check Your Product Knowledge

1. Name the three main groups of modern-day travelers.
2. What is the purpose of dividing travelers into these groups?
3. List the characteristics of each group.

VACATION AND LEISURE TRAVELERS

Imagine that you're a travel agent in a retail travel agency. A woman, who appears to be in her late thirties, comes into your office. She introduces herself as Mrs. O'Neill and says she wants help planning a trip to Mexico. You begin to reach for the brochures describing a family vacation in Mexico, but Mrs. O'Neill says she'll be traveling without her family. You then ask if she's seeking a sun vacation on the Mexican Riviera, but that's not it either. Mrs. O'Neill tells you she's bored with the routine of everyday life. What she really wants is a vacation experience that will challenge her mind and imagination. After thinking for a moment, you suggest that she go to Mexico to study the architectural ruins of the Aztec Indians. Mrs. O'Neill thinks that is a wonderful idea.

Discovering a vacation traveler's motivation, or reason, for traveling is very important. A travel agent needs this information in order to sell the client the right travel product for his or her needs. In the case of Mrs. O'Neill, a family vacation tour or a resort vacation would clearly have been the wrong product.

To define the product further, the travel agent needs to ask questions related to the client's background and lifestyle. You would ask Mrs. O'Neill questions such as:

Do you want to travel alone or with a group? What kind of accommodations do you want? About how much money do you want to spend? How long do you want to stay? After discussing these questions, you and Mrs. O'Neill might agree that she should join a study tour to Mexico that is being organized by the Smithsonian Institution in Washington, D.C.

Why Do They Travel?

In the dining room of a resort hotel in Balestrand, Norway, the guests are enjoying a Sunday evening smorgasbord. If you were to ask each traveler why he or she came to Norway, you would get several different responses. For example, Vern Olson, a dairy farmer from Wisconsin, wants to visit the village from which his ancestors emigrated. He's also interested in learning more about Norwegian folklore and music. Recently widowed, Dora Larson is seeking companionship from other members of her tour group. Travel posters showing magnificent mountains and fjords convinced Brian and Melissa West to make a trip to Norway. Peter Holm, a college student from Nebraska, wants to hike up to the glaciers. And, after teaching junior high students for nine months, Bill Weber is hoping this trip will restore his frazzled nerves.

Underlying stated objectives such as these may be deeper, psychological motives. For example, Andrea Stevenson enjoys the feeling of importance she gets when people wait on her. Ray and Maryann Kerncamp decided to go to Norway because last year their neighbors made a similar trip. And Mark Williams, a middle-aged bachelor, is secretly hoping to find romance.

There are many reasons for vacation and leisure travel, and travel experts have many ways of listing or describing them. In recent years, however, two theories have gained widespread acceptance in explaining travel motivation. One theory is offered by psychologist Stanley Plog, and the other by sociologist Abraham Maslow.

Stanley Plog. According to Plog's theory, an individual's personality determines his or her motivation for travel and choice of destination. Plog uses a continuum to describe vacation and leisure travelers (Figure 2-2 shows the continuum, along with possible destinations for each personality type).

At one end of the continuum is the *allocentric personality* (allo means "varied in form"). Allocentric personalities seek adventure, variety, and excitement. They want to experience totally different cultures and environments. They might choose to visit an isolated hill tribe in India and stay in native lodgings, eat native food, and participate in native dances and ceremonies. Allocentric personalities shun traditional destinations and modes of transportation. They may be seen driving a jeep across the Sahara or paddling a dugout canoe on the inland waters of Panama. Allocentric personalities are trendset-

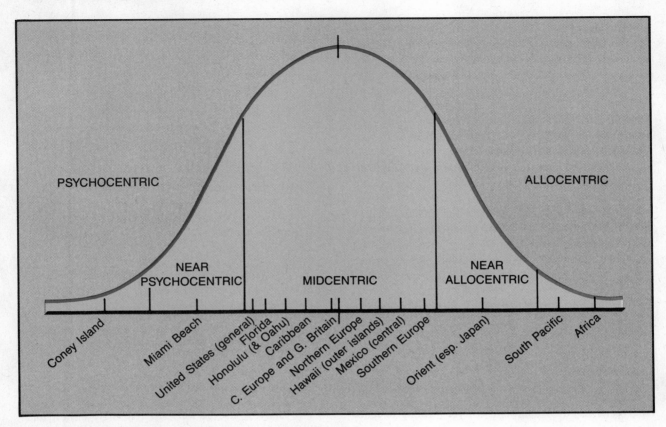

Figure 2-2 Plog's Continuum of Vacation and Leisure Travelers

ters—they help to establish new destinations. When those destinations become popular with other travelers, then allocentrics move on to explore new territory.

At the opposite end of the continuum is the *psychocentric personality* (psyche means "self"). Psychocentric personalities, who tend to focus their thoughts on themselves and their families, don't travel much. When they do go away, they don't venture too far from home. For example, if they live in the South, they might travel to New Orleans, Nashville, or Miami. Psychocentric personalities need consistency and reliability in their travel products. Often, they return to the same place year after year. They don't want to experiment with accommodations, food, or entertainment. Nor do they want to experience personal stress or encounter unusual situations.

Falling between these two extremes is the *midcentric personality*. Most vacation and leisure travelers fit into this category. Midcentric personalities travel in order to obtain a break from their everyday routine. They want to strike a healthy balance between work and recreation. Midcentric personalities aren't afraid to try new travel experiences as long as these experiences are not too bizarre or challenging. The environment can't seem too foreign—a fast-food restaurant in the midst of seventeenth-century buildings is reassuring to them. Midcentric personalities often go where their friends have gone.

They tend to travel to familiar destinations, such as the Caribbean, Hawaii, and Great Britain. They might go to Hong Kong, Tokyo, and Manila, but most places in the Far East are too extreme for them.

Abraham Maslow. Maslow's theory centers on the belief that needs satisfaction motivates human behavior. Maslow developed five areas of human needs and arranged them in a hierarchy. (Figure 2-3 shows Maslow's hierarchy of human needs.) Like climbing a ladder, individuals start at the bottom of the hierarchy and work their way up. The needs at a lower level must be met before the individual can proceed to a higher level. In other words, individuals must first satisfy their needs for food, shelter, and clothing before seeking safety and security. When their needs for safety and security have been met, then they are free to seek love and the company of other people, and so on.

As applied to travel, Maslow's theory suggests that vacation and leisure travelers are motivated by the desire to satisfy needs. People who lack money for food, shelter, and clothing can't travel for pleasure. But, after basic physical and emotional needs have been met, travel meets people's needs for esteem, respect, and self-actualization. (Self-actualization is Maslow's term for the highest level of personal fulfillment.)

Travelers who feel a need to be with other people may purchase an escorted group tour or a cruise with many planned activities. Travelers who feel a need for respect may purchase a travel product that will impress their friends and associates. This might be a trip to an exotic destination or a stay in a ritzy resort or hotel. Travelers who feel a need for self-actualization are beyond trying to impress their friends. Instead, they want a travel product that will help them develop physically, mentally, or spiritually. They might choose a bicycle tour through Ireland, a study tour of France's chateaus, or a trip to Mecca.

Maslow's hierarchy of needs operates on different levels for different activities at different times. The hierarchy also operates within a single travel experience. For example, sudden terrorist activities at a destination will bring a vacation back down to the level of safety and security—needs for esteem, respect, and self-actualization must be set aside. While on vacation in Europe, a traveler may receive news that a family member has become seriously ill. The traveler's needs then shift to a basic emotional level, as he or she attempts to deal with the crisis.

In addition to planning travel products and services to meet human needs, travel professionals must recognize when needs change and adapt products and services accordingly. In the case of a traveler with a critically ill relative, a hotel manager might arrange for long-distance telephone calls, and the tour escort might arrange for quick transportation back home.

Who Are the Travelers?

Modern-day travelers are a diverse group of people, with varying MNEs. Consequently, the travel industry doesn't create one product and try to sell it to everybody. The industry recognizes, for example, that young, single persons comprise a market different from senior citizens or young families. The concept that the travel market is really many submarkets is known as *market segmentation*.

Thousands of market segments exist, and there is no standard classification system. As you've seen, a general classification system is that of vacation and leisure traveler, business and professional traveler, and traveler visiting friends and relatives. But each of these can be further divided into segments according to travel habits and preferences, kind of transportation used, how travel arrangements are made, class of service purchased, and many other factors. Furthermore, each component of the travel industry may have one or more ways of segmenting its own market. For example, airlines classify their customers into first class, business class, and economy class. But they also categorize them according to destinations and routes.

The travel industry depends on two kinds of marketing research in identifying and describing each market segment. *Primary research* is carried out by the travel industry itself. For instance, airlines, buses, and cruise

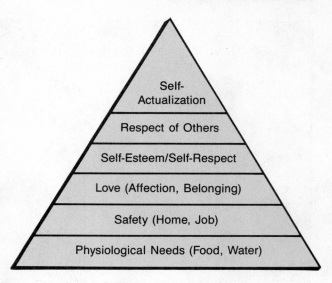

Figure 2-3 Maslow's Hierarchy of Needs

Source: "Hierarchy of Needs" from MOTIVATION AND PERSONALITY, by Abraham H. Maslow. Copyright 1954 by Harper & Row, Publishers, Inc. Copyright © 1970 by Abraham H. Maslow. Reprinted by permission of HarperCollins Publishers.

ships—or marketing firms hired by them—conduct onboard surveys of passengers. Hotels leave questionnaires in guests' rooms and periodically review their guest ledgers. Airlines and hotels interview travelers at airports and resorts. Another kind of research, called *secondary research*, is based on information from other sources, such as a census conducted by the federal government or a study conducted by the United States Travel Data Center.

The travelers in a particular market segment are assumed to have similar purchasing habits. With the information gathered in market research, the travel industry can tailor specific products for that segment and plan specific marketing strategies. The information collected is in the form of demographics or psychographics.

Demographics. *Demographics* are statistics and facts that describe a human population. They include age, income, sex, marital status, size of family, education, occupation, residence, ethnic origin, and religion. Based on demographic information, the travel industry can describe vacation and leisure travelers with statements such as the following:

- More urban dwellers travel than do rural dwellers.
- People with college degrees are more likely to travel than are people without college degrees.
- Blue-collar workers tend to prefer group travel, whereas executives and professional-level workers tend to prefer more individualized travel.
- There is a strong relationship between travel and age—approximately 71 percent of the 18-to-24 age group travels, 70 percent of the 25-to-49 age group, 64 percent of the 50-to-64 age group, and 38 percent of the 65-and-over age group.

■ People with a high income and a high level of education tend to travel by air and stay in hotels, whereas people with a lower income and less education tend to travel by car or bus and stay with family and friends.

■ The majority of overseas travelers have traveled abroad in the past.

Demographic information can also uncover potentially lucrative markets for the travel industry. For instance, recent data reveal that there are approximately 37 million physically handicapped people in the United States. Many of these people would be willing to travel if the travel industry would provide products and services to meet their needs. Travel enterprises are now reaching out to this market segment by modifying structures to allow for wheelchair access (wider hotel-room doors, ramps at the entrance of buildings), allowing an aide to travel at a reduced price, or offering tours geared to the handicapped. Winter Park, Colorado, offers special ski programs for blind people and other handicapped vacationers.

Psychographics. Demographics, which provide objective information, can't fully describe market segments. *Psychographics* furnish more subjective information. Psychographic research asks travelers to reveal their activities, interests, and opinions. Such information might suggest, for instance, that young people travel to experience excitement, independence, and new environments.

Psychographic information also relates an individual's life stage, or position in the life cycle, to travel. Because they have more time and money, young, single people and young, newly married, childless couples tend to travel more for pleasure. Married couples with dependent children, or single parents, tend to travel less. When they do travel, they go by car or camper and stay with friends and relatives. Recently retired people and married, older couples with no dependent children return to pleasure travel—buying air transportation and cruises.

While uncovering the attitudes of travelers, psychographic information is also useful in uncovering the attitudes of nontravelers. A great many people do not travel, even though they have the time and money. Barriers to travel may include fear of the unknown, fear of flying, lack of interest, or even uneasiness about how to tip in a restaurant. Once such barriers are revealed, products and services can be designed to overcome them. Airlines, for example, introduced in-flight movies partly to keep nervous passengers from thinking about their fear of flying. Nontravelers represent a vast, untapped resource for the travel industry.

Psychographics show what travelers expect from their vacation experience. The travel industry seeks to market its products and services based on these expecta-

tions. If a traveler seeks glamour and romance, then the product might be a trip to Paris, with accommodations in an elegant hotel. If a traveler seeks outdoor adventure, then the product might be a white-water rafting trip in Colorado.

Check Your Product Knowledge

1. Why is it important for the travel professional to understand why people travel?
2. According to Stanley Plog, what determines an individual's choice of travel experience and destination?
3. Why does the travel industry divide the travel market into segments?
4. What two methods of research are used to obtain information about travelers?
5. What is the difference between demographic information and psychographic information?

DOMESTIC VACATION TRAVEL

Where do vacation and leisure travelers go? The majority of United States travelers visit destinations within the United States. In 1988, United States citizens spent $542 billion on domestic vacation trips.

See the United States of America

A few years ago, an often-repeated travel slogan was "See America First." This campaign was in response to the fact that growing numbers of Americans were traveling to Europe. However, domestic travel has always been popular among vacation and leisure travelers.

Because of its vast size, the United States offers a diversity of travel experiences. Travelers can enjoy the seashore of Virginia, the plains of Kansas, the mountains of Colorado, or the deserts of Arizona and Nevada. The Grand Canyon, Niagara Falls, and Old Faithful are just a few of this nation's natural wonders. The climate also varies widely in the United States. The tropical climate of Hawaii, the hot and dry weather in New Mexico, and the cold, snowy winters of Minnesota have created different and interesting lifestyles and activities. Many regions of the United States have maintained the ethnic traditions of the people who settled there. The upper Midwest, for example, demonstrates a strong Scandinavian influence, while the Southwest continues Spanish traditions. Thus, the United States can provide samples of the food, music, and customs of cultures from all over the world.

Many Americans, especially families with young children, find it less expensive to travel within the United

Illus. 2-3 *Because America is so large, it offers a variety of sights, climates, and cultures to the domestic traveler.*
Source: (top) Niagara Falls Convention and Visitors Bureau, Inc. (bottom) Colorado Tourism Bureau

States. Vacationers can usually save money traveling by passenger car or recreational vehicle. An excellent system of roads, with restaurants and motels along the way, makes highway traveling pleasant. In fact, highway travelers represent the largest segment of this country's tourists.

Many Americans also find domestic traveling more convenient. Travelers who stay in the United States don't have to apply for passports, get shots, or exchange their currency. They don't have to worry about not understanding the language.

Recognizing the economic benefits of tourism, most states are developing even more of their resources to entertain domestic travelers. State tourism offices are vigorously promoting their states' attractions—especially through television advertising in neighboring states. For 1989–1990, travel office budgets for the 50 states totaled over $340 million, as compared with under $90 million for 1980. Hawaii, New York, and Illinois rank as the top

three states in spending for tourism promotion.

In addition to these reasons for domestic travel, world events influence the travel plans of vacationers. In the early 1990s, the war in the Persian Gulf and threats of terrorism against Americans caused many Americans to cancel overseas travel plans. Also, when the value of the dollar declines abroad, as it did in the early 1990s, Americans tend to stay home.

Where Do Travelers Go?

The California redwoods. Disneyland. The White House. Colonial Williamsburg. The Empire State Building. The Everglades. Mount Rushmore. Wrigley Field. The Blue Ridge Mountains. These are just a handful of America's numerous tourist attractions. Chapter 9 will give you an overview of the wide variety of public and commercial tourist attractions in the United States.

A DAY IN THE LIFE OF
Three Travelers

Woman Business Traveler:
I spend about 15 days out of each month traveling for business. Usually I know my travel plans well in advance, so my travel agent can get good flights and prices for me. Last week, for instance, I spent three days in Los Angeles. I arranged that trip six weeks ago, and my agent got discount rates for me. Nowadays, there can be a penalty for cancellations, so I have to make sure that I know exactly what I'll be doing. Sometimes, of course, I need to make last-minute plans or make changes during a trip. The agency's toll-free number helps when I have to make changes from far away.

My travel agent keeps a file on me. She knows that I prefer to fly business class, and that I prefer certain airlines because I have some frequent flier bonuses to build on. She even knows that I prefer an aisle seat. When she books a flight for me, she gets a seat assignment and boarding pass in advance so that I don't have to stand in line when I arrive at the airport.

My agent also knows my hotel needs and makes the necessary reservations. She knows that my first requirement is that the hotel be near my meeting location. But I insist on certain standards. I don't like eating alone in a hotel restaurant, so room service is important, especially since I often have to spend the evening before a meeting reading papers and preparing. Sometimes I have to meet with clients in my hotel room. When I know that will happen, I ask my agent to book a suite for me. I also like to exercise while I'm away, so I want a hotel with a swimming pool and an exercise room.

The primary thing I look to my travel agent for, though, is a trouble-free trip: direct flights or good connections, a comfortable hotel, and no surprises.

Emergency Travelers:
Recently my husband and I had to make an unexpected trip to Los Angeles to attend my uncle's funeral. Since I was appointed executor of his will, we also had to spend some time there sorting matters out. We had only two days' notice before the trip, but our travel agent was able to make good arrangements.

In our case, we had little flexibility—we had to get from Chicago to Los Angeles as quickly as possible. We also needed a rental car. I was pleased that the travel agent saved us money by finding a discounted airfare for our flight and by getting us a subcompact rental car. We had only two suitcases, and all we needed the car for was to get us around town. It certainly wasn't a pleasure trip, and we didn't expect to do any sightseeing.

Our agent was also helpful in suggesting that we should not book a round-trip flight. Sure enough, the settlements didn't go quite as smoothly as we had hoped, and we had to stay a day or two longer than we'd anticipated. Waiting to book the flight until we knew our departure date was a good idea.

An experienced travel agent made an unpleasant trip a lot easier. The agent's understanding of the purpose of our trip and our traveling needs really helped us out. The next time we take a vacation, I know where we'll go to make our travel arrangements.

Family Vacation Travelers:
Finally, our family was to take the vacation we'd been planning for some time—a trip to Disneyland. It was a package tour with the flight to Los Angeles, the bus trip to Anaheim, and the accommodations all included in one price. Our travel agent suggested this particular package when we told her we wanted to go to Disneyland. It was a good choice. It gave us enough structure to have something to do when we wanted it, and enough freedom to explore other avenues if we wished.

The flight was our kids' first, and the airline we were booked on seemed to take a special interest in children. The hotel we stayed in was fantastic—two well-guarded swimming pools, several game rooms, shuttle service to Disneyland, and state-certified child care for a nominal fee—a great help for our one "parents' night out." We would never have found such a perfect place on our own.

I really have to hand it to our travel agent, in fact, for sizing up the family and its needs after only a short conversation. We've never had a better time on a vacation; of course, there's always next year.

Photo Source: © THE WALT DISNEY COMPANY

Although almost every area of the United States has fascinating tourist attractions, vacation and leisure travelers visit certain states more frequently than they do others. For beautiful scenery—mountains, lakes, seashores, parks—and peaceful, quiet locations, vacation travelers favor the Rocky Mountain states and the New England states. For sunshine and outdoor sports—swimming, sailing, horseback riding, surfing, tennis—travelers head for Florida, California, Texas, and Hawaii. In fact, these four states account for more than one-quarter of the nation's domestic tourism receipts. For fine dining, shopping, historical sites, and cultural activities—theater, opera, ballet, concerts, museums, and art galleries—travelers visit Los Angeles, Chicago, New York City, Boston, New Orleans, and Washington, D.C.

Check Your Product Knowledge

1. What is meant by domestic tourism?
2. What factors favor domestic tourism in the United States?
3. Which states tend to draw the most vacation and leisure travelers? Why?

FOREIGN VACATION TRAVEL

The United States has much to offer vacation and leisure travelers. But there are certain sights and experiences that are available only through travel to foreign countries. There is just one Eiffel Tower, and people must go to Paris to see it. Only India has the Taj Mahal. For many people, books and television documentaries about foreign countries can't replace the excitement of experiencing a different culture firsthand. Many Americans dream about going to faraway places and consider their lives to be incomplete until they've traveled abroad.

In 1990, more than 44 million Americans visited foreign countries (see Table 2-1). Of this number, about 16 million traveled overseas, 13 million traveled to Canada, and 16 million traveled to Mexico. The overseas destinations most frequently visited were the United Kingdom, France, Germany, Italy, and Japan.

Compared with domestic tourism, travel to other countries usually requires far more preparation. Travelers must prepare various documents, obtain traveler's checks or exchange currency, take precautions to safeguard their health, and inform themselves about customs regulations. There are several free United States government publications that highlight the concerns of the foreign traveler. These pamphlets include *Know Before You Go* from the United States Customs Service and *Traveler's Tips* from the United States Department of Agriculture. As a travel professional, you can assist travelers with special aspects of foreign travel so that they have a safe and pleasant trip.

Documentation

Documentation refers to government-issued papers used to identify travelers. These documents include passports, visas, tourist cards, and vaccination certificates. When travelers enter or leave a country, immigration officials

Destination	Departures (in thousands)	Percent Change 1990/1989	Percent Change 1990/1985
Canada	12,664	-2%	5%
Mexico	15,560	9%	49%
Overseas	15,849	7.2%	25%
Europe	7,465	8%	16%
Caribbean	3,941	6%	24%
Asia	2,073	7%	41%
South America	817	-4%	47%
Central America	720	20%	84%
Oceania	583	12%	76%
Middle East	200	-2%	-20%
Africa	50	4%	-56%
Total All Countries	44,073	6%	25%

Table 2-1 American Travelers Abroad, 1990
Source: U.S. Travel and Tourism Administration

ask to see these papers. Documentation enables governments to regulate travel.

Passport. A *passport* enables travelers to pass through ports, that is, to enter a foreign country and to return to their native country. By means of passports, governments approve the travel of their citizens and request protection for them while they travel abroad.

Countries that do not have diplomatic relations with each other do not honor each other's passports. If a country is experiencing political upheaval or terrorism, or if there is some other condition that would make travel difficult, such as a shortage of hotel rooms, the United States Department of State will issue a travel advisory for that area. For example, in the early 1990s, the State Department advised Americans against traveling to the war-torn countries of the Middle East. In some cases, the government will ban travel altogether—any citizens traveling to the restricted area do so at their own risk. These travel advisories are made available to travel agents through the trade press and through the agency computer system.

Every individual must have his or her own passport—family passports are no longer issued. To obtain a United States passport for the first time, a citizen applies in person at a passport agency, state or federal court building, or post office. Along with the completed application, the person submits:

- Proof of citizenship (a birth certificate or certificate of naturalization—not a driver's license).
- Two recent photos (2" x 2").
- Proof of identity (a driver's license or a document not used for proof of citizenship that bears the applicant's signature and physical description).
- Fee (for adults 18 years and older, currently $55 plus a $10 execution fee).

Since it can take two months to process an application, travelers should apply for their passports well ahead of their scheduled departure. Passports are valid for ten years and may be renewed by mail.

A passport is in the form of a wallet-sized booklet. Travelers should carry their passports with them at all times. If they lose any of their documentation while traveling overseas, they should go immediately to the nearest United States embassy or consulate and report the loss. There is a United States embassy in most major world capitals. Each *embassy* is the official residence of the United States ambassador for that country. It also houses diplomats and other officials. *Consulates* are like branch offices of embassies and are located in major cities other than the capital. Just as the United States has embassies in the capitals of foreign countries, so those countries have embassies in Washington, D.C. Both embassies and consulates can assist tourists traveling in foreign countries.

Illus. 2-4 *A visa is one of several ways a government regulates travel in and out of its country.*

Visa. While a passport is issued by the traveler's own government, a *visa* is issued by a foreign government. A visa is a stamp or endorsement placed in the traveler's passport, specifying the conditions for entering a country.

Vacation and leisure travelers apply either for a transit visa, which allows them just enough time to pass through a country, or for a tourist visa, which allows them to stay in the country for a specific period of time. Travelers to the Soviet Union, for instance, can obtain a one-month tourist visa for between $15 and $25. Tourist visas generally permit multiple entries—that is, travelers can leave the country on side trips and then return. Other types of visas may be required for travelers who intend to conduct business in a foreign country, for students who will attend school in a foreign country, or for people who plan to establish long-term residence in a foreign country.

About 60 percent of the world's countries still require visitors to have tourist visas. This is beginning to change, however. American citizens no longer need tourist visas to travel to most countries in Western Europe. Travelers can obtain visas directly from a foreign country's embassy or through a travel agency or a visa service. Since visas are stamped into travelers' passports, the passport must be sent along with the visa application. This means that the process for obtaining a passport should be started even earlier when one or more visas are needed.

Proof of Citizenship. When relations are friendly between certain countries, such as between the United States and Canada, a passport is not necessary. Instead travelers on vacation who stay less than six months may simply carry some *proof of citizenship*. An expired passport, a birth certificate, a naturalization certificate, or a voter registration card may be used to show allegiance. A driver's license, however, is not proof of citizenship.

Tourist Card. Another type of document is a *tourist card*. Along with proof of citizenship, it can be used instead of a passport in some countries, such as Mexico. Travelers can obtain tourist cards from the foreign government's embassy or through a travel agency or an airline.

Vaccination Certificate. For travel to certain countries, travelers need immunizations, or shots, to protect themselves from various diseases and to prevent the spread of diseases. An *International Certificate of Vaccination* verifies that a traveler has received the proper immunizations. The certificate is a passport-sized yellow pamphlet with space to list the date of each vaccination and its date of expiration. Many travelers use this "yellow card" to record other health information, such as any medications that must be taken frequently.

Immunizations are no longer required for direct travel between the United States and developed nations, such as Japan and the countries of Western Europe. Even so, health officials recommend that travelers be sure they have received routine childhood vaccinations and have kept up with booster shots. For instance, adults should have a diphtheria-tetanus booster every ten years.

Some countries in Africa and Asia may require cholera vaccinations. Countries in Africa and South America may require yellow fever vaccinations. To help prevent hepatitis, an injection of gamma globulin is recommended for travelers who will be visiting the rural areas of underdeveloped countries, where sanitary conditions are often poor.

Since vaccination requirements change depending on the current health situation, travelers should get up-to-date information from public health departments. The Centers for Disease Control in Atlanta, Georgia, can also advise them on health conditions in various parts of the world.

Customs

Just as governments regulate who may leave and who may enter their countries, they also regulate what goods may be brought in and what goods may be taken out. This type of regulation is referred to as *customs*. Immigration and customs are usually handled as a single process, although they may involve two or more government bureaus or agencies working together. In the United States, the immigration procedures are handled by the Immigration and Naturalization Service; passports are issued to United States citizens by a special bureau in the United States Department of State.

Outgoing customs checks seek to prevent travelers from taking certain items out of a country. For example, some countries prohibit travelers from removing an archeological treasure, even if the traveler has paid for it. Incoming customs checks seek to discourage travelers from purchasing too many foreign-made items at the ex-

pense of domestic manufacturing. These checks also seek to prevent the importation of items harmful to humans, animals, or plants. In the United States, responsibility for customs checks resides with the United States Customs Service, a branch of the Treasury Department.

Duty-Free Purchases. Travelers pay a *duty*, or tax, on items purchased abroad. However, under present United States Customs Service regulations, travelers returning to the United States are allowed $400 worth of *duty-free* purchases. They do not have to pay any taxes on those goods. The travelers must have been out of the country for more than 48 hours, and they can take the exemption only once every 30 days. (If these requirements are not met, only $25 worth of items are duty-free.) The items must be taken through customs by the traveler and must be for his or her personal use. Travelers may be required to show receipts for expensive purchases.

After the $400 exemption, the next $1,000 worth of items is assessed a flat duty of 10 percent. Thus, if a traveler spent $1,400 for foreign goods, the duty would be $100. The amount of duty is variable beyond the $1,000 level.

Under the Generalized System of Preferences (GSP), no duty, or a lower duty, is charged on goods purchased in developing countries. The Caribbean Basin Recovery Act is similar to the GSP for designated Caribbean and Central American countries. The purpose of these programs is to stimulate the economies of poorer countries by making their goods seem more attractive to visitors.

Duty-Free Shops. Located in international airports, duty-free shops sell merchandise at reduced prices to departing travelers. Many travelers believe that they won't have to pay duty on items purchased in these shops. This is not true—items purchased in foreign duty-free shops are subject to customs regulations upon the traveler's return home. "Duty-free" means that the seller hasn't been required to pay a duty on the merchandise and thus can sell it at reduced prices. In addition, the traveler does not have to pay sales tax on the merchandise.

Departure Taxes. Most countries charge some kind of *departure tax*. Visitors to a country are expected to pay this tax when they leave. Usually it is not a large sum— the equivalent of between $2 and $25. The United States departure tax is $6. Governments use the revenues from departure taxes to help fund their work in promoting and regulating tourism.

Forbidden and Restricted Purchases. Animals and plants officially listed as endangered may not be brought into the United States. This is also true of products made from endangered species. These products include ornaments and clothing made from crocodile skin, lizard skin, the shells of sea turtles, the skin of spotted cats, and the tusks of Asian and African elephants. Thus, if a person purchased a leopard-skin coat while traveling abroad, United States Customs officials would confiscate it without reimbursement—even though the person purchased the coat legally. To avoid losing hundreds of dollars in purchases, travelers should know what animals are on the list of endangered species.

Most agricultural products are also forbidden, since they may bear diseases or pests. Even seemingly innocent items such as a mango or a salami may be dangerous. The Mediterranean fruit fly, which caused an agricultural crisis in California in 1980, may have been introduced to this country through a single imported orange. Besides confiscating prohibited items, the United States Department of Agriculture (USDA) also collects fines. At some international airports, USDA officials use "beagle brigades" to check the baggage of overseas travelers. These beagles have a keen sense of smell and have been specially trained to sniff out meat and fruit hidden in baggage.

Some items may be brought into the United States only if travelers obtain permits and follow strict regulations. These include:

- Automobiles.
- Pre-Columbian artifacts.

- Firearms and ammunition.
- Medicines containing narcotics.
- Merchandise from certain countries, such as North Korea, Vietnam, Cambodia, and Cuba.

Common Health Problems

Any travelers going out of their own country should think about medical care before they leave. This is especially true for those who have a preexisting medical condition that might flare up while they are away. Travelers can prepare for such an emergency by getting a directory of doctors throughout the world. A list can be obtained from the International Association for Medical Assistance to Travelers (IAMAT), the World Medical Association, or the International Health Care Service.

Diarrhea. Whether it's called Montezuma's Revenge or Delhi Belly, diarrhea ranks as one of the most common illnesses of people traveling abroad. The cause is usually an unfamiliar intestinal bacteria picked up from untreated water or unclean food. Symptoms may also include fever and vomiting.

Travelers can help prevent diarrhea by watching their eating and drinking habits. They should avoid dairy

Illus. 2-5 *Governments use the customs regulation to control the importation of goods that are potentially harmful to humans, animals, or plants.*
Source: *Miami International Airport*

products unless they're sure the milk or cream in the product was pasteurized. They should also avoid "cold" food, such as sliced meats or hard-boiled eggs, unless they're certain of the refrigeration. Raw or undercooked meat and raw fruits and vegetables may also cause problems. Most travelers have heard "Don't drink the water," but not all travelers realize that they must be careful about the ice added to beverages. In addition, travelers should be sure not to swallow any water when brushing their teeth.

If diarrhea does occur, it's vital to prevent dehydration. Diarrhea victims should drink plenty of liquids—tea, bottled water, soda pop, or broth. An over-the-counter diarrhea medicine may be taken. If symptoms persist longer than three days, a physician should be consulted. The nearest American embassy or consulate will have a list of local doctors who speak English.

Dysynchronosis. The symptoms of this traveler's disease are irregular sleeping and waking and physical exhaustion. Dysynchronosis (meaning "time out of sync") sounds frightful until you hear its common name—jet lag.

Jet lag results from transatlantic and transpacific flights. Because travelers pass through several time zones in a short period of time, the body's natural biological clock becomes confused. For instance, passengers might take off from Chicago at 5:30 P.M. and fly nonstop to London. They arrive at 1:00 A.M.. Chicago time, but it's already 7:00 A.M. London time. The travelers are ready for bed, while Londoners are ready for a full day's activities. It will take two or three days for the travelers' biological clocks to reset themselves to the new time schedule.

To minimize the effects of jet lag, some authorities suggest that, before departing, travelers gradually adjust their eating and sleeping schedule to that of their destination. However, this is often difficult to do, especially in the busy and exciting week before departure. Travelers should try not to become overtired on the day of departure. During the flight, they should drink plenty of non-alcoholic liquids and try to doze for a while. Sleeping pills, motion sickness medicine, tobacco, and caffeine tend to aggravate jet lag.

Once arrived at their destination, travelers should not attempt a full day of sightseeing. Nor should they sleep themselves out, or they will be wide awake at the wrong times. Instead, they should rest for two or three hours and then force themselves to get up and pursue some activity, such as a short sightseeing trip.

Sleepy travelers should not try to drive a car the first day or two. This would be especially hazardous in the British Isles, where Americans must adjust to driving on the left side of the road!

Motion Sickness. In the movies, motion sickness is often treated with humor. The audience laughs at passengers on a cruise ship moaning and groaning in their berths or turning green and hanging their heads over the railing. But in real life, motion sickness is miserable.

Motion sickness is caused by the effect of motion on the fluid in the inner ear. Its symptoms are dizziness, nausea, vomiting, and fatigue. Travelers can become sick while riding in an airplane, car, train, or boat.

Prescription and over-the-counter drugs are available to minimize the effects of motion sickness. A popular prescription medication is in the form of a small adhesive patch, which the traveler places behind his or her ear. The medication is slowly released into the bloodstream for 72 hours. The patch must be applied from 4 to 16 hours before exposure to motion. Acupressure wristbands have also gained popularity in recent years.

Altitude Sickness. Travelers to Mexico City (altitude 7,349 feet), La Paz, Bolivia (altitude 12,200 feet), and other destinations with high altitudes may experience breathlessness, headache, heart pains, nausea, and severe fatigue. Altitude sickness develops when the body doesn't receive enough oxygen. Although sea-level air and high-mountain air contain the same percentage of oxygen, the reduced air pressure at higher altitudes makes oxygen less available to the lungs.

After two to six days, the traveler's lungs and heart will become accustomed to the higher altitude. To prevent acute altitude sickness, vacationers should rest during the first day, eat and drink with moderation, and have their main meal at midday. Stopping to rest during the ascent or descent—even staying overnight at a lower altitude—helps the body adjust to the change in altitude. Skiers and mountain climbers should limit strenuous activity to half a day during the first 24 to 48 hours. For people who must travel directly to high altitudes, a prescription drug called acetazolamide is available.

Foreign Currency

Travelers should be familiar with the currency used in countries they plan to visit and its value in United States dollars. A money-conversion chart or a small programmable exchange calculator would be handy for travelers to take with them.

When exchanging dollars, travelers are actually buying a foreign currency. How much foreign currency United States dollars will buy depends on the current rate of exchange. Today, 1 United States dollar might buy 5 French francs. In two months, 1 dollar might buy 8 francs. But in four months, 1 dollar might buy only 4 francs. Political, social, and economic factors contribute to fluctuating exchange rates.

The rate of exchange often determines where travelers go. American travelers tend to go to places where the dollar buys more and to stay away from places where the dollar buys less. Since the mid-1970s, Mexico has been a travel bargain for Americans because of the continuing devaluation of the peso. (In early 1991, the Mexican peso had fallen to about 2,960 to the dollar and was expected to continue to decline.) Sometimes the exchange rate can change drastically while travelers are on vacation, and they may either run out of money or find themselves with more money to spend.

There are four ways to exchange money, and travelers will probably want to use a combination of these methods:

- Obtain foreign currency before departure. It's a good idea to purchase a small amount of foreign currency before leaving home. On arrival at their destination, travelers will be able to pay for a taxi or a telephone call immediately. This is an especially good idea if they will be arriving at night or on the weekend, when banks and exchange offices are closed.
- Use a credit card and be billed later in United States dollars. By paying for major purchases, such as hotels and airfare, with a credit card, travelers can spread the cost of a trip over time. The exchange rate is the rate in effect the day the bill is posted and may or may not be similar to the rate in effect the day of the purchase.
- Buy traveler's checks in foreign currency before departure. When cashing these abroad, travelers won't be charged a conversion fee. Foreign traveler's checks and currency are available from the international banking department of a major bank or from a foreign exchange company.
- Buy traveler's checks in United States dollars and exchange for cash as needed. These are good anywhere and any leftover traveler's checks can be used when travelers return home.

In addition to knowing *how* to exchange their money, travelers should know *where* to exchange money overseas. For example, banks offer the best exchange rates, but they have limited hours, and travelers often have to stand in line and go through a formal procedure. On the other hand, they can cash traveler's checks at their hotel, which is convenient, but hotels charge a service fee.

Finally, travelers must know if a country limits the amount of currency that may be brought in or if a country forbids the export of its currency. United States Customs requires that travelers departing or arriving with more than $10,000 in any kind of monetary form (United States or foreign currency or coin, traveler's checks, money orders, investment securities) report this on Customs Form 4790. Some countries require travelers to purchase in advance set amounts of nonexportable currency.

Foreign Languages

Some travelers worry about being able to communicate in a foreign country, while others consider this part of the fun of traveling abroad. Since English is widely spoken in developed nations, communicating is generally not a major problem—especially if travelers are part of a tour group, where selected hotels and attractions cater to American tourists. Signs using pictographs also guide travelers to restrooms, exits, subways, and other important destinations.

However, tourists will find that they are well received if they can speak at least a few words of the native tongue, such as "Good morning," "How are you?" and "Thank you." Being able to identify foreign words on menus and street signs will make traveling safer and more pleasant. Foreign-language dictionaries are available to help travelers learn the meaning of important words and phrases. Also, in many parts of the United States, foreign-language classes geared to the needs of travelers are available.

Travelers who intend to rent a car should learn international road signs before leaving home—not while they're driving on the autobahn (German expressway) for the first time! And, since most of the world follows the metric system, travelers should carry a conversion chart with them. Then, when they see "Neustadt/78 km" on a road sign, they'll have a better idea of the distance to the next town.

Check Your Product Knowledge

1. Name five types of documentation. What is the purpose of each?
2. What are the two purposes of customs regulations for travelers entering the United States?
3. Name four health problems common among international travelers.
4. What are four ways to exchange money?
5. List categories of foreign words and phrases a traveler should know.

INBOUND TOURISM

What do you know about the lifestyle of a British working-class person? Can you speak French? What type of food does a German prefer? How do Japanese customs differ from United States customs?

As a travel professional, you will help United States citizens to travel domestically and internationally. But you may also have an opportunity to assist people from other countries who visit the United States. *Inbound tourism,* or vacation and leisure travel to the United States, is a rapidly growing segment of the travel market. Figure 2-4 shows the growth of inbound tourism in recent years, while Figure 2-5 shows the growth of outbound tourism. To design appropriate products and services for inbound tourists, travel professionals must get to know the needs of these travelers as well.

Who Are the Travelers?

Between 1985 and 1990, the number of foreign visitors to the United States increased by more than 50 percent. In 1990, approximately 40 million foreign travelers visited

the United States, spending more than $44 billion. There were 17 million visitors from Canada, 8 million from Mexico, and 15 million from overseas (see Table 2-2). Of European visitors, most were from the United Kingdom, and of Asian visitors, most were from Japan.

For the most part, these visitors are from highly developed, industrialized countries, where there is a high standard of living and people have time and money to travel. For example, 95 percent of England's blue-collar workers receive four weeks of paid vacation annually. Along with the rise in personal affluence, the decline of the United States dollar and low transoceanic airfares make travel to the United States

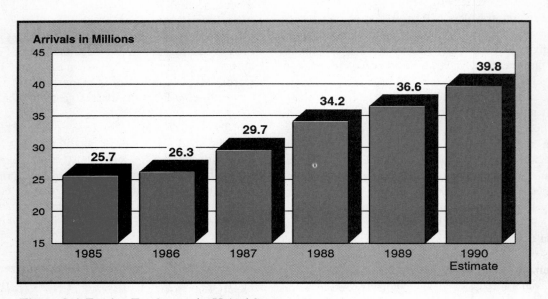

Figure 2-4 Foreign Tourism to the United States
Source: U.S. Travel and Tourism Administration

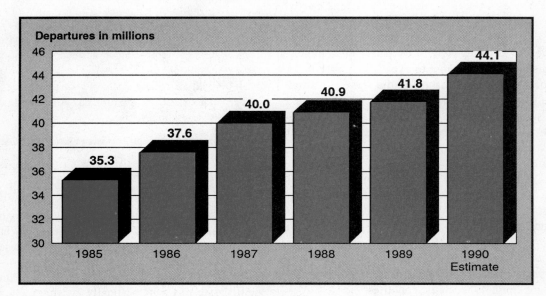

Figure 2-5 Outbound Travel by Americans
Source: U.S. Travel and Tourism Administration

Origin	Arrivals (in thousands)	Percent Change 1990/ 1989	Percent Change 1990/ 1985
Canada	17,179	12%	58%
Mexico	7,745	7%	6%
Overseas	14,849	6%	97%
Europe	6,544	5%	125%
Asia/Middle East	4,689	7%	75%
South America	1,264	12%	62%
Caribbean	1,144	3%	57%
Oceania	658	9%	92%
Central America	412	7%	44%
Africa	137	0%	5%
Total All Countries	39,772	9%	55%

Table 2-2 Foreign Visitor Arrivals, 1990

Source: U.S. Travel and Tourism Administration

feasible for thousands of tourists. For Europeans, a visit to the United States now costs only a little more than a trip in their own hemisphere. Visits from Canadians and Mexicans are even less expensive because their countries are closer.

Why Do They Travel?

Vacation and leisure travelers from abroad visit the United States for some of the same reasons Americans travel domestically. They enjoy the diversity of climate, culture, and scenery. The image of the United States as a land of plenty excites the imagination of international travelers and makes them want to see the country for themselves.

A kind of reverse motivation also exists. Whereas Americans may journey abroad to find their ancestral roots, foreign tourists want to see the land to which their relatives emigrated. Reunions with family members are a common reason for visiting the United States. Whereas Americans travel abroad to see old castles, cathedrals, and fortresses, foreign tourists are attracted by this country's youthfulness. They want to see America's architecture, technology, and pace of life. Even though the United States is relatively young, its history—especially the history of the Old West and the American Indian culture—fascinates foreign tourists.

Where Do They Travel?

If you live in the interior of the United States, you may not believe that over 38 million foreign travelers now visit this country each year. You probably haven't seen many of these visitors because their principal ports of entry are New York City, Miami, Honolulu, and Los Angeles, and their top four destinations are California, New York, Florida, and Hawaii.

Receptive Operators. Just as a trip abroad represents a dream come true for United States travelers, so, too, does a trip to the United States for foreign travelers. The *receptive operator* is primarily responsible for seeing that the dream of international visitors doesn't become a nightmare.

Receptive operators are travel professionals who specialize in arranging tours for visitors from other countries. They usually work in cooperation with overseas operators to plan and market the tours. In addition to handling the usual details of a tour—checking the itinerary; making arrangements with hotels, bus companies, restaurants, and tourist attractions; pricing out the tour—receptive operators arrange for the special needs of the tour group, such as multilingual guides and interpreters. Foreign countries can set up their own receptive services in this country (Japan, for example, has operators on the West Coast), or United States travel agencies can specialize in this service. With the number of visitors increasing, the receptive operator is growing in importance.

Until recently, foreign vacation and leisure travel in the United States consisted of a customary grand tour. Travelers typically visited Washington, D.C., New York City, Niagara Falls, Los Angeles, and an ethnic destination, such as Chinatown in San Francisco. Receptive operators were mainly located in major cities on the East and West coasts.

This situation is beginning to change. Today, international visitors are looking for new destinations between the coasts. They want to go further inland and see

Illus. 2-6 *Inbound tourists visit the United States for many reasons.*

Source: ©Margaret Granitsas/The Image Works

America. Yours to Discover.™

United States Travel and Tourism Administration

How many foreign visitors come to the United States each year? Where do they stay? How much money do they spend? How can the government help the American tourism industry attract more foreign travelers? To answer these questions, the federal government established the U.S. Travel Service in 1961 as an agency of the U.S. Commerce Department. In 1981, the Travel Service was replaced by a new agency, the United States Travel and Tourism Administration (USTTA). The primary task of the agency is to increase American export earnings by promoting American tourism abroad. In other words, the USTTA is supposed to get more foreign travelers to come to the United States and spend their money here. It is an important assignment. In 1990, the USTTA estimated that 41 million foreign visitors entered the United States and spent nearly $50 billion here.

Today the USTTA maintains offices in nine foreign countries—Canada, Mexico, Great Britain, France, Germany, Japan, Australia, the Netherlands, and Italy. It also has regional offices in New York, Florida, Texas, and Washington, D.C. The United States competes with many other countries for tourism dollars. The USTTA's role is to help American tourism companies compete as effectively as possible. Here are some of the means by which the USTTA attracts foreign visitors:

■ **Information Centers.** The USTTA's Travel Information Centers in foreign countries advise travelers about what to see and do in the United States. Their counselors provide information and advice to thousands of customers who call, write, or visit the centers every day. The counselors try to convince travelers to come to the United States. They also try to provide the most accurate information and best advice they can so that the travelers will know what to expect from a vacation in America.

■ **Travel Brochures.** The USTTA has developed its own set of travel brochures to inform visitors about places to visit and sights to see in the United States. Some brochures focus on different regions of the country because most visitors confine their travels to a specific area. The brochures are published in

several languages: English, German, French, Italian, Japanese, and Spanish.

■ **Visit USA Committees.** The USTTA estimates that about 85 percent of all foreign travelers to the United States come from the nine countries in which it has Information Centers. The United States also receives a large number of visitors from 18 other countries. In each of those countries, the USTTA has established Visit USA committees made up of representatives of various United States travel industry components such as hotels, tour operators, and airlines. The committees work together to market their products to travelers within each country.

■ **Advertising.** The USTTA plans and carries out extensive advertising campaigns in cooperation with the tourism industry. It has joined with companies such as Pan American Airlines and American Express as well as with regional and state tourism agencies to advertise America's attractions abroad. In 1991, its slogan was "America—Yours to Discover."

■ **Seminars, workshops, and trade shows.** The USTTA organizes dozens of seminars and workshops each year. Some of the workshops are intended to inform foreign travel agents about American destinations. For example, the USTTA might cosponsor a visit by British travel agents to the Orlando, Florida, area so they can learn about its attractions. The USTTA is a cosponsor of the annual Discover America International Pow Wow, the largest trade show aimed solely at attracting foreign visitors to the United States. In 1989, the USTTA estimates, the Pow Wow generated more than $1 billion in business for American companies.

■ **Research.** One of the USTTA's most important tasks is to gather reliable statistics about foreign travel to the United States. It conducts many studies aimed at determining how many visitors come to the United States, where they spend their money, and what they like and don't like about America. The USTTA's research is invaluable to America's tourism industries as they plan for the future.

Photo Source: United States Department of Commerce

how people in this country live. The opening of international airports in St. Louis, Houston, Dallas, Minneapolis/St. Paul, and other interior cities has made travel to the center of the United States more feasible. This interest in destinations also brings more opportunities for regional receptive operators. Compared with operators on the coasts—especially those established by foreign countries—regional operators know the area better and can plan more efficient and interesting tours.

Increasing Marketability. Inbound tourism represents a lucrative market—an important source of jobs and revenue. To capture and maintain this market, the travel industry and the United States public must overcome this country's shortcomings as a tourist destination.

Language is perhaps the biggest barrier to overcome. When traveling to well-developed destinations overseas, people from the United States expect to encounter English-speaking personnel in hotels, restaurants, and tourist attractions. The reverse is not true for the international traveler to the United States. To minimize language difficulties for foreign visitors, the travel industry might take the following steps:

- Use internationally recognized pictographs in restaurants, hotels, and bars.
- Print menus in other languages, or provide photos.
- Provide multilingual travel personnel, and encourage more citizens to become multilingual, especially at popular tourist destinations.
- Provide a public translating service at travel destinations. Foreign visitors could bring printed materials to the service center for translation. Hotels, restaurants, and receptive operators could also send menus, itineraries, and general instructions to the center for translation into the appropriate language.

Other improvements that might be made include the following:

- Make the exchange of money easier at airports and in banks and hotels.
- Explain tipping customs and sales taxes.
- Improve the intercity railroad system, since foreign visitors are accustomed to rail travel.
- Have conversion tables for the metric system available.
- Train waiters, waitresses, bellstaff, bartenders, salespeople, and others to be friendly and patient in assisting international travelers.

The United States public needs to realize the extent and importance of inbound tourism. All citizens, and not just travel professionals, need to assume the role of gracious host in welcoming foreign guests.

Check Your Product Knowledge

1. From what countries do the majority of our international visitors come?
2. What circumstances are contributing to the increase in foreign travel to the United States?
3. List four reasons why people from other countries want to visit the United States.
4. Why are regional receptive operators becoming more important?
5. What improvements could be made in the United States to minimize difficulties for foreign visitors?

Summary

- People have traveled throughout history for a variety of reasons. For most of history, travel has been difficult and dangerous.
- For travel to flourish, there must be an efficient system of transportation and protection for travelers. Pleasure travel also requires that people have leisure time and money to spend.
- Largely because of economic prosperity, more people in industrialized societies are traveling than ever before. For them, travel has become a symbol of the good life.
- Modern-day travelers form a diverse group. Travel professionals must match appropriate products and services to each traveler's motivations, needs, and expectations (MNEs).
- There are three main groups of travelers. For vacation and leisure travelers, travel is discretionary, or voluntary. For business and professional travelers, it is nondiscretionary. For travelers visiting friends and relatives, travel may be discretionary or nondiscretionary.
- Many types of experiences—such as learning about other cultures, participating in sports, and being with other people—give vacation and leisure travelers pleasure. According to Stanley Plog, an individual's personality (allocentric, psychocentric, or midcentric) determines travel motivation and choice of destination. Applying Abraham Maslow's theory of needs satisfaction, people travel for pleasure in order to satisfy needs for social interaction, self-esteem, respect, and self-actualization.
- The travel industry designs products and services to meet the needs of a particular market segment. Demographics (statistical information) and psychographics (information on interests and attitudes) help the industry understand the marketplace.

- The majority of American vacation and leisure travelers take trips within the United States. States offering beautiful scenery, sunshine, and culture attract the most visitors.
- Vacation and leisure travel abroad offers unique experiences. International travel, however, requires more preparation, such as obtaining documentation, learning customs regulations, taking measures to safeguard health, exchanging currency, and learning some basic phrases in a foreign language. Travel professionals must be able to assist travelers with these preparations.
- Inbound tourism has been increasing. To maintain this market segment, travel professionals must also become familiar with the MNEs of international visitors.

Key Terms

discretionary travel
nondiscretionary travel
allocentric personality
psychocentric personality
midcentric personality
market segmentation
primary research
secondary research
demographics
psychographics
documentation
passport
embassy
consulate
visa
proof of citizenship
tourist card
International Certificate of Vaccination
customs
duty
duty-free
departure tax
inbound tourism
receptive operator

What Do You Think?

1. What are some current examples of people traveling to meet the basic need for survival?
2. According to Plog's theory, what type of personality is Mrs. O'Neill (see page 32)? What needs is she satisfying according to Maslow's theory? Explain your point of view.
3. How might a tour to New York City for senior citi-

zens be different from a tour for young singles to the same destination?
4. In arranging an international journey for a client, what are the responsibilities of the travel agent?
5. How do customs regulations reflect the views of a government?
6. What is the purpose of confiscating products made from endangered animals?
7. In promoting inbound tourism, how does the United States government compare with the governments of other developed nations?
8. What can be done to encourage more people who live in the United States to become multilingual? Which languages should be stressed?

Dealing with Product

Travel and tourism products do not exist in a vacuum. They are often affected by events that take place half a world away. Consider the following:

In 1990, Iraq invaded Kuwait. After several months of negotiations, the United States and its allies launched a war against Iraq, with the intent of driving Iraq out of Kuwait. Many countries were involved in the war, including Great Britain, France, Italy, and Saudi Arabia.

What impact did this fighting have on international travel? Did each of the three primary types of travelers react in the same way? What impact did this fighting have on domestic travel? In what ways might a war on the other side of the world cause changes in the price of travel products in Yourtown?

Dealing with People

It is often said that the three most important ingredients in pleasure travel are time, money, and education. The more of each the better. Unfortunately, most of us either never seem to have enough, or have plenty of one and not enough of the others. First, let's look at time and money.

How would you describe the following prospective travelers in terms of time and money? What type of vacation and leisure travel product would you recommend for these travelers?

1. A college student
2. A dairy farmer
3. A high school teacher
4. An orthopedic surgeon
5. A factory worker
6. The owner of a laundry and dry cleaning company

Now—how do you think that education affects a person's travel plans? Can you find any relationship between education and the profiles provided by Plog and Maslow?

Name _____

WORKSHEET 2-1   FOREIGN TRAVEL: FAM TRIP

The decline of communism in Eastern Europe has opened up new and exciting opportunities for travel. Imagine that your travel agency has sent you on a FAM trip to Prague, Czechoslovakia. Use the space below to record your findings.

1.   How to get there from Yourtown

_____

_____

_____

_____

2.   How to obtain a visa

_____

_____

_____

3.   Currency used and exchange rate in dollars

_____

_____

_____

4.   Customs rules

_____

_____

_____

_____

5.   What type of clothes to pack

_____

_____

_____

_____

6.   Where to stay

_____

_____

_____

_____

7.   Recommended restaurants

_____

_____

_____

_____

8.   Things to see and do in the city

_____

_____

_____

_____

9.   How to get around the city

_____

_____

_____

10.   What to do in case of a medical emergency

_____

_____

_____

11.   Additional tourist information

_____

_____

_____

_____

Name _____

WORKSHEET 2-2   TRAVEL USA: TOURIST ATTRACTIONS

The United States has a variety of tourist attractions. Some attractions provide breathtaking scenery, others provide fun and relaxation, and still others provide a glimpse of our nation's history. The chart below lists a few of this country's outstanding tourist attractions. Use travel guides and encyclopedias to help you locate and describe each attraction.

INDEPENDENCE HALL NATIONAL HISTORIC PARK

Location _____

Description _____

_____

_____

_____

GRAND CANYON

Location _____

Description _____

_____

_____

_____

BADLANDS

Location _____

Description _____

_____

_____

_____

NATIONAL AQUARIUM

Location _____

Description _____

_____

_____

_____

EPCOT CENTER

Location _____

Description _____

_____

_____

_____

MOUNT McKINLEY

Location _____

Description _____

_____

_____

_____

SMITHSONIAN INSTITUTION

Location _____

Description _____

_____

_____

_____

MAUNA LOA

Location _____

Description _____

_____

_____

_____

Name _____

WORKSHEET 2-3   INBOUND TOURISM

Travelers to the United States have different motivations, needs, and expectations. Based on the information given, draw up suitable itineraries for the following travelers:

1. Inge Edberg and Katerina Petersen, two university students from Sweden, want to go hiking, visit a friend in San Francisco, and meet American students—all on a low budget; one month.

_____
_____
_____
_____
_____
_____
_____
_____
_____
_____

2. Dr. Mario Alvarez, a doctor from Venezuela, is attending a convention in Atlantic City. His wife and daughter are accompanying him. After the convention, his wife wants to do some shopping and see a musical, and his daughter wants to visit Disney World; one week.

_____
_____
_____
_____
_____
_____
_____
_____

3. A group of 12 French tourists wants to see the United States from coast to coast in three weeks.

_____
_____
_____
_____
_____
_____
_____
_____
_____
_____

4. James Chang, an architect from Hong Kong, wants to see the monuments of modern American architecture and to visit family in Washington, D.C.; two weeks.

_____
_____
_____
_____
_____
_____
_____
_____

Name _____

WORKSHEET 2-4   MOTIVATIONS, NEEDS, AND EXPECTATIONS

An important part of a travel professional's job is to understand the motivations, needs, and expectations of different travelers. Using the information provided below, complete the profiles of the travelers described. The motivations are given; fill in the needs and expectations.

1. The Burkowskis, a retired couple living in Tucson, Arizona, want to visit London, see the main tourist sights, and go to the theater. They have never been abroad before and are a little unsure about how they should make the arrangements for the trip.

    Motivation   *To visit a foreign country now that they have some time.*

    Needs

    Expectations

2. Jill Dillon, an executive from Little Rock, Arkansas, has to attend a sales meeting in Charleston, South Carolina. The meeting starts on Sunday evening, but Jill would like to spend the weekend with a friend in Atlanta, Georgia. She also needs to be in St. Louis, Missouri, for a meeting on the Thursday morning before the weekend.

    Motivations   *Business travel with a personal side trip.*

    Needs

    Expectations

3. Alicia Valdez of Philadelphia wants to visit her sick mother in Austin, Texas. She will be taking her two children, ages one and three, and will need a place to stay that is inexpensive.

    Motivation   *To visit a sick relative.*

    Needs

    Expectations

"Free market competition, freely advertised, is consumerism at its best."
—*J. Kesner Kahn*

Objectives

When you have completed this chapter, you should be able to:

- Explain how travel retailers differ from retailers in other industries.
- Distinguish between the three different systems of distribution.
- List the primary printed references available to travel professionals.
- Distinguish between the informational functions of a computer reservations system and its transactual functions.
- Outline the development of automated reservations systems.

- List the major domestic CRS vendors.
- Describe the relationship between host vendors and cohosts.
- Discuss the issue of bias.
- Distinguish between teleticketing machines and satellite ticket printers.
- Show how automated back office systems can facilitate a travel agency's internal operations.
- Explain how hotel and car rental reservations systems differ from airline CRSs.

Every industry has products that it attempts to sell to consumers at a profit. Most industries sell tangible products. The automobile industry sells cars and trucks, the garment industry sells clothes, the food processing industry sells food products. The product of the travel and tourism industry is usually intangible, such as a flight on an airplane, a stay at a hotel, the use of a rental car, or a complete tour package.

Travel products are perishable. They must be sold within a certain period of time or else they become worthless. An empty seat on an airplane can never be sold once the flight has taken off. Some travel products are also seasonal. They are in great demand during certain times of the year and unattractive at others. A trip to the Maine seashore is an example of a seasonal product.

Like other industries, the travel industry uses a system of distribution to move its products and services from producer to consumer. Manufacturing industries typically use wholesalers and retailers as *intermediaries*, or links, between the producer and the consumer. The wholesaler purchases products from the manufacturer and sells them to the retailer. The retailer in turn sells the products to the consumer. The sales distribution system of the travel industry also involves intermediaries, such as wholesalers or tour operators and retail travel agents.

An important difference between the travel industry and other industries is the status of the retailer. A traditional retailer buys goods and services and sells them to the consumer with markup. Travel retailers, however, do *not* buy goods and services, nor do they mark up the price. Instead, they are paid a *commission*, or a percentage of the selling price, by the supplier or wholesaler. It is for this reason that travel retailers are most commonly called travel "agents"; they act as agents for the supplier or wholesaler. Another difference between the travel industry and most other industries is that the consumer can bypass the intermediaries and purchase the product directly from the supplier.

In this chapter, you'll learn how the different channels of distribution used in the travel industry are structured. You'll also learn about the increasing use of automation in getting the travel product from the supplier to the consumer.

CHANNELS OF DISTRIBUTION

There are three main channels of distribution in the travel industry, which can be defined by level of complexity:

- Unilateral, involving no intermediaries between supplier and consumer.
- Bilevel, involving one intermediary.
- Multilevel, involving two or more intermediaries.

Consumers are free to choose the channel they prefer. Regardless of whether they buy a travel product directly from the supplier or through an intermediary, identical products usually cost the same. This feature is unique to the travel industry.

Unilateral Distribution System

The unilateral system is the simplest of the three distribution systems (see Figure 3-1). It involves the direct sale of travel products and services from supplier to consumer. Suppliers include airlines, railroads, bus companies, cruise lines, car rental firms, hotels, resorts, sightseeing companies, and so forth.

Customers can either telephone the supplier to make a reservation or go in person to the ticket or sales outlet. Most major suppliers in the travel industry maintain national and regional sales offices. Some own or lease counter space in airports, hotels, convention centers, and other high-visibility locations.

In recent years, suppliers have begun to experiment with automated methods of direct distribution. Automated ticketing machines (similar to automated bank-teller machines) have been installed at airports, railway stations, and major city ticket offices. It is expected that they will become widely available in the near future. Teleshopping—the use of personal computers for obtaining flight information and for making reservations—is already accessible through several software packages, including Prodigy and CompuServe. Though still in its early stages, teleshopping is likely to have far-reaching effects on the way travel products and information are distributed in the future.

The unilateral system of distribution is ideally suited for simple travel arrangements, such as domestic airline reservations and hotel bookings. More complex arrangements, such as cruises and tour packages, generally require the assistance of a travel agent or other sales intermediary.

In fact, the greatest advantage of the unilateral system is its simplicity. Suppliers deal directly with consumers, thereby minimizing the misunderstandings that are possible when a third party is involved. Many clients prefer to talk directly to the supplier because they feel that this allows them greater personal control over the transaction.

Suppliers make a greater net profit per unit sale if they sell directly to the traveler. Suppose, for example, that Annette Carson wants to fly from New York to Los Angeles on United Airlines. The quoted fare is $300. If she buys the ticket directly from United, she will pay the airline $300. If she decides to book the flight through a travel agency, it will still cost her the same amount, but United will not receive the full $300. The reason is that airlines (and other suppliers) have to pay a commission to travel agents to compensate them for making the booking. If United pays 10 percent commission, then the travel agency will receive $30. In other words, United earns only $270 on the sale instead of $300. You can understand why airlines like to sell directly to the traveler.

The unilateral system also offers the supplier the opportunity to make additional sales. If United Airlines talks directly to Annette Carson, the company might be able to encourage her to book her return trip to New York on United or to upgrade her seat from economy to first class.

Bilevel Distribution System

Two main forces work against the unilateral system of distribution. First, many suppliers cannot afford to maintain regional sales offices and must therefore rely on intermediaries to get their product to the consumer. In addition, many travelers would rather make their travel arrangements through a retail agency than deal directly with the supplier.

The bilevel distribution system most commonly involves a travel agent as intermediary (see Figure 3-2). The agent represents the suppliers and sells their travel services to the consumer. Suppliers also use business travel departments (BTDs) and scheduled airline ticket offices (SATOs) as distribution channels. In-house BTDs sell travel products and services to employees of large corporations. SATOs are located on military bases and posts and sell tickets to members of the United States Armed Forces. Tour operators may also serve as intermediaries, buying travel products from various suppliers and packaging them for sale directly to the consumer.

Figure 3-1 Unilateral Distribution System

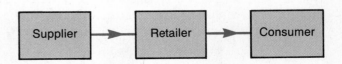

Figure 3-2 Bilevel Distribution System

A recent development has been the use of supermarkets, department stores, and other retail outlets as distributors of travel products (especially airline tickets). Some United States supermarket chains sell certificates that are redeemable for discounted airline tickets. A supermarket in the Netherlands has even experimented with selling package tours in cans. The cans contain tickets and travel itineraries and are placed on the shelves alongside more traditional grocery products. It is conceivable that suppliers will look to similar retail outlets to distribute an ever-widening variety of travel products. This will make it more convenient for consumers to shop for travel, but may eventually take business away from travel agencies.

The recent success of *video marketing*—whereby television cable channels show a catalog of items on the screen—has not gone unnoticed by the travel industry. In fact, The Travel Channel in New York City is an all-travel video marketing channel. The channel shows travel films and promotes tours and other travel products.

For the consumer, the bilevel system's greatest advantage is that most travel intermediaries can provide professional assistance and personalized advice. In the present deregulated marketplace, the traveler is confronted by a baffling maze of airfares. One airline may offer a bargain fare to Chicago, but only if you book a month in advance, travel on a Wednesday, and return on a Monday. Another airline offers an unbeatable fare to Miami, but the fine print reveals that you can fly only from Denver and must stay in Miami for a minimum of seven days. Professional travel agents have the expertise to make sense of the airfare maze and to recommend arrangements to suit the needs and budgets of individual travelers.

Travel intermediaries can also provide the traveler with information on a greater variety of travel options than can any single supplier. An example will illustrate this point. John Martinez wants to take his family to Disney World for a week's vacation, but he is not sure where to stay. If he has the time, patience, and money for long-distance telephone calls, Mr. Martinez can call several hotels and motels in the area to find suitable accommodations. His other option is to call or visit a local travel agency and explain his specific needs. The agent will be able to eliminate those hotels that are beyond his budget or unsuitable for other reasons. If Mr. Martinez plans to fly to Disney World, the agent will also be able to make the necessary flight arrangements and possibly reserve a rental car for the family's use. In other words, Mr. Martinez can make all his travel plans in one simple step, instead of calling a host of different suppliers.

Since travel retailers do not charge clients for their services, John Martinez is not paying any extra for his family's trip. Only if the agent has to make overseas phone calls, or if a particularly complicated itinerary is involved, will the customer be charged.

Travel intermediaries usually have more influence with suppliers than do individual travelers. Suppliers value retail intermediaries as an important source of volume bookings and generally give preferential treatment to these customers. If space is limited—as is often the case during peak seasons—the traveler who books through an intermediary is more likely to get a seat on a plane or a room in a hotel than is a traveler who books independently. Suppliers cannot afford to disappoint the intermediaries. You might have heard of travelers who have been "bumped" from flights or who turn up at a hotel to find that the front desk has no record of their reservation. Often, these are clients who have booked independently.

It is clear that the bilevel distribution system offers a number of distinct advantages for the consumer. What about the supplier? Travel intermediaries can serve as an extension to the supplier's existing sales force or, in some cases, they can be the sole sales force. In the latter case, the supplier has no sales overhead except for the commission that must be paid to the retailer. Many suppliers prefer to pay commissions to travel agents rather than maintain a network of sales offices with full-time reservations staffs. This is particularly true of smaller suppliers.

Airline commissions are the major source of travel agency revenues, accounting for almost two-thirds of total receipts. Since deregulation, suppliers have been free to choose how much commission they pay, although 10 percent remains the standard rate. Some suppliers also offer *overrides* to travel agents in addition to regular commissions. The override is a volume incentive and is usually paid on a graduated scale (for example, 1 percent for sales between $10,000 and $20,000, 2 percent for sales between $20,000 and $30,000, and so on).

Multilevel Distribution System

The multilevel system is the most complex distribution system. It involves the intervention of two or more intermediaries between the supplier and the consumer (see Figure 3-3). The system is most commonly used for the distribution of tour packages. Suppliers sell their products and services to wholesalers or tour operators, who package the various components into a tour (transportation, accommodations, meals, sightseeing services, transfers, and so forth). The wholesaler then sells the tour to the consumer through a retail outlet (usually a travel agency).

An additional intermediary is sometimes involved in the planning of a tour package. The intermediary can be an incentive travel company, a meeting/convention planner, a travel club, or some other *specialty channeler*. All intervene between the retailer and the consumer.

The multilevel system offers the consumer similar

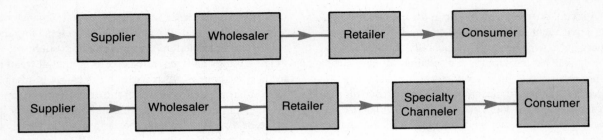

Figure 3-3 Multilevel Distribution Systems

advantages to those offered by the bilevel system. An additional advantage results from the intervention of the wholesaler in the distribution process. Wholesalers buy travel services and products in bulk from suppliers. Advance sales, combined with the savings that come from bulk buying, enable suppliers to offer their services to wholesalers at substantially reduced prices. Unlike the retailer, the wholesaler is not paid a commission by the supplier. Instead, wholesalers make their profits by marking up the price of the product. The markup must be high enough to cover overhead and commissions paid to travel agents or other retailers. Even after markup, the final package is still cheaper for the traveler than buying the various components directly from the suppliers.

As we have seen, the multilevel system involves the greatest number of distribution channels. Occasionally, one company acquires several different channels of distribution. Each channel might then promote the services or products supplied by other channels within the group. This concept is known as *vertical marketing*. One of the first companies to form a vertical marketing operation was Canadian Pacific Ltd. Canadian Pacific owned and operated an airline (CPAir), a railroad (CPRail), a shipping line, and a hotel company. CPAir is now part of Canadian Airlines International.

In many cases, a single member of the distribution channel will sell products from other suppliers as well as its own products. Most of the large airlines, for example, sell hotel rooms, car rentals, and tour packages in addition to airline tickets. Similarly, American Express sells airline tickets and hotel accommodations as well as escorted tours. Cruise lines sell airline tickets as well as cruises. This means that a traveler can usually buy a package of two or more products from almost every member of the distribution channel.

Check Your Product Knowledge

1. What advantages does the unilateral distribution system offer to consumers and to suppliers?
2. How might the use of automated ticketing machines, personal computers, and supermarkets as channels of distribution affect the role of travel agents?
3. What is the difference between the bilevel system of distribution and the multilevel system?
4. What is meant by vertical marketing?

NONAUTOMATED SYSTEMS OF INFORMATION

For successful operation, the travel industry depends on a continuous flow of information from supplier to consumer. The information must be accurate and up-to-date, especially since fares and schedules can change overnight. What is this information and how do travel retailers and consumers have access to it? We'll answer these two questions in this section. Although almost all travel agencies now use automated systems of information, it is still important for today's travel professional to know about nonautomated systems. That way, in the event of a breakdown in the computer system or similar problem, the travel professional will still be able to obtain current information. Let's take a look at how travel agencies operated before automated systems were widely used.

Types of Information

Daralyn Walker wanted to fly from Detroit, Michigan, to Omaha, Nebraska. In the past, she made travel arrangements through a local agency—let's call it Alpha Travel. She was always happy with their service and decided to use them again to make her reservation. Having established where Ms. Walker wanted to go (Omaha) and where she wanted to fly from (Detroit), the agent at Alpha Travel had to determine:

- Which airlines had flights from Detroit to Omaha.
- The seat availability on these flights.
- The comparative fares of the flights to Omaha.
- When the flights left Detroit and arrived in Omaha.
- How the flights got to Omaha—were they direct, or was a connecting flight necessary?

Anne Marie Powell

When Anne Marie Powell started out as a freshman at Niagara University in 1974, she had no idea that she would end up in the travel industry. In fact, she started out wanting to be a nurse, but she soon changed her mind and switched her major to travel and tourism. Today Powell is senior vice president and general manager of the American Society of Travel Agents (ASTA), the world's largest professional association for travel agents and other travel suppliers.

ASTA is a nonprofit professional organization that serves the suppliers, wholesalers, and retailers of travel products. It has 21,000 members in the United States and 128 other countries. ASTA's main purpose is to promote the interests of travel agents and other travel suppliers. It deals with many of the legal, political, and financial aspects of the travel business.

As one of the top executives at ASTA, Powell is in charge of the service division of the association. This division includes public relations, consumer affairs, educational programs, conferences and workshops, and sales and marketing. Powell directs a staff of 50 people, including five directors and vice presidents.

Powell chose travel and tourism in college because she was attracted by the "glamour" of it. After working in the industry for several years, she says she still thinks there's an element of glamour in it, but that it also requires a lot of hard work and perseverance. She recommends that anyone considering a career in the travel industry take college courses in business management, accounting, and writing skills. She also recommends that someone starting out in the travel business begin as a tour director. "Tour directors deal with all the components of the travel business—airlines, hotels, bus operators, restaurants, attractions," she said. "It's a great place to really get a feel for the business."

Powell joined ASTA in 1980 as a training manager in its education department. She spent about a year and a half on the road giving seminars and workshops to travel agents all over the country. Her department was also responsible for updating ASTA's correspondence course for travel agents and for creating various operating manuals and handbooks for travel agency owners and managers. Powell says that, although students cannot learn everything they need to become a travel agent from ASTA's correspondence course, they can use it to determine whether a career as a travel agent is right for them.

According to Powell, most of ASTA's educational programs are concerned with the business aspects of the profession, such as finances and personnel management, rather than with specific products. "We leave the selling of products up to the suppliers themselves because we feel they can do a better job of it than we can," she said. The one exception is ASTA's Cruisefest, which brings 500 travel agents to a major cruise ship port for a weekend each year. The agents tour five or six ships and attend workshops on how to sell cruises to their clients.

In 1986, Powell took over the convention department, which sponsors a large international conference and several regional conferences for travel agents each year. One of her duties is to oversee the planning of the annual ASTA World Travel Congress. This international convention attracts about 7,000 travel agents, airlines, tour operators, hotel operators, and others. The 1990 conference was held in Hamburg, Germany. According to Powell, most of the workshops at the annual conference deal with such topics as labor relations, financial planning, sales and promotion, bookkeeping, and management techniques.

Although ASTA started 60 years ago as an association of travel agents, Powell says that one of its greatest strengths is that it helps pull all the elements of the travel industry together. "Restaurants think only of their own and airlines think only of their own and hotels think only of their own," she said. "ASTA helps them join forces and make people aware of the economic impact of the entire travel industry."

Powell, who lives in Alexandria, Virginia, near ASTA's headquarters, says she loves her job and doesn't plan to do anything else. Her career at ASTA, she says, is challenging and satisfying. It has taken her to six of the seven continents and enabled her to meet hundreds of interesting people from all over the world.

Where could the agent find the relevant flight information? If Daralyn Walker also wanted to arrange hotel accommodations and to rent a car in Omaha, where could the agent find information on hotel and rental car availability and rates?

Alpha Travel was a nonautomated agency—that is, it did not have access to a computer reservations system. As a result, the agent had to rely on printed reference sources and on telephone inquiries to suppliers.

Primary Printed References

A nonautomated travel agency needed a large number of printed reference works. All of these works had to be updated regularly.

Airlines. There are three main sources of information on flight schedules and fares:

- Timetables and fare sheets.
- Airline guides.
- Tariffs.

Timetables and fare sheets are published by all major airlines and distributed to travel agencies on a regular basis. The material must be updated every time there is a change of schedule or change of fare. Individual timetables and fare sheets show information for only the issuing carrier. To get a comparative picture of all the available schedules from a single source, the agent must consult an airline guide. The *Official Airline Guide (OAG)*, published by Official Airline Guides Inc., is available in North American and worldwide editions. It lists all scheduled flights. The North American edition is updated every two weeks; the worldwide edition is updated once a month.

Tariffs list scheduled airfares and provide a summary of rules and regulations that apply to the flights. There are two main types of tariff. The *ATPCO Tariff*, issued by the Airline Tariff Publishing Company, lists domestic flights. International tariffs are published by individual international carriers such as Lufthansa, Swissair, and SAS, or by a consortium of foreign airlines. Of all printed reference sources, tariffs are the most likely to become fully automated. Since passage of the Airline Deregulation Act in 1978, domestic carriers have been allowed to set their own fares. It is much easier to update a computer every time a fare changes than it is to reprint a tariff. As a result, printed tariffs are rarely used by the travel industry today. (Note: domestic carriers are no longer required to file tariffs with the government; international carriers, however, must still file them with the United States Department of Transportation.)

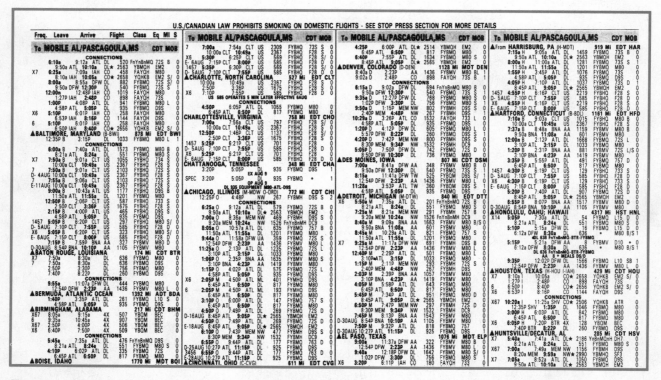

Illus. 3-1 *Printed references are essential sources of transportation schedules and fare information for nonautomated travel agencies. Shown here is a portion of the Official Airline Guide.*

Ground Transportation. Ground transportation includes railroads, intercity buses, rental cars, and mass transit and public transportation systems. Information on schedules and fares can be found in the following sources:

■ Timetables.
■ Rail and bus guides.
■ Car rental rate sheets.

All ground transportation companies publish timetables that are updated as schedules change. The *Official Railway Guide* is the primary source for Amtrak schedules and fares. It also contains information on commuter rail services in major United States cities. Rail services worldwide are listed in the *Thomas Cook Overseas Timetable.*

Russell's Official National Motor Coach Guide lists domestic long-distance bus schedules. Car rental companies clearly have no need to publish timetables but they must distribute information on rates to travel intermediaries. Car rental rate sheets issued by individual companies, such as Avis and Hertz, serve this purpose.

Cruise Lines. The major printed reference sources for information on cruises are:

■ Brochures.
■ Official cruise guides.

Cruise lines rely heavily on retailers for the distribution of their product. (Travel agents account for 95 percent of total cruise sales.) Individual companies supply agencies with lavish brochures detailing the season's cruise offerings, complete with sailing times, deck plans, rates, and related information. Official publications include the *Official Steamship Guide International* and the *Worldwide Cruise and Shipline Guide.* Both contain listings of cruise schedules throughout the world.

Hotels and Resorts. Information on hotel and resort rates and services is available from two types of printed sources:

■ Brochures.
■ Guides and manuals.

Hotel brochures serve a function similar to cruise brochures. They not only provide information on individual properties but are also used as a selling tool. Brochures stress the hotel's most attractive features in the hope that travelers will be encouraged to stay at the property.

A more objective viewpoint is provided by the various official guides and manuals. These include the *Hotel and Travel Index*, the *Official Hotel Guide*, and the *OAG Travel Planner Hotel and Motel Red Book.*

Illus. 3-2 *Tour brochures are informative marketing tools that contain attractive photographs with listings of rates and itineraries.*
Source: *Sara G. Matthews*

Tours. There are four sources of information on tour packages:

■ Brochures.
■ Tour manuals.
■ Catalogs.
■ Tariffs.

Most of the major tour operators, such as American Express and Thomas Cook, put out glamorous brochures each season with listings of rates and itineraries. A variety of tours are described in the *Consolidated Tour Manual* and the *Official Tour Directory*. A recent innovation in the United States is the use of mail-order catalogs listing tour packages. Catalogs have been used successfully in Europe for many years.

Travel agents have access to tariffs, which quote net tour prices. The net price is a noncommissionable price that the supplier charges the retailer. The retailer then adds a markup before quoting the price to the client. Confidential Tariffs are issued by individual tour operators. These provide listings of tours and excursions, giving net prices.

Telephone Service and the Reservations Center

With a nonautomated reservations system, once the travel agent obtained the relevant information and discussed options with the client, he or she would be ready to make the reservation. Let's return to our earlier example. You will recall that Daralyn Walker wanted to fly from Detroit to Omaha. The agent at Alpha Travel informed her that three airlines had flights to Omaha on the day she wanted to travel. Ms. Walker chose the 9:30 A.M. American Airlines flight because it was the least expensive.

The agent could then telephone the American Airlines reservations center to determine if there was a seat available on the preferred flight. If there was, Daralyn Walker's name would go on the *manifest*, or passenger list. If the flight was full, her name could be placed on the *wait list*. (The wait list is like the numbering system used in a bakery or delicatessen. As each passenger on the list is accommodated, or cancels, the others move up one place.) Daralyn Walker could take her chances with the wait list, or she could decide to fly at a later time or with a different airline.

When the agent called American Airlines, he or she probably dialed a toll-free number. Most of the major suppliers—particularly airlines, hotel chains, and car rental companies—have a toll-free number. This number allows consumers and retailers to call the reservations center free of charge from anywhere in the country. It is a valuable marketing tool for the supplier. A supplier without a toll-free number—such as a small, independently owned hotel—is at a distinct disadvantage.

Toll-free numbers not only help the suppliers but could also present considerable savings to the travel agent. During the course of a working day, a travel agent in a nonautomated setting might make more than 100 calls to suppliers. Bills for long-distance telephone calls could soon add up, eating into an agency's profits. If the 100 calls were all to toll-free numbers, they wouldn't cost the agency a cent.

Once a reservation was made and a fare or rate established in a nonautomated setting, some sort of document would be issued. These documents included standard airline tickets, rail and motorcoach tickets, and vouchers or coupons that could be exchanged for car rentals, package tours, cruises, and hotel accommodations. In a nonautomated agency, the ticketing process was often done manually.

Check Your Product Knowledge

1. What type of information does an agent need before he or she can book a flight?
2. In a nonautomated setting, where could an agent find information on (a) ground transportation, (b) hotels, and (c) tours?
3. How are toll-free numbers useful for (a) suppliers and (b) travel agents?

AUTOMATED SYSTEMS OF INFORMATION

The past fifteen years have witnessed a tremendous growth in the automation of travel industry operations. When we talk about automation in the travel industry setting, we refer primarily to the use of airline computer systems. These systems have been developed to facilitate operations in two distinct areas:

- External functions, which relate directly to the consumer (such as reservations and ticketing).
- Internal functions, which relate to the efficient operation of the company (such as accounting and management).

In this section, we will look closely at the external functions of the computer systems.

The Computer Reservations System

A *computer reservations system* (*CRS*) can be visualized as a huge general store that stocks an almost unlimited variety of travel products and services in one central location. The owner of the store is most commonly an airline. The airline sells not only its own products, but also the flights of other airlines, as well as the products of travel suppliers such as hotels, car rental companies, and tour operators.

It is estimated that between 98 and 99 percent of travel agencies now use CRSs. To understand why CRSs are so popular, we must first establish what they are capable of doing. A CRS provides both informational and transactual functions. Informational functions allow the travel agent to obtain up-to-date information on schedules, availabilities, and fares. In this way, the CRS replaces the printed reference sources. Transactual functions allow the travel agent to print tickets, invoices, and itineraries, and book reservations. A number of travel agents have joined the Travel Agents Computer Society (TACOS), which provides information on system suppliers and vendors.

CRS vendors typically lease computer hardware to travel agencies for a monthly fee. The hardware includes keyboard, video screen or CRT (cathode ray tube), modem, and printer. Using this equipment, the agent can communicate directly with the system's CPU (central processing unit) and memory.

More recently, many travel agencies have purchased their own personal computers (PCs) to access their CRS vendor. In the past few years, "intelligent" PCs have been quickly replacing the old "dumb" terminals. PCs are more versatile than dumb terminals because they can be used for many functions, including accounting and management. According to one survey, almost 50 percent of travel agencies now use PCs.

Illus. 3-3 *By using the CRS, travel agents can obtain information on flight schedules, fares, and availability; make reservations; and even print tickets and travel documents at the touch of a button.*
Source: *American Society of Travel Agents*

An agency's in-house computer consolidates the many steps that must be taken in making manual reservations. You will recall that our Alpha Travel agent, working in a nonautomated setting, first had to consult printed reference sources, then call the airline to confirm availability and make the reservation. An agent in today's automated agency can communicate directly with the CRS through the computer keyboard. Information on routes, schedules, fares, and availabilities of participating airlines will be displayed instantly on the screen. The agent can make the reservation with the push of a few keys and create a *passenger name record* (*PNR*) for the client. The PNR is a complete record of the client's travel plans, which can be retrieved at any subsequent time for additions, changes, or cancellations. Its equivalent in the nonautomated system was the reservations card.

If the computer is linked to an in-house printer, it can automatically print airline tickets, boarding passes, and invoices or itineraries as soon as the flight reservation is made. Reservations for hotels, rental cars, and other services can also be made at the same time through the same CRS. The additional data is stored on the PNR.

The obvious advantage of using the computer reservations system is the savings in time it allows. An agent can complete the reservation and ticketing process in a fraction of the time it used to take working manually, allowing for increased productivity and a greater percentage of sales.

The Airline as Vendor

The airlines were the first organizations to develop automated reservations systems, and they have remained firmly in the forefront as vendors of CRSs. As *host vendor*, the operating airline receives revenue from three main sources:

- Participating airlines that pay to have their schedules displayed through the CRS.
- Nonairline suppliers, such as hotels and car rental agencies, which pay to have their services displayed.
- Travel agencies that subscribe to the CRS.

Each CRS allows access only to those suppliers that have agreements with the host vendor. Information on bookings with nonparticipating suppliers must be secured by other means.

Before we consider the different systems available, we'll look briefly at the way airlines developed their own CRSs.

History of Automation. Airlines recognized the potential of applying computer technology to the reservations process as early as the 1950s. Individual carriers first began to use in-house computers to keep track of the number of seats available on certain busy flights. The next stage was to develop reservations systems to which travel agents could have direct access. The problem was that each airline used a different automated system, which made it impossible to coordinate the entire reservations network.

An agency clearly couldn't afford to purchase a computer terminal for each of the airlines it needed to contact. What was needed was a common automated reservations system that incorporated the schedules and fares of all the major airlines. The American Society of Travel Agents (ASTA), the largest agency trade group in the United States, launched a joint agent-carrier project to test the feasibility of a multiaccess system. The plan collapsed in 1976.

That same year, United, American, and TWA began installing their own competing reservations systems in travel agencies throughout the United States. These sophisticated CRSs differed from earlier systems in that they allowed access to several airlines, not just to the host airline, as well as to nonairline suppliers. Most agencies today subscribe to one or more of the major airline CRSs.

Major Domestic CRS Vendors. The original airline CRSs introduced in 1976 were APOLLO (United), SABRE (American), and PARS (TWA). They were later joined by DATAS II (Delta) and System One (Eastern). Recently, several mergers have created major changes in the CRS industry. In 1987, Northwest teamed with TWA as a co-owner of PARS. Then in 1990, PARS and DATAS II joined forces to create WORLDSPAN, a new CRS.

Worldspan

It is now possible for a travel agent to switch on a computer and find the cheapest airfare to Acapulco, Mexico, show a client the floor plan of a cruise ship, and book a tour, hotel room, and rental car—all within a matter of seconds.

Thanks to increased competition, the services provided by computer reservations systems (CRSs) are getting better and better. A major development among American CRSs occurred in 1990 when three airlines—Northwest, Delta, and TWA—formed an independent company to produce and market a new computer reservations system.

The new company, WORLDSPAN Travel Agency Information Services, is spending millions of dollars to develop a new state-of-the-art CRS. The new company is made up of two existing CRSs, DATAS II (Delta Automated Travel Account System) and PARS (Programmed Airline Reservations System). WORLDSPAN's 10,000 clients will continue to subscribe to PARS or DATAS II until the new system is operational. The company is building a new data center in Atlanta, Georgia, which it expects to occupy in 1993.

The creation of WORLDSPAN has had an enormous impact on the CRS industry. The merger of PARS and DATAS II reduced the number of United States CRSs from five to four. At the same time, it has created a stronger CRS industry, allowing the four companies to compete against one another more evenly. DATAS II had been the smallest CRS company among the five, with only 3,500 clients. The joining of DATAS II and PARS has made WORLDSPAN the third largest CRS in the United States. SABRE, owned by American Airlines, is the largest CRS; APOLLO is the second largest; and System One is the fourth largest.

Many travel agents expect to see much more competition among the four CRS companies in the 1990s. The payoff, for travel agents and their clients, will be more and better services in the coming years. The four companies are developing or already have produced several new programs that enable travel agents and airlines to better serve their clients.

WORLDSPAN will be a completely neutral CRS. Although WORLDSPAN is principally owned by three airlines, the new company promises to offer equal access to all suppliers of travel products and services, including rival airlines. In a move toward increasing globalization, WORLDSPAN recently purchased a 5 percent ownership share in Abacus, an Asia/Pacific Region CRS. In turn, the Singapore-based Abacus purchased a 5 percent ownership share in WORLDSPAN. This agreement will allow both companies to capitalize on the increase in international travel that is expected to continue throughout the decade.

With the improved services offered by WORLDSPAN and the other CRSs, travel agents have a great deal of information about major airlines, hotel chains, car rental agencies, tour operators, and cruise lines at their fingertips. They can serve their clients quickly and efficiently, and they can be certain that they are assembling the lowest cost package for each client.

CRSs are improving in other ways as well. They already offer a program that searches out the lowest fares before and after a selected travel time. This enables clients to fly more cheaply if they are willing to leave a few hours earlier or later than planned. The CRS companies are also working to speed up the booking and confirmation process for airlines and hotels. All four CRS companies offer a computer service provided by THISCo—The Hotel Industry Switching Company. This service enables travel agencies and airlines to book rooms for customers in 15 major hotel chains. While the ability to book hotel rooms is not new, the THISCo program allows travel agents to confirm reservations at an amazing speed—within three seconds.

Another factor that will spur competition among CRSs is a proposed government rule that will limit contracts between the CRS companies and their clients to three years instead of five. If a travel agent feels his or her current CRS vendor isn't keeping up with new developments, the agent will be free to switch to a new company after three years. The proposed rule would encourage CRS companies to continue to look for new ways to better serve their clients.

Photo Source: WORLDSPAN

SABRE (Semi-Automated Business Research Environment) is the world's largest private real-time computer network and travel information data base. It is the most popular CRS among travel agencies, with about 14,000 United States subscribers. The heart of the SABRE network is the Tulsa Computer Center in Tulsa, Oklahoma, which processes a staggering 107 million transactions a day. Using SABRE, an agent can check schedules for 650 airlines worldwide, make reservations for more than 300 airlines, book rooms at more than 22,000 hotel properties, and reserve vehicles from 60 car rental agencies. The system also allows agents to buy Amtrak and Eurail tickets, tour packages, cruises, and tickets to Broadway shows. You can even charter a private jet through SABRE.

APOLLO is just behind SABRE in popularity, with approximately 11,500 travel agency subscribers in the United States. It has similar capabilities to those of the SABRE system. APOLLO allows direct access to most major air carriers, 19,000 hotel properties worldwide, and 35 car rental agencies. Other system participants include rail, limousine, entertainment, and tour companies.

WORLDSPAN is the newest major CRS vendor. With the combined total from PARS and DATAS II, WORLDSPAN has 10,000 agency subscribers. The new CRS is operated by WORLDSPAN Travel Agency Information Services, an independent company.

WORLDSPAN has the combined capabilities of the PARS and DATAS II systems.

System One is the smallest CRS, with 7,100 agency users in the United States. With System One, travel agents have direct access to 42 airlines worldwide, 135 hotel chains representing 18,000 properties, 40 car rental companies, and 20 other suppliers, including cruise lines and tour operators.

Most of the major vendors are developing second-generation computer products to further upgrade capabilities. Focalpoint (Covia) and WORLDSPAN LAN are two examples. These systems are intended to supplement the existing systems rather than to replace them.

Major Foreign CRS Vendors. United States CRSs have been successfully exported overseas, but there are also a number of foreign airlines that sell their own CRSs. These include:

- Gemini (Canada).
- ResAid (Scandinavian Airlines).
- TraviSwiss (Swissair).
- Jalcom-3 (Japan Air Lines).
- Resana (All Nippon Airways).
- Galileo Distribution Systems (Alitalia, British Airways, KLM, and Swissair).
- Amadeus Consortium (Air France, Iberia, Lufthansa, and SAS).
- Abacus (Cathay Pacific, Singapore Airlines).
- Fantasia (Qantas).
- INFINI (Abacus, All Nippon).

The use of United States systems in overseas markets has been a cause of concern for foreign airlines, particularly in Europe. European CRSs can offer more complete local listings, but they cannot match the worldwide information listings and reservations capabilities of SABRE, APOLLO, and WORLDSPAN.

In order to avoid losing control of their distribution network and millions of dollars in revenues, in the mid-1980s European airlines started to develop a joint-venture reservations system to compete with the United States CRSs. After that plan fell through, some of the foreign CRS vendors formed alliances with United States CRS vendors.

Cohosts and Shared Data Bases. An airline that does not have its own CRS can participate in a computer reservations system in one of four ways:

1. The least-expensive level permits a display of the airline's schedules but not of availability.
2. The next level of participation permits a display of schedules and availabilities, but reservations cannot be confirmed instantly.
3. The third level allows the airline to provide instant confirmation of reservations.

Illus. 3-4 *The Tulsa Computer Center in Tulsa, Oklahoma, is the heart of the SABRE network.*
Source: *American Airlines*

4. The most-expensive level allows the participating airline to provide the same information and services as those offered by the host airline.

An airline that participates at the fourth level is known as a *cohost*. Cohosts pay part of the cost of developing the system. In return, they share the data base and their flight listings are given preferential display over other carriers.

The Issue of Bias. *Bias* has been a hot topic in the automated travel industry ever since the first CRSs were introduced in 1976. Bias refers to the preferential display of host-carrier flight schedules on the CRT over the schedules of competing airlines. A hypothetical example will illustrate the point.

A travel agent using SABRE requests flight availability between Los Angeles and Miami on a specific date. There may be 30 flights to Miami on that day, but the CRT can display only 6 to 8 flights at a time. Because SABRE is owned by American Airlines, it is clearly in their interest to display their own flights first. Let's imagine that American has seven flights available to Miami: they could all be shown on the first display. The agent can request to see the second, third, and fourth displays for additional flights, but studies indicate that most bookings are made from the first display. If American did display its own flights first, as in this example, the company would be guilty of bias.

In response to the problem, the Civil Aeronautics Board (CAB) issued a series of rules in 1984 to eliminate bias from the reservations system. Host carriers were no longer permitted to display their own flights preferentially, nor those of cohost carriers. The CAB rulings have not been entirely effective, however, and bias remains a problem in the computerized travel industry.

Teleticketing

Teleticketing, in use since 1960, is the simplest and least-expensive form of automation available to travel agents. It permits subscribers to have airline tickets printed on a machine in the agency office. The teleticketing machine, which can be leased or purchased, is linked to the airline CRS by telephone lines. When an agent makes a reservation by phone, he or she can ask for the ticketing information to be relayed directly to the in-house teleticketing machine. Unlike automated reservations systems, teleticketing only allows one-way communication—from the airline system to the agency. (CRSs allow two-way communication between the airline and the agency.)

Teleticketing machines are useful for small agencies that do not have the volume of business to warrant the expense of a CRS. Larger agencies that have subscribed to CRSs since 1976 usually hang on to their teleticketing machines, especially if they own them. Even though CRSs linked to printers have made teleticketing machines obsolete, they still come in handy if the in-house computer breaks down.

Satellite Ticket Printer

The *satellite ticket printer* (*STP*), another form of travel agency automation, made its first appearance in 1986. STPs allow travel agents to deliver tickets electronically to a client's premises. The communication process is similar to teleticketing. STPs, however, are run by travel agents, not by airlines. The machines have proved particularly popular for in-plant industrial locations, such as those in industrial parks. With a growth rate of almost 79 percent in 1989, STPs are the fastest-growing category of travel agency location. There were 3,840 STPs at the end of 1989, with locations in all 50 states (see Figure 3-4).

Electronic Ticket Delivery Network

One of the most recent innovations in automation is the *electronic ticket delivery network* (*ETDN*). These ticket printers enable travel agents to make deliveries to travelers, especially business travelers, who need same-day or next-day tickets. ETDNs are similar to STPs but differ in that they are not owned by travel agencies. ETDN vendors expect to have the ticket printers in such varied locations as hotels, shopping malls, office buildings, and supermarkets in the near future.

Automated Ticketing Machine

Automated ticketing machines (*ATMs*) directly connected to a CRS are another recent development. Unlike

Illus. 3-5 *The satellite ticket printer is the fastest growing category of travel agency location.*

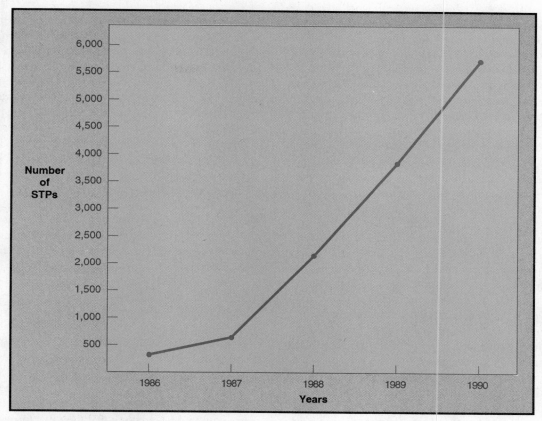

Figure 3-4 Growth of Satellite Ticket Printers
Source: Airlines Reporting Corporation

STPs, ATMs are owned and operated by individual airlines. By inserting a credit card into the ATM, a customer can gain access to flight information, make a reservation, and receive a ticket and boarding pass. ATMs can be found primarily in major airports, but industry analysts predict that self-service machines will eventually be installed in supermarkets, shopping centers, hotel lobbies, banks, and elsewhere. We might also expect to see machines that are shared by a number of different suppliers. Such machines might allow consumers to buy a complete travel package from a single automated location.

Check Your Product Knowledge

1. Why do travel agencies subscribe to computer reservations systems?
2. Name the four major computer reservations systems available in the United States.
3. What is meant by *bias*?
4. How do teleticketing machines, STPs, ETDNs, and ATMs differ?

OTHER USES OF AUTOMATION

So far, we have focused on the uses of automation for information, reservations, and ticketing functions, with specific reference to airline CRSs. In this section, you will learn how computer technology has been applied to back office functions. You will also read about the CRSs of nonairline suppliers, such as hotels and car rental agencies.

Back Office Systems

As the name suggests, *back office systems* involve functions performed behind the scenes—literally in the "back office." These functions are concerned not with the customer but with the efficient operation of the agency.

Back office systems are sometimes known as "computerized accounting systems" and "travel agency management systems." This will give you an idea of what the systems are primarily used for—to perform accounting functions and to prepare management reports.

Accounting functions include listing accounts receivable and accounts payable, writing checks, general ledger bookkeeping, and preparing balance sheets and financial statements. Some packages also include programs for maintaining agency payrolls.

Management functions of the automated back office systems allow reports to be compiled for the use of the agency management. These might be reports on productivity per employee, reports showing the source of all commissions earned, reports on the volume of business with individual suppliers, projections for future sales, and so forth. Many back office packages also feature programs for word processing and compiling mailing lists.

The advantages of using an automated back office system are similar to those of using a computer reservations system. They include considerable time savings, increased efficiency, and increased productivity. Agencies have been slower to automate back office functions than those directly relevant to the consumer, such as reservations and ticketing. More than half of all domestic travel agencies currently use computerized accounting and management systems (compared with 98 percent using CRSs). Most vendors are, however, reporting rapidly increasing sales of software packages.

Back office systems are available both from vendors of CRSs and from independent companies. One of the first systems to be developed was ADS (Agency Data-Systems), marketed by American Airlines (the same airline that sells the SABRE reservations system).

Most automated back office systems *interface* with one or more CRSs. This means that information can be transmitted from the reservations system to the accounting/management system. Suppose that an agency subscribes both to SABRE and to ADS. When an agent makes a reservation and a ticket is printed through SABRE, the information is automatically relayed to ADS. The back room system records the sale, notes the commission, credits the agent who made the sale, and compiles reports from the data supplied. In this way, the front room reservations system and the back room system come together.

Uses of Automation by Nonairline Suppliers

Earlier in this chapter, you read that airline CRSs can display the products and services of nonairline suppliers. A travel agent with access to a computer reservations system can, for example, make room reservations for most major domestic hotel chains.

In addition, some suppliers, particularly hotels and car rental agencies, have developed their own automated reservations systems. Holiday Inn's Holidex system, introduced in 1964, was a pioneer in hotel CRSs. Holidex links 1,600 Holiday Inn properties worldwide with a central computer in Memphis, Tennessee. About 40 percent of all Holiday Inn reservations are made through Holidex.

Reservations systems have also been installed by chains such as the Sheraton Corporation (Reservatron), Hilton (Hiltron), Westin (Westron), and Quality Inns (Sunburst).

Hotel reservations systems are accessed by hotel employees, through phone or in-person contact with guests. All hotel reservations systems operate on a single level, which means that only the services of the host vendor can be booked on individual CRSs. For example, reservations for a room in a Sheraton hotel cannot be made using the Holidex reservations system. Nor can a flight reservation be made using the hotel system. This is an important difference between airline CRSs and hotel CRSs. The advantage of making a hotel reservation through a hotel system is that the hotel CRS has the most up-to-date information on room availability. Airline systems are not usually updated automatically every time a reservation is made through the hotel CRS.

Car rental reservations systems function at the same level as hotel systems. Avis's Wizard Direct Input Reservation System, for example, can be used for booking Avis rental cars only.

Amtrak also has its own automated reservations system, known as ARROW. Initially, ARROW was purely informational, providing travel agents with information on train schedules, fares, and so forth. Travel agents are, however, now allowed to print Amtrak tickets, using the same standard ticket stock that they use for issuing airline tickets. Like the hotel and car rental CRSs, ARROW is a single-level system.

Illus. 3-6 *A hotel reservations agent uses computers to check room availability and book reservations at the request of customers, travel agents, and airlines.*
Source: *Marriott Hotel and Resorts*

A DAY IN THE LIFE OF
Airline Reservation Agent

If you're planning a trip that involves flying, I may be the first person you contact. I'm a reservations agent with a major airline. The telephone and the computer are the main tools of my trade. In many ways, I am the airline's "voice." I represent the airline every time I answer the phone and deal with a caller. Every caller is a potential customer, whether that person is a travel agent, an individual passenger, or someone from a business travel department.

It's my job to make sure that callers become customers. To many callers, I am the first contact they have with the airline. So it's very important that I deal with every call professionally, efficiently, and courteously.

In addition to knowing when and where we fly, I also have a host of information available about flights offered by other airlines and about rental cars, tours, and hotels and motels. Many people who call for flight information are pleasantly surprised to discover that I can also arrange for rental cars and accommodations. I can even book them onto sightseeing tours. Our prices for these services are very competitive, since the airline negotiates bulk discounts with the rental car companies, tour operators, and hotels and motels. Individuals might pay a lot more if they dealt with the suppliers themselves. So in addition to representing the airline and helping callers book seats on flights, I also sell the other services we offer. These telephone sales are an important aspect of my job.

The computer I use at work enables me to access all the information I need to help callers. All the information about our flights, fares, arrivals, departures, and other services is entered into the computer. I can find out anything I need to know at the touch of a few keys. With a typical call, I first find out where the person wants to go and when he or she wants to depart. I also need to know the length of stay at the destination so that I can check to see whether we can offer special fares. Once I have that information, I can give the cost of traveling in first, business, and economy class. I also explain any special fares.

The APEX fares, for example, are cheaper than the economy fare, but they have several restrictions, including an advance payment requirement and no cancellations.

To make a reservation for a caller, I type the caller's name, address, and phone number into the computer. This file is called the passenger name record, or PNR. I specify the flight the caller is taking, noting the flight number, departure date and time, and arrival time. I also handle seat assignments. Passengers may request an aisle or a window seat. Still others want to know what type of plane they will be flying. On our 747s, passengers who want more room can elect to sit in the back of the plane where the side rows contain only two seats. Others may request seats at the front of each section where there is more leg room. If there will be any small children traveling, I make special arrangements for them. Finally, I make arrangements for other passenger requests such as special meals or a wheelchair to and from the aircraft. It's my job to process this information properly to ensure that the passenger has the best possible flight.

Since our airline provides reservations information 16 hours a day, 7 days a week, 365 days a year, I work several different shifts. I like the flexibility that gives me, and I enjoy sometimes being off during the week when everyone else is working. While I enjoy my job, I like being part of a large organization that offers me several different career paths. I have the opportunity to build on what I have learned as a reservations agent or I can continue in my present position. Reservations agents can go on to become sales representatives or senior agents who supervise shifts and help set policy for the entire department.

I like helping people plan their business trips and vacations. I am always pleased when they benefit from all of the extras the airline has to offer, such as our discount accommodations and tours. A good reservations agent helps thousands of travelers get off to the right start each year. That's a big responsibility, but it's an interesting and challenging way to earn a living.

CAREER OPPORTUNITIES

All the major suppliers employ large staffs of reservations agents. In this section, we will look at the nature of the work of those who book reservations in the airline industry, the accommodations industry, the car rental industry, the tour industry, and the cruise line industry.

The reservations systems of most suppliers are now computerized. Job applicants are expected to have a working knowledge of computers and computer terminology. Some of the larger suppliers offer training courses for new reservations agents to familiarize them with the CRS. Keyboarding skills are necessary for reservations agents and office experience is helpful. Some suppliers prefer to hire applicants who have two years of college experience; for others, a high school diploma is sufficient.

Airline Reservations Agents. Airline reservationists typically work at large central offices, spending much of their time in front of computer screens. They handle telephone calls from travel agents and consumers who want to book flights. Using the computer keyboard, reservations agents check flight schedules, availabilities, and fares and then reserve seats for passengers.

Hotel Reservations Agents. Hotel reservationists, working in reservations centers, answer telephone calls from travel agents, airlines, and members of the public requesting room reservations. Agents check room availability on the computer screen and book accommodations accordingly.

Car Rental Reservations Agents. Car rental reservationists also work over the phone with travel agents, airlines, and the public. These reservationists check the availability of cars at the location requested. When making the reservation, they enter the length of time the car will be rented as well as the location to which the car will be returned (rental cars do not have to be dropped off at the same place they are picked up). Any relevant flight information must also be recorded.

Most car rental reservations systems are centralized. Avis reservations agents, for example, work at the central Avis reservations office in Tulsa, Oklahoma.

Tour Operator Reservations Agents. Reservations agents employed by tour operators work in a similar way to other reservations agents. They check the availability of tours and confirm reservations over the telephone.

Cruise Line Reservations Agents. Reservations agents working for cruise lines explain to clients what the cruise line offers and when the various cruises take place. They also take reservations and handle routine inquiries. Most cruise line reservations agents work with travel agents, not directly with consumers.

Computer Careers. The number of jobs available for reservations agents is expected to decline as a result of automation. Fewer agents are required to operate the computers. At the same time, however, automation has opened up a whole new field of computer-related career opportunities in the travel industry. CRS vendors employ people to train potential users of their systems. They also employ programmers, equipment installers, service professionals, and sales and marketing representatives. All of these jobs generally require some experience with travel agency operations of airline reservations systems.

Summary

- The travel industry uses three main systems of distribution to move its products from producer to consumer.
- Regardless of the system used, identical products will usually cost the consumer the same amount.
- The unilateral system involves the direct sale of travel products and services from supplier to consumer.
- The bilevel system most often involves a travel agent as intermediary. The agent is paid a commission by the supplier.
- The multilevel system involves the intervention of two or more intermediaries, most often a tour wholesaler and a retail travel agency.
- A single member of the distribution channel can sell products from other suppliers as well as the member's own products.
- The travel industry depends on a continuous flow of up-to-date information from supplier to consumer.
- In a nonautomated agency, travel agents have access to information through printed reference sources. Reservations are made by telephone.
- In an automated agency, travel agents have access to information through a computer reservations system. Printed reference sources are used for supplementary information.
- A CRS allows travel agents to make reservations and to ticket electronically.
- Airlines are the principal vendors of computer reservations systems.

- The four major domestic reservations systems are SABRE, APOLLO, System One, and WORLDSPAN.
- CRSs allow access to participating airlines and nonairline suppliers.
- Tickets can be delivered electronically to various locations by teleticketing machines, satellite ticket printers (STPs), electronic ticket delivery networks (ETDNs), and automated ticketing machines (ATMs).
- Automated back office systems, marketed by CRS vendors as well as independent companies, have been developed to perform travel agency accounting and management functions.
- Back office systems interface with one or more reservations systems.
- Many hotel chains and car rental agencies have their own automated reservations systems.

Key Terms

intermediary

commission

teleshopping

video marketing

override

specialty channeler

vertical marketing

manifest

wait list

computer reservations system (CRS)

passenger name record (PNR)

host vendor

cohost

bias

teleticketing

satellite ticket printer (STP)

electronic ticket delivery network (ETDN)

automated ticketing machine (ATM)

back office system

interface

What Do You Think?

1. Retail outlets such as supermarkets and department stores are being used as distribution points for travel products. Automated ticketing machines (ATMs) and personal computers are being used for direct ticketing and direct reservations. What effect do you think that these developments might have on the travel industry as a whole and on travel agencies in particular?
2. Why do you think that it has proved so difficult for United States airlines to come to an agreement on a neutral reservations system?
3. Do you think that CRS vendors should be allowed to display their own flights preferentially?
4. Why might a travel agency choose to subscribe to more than one computer reservations system?
5. Why do you think that airlines have played such a prominent role in the development of automated reservations systems?

Dealing with Product

The word *perishable* seems appropriate for describing dairy products and fresh-cut flowers, but how can this term apply to travel products as well? After all, most hotels are made with iron girders and tons of brick and mortar, ocean liners weigh thousands of tons, and airplanes are crafted from the strongest metals. Nevertheless, many marketing specialists will tell you that few products are as perishable as an airplane seat, a hotel bed, or a berth in a cruise ship. What do you suppose they mean by *perishability*? In what ways are travel products seasonal? How does seasonality affect the supply, demand, and cost of a travel product? What impact do you think nonrefundable cancellation penalties will have on perishables?

Dealing with People

You are a regional sales manager with a major airline. You have just received a telephone call from the president of a ski club in Yourtown. It seems the club plans to promote a ski group this winter and they would like to use your airline. You can expect at least 75 passengers, and perhaps as many as 100 will participate—that's a good day's work!

The president of the ski club has assured you that no travel agency is involved; in fact the club has always dealt directly with air carriers and has never used a travel agency. There are ten travel agencies in Yourtown, each one well qualified to handle this group. Should you recommend that the president use a travel agent, who might be able to get better flights with another airline? Will you just accept the order and thereby increase your profit margin? What will you tell the travel agency managers when they hear of this group?

Name _____

WORKSHEET 3-1   PERISHABLE PRODUCT

You have read about the perishable nature of travel products. One kind of intermediary that takes advantage of this perishability is the travel club. Travel clubs offer discounted travel products, such as seats on a charter airplane or cabins on a cruise ship, on very short notice. Look in a local magazine or the travel section of a newspaper and find an ad for such a travel club. Contact the club and get the following information:

Name of travel club

Annual membership fee

Services offered

How members find out what is available

How far in advance members can make plans

Possible savings

What characteristics identify people who can take advantage of clubs like this? What groups of people have these characteristics?

Can you think of any ways to extend the advantage of last-minute buying to other travelers?

The Yourtown Chamber of Commerce has asked you for your ideas to extend the tourist season. Lower airfares to your area and the absence of crowds are two advantages of off-season travel. What existing but underappreciated aspects of Yourtown's off-season life could you publicize? What special events or activities could Yourtown offer to attract visitors beyond the usual tourist season?

WORKSHEET 3-2   SPECIALTY CHANNELER

Imagine that you work as a specialty channeler who creates packages and tours for special-interest groups. Use brochures, tour manuals, catalogs, and other printed references to find a package or tour for each of the following groups. In the space provided, briefly describe the package or tour and the reference you used.

1. White-water rafting enthusiasts

2. Theatergoers

3. Physically disabled campers

4. Avid baseball fans

5. Young singles

6. Families who want to experience a cruise

7. Novice skiers

8. Wine connoisseurs

9. Mystery lovers

10. United States history buffs

WORSHEET 3-3   DISTRIBUTING THE TRAVEL PRODUCT

As you read in Chapter 3, there are three main channels of distribution: unilateral distribution system, bilevel distribution system, and multilevel distribution system. Read each situation below. On the line to the left, write the type of distribution system being used to bring travel products to the consumer.

_____ 1. When Al Isaacs was stationed in the U.S. Army in Japan, he relied on the SATO on base to make his travel arrangements.

_____ 2. Gary Nakata called an 800 number to reserve a room at the Holiday Inn in Eau Claire, Wisconsin.

_____ 3. Kathy Ernst had to fly to Denver at the last minute for a business meeting. She was able to purchase a ticket from an automated ticketing machine in the airport terminal.

_____ 4. While shopping at the mall one Saturday, Cindy and Mark Pfeifer bought a new washing machine and two airline tickets to Mexico City.

_____ 5. After browsing through a tour catalog of summer trips, Jane Oram decided to go on the 17-day Grand Alpine tour. Mercury Travel, a small travel agency in the mall, helped her make the arrangements.

_____ 6. Bradley Ortiz stopped in at Amtrak's downtown office to pick up tickets for his trip to Seattle.

_____ 7. Anne Vaughn purchased a home-shopping system for her personal computer. She can use it to check the balance in her checking account, get the latest stock-market reports, and even make airline reservations.

_____ 8. African Safaris, Inc., helped Troy and Amanda Burton plan their adventure trip to Kenya.

_____ 9. When Pete Hernandez booked a flight to San Francisco, the airline reservations agent also reserved a rental car and a hotel room for him.

_____ 10. Jack Trotter works for a large corporation. He makes all his travel arrangements—business and pleasure—through the company travel department.

WORKSHEET 3-4   TRAVEL INDUSTRY SPECIALISTS

You are the owner of a medium-sized travel agency in a small city. To which travel industry specialists would you go for the following?

A small color ad for a travel magazine

An illustrated brochure advertising a special tour to Disney World

A 30-second television commercial

Specialized travel industry publications are an important means of communicating information relevant to travel professionals.

1. You are a vice president of a large car rental chain, with facilities in all major United States cities and several foreign cities. Name two kinds of information you would want to find in travel publications.

2. You are the owner of a small, successful bed and breakfast in the California wine country. Name two kinds of articles you would want to read in the travel industry newsletter to which you subscribe.

3. You arrange wilderness adventures for high school students. What kind of information from specialized newsletters would be critical to your work?

4. You are a writer for a travel industry newsletter. Select a specific branch of the travel industry as your audience and outline an article you would like to write.

PART 2

TRANSPORTATION AND ACCOMMODATIONS

"Aviation was the combination of an undeveloped science with an art, resulting in adventure for the mind and body that brought stimulation to the spirit."

—Charles Lindbergh

Objectives

When you have finished this chapter, you should be able to:

■ Name aircraft and events significant in the development of the airline industry.

■ Distinguish between types of aircraft in service today.

■ Define air carrier aviation and general aviation and describe the types of services each provides.

■ Identify the parts of an airport.

■ Describe types of air routes.

■ Compare multilateral agreements with bilateral agreements and explain how they make the international air system work.

■ Discuss the role of the International Air Transport Association.

■ Summarize federal regulation of the United States airline industry since 1925.

■ Discuss the effects of the 1978 Airline Deregulation Act.

■ List factors that influence airfares.

■ Explain how IATA calculates international airfares.

In 1914, Tony Jannus flew passengers, one at a time, across Tampa Bay, Florida, in his seaplane. He charged five dollars for the 22-mile trip from St. Petersburg to Tampa. Jannus's operation was the first scheduled airline, or air transportation system, in the United States. Since then, this country's domestic airline industry has grown tremendously. In contrast to Jannus's one-man company, the airline industry today employs thousands of people to fly passengers and cargo to destinations throughout the United States.

International aviation—involving planes that leave the airspace of one country and enter the airspace of another—has grown simultaneously with domestic aviation. As a result, almost every part of the world is now accessible to aircraft. The growth in air travel has been the single most important factor in the development of the modern travel industry. It is the central ingredient on which so much else depends, including the hospitality industry, the tour industry, the cruise industry, and the car rental industry.

A BRIEF HISTORY OF GLOBAL AVIATION

Navigating the air to transport passengers and cargo has been possible, practically speaking, only in the last 60 years. But human beings have dreamed of flying since ancient times. The first successful flight of a manned aircraft occurred in 1783 when two Frenchmen floated 300 feet above Paris in a hot-air balloon. Important milestones in the history of aviation are shown in Figure 4-1.

Subsequent experiments with hot-air balloons led to the development of the airship, a lighter-than-air aircraft. For a time in the 1920s and 1930s, airships fitted with engines and propellers seemed to offer a viable means for long-distance air transportation. With the explosion of the German-built *Hindenburg* in 1937, however, interest in airships as passenger carriers declined.

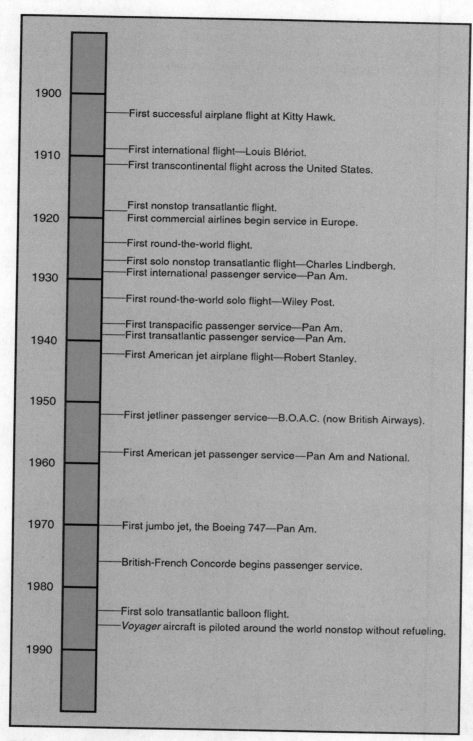

Figure 4-1 Milestones in Aviation History

The timeline shows:

1900

First successful airplane flight at Kitty Hawk.

1910

First international flight—Louis Blériot.
First transcontinental flight across the United States.

1920

First nonstop transatlantic flight.
First commercial airlines begin service in Europe.

First round-the-world flight.
First solo nonstop transatlantic flight—Charles Lindbergh.
First international passenger service—Pan Am.

1930

First round-the-world solo flight—Wiley Post.

First transpacific passenger service—Pan Am.
First transatlantic passenger service—Pan Am.

1940

First American jet airplane flight—Robert Stanley.

1950

First jetliner passenger service—B.O.A.C. (now British Airways).

1960

First American jet passenger service—Pan Am and National.

1970

First jumbo jet, the Boeing 747—Pan Am.

British-French Concorde begins passenger service.

1980

First solo transatlantic balloon flight.
Voyager aircraft is piloted around the world nonstop without refueling.

1990

Early Airplanes

Early experiments with airplanes were to prove of much greater significance in the development of air transportation. The earliest planes were gliders—aircraft without engines. The first successful manned glider flights were made during the 1890s by pioneers such as Otto Lilien-thal of Germany and Octave Chanute of the United States. Their achievements inspired Americans Orville and Wilbur Wright to turn their attention from manufacturing bicycles to building gliders. The Wright brothers developed a glider that could be controlled in flight, then added a 12-horsepower gasoline engine to create the first airplane (the *Flyer*).

The historic first flight, lasting just 12 seconds, was made on December 17, 1903, at Kitty Hawk, North Carolina. The entire 120-foot flight could have been made within the cabin of a Boeing 747. By 1905, the Wright brothers had developed a fully maneuverable biplane (a plane with two pairs of wings) that could stay in flight for more than half an hour. Experiments in other countries led to the development of monoplanes (with one pair of wings), four-engine planes, and planes of monocoque construction (a tubelike design that eliminated the need for body braces).

World War I greatly advanced the development of the airplane, as warring nations manufactured fighter planes and bombers equipped with more powerful engines and all-metal bodies. During the course of the war, average airplane speed increased from 65 miles an hour to 130 miles an hour.

Between the Wars

Organized airline service developed rapidly in Europe after World War I. At first, the airlines used surplus warplanes. Then they began to incorporate newer model transports such as the trimotor. Government subsidies accelerated the growth of airlines, and by 1921 Europe's major cities were linked by ten airlines.

Commercial airline service did not get underway in the United States until 1926, when the government began offering subsidies to private airline companies to carry mail. The Ford Trimotor, introduced the same year, was the first United States aircraft designed primarily to carry passengers (a maximum of ten per flight).

The pioneering flights of Charles Lindbergh, Amelia Earhart, and others captured the imagination of the United States public and created wider acceptance of the airplane. Between 1926 and 1930, the number of people traveling by air each year increased from 6,000 to 400,000. The introduction of the 21-person-capacity Douglas DC-3 in 1936 further accelerated the growth of air travel. Incorporating all the major technological advances of the time, this 170-mile-per-hour twin-engine transport acquired a reputation for incomparable comfort and safety. For a while, the DC-3 was to the airline industry what the Model T Ford was to the automobile industry: it enabled airlines to make a profit. The DC-3 is still used in many parts of the world today.

By the late 1930s, the United States had assumed world leadership of commercial aviation. American Airlines, Eastern Airlines, TWA, and United Airlines were the big names in domestic operations, while Pan Am was the major international carrier, flying routes from Alaska to South America. Pan Am introduced transpacific passenger service to Asia in 1937 and transatlantic service to Europe two years later.

World War II to the Present

World War II played a major role in promoting the growth of the commercial airline industry. As in World War I, warfare accelerated the research into and development of

Illus. 4-1 *The DC-3 aircraft was introduced to the airline industry in the 1930s, and it accelerated the growth of travel.*
Source: McDonnell Douglas Photo/Harry Gann

Illus. 4-2 *The Concorde, a supersonic transport, is characterized by a beaklike nose and exceptionally fast speed.*
Source: © Douglas/The Image Works

more advanced airplanes that could fly faster, higher, and further without refueling. After the war, these improvements were applied to commercial planes. In 1947, United Airlines and American Airlines inaugurated coast-to-coast United States service with the Douglas DC-6—a plane with a capacity of 55 passengers and a cruising speed of 300 miles per hour at 20,000 feet. Nonstop transoceanic transports such as the Douglas DC-7, Boeing 377 Stratocruiser, and Lockheed Super-Constellation were developed, all of which could carry 100 passengers at similar speeds.

In addition to improved airplane design, the war produced trained pilots anxious to transfer their skills to commercial aviation. Surplus warplanes, which could be purchased cheaply, enabled many airline companies to start up, especially smaller regional airlines and charter companies. One further effect of the war was to increase public confidence in the airplane as a means of transportation.

The Jet Age. Although privately owned United States airline companies continued to dominate the air, by the 1950s there was an increase in the number of foreign airlines flying international routes. Most of these airlines were government owned and operated. Foreign manufacturers, most notably the British, led the way in the development of jet airliners for commercial use. The Vickers Viscount (the first turboprop) and the De Havilland Comet (the first turbojet) were introduced in 1952.

The United States did not have a jet transport in commercial service until 1958, when Pan Am launched the Boeing 707 on transatlantic routes and National inaugurated DC-8 flights on domestic routes. The 707, with its 180-person capacity, was to have a revolutionary effect on the growth of international tourism. At a speed of 590 miles per hour, the turbojet could fly from New York City to Europe in just over seven hours. The fastest propeller-driven plane took 18 hours. A comparable trip on an ocean liner took four days. Faster flights meant that airlines could offer more flights. Increased passenger volume in turn reduced airfares and expanded flight schedules.

The expansion of jet service signaled the decline of ocean-going passenger ships as a means of point-to-point international travel. Jets also undercut rail and bus service for domestic travel. By the late 1960s, all the major airlines were operating with large jet-powered planes, and many of the smaller airlines were using small- to medium-range jets.

Jumbo Jets, Airbuses, and Supersonic Transports. Improvements in jet performance and comfort led to the development of huge, wide-bodied jets in the early 1970s. The first jumbo jet—the four-engine Boeing 747—was put into service by Pan Am in 1970. It could carry as many as 500 passengers. Europe's answer to the jumbo jet was the Airbus, launched in 1974. Built for fuel efficiency as well as passenger capacity, the Airbus

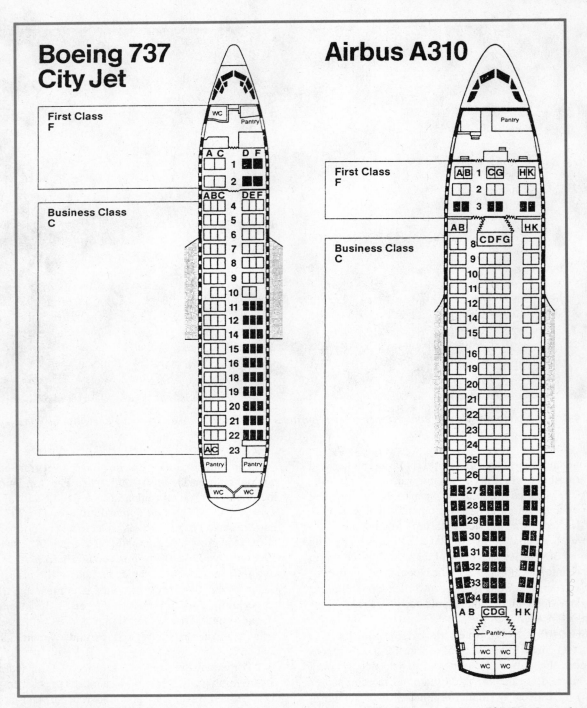

Illus. 4-3 *Note the comparative sizes and seating configurations of Lufthansa's Boeing 737 City Jet and Airbus A310.*
Source: Lufthansa Airlines

A-300 was the first twin-engine, wide-bodied jet. It was produced by Air Industrie, a consortium of West European companies.

International cooperation—between Britain and France— produced the Concorde, a supersonic transport (SST). Distinguished by its beaklike nose, the Concorde carries 125 passengers at a speed of 1,350 miles per hour—faster than the speed of sound. The British-French SST began passenger service in 1976, shortly after the Russian SST, the Tupolev-144, had been introduced. The manufacture of an American SST was halted in 1971 when the United States Senate refused to grant further funds. The refusal followed public protests against the loud sonic booms caused by the fast-flying SSTs.

The 1980s and Beyond. In the history of the airplane, bigger, faster, and higher have been the key terms. This trend may continue—designers and manufacturers are considering a hypersonic transport, a plane that would travel six times the speed of sound at an altitude of 120,000 feet. On the other hand, economic circumstances may dictate that fuel efficiency be given priority in future designs. Faced with rising costs and falling profits, many airlines are turning to cheaper, more fuel-efficient planes that require fewer people to operate and maintain them. The MD-80; Boeing 737-300, 757, and 767; and Airbus 310 are examples of jets that have been designed for fuel-efficient operation in recent years. Each of these aircraft, designed to carry 180 or more passengers, is powered by two engines and flown by only two flight officers. The 767 can make international long-haul flights.

Another trend is toward increasing privatization of overseas airlines. Airlines in the United States have long been privately owned; now a number of foreign governments are transferring airline ownership and operation from the public to the private sector. British Airways is an example of a government-run airline that has passed into private hands.

Types of Aircraft

In this book, aircraft will be described in two ways: by type of engine and by purpose.

Engine Type. Modern airplanes either have jet engines or they are propeller-driven. Both types are in service worldwide.

Jet aircraft, powered by turbine engines producing tremendous thrust, can cruise at 500 miles per hour. Cabins are pressurized so that the aircraft can fly at high altitudes (30,000 feet and above). *Pressurization* means an artificial increase in the cabin air pressure so that it is almost the same as air pressure at ground level. Because jets provide speed and comfort, they are used for long-distance and medium-range domestic and international flights. With fewer moving parts, the jet engine requires less maintenance than the gasoline-powered, piston engines that propeller planes use, and jets can be operated for more hours per day.

The turbojet was the first successful jet engine. Although it is still used on some planes, it has been superseded by the turbofan engine, which operates more efficiently (and more quietly) at low speeds.

More than 6,000 jet aircraft are currently in operation worldwide. Most of them were manufactured in the United States by the Boeing Company and the McDonnell-Douglas Corporation. In recent years, European manufacturers such as British Aerospace and Airbus Industrie have begun to offer strong competition to these two United States giants of the jet aircraft industry.

Propeller-driven airplanes, or props, fly more slowly and at lower altitudes than jets. Props can be divided into two categories: those with piston-powered engines plus one or more propellers (small airplanes); and those with turbine engines plus propellers, known as turboprops (medium-sized planes). Most turboprops and some piston-powered aircraft are pressurized. However, several models are not pressurized and must therefore fly below 12,000 feet, often in the weather rather than above it.

For the first 50 years of modern aviation, all airplanes were piston powered. Airplanes powered by turboprop engines entered commercial service in the 1950s. Jet aircraft replaced turboprops for long-distance flights during the 1960s, but many turboprops are still in use over shorter distances (400 miles or less). Some turboprops are pressurized and fly above bad weather. New propeller-driven aircraft are being designed for the growing regional and commuter airlines. Foreign manufacturers are earning a large share of this market. For example, Embraer's Bandeirante, a twin turboprop light transport, made in Brazil, has been sold to 21 countries. Other manufacturers include De Havilland of Canada, Casa of Spain, Fokker of the Netherlands, and Short Brothers of Northern Ireland.

Purpose. Aircraft can be further classified according to the particular market they are designed to serve.

- *Short-haul flights.* The regional/commuter market is served by a variety of single- and twin-engine planes carrying between 19 and 60 passengers on short-haul flights of 100 miles or less.
- *Short- to medium-range flights.* Twin-jets, such as the McDonnell-Douglas DC-9 and the Boeing 737, operate within the short to medium range (1,000 miles or less) and usually carry between 100 and 160 passengers. There are more 737s flying today than any other type of commercial aircraft. The Boeing 727, a three-engine jet, usually provides service on flights of 2,000 miles or less and carries up to 180 passengers.
- *Long-haul flights.* The long-haul transcontinental and intercontinental market is served by the largest jets of all. They include twin-jets (the Boeing 767 and Airbus A-300), tri-jets (the DC-10, McDonnell-Douglas MD-11, and Lockheed L-1011), and four-engine jets (the Boeing 747 and McDonnell-Douglas DC-8). These planes vary in capacity from 180 to 500 passengers and fly within the range of 3,000 to 7,000 miles.
- *Special purpose.* One final category is the special-purpose aircraft. This category includes helicopters, seaplanes, and amphibian vehicles. There are several all-helicopter and all-seaplane airlines both in the United States and overseas.

The Boeing Company

Boeing is the world's leading manufacturer of airplanes for commercial travel. It was founded in 1916, only 13 years after the Wright brothers made their first flight. In those days, airplanes were still very crude handmade machines. William E. Boeing, the son of a wealthy lumber company owner, took up flying as a hobby when he was 34. He quickly became dissatisfied with the planes he was flying and decided he could build a better plane himself.

Boeing set to work with an associate, G. Conrad Westervelt, to construct two airplanes at a Seattle, Washington, shipyard. They finished the first plane, which they called the B&W, in 1916. It was a bi-wing float plane with an open cockpit. The B&W was the beginning of the Boeing Company.

The following year, 1917, the United States entered World War I. The U.S. Navy, which had a sudden urgent need for training planes, ordered 52 planes from Boeing. Those planes, an improved version of the B&W, were called Model Cs. The planes were assigned a Navy serial number, 699, so they became known as C-699s. When Boeing built an additional Model C for himself, he named it the C-700. The Boeing Company still uses numbers in the 700s to designate its jetliners. If you have flown on a commercial airline, you have probably flown on a Boeing 707, 727, 737, 747, 757, or 767.

In 1927, Boeing won a contract to fly airmail between San Francisco and Chicago. His company produced 24 new airplanes, Model 40As, in six months to begin the new service. The Model 40As were open cockpit biplanes with wheels rather than pontoons. They could carry 1,200 pounds of mail. However, tucked away under the wings was a small closed compartment that could carry two very brave passengers. The Model 40As were the first planes to be used for regular long-distance passenger and mail service.

The Model 40As were soon outdated, however. In 1928, Boeing produced a greatly improved passenger plane called the Model 80. This plane was still a bi-wing, but it had three engines and a cabin large enough to carry 12 passengers. The cabin included upholstered seats, a toilet, running water, and reading lamps. By the standards of the time, the Model 80 was the state of the art in luxury and comfort. The new plane also included two other innovations in air transportation: an enclosed cockpit for the two-person crew and registered nurses—the first flight attendants—to wait on the passengers.

From the 1930s to the present, the Boeing Company has continued to develop new, improved airplanes, both for commercial airlines and for the military. These include the famed Pan American clipper ships in the 1930s, the Stratacruiser airliners in the 1940s, and the Dash 80, the first jet airliner, in the 1950s. During World War II, 12,000 Boeing B-17 bombers—the famed Flying Fortresses—were produced to meet the needs of America's war effort. Boeing now builds Chinook helicopters for the military.

William Boeing died in 1956, but the company he built has continued to grow and prosper. Today, Boeing produces more commercial airplanes than all other aircraft companies combined. Boeing's Everett, Washington, plant is the largest building in the world. The Everett site covers 1,000 acres and employs a total of 24,000 workers.

The Everett plant normally produces five jumbo 747s and five wide-body 767s each month. Boeing delivers nearly two airplanes per working day to airlines in countries such as Singapore, Britain, Algeria, Japan, and Brazil. The company has also been awarded contracts to design and build pressurized modules for the proposed NASA space station that is scheduled to be completed in the mid-1990s. These modules will provide living and work space for future astronauts. Perhaps someday Boeing airships will fly passengers to space stations for vacations that would truly be "out of this world."

Photo Source: Boeing Commercial Airplane Group

Illus. 4-4 *Foreign manufacturers are designing new propeller-driven aircraft for the growing regional and commuter airlines.*
Source: © *Earl Dotter*

Check Your Product Knowledge

1. How did World War II influence the development of the commercial airline industry?
2. What effects did the inauguration of passenger jet service in the 1950s have on the travel industry?
3. What is the main difference between United States airlines and foreign airlines?
4. Name four types of airplane engines.

TYPES OF AIR SERVICE

Within the United States, airplanes and other aircraft provide services in two broad areas—civilian and military. Civilian services can be further divided into air carrier aviation and general aviation.

Air Carrier Aviation

Air carrier aviation consists of privately owned companies that produce for-hire public transportation of passengers, cargo, and mail. There are approximately 250 domestic airline companies in the United States at the present time. An air carrier, also known as a *common carrier*, can be a small company with 100 employees and a dozen aircraft, or it can be a huge conglomerate with 40,000 employees and hundreds of aircraft. Airlines such as United and USAir belong to the category of air carrier aviation.

Some airplanes are designed to transport passengers only. Others—with removable seats, extra-wide doors, and machinery for loading and unloading—can transport either passengers or cargo. Still others are designed solely to transport cargo. These airplanes look like passenger airplanes, but they have no windows. The largest cargo planes, such as the Boeing 747F, can carry 100 tons 4,000 miles nonstop. Typical airline cargo includes goods that must be delivered quickly (flowers, fruits, vegetables); lightweight, expensive goods (electronic equipment, machine parts); and business documents. In recent years, small-package carriers that guarantee overnight delivery to major cities across the United States have found a lucrative market. These include Federal Express, UPS, Purolator, and Emery.

Air carriers provide services on either a scheduled or a nonscheduled basis. Most airlines are *scheduled airlines*, that is, each flight is scheduled to depart and arrive at certain times. Timetables are extremely important, and most carriers achieve on-time departures and arrivals throughout 90 percent of their schedules. Nonscheduled airlines, also called *supplemental airlines* or *charter airlines*, provide air travel at lower rates than regular fare on scheduled airlines. Planes can be chartered from supplemental airlines or from airlines operating scheduled flights.

Classification Systems. Prior to the Airline Deregulation Act of 1978, the Civil Aeronautics Board (CAB) awarded "certificates of convenience and necessity" to domestic airlines; these certificates assigned airlines to specific routes. Northwest Orient, for example, was given control of the route from Minneapolis/St. Paul to Seattle. To indicate their size and scope, certified air carriers, providing scheduled services, came to be classified along geographical lines:

- *Trunk lines.* The heart of the airline industry, these were the large airlines (such as American, United, and Delta) with long-distance routes between major metropolitan areas and medium-sized cities and some international flights.
- *Intra-Hawaiian and intra-Alaskan.* These airlines operated only within Hawaii or Alaska.
- *Regional.* These airlines served a specific area of the country. For example, Allegheny Airlines served the northeastern United States, while Southern served the South. Regionals were feeders for the trunk lines.
- *Local and/or commuter.* These smaller airlines flew to the smaller communities that the regionals could not serve profitably.

Since deregulation, these geographical distinctions have become blurred. For instance, airlines formerly allowed to operate only within Hawaii now provide service to the mainland. Former regional airlines have developed service between major cities in competition with trunk airlines. Consequently, air carriers are now classified on the basis of revenue or annual earnings.

- Major air carriers earn $1 billion or more yearly.
- National air carriers earn $75 million to $1 billion yearly.
- Large regional/commuter carriers earn $10 million to $75 million yearly.
- Medium-sized regional/commuter carriers earn less than $10 million yearly.

A classification system based on revenue is more realistic and flexible and more accurately describes what is happening in the industry. If business is brisk, a regional carrier could be a national carrier next year. Conversely, a major carrier could drop to a national carrier if sales are low.

It should be noted that every major air carrier in the United States, and even some of the national carriers, are also international carriers, that is, they operate scheduled service to foreign nations.

International Air Carriers. No nation has as many airlines as does the United States; indeed most have only one. Even the leading industrial nations rarely have more than three carriers. They might have one long-haul/international, one regional/commuter, and one all-charter operator. Switzerland, for example, is represented by Swissair (long haul), Crossair (regional), and Balair (charter).

General Aviation

General aviation applies to all civilian aircraft except those used by the commercial airlines. In terms of revenue, general aviation is far less important than air carrier aviation. In terms of number of aircraft, however, it is of far greater significance. More than 95 percent of the 224,000 aircraft in the United States are classified as general aviation aircraft. Of these, more than half are single-engine, propeller-driven planes, seating from one to six passengers. Few general aviation aircraft fly in the jet routes that begin at 18,000 feet.

Categories of Aircraft. General aviation aircraft provide a mix of public (for-hire) and private services. They can be divided into six broad categories, according to use:

- Air taxis operate on a charter, contract, or demand basis and provide access to almost 14,000 United States airports (whereas the air carriers offer scheduled service to only about 600 airports). They range in size from single- and twin-engine propeller-driven aircraft to small jets.
- Corporate airplanes fly a company's managers, salespersons, and other employees to out-of-town meetings and assignments. Nearly all of the Fortune 500 companies (the leading United States corporations), operate their own private fleets. Aircraft include business jets such as the Lear jet and Cessna Citation, as well as light twins and helicopters.
- Special-services planes are used for aerial photography, pipeline and power line patrol, fire prevention and fire fighting, law enforcement, emergency medical services, traffic reporting, crop dusting and spraying, conservation, and much more.
- Flight instruction aircraft range from primary two-place trainers to complex aircraft used for professional pilot training and proficiency programs.
- Privately owned planes are used for personal transportation (for business and pleasure).
- Sports planes, such as the 250-pound ultralight, provide recreation for their owners.

General aviation is seldom as well developed or diversified in other countries as it is in the United States.

Edwin Colodny

Edwin Colodny was born in Burlington, Vermont, in 1927, the son of a grocer. As a youngster, he bagged potatoes, delivered groceries, and waited on customers in his father's store. This early work experience taught him that one of the best ways to succeed in business is to provide good service to your customers. Until his retirement in mid-1991, Colodny applied that same principle in his role as the chairman of the board and president of USAir, one of the largest airlines in the United States.

Colodny graduated from Harvard Law School in 1951. After law school, he served three years in the U.S. Army Judge Advocate General Corps, the legal department of the Army. In 1954, Colodny took a job with the Civil Aeronautics Board (CAB). This was the federal agency that monitored the airline industry before deregulation in 1978. As a CAB counsel, it was Colodny's job to represent the public interest in hearings when rival airlines applied for a new air route and to recommend a candidate to the board.

In 1956, Colodny was hearing a case involving Allegheny Airlines and three other competitors for a new route when he met Allegheny's president, Leslie O. Barnes. In 1957, Barnes was looking for an experienced lawyer to help the airline deal with the CAB, and he offered Colodny the job. Colodny accepted and became Allegheny's one-man legal department.

In the 1960s and 1970s, Colodny climbed steadily through the airline's ranks. He was named executive vice president for law and marketing services in 1969 and president of the company in 1975. Three years later, shortly after Colodny became chairman of the board, Allegheny changed its name to USAir. During his tenure as the chief executive of USAir, Colodny tried to provide top-quality service to the airline's customers. He frequently toured USAir stations to talk to employees and passengers and to inspect the facilities. While flying on USAir planes, he liked to spend his time talking to passengers and crew members.

When the federal government deregulated the airline industry in 1978, Allegheny was still a small regional airline. It did not enjoy a great reputation among passengers, but it succeeded by flying the shorter, less profitable routes that the larger airlines shunned. A passenger who wanted to go to New London, Connecticut, or Erie, Pennsylvania, had little or no choice but to fly Allegheny.

Colodny's background as a regulator led him to believe that the small airlines, like USAir, needed some government protection to be able to compete with the large airlines and to ensure that airlines provided efficient service to their customers. Under deregulation, airlines of all sizes were left to succeed or fail on their own with no help from the government. As a result, some small airlines have grown large, some have been acquired by larger carriers, and some have folded.

Despite Colodny's reservations, USAir has fared well under deregulation. Colodny continued USAir's emphasis on domestic flights and kept the company operating profitably while he gradually expanded it. In 1987, USAir acquired Pacific Southwest Airlines and Piedmont Airlines. These mergers nearly doubled the size of USAir. By 1989, it had become the fourth largest airline in the United States in number of passengers served.

The mergers, however, created many unexpected problems. Colodny, the man who prided himself on personal service, suddenly had to deal with delayed flights, lost luggage, long lines, confused employees, and irate passengers. It took USAir more than a year to straighten out its post-merger problems.

In the meantime, the United States was struck in 1990 by a recession, or economic downturn, that reduced profits for USAir and most other airlines. Despite these setbacks, Colodny's conservative, service-oriented approach to airline operations helped to make USAir a solid, profitable carrier likely to survive for some time to come.

Relation to Air Carrier Aviation. Although travel professionals are primarily interested in air carrier aviation, a knowledge of general aviation is important for several reasons. First, general aviation aircraft provide access to air travel for people in areas of the country that are not served by scheduled airlines. Second, general aviation is a nationwide training school for pilots, mechanics, and technicians. Third, many domestic airlines, especially scheduled regional and commuter airlines, evolve out of general aviation. Finally, general aviation provides a career path. Many workers gain experience in general aviation and then move on to employment in air carrier aviation.

Check Your Product Knowledge

1. What is the difference between air carrier aviation and general aviation?
2. Why did airline classification change from a system based on geography to a system based on revenue?
3. How is general aviation important to air carrier aviation?

AIRPORTS: TRANSPORTATION TERMINALS FOR THE SKIES

The world's major airports are international crossroads, handling thousands of passengers and hundreds of flights each day to every corner of the globe. Figure 4-2 lists the world's ten busiest airports. At Chicago's O'Hare International Airport, the world's busiest, a plane takes off or lands every 23 seconds. Some international airports resemble cities. Germany's Frankfurt-Main Airport, for example, features 12 restaurants, 10 snack bars, a variety of boutiques, medical and dental offices, banks, a supermarket, a disco, and 4 movie theaters.

At the opposite extreme are the thousands of small, private airfields with no scheduled flights, limited facilities, and little daily activity.

Types of Airports

The Federal Aviation Administration (FAA) classifies United States civilian airports into two types: air carrier airports and general aviation airports. Air carrier airports, numbering approximately 570, are used by the airplanes of scheduled airlines—the majors, nationals, and regionals. Air carrier airports can also serve general aviation air-

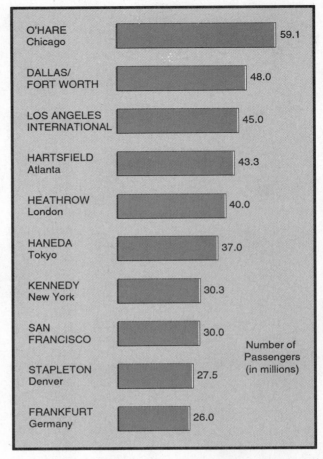

Figure 4-2 The World's Ten Busiest Airports, 1989
Source: Airport Operators Council International

craft, especially corporate airplanes. The 12,400 general aviation airports—often unpaved and unlighted—serve all types of aircraft, except scheduled airline planes.

Airport Ownership

In the United States, a railroad company not only owns the trains it operates but also the tracks and stations its trains use. Bus companies, too, generally own the stations out of which their buses operate. The same is not true for airports; very few airlines own and operate the airports they serve. Instead, they rent space.

The majority of airports are small, privately owned facilities. Their owners primarily serve the recreational flyers who are part of general aviation. There are, however, more than 5,000 publicly owned and operated airports in the United States. These include all large airports serving metropolitan areas. Publicly owned airports are administered by state, county, or city governments.

Airports often enter into a contract with a *fixed-base operator (FBO)*. The FBO sells fuel, rents hangar space to aircraft owners, provides maintenance and repairs, and gives flying lessons. The FBO pays rent (and usually a percentage of gross revenue) to the airport.

Air carriers pay for use of the airport through landing fees, rent on counter and office space, and fuel and registration taxes. As landlord, the governing authority also charges rent to car rental companies, coffee shops and stores, and other concessions in and around the terminal building.

Airport Location

Because of the space required by runways, even the smallest airport needs four acres of land. Medium-sized airports require 500 to 1,500 acres, while large airports require 15,000 acres. The Dallas-Fort Worth Airport, the largest airport in the United States, covers 17,500 acres of land—more than 27 square miles.

The large amount of land required by airports makes them difficult to site and construct. The rapid growth of airline traffic and the increase in the size of airplanes have created a constant demand for more space. Whereas train and bus stations can be placed in downtown areas, airports must usually be situated in outlying districts. In the 1940s and 1950s, airports were constructed on what were then the outskirts of metropolitan areas. Airports remained on these sites while suburbs sprang up around them in the 1960s and 1970s. As a result, many communities today must contend with the noise and congestion caused by nearby airports.

Illus. 4-5 *The largest airport in the United States is Dalls-Ft. Worth, which occupies 17,500 acres.*

Source: American Airlines

The Layout of an Airport

Airports vary in layout depending on their size and the time they were built. Early airports were far simpler in design than those built today.

The Terminal Building. The terminal building is the heart of the airport complex. It is the place where passengers purchase or present their tickets, check in or retrieve baggage, and board an airplane or deplane. In addition to ticket counters and waiting areas, the terminal building includes a weather station, briefing room for pilots, dispatch office for communicating with ticket counters and planes, and the office of the airport manager. The terminal buildings at major airports also offer the services of car rental agencies, shops, restaurants, cocktail lounges, and banks.

The first air terminals were long, straight buildings. People entered in the front and walked out to airplanes parked in back. With the growth of air traffic, pierlike extensions, flanked by parking bays, were added to the back of the terminal building. This configuration allowed the airport to increase the number of gates for boarding and deplaning. Most major airports follow this type of terminal design.

To avoid long walks along piers, the satellite design was introduced in the 1960s. Passengers check in at ticket desks in a main terminal building. Then they go by way of moving sidewalks or underground trains to satellite buildings to board their flights. The Seattle-Tacoma International Airport follows this arrangement. Another design features a row of terminals shaped like rings or horseshoes. Passengers enter the terminal at the gate marked for their flight and walk only a short distance.

Other Parts of an Airport. In addition to the passenger terminals and parking lots, major airports have the following areas:

- The *cargo terminal*—one or more separate buildings where mail or freight is processed.
- The *control tower*—the nerve center of the airport, usually adjacent to the passenger terminal. From the glass-enclosed top level, or cab, air-traffic controllers use radar, radio, and signal lights to direct traffic in the air and on the ground.
- *Hangars*—the places where planes are stored and repaired. The hangars must be far enough from the runways to avoid interference.
- *Runways*—the strips of land on which airplanes land and from which they take off. Runways must be long enough and wide enough to accommodate the airplanes using them. The FAA sets size specifications. There must also be a clear zone at either end of the runway. To accommodate a jumbo jet, a runway with its clear zone might be four miles in length.

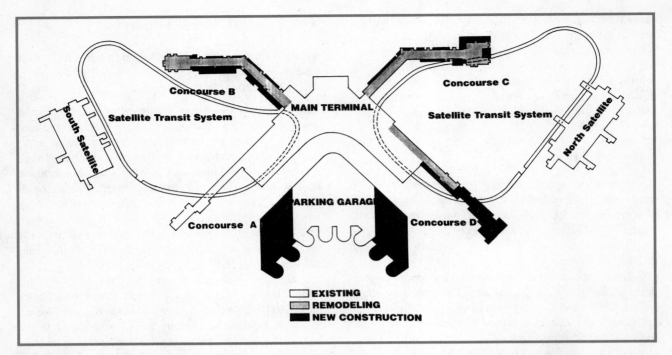

Illus. 4-6 *The layout of the Seattle-Tacoma Airport shows the south and north satellites and the routes for reaching them.*
Source: Seattle-Tacoma International Airport

- The **loading apron**—the parking area at the terminal gate where the airplane is refueled, loaded, and boarded.
- *Taxiways*—lanes for the airplane to use when going from the apron to the runway or from the runway to the hangar.

Airports and Route Structures

An airline route is the path an airplane takes in delivering its services. Airports are the delivery points along the path. To make the most efficient use of their airplanes, airline managers plan routes carefully, using three main patterns or structures.

When an airplane flies to a destination in one direction and then turns around and repeats the flight in the opposite direction, it has completed a *linear route*. A linear route can have intermediate stops that generate additional traffic and revenue at marginal costs.

On a *hub-and-spoke route*, a major airport becomes the center point for arrivals from and departures to all directions. The airport is like the hub of a wagon wheel; the smaller airports that surround it form the rim; and the flights that connect the hub and the rim are the spokes. These route structures can be overlapped to create an ever-widening air-route system. For example, the airport at Syracuse, New York, could be the hub for flights to small cities around it. In turn, Baltimore could be a hub city with Syracuse on its rim. Then Atlanta could be the hub city with Baltimore on its rim. Finally, London could

be the hub city with Atlanta on its rim. In this case, the airport at Atlanta becomes a *gateway airport* because it services scheduled international flights. With the increase in international tourism, many cities have had to expand their airport facilities and some now have more than one airport. In New York City, for example, Kennedy Airport handles long-distance international flights, while LaGuardia and Newark handle domestic flights and some international flights.

A third type of route combines the linear with the hub-and-spoke. As many flights as possible are scheduled to arrive in a particular city (the hub) at the same time. The same planes depart one hour later on a linear route to their originating cities after picking up passengers from the other flights who need connecting flights to particular destinations. For example, Passenger 1 arrives in Chicago on Flight A from Denver. She immediately boards Flight C, which is returning to Miami, while Passenger 2, who just got off Flight B from New York, catches Flight A for the return trip to Denver.

Security at Airports

While international airports have become global crossroads, they have also become killing grounds for disputes half a world away. Bombings, shootings, and hijackings have prompted governments and airport officials to tighten security at international airports.

Following the terrorist hijacking of a TWA jet shortly after takeoff from Athens Airport in June 1985,

Illus. 4-7 *To reduce the danger of skyjacking, all airports have installed rigorous security check systems.*
Source: *Doug Goodman/Monkmeyer Press Photo Service*

the FAA imposed stricter security measures, focusing on thorough inspection of passenger baggage. Individual airports have instituted further precautions such as requiring all passengers to pass through metal detectors before boarding. Some have also hired security coordinators to monitor the servicing and loading of planes and to use dogs to sniff out explosives. At some airports, police in armored trucks meet and dispatch airplanes from nations associated with terrorists.

Some analysts predict that airports of the future will be located in isolated areas surrounded by electrified barbed-wire fences. Terminals may be designed so that passengers funnel through checkpoints. Lockers, rest rooms, restaurants, and other potential hiding places may be placed behind secure checkpoints.

Check Your Product Knowledge

1. What are the FAA classifications for civilian airports?
2. Who owns the airports in the United States?
3. List the main parts of an airport.
4. What are three types of airline route structures?

REGULATION

Governments have been involved in the regulation of the airline industry since the early days of aviation. We can identify three different levels of regulation. On the highest level, commercial flights between countries are regulated by international agreements. On a second level, individual governments enforce economic and air safety regulation within each country. And on a third level, governments regulate international travelers by requiring them to carry documentation and observe health and customs regulations. The regulation of international travelers was discussed in detail in Chapter 2.

How the International System Works

In August 1983, Korean Air Lines flight 007 was returning to Seoul when it wandered into Soviet airspace. A missile-firing Soviet interceptor shot the plane down, killing all 269 persons aboard. Throughout the world, people were outraged. By launching a military attack on a defenseless civilian airplane, the Soviet Union had violated a basic rule of the air.

Early in the development of international aviation, governments realized that uniform rules would be necessary to ensure the smooth operation of airlines between countries. Over the years, a system for conducting international aviation has evolved through three channels:

- Multilateral agreements reached at worldwide conferences.
- The negotiation of bilateral agreements.
- Membership in international organizations.

At the present time, the international system is a compromise between total government control and totally independent decision making by the airlines.

Worldwide Conferences. Just as each nation claims ownership of the soil within its boundaries or the sea close to its borders, each nation also claims ownership of the sky above it. The fundamental principle of sovereign skies, first affirmed at the Paris Convention on the Regulation of Aerial Navigation in 1919 and reaffirmed at subsequent conventions, explains why countries have to negotiate the mutual use of airspace. According to this principle, a country must be invited to fly through the airspace of another. Thus, when the Soviets shot down KAL 007, they did have the right to regulate the entry of a foreign aircraft into their territory. But they did not—by international custom—have the right to do it in such a drastic manner.

Another important principle resolved at the Paris Convention was that every aircraft must have a nationality. In other words, an aircraft must be validly registered in a specific nation and accountable to that nation for its operations. This principle is especially important in the event of an infraction of international air law.

The Havana Convention of 1928 resulted in the standardization of operating procedures, such as issuing tickets and checking baggage. The agreement enabled international airlines to work together more easily.

The 1929 Warsaw Convention on International Carriage by Air established limits of liability if a passenger is injured or killed, and if baggage or cargo is lost or damaged. The agreement was amended in 1955 by The Hague Protocol and again in 1971 by the Guatemala City Protocol.

The agreements reached at these conventions are multilateral, or many-sided. They involve more than two nations and are equally binding on all nations that sign them. In recent years, further conventions have established procedures for dealing with hijacking and other crimes committed aboard international flights.

The Freedoms of the Air. Toward the close of World War II, representatives of all the member countries of the United Nations, except the Soviet Union, gathered in Chicago to renew the principles of international air law. Among other accomplishments, the Chicago Convention of 1944 formulated the Five Freedoms, which have greatly affected international aviation. Also called the Flying Freedoms, these statements categorized the ways in which a carrier of one nation can pass through, land in, and depart from the sovereignty of another nation. They provide a basis for international negotiations. Over the years, three unofficial freedoms have been added to the list.

Figure 4-3 summarizes the eight freedoms and gives an example of each. The first two freedoms are called

transit rights and have been widely accepted on a multilateral basis. Freedoms three, four, five, and six are called traffic rights and have not been completely accepted. The seventh and eighth freedoms are allowed only under special circumstances.

Bilateral Agreements. Shortly after the Chicago Convention, nations began to realize the need for bilateral, or two-sided, agreements. A bilateral aviation agreement is an agreement between two nations regarding air service between them. In 1946, the United States and the United Kingdom negotiated a bilateral agreement that became a model for subsequent agreements. Signed in Bermuda and referred to as the Bermuda system, this agreement incorporates the spirit of the Flying Freedoms.

Negotiating an airline agreement between nations is similar to negotiating a trade pact or a peace treaty. During the negotiations, the governments decide on the routes to be served and the airports to be used. The frequency and capacity of flights and restrictions for taking off and landing are also determined. In addition, the agreement specifies the procedure for the approval of fares and tariffs. Usually the airlines are asked to consult about fares with the International Air Transport Association (IATA). In the United States, the government decides which airline or airlines get the new routes established through a bilateral agreement.

International Air Transport Association. IATA is an airline service organization. It was founded in 1919 by a group of European airlines and reorganized in 1945. Today, approximately 200 of the world's airlines belong to IATA, either as full members or as associate members. Although more Third World airlines are joining, IATA is basically controlled by its European members.

IATA performs several important functions for members. The purpose of the organization is to:

- Provide a forum for airlines to meet and discuss mutual concerns.
- Recommend fares and tariffs for government approval.
- Represent the airlines in travel agency affairs.
- Promote air safety.
- Encourage worldwide air travel.

Another important organization is the International Civil Aviation Organization (ICAO). Founded by the Chicago Convention, the ICAO is an agency of the United Nations. When the Soviet Union joined in 1970, membership became almost universal. ICAO is primarily concerned with setting standards for aviation equipment and operations. It also organizes world conferences and can mediate disputes between members.

Traffic Conferences. To make air travel easier to describe and organize, IATA has divided the global airline community into three areas (see Figure 4-4).

The United States and IATA. The United States has frequently disagreed with the airfares established by IATA and has conducted bilateral pacts to bypass them.

Most of IATA's members are *flag carriers*, or national airlines representing an individual nation. For example, El Al is the flag carrier for Israel and Japan Air Lines (JAL) is the flag carrier for Japan. Scandinavian Airlines (SAS) is the exception, since this carrier is a cooperative venture involving Norway, Sweden, and Denmark. Therefore, the flags of all three nations are

First Freedom. The right of an airline to overfly one country to get to another.
Second Freedom. The right of an airline to land in another country for a technical stopover (fuel, maintenance, etc.) but not to pick up or drop off traffic.
Third Freedom. The right of an airline, registered in country X, to drop off traffic from country X into country Y.
Fourth Freedom. The right of an airline, registered in country X, to carry traffic back to country X from country Y.
Fifth Freedom. The right of an airline, registered in countryX,tocollecttraffic in country Y and fly on to country Z, as long as the flight either originates or terminates in country X
Sixth Freedom. The right of an airline, registered in country X, to carry traffic to a gateway—a point in country X—and then abroard. The traffic has neither its origin nor ultimate destination in country fX.
Seventh Freedom. The right of an airline, registered in country X, to operate entirely outside of country X in carrying traffic between two other countries.
Eighth Freedom. The right of an airline, registered in country X, to carry traffic between any two points in the same foreign country.

Examples of Freedoms of the Air

First Freedom. Delta Airlines departs from Atlanta and overflies Canada en route to London.

Second Freedom. Japan Airlines departs from Copenhagen, Denmark, and lands in Anchorage, Alaska, en route to Tokyo. The stop in Alaska is for fuel and a crew change. Japan Airlines is not allowed to carry passengers or cargo to or from Anchorage.

Third Freedom. Delta Airlines departs from Atlanta and carries U.S. citizens to London.

Fourth Freedom. Delta Airlines departs from London and carries British subjects to the U.S.

Fifth Freedom. Delta Airlines departs from Atlanta, stops en route in London, and boards passengers there for its continuation to Frankfurt, Germany.

Sixth Freedom. Northwest Airlines, carrying Norwegian passengers from Oslo bound for Tokyo may stop over in Minneapolis/St. Paul, Minnesota, a gateway city.

Seventh Freedom. British Airways flies nonstop from Frankfurt, Germany, to Washington, D.C., without stopping in Great Britain.

Eighth Freedom. Air France, a French carrier, carries traffic between Frankfurt and Berlin—all within Germany.

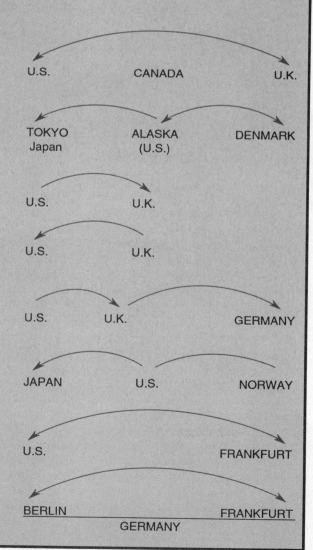

Figure 4-3 The Eight Freedoms of the Air

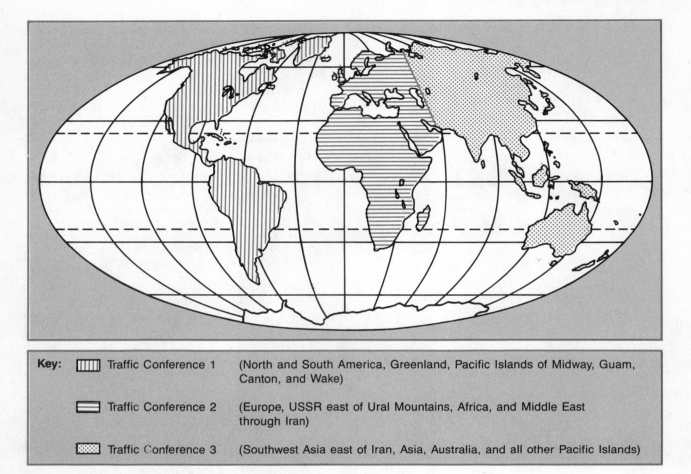

Key:

    ▥ Traffic Conference 1   (North and South America, Greenland, Pacific Islands of Midway, Guam, Canton, and Wake)

    ▤ Traffic Conference 2   (Europe, USSR east of Ural Mountains, Africa, and Middle East through Iran)

    ▨ Traffic Conference 3   (Southwest Asia east of Iran, Asia, Australia, and all other Pacific Islands)

Figure 4-4 The World Traffic Conferences

painted on the tail of SAS aircraft. All carriers registered in other nations are known in the United States as *foreign flags*. A large number of flag carriers are government owned or government subsidized. Because they receive funding from their governments, flag carriers can offer lower fares, even though this might mean operating at a loss. Also, when flag carriers go to an IATA rate-setting meeting, they know in advance what rates their governments will accept. The privately owned airlines of the United States believe that this situation is unfair and damaging. To be competitive, the United States reserves the right to disallow airfares to and from this country that are unrealistically low.

Pressures on IATA. During the 1970s, several airlines dropped their membership in IATA because of the organization's inability to control several forces in the marketplace. One of these forces was the growth of nonscheduled or charter flights. A second force was the increase in the sale of discount package tours by wholesalers. Both nonscheduled airlines and wholesale distributors are outside the international regulatory framework. A third force was overcapacity in some parts of the world. With wide-bodied jets in use and more airlines offering long-distance

service, there were often too many seats and not enough passengers. To fill the seats, a few airlines were bending the rules. Because of these regulatory problems, some critics have suggested that IATA—and bilateral agreements—should be dismantled so that the world's airlines can be free to become more competitive.

Regulating Domestic Service

Although airlines of the United States are privately owned, they are subject to regulation by the federal government. The primary justification for this control is that the airlines use federal airways and engage in interstate commerce.

Federal regulation of the airlines began in 1925 with the Kelly Act, which awarded contracts for air mail delivery to private carriers. Since then, regulations have been enacted primarily in the areas of economics and safety.

Economic Regulation: Civil Aeronautics Board. To regulate the economics involved in airline service, the government decided which routes airlines could operate, when they could schedule flights, and how much they could charge for their services.

The Civil Aeronautics Act of 1938 was the most influential piece of legislation in establishing economic regulation. The act led to the creation of the Civil Aeronautics Board (CAB), a five-member board with the following powers:

- Granting route authorizations.
- Establishing a uniform system of rates and fares.
- Ruling on mergers and acquisitions.
- Ruling on unfair competition.

As a result of exercising its authority, the CAB established the system of trunk lines and feeders, which lasted 40 years, from 1938 to 1978.

Deregulation. With the growth of the airline industry, a new generation of lawmakers began to reevaluate governmental policy on economic regulation. Proponents of *deregulation* argued that the CAB had become too powerful and that airlines should have the right to choose new markets and abandon unprofitable ones. A free marketplace would promote better air service, a wider selection of flights through an expanded route system, and lower airfares.

For the most part, economic regulation ended with the passage of the Airline Deregulation Act of 1978. This legislation allows air carriers freedom to enter and leave the marketplace; that is, they can establish service wherever they want to and drop it wherever they want to.

The Airline Deregulation Act also provided for the gradual phasing out of the CAB (known as "sunset legislation") and the orderly transfer of remaining federal authority to other agencies, such as the Department of Transportation and the Department of Justice. By virtue of the sunset clause of the deregulation act, the CAB ceased operations at midnight on December 31, 1984.

The New-Entrant Carriers. With the almost immediate access to the marketplace provided by the new law, more than 150 carriers have chosen to compete with the established scheduled airlines. These *new-entrant carriers* are classified into four types:

- *Interstate carriers.* Airlines formerly operating within a state, such as Air California, became interstate carriers by expanding their routes across state lines.
- *Supplemental carriers.* Companies such as Transamerica Airlines, formerly offering domestic all-charter flights, began to provide scheduled service.
- *Commuter carriers.* Deregulation plus new rules permitting commuter carriers to fly larger airplanes brought about enormous growth in this segment. Many nonscheduled air taxi operators chose to leave general aviation and compete as scheduled commuter carriers.

- *Brand-new entrants.* These airlines did not exist in any form prior to 1978. By offering cut-rate prices as a means of entering the marketplace, the brand-new entrants have had a great impact on the travel industry. The lower airfares of airlines such as America West were originally achieved by operating used aircraft, employing nonunion workers, and offering "no-frills" flights.

Effects of Deregulation. Deregulation means that airlines now compete with each other for passengers. With the new-entrant carriers, competition has become even more fierce, frequently resulting in price wars. In some instances, an airline ticket has been cheaper than a bus ticket to the same destination. In their attempts to get ahead of the competition, airlines have looked for new places to sell tickets, new ways to advertise them, and new ways to package them.

Some airlines have entered into *code-sharing* partnerships. In a code-sharing agreement, a small regional airline flies under the code of a major airline. That way, the major airline can serve the smaller cities that generate too little traffic to fill its own larger planes. For example, Continental Airlines has a code-sharing agreement with Rocky Mountain Air. Travelers who book onto a Continental Airlines flight to Aspen, Colorado, may find that they have to transfer to Rocky Mountain Air for the last part of the journey. This often involves transferring from a large jet transport to a small turboprop commuter airliner. About 50 regional/commuter airlines have entered into code-sharing arrangements.

Deregulation has benefited the public by providing, for the most part, reduced airfares and expanded routes. More airplanes are flying now than ever before. Critics of deregulation, however, say that this growth has created congested airports and airways and increased the likelihood of accidents. The deplorable on-time performance and the increase in canceled flights has brought forth stern warnings to the airlines from the federal government. Critics also point to the reduction of services on many low-traffic routes. Several carriers have abandoned unprofitable routes to and from smaller communities, concentrating instead on flights in the high-density corridors. As a result, some communities now have fewer flights than before deregulation.

Many airlines, among them some of the oldest and most established companies, have experienced severe economic turbulence in the deregulation marketplace. Eastern and Braniff, for example, have declared bankruptcy and ceased all flight operations; many more have merged with other airlines.

Safety Regulation: Federal Aviation Administration. While economic regulation has largely ceased, federal regulation of aircraft safety continues. As with economic regulation, the 1938 Civil Aeronautics Act strengthened the government's power to regulate air safety. This legislation created the Air Safety Board and authorized it to grant certificates of airworthiness. In 1958, the Air Safety Board was superseded by the Federal Aviation Agency, an independent agency in charge of air safety. When the Department of Transportation was created in 1966, the Federal Aviation Agency was made a part of it and renamed the Federal Aviation Administration.

The primary responsibility of the FAA is to direct air traffic in the federal airways so that accidents do not occur. Comparable to the interstate highway system, the federal airway system covers 350,000 miles. Beginning at ground level, the airways extend 75,000 feet above the earth's surface. All aircraft flying between 18,000 feet and 75,000 feet are constantly monitored by ground-based radar control. Aircraft flying below 18,000 feet usually fly by a system of visual rules and are not necessarily monitored by the FAA.

Other responsibilities of the FAA include:

- Establishing and enforcing safety standards.
- Certifying and monitoring the skills and health of pilots.
- Certifying the safety of aircraft.
- Investigating accidents (along with the National Transportation Safety Board [NTSB]).
- Setting standards for designing and building new aircraft and equipment.

Industry Regulation. Both the scheduled air carriers and the regional and commuter air carriers are represented by associations located in Washington, D.C. The scheduled air carriers of the United States are represented by the Air Transport Association (ATA). ATA lobbies federal and local government on behalf of the scheduled airlines and actively promotes airline travel. The nation's regional and commuter air carriers are represented by the Regional Airlines Association (RAA), which lobbies and promotes their interests.

The Airlines Reporting Corporation (ARC) was established by ATA in 1984. ARC serves as a link between the United States airlines that belong to ATA and the 37,000 retail travel agencies that are accredited to sell the airlines' tickets. The role of ARC as well as that of the International Airline Travel Agency Network (IATAN), the international counterpart of ARC, will be discussed in greater detail in Chapter 13.

Check Your Product Knowledge

1. What are the three main channels for regulating the international air system?
2. Why are the Flying Freedoms important?
3. Name two organizations that help to regulate the international airline industry.

4. Why was the United States airline industry deregulated in 1978? What were the results?
5. What are the responsibilities of the FAA?

THE PRODUCT

Every industry has a product. The product of the airline industry is a flight on an airplane. A travel professional must determine the motivations, needs, and expectations (MNEs) of travelers and then sell them the right product.

Factors Affecting the Price of the Product

Matching each traveler with the right product at the right price is not always easy, especially since deregulation. In the deregulated marketplace, there may be 199 different types of airfares for a trip from New York to Los Angeles. In some instances, it is less expensive to fly from coast to coast than to a city 1,000 miles away. The price of a ticket is no longer based solely on the distance of the trip. Instead, the type of journey, the type of flight, the type of service, and whether or not the flight is restricted all influence the airfare.

Type of Journey. There are four types of journey. A *one-way trip* begins in an originating city and ends in a destination city (for example, Dallas to Los Angeles). A one-way journey can be made on more than one flight, as in Dallas via Salt Lake City to Los Angeles.

A *round trip* begins in an originating city, goes to a destination city, and returns to the originating city. The routing must be the same in both directions. Such a trip might be Boston to New York to Boston. Buying a round-trip ticket is often cheaper than buying two one-way tickets.

A *circle trip* is similar to a round trip, with an important difference: the outbound journey differs from the return journey, either in terms of the routing or the class of service. Routing: Minneapolis via Chicago to St. Louis and returning from St. Louis to Minneapolis nonstop. Class of service: Minneapolis to St. Louis first class, return trip economy class.

An *open-jaw trip* is interrupted by surface travel. A traveler may, for example, proceed from New York to Richmond, Virginia, by air; from Richmond to Washington by rail; and from Washington to New York by air. An open-jaw trip can also be a journey with a return destination other than the originating city. Such a trip may take a traveler from San Francisco to New York, then from New York to Los Angeles.

Type of Flight. There are four types of flights. One type is nonstop service with no scheduled stopovers en route.

A second type is direct or through service. There can be one or more intermediate stops en route, but the passenger remains aboard the same plane.

A third type is a connecting flight. With an *on-line connection*, the passenger changes airplanes, but remains on the same airline. Continental for example, can offer a flight from Salt Lake City to Denver connecting with another Continental flight from Denver to Kansas City. An airline can change planes for any number of reasons, including mechanical difficulty and seating capacity. With an *interline connection*, the passenger changes both airplanes and airlines. A passenger can fly Northwest Airlines from Seattle to Minneapolis/St. Paul, and United Airlines from Minneapolis/St. Paul to Cleveland.

Agreements among airlines to honor the tickets of other carriers make interline connections, or *interlining*, possible. Rather than having a separate ticket for each flight, interlining permits the use of one standard ticket; the system also enables baggage to be checked through to its final destination. Interlining is an international as well as a domestic practice. Some new entrants and regional commuters in the United States market, however, do not participate in interlining agreements.

Intermodal ticketing, which simplifies the coordination of different modes of travel, has become another popular travel product. In a system similar to interlining, the passenger buys one ticket for through travel using an airplane and a bus, an airplane and a cruise ship, or an airplane and a rental car.

A fourth type of flight is the *stopover*. In a stopover, the passenger requests a deliberate interruption of a trip at some intermediate point for 12 or more hours. A passenger can choose to fly from Denver to Dallas on Monday, remain in Dallas until Wednesday evening, then fly on to El Paso.

Type of Service. Forty years ago, in-flight service on a domestic airliner consisted of a cold box lunch and a pack of chewing gum to relieve pressure on the eardrums. Today, passengers eat hot meals, drink cocktails, listen to music, and watch movies.

The type of service passengers receive depends on where they sit in the cabin of the plane, and they often pay accordingly. The most common *configuration*, or seating arrangement, on a plane consists of a first-class ("F class") cabin and a coach or economy-class cabin, but an airplane could have all coach seats or, less frequently, all first-class seats. Large jets can have several coach cabins. Aircraft cabins are further classified as narrow body (one aisle) and wide body (two aisles).

The most expensive class of service, "R class," is available on Concorde flights only. This is an example of an all-first-class configuration; there are no coach seats on board the Concorde. R class tickets cost 20 percent more than the first-class fare. Some airlines are experimenting with business or executive class ("Y class");

halfway between first-class and coach in amenities, business class was developed for people who want a quiet place to work and who expect greater service than do those passengers flying on a discounted ticket.

Passengers in first class receive elaborate meals served on fine china, complimentary alcoholic beverages and movies, and individualized service. They also ride in more comfort. First-class seats are at the front of the plane, farther away from engine noise. They are also wide and have plenty of legroom (greater pitch, or distance between the knees and seatback). Seats in coach class are closer together and narrower, and they vary in comfort depending on their location in the cabin. Although coach passengers often receive complimentary meals, they can pay extra for alcoholic beverages and for headsets in order to listen to music or watch in-flight movies.

Airlines usually provide in-flight services for passengers with special needs. Flight attendants are trained to assist handicapped travelers in boarding and to take particular care of children traveling alone. Airlines will also cater to passengers with special dietary needs (for example, those who require vegetarian or kosher meals) if they are given advance notice. The provision of such special services does not affect the airfare.

Unrestricted and Restricted Airfares. With an unrestricted airfare, also called a nondiscounted airfare or normal airfare, a passenger can board any plane going to his or her destination that has an available seat. People must pay extra for the convenience of an unrestricted airfare.

Illus. 4-8 *Flight attendants are trained   to assist passengers with special needs.*
Source: America West Airlines

Restricted airfare—also called promotional airfare, discounted airfare, or excursion airfare—is the airlines' version of a sale or a bargain. The less expensive the airfare, the greater the restrictions. They can include some or all of the following:

- Advance purchase requirement (up to a month prior to departure).
- Minimum/maximum length of stay at destination.
- Fixed itinerary and departure times (no last-minute changes).
- Limited departure dates (good only on certain days of the week).
- Nonrefundable cancellation penalty.
- Capacity control (only a limited number of seats available on any given flight at the discounted fare).
- Nontransferable ticket (one airline may not honor certain excursion-fare tickets from another airline).

Because they generally have more flexible schedules, vacation travelers or persons visiting friends and relatives (except in emergency situations) are more likely to purchase restricted airfares than are business travelers.

With deregulation, airlines found themselves promoting discounted tickets in order to fill seats that would otherwise remain empty; the philosophy is that half a fare is better than no fare. The result is that the passengers in the coach cabin on any flight may have spent varying amounts of money for the same type of seat and service, depending on whether or not they purchased a restricted ticket. Thus, restricted airfares have in effect done away with the two-tier pricing system and replaced it with a three-tier system: first-class, economy, and excursion fares.

Financial penalties for cancellations have been introduced by a number of airlines in an effort to combat *no-shows*. No-shows are people who make a reservation but, for whatever reason, fail to use it. There are always more no-shows when no penalty is involved. Another way airlines protect themselves against no-shows (and, consequently, too many unsold seats) is to *overbook*, or sell more seats than they actually have. However, when an airline overbooks and no one cancels, the airline is liable and must compensate the passengers who are denied boarding. This compensation can be a cash settlement plus transportation on the next available flight or a free upgrade in class of service.

International Airfares. IATA members hold conferences to discuss international airfares. On the basis of rules and principles developed by the organization, IATA decides on rates for city-pair combinations throughout the world. To reduce the complexity of calculating airfares in different currencies, all international airfares are expressed in Fare Construction Units (FCUs). A formula converts FCUs into specific currency for actual transactions.

As with domestic airfares in the United States, IATA calculates the price of a ticket on the basis of distance flown, type of service, and whether the fare is restricted or unrestricted. Many IATA airfares are based on the mileage principle. The actual mileage flown between destinations is measured and then compared with a maximum allowable mileage, usually about 20 percent greater than the actual mileage. This bonus mileage enables the passenger to make stopovers at intermediate cities along the route of travel. This process of computing international airfares is called *fare construction*.

The cost of an international airline ticket, then, is usually directly related to the number of miles flown. This means that a trip from Washington, D.C., to Paris (3,829 miles) should cost more than a trip from Washington, D.C., to Caracas (2,059 miles). However, various factors in the marketplace can actually make a longer trip less expensive. More people want to fly to Paris than to Caracas. There is also more competition on the Washington-to-Paris route. In addition, the French government may have authorized a lower promotional airfare in order to encourage travel and tourism. As a result, an airline ticket from Washington, D.C., to Paris will generally cost less than a ticket to Caracas, even though the distance flown is greater.

Marketing in the Jet Age

Prior to the Airline Deregulation Act of 1978, airline marketing focused on service. To lure passengers, airlines promoted in-flight amenities and friendly skies. There were even drawings for free car rentals, shows by magicians and guitarists, and wine-tasting parties. Following deregulation, marketing centered on pricing. Discounted, advance-purchase airfares, such as the Super Apex, made people realize that they could travel greater distances at reasonable prices. In 1982, approximately 75 percent of United States passengers flew cut-rate. In recent years, however, there is some indication of a return to service-oriented marketing. Business-class service and all-first-class service are examples of this trend.

Check Your Product Knowledge

1. Describe the four types of journeys.
2. How does seat location influence the airfare?
3. List five typical restrictions on a discounted airfare.
4. How do airlines protect themselves against no-shows?

CAREER OPPORTUNITIES IN THE AIRLINE INDUSTRY

The domestic air carrier industry employs about 720,000 persons in a wide variety of jobs requiring differing levels of education, training, and experience. Airline pilots and flight attendants are the most visible employees, but there are many others working behind the scenes. Delta Air Lines, one of the largest domestic employers with a payroll of 64,000, estimates that it takes an average of 156 employees to put one of their planes in the air.

Positions are available both in the private sector (working for the individual airline companies) and in the public sector (working for the local, state, and federal governments, which own and operate the larger airports or regulate the airways system).

Employees in the international airline industry can work in a gateway airport in the United States or in an airport station in a foreign country. (Note: United States citizens often find it extremely difficult to obtain employment as pilots or flight attendants with foreign airlines because of visa restrictions.) In addition to the training required of domestic airline employees, international airline employees, especially those in direct contact with the public, may need to be bilingual or multilingual. Persons working for an international airline should be informed about and accepting of different cultures.

Jobs in the airline industry can be classified into two main categories: flight crew and ground crew. The flight crew consists of those persons who operate the airplane and provide in-flight service, while the ground crew or staff consists of those persons who keep the plane airworthy and fill it with passengers.

Flight Crew

The flight crew, in turn, can be separated into two groups. The pilots who fly the airplane make up the flight deck crew or cockpit crew, and the attendants who provide in-flight service and passenger safety make up the cabin crew.

Flight Deck Crew. There are usually two or three pilots, depending upon the type of aircraft. In larger aircraft that use three pilots, the cockpit crew generally consists of: the captain, or senior pilot, who makes flight plans, operates the airplane, and supervises other crew members; the first officer, or copilot, who assists the captain, charts the airplane's route, and computes flying time; and the second officer, or flight engineer, who inspects the airplane before it takes off and after it lands, monitors all instruments and gauges during flight, and calculates the amount of fuel needed. The latest models of aircraft are designed for a two-person crew in which the second officer is not required.

As nearly all airlines are unionized, a pilot's career is influenced by the seniority system, which determines promotions. New pilots for a large airline begin as second officers; in five to ten years they might become first officers. It might take 20 years to reach the rank of captain. Promotions for the new entrants tend to be faster since they are largely nonunionized.

The employment outlook for pilots is good. The rapid growth of air traffic and the expansion of airline fleets, especially among the regional and commuter airlines, are contributing to the need for more pilots. There are also excellent opportunities for pilots to fly aircraft owned by private corporations and air taxi operators. In particular, airlines are looking to hire more women as pilots.

Cabin Crew. While there are usually three persons in the cockpit crew on a long-distance flight, there can be as many as 16 in-flight attendants, depending on the size of the airplane and the proportion of first-class to coach passengers. Flight attendants provide for the comfort and safety of the passengers. Among other duties, they serve in-flight meals and beverages, demonstrate safety equipment, check seat belts, and cope with medical emergencies. Flight attendants personally represent the airline and, in a sense, personify the product. The employment outlook for flight attendants should remain good.

Cross-Training. In nonunion airlines, members of the flight crew might also perform the duties of the ground crew. For example, flight attendants might work in customer service positions, while flight officers might have scheduling and dispatching duties. Cross-training is more common among the new entrants.

Ground Crew or Staff

A commercial airplane flight would not be possible without the work of hundreds of people in the ground crew. Jobs on the ground are found in the areas of reservations, passenger services, aircraft and building maintenance, safety regulation and airline security, in-flight services and freight services, and management and sales.

Reservations. An airline reservations agent is usually the first contact a prospective passenger has with the airline. At the request of customers, airline reservations agents answer questions about flight schedules, check the availability of flights, and book passengers. As the reservations system becomes more automated, fewer agents are likely to be needed.

Passenger Services. This group of employees works mainly in the terminal building. Airline ticket agents sell tickets and keep records, tag luggage, assign seats, announce flight arrivals and departures, and board passengers. Customer service agents deal with passengers with special needs, such as handicapped travelers and children

Illus. 4-9 *The airline reservations agent is the first contact a potential passenger has with an airline.*
Source: *© Richemond/The Image Works*

traveling alone. Ramp agents see that passengers' baggage is loaded on the correct flight.

Maintenance. Maintenance employees work either for a specific airline or for the local governmental authority that runs the airport. Plumbers, carpenters, electricians, and painters maintain airport buildings. Other maintenance workers plow snow and clear debris from the runways.

Probably the most important maintenance workers are the mechanics and engine specialists who service and repair airlines. As the FAA raises safety standards and as airplane traffic increases, there will be more jobs for mechanics.

Other Personnel. Airline dispatchers schedule flights for an airline and are responsible for ensuring that FAA regulations are enforced. Airports that allow general aviation aircraft to use their facilities can employ a fixed-base operator (FBO). The FBO provides small-aircraft operators with flight information, fuel, and hangar space.

Security officials inspect baggage and electronically search passengers. Most uniformed security personnel are employed by private security companies that are in turn hired by the airport authority.

Flight-kitchen or catering personnel prepare passenger meals. Aircraft cleaners supply the airplane with items such as clean towels, fresh water, and magazines. Freight handlers process cargo and air freight and load and unload it.

FAA Employees. Air traffic controllers coordinate the flights of airplanes to prevent accidents and minimize delays in accordance with FAA rules and regulations. Some controllers give pilots permission to take off and land (airport traffic controllers); others instruct pilots en route between airports (air-route traffic controllers).

With airspace becoming more congested and with the rapid turnover among controllers, opportunities for employment should remain high.

Station Manager. Every airline operating a scheduled service has a station at the airport, which is run by a station manager. It is his or her responsibility to see that flights are coordinated and that the weight, balance, and load of each departing flight is calculated. The station manager is employed by the airline.

Airport Manager. Every airport has a manager who deals with the airlines, oversees maintenance of the buildings and runways, monitors businesses operating in the airport, handles public relations, and makes sure that FAA regulations are enforced. The airport manager is employed by the governmental authority that runs the airport.

There may be assistant managers in charge of specific areas, such as cargo services. Although the number of airports is growing, airport management is a relatively small career field and openings are limited.

General Office (GO). Major airlines maintain a general office that serves as the corporate headquarters. Delta, for example, has its general office in Atlanta; USAir's is in Arlington, Virginia. The GO is the center for administrative and technical departments, major maintenance, and training. Most public relations and advertising work is also carried out at the general office.

Sales Offices. Most United States airlines operate sales offices. These should not be confused with the city ticket offices or airport ticket counters. Very few passengers buy their tickets from an airline sales office. Rather, the sales representatives who work out of these offices are responsible for calling on the intermediaries and decision makers—travel agencies and business travel departments.

Flight Attendant

People think of my job—a flight attendant for an international airline—as glamorous and exciting. And it is. I get to travel to other countries and to meet interesting people. But it's a lot of hard work too. Flight attendants are the airline employees passengers see the most of. That means they are often the employees passengers remember most clearly. I think of myself as an ambassador of goodwill for the airline. If I do my job well, people will travel with our airline again.

Most of what I do falls into one of two categories: safety and service. I think the most ignored speech in the world is the one I give at the beginning of each flight when I point out the emergency exits, explain the use of the oxygen masks, and tell where the life jackets are found. Flying is so safe today that most people take an uneventful flight for granted. In fact, I've never been in an accident myself. Still, simulators train us for emergencies. We learn how to evacuate passengers quickly, safely, and calmly. A flight attendant has to stay calm—especially when passengers are panicking.

I'm also trained in simple first aid procedures. I have a friend who actually attended at a birth on a flight. Fortunately, there happened to be a doctor on board who did the actual delivery. One time, a passenger on my flight had a heart attack—and there was no physician aboard. I was able to help the person until we could make an emergency landing.

Service is the other major part of a flight attendant's job. Service involves everything from serving meals and drinks to calming nervous fliers to coping with belligerent passengers. Basically, I have to be "people conscious"—often I can sense a passenger's need before he or she voices it.

Some of the neediest passengers are children who are alone on a flight. Frequently parents will see a child onto the plane and arrange for someone—say, a grandparent—to meet the flight at the destination. The airline I work for treats these small passengers with extra care. They get a special badge and the flight attendants keep an eye on them during the whole trip. Sometimes a child

is frightened or lonely, and I'm sort of a friend, nurse, and parent all rolled into one. I especially feel like a parent when someone asks me for the twentieth time: "Are we there yet?" But part of my job is to answer the question politely and with a smile—every time.

As I said earlier, the airline I work for flies international as well as domestic flights. I speak French fluently—a real advantage for me on overseas flights. Most of the other attendants speak either French, Spanish, or German in addition to English. On a flight several weeks ago, a French businessman broke his only pair of reading glasses during the flight. He was so upset that even though he spoke English well, he wasn't able to communicate in it at the time. In French, I assured him that on landing we could guide him to an optometrist who would replace his glasses.

A second language also helps during layovers—the nights and days I spend away from my home base in New York City. On international flights, layovers are at least 12 hours, sometimes as long as 36 hours. I may be away from home a week or so at a time when we lay over in several European cities in a row. During a layover, my food, lodging, and transportation are paid for by the airline. Layovers are forced "R&R"—rest and relaxation. I sightsee, visit friends I've made on previous flights, or just relax.

On my last flight, we had a two-day layover in Paris. I'd already seen the Eiffel Tower, Notre Dame, and all the other Paris sights. This time I rented a car and visited the chateau region along the Loire River. It's an easy day's drive from Paris. The two days left me refreshed and ready to give "service with a smile" on the way back to the United States.

Of course, during my real vacation time I can take advantage of the low-cost flights offered by my airline or by others we have reciprocal agreements with. Then I sit back and enjoy being the passenger. Believe it or not, I even listen to the flight attendant's speech about oxygen masks and life jackets—you can never know too much in an emergency!

Photo Source: Courtesy of Delta Air Lines, Inc.

Summary

- The airplane evolved as the result of experimentation with lighter-than-air and heavier-than-air craft.
- Domestic and international airline industries began to grow rapidly following World War II. The development of bigger, faster, and more comfortable planes increased the popularity of air travel.
- Modern aircraft either have jet engines or are propeller driven.
- Civilian air services in the United States are divided into air carrier aviation and general aviation. Air carrier aviation specializes in carrying passengers and/or cargo on a large scale.
- Major airports are publicly owned and require large amounts of land. General aviation airports are privately owned.
- Airlines plan their routes for maximum efficiency, either by the linear concept or the hub-and-spoke concept.
- International aviation is more complex than domestic aviation because governments must negotiate the use of sovereign airspace.
- Multilateral agreements reached at worldwide conferences have helped define the use of airspace.
- Bilateral agreements are used to work out the specific details of traffic rights between two nations.
- The International Air Transport Association (IATA) helps to regulate the international air system.
- Until 1978, the government controlled the routes, schedules, and rates of domestic carriers. Economic regulation ended with the Airline Deregulation Act. Safety regulation continues under the Federal Aviation Administration (FAA).
- Factors influencing the price of an airline ticket include the distance flown, type of journey, type of flight, and level of service.
- Air travelers can buy reduced-price tickets if they are willing to follow various restrictions.
- Thousands of airline employees, both flight crews and ground crews, aid in the transportation of passengers and cargo.

Key Terms

pressurization
common carrier
scheduled airline
supplemental airline
charter airline
fixed-base operator (FBO)
cargo terminal
control tower
hangar
runway
loading apron
taxiway
linear route
hub-and-spoke route
gateway airport
flag carrier
foreign flag
deregulation
new-entrant carrier
code sharing
one-way trip
round trip
circle trip
open-jaw trip
on-line connection
interline connection
interlining
stopover
configuration
no-show
overbook
fare construction

What Do You Think?

1. What might happen if airlines owned airports?
2. Do you think the United States government should subsidize airline companies to make them more competitive in international markets? Explain your point of view.
3. How might increased security against international terrorism damage the airline industry?
4. Do you think that deregulation has had positive or negative effects on the domestic airline industry? Explain your point of view.
5. Do you think the United States should advocate a policy of open skies, as opposed to sovereign skies? Explain your point of view.
6. Compared with other means of transportation, what are the advantages and disadvantages of airplanes for transporting passengers and cargo?
7. What would be the advantages and disadvantages of having just one type of in-flight passenger service?

Dealing with Product

How fair are airfares? Consider the following scenario. Flight 123 is scheduled to leave Denver at 7:30 A.M. and to fly nonstop to Pittsburgh, where it will land at 12:30 P.M. Mr. Blue, Mrs. Green, and Dr. Brown have been assigned to seats 3A, 3B, and 3C. Each of these travelers will be served an identical complimentary breakfast, and each passenger has checked two pieces of baggage on to Pittsburgh. In other words, each of these passengers will receive exactly the same service as his or her seatmates.

Somewhere above Kansas, at 35,000 feet, the seatmates compare their airfares. Mr. Blue paid $400 for his round-trip ticket, while Mrs. Green paid only $299 for her flights to and from Pittsburgh. Imagine their reaction when Dr. Brown announces that he paid only $199 for his passage.

Each passenger has bought what seems to be a similar product—a round-trip ticket from Denver to Pittsburgh and return. Why do you think the fares varied so much? Do you think the airlines are justified in having many different fare structures? Why or why not? What methods can you think of for simplifying airfares?

Dealing with People

You are a newly hired employee with a major airline. You have just completed four weeks of training, and today is your first day on the job. You have been assigned to the ticket counter, and the first voice you hear is not a pleasant one. Your supervisor is busy with a conference call and the senior agent has just gone to lunch, so you are all alone with a very irate passenger.

It seems that this passenger just arrived from Los Angeles, but his baggage did not. Furthermore, he is doubly furious because he arrived at Yourtown airport aboard a code-sharing regional aircraft. He is threatening to sue you and your airline not once but twice—first for losing his baggage and ruining his trip, and a second time for false advertising. He thought that because his ticket was issued on your airline and that he left Los Angeles on a large jet, he would fly all the way to Yourtown on a "big bird." Instead, he flew the last leg of his journey on a small, 19-passenger turboprop. How can you help solve this passenger's problems and convert him into a frequent flyer?

Name _____

WORKSHEET 4-1   AIRPORT CODES

Every major airport worldwide is designated by a code that is recognized internationally. This code is used to identify the airport on tickets, baggage, freight packages, and so on. Use the appropriate *Official Airline Guide* (see Chapter 3) or a similar reference guide to obtain the codes for the airports in the cities listed below. If there is more than one airport in a city, give the codes for all the airports.

THE UNITED STATES

New York, NY	_____	Houston, TX	_____
Atlanta, GA	_____	Lincoln, NE	_____
Boston, MA	_____	Denver, CO	_____
Newark, NJ	_____	Phoenix, AZ	_____
Philadelphia, PA	_____	Salt Lake City, UT	_____
Portland, ME	_____	Tulsa, OK	_____
Miami, FL	_____	Albuquerque, NM	_____
Montgomery, AL	_____	Boise, ID	_____
New Orleans, LA	_____	Las Vegas, NV	_____
Chicago, IL	_____	Los Angeles, CA	_____
Detroit, MI	_____	Seattle, WA	_____
Minneapolis, MN	_____	Portland, OR	_____
Cleveland, OH	_____	San Francisco, CA	_____
Washington, DC	_____	Anchorage, AK	_____
Richmond, VA	_____	Honolulu, HI	_____

THE WORLD

Edmonton, Canada	_____	Rome, Italy	_____
Mexico City, Mexico	_____	Paris, France	_____
Port-au-Prince, Haiti	_____	Copenhagen, Denmark	_____
Lima, Peru	_____	Athens, Greece	_____
Rio De Janeiro, Brazil	_____	Warsaw, Poland	_____
Bogotá, Colombia	_____	Dublin, Ireland	_____
Santiago, Chile	_____	Berlin, Germany	_____
Buenos Aires, Argentina	_____	Moscow, USSR	_____
Cairo, Egypt	_____	Tel Aviv, Israel	_____
Lagos, Nigeria	_____	Bombay, India	_____
Nairobi, Kenya	_____	Seoul, Korea	_____
Sydney, Australia	_____	Tokyo, Japan	_____
London, England	_____	Beijing, China	_____

WORKSHEET 4-2   YOURTOWN AIRPORT

Find out the following information about an air carrier airport in or near Yourtown. Write your findings in the space provided.

Name of airport

Location

Acreage

Ownership/governing body

Number of air carriers currently using facilities

Names of air carriers

Annual volume of air traffic

In some communities, citizen groups monitor the environmental impact of local airports. Find out if such a group exists in Yourtown. In the space below describe the activities of the group (for example, lobbying against airplane noise).

Imagine you are a travel agent. You have just sold B. P. Walter a round-trip airline ticket on one of the major carriers that serves Yourtown airport. Mr. Walter is new to Yourtown and has never been to Yourtown airport. In the space below, provide Mr. Walter with information about how to get to the airport, where to park, where to check in, where to find his gate, etc. Obtain a map of the layout of Yourtown airport to help you with your explanation.

WORKSHEET 4-3   TRAVEL ARRANGEMENTS

You are a travel agent. What travel arrangements and airfares can you offer the following customers? Use nonautomated information systems to help you arrange their travel.

1. A university professor in Stanford, California, wants to attend an international conference in Sydney, Australia. The conference will be held in six months. The university will pay for the professor's trip, but funds are limited.

2. A couple are planning their honeymoon, three months away. They want to fly from St. Louis, Missouri, to Miami. They want to stay for a few days, then board a ship to cruise the Caribbean for ten days. They will fly from Miami to St. Louis the same day the ship returns. The trip is a wedding present from the bride's wealthy father, so money is not a major factor.

3. A 60-member high school marching band from Cleveland wants to tour several cities in Germany this summer. They would begin and end their tour in Frankfurt. Although band members have been working for months to raise money for their trip, they must travel as inexpensively as possible.

4. A businessman must fly out of New York City tomorrow morning to arrive as early as possible in Washington, D.C. He wants to return to New York as soon as possible after 8 P.M.

5. A Chicago couple and their two preschool-age children want to visit family in Dallas for Christmas. It is now mid-October. They are flexible about when they fly, plan to stay about two weeks, and want to fly back to Chicago from Houston. They would prefer not to change planes, but flying as cheaply as possible is their priority.

6. An 80-year-old woman wants to go from Boston to Los Angeles two weeks from now. It is difficult for her to walk, so she does not want to change planes. She wants to travel first class.

Name _____

WORKSHEET 4-4   SPECIAL NEEDS

Providing services to passengers with special needs is important for an airline's success. Contact two major airlines that service the city nearest to Yourtown and find out what services are available for the passengers listed below.

Airline   _____   _____

A handicapped traveler   _____   _____

                                                      _____   _____

                                                      _____   _____

A passenger who does not speak English   _____   _____

                                                      _____   _____

                                                      _____   _____

A child flying alone   _____   _____

                                                      _____   _____

                                                      _____   _____

A passenger traveling with an infant   _____   _____

                                                      _____   _____

A passenger requiring a low-salt diet   _____   _____

                                                      _____   _____

                                                      _____   _____

What additional services could the airlines offer?

What other kinds of passengers might require special attention? What services would help them?

CHAPTER 5 THE SURFACE TRAVEL INDUSTRIES

"My heart is warm with the friends I make,
And better friends I'll not be knowing;
Yet there isn't a train I wouldn't take,
No matter where it's going."

—Edna St. Vincent Millay

Objectives

When you have completed this chapter, you should be able to:

■ Trace the rise and decline of the United States railroad industry.

■ Describe the government's role in revitalizing passenger rail service through Amtrak.

■ Describe the different types of accommodations and services offered by Amtrak.

■ Compare the importance of the passenger train in the United States with that of trains in other nations.

■ Give reasons for the growth of the charter and tour business in the motorcoach industry.

■ Discuss the effects of deregulation on the motorcoach industry.

■ List and describe the types of motorcoach tours now available.

■ Describe the close connection between the car rental and airline industries.

■ Explain why it is easier to enter the car rental industry than other sectors of the surface transportation industry.

■ Describe the various urban public transportation systems, the needs they fulfill, and the problems they alleviate.

Despite the advent of air transportation, travel by land is still the major way to get from here to there. The various sectors of the surface travel industry—railroads, motorcoaches, car rentals, and mass transit—all play a vital role in modern transportation, both in the United States and abroad. With the exception of the car rental industry, however, all have experienced periods of decline in the United States in the postwar period. They have lost passengers to the airlines and, more importantly, to the private automobile. (Car transportation now accounts for almost 85 percent of all intercity passenger miles traveled in the United States.) Still, the United States passenger rail industry has managed to stay alive through reorganization, and the motorcoach industry has turned to the charter and tour business to offset the decline in scheduled services. These new services, along with the traditional ones, show an industry adjusting to supply the needs of travelers in a changing world.

THE RAILROAD INDUSTRY

For many people in the United States, trains are an important method of transportation. Some people use them every day to get to jobs in the city. Businesspeople take high-speed trains, such as the Metroliner between New York and Washington, because the trains are a fast, comfortable, easy way to travel from one city center to another. Families travel on special family excursion fares to visit relatives. College students take the train to go home during a school break. Retirees planning to spend the worst of the winter in Florida travel south in Auto Trains that transport passengers and their cars. Trains, then, can satisfy the motivations, needs, and expectations (MNEs) of many different kinds of travelers.

United States trains may not be as glamorous as they once were, but they are still a useful way to travel.

In addition, there are many people who are attracted to the special mystique of train travel. Traveling by air may be fast, but there is little to see on the way. The leisurely pace of rail travel gives passengers time to sit back and enjoy the passing scenery. For many, a train trip is more than a matter of reaching a destination promptly; "getting there" is part of the experience.

As a travel professional, you will need to know how to obtain information about train routes and schedules for both American and foreign trains. You will also need to know how to make reservations.

In this section, you will learn something about railroads past and present—their proud history and their problems today. You will also learn about railroads in other countries and the great trains of the world.

A Brief History of the Railroads

The history of railroads goes back a long time. As early as the sixteenth century, a primitive railroad powered by horses was used to haul coal and iron ore on wooden tracks. But the real ancestors of the modern railroads appeared in the early 1800s, following the invention of the steam engine. In 1804, the world's first successful steam-powered locomotive chugged along a nine-mile track in England at a speed of five miles per hour—little faster than a person could walk.

The idea of steam locomotion crossed the Atlantic, and work on the South Carolina Canal and Railroad started in 1829. This railroad, the first scheduled passenger line in the United States, ran from Charleston, South Carolina, to Hamburg, Georgia, a distance of 136 miles. It was the wonder of the day.

Though few people believed that railroads could compete successfully with canal transportation, far-sighted entrepreneurs proceeded to build railroads and then to expand existing lines. By 1835, there were 1,000 miles of track in operation; by 1850, the figure had risen to 9,000. Most of these early railroads were concentrated in New England and the mid-Atlantic states and were built to serve local needs.

All this began to change in 1850, when the federal government initiated a policy of offering land to states for railroad development. The states distributed the land to local railroad companies, which sold some of the acreage to settlers to pay for rail construction costs. Lines were extended into unsettled areas in the West, and wherever tracks were built, new communities sprang up.

Transcontinental Line. On May 10, 1869, at Promontory Point, Utah, a crowd of dignitaries and railroad workers cheered as the governor of California hammered in a golden spike that marked the joining of the Union Pacific and Central Pacific rail lines. The transcontinental railroad was completed. Now it was possible to travel from New York to San Francisco by rail in six days, a journey that used to take months. By the end of the century, four more lines stretched across the country, linking the East and West coasts and bringing isolated communities into the national transportation network.

The Golden Age of Railroads. In the following years, trains became safer, faster, and more comfortable. Some were luxurious. By 1900, railroads could offer all the amenities of modern living, including electric lighting and steam heat, sleeping cars, dining cars, and washroom facilities. Train travel was no longer a matter of getting from point A to point B. It had become a distinctly pleasurable experience. On trains with names like the Twentieth Century Limited, Super Chief, and the Empire Builder, passengers were pampered as they were transported to their destinations. Railroad companies made huge profits, and route mileage reached a peak of 254,000 miles in 1916.

Competition. Though the railroad industry enjoyed a period of relative prosperity in the 1920s, it also faced serious competition from other forms of transportation. The growth of automobile ownership and the development of intercity bus services cut into the railroad's passenger business. At the same time, the trucking industry challenged the railroads' monopoly of freight traffic. During the Depression, railroads lost huge sums of money, and several companies went out of business. World War II brought a temporary upturn, but in the years since then the railroad industry has faced hard times.

Industry in Decline. In the 1950s and 1960s, intercity passenger services on railroads declined dramatically. Table 5-1 shows where the passengers went. By 1980, the railroads' share of passenger miles (including those traveled by car) had fallen below 5 percent. During the same period, the number of passenger trains in operation plummeted from 20,000 to fewer than 500.

The major factor in the decline of rail travel has been, undoubtedly, the increase in car ownership. In 1929, one out of five people in the United States owned a car. Today, the figure is one out of two.

Another important factor in the railroads' decline has been the continued growth of the airline industry. After long-distance air routes came into service, it was much quicker and sometimes less expensive to travel by plane than by train. Only on the heavily traveled Northeast Corridor, between Boston and Washington, and on a few other medium-distance routes could train travel remain competitive.

A third factor in the decline of the railroad industry has been its financial structure. The fixed costs of railroads are much higher than those for other surface transportation industries. Railroads have to spend large sums on equipment, maintenance, and labor. Political conflict over the roles of government and private enterprise in the industry has also been a problem.

Passenger Miles (in millions) and Percentage of Total									
Year	Railroads	Percent	Buses	Percent	Air Carriers	Percent	Inland Waterways	Percent	
1929	33,965	77.1	6,800	15.4	NA	—	3,300	7.5	
1939	23,669	67.7	9,100	26.0	683	2.0	1,486	4.3	
1944	97,705	75.7	26,920	20.9	2,177	1.7	2,187	1.7	
1950	32,481	47.2	26,436	38.4	8,773	12.7	1,190	1.7	
1960	21,574	28.6	19,327	25.7	31,730	42.1	2,688	3.6	
1970	10,903	5.7	25,300	14.3	109,499	77.7	4,000	2.3	
1975	10,100	5.7	25,400	14.4	136,900	77.6	4,000	2.3	
1980	11,000	4.5	27,400	11.3	204,400	84.2	NA	—	
1985	12,000	3.8	25,500	8.1	277,200	88.1	NA	—	
1988	13,000	3.4	23,000	6.0	346,000	90.6	NA	—	

Table 5-1 Volume of Passenger Traffic
Source: U.S. Bureau of the Census, Statistical Abstract of the United States: 1990.

Faced with heavy annual losses, many railroad companies went out of business in the 1950s and 1960s. Others survived only by dropping unprofitable services, which in most cases meant passenger routes. Pessimists predicted the end of all passenger service by the 1970s. It was plain that something had to be done to save the ailing passenger train.

There were those who believed that the federal government should *nationalize*, or take over control of, the railroad industry. Opponents of this plan pointed to the heavy losses that had been sustained by nationalized railroads in other countries. In the end, there was a compromise.

United States Passenger Railroads Today

When the government created the semipublic, federally subsidized National Railroad Passenger Corporation in 1970, United States railroads got a new lease on life. The corporation, better known as Amtrak, was to be financed jointly by payments from participating railroads and by federal subsidies. The goal was to restore public confidence in rail travel by improving service and eliminating unprofitable routes.

Amtrak. Amtrak took over almost all of the nation's intercity passenger networks in 1971. Eighteen of the twenty-two largest passenger railroads joined the corporation when it started operation. (The other four joined in 1983.) As a first step, routes and services were cut in half. Service was concentrated along high-density corridors, such as Boston-New York-Washington, Los Angeles-San Diego, and Miami-Orlando-Tampa.

Initially, the outlook for the new corporation was not very promising. But Amtrak began an ambitious modernization program. It ordered new locomotives and improved tracks. It also introduced a national reservations system. In the mid-1970s, Amtrak and passenger rail lines in general received a boost from the gasoline crisis. As the price of gas went up, increasing numbers of motorists decided to travel by train. In the first ten years of Amtrak's operation, passenger miles traveled went up 60 percent, and total revenues increased by more than 300 percent.

Despite the impressive rise in passenger use, Amtrak still depends on federal subsidies for 28 percent of its total operating budget. While government subsidies have been cut back—from $896 million in 1981 to $635 million in 1990—plans to eliminate all federal financing seem optimistic. Despite its problems, Amtrak has been able to expand some of its routes in California, Texas, and Florida. And, in 1989, it introduced daily rail service between Philadelphia and Atlantic City.

As a travel professional, you will need to know about the different types of Amtrak trains and special services:

- Standard coaches are used for day travel on Amfleet, Superliners, Metroliners, and Turboliners across country.
- Metroliners are high-speed, first-class, all-reserved trains that travel between New York and Washington, D.C.
- Club Service offers extra space; reserved, private cars; and personalized service on many trains on the Northeast Corridor.
- Custom Class, available on Empire Service trains, offers reserved seating and reclining seats.

- Superliners provide luxurious, long-distance service in double-decker cars between Chicago and New Orleans and the West Coast.
- The Heritage coach cars, equipped for overnight travel, are used for long-distance routes in the East.
- The Vista-Dome Car offers panoramic views on eastern, midwestern, and southwestern long-distance trains.
- The Auto Train carries travelers and their cars between the Washington, D.C., area and Florida.

Federal Regulation. In 1887, Congress established the Interstate Commerce Commission (ICC) to regulate competition between railroads and to ensure reasonable passenger and freight rates. The ICC still oversees the railroad industry today, but its powers have been sharply reduced—first by the Regional Rail Reorganization Act of 1973 and then by the Staggers Rail Act of 1980. These laws have allowed rail companies greater freedom to set their own fares and to abandon unprofitable lines. Through deregulation, the government hoped to help the railroads operate at a profit and to reduce the need for government subsidies.

The Department of Transportation (DOT) is also involved in the railroad regulatory process. The DOT and Amtrak work with Congress and local government to make decisions about routes and the number of trains per route. The Federal Railroad Administration, a division of the DOT, sets safety standards for the industry and in-spects rolling stock (locomotives and cars), tracks, and signal systems.

Foreign Railroads

In many countries outside of the United States, railroads are still a major form of transportation. Most of these railroads are owned and operated by the government.

Canada. The Canadian government plays a leading role in the Canadian railroad industry. One of the country's two major railroads, Canadian National Railways, is government owned. The other, the Canadian Pacific Railway, is privately owned but is run by VIA Rail Canada, a government corporation that took over the management of Canadian passenger rail services in 1978. Recently, Canada announced that it would make major cutbacks in its rail network, reducing the size by more than half.

Currently, major rail lines extend from coast to coast, serving most cities in southern Canada. However, the Transcanada, which ran between Montreal and Vancouver, has been closed. Rapido trains, including the new high-speed LRC (Light Rapid Comfortable) trains, provide express service between the major cities. The routes of VIA Rail and Amtrak connect at various points, providing north-south rail service between the United States and Canada. Amtrak trains such as the Adirondack and the Montrealer start in New York City, cross the border,

Illus. 5-1 *Amtrak's Superliners provide luxurious service in double-decker cars operative on long-distance routes in the West.*
Source: *Amtrak Photo*

and carry passengers directly to Montreal. Passengers from Chicago or Cleveland can travel on the International through to Toronto.

A Canrailpass allows unlimited travel on VIA Rail trains in designated areas—all Canada, Winnipeg and Eastern Canada, Winnipeg and Western Canada, or the Quebec City-Windsor/Sarnia Corridor—for a fixed rate for periods of 8, 15, 22, or 30 days.

In Canada, railroads are a much more important means of surface transportation than in the United States. The rail services of each country carry about the same number of passengers annually, but of course the United States has about ten times as many people as Canada.

Europe. While the rail passenger industry has been struggling to survive in the United States, the passenger train has remained a major form of transportation in Europe. Most railroads are government owned and operated, and although few make a profit, European governments consider efficient and extensive passenger railroads an essential service.

There are other factors besides government subsidies that account for the survival of the passenger train in Europe.

- *Private car ownership.* Although the number of Europeans owning cars has increased in recent years, it is still well below the level in the United States.
- *Price of gasoline.* Gasoline is much more expensive in Europe than in the United States.
- *Proximity of major cities in Europe.* Few Western European capitals are as far apart as the major population centers in the United States. It takes about the same time, for example, to travel from Geneva to Paris by train as it does to fly. In general, train travel in Europe is more comfortable than air travel, less expensive, and less subject to traffic or weather delays. It is also more convenient in that it goes from one city center to another.
- *Reliability of rail services.* Throughout Europe, trains almost always depart and arrive on schedule.
- *Price of air travel.* In Europe, it is almost always much less expensive to take a train than a plane to a given destination.

There is a great deal of cooperation and coordination between European railroads. The national systems of each country are integrated into the International Inter City network (formerly the Trans-European Express network), which provides first class rail travel through nine Western European nations. In 1993, the opening of the English Channel tunnel will mark a milestone in the history of European railroads. The "Chunnel" will enable people to travel by rail between England and France.

Illus. 5-2 *The French TGV Atlantique is one of the fastest trains in Europe, traveling at 186 miles per hour.*
Source: © Mark Antman/The Image Works

Another example of cooperation between the railroads of different countries of Europe is the *Eurailpass.* First introduced in 1959 to promote train travel by non-European tourists, the Eurailpass is good for unlimited first-class travel throughout the 16 participating countries: Austria, Belgium, Denmark, Finland, France, Germany, Greece, Ireland, Italy, Luxembourg, the Netherlands, Norway, Portugal, Spain, Sweden, and Switzerland.

The Eurailpass can also be used on certain ferry and intercity bus services. Eurailpasses are valid for periods of 15 or 21 days, or for one, two, or three months. They are sold only outside of Europe, and people living in Europe are not eligible to use them. Eurail Youthpasses are available to people under the age of 26 at a reduced rate.

Great Britain does not participate in the Eurailpass program. It offers a separate *BritRail pass* for rail travel in the British Isles. The BritRail Seapass, an extension of the BritRail pass, allows holders to sail from Britain to Ireland or to continental Europe, where they can connect with the Eurail system. Both the Eurailpass and the BritRail pass have been big successes. Every year, thousands of people from the United States take advantage of the reduced rates to see Europe by train.

European trains differ from American trains in several ways. To begin with, most European trains are divided into first- and second-class sections. The difference between the two classes is one of price and one of comfort—more room and generally fewer passengers in first class. Another distinctive feature of European trains is that many railroad cars are divided into compartments

The Chunnel

In 1993, it will be possible to board a train in London and arrive in Paris—about 300 miles away—in less than three hours. In the summer of 1993, workers are expected to complete a 31-mile train tunnel under the English Channel, creating the longest undersea tunnel in the world. The channel tunnel will connect the Britain Isles to the rest of Europe for the first time since the last Ice Age.

The channel tunnel, or Chunnel as it has been nicknamed, is the fulfillment of a 200-year-old dream dating back to the Napoleonic Wars. At that time, the French Emperor Napoleon talked of digging a tunnel under the channel so his army could invade England. In the nineteenth and twentieth centuries, others envisioned and even attempted to dig a channel tunnel for commercial travel, but all their attempts were unsuccessful.

In 1986, a group of British and French investors started a new company, Eurotunnel, to raise money and begin work on a new attempt to dig a channel tunnel. Eurotunnel sold more than $2 billion in stock in the company and took out another $10 billion in loans, making the Chunnel the most expensive privately financed construction project in the world. By the time it is finished, it will have cost more than $14 billion due to delays and cost overruns.

The Chunnel is also one of the most ambitious building projects in the world. It will consist of three tunnels—two rail tunnels and a middle service tunnel. As work proceeds, huge, 1,500-ton boring machines are chewing out more than 10 million cubic feet of chalk from the bed of the channel.

Although the tunnel will not be completed until 1993, it is already a reality. At the end of 1990, French and English workers cut through to one another in the central service tunnel and happily shook hands. The boring machines which had started out from England and France were a mere 20 inches out of alignment when they met near the center of the channel.

Once the Chunnel goes into operation, trains will depart from Folkestone, England, and Calais, France, every 10 to 15 minutes. Train passengers can ride all the way from London to Paris, and their travel time will be cut from 12 hours to less than 3 hours. Motorists and truckers can drive to Folkestone or Calais and then put their vehicles aboard double-decker shuttles for the journey across the channel. The trains and vehicle shuttles will travel at 75 miles an hour and will take about half an hour to make the underchannel crossing. By the year 2003, the Chunnel is expected to carry more than 120,000 passengers a day across the English channel.

As construction proceeds on the Chunnel, it is also proceeding on several other rail lines throughout Europe. France is beginning construction of a high-speed train line between Paris and Brussels, Belgium, while Spain is completing a high-speed rail line between Madrid and Seville. Germany already operates a 150-mile-per-hour bullet train between Hanover and Wurzburg. In the meantime, Denmark, Sweden, and Germany are building a multibillion dollar system of tunnels and bridges to link up train service in those three countries. Great Britain is also planning a new high-speed line from London to Folkestone to be completed by the end of the decade.

These rail lines will provide the European Community (EC) with the finest high-speed train system in the world. For tourists, the new rail system will enable travelers to see more of Europe in much less time. They will be able to enjoy traveling in some of the fastest and most modern trains in the world. The Chunnel will also enable travelers who prefer to drive to get around Great Britain and Europe much more easily.

The year 1992 marks the time when the 12 nations of the European Community become one big, borderless nation for purposes of travel and trade. The Chunnel is an important symbol of that unity.

Photo Source: British Information Service

with six or eight places. On long trips, it is possible to reserve a seat in advance for either first or second class for
a small surcharge. For overnight trips, there are a number
of options. Passengers can sleep in the regular seats, or
they can reserve—and pay a supplement for—a
couchette, which is a bunk in a second-class compartment. *Wagon-lits* are coaches containing private sleeping
compartments for one or two persons.

Overnight train travel offers a number of advantages. For example, John Kelly, an American tourist in
France, could enjoy dinner in Paris and then board an
overnight train to the Riviera. He could sleep in a
couchette, wake up in Nice in time for breakfast, and
then spend the day at the beach or exploring the back-
country. Mr. Kelly has saved money by traveling by train
instead of plane and by spending the night in a couchette
instead of a hotel. And instead of wasting the better part
of a vacation day traveling, Mr. Kelly can enjoy the sites
at his destination.

Most long-distance trains in Europe travel considerably faster than their United States counterparts. The
French *TGV* (train à grande vitesse), the fastest, cruises
at speeds of 160 miles per hour. The TGV makes the trip
from Paris to Lyons, for example, a distance of 265
miles, in a mere 2 hours and 40 minutes. The new French
TGV Atlantique is even faster, traveling at an amazing
186 miles per hour.

The French TGV has inspired an American counterpart. The state of Texas is currently developing the first
rapid rail in the United States—the Texas TGV. The new
train will travel at speeds similar to that of the French
TGV and is expected to make the trip between Dallas
and Houston in 90 minutes.

Other Foreign Railroads. Railroads are a major form of
passenger transportation in Latin America, Asia, Africa,
and Australia. As in Europe, most of the railroads are
government owned and operated. Few, though, are as advanced as the European system.

The Soviet Union has the largest rail system in the
world and is one of the few industrialized nations that is
still building railroads. Soviet railroads carry about 50
percent of intercity passenger traffic and as much as 75
percent of the country's freight.

The government-owned Japanese National Railways
operates most passenger services in Japan, but Japan also
has some private railroad companies. Experts consider
the Japanese passenger train system to be the finest in the
world. Service is so fast, comfortable, and reliable that
domestic airlines have made little headway.

The Shinkansen bullet trains, introduced in 1964,
cross the densely populated country of Japan at speeds in
excess of 125 miles per hour. Japanese engineers are currently working on a new high-speed train called the
Maglev. In test runs, it has reached speeds of 300 miles
per hour. The Maglev uses electromagnetism to glide

Illus. 5-3 *The Japanese bullet train cruises at 125 miles
per hour or more. An even faster train is being
developed.*
Source: *Sumimoto Metal America Inc.*

over a single rail. If it becomes operational, the Maglev
promises to revolutionize the rail industry in Japan and in
the rest of the world.

Great Trains of the World. Most people have heard of
the fabled Orient Express. Called "the Train of Kings,
the King of Trains," it is perhaps the most famous train in
the world. In its day, it was the epitome of luxury and it
still stands for the ultimate in the romantic travel experience. Inaugurated in 1833, the Orient Express carried the
rich and powerful from Paris to Istanbul over a spectacu-
larly scenic route. The trip took four days, but in the elegant setting and with food fit for royalty and service to
match, the time passed quickly.

In 1977, the Orient Express—a shabby, forgotten
shadow of the old train—made its last run. But five years
later, the Venice Simplon-Orient-Express was inaugurated, featuring many of the train's original 1920s
coaches restored to their former splendor. Orient-Express
passengers today can start their journey in London or
Paris. After crossing France, the train winds through the
Swiss and Austrian Alps, cuts through the Brenner Pass
to Italy, and arrives in Venice in time for cocktails and
dinner.

Other glamorous trains include:

- The Trans-Siberian Special, which makes a leisurely 19-day voyage from Moscow to Mongolia.
- The Blue Train, which provides a 24-hour luxury
  trip from Cape Town to Pretoria, South Africa.

■ The Royal Scotsman, which meanders through the Scottish highlands in renovated Victorian and Edwardian railroad cars. The staff, of course, wear kilts.

Channels of Distribution

In the Golden Age of Rail, the railroads did not have to worry too much about promoting and selling themselves. Nowadays, though, Amtrak has to work hard to promote itself against stiff competition from the airlines. With catchy slogans, such as "All Aboard Amtrak," "America's Getting into Training," and "Discover the Magic—Amtrak," Amtrak has tried to convince the public that trains are once again a good way to get around the country. Amtrak has also had to modernize its reservations and ticketing systems.

The Reservations System. Reserving tickets on Amtrak has never been easier. Amtrak inherited an antiquated reservations system when it took over passenger services in 1971. Since then, the system has been completely computerized. Amtrak now has a nationwide reservations and information telephone network on which passengers can book seats directly. Amtrak has encouraged the sale of tickets through travel agencies, which now sell about 39 percent of the total. Amtrak's reservations system is linked to airline CRSs and to ARC standard ticket stock, and almost all travel agencies are now equipped to sell and issue Amtrak tickets by computer.

VIA Rail Canada reservations can be made through travel agents, or directly with VIA Rail Canada. Tickets can be purchased at Amtrak stations. Eurail and BritRail passes can be reserved through travel agents using airline CRSs.

Types of Fares. Amtrak has tried to lure passengers back to trains by offering competitive fares. As a travel professional, you will need to know about Amtrak's fare structure. The basic fare covers what Amtrak calls coach service. Special service and accommodations—such as club cars, slumbercoaches, roomettes, and bedrooms—are available on some routes at additional cost.

Amtrak also offers discount fares to encourage group and family travel, short-term promotional fares, and a USA rail pass that allows unlimited travel throughout the country for a fixed period of time. Amtrak has entered the tour market as well. Tour packages include hotel accommodations plus train travel. Some packages also include car rental, bus tours, or sightseeing. In addition, Amtrak offers *rail/sail packages*, which are vacation packages that include both train fare and cruise ticket. Train travelers can set sail from several ports, including New York and Miami.

Publications. Detailed information on the fares, schedules, and services of railroads in the United States and around the world can be found in a number of publications. For information about United States trains, the *Official Railway Guide (ORG)* is invaluable. Appearing eight times a year, the guide contains information on both Amtrak and the commuter rail services operated by transit authorities in major cities of the United States. In addition, the guide includes schedules for VIA Rail Canada, and a selection of important international routes.

The *Rail Traveler's City Planner* is a useful guide for the domestic traveler, containing information about each Amtrak station and about the connecting transportation and car rental services available.

A number of publications provide information about international rail services. The *Thomas Cook Continental Timetable* and *Thomas Cook Overseas Timetable* both contain exhaustive listings of routes and schedules; country maps with train routes; and information about visa requirements, time zones, and so on. *The Eurail Guide: How to Travel Europe and All the World by Train* includes a description of recommended excursions from cities around the world. Fodor's *Railways of the World* is a comprehensive tourist guide to travel by train.

Check Your Product Knowledge

1. What effect has increased car ownership had on the United States railroad industry?
2. How did the federal government act to save rail passenger service in the United States in the early 1970s?
3. What role does the Interstate Commerce Commission play in the railroad industry?
4. Why has the rail passenger industry been able to survive in Europe?
5. Describe the ways Amtrak is trying to encourage more people to ride trains.

THE MOTORCOACH INDUSTRY

The motorcoach, more commonly known as the bus, has played a major role in the surface travel industry throughout the world. In the United States, the motorcoach is the most widespread and the least-expensive form of public transportation. Covering a vast network of intercity and urban routes, motorcoaches carry more people and serve more communities than do either trains or planes.

Travelers use motorcoach service for a variety of reasons, depending on their MNEs. A business traveler staying in New York City might take a chartered motorcoach to a trade show at the Meadowlands in East

Rutherford, New Jersey. In this way, she could avoid the hassle of riding the train and then switching to a bus or taxi. A college student on summer vacation who wants to see something of the United States—without spending too much money—might take a cross-country motorcoach tour. An elderly man who doesn't like to fly or drive a car could travel by bus to a small town in Texas for a family reunion.

Because buses travel over many highways and byways in this country, the bus industry is well-equipped to serve the needs of travelers heading for remote areas or small towns. It is also the most fuel-efficient form of intercity travel.

The Origin of Motorcoaches

The motorcoach, which first appeared in the 1890s, is really a descendant of the horse-drawn stagecoach. Stagecoaches began passenger service in Europe in the seventeenth century (service between London and Edinburgh started in 1670) and in the United States in the eighteenth century. The name *stagecoach* came from the fact that the coaches traveled in stages, stopping at scheduled places along the route to change horses.

Horse-drawn coaches were used for intercity travel in Europe and the United States until the 1890s, when the gasoline engine was developed. The first gasoline-powered buses were built in Germany, and in the early 1900s, urban bus services were started in London and New York. Motorcoaches were also used for intercity travel.

The first intercity service in the United States was started in Oregon.

The intercity network expanded rapidly with improvements in road conditions and in bus design. Transcontinental bus service began in the United States in 1928, and in the 1930s, buses were a common sight on highways around the country. The earliest motorcoaches carried about 20 passengers on hard bench seats. The buses ran on solid tires and often had no springs. After 1920, a number of refinements were made. These included more comfortable seats, air-filled tires for a smoother ride, improved brakes, engines, and transmissions, and a lower floor that made it easier for passengers to get on and off the bus.

Such improvements encouraged more people to ride buses. By the 1930s, the bus industry was challenging the railroads' monopoly of public passenger transportation in the United States. In 1939, there were almost 1,000 bus companies, carrying about 300 million passengers. World War II brought a rapid growth in intercity bus travel, and by 1945, the number of companies had risen to 2,600. That year, ridership on buses soared to over 1 billion passengers.

The Motorcoach Industry Today

The motorcoach is still the most accessible form of transportation in the United States. Intercity buses carry more passengers and serve far more communities than do airplanes and trains combined. For thousands of communi-

Illus. 5-4 *The domestic motorcoach tour is a vacation alternative.*
Source: Tony Freeman/Photoedit

ties, buses provide the only form of public transportation.

The pattern of bus use has changed dramatically in recent decades, however. Since the end of World War II, there have been two major trends in the motorcoach industry: regularly scheduled passenger services have declined and the bus charter and tour business has expanded.

Scheduled Services. Except during the gas crisis years of the 1970s, scheduled intercity bus travel has declined every year since 1945. As with rail travel, the boom in automobile ownership in the postwar years contributed to a decrease in bus travel. Increasing competition from the airline industry also played a role in the decline in bus travel, especially on long-distance routes.

The number of operating intercity bus companies plummeted to around 1,000 by the early 1970s. The gas crisis of 1973–1974 provided a temporary reprieve for the industry, when people rediscovered the bus as the economical alternative to their cars. But when gas prices fell, many returned to private transportation.

In 1977, 325 million passengers rode the nation's intercity buses, the lowest number since 1939. In just five years, scheduled route service had declined 54 percent. When the second gas crisis rocked the country in 1979, doubling gas prices, the Department of Energy urged the public to make greater use of intercity bus service in order to lessen the nation's dependence on foreign oil. The bus was the most energy-efficient alternative to the automobile. As during the previous oil crunch, ridership increased, but since 1981 it has continued its decline.

Charters and Tours. The one bright spot for the motorcoach industry in recent years has been the dramatic growth of the charter and tour business. Although motorcoach tours have been in operation since 1926, they had little impact on the travel market before World War II. In 1939, charters accounted for only 3.4 percent of all bus revenues.

In recent years, many new bus companies have been formed (there were about 2,800 in 1990), and the vast majority of these companies have entered the charter and tour field. This increase is due mostly to deregulation (discussed in the following section) and to a change in the vacation patterns of the American public. Until the first gas crisis, many Americans scorned the idea of taking a vacation by bus in the United States. Instead, they preferred to travel abroad on package tours. But in 1974, travel to Europe and other overseas destinations became too expensive for many United States citizens, and the domestic bus tour emerged as a vacation alternative. Even when foreign vacations again became affordable, bus charters and tours continued to attract customers. In 1974, the motorcoach industry carried 131 million chartered passengers; fifteen years later, the figure had risen to 300 million.

Deregulation. Government regulation of the bus industry was introduced with the passage of the Motor Carrier Act of 1935, which gave the ICC control over all motor carriers. At first, the industry was tightly controlled: the ICC set motorcoach fares and told companies which routes they were required to operate. This practice often meant that companies had to continue unprofitable routes. New companies could not break into the intercity market unless they could show a public need for the services they proposed.

Regulation was relaxed somewhat in later years, and then was eliminated completely with the passage of the Bus Regulatory Reform Act. When President Reagan signed the act into law in September 1982, with little opposition and no fanfare, he opened up the industry to competition and to the possibility of expansion. Unlike the Airline Deregulation Act, no one hailed the Bus Regulatory Reform Act as a milestone, but it changed the motorcoach industry dramatically.

Since deregulation, bus companies have had much greater freedom. They can set their own fares and decide which routes they want to operate. These changes have resulted in a general reduction in bus fares. Deregulation has also made it easier for new companies to enter the bus market and for existing companies to extend their operating authority. Hundreds of new charter and tour companies have come into existence since 1982. Many of these new tour operators cannot afford to buy a whole fleet of buses, which can cost more than $150,000 each. Instead, they lease buses for about $500 a day. Leasing means that a new company does not necessarily need a huge initial capital outlay to go into business.

The inevitable result of the rise in the number of companies has been increased competition. Many of the new companies have adopted aggressive marketing and advertising programs to sell their charters and tours. Some of the older companies have been unable to adjust to the new conditions of the highly competitive market and have gone out of business. There is also the problem of insurance. The skyrocketing cost of insurance has threatened the future of many bus companies—both old and new. Many smaller companies have been forced out of business by high insurance premiums.

Greyhound and Trailways. The two giants in the scheduled intercity bus travel industry merged to become Greyhound and Trailways Lines. The company operates 3,900 buses and serves all 48 contiguous states and Canada.

In addition to Greyhound and Trailways Lines, there are thousands of smaller companies that provide local scheduled intercity service and/or charter and tour service. Table 5-2 shows the top ten motorcoach operators in the United States. Greyhound and Trailways Lines has also been offering charters in recent years in an attempt to survive in the competitive industry.

Company	1988 Sales (in millions)	1987 Sales (in millions)	Number of Buses in 1988
1. Greyhound Travel Services (Dallas)[1]	$87	$73.9	4,000
2. Blue Bird Coach Lines (Olean, NY)	32	30	145
3. Kerrville Bus Co. (Kerrville, TX)	29	26	180
4. Peter Pan Bus Lines Inc. (Springfield, MA)	20	18.5	145
5. Jefferson Tours (Minneapolis)	17	16	134
6. Alaska Sightseeing Tours (Seattle)	16	13	92
7. Gray Line of Alaska (Seattle)	15	14.3	170
8. Gray Line of Seattle (Seattle)	14	13	100
9. Martz Coach Co. (Wilkes-Barre, PA)	13	13	83
10. A-1 Bus Lines Inc. (Miami)	12	11	91

[1] Charter business only

Table 5-2 Motorcoach Operators

Source: Travel Industry World Yearbook, 1990 produced by Child and Waters, Inc., New York

The future of Greyhound and Trailways Lines is uncertain. In 1990, the company filed for bankruptcy in an effort to prevent its creditors from seizing some of its buses. The bankruptcy was due in large part to losses the company suffered from a drivers' strike that lasted for three months.

Sightseeing Companies. Gray Line, the world's largest sightseeing company, offers about 1,500 excursions daily. Gray Line is an association of about 200 independently owned and operated companies, with offices throughout the United States and Canada and in major cities overseas.

American Sightseeing International is the number two sightseeing company, with representation in about 50 cities in the United States and in about 50 cities in other countries. Both companies have grown impressively in the past 35 years. Together, they account for a large percentage of the sightseeing market. In addition to long-distance and local sightseeing tours, both have expanded their services to include charters, limousine service, and transfer transportation.

Information about the services of the two companies can be found in the *Gray Line Sales and Tour Guide*, the *American Sightseeing International World Tariff*, and the World Association of Travel Agents (WATA) *Master Key*.

Bus Service in Other Countries. Intercity services in most foreign countries are provided by government-owned bus lines as well as by independent companies. Government-run buses often operate in conjunction with the national railroads.

Motorcoach as Product

The motorcoach industry in the United States earns billions of dollars each year carrying travelers to out-of-the-way places and over short distances. For many people in the United States, bus service is the only form of public transportation. For some, it is indispensable.

In recent years, the motorcoach industry has focused on the development of tour programs.

Types of Tours. To attract more passengers, many bus companies offer package tours and chartered motorcoach services. Several types of tours are available:

■ *Charter tours.* A charter tour is a tour taken by a club, organization, school party, or other preformed group. Any group can charter, or hire, a bus from a charter operator for a day trip to a sports event, museum, shopping center, or casino, among other places. Holiday packages lasting a week or more are also available. These usually include accommodations, meals, and sightseeing trips in addition to the bus ride. A tour escort does not accompany the group on a charter trip.

■ *Escorted tours.* These are scheduled group tours that travel from major cities in the United States and Canada to tourist destinations throughout North America. Popular destinations include national parks, the Rocky Mountains, New England, the Pennsylvania Dutch country, and the California and Canadian coastlines. Many United States companies also offer escorted tours in Europe. Escorted tours, which can last anywhere from five days to four weeks, include quality hotel accommodations and most meals. A trained tour escort travels with the group for the entire trip.

■ *Independent package tours.* These tours visit several cities or places of interest on regular scheduled buses. Hotel accommodations and sightseeing are included.

■ *City package tours.* These are similar to independent package tours, but visit only one city.

■ *Intermodal tours.* A recent trend in the industry has been the development of motorcoach tours that tie in with other forms of transportation. The idea for intermodal tours began in 1974 with a ticketing agreement between Greyhound and Amtrak to connect nine of Greyhound's routes with Amtrak services. Trailways and TWA later introduced air-motorcoach tours within the United States and abroad. Cruise-motorcoach tours have also become popular. Such a tour might feature a one-week motorcoach tour from New York to Florida, and then a one-week Caribbean cruise.

Buses as Transfer Transportation. The term *transfer* refers to any change in transportation in the course of a journey. Buses are used extensively to provide transfers for passengers between airports and hotels or city centers. There are many companies offering this service in the United States, either as independent operators or as divisions of larger transportation companies. Many companies also provide van service to small towns and rural areas. In addition, hotels and motels may offer their own complimentary bus service to and from the airport.

The Motorcoach vs. Other Modes of Travel. The major attraction of the motorcoach has long been its low cost in comparison with other forms of public transportation. However, while the bus is still generally cheaper than the train, airfares have been reduced sufficiently in recent years for the airlines to compete with bus companies, especially on trips of more than 500 miles. Rather than continue to compete for passengers with the airlines, several bus companies have decided to join them by offering intermodal tickets. An airline, for example, might offer a ticket that combines air passage to a major airport with bus service for passengers traveling from the airport to a more remote destination.

Many people are reluctant to travel any significant distance by bus because they believe that buses are uncomfortable. Modern long-distance buses, however, are much more luxurious than earlier models. Air conditioning and restroom facilities are standard features. Many buses now have wider seats, soundproofing, improved lighting, and large picture windows for sightseeing. Some even offer video screens on seatbacks for viewing television and movies.

In an attempt to lure travelers away from airplanes, many bus companies have stepped up their promotion efforts. Some bus lines offer passes that enable a passenger to tour the country at a discount price. Many of these tours are only promoted overseas to attract inbound tourism, while others have been advertised in the United States to attract domestic tourism.

Channels of Distribution

Bus tickets can be obtained through several channels of distribution. Many short-distance passengers buy their tickets at the bus station just before boarding or from the bus driver. However, travelers who plan to take a long trip or who are going on a tour offered by the bus line can purchase their tickets in advance from the bus company. Many bus companies subscribe to a computer reservations system and can accept reservations and issue tickets before the departure date. Travelers can also purchase tickets for bus trips, escorted tours, charter tours, package tours, and intermodal tours from travel agents. Tours can be booked through a tour broker as well.

Motorcoach tour information is distributed through various printed materials, such as tour brochures, tariffs, and guides. Detailed information on fares, schedules, and other aspects of motorcoach tours is given in *Russell's Official National Motor Coach Guide.*

Associations

Two major associations represent the motorcoach industry. The American Bus Association (ABA), a national organization of bus-operating companies, services the intercity bus industry and is the prime source of industry statistics. The United Bus Owners of America (UBOA) is the largest trade association serving intercity bus owners. It offers programs in safety, credit, insurance, lobbying, and computer services.

Because bus companies and tour operators often work together on tours and charters, the National Tour Association (NTA) and the UBOA agreed, in 1984, to exchange certain membership benefits.

Check Your Product Knowledge

1. How have the patterns of bus use changed in recent decades?
2. In what way is the intercity bus a more essential form of transportation than either the train or the airplane?
3. What have been the main results of deregulation of the bus industry?
4. What are the five main types of tours offered by bus companies?

THE CAR RENTAL INDUSTRY

A business traveler flies from Houston to Miami for a four-day sales trip. He rents a car to make numerous sales calls at companies in the area. A family flies from New York to Los Angeles for a two-week vacation. They rent a car and drive up the coast to San Francisco, stopping to admire the scenery and visit the tourist attractions along the way. A retired couple flies from Minneapolis to Phoenix to see their grandchildren who live just outside the city. They rent a car to explore the Phoenix/Tucson area and to visit the Grand Canyon.

These examples illustrate how the car rental industry meets the MNEs of all types of travelers. The car rental industry is different from other transportation industries in that it allows travelers complete control over their schedules and itineraries. Travelers are free to venture to a remote destination not accessible by public transportation, to find a quaint out-of-the-way country inn, or to make a spontaneous change in travel plans.

A Brief History

The car rental industry is almost as old as the automobile itself. Car rentals began back in 1916, when the Saunders brothers of Omaha, Nebraska, borrowed a car when their own car broke down. The brothers reasoned that there must be others who needed a car for a limited period of time, so they bought another car and went into the rental business. They charged 10 cents a mile with a three-mile minimum. Business grew; they bought more cars; and by the time they merged with another firm in 1925, the company had offices in 21 states. Hertz—today's largest car rental firm—started in 1918. Avis began in 1946 and National in 1947.

The car rental industry really took off when the first commercial jet airliners came into service in 1958. As the volume of air travel increased, more and more people—especially businesspeople—needed a rental car when they arrived at their airport destinations. A car provides business travelers with the mobility they need to conduct business without having to rely on taxis and other forms of public transportation.

The idea of operating car rental desks at airport locations was pioneered by Warren E. Avis, founder of Avis. From the late 1940s on, the car rental business was closely connected with the airline industry. By the late 1950s, rental counters could be found at all the major airports.

The Car Rental Industry Today

The car rental industry has expanded impressively, both in terms of revenue and number of rental cars on the road. As of 1989, Hertz and Avis continued to dominate the field, with National number three and Budget number four. Although these four are the largest and probably the best-known car rental companies, there are actually about 5,000 companies in operation in the United States today. This number is growing every year. Aggressive companies, such as Dollar, Alamo, and Thrifty, have won a greater share of the market in recent years. Table 5-3 shows the fleet sizes and number of locations of the top car rental firms in the United States.

The economics of the car rental industry are quite different from those of other sectors of the transportation industry. Small companies can enter the market with relative ease. No large initial capital investment is needed. Individuals with good credit rating can obtain financing

Company	U.S. Fleet Size	Number of U.S. Locations	Estimated 1989 Revenue (in millions)
Hertz	205,000	1,400	$1.530
Avis	190,000	1,300	$1.300
National	125,000	1,000	920
Budget	125,000	1,241	825
Alamo	80,000	86	525
Dollar	50,000	762	255
Thrifty	30,000	375	235
American International	26,000	106	175
Value	25,000	28	N/A
General	20,000	100	190

Table 5-3 Top Ten Car Rental Agencies, 1989
Source: Auto Rental News

Henry Ford

Henry Ford, the founder of one of the world's largest automobile companies, was born in 1863 on a farm near Dearborn, Michigan. The oldest of six children, he showed an early interest in machinery, claiming later that the sight of a steam-powered wagon cemented his destiny at the age of 13.

When he was 15, Ford dropped out of school and became a machinist's apprentice in Detroit. Ford's father had wanted him to run the family farm, but Ford had no intention of becoming a farmer. After completing his apprenticeship, Ford began working as an engineer for the Edison Illuminating Company in Detroit. He spent his spare time tinkering, trying to build an automobile with an internal combustion engine. He succeeded in 1896.

Ford left the Detroit Edison Company to form the Detroit Automobile Company. This was the first automobile company to be established in the city whose name would become synonymous with automobile manufacturing. Unfortunately, Ford's company folded in a little over a year. After that, Ford achieved some renown as a manufacturer of racing cars.

In those days, automobiles were the playthings of the wealthy. Ford dreamed of changing that. He wanted to produce a low-priced car that most people in the United States could afford. With that aim in mind, he founded the Ford Motor Company in 1903. He began production with the Model A, followed by Models B through S, and received a favorable response from the public.

In 1908, the Model T appeared. Dubbed the "Tin Lizzie," it was durable and easy to operate, What's more, it was economically priced at $825. At the time, it came in only one color—black. (Other colors came later.) The Model T's popularity convinced Ford to limit his production to the Model T. This concentration allowed Ford to standardize production and make one of his most far-reaching contributions to modern industry—the moving assembly line. Instead of having employees go to their work, Ford had their work come to them on a moving conveyor belt.

By 1914, Ford was producing over 250,000 cars each year. The price of the Model T went down to $440. (It was to go even lower during the Depression.) Ford surprised the auto industry by raising his workers' wages to $5 a day, almost double the average industry wage. Part of his strategy, however, was to increase his worker's spending power so that they would buy more cars—Model Ts, of course.

Ford became the sole owner of the Ford Motor Company in 1919. In the early 1920s, the Model T was unchallenged by rivals, commanding an impressive 57 percent of the automobile market. Later in the decade, however, advances by Ford's competitors caused the Model T to become outmoded. Bowing to pressure, Ford brought out a new Model A in 1927—with huge success. The Depression, however, caused the automobile market to collapse in the 1930s.

Ford's final years were ones of frustration. Never an easy man to work with, he ran the company in an increasingly dictatorial manner. He distrusted and undermined his son Edsel's handling of the company. He also fought bitterly against unionization of his plants. After an initial pacifist stance in World War II, he threw Ford Motor Company's energies into the production of war supplies such as aircraft engines. As the company's health improved, however, Ford's declined. He died in 1947 at the age of 83.

Henry Ford's contributions were not so much to the development of the automobile as to its methods of production and promotion. Ford's assembly line brought the purchase of an automobile within the reach of middle-class Americans and opened up isolated rural areas that were inaccessible by train. More cars created a demand for more and better roads, leading to the excellent highway system we enjoy today. And more travel contributed to the growth of the domestic travel industry. Through his innovations, Henry Ford was instrumental in the creation of a new system of transportation that changed the lives of millions.

for the cars from banks, and can lease rental counter space and garage facilities. Most companies starting out in the car rental business become part of a chain. They give a percentage of their income to the chain in exchange for the benefits of the chain's name and backup services. Rental firms can respond to the demands of the market, selling cars when business is slack and buying more when it picks up.

The car rental industry is still heavily oriented toward the business traveler, but the leisure market is expanding rapidly, from 10 percent in 1971 to about 35 percent in 1989. The growing popularity of *fly/drive packages*, which are vacation packages that include both airfare and car rental, has been a major factor in this growth. The popularity of these packages has been stimulated by lower airfares and cut-rate rental prices. *Train/drive packages*, similar to fly/drive packages but with train fare included instead of airfare, are also now available. It is predicted that the leisure market will continue to be the major growth area in the car rental industry.

Car Rental Companies

The car rental industry has always been highly competitive, but with the arrival of many new companies during the 1980s, the competition has intensified. The larger companies have been forced to reduce prices and offer other promotional inducements in an attempt to hold their share of the market.

Types of Company. Car rental companies have two main types of operations: corporate and licensee. Most of the larger firms, including Hertz, Avis, and National, have mostly corporate operations. They purchase the cars and rent them to consumers. After the cars have been driven 18,000 to 25,000 miles, these companies resell them at used-car prices, either directly to consumers or to used-car dealers. However, under the more recent "buy back" programs, the used cars revert to the original car manufacturer instead of being resold. Licensees are usually part of a chain operation. They often lease the cars from larger companies rather than purchase and resell them.

Location. Large car rental firms have both in-town and suburban locations, but most business is still conducted at airports. In the late 1980s, Hertz accounted for about 32 percent of airport business, Avis for 28 percent, National for 17.5 percent, and Budget for 17.5 percent. The location of a car rental company affects the car rental rates and the convenience with which renters can pick up their cars.

Car rental companies with counters at airports must figure the often steep cost of leasing airport space into the car rental rate. Consequently, their rental rates are usually higher than those of companies without airport locations. The consumer, however, benefits from the convenience of being able to step off the plane and right up to the rental counter. Most of the larger car rental companies, including Hertz, Avis, and National, have rental locations or facilities at almost all major airports.

In the past, many of the smaller car rental companies kept their costs down by not having airport counters and by keeping their cars at off-airport locations. Most of these companies provided free transportation from the airport to their location. Clients were compensated for their slight inconvenience by the lower rental rates that

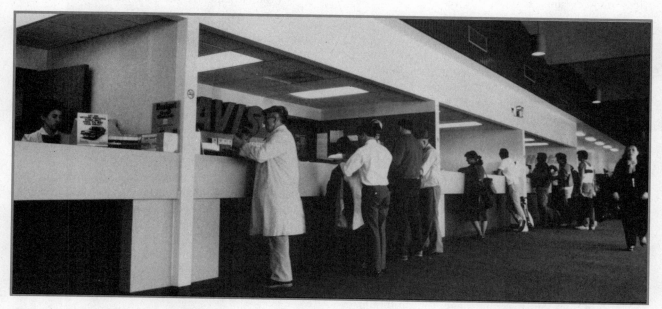

Illus. 5-5 *Travelers generally have a choice of car rental companies when they arrive at a major airport.*
Source: © Daemmrich/The Image Works

these companies charged. This is beginning to change, however, because many airports now charge the off-airport companies for being allowed to enter the airport to pick up customers. More than 20 states now allow airports to charge these fees.

Advertising. Advertising has had a remarkable effect on the car rental market. Back in the 1960s, Avis launched its "We Try Harder" campaign in an attempt to challenge Hertz's domination of the industry. Hertz responded with their "We're #1" slogan, and now most companies spend substantial amounts on national advertising. A few years ago, Hertz used sports stars O. J. Simpson and Arnold Palmer in the company's "Superstar in Rental Car" campaign.

Clubs. Many car rental companies offer free club memberships to car renters in an attempt to promote customer loyalty and to service frequent renters. These clubs, such as Hertz #1 Club, Wizard of Avis, and National's Privilege Club, are computerized information systems that help car rental companies keep track of client names, credit information, and preferences. In this way, firms can provide club members with faster, more efficient service. Some clubs provide express service for members. Express service allows members to avoid the rental counter and go directly to the courtesy bus, which will take them to their car.

The Rental Process

As a travel professional, you should know all aspects of the car rental process so that you can better assist travelers. Travelers should be aware that there are certain qualifications they must meet before renting a car. They should also know of the various rental rates, makes and models of cars available, and extra charges that they may incur.

Qualifications. Car rental is quite different from most other transportation services. Planes, trains, and buses are operated by trained employees of transportation companies. Rental cars, however, are operated directly by the travelers. The moment the car rental company hands over the car keys, it is surrendering control of the vehicle. It is not surprising, then, that car rental companies have strict requirements of those who rent their cars. To qualify to rent a car, clients usually must:

- *Have a valid driver's license.* Some foreign countries require an international driver's license, which can be obtained from an automobile club.
- *Be of a certain age.* In the United States, the minimum age is usually 25. In some countries there is a minimum and maximum age; the minimum is usually 25 and the maximum may be 65.
- *Have a major credit card.* If travelers do not have

credit cards, they must be cash qualified; in other words, they must put down a cash deposit equal to the expected rental amount plus a specified percentage.
- *Be personally responsible.* Client must have verification of address and employment (if they do not have a major credit card).

Rates. Several years ago, companies charged a flat-rate daily fee with an additional charge for the number of miles driven. As competition between companies increased, many firms began to offer *unlimited mileage* plans that allowed clients to travel as far as they wanted for a flat fee within the allotted rental period. More recently, the four major companies started placing mileage caps on car rentals in an effort to cover their costs as rental rates declined. With a *mileage cap*, clients are allowed a certain number of free miles each day and are charged from 20 cents to 30 cents extra for each additional mile driven. Most of the smaller companies still offered unlimited mileage plans so that they could compete with the larger firms. In 1989, however, the leading companies returned to offering unlimited mileage plans in an effort to obtain a larger portion of the leisure market.

Rates vary according to the size of the car and do not include gasoline, tax, or charges for extra services. Many companies offer the following types of rates:

- Regular rate—A standard charge for the day, usually with an added amount for miles driven.
- Special rate—A discount rate for weekends or holidays. A special rate can also include an unlimited mileage plan.
- Corporate rate—A discount rate for employees of companies with a high rental volume.

Makes and Models. Thirty-five years ago, each rental company concentrated on cars from just one United States manufacturer, such as General Motors or Ford. Usually, only three or four models were offered to customers. Today, the choice is much greater. Although some car rental firms still supply cars from only one manufacturer, many different models are available, as are vans, trucks, and even chauffeur-driven limousines. Other car rental companies offer both foreign and domestic models. Travelers with special requirements, such as handicapped drivers needing cars with hand controls or other specially equipped vehicles, or travelers requesting wagons or recreational vehicles, can be accommodated by many rental car firms.

Many rental firms provide charts showing which cars are available within each class. The following are the four basic classes of rental cars and examples of each:

- *Subcompact*—A small car. Examples include Ford

Escort, Dodge Shadow, Nissan Sentra.

- *Compact*—An average-size car. Examples include Chevrolet Cavalier, Ford Tempo, Toyota Corolla.
- *Standard*—A full-size car. Examples include Ford Thunderbird, Chrysler Le Baron, Subaru Legacy.
- *Deluxe*—A large luxury car that usually comes equipped with many extras. Examples include Lincoln Town Car, Cadillac Sedan de Ville, Buick Century.

If a customer has a reservation and a car in the requested class is not available, most companies will provide an upgrade to the next higher class at no extra charge.

Charges. Most car rental companies charge fees not included in their regular rates for any extra services that they provide, including the following:

- Drop off—It is not always convenient for a renter to drop off a car at the place where it was rented. Many companies allow clients to drop off their cars at any location owned by the same company. However, there is usually an additional *drop-off charge* for this service.
- Gas—Car rental firms usually charge clients for gasoline when cars are returned with less than a full tank. The prices are much higher than those charged at most gas stations, so clients usually save money by filling the tank before returning the car.
- Insurance—Clients are liable for a specified initial amount of damage to the car. Car rental firms offer clients a *loss/damage waiver (LDW)* for a fee of about $13 per day. An LDW is not insurance, but it relieves clients of their liability for this initial amount of damage. It also provides coverage for loss of the use of the rental car should an accident occur. For an additional fee, car rental firms also offer *personal accident insurance (PAI)*, which provides coverage in case of bodily injury to the client. The charges for LDW and PAI are a means by which car rental firms create additional revenue. LDWs are quite controversial, however, and some states no longer allow car rental companies to sell them.
- Lost keys—A fee is charged if clients lose the keys to the rental car.

The Industry Abroad

The 1950s witnessed a period of rapid growth in the car rental industry throughout the world. United States companies began to enter the overseas market in the 1960s and now are represented in almost every country, even the Soviet Union and China. Many countries also have their own car rental companies.

United States Companies Abroad. Hertz, with offices in over 120 countries, dominates the market. Many other large United States companies also have offices abroad. In spite of the expansion of overseas operations, the United States car rental market is still larger than that of the rest of the world combined.

Foreign Companies. In addition to American car rental companies operating abroad, foreign car rental firms also service the needs of travelers wanting to rent a car overseas. These car rental companies include Tilden (of Canada) and Europcar, Auto Europe, and Europa Rent-a-Car (of Europe). Some firms offer both American and foreign-made cars.

Driving Abroad. Travelers who rent cars abroad should be aware of the different driving conditions and practices in some countries. For instance, in Great Britain, the Bahamas, and a few other countries, driving on the left side of the road is standard. The steering wheel is on the right side of the car, and shifting must be done with the left hand instead of the right. In most countries abroad, cars tend to be smaller than those in the United States. In Europe, most rental cars have manual transmissions. Travelers who want a car with an automatic transmission must request it specifically and usually pay more.

Speed limits abroad are usually posted in kilometers, so a conversion chart or a knowledge of the metric system is useful. Speed limits vary from country to country, but they tend to be higher in foreign countries than they are in the United States. For example, the speed limit on many roads in France is 110 kilometers per hour (66 miles per hour). The expressways (autobahns) in Germany have no real speed limit, and some cars race along at speeds of 80 to 100 miles per hour.

Channels of Distribution

Several channels of distribution are used in the car rental industry, including travel agencies, business travel departments (BTDs) and car rental central reservations offices. Recently, travel agents have begun to play an increasing role in the car rental business. Rentals through travel agents were negligible 25 years ago; now they account for about 50 percent of car rental business. Reservations for employees of large companies are often made through BTDs; these clients usually receive the car rental firm's corporate rate.

Because most travel agents depend on airline CRSs for obtaining current information on car rental availability, smaller car rental companies that don't appear on the computer screen may suffer by not being as accessible. Travel agents often make car rental reservations on the CRS as part of a package, along with an airline ticket and a hotel room. Reservations can also be made by calling the toll-free number of the car rental company's central reservations office. Travel agents earn commissions from car rental firms just as they do from other travel and tourism suppliers.

MASS TRANSIT SYSTEMS

The term *public transportation* refers to any organized passenger service available to the general public within a small geographic area. Commuter buses, trains, and subways are the most important components of a public transportation system. They carry millions of people back and forth to work each day, either within a city or between a city and its suburbs. Public transportation systems provide an essential service for people living in urban areas. Most systems are heavily subsidized by local, state, or federal governments. The term *mass transit* refers more specifically to the movement of people in large metropolitan areas. The most important forms of mass transit are urban buses, subways, and taxicabs.

As a travel professional, you may be called on to provide information on mass transit in United States and foreign cities. You may be asked the best way to get from the Brussels airport to the central railroad station in downtown Brussels, or how to travel on the BART system in San Francisco, or how to reserve a limousine in Dallas.

In this section, you will learn of the history of urban mass transit, about getting around in United States cities, and about the transportation systems in some key cities of the world.

The Development of Mass Transit

In 1662, the French philosopher and mathematician Blaise Pascal was instrumental in starting a horse-drawn coach service in Paris. This may or may not have been the first urban transportation system in the world. In any case, it seems to have suffered a fate shared by many mass transit systems. When the fare was raised (in this case from no charge to a charge), ridership dropped sharply and eventually the service was discontinued.

Urban mass transit really got started in New York City, London, and Paris in the early part of the nineteenth century. Horse-drawn coaches, known as omnibuses, picked up and discharged passengers along set routes. In 1836, the first subway system was opened in London. Built to ease the congestion caused by horse-drawn surface traffic, the 3.7-mile underground line was an instant success. New York City built its first subway line in 1870, but it lost money and was soon abandoned. In 1897, Boston opened its first subway line, and the present New York City subway system was inaugurated in 1904.

In the late nineteenth century, electric streetcars, or *trolleys*, came into their own. They ran on tracks that were often laid down the middle of the street, and were powered by overhead wires. Trolleys were introduced in many cities in the United States and abroad.

The development of the gasoline engine led to the advent of the motor bus. The early buses were elongated automobiles that seated 12 to 20 people. Regular urban bus service began in London in 1904 and in New York City a year later.

Urban Buses and Trolleys

Today buses are the primary form of urban mass transit. An *urban bus* is one that operates over short distances within a city. Of the 950 cities in the United States with some form of public transportation, the majority have bus service only.

In the 1970s, federal programs for planning, financing, and operating public transportation gave urban bus service a new lease on life. Recognizing that buses are a much more energy-efficient form of transportation than cars, several cities have introduced special traffic lanes in downtown areas reserved for buses. By speeding up bus service in this way, cities hope to encourage car owners to leave their cars at home and take the bus.

In many metropolitan areas, privately operated buses or vans or extended cars, often called *airport limousines*, provide passenger service between airports and city centers. Airport limousine service usually operates at fixed intervals and is regulated by the airports. In many cities, large hotels have their own cars or vans to take hotel guests to and from the airport. Local city buses may also provide service to airports.

A growing number of United States cities are bringing back trolleys. Formally known as *light-rail transit*, trolleys carry some 500,000 passengers a day in such cities as Boston, Buffalo, Philadelphia, New Orleans, Los Angeles, and San Francisco. Trolleys are more reliable than buses and, running on their own tracks on the side of the street, can bypass a lot of city traffic. They are also nonpolluting. City planners of Los Angeles have great hopes for trolleys in breaking through the city's gridlock.

The famous cable cars of San Francisco were recently overhauled and once again carry passengers up and down the city's steep streets. This picturesque but practical form of transportation is on the must-see list of every tourist who visits San Francisco.

To cope with traffic congestion in downtown areas, a few cities have even tried the *monorail*, an elevated urban transit system that runs on one rail. Miami opened a monorail called the Metromover in 1986. The following summer, Detroit inaugurated the People Mover, a 2.9-mile monorail that runs 20 feet above ground.

Subways

A *subway* is a rail transportation system that provides local rapid-transit passenger service either wholly or partially underground. Subway systems are in operation in New York City, Boston, Philadelphia, Chicago, Atlanta, San Francisco, and Washington, D.C. Baltimore recently opened a subway as well.

Subways provide a way of moving many people around town quickly, inexpensively, and without polluting the atmosphere. The most recently built lines are clean, quiet, and efficient. Many travelers find subways the fastest and easiest way to get around a city, once they overcome their initial reluctance to figure out the system.

A number of cities in the United States have developed subway or rail links from the airport to the city center. New York City inaugurated the JFK Express connection in the 1970s; Philadelphia and Cleveland also have direct rail connections to their airports.

Taxicabs and Limousines

Taxis and, to a lesser extent, limousines play an important part in public transportation systems in most cities. Known as *on-demand public transportation*, this kind of service does not have regular schedules. Passengers arrange individually for service. In some cities, you get a taxi by hailing it in the street or at a cab stand. In other areas, a taxi is summoned by phone.

Limousines are privately owned and operated chauffeur-driven cars often hired for special occasions or for business purposes. Limousines are ordinarily reserved by phone. Fees can be calculated on a per-hour basis or on distance traveled.

In most cities, cab fares are indicated on a meter according to distance traveled. But fares may also be calculated by zone, as in Washington, D.C.

For tourists and business travelers unfamiliar with a city, taxis are an extremely convenient way to get around. They also provide an essential link between the railroad station or airport and the traveler's destination in the city.

Illus. 5-6 *The Washington, D.C., subway is quiet, clean, and efficient. Many of its operations, including ticket sales and collections, are automated.*
Source: *Washington Metropolitan Area Transit Authority*

Taxis and limousines form an integral part of airports and railroad stations. For the traveler who has just gotten off a plane, a taxi provides a transfer to the city center. The plane-taxi combination is yet another example of intermodal transportation.

Mass Transit in Foreign Cities

One of the first things a traveler arriving in a foreign city has to find out is how to get around that city. Will a taxi be the fastest and easiest way to go from the hotel to the trade show on the outskirts of town? Or is there a subway line that makes the trip without too much hassle and avoids the rush-hour traffic?

Transportation facilities, conditions, customs, and relative costs vary a great deal among the cities of the world. Buses in Switzerland, for example, operate more or less on the honor system. Passengers board the bus with tickets they have punched in a machine at the bus stop. Occasionally, a conductor comes through a bus to check tickets.

Some highlights of mass transit systems in cities around the world follow:

■ *Montreal.* Montreal has one of the most modern subway systems in the world. The trains run on rubber tires, which provide a quiet, comfortable ride.

■ *London.* The legendary cabbies of London have to pass a test to demonstrate their knowledge of the city's streets. London cabbies drive old-fashioned-looking black taxis that offer old-fashioned comfort with lots of headroom. The London Underground, known locally as the "Tube," has a repu-

tation for dependability, cleanliness, and civility. A line now runs directly to Heathrow Airport. Last, but not least, are the famous red double-decker buses. Double-deckers may not get to the destination faster, but the view from the upper level makes bus travel in London a tourist's delight.

■ *Paris.* The Paris Metro, built in 1900, is considered by many to be the finest subway system in the world. It is certainly the fastest, with trains averaging over 60 miles per hour on its newest line. Subway cars, which run on rubber tires, are divided into first- and second-class sections. Major stations have metro maps, which light up when you push a button, to show the best route to your destination.

■ *Moscow.* Moscow takes the prize for the world's grandest subway. Marble columns, glittering chandeliers, and paintings adorn the subway's stations. The subways also run meticulously on schedule.

■ *Tokyo.* Tokyo's subway qualifies as the most heavily used in the world. To pack as many riders as possible into each car during the rush hours, the subway employs white-gloved "pushers."

Channels of Distribution

Tickets and tokens for mass transit are usually sold directly at the point of departure. The traveler to New York City buys subway tokens at a subway station on arrival in the city. But the traveler may have obtained a subway map ahead of time. In this case, the channels of distribution serve as sources of information rather than for reservations or tickets.

Information about the mass transit system of a city is usually available from the local tourist office or chamber of commerce. Subway maps, information on bus routes, and tips on using taxis can also be found in guidebooks to the particular area, whether it is Paris, Mexico City, or Washington, D.C.

Illus. 5-7 *The double-decker bus is a familiar sight on London streets and is a great favorite among tourists.*
Source: *Courtesy of the British Tourist Authority*

Check Your Product Knowledge

1. What forms of mass transit carry travelers between airports and city centers?
2. Explain why many cities are building trolley lines today.
3. Which United States cities have subway systems? What advantages does a subway system offer?

CAREER OPPORTUNITIES

The career opportunities in the surface transportation industries are varied. Many require mechanical expertise or driving skills. Others involve sales and promotional abilities.

Careers in the Railroad Industry

Probably the best-known jobs in the railroad industry are those of engineer (train driver) and conductor. Engineers are responsible for the safe operation of the train, while conductors oversee the safety of the passengers. Other occupations in railroad operations include brake operator; signaler and signal maintainer; and track worker.

Some careers in the railroad industry involve public contact and/or sales and service. These include reservations clerk, sales representative, and station agent (the railroad's representative with the public). There is also a wide range of clerical positions.

Railroad employment has fallen from a high of 2 million in the 1920s to less than 300,000 in 1990. This sharp decrease can be attributed to a general decline in the industry and the increasing use of automation on the train, in the yard, and in the office. At the present time, career opportunities in the railroad industry are limited.

Careers in the Motorcoach Industry

Bus operators may be intercity drivers (city to city), local transit operators (public transportation within cities), or special-service drivers (charters, tours, and sightseeing). Dispatchers assign drivers to buses and coordinate the movement of buses in and out of the bus terminal.

Careers involving public contact and/or sales and service include ticket agent, tour manager, tour representative, and sales representatives. Clerical and general office positions are also available.

Employment prospects in the charter, tour, and sightseeing business have improved considerably since deregulation.

Careers in the Car Rental Industry

Preparing the car for the customer is an important part of the car rental service. The maintenance and service worker and the mechanic make sure that each car is clean and in good working order.

Other careers in the car rental industry, such as reservations agent and customer service representative, involve contact with the public. Station managers run the rental office and supervise the rental representatives; sales representatives sell the services of their company to airlines, travel agents, and business accounts.

The number of car rental companies increases each year, and career opportunities in the industry are expected to remain good.

Careers in Mass Transit

Careers in mass transit include drivers of taxicabs, limousines, urban buses, trolleys, and subways. Subway operators open and close subway doors and announce the stops. Bus and subway dispatchers regulate the flow of bus and subway traffic. Attendants in subway stations sell tokens or tickets to the public.

Summary

- The first public railroads came into service in England and the United States in the early nineteenth century.
- The private automobile, intercity buses, and airlines began to challenge the railroads in the 1920s. After World War II, the United States railroad industry declined rapidly.
- Amtrak, a semipublic railroad corporation, took over and revamped the intercity railroad passenger network in the United States in 1971.
- Railroad systems in Canada, Europe, and throughout the world continue to provide extensive service.
- The first motor buses appeared at the start of the twentieth century, and by the 1930s buses were a common sight on highways around the United States.
- Scheduled motorcoach passenger service declined after World War II as car ownership and air travel increased.
- The deregulation of the motorcoach industry in 1982 resulted in the entrance of many newly formed companies into the growing charter and tour business.
- The car rental industry began to grow rapidly during the late 1950s, a boom that continues today.
- The success of the car rental industry is closely related to the growth of air travel and, in particular, business travel.
- Mass transit systems are an essential part of life in urban areas, helping to ease traffic congestion and air pollution.

A DAY IN THE LIFE OF
A Car Rental Agent

Some people think my job as a car rental agent is routine and easy. In some ways, I guess it is, but I help provide a very important service to many travelers and I am proud of my work. The car rental agency I work for has a desk in the baggage claim area of a large airport. When people know they are coming to my city and will need to rent a car, they usually reserve one over the telephone. I also receive many calls from travel agents who want to reserve cars for their clients. When customers arrive at the airport and pick up their luggage, they simply walk over to my counter to get the car they have reserved.

It is my job to process the necessary forms so people can rent cars from my agency. I explain the terms of the rental to the customers and have them sign a rental agreement. I also tell them about the types of insurance that are offered. Customers must either leave a cash deposit or provide a credit card so I can bill the rental to their credit card account. Most customers use credit cards rather than cash.

I must make sure that the car that the customers have ordered is clean, filled with gas, and available for use. Some car rental agencies charge just a flat daily fee for the use of their automobiles. Other companies, like mine, charge that fee plus an additional charge per mile. For example, a typical fee at my agency is $29 per day plus 22 cents per mile for a compact car. When people rent a car, part of my job is to verify the mileage so that the agency will know how much to charge for mileage when the car is returned.

I also check in cars when they are returned. This involves checking the mileage and condition of the car and computing the renter's bill. Since most people pay by credit card, I process the credit card charge and provide the customer with a receipt. Many customers rent automobiles while on business trips, and they need the receipts to get reimbursement for their expenses from their companies.

A car rental agent is an entry-level job. That means that it is the first job that many people take in a particular business or industry. I have been a car rental clerk for a year. I hope to be promoted to station manger in another year or two. A station manager directs all operations at a car rental office or at a rental station in an airport, bus depot, or train terminal. The station manager is in charge of supervising the employees, running the desk or building, and managing the cars assigned to his or her station. I could also be promoted to customer service representative. In that position, I would handle customers' problems or complaints.

In order to qualify for a job as a car rental agent, I had to be a high school graduate. After I was hired, I took a four-week training course. I learned how to fill out forms, process credit cards, take reservations, greet the public, and so on. Car rental agencies strive to be very professional organizations. The company I work for provides its employees with attractive, businesslike uniforms. The company makes sure that all employees treat customers with great courtesy and respect.

You may not think my job requires many skills, but there are several things that I need to do well. I need a good command of the English language, of course, since I work at an American airport. Sometimes I wish I spoke another language as well since many of our foreign visitors are not fluent in English. Some of my co-workers can speak Spanish, French, or German. They are very handy to have around when I have difficulty communicating with a foreign customer.

I need to be able to operate a computer so that I can take reservations and fill out forms. I must also be able to write legibly and spell accurately since other people will be following my handwritten work orders. Most of all, I must have excellent math skills and be able to use a calculator because I spend a good deal of time working with figures. Much of my work involves adding up bills and calculating mileage charges.

I got my job by answering an advertisement in my local newspaper. Some of my co-workers applied directly to the car rental agency, and some found out about their job from a college placement office. Many new car rental agencies have started up in recent years so there are a lot of new jobs in the field. In addition, jobs as rental agents open up all the time as people are promoted or change jobs. A car rental agent does not receive a high salary, but there are frequent opportunities for advancement to better-paying jobs.

CHAPTER FIVE The Surface Travel Industries

Key Terms

nationalize
Eurailpass
BritRail pass
couchette
wagon-lit
TGV
rail/sail package
charter tour
escorted tour
independent package tour
city package tour
intermodal tour
transfer
fly/drive package
train/drive package
unlimited mileage
mileage cap
subcompact
compact
standard
deluxe
drop-off charge
loss/damage waiver (LDW)
personal accident insurance (PAI)
public transportation
mass transit
trolley
urban bus
airport limousine
light-rail transit
monorail
subway
on-demand public transportation
limousine

What Do You Think?

1. How important do you think it is to maintain inter-city rail passenger service in the United States? Give reasons for your answer.
2. Do you think that motorcoaches and trains should compete for the same intercity routes? What would be the advantage of competition? What would be the disadvantage?
3. Do you think that deregulation has had a beneficial effect on the motorcoach industry? Why or why not?
4. If someone asked you to recommend a car rental company, how would you go about choosing one?
5. What steps might be taken by mass transit systems to encourage more people to use their services?

Dealing with Product

Amtrak, which was created by the Rail Passenger Act of 1970, is one of the most controversial components of the travel industry. Many people mistakenly believe that Amtrak is a nationalized company, totally owned and operated by the federal government. In fact, Amtrak is a private, for-profit corporation, although the federal government does own Amtrak stock. In addition, five of the nine members of the Amtrak's board of directors either are appointed by the president and confirmed by the Senate, or are otherwise chosen by the government.

Imagine that you have been appointed to lead a fact-finding commission into the railroad system. You are to examine and report on the need for a national rail passenger system. Is there a need for this product in the United States? Should the federal government be involved in the funding and running of the system? Should Amtrak be treated differently from the way other modes of transportation are treated?

Dealing with People

You are a travel counselor with a dilemma. It seems you have just sold four students from Yourtown Community College a tour to Fort Lauderdale for the spring vacation. The package includes round-trip airfare, a shared room at a beachfront motel, and transfers to and from the Fort Lauderdale airport. So far, so good.

Now for the challenge. The students have requested that you also reserve a rental car for seven days. You know that none of them is old enough to rent a car legally, and you also doubt whether they can meet the other criteria for car rental. When you raised the question of age, one of the students told you not to worry, because he planned to borrow some identification from his older brother. What will you do? What are your responsibilities as a professional travel counselor? What will you do if the group threatens to cancel their trip and take their business elsewhere if you refuse to reserve the rental car?

Name _____

WORKSHEET 5-1   RAILROADS

Select a country with at least a small railway system. Use Fodor's *Railways of the World*, the *Thomas Cook's Timetable* books, or other tour or source books to get the following information.

OVERVIEW

Miles of track

Cleanliness

Number of scheduled trains

Safety

Passenger capacity

Classes of travel

Yearly passenger load

Services offered

Speeds reached

Other countries system connects to

Dependability

Additional information

PLAN A TRIP ON THIS RAILROAD SYSTEM

Departure (place/time)

Class you will travel

Arrival (place/time)

Services you will use

Number of miles traveled

Approximate cost

WORKSHEET 5-2   INDIVIDUAL BUS TOUR

Pick a region of the United States and plan a two- or three-week bus tour of it. Decide where you will stop over, for how long, what you will see and do. Be sure there is bus service all along your route. Estimate travel time and cost.

Region _____   Other expenses _____

_____   _____

_____   _____

_____   _____

Bus line(s) _____   Stopovers (where and how long) _____

_____   _____

_____   _____

_____   _____

Bus route/itinerary _____   _____

_____   Kind of accommodations (each stopover) _____

_____   _____

_____   _____

Miles traveled (each part) _____   _____

_____   Expenses (each stopover) _____

_____   _____

_____   _____

_____   Attractions or activities (each stopover) _____

Cost of ticket (each part) _____   _____

_____   _____

_____   _____

_____   _____

WORKSHEET 5-3   GROUND TRANSPORTATION AND SIGHTSEEING

Use the OAG *Travel Planner Hotel and Motel Redbook* or a similar publication to describe the various ways to get from the airport near each of the following cities to the city's downtown area. If there is more than one airport near any city, select one and identify it.

Austin, TX

Chicago, IL

Lincoln, NE

Los Angeles, CA

Miami, FL

Milwaukee, WI

Montgomery, AL

Use *Gray Line Sales and Tour Guide, American Sightseeing International World Tariff*, or similar publications to select a sightseeing tour of each city. Describe it briefly below. Include highlights, duration, and cost.

Austin

Chicago

Lincoln

Los Angeles

Miami

Milwaukee

Montgomery

WORKSHEET 5-4   RENTING A CAR

You are a travel agent. You have just finished arranging a round-trip flight from Yourtown to San Francisco for Rosalind Burton. While in California, Ms. Burton plans to rent a car and tour the redwood forests in the northern part of the state. She would like to drive a compact car with automatic transmission. Ms. Burton has never rented a car before and is somewhat apprehensive about the rental process.

Reserve a rental car for Ms. Burton. Choose a car rental company and find out the rates and charges for the type of car she wants. Also find out the company's procedures for renting a car. Record your findings on the form below.

Name of car rental company _____
_____
_____

Information needed before renting a car _____
_____
_____
_____
_____

Rates _____
_____

Makes and models available in compact size _____
_____
_____
_____
_____

Charges _____
_____
_____

Insurance price and information _____
_____
_____
_____

Where to pick up car _____
_____
_____
_____
_____
_____

What to do in case of mechanical failure or accident
_____
_____
_____
_____
_____
_____
_____

What to do before dropping off car _____
_____
_____
_____
_____
_____
_____

Where and how to drop off car _____
_____
_____
_____
_____
_____
_____

CHAPTER 6 THE CRUISE AND STEAMSHIP INDUSTRY

"I must down to the seas again,
To the lonely sea and the sky,
And all I ask is a tall ship,
And a star to steer her by."

—John Masefield

Objectives

When you have completed this chapter, you should be able to:

- List the highlights in the history of sailing ships and steamships.
- Give reasons for the decline of point-to-point passenger service and the rise of the cruise industry.
- List the most popular cruising areas of the world.
- Give examples of theme cruises.
- Explain the differences between freighter cruises and standard liner cruises.

- Describe some key marketing techniques used by contemporary cruise companies.
- Evaluate the fly/cruise and land/cruise packages.
- Discuss the concept of the cruise ship as a floating hotel.
- Describe the layout of a cruise ship.
- Identify the factors that affect the price of a cruise.
- Outline the regulations affecting cruises.

The cruise is widely regarded as the most glamourous of all travel products. *Romance*, *excitement*, and *adventure* are all words that spring to mind when we think about cruising.

The romance of the seas is nothing new, of course, but the cruise industry is. The rich and famous have been taking cruises since the 1920s, but mass-market cruises have been available only since the early 1960s. Shipping companies developed the concept of the contemporary cruise in response to their decline in passenger traffic following the advent of the jet age. The contemporary cruise was a remarkable marketing achievement. The ship was no longer simply a means of transportation but a destination in itself. Cruising became a total vacation experience.

The success of the young cruise industry has been phenomenal. Between 1980 and 1990, the number of people taking cruises each year has nearly tripled. The cruise industry is also the fastest-growing segment in travel and tourism. Cruises are offered on oceans and waterways throughout the world, on ships ranging in size from the luxury liner that carries 2,000 passengers to the small yacht carrying just a dozen.

In this chapter, you will learn about the development of the cruise industry and about the different types of cruises that are available. You will read about the cruise program and about the physical layout of a cruise ship. You will also learn how cruise companies have successfully broadened the appeal of cruises through aggressive marketing techniques.

THE ORIGINS OF THE CRUISE INDUSTRY

Ships have played an important role in human history ever since the Egyptians invented the sail about 3200 B.C. Greeks, Romans, and other early seafarers made various technological advances in shipbuilding, improving the seaworthiness of sailing ships and increasing their speed. They did little, however, to make the vessels more comfortable for the people on board. Early sailing ships were used primarily for trade and warfare, not for transporting passengers.

With the development of the compass and navigation charts in the twelfth century, ships began to venture out to sea on longer ocean voyages. The invention of the rudder made it easier to steer a ship and allowed for the construction of heavier, sturdier vessels. The period between 1400 and the late 1800s was one of constant improvement in sailing ship design. This was the age of overseas expansion, when sea routes were opened up from Europe to the Far East and across the Atlantic Ocean

to the New World. Trade was still the primary motivation for the shipping industry, but passenger transportation began to increase in importance (see Figure 6-1).

Regularly scheduled transatlantic passenger service was introduced in 1818 by the Black Ball Line of the United States. As the pace of immigration quickened, other United States lines began to offer scheduled service

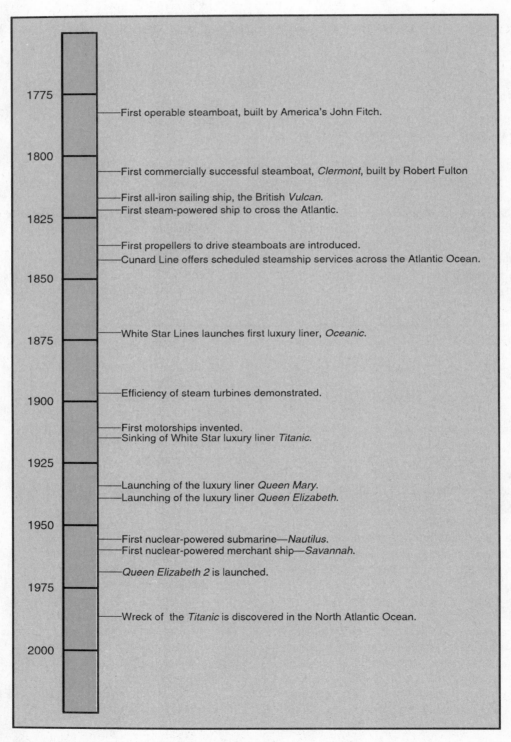

Figure 6-1 Milestones in Maritime History

between England and the United States. Rival companies competed with each other to increase speed of passage. By the 1840s, crossing time between Liverpool and New York City was about three weeks. Competition also led to some improvements in passenger comfort, though accommodations were still far from luxurious.

Passengers (and cargo) were carried on longer routes by the legendary clipper ships, introduced in the mid-nineteenth century and designed for maximum speed. Clippers carried gold prospectors from the eastern United States, around the tip of South America, to the California goldfields on the famous "round the Horn" journey. They reached their destination in three to four months—half the time it would take by the overland route. By the late 1860s, however, clippers were obsolete. The steamship had appeared.

The Age of Steam

The use of steam engines on ships marked the greatest revolution in water transportation since the invention of the sail. Robert Fulton's *Clermont* made its maiden voyage up the Hudson River from New York City to Albany in 1807. Within a few years, hundreds of steamboats were carrying passengers on inland waterways throughout North America.

Steamships were soon introduced on transatlantic routes. In 1819, the *Savannah* became the first steamship to cross the Atlantic. In 1840, the famous Cunard Line became the first to offer scheduled steamship service across the Atlantic. Cunard, White Star, and other British lines were the leaders in transatlantic passenger service in the early years. Germany's North German Lloyd and Hamburg-American lines began to provide stiff competition by the 1870s. French and Dutch companies had also entered the transatlantic passenger race by the end of the century. The United States turned its attention to the Pacific, and the Pacific Mail Steamship Company began passenger service in 1867.

As the rivalry among the European shipping companies intensified, each line tried to outdo the others with larger ships, faster crossings, and more luxurious accommodations.

In spite of the improvements in comfort, most passengers continued to travel in *steerage*, the lowest class on board. Steerage passengers occupied cramped, communal quarters on the lowest deck, near the ship's engines. The low price of steerage-class travel encouraged millions of Europeans to emigrate to the United States. A typical steamship of the period might carry 50 cabin passengers, but ten times that number in steerage. Separate cabins with plush interiors, ventilation, and steam heat were only for the privileged few who could afford them. Already, you can see the different motivations, needs, and expectations (MNEs) of different travelers. The rich

traveled for pleasure and expected luxury. Steerage passengers traveled to get to their destination, could only afford inexpensive accommodations, and had limited expectations.

Significant improvements continued to be made in shipbuilding. Iron hulls replaced wooden hulls, propellers replaced paddle wheels, and steam turbines and later diesel engines replaced steam engines. Two of the most important maritime advances occurred on land: the opening of the Suez Canal (1869) and the Panama Canal (1914), both of which saved thousands of miles and dozens of days at sea.

The Age of the Ocean Liners

The late nineteenth century and first half of the twentieth century comprised the great age of the ocean liners. A *liner* is an oceangoing passenger vessel that runs over a fixed route on a fixed schedule. The term is generally applied to those large luxury ships that came into transatlantic service about 1885. Liners also sailed on other routes throughout the world, but the largest and fastest were those built for passenger service between the United States and Europe. They include such great names as the *City of Paris*, the *City of New York*, the *Mauretania*, the *Lusitania*, and the *Titanic*.

By the early twentieth century, the luxury of onboard accommodations had been raised to an extremely high level. In fact, many of the ships had all the comforts of a five-star resort hotel, with hot and cold running water, private baths, sumptuous meals, and lavish public rooms. The emphasis on luxury was meant to appeal to the growing number of wealthy United States citizens traveling to Europe either on business or for pleasure. By the early 1920s, 80 percent of all steamship passengers were United States citizens. Steerage traffic was on the decline and there was a new breed of passenger—the tourist. A new class—tourist third class—was created to accommodate the thousands of United States citizens eager to see the wonders of Europe. The number of passengers crossing the Atlantic rose sharply—from 200,000 in 1902 to more than 1 million in 1929.

During the 1920s, some shipping companies began to offer the first world cruises and winter cruises in the warm waters of the Caribbean and the Mediterranean. During the summer, they returned to regular scheduled passenger service.

The rivalry among the shipping lines continued through the 1920s and into the early 1930s. Liner size continued to increase, reaching its peak during the 1930s with the French Line's *Normandie* and Cunard's *Queen Mary*. Both could carry over 2,000 passengers and were capable of 30 knots. Crossing time was reduced to just over four days. At the end of the decade, the *Queen Elizabeth*, the largest liner ever built, was launched by Cunard.

The Modern Age

The passenger ship business continued to thrive for 13 years after World War II, largely due to the boom in tourism. Immigrants, business executives, and the wealthy continued to use the service, but the largest group of travelers consisted of American tourists. By 1958, there were 25 companies and 70 ships operating on transatlantic routes.

It is ironic that although most of the passengers were from the United States, most of the shipping lines were European owned and operated; by the late 1950s, the United States had priced itself out of the passenger market because of high labor costs. American crew members demanded much higher wages than their foreign counterparts. The problem has continued to plague United States cruise companies to the present day. This explains why so many ships are foreign flag vessels, registered in other countries. By registering in a foreign country, American shipowners can pay wages lower than those required by unions in the United States.

Some United States lines have survived, however. These include the United States Line (serving Europe), Matson Lines (Hawaii, the South Pacific, Australia, and New Zealand), Moore-McCormack (South America), and American President Lines (the Orient).

The Birth of the Cruise Ship

In 1958, the first commercial jet airliner flew nonstop across the Atlantic. This flight marked the beginning of the end for the passenger ship industry. The airlines had been carrying an increasing number of passengers since the late 1940s. By 1958, as many people were crossing the Atlantic by air as by sea. Just one year later, 63 percent of all transatlantic passengers traveled by air. It was a dramatic turnaround. Only 15 years earlier, virtually all transatlantic passengers had crossed by sea.

Shipping lines tried to hold on to their share of the passenger market by emphasizing that "getting there is half the fun." But travelers wouldn't buy it. It was understandable that business travelers would prefer to cross the ocean in eight hours by plane rather than in four or five days by ship. What is interesting is that vacationers and travelers visiting friends and relatives also chose to fly. Evidently, they placed more importance on spending time at their destination than on having fun getting there. The jet succeeded at the expense of the liner because it could better satisfy the MNEs of all types of travelers.

As the volume of air traffic increased, a number of the great liners had to withdraw from passenger service. They could not afford to operate half-empty. Some were junked for scrap; others began new lives as freight carriers; a few were docked as tourist attractions; but most significantly, many were converted into cruise ships.

The development of the modern cruise is a classic example of necessity being the mother of invention. If the shipping companies could not compete with the airlines, they would compete with the resort hotels by offering the cruise as a complete vacation. "Getting there is half the fun" gave way to "Being here is *all* the fun."

Earlier cruises had catered to a small, rich elite. The "contemporary" cruise that was developed in the early 1960s was targeted at a much larger segment of society—the tourist market. To widen the appeal of the cruise, the traditional three-class division (first, cabin, and tourist) was abandoned in favor of a single, high-class accommodation.

Shipping companies began converting their passenger liners into tropical cruise ships in the early 1960s. Some could be transferred to the cruise trade with comparative ease. Others were sold, modernized, and later reborn as cruise ships under a new name. The *France*, for example, became the *Norway*, flagship of Norwegian Cruise Line (NCL). Not all of the older superliners could be adapted for the cruise business. Giants such as the *Queen Mary*, *Queen Elizabeth*, and *United States* proved uneconomical to operate and were withdrawn from service by 1970.

The established companies continued to build luxury superliners throughout the 1960s, but these were to serve a dual purpose. During the summer, they served as **point-to-point** liners; that is, they took passengers from one destination to another. During the winter, they served as warm-water cruise ships. Cunard's *Queen Elizabeth 2* (*QE2*), which made its maiden voyage in 1969, was the most notable example. Built as a replacement for the *Queen Elizabeth*, the 65,000-ton liner reflected the demands of the new cruise market. Its on-board facilities included four swimming pools; bars, lounges, and shops; a nightclub; and a children's playroom. All cabins were fitted with air conditioning and private bath or shower. The liner had a passenger capacity of 1,700 and a crew of 900. This 2:1 passenger-to-crew ratio was to become standard on most cruise ships.

The next phase was the development of the year-round cruise. NCL was a pioneer, packaging the first mass-market, year-round cruises from Miami to the Bahamas in 1966. Miami was rapidly replacing New York as the number one port in the United States as the Caribbean became the major cruising area. New companies such as Royal Viking Line and Royal Caribbean Cruise Line introduced fleets of ships specifically designed for Caribbean cruising.

The focus of technological improvements in earlier times had been on increased speed and increased ship size. With the development of the cruise ship, the emphasis shifted to fuel efficiency, low operating costs, and continued improvements in passenger comfort. The use of aluminum for a ship's superstructure (that part of the ship above the main hull) meant that the new cruise ships

Illus. 6-1 *The* QE2 *provides both point-to-point sailings and warm-water cruises.*
Source: *Cunard Line*

were considerably lighter than the earlier liners. As a result, they consumed less fuel. (The use of aluminum also allowed for the addition of more decks.) Fuel costs were further reduced by the widespread use of diesel engines.

Passenger comfort was greatly increased by the introduction of *stabilizers*, which minimize the effects of a ship's side-to-side roll. The development of radar meant that ships could steer clear of the worst storms. As more and more vessels were built for cruising, on-board amenities were greatly improved. Cabins were standardized, with private bathrooms and air conditioning throughout. More space was given over to public rooms and outdoor open decks. Dining rooms were located higher in the ship so that passengers could view the sea while dining.

Check Your Product Knowledge

1. List five important technological improvements made in shipbuilding in the last 1,000 years.
2. What was the new breed of passengers that appeared during the 1920s? How did they differ from earlier types of ocean travelers?
3. What effect did transatlantic jet travel have on the passenger ship industry?
4. How do modern cruise ships differ from the luxury ocean liners?

CRUISES OF TODAY

The cruise industry had established itself as a major force in the tourist industry by the early 1970s and has continued to grow to the present day. By the mid-1970s, existing cruise ships were operating at maximum capacity and more were being built. Between 1980 and 1986, $3 billion was spent on cruise ship construction, doubling the world's cruise fleet. New ships were built and old ones were modernized—some by being cut in half and then welded back together with a larger midsection. In 1990, several cruise lines, including Carnival and Chandris Fantasy Cruises, introduced new, larger ships to their fleets.

The rise in the number of passengers taking cruises has been equally spectacular—from 1.4 million in 1980 to nearly 4 million in 1990. About 70 percent of all passengers are from North America. In just 15 years, Carnival Cruise Lines, a leader in the Caribbean with nine ships, has seen its number of passengers increase from 100,000 to nearly 1 million a year.

A few of the older shipping companies (most notably Cunard, Holland America, and P&O) have successfully made the transition from point-to-point service to the cruise trade. But most cruise lines have been in operation for less than 25 years. Today, there are about 50 companies offering a wide variety of cruises on about 190 passenger vessels. More than half of the lines belong to the Cruise Lines International Association

S.S. Norway

The *S.S. Norway* is one of the largest passenger ships in the world. Built as a transatlantic ocean liner, it now plies the waters of the Caribbean as a cruise ship carrying more than 2,000 passengers a week from Miami to the Virgin Islands and back. The *Norway* is owned by the Norwegian Cruise Line (NCL), which also operates four smaller cruise ships in the Caribbean and one in California.

The *S.S. Norway* started life as the *S.S. France*. The ship was built in the late 1950s to carry passengers across the Atlantic Ocean just as people began to desert ocean liners for air travel between Europe and North America. The *France* was one of the last of the large, luxurious ocean liners ever built. Its silhouette, with two stately winged smokestacks, became very familiar on travel posters and in travel magazines in the 1960s. Although ocean liner travel was declining, the *France* continued to carry passengers from the United States to France and back until the French government took the ship out of service in the early 1970s.

The Norwegian Cruise Line purchased the *France* and renamed it the *Norway* in 1979. The liner had to be refurbished and converted from an enclosed ship, suitable for sailing the frigid North Atlantic, to an outdoor ship, open to the balmy breezes of the Caribbean. NCL altered the *Norway's* classic lines by adding two huge davits, or cranes, on the foredeck to hold two large tenders, each capable of carrying 400 passengers between ship and shore. It also added two large "Norway" signs between the smokestacks.

In recent years, the *Norway* has been assigned to seven-day cruises from Miami to St. Maarten, St. John, and St. Thomas in the West Indies. It also stops for one day at Pleasure Island, which is owned by NCL. The *Norway's* passengers can enjoy a day of snorkeling, swimming, beachcombing, sunbathing, and beach games on the island.

The sheer size of the *Norway* is one of its most fascinating features. It weighs about 75,000 tons. It has 12 decks and more than 65,000 feet of sun decks and walkways. Its engine room is 800 feet long and seven stories high. It would take more than an hour to descend by stairs from the top to the bottom of the ship. In order to help passengers find their way around, NCL has painted the forward areas of the ship turquoise and the aft areas pink.

Because it is so large, the *Norway* can offer passengers an enormous variety of shipboard activities. The ship's facilities include two pools, a 6,000-square-foot Roman spa, a health and fitness center, two large dining rooms, a gambling casino, a video game room, a library, a nursery, a children's activity room, several shops, and many nightclubs and bars.

On board, passengers can enjoy playing a wide variety of sports, such as basketball, racquetball, volleyball, or shuffleboard. They can take classes in aerobics, swimnastics, and cooking. They can learn ice carving, attend a fashion show, participate in a wine-tasting, practice playing golf on the ship's driving range, or try their hand at trap shooting. In the evening, passengers can choose between concerts, dancing, a comedy revue, or a Broadway-type show.

The *Norway* has something for everyone, including children. Some of the many supervised activities for children include ice cream and cookie parties, movies, story times, and crafts. Children can even take their own guided shore trips while their parents are off shopping and seeing the sights.

Since 1983, the *Norway* has been host to an annual floating jazz festival each fall. The festival brings together jazz fans and many of the leading jazz performers for a week of music and sun. NCL has also added several other kinds of theme cruises to the *Norway's* schedule including a comedy cruise, a country and western music cruise, a magic cruise, and a big band cruise.

NCL also offers a series of sports cruises on the *Norway*. These cruises are intended to bring fans together with big names in professional sports. In recent years, NCL sports cruises have featured football star Larry Csonka, basketball great Michael Jordan, NHL hockey player Brad Park, and baseball player Joe Morgan.

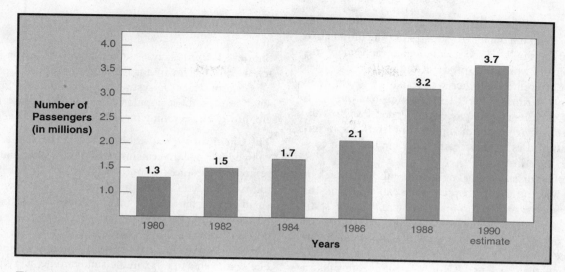

Figure 6-2 Cruise Line Passengers
Reported by CLIA Member Lines (U.S., Puerto Rico, and Canada)
Source: Cruise Lines International Association

(CLIA), a regulatory and promotional organization founded in 1975. Figure 6-2 shows the increase in passengers carried by CLIA member ships between 1980 and 1990. (CLIA is discussed in detail later in this chapter.)

The number of cruise lines in operation has increased considerably in the past decade. Some of the new lines are owned and operated by United States companies, but the majority are in European hands. Greek, Italian, Norwegian, Dutch, and British lines dominate the industry. Soviet companies have expanded their country's cruise fleet in recent years and have succeeded in penetrating the Western market by offering cheaper rates than European and United States lines. Figure 6-3 shows how domestic and international cruise revenues increased during the 1980s.

You can't always tell who owns a ship by the flag it is flying. A number of cruise ships fly what is known as a *flag of convenience*. This flag signifies that a ship of one nation is registered under the flag of another. The ships of the United States-owned Carnival Cruise Lines, for example, sail under the Liberian flag. You read earlier that foreign registry enables shipping lines to cut labor costs. It also allows them to avoid strict controls and high taxes imposed in their country of origin.

A Wide Array of Cruises

The cruise industry has responded to the varying MNEs of travelers with a diversity of cruise types and cruise destinations. Cruise lines sail to every conceivable maritime location, from the spectacular coast of Alaska to the icy waters of Antarctica. There are cruises to fit every need and pocketbook, with sailings of almost any time length. Travelers can choose from weekend jaunts to the Bahamas, six-day journeys along the rivers of Europe,

two-week cruises of the Mediterranean, six-week sailings around South America, and, of course, the three-month world cruise.

World Cruises

A world cruise is the ultimate journey, the vacation of a lifetime for those who can afford the time and the expense. For three months, passengers are pampered with first-rate personal service, superb cuisine, international entertainment, and shore excursions to exotic ports of call. The cost can be staggering, ranging from about $25,000 to over $125,000 for a deluxe suite on the *Queen Elizabeth 2*. At those prices, it's hardly surprising that the market for world cruises is relatively limited.

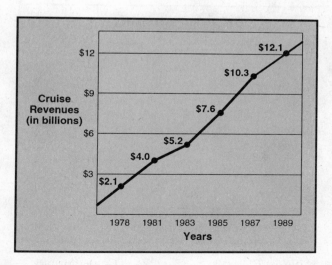

Figure 6-3 Total Domestic and International Cruise Revenues
Source: Louis Harris and Associates, Travel Weekly

Cunard offered the first official world cruise aboard the *Laconia* in the winter of 1922–1923. The ultradeluxe *QE2* and the smaller *Sagafjord* maintain the Cunard tradition on the world cruise circuit today. World cruises are also offered by another well-established shipping company—Britain's P&O Line, which has over 100 years of experience as a passenger carrier. P&O's *Canberra* (sailing from Southampton, England) was originally designed as a transoceanic liner but has been converted to the cruise trade.

World cruises usually begin during the first week of January and end in early April. Some call at as many as 30 ports on the way. All ships travel in an east-west direction, generally crossing from the North Atlantic to the Pacific via the Panama Canal, then on to Asia and the Indian Ocean, through the Suez Canal into the Mediterranean, and then back to the North Atlantic. A few take a more southerly route, sailing around the tip of South America and South Africa. *Sagafjord's* 1992 world cruise itinerary is shown in Table 6-1.

Cruise lines sell not only the complete world cruise but also segments of the trip. In this way, they cater to travelers who want to savor the luxury and excitement of a world cruise but who cannot afford the whole trip. Once again, a supplier identifies a customer need and markets a product to satisfy that need. Typical segments include New York to Los Angeles, Los Angeles to Singapore, Hong Kong to Singapore, Singapore to Rio de Janeiro, and Southhampton to Barbados. To encourage travelers to sign up for portions of world cruises, cruise lines offer generous credits for air travel to the port of *embarkation* (the boarding of passengers onto a ship) and back from the port of disembarkation.

Depart from FORT LAUDERDALE—January 6, 1992	
LIMA, PERU	BANGKOK
BUENOS AIRES	HONG KONG
RIO DE JANEIRO	SHANGHAI
DURBAN, SOUTH AFRICA	TOKYO
MOMBASA, KENYA	HONOLULU
MADRAS, INDIA	ACAPULCO
SINGAPORE	ARUBA
Arrive in FORT LAUDERDALE—April 22, 1992	
Fare: $30,340 per person, double occupancy	

Table 6-1 Cunard's *Sagafjord* World Cruise Itinerary, 1992
Source: Cunard Line

Shorter Sea Cruises

Shorter sea cruises are the mainstay of the cruise industry, accounting for by far the largest number of passengers. Warm-water cruises, with the emphasis on "fun and sun," are the most popular. The Alaskan cruise routes are, however, becoming increasingly well traveled.

The Caribbean. The Caribbean became the first area developed for modern cruising during the 1960s, and it has remained the most popular region for United States tourists. It offers a wealth of tropical islands within a small geographic area. As many as five or six islands can be visited during a one-week cruise. A typical Caribbean cruise is shown in Figure 6-4.

The Caribbean cruise appeals primarily to the traveler who wants to relax in the sun en route, and then experience a little local culture at the destinations. Although the Caribbean offers exotic attractions, it is still familiar and "safe" enough for the traveler who does not want to experience a totally foreign culture.

The islands of the Western Caribbean are within a day or two's sailing of Florida ports such as Miami, Fort Everglades/Fort Lauderdale, and Tampa. Nassau, in the Bahamas, is one of the most frequently visited destinations. San Juan, Puerto Rico, serves as a base for cruises to the Virgin Islands, Guadeloupe, Martinique, Barbados, and other Eastern Caribbean Islands.

Another popular cruise destination is the island of Bermuda. One-week cruises to Bermuda, with three days of sailing and four days in port, leave from New York City. Bermuda cruises are so popular that Bermuda's government has placed strict limits on the number of ships allowed to enter the port. This is a means of minimizing the negative effects of tourism on the environment.

In the early days, cruise ships sailed to the Caribbean only during the winter months, generally on seven-day voyages. The winter season is still the busiest, but many Caribbean lines now operate year-round, offering cruises that vary in length from two to fourteen days. Three- and four-day trips have become increasingly popular in recent years.

More than 30 cruise lines operate in the Caribbean. Carnival Cruise Lines, launched in 1973, is one of the most aggressive companies in the Caribbean. The company bills itself as "the most popular cruise line in the world." With its casual atmosphere and action-filled onboard program, the emphasis on a Carnival cruise is unmistakably on recreation. (Its nine ships are even billed as the "Fun Ships.")

The Mexican Riviera. The Mexican Riviera is the most popular destination for cruises from West Coast ports in North America. This destination has been one of the fastest growth areas in the cruise trade in recent years. More than a dozen lines now run regular cruises to the

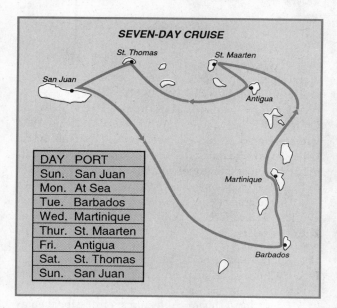

SEVEN-DAY CRUISE

DAY	PORT
Sun.	San Juan
Mon.	At Sea
Tue.	Barbados
Wed.	Martinique
Thur.	St. Maarten
Fri.	Antigua
Sat.	St. Thomas
Sun.	San Juan

Figure 6-4   A Typical Caribbean Cruise Route
Source: Norwegian Cruise Line

Illus. 6-2   *Spectacular scenery such as this makes Alaska cruises the fastest-growing sector of the cruise market.*
Source: Royal Viking Line

Mexican West Coast, offering fun in the sun with the added attraction of ports such as Mazatlan, Puerto Vallarta, and Acapulco. Most cruises last seven days or longer and depart from Los Angeles in winter and spring.

Trans-Canal. A number of cruise lines offer both the Mexican Riviera and the Caribbean on the same cruise. As well as experiencing two popular cruise areas, passengers also get to pass through the Panama Canal (hence the name Trans-Canal cruises). Typical cruises last about ten days and sail between Los Angeles or Acapulco and Fort Lauderdale. Longer cruises terminate or begin at Vancouver.

Alaska. Ships that sail south from Los Angeles during the winter season often head north to Alaska in summer. Alaska cruises are currently the fastest-growing sector of the cruise market. They are targeted at a different market from the "fun-in-the-sun" cruises. The passenger list might include naturalists, whale watchers, and other adventurers for whom natural wonders are more important than sun.

Seven-day cruises from Vancouver sail up the protected waters of the Inside Passage to the spectacular Glacier Bay National Monument, calling at such far northern ports as Ketchikan, Skagway, Juneau, and Sitka. Fourteen-day Alaska cruises depart from Los Angeles and San Francisco.

The Hawaiian Islands. At present, there are no round-trip cruises from the mainland United States to Hawaii. Honolulu, however, is often a port of call on long South Pacific trips departing from Los Angeles or San Francisco.

American Hawaii Cruises, launched in 1979, operates year-round seven-day cruises of the Hawaiian Islands, calling at all the major ports. The line offers air/cruise packages to encourage people to fly out to Honolulu, the port of departure and return.

The Eastern United States. The coastal waters of New England have attracted many people, particularly senior citizens. Cruise ships operating in this area are small, with a maximum capacity of 100. Their size enables them to get in and out of ports that are too small for larger vessels. Coastal cruise ships are generally quieter than the luxury liners that cruise the Caribbean and Mexican Riviera. They have a greater proportion of elderly passengers on board, and there is little demand for the type of entertainment offered by lively discos, for example. Again, notice the principle of different travelers having different MNEs.

Seasonal cruises operate along the entire Eastern Seaboard from Maine to the Florida Keys. A complete cruise along the length of the East Coast takes from two to three weeks. The focus is on scenery and historic coastal towns. Shorter cruises of New England, the Chesapeake Bay, the Intracoastal Waterway between Baltimore and Savannah, and the Florida coast are also available. Many of the vessels that serve the East Coast in summer go south to the Caribbean in winter.

The Mediterranean. The Mediterranean is the major cruising area in Europe and the most popular destination after the Caribbean. Cruise lines usually concentrate on either the Eastern or the Western Mediterranean. A few lines operate cruises throughout the entire region.

The Eastern Mediterranean offers benefits similar to those of the Caribbean: sun and a rich diversity of islands grouped closely together. The area is also steeped in history. Culture can be as strong a motivator as lying in the sun for travelers on Mediterranean cruises.

Piraeus, the port of Athens, is the major point of departure for the Greek cruise lines that dominate the Eastern Mediterranean. As in the Caribbean, cruise companies have begun offering more three- and four-day sailings in an attempt to attract first-time cruise passengers.

Western Mediterranean cruises usually depart from Genoa and call at Barcelona, Majorca, Minorca, Gibraltar, and ports on the North African coast.

Northern Europe. Norway's North Cape is to Europe what Alaska is to the United States. As in Alaska, the main attraction is the scenery—in this case, the spectacular fjords of Norway's western coast. Cruises lasting seven, ten, or fourteen days leave from ports such as Copenhagen, Hamburg, Bergen, and Bremerhaven during the short June–August season. Ships sail up the Norwegian coast as far north as Tromso and Hammerfest. Some cruises continue farther north into the Barents Sea.

Copenhagen and Hamburg are also departure points for cruises into the Baltic Sea. Here the emphasis is less on scenery and more on the actual ports visited—ports such as Leningrad, Helsinki, and Stockholm.

Repositioning Cruises. A final noteworthy, shorter sea cruise is the *repositioning cruise*. Because of the seasonal nature of the cruise industry, many cruise lines transfer ships from one cruising area to another between seasons. A line can have a ship that cruises in the Caribbean in winter and in the Mediterranean or Northern Europe in summer. Rather than running an empty ship across the Atlantic at the end of the winter, the repositioning voyage is marketed as a special cruise. Repositioning cruises are also common between the Mexican Riviera and Alaska, and between the Caribbean and the East Coast.

Theme Cruises/Special-Interest Cruises

Many of the larger cruise companies try to vary their cruise program by occasionally offering cruises structured around a particular theme. French-owned Croisieres Paquet pioneered the theme cruise in 1968 with the first of its many classical music festivals at sea. Other lines were quick to realize the value of the theme cruise as a marketing tool and began to develop cruises to fit a wide range of special interests.

Theme cruises can be broken down into several categories, each reflecting the different motivations of different travelers:

- Recreational (sports, backgammon, bridge).
- Cultural (classical music, opera, the Big Band sound, film and theater festivals).
- Educational (historical lectures, professional study programs, financial planning).
- Health-oriented (diet and exercise).
- Hobby-oriented (stamp collecting, photography, gourmet cuisine, wine tasting, murder mysteries).

Most of the lines try to hire top-name celebrities to lecture and perform on theme cruises. Paquet, for example, planned to feature such renowned international performers as violinist Isaac Stern and flutist Jean-Pierre Rampal on its thirty-fifth music festival cruise in 1991.

In addition to companies that offer occasional theme cruises, there are a number of smaller companies that run nothing but adventure and academic cruises. The emphasis is on exploration and/or study. Guest scholars lecture on history, zoology, botany, archaeology, anthropology, and related topics. Instructors can even require their student passengers to complete homework assignments. Quite a contrast to the "fun-in-the-sun" type cruise! Clearly, these highly specialized cruises are targeted at a completely different market than are the warm-water cruises.

Ships for adventure and academic cruises usually accommodate fewer than 150 passengers and are designed to reach out-of-the-way areas not served by the larger cruise liners. A number of United States companies have stepped into the market and operate a variety of cruises to exotic locations. These companies include Society Expeditions and Special Expeditions.

Freighter Cruises

The world cruise fleet is supplemented by about 80 freighters that provide accommodations for a limited number of passengers on worldwide itineraries. As the name suggests, freighters are principally engaged in cargo transportation, but passengers can be an important source of additional income.

Freighter cruises are an alternative for those travelers who prefer to avoid the crowds of people on large cruise liners. Freighters usually carry a maximum of 12 passengers. (If they carry more, they are required to have a doctor on board.) Cruises last anywhere from one to four months. Travelers who cannot spare that much time can purchase segments of longer cruises. A major attraction of freighter cruises is that they often put in at ports not usually visited by the scheduled cruise lines.

Freighter cabins are as large and as comfortable as those found on cruise ships and are often more moderately priced. On the negative side, on-board entertainment and amenities are extremely limited. Schedules and itineraries are also subject to change at short notice. While every effort is made to make the cruise as enjoyable as possible, the ship's major business is carrying freight, not pampering guests. For these reasons, freighter cruises are only for the more adventurous travelers, those with different MNEs than, for example, Caribbean cruise passengers.

River Cruises

The river cruise has much in common with the coastal cruise that you read about earlier. On both types of cruise, the vessel never leaves sight of shore. There is always something for the passenger to see, which means that on-board distractions don't have to be as numerous as on oceangoing cruises. The river cruise, like the coastal cruise, tends to appeal more to the over-55 age group.

The Mississippi is the most popular river for cruising in North America. At the height of the steamboat age, thousands of paddle wheelers plied the Mississippi. Today, the two well-known riverboats in service are the *Delta Queen*, last of the old-time steamboats, and its modern sister ship, the *Mississippi Queen*. Both are operated by the Delta Queen Steamboat Company, which offers year-round (excluding January) three- to twelve-night cruises of the Mississippi and Ohio rivers. Shorter cruises depart from New Orleans and call at antebellum mansions and at the historic riverboat towns of the lower Mississippi, including Baton Rouge, Natchez, and Vicksburg. Longer cruises may include stops at other cities, such as Memphis, St. Louis, and St. Paul on the Mississippi, and Cincinnati and Pittsburgh on the Ohio.

A recent addition to river cruises is riverboat gambling. Some Illinois and Iowa cities along the Mississippi River have revived riverboat gambling on board several "floating casinos."

Seasonal cruises are also offered on the Hudson, the St. Lawrence, and rivers of the Pacific Northwest.

The waterways of Europe are well traveled by cruise vessels between the months of April and October. Luxury liners carrying up to 200 passengers cruise the Rhine, Moselle, Danube, Volga, and Don rivers. Tiny barges chug along smaller rivers and canals of England and France.

More exotic riverboat cruises are available in Egypt and South America. These appeal to the same type of traveler who takes ocean-going adventure cruises. Hilton International has year-round sailings up the Nile, where

Illus. 6-3 *One of the original paddle wheelers, the* Delta Queen *is a piece of living history as it continues to ply the waters of the Mississippi River, providing pleasure for thousands of passengers.*
Source: *Delta Queen Steamboat Company*

the tombs and temples of the pharaohs are the major attractions. Sun Line Cruises' 620-passenger *Stella Solaris* sails to one of the most exotic of all cruise destinations—the Amazon.

Yacht Charters

Yachts can be chartered either with or without a crew. In the first category, the group of people chartering the yacht decide the itinerary but leave the actual task of sailing to a professional crew. Passengers are, however, sometimes given sailing lessons. In the second category, the yacht is chartered by a group of experienced sailors who operate the vessel themselves.

The Caribbean is the main charter area. Yachts can also be chartered in the Greek Islands and off the New England coast. The Charter Yacht Brokers' Association represents yacht owners in the United States and abroad. The association acts as a wholesaler of charters.

Point-to-Point Crossings

The cruise trade has clearly been the major growth area of the shipping industry in the last 25 years. But point-to-point liner crossings (also known as port-to-port crossings) have not disappeared entirely. Admittedly, such services have been greatly reduced since the early 1960s, when there were as many as 100 passenger ship companies offering ocean crossings throughout the world. Only about a dozen of these companies survive and only a few lines provide service across the Atlantic. Cunard Line has maintained the tradition of regular transatlantic crossings since the mid-nineteenth century, firmly believing that there will always be passengers who prefer sea travel to air travel. Cunard's *QE2* currently makes regular five-day crossings between Southampton and New York from April to December.

It remains to be seen whether long-distance, point-to-point passenger crossings will disappear entirely. Although air travel is much faster than sea travel, point-to-point crossings do still offer a number of distinct advantages. At the simplest level, they are the only alternative on transoceanic routes for people who don't like to fly. Also, passengers are free to take much more baggage by sea than by air, an important consideration for those planning an extended stay at their destination. (Even large items such as cars and furniture can accompany the passenger by sea.) And for those who have the time, the crossing is a minivacation in itself. The cost of a transatlantic crossing is not much more than first-class airfare, quite a bargain when you bear in mind that all meals and accommodations are included.

Ferries. Ferry boat service is the one form of point-to-point water transportation that has been largely unaffected by the increase in air traffic. One reason is that ferry routes tend to be short and comparatively inexpensive. Another reason is that ferries often operate on routes that are poorly served by air. Some destinations are only accessible by ferry. Not all ferry routes are short, however. Some ferries steam for several hours and offer cabins, restaurants, and recreation rooms. In spite of these creature comforts, ferry companies do not pretend to be in the cruise business; their priority is transportation from point A to point B.

Some ferries are intermodal. In addition to passengers, they carry cars, trucks, and even railroad cars. Intermodal ferries can be as large as cruise ships.

Ferry boats are in operation throughout the world. They connect, for example, Alaska and the western United States; the Maritime Provinces of Canada; the Japanese islands; and Great Britain and continental Europe. Currently, the English Channel is one of the busiest ferry routes in the world. A staggering 50 million passengers a year cross between Southern England and Northern Europe. Of course, the opening of the English Channel tunnel in 1993 will greatly decrease the number of ferry-boat passengers. Nonetheless, the ferry business is an extremely important segment of the passenger shipping industry.

Check Your Product Knowledge

1. Why are the Caribbean and Mediterranean such popular cruise areas?
2. Name three cold-water cruise areas.
3. Explain how a repositioning cruise works.
4. Give two advantages and two disadvantages of cruising by freighter.
5. What are some of the attractions of a point-to-point crossing?

CRUISE MARKETING

Although the number of people taking cruises has increased significantly over the 30-year period of the modern cruise industry's existence, approximately 96 percent of the population of the United States has never taken a cruise. This means that there are almost 240 million people in this country ready to become first-time cruisers! In this section, you will read about the ways the cruise industry is trying to tap this vast potential market.

Broadening the Appeal of Cruises

There are two main reasons why the cruise industry has not been able to capture a larger share of the travel market:

Robert Dickenson

When Bob Dickinson joined Carnival Cruise Lines in 1973, the company owned only one ship and was bordering on bankruptcy. Dickinson was hired to direct the floundering company's sales and marketing division, something he admitted he knew little about. Nevertheless, Dickinson's sales and marketing ideas have transformed the cruise industry and helped make Carnival the largest and most popular cruise line in the world.

Dickinson graduated from John Carroll University in Ohio in 1965 and studied two years toward a master's degree in business administration at Duquesne University. Before joining Carnival, he worked for the Ford Motor Company and for RCA. Then he joined the American International Travel Service (AITS), which was then the parent company of Carnival Cruise Lines. In all those jobs, Dickinson's work focused on finance, not on sales and marketing.

When it came to selling cruises, Dickinson has said, "I had no perspective and no experience." Not only did he learn how to sell cruises, he practically reinvented the cruise industry. When he started out with Carnival, the modern cruise industry was in its infancy. The people who then took cruises were mainly older, wealthy people who saw cruising as a quiet, elegant way to travel to their vacation destinations.

One of Dickinson's first innovations was to develop the "Fun Ship" concept—the idea that a cruise was not just a way to get from port to port but an entire vacation in itself. The "Fun Ship" concept was also a way to let people know that cruises were not just for older travelers but for families, young couples, and singles looking for romance. Along with the "Fun Ship" concept, Dickinson also sought to change the image of cruises as being too expensive for the average person. His idea was to offer cruises as an entire vacation package at a price that was competitive with any other type of vacation or tour package.

Dickinson's strategies worked so brilliantly that within three years, Carnival had made enough profit to purchase a second ship, the *Empress of Britain*, which was renamed the *Carnivale*. In 1978, Carnival added a third ship to its fleet—the *Festivale*. The three ships made week-long round-trip cruises from Miami to vari-

ous Caribbean ports. In 1979, Dickinson was named Carnival's senior vice president for sales and marketing.

Early on, Dickinson recognized the value of using travel agents to market Carnival cruises. Here was a ready-made, in-place sales force, with thousands of locations throughout the United States. At the time, many travel agencies were little more than ticket offices—places where customers would go to buy airline tickets and pick up brochures about vacation destinations. Many agencies were uninviting offices whose employees were not necessarily interested in trying to *sell* anything to their clients.

Dickinson believed that the best way for Carnival to sell its cruises was to change the way travel agents did business. He envisioned travel agencies as vacation stores where people could go and shop for a vacation to fit their interests and budgets just as they shopped for any other goods and services. He wanted travel agents to sell cruises, but not through high pressure sales tactics. Instead, he wanted them to learn to match the customers' needs and expectations with the products that Carnival had to offer.

To help travel agents learn how to sell cruises, Dickinson's department developed a staff of sales representatives who, by the early 1990s, numbered more than 75. Each sales representative serves more than 500 travel agents a year, providing help, suggestions, and information on new products and services. The department also produced a series of short, entertaining videotapes to help educate and motivate travel agents to sell Carnival cruises. In addition, the company has a firm policy of supporting travel agents by not participating in any discount programs that would cut out the travel agents and their commission.

Coupled with an extensive television commercial campaign to attract consumers, Dickinson's marketing strategies have paid off handsomely. Carnival's bookings and profits have grown steadily each year. The Carnival fleet has grown to nine "Fun Ships," and the company also owns two other cruise lines. While other cruise companies have sought to duplicate Dickinson's formula, his rivals concede that he is still the man to beat when it comes to selling cruises.

Photo Source: Carnival Cruise Lines

■ Lack of public awareness about the range of cruise products available.
■ Misconceptions about cruising.

Individual cruise companies and Cruise Lines International Association (CLIA) have addressed the first problem by targeting major advertising campaigns and other promotional efforts at potential cruisers.

To understand the misconceptions that exist about cruising, we must return to the distinction between traditional and contemporary cruises. Far too many people in the United States still think of cruises in terms of traditional cruises—that they are only for the rich and the elderly, that they last for several weeks, and that they are expensive, upscale, and formal. A few modern cruises can still be characterized as traditional cruises, but by far the greater number are now contemporary cruises; that is, they are of shorter duration, have lower costs, and are organized to appeal to a much wider market.

A key marketing tool used by contemporary cruise companies is the three- and four-day cruise. By introducing the shorter vacations, cruise lines have been able to attract many first-time passengers who otherwise might not have thought of taking a cruise. About 90 percent of all passengers on three- and four-day cruises are first-timers. Once passengers have experienced and enjoyed the shorter cruise, they are more likely to take longer cruises with the company in future years (see Table 6-2). Some cruise lines even promote one-day cruises to nowhere to get people into the swing of cruising.

The three- and four-day cruises have proved particularly popular with the under-40 age group. Carnival Cruise Lines caters heavily to the younger market with activities such as singles' parties. Other lines attract young married couples with honeymoon cruises. Families with young children can take advantage of babysitting services, and many lines now offer programs for young children and teenagers. Substantially reduced rates for children sharing their parents' accommodations

are also an incentive. All these measures have served to reduce the average age of the cruise passenger. Today, there are almost as many passengers in the 25-40 age group as in the 60-and-older category. More than 40 percent of all first-time passengers are under 40.

Cruise companies have begun to appeal to more specialized markets by developing theme and special-interest cruises. The theory is that people are more likely to take a cruise if it is focused on something that strongly interests them. Classical music lovers, for example, might be more inclined to take cruises if there is a program of on-board concerts.

Many cruise companies are also pursuing commercial business. Several ships are now equipped with facilities to handle meetings and conventions, and cruises are being used increasingly for incentives (incentive travel is discussed in detail in Chapter 12).

Fly/Cruise Packages. Cruise lines have also succeeded in reaching a larger market by marketing cruises over a wide geographic area. In the early days of cruising, Caribbean cruises sailing from Florida ports were marketed only in the Southeast. West Coast cruises departing from Los Angeles were marketed only in California. This meant that if you lived in Topeka, Kansas, you probably wouldn't think of going on a cruise.

All that has changed, and cruises of all types and to all destinations are now marketed throughout the United States. What has made this development possible is the introduction of the fly/cruise concept. *Fly/cruise packages* (or air/sea packages, as they are sometimes known) are used to fly passengers to and from the port of embarkation of hundreds of destinations all over North America. The airfare is often included in the package price and can be greatly reduced. Cruise lines arrange air transportation on scheduled or chartered airlines. They can also issue passengers an air travel credit; passengers then make their own travel arrangements. The credit is deducted from the cruise fare.

As the market becomes more competitive, particularly in the Caribbean, the fly/cruise package is an increasingly important promotional tool for the cruise lines. Fly/cruise packages now account for almost 75 percent of all cruise bookings. Fly/cruise options have proved very successful in attracting first-time passengers, especially those who live far from the major cruising ports. The resident of Topeka, Kansas, is now much more likely to consider a cruise as a vacation option.

Fly/cruise packages are most often used to transport passengers to warm-water ports like Miami, Fort Lauderdale, and Los Angeles. The advantage for passengers is that they spend their whole vacation at sea in warm weather. On the most practical level, it means that they need only bring one wardrobe instead of two. Imagine, by contrast, a December sailing from New York City to St. Thomas. The passenger has to endure two days of

Length of Cruise	Passengers (in thousands)		Percent of Growth
	1980	1989	
3-5 Days	347	1,109	+220%
6-8 Days	846	1,790	+112
9-17 Days	221	365	+ 65
18+ Days	17	22	+ 29
TOTAL	1,431	3,286	+130%

Table 6-2 Growth by Length of Cruise
Source: Cruise Lines International Association

cold weather and rough seas on the southbound journey to the Caribbean, and more of the same on the way back. The alternative is a flight of less than three hours to Miami and almost four extra days at sea in the sun.

The fly/cruise concept also has another application. This is the "fly one way, cruise the other" package. This type of package was first introduced on transatlantic routes in the early 1960s. Cunard and British Airways have maintained the tradition with an outward journey from New York on the *QE2* and a return flight by Concorde. The chief advantage of this type of package is that it reduces point-to-point travel time, allowing passengers to custom-tailor their vacation. For example, a passenger may wish to cruise from Los Angeles to Acapulco. The complete round-trip cruise, including shore excursions, will take about two weeks. If the passenger has only one week to spend, he or she can cruise to Acapulco, then fly back to Los Angeles.

Land/Cruise Packages. The *land/cruise package* is another marketing tool that has been developed by many contemporary cruise lines. The land section of the package typically involves a short stay in a hotel at or near the port of embarkation. It can be taken either immediately before the cruise begins, or after it is over. American Hawaii Cruises, for example, gives passengers booking their seven-day Hawaiian Islands cruise the option of a three-day/two-night vacation at an island hotel.

It was a stroke of marketing genius that packaged a four-night Bahamas cruise with a three-day Disney World vacation. Premier Cruise Lines—"The Official Cruise Line of Walt Disney World"—pioneered this concept. It has become one of the most popular of all land/cruise options. The Disney World segment typically includes accommodations at an Orlando hotel; admission to the Magic Kingdom, EPCOT Center, and Disney-MGM Studios; a tour of the Kennedy Space Center; and the use of a rental car.

Cruise Pricing

Cruise ships have the highest overheads in the travel industry. To cover operating costs, cruise lines must achieve 80 to 90 percent occupancy rates. (By contrast, airlines can break even at 60 to 65 percent, and hotels at 55 to 60 percent.)

Pricing is the key to making sure that a cruise ship leaves port as full as possible. All cruise lines offer tiered pricing to attract passengers across a wide range of income levels. There can be more than a dozen price categories on a single cruise. The most expensive category (deluxe) can be twice as high as the least expensive (economy). For the extra money, the cruise passenger gets a better cabin.

Cruise lines also offer discount fares as passenger incentives. Many lines have off-season rates and reduced rates for clients who book well in advance. Others offer discounts for repeat cruisers. Accommodating the third or fourth person in a cabin at a reduced rate is another promotional pricing technique.

Check Your Product Knowledge

1. What are three image problems that contemporary cruise companies face? What measures have the lines taken to address these problems?
2. Explain how the fly/cruise concept works. What are two advantages of fly/cruise packages?
3. What pricing techniques do cruise lines use to achieve high occupancy rates?

THE CRUISE AS PRODUCT

The cruise is a unique travel product, one that combines both transportation and destination. This section will focus on the cruise ship as destination. You will read how the ship functions as a "floating hotel" and how the cruise program is structured. You will also look at the physical layout of a cruise ship and at the factors that affect the price of a cruise.

The Ship as Hotel

Almost every cruise ship calls in at one or more ports during the course of its journey. This represents the transportation element of the cruise product. Yet on most cruises, the ship itself is the main attraction. A headline

Illus. 6-4 *Premier Lines Cruise, Disney/Bahamas land/cruise package is immensely popular with both kids and adults.*
Source: © 1991 Premier Cruise Lines

in a recent Costa Lines' cruise brochure made the point very well: "Even if she never left home port, the *Carla Costa* would be a fabulous vacation destination by herself." In the same brochure, the *Costa Riviera* was referred to as "a floating European island."

A "floating island" may be stretching the point a little far, but the cruise ship is certainly a "floating hotel." For the vacation traveler, the ship must provide all the services of a resort hotel and the amenities of a vacation on dry land. For the business traveler, the cruise ship must be able to offer all the facilities of a convention hotel or convention/conference center. (Note that cruise ships have limited appeal for our third type of traveler—the person who is visiting friends and relatives. This type of traveler usually travels by air or by land. An exception would be if his or her friends and relatives were traveling on the same cruise.)

Meeting Passengers' MNEs. Because passengers cannot leave the ship while it is at sea, the cruise line must ensure that everything they might need or want is on board. A passenger's most basic needs, of course, are food and a place to sleep. Many will require the services of a laundry and a hairstylist. Others might expect to find a gymnasium or health center on board. Some will want to attend religious services. Business executives may need to keep in touch with the outside world by telephone or fax machine. They may also want access to a computer while on board. In short, the ship must provide a wide array of services, particularly on longer voyages.

Then there is the question of how to amuse the passengers while they are on board. A few will be content to laze in the sun all day. But most will expect a variety of on-board activities and nightly entertainment.

It is hardly surprising, then, that most ships have such a large crew on board. There is a division between the ship's crew, or ship's company, and the hotel crew, or staff. The ship's crew includes:

- Captain.
- First, second, and third officers (or "mates").
- Engineering officers.
- Radio officers.
- Medical officers.
- Purser.
- Ordinary and able seamen.

The hotel crew comprises:

- Hotel manager.
- Cruise/social director.
- Steward department (cabin stewards, dining room stewards, wine stewards, night stewards, deck stewards).
- Kitchen/galley department.
- Bartenders.
- Service department (barbers, hairstylists, launderers, librarians, masseurs, photographers, printers, shop assistants).
- Entertainers, instructors, lecturers.

Cruise guides and manuals often indicate the ratio between the total number of passengers and the number of hotel-crew members. Many cruise ships have one crew member for every two passengers: this gives a crew ratio of 0.5. In general, the higher the crew ratio, the better the level of passenger service.

Handicapped Passengers. The handicapped cruise passenger has special needs. He or she may require individualized attention and supervision, as well as special facilities. Some cruise ships are fitted with ramps, elevators, and other devices that minimize obstacles for the handicapped traveler. There may be one or two cabins on board that have been modified for wheelchair-bound passengers. Not all cruise lines, however, have the facilities to accommodate the handicapped. Many state in their brochure that they "reserve the right to refuse passengers who require treatment, care, or attention beyond that which on-board facilities can provide, or whose mental or physical condition may make them incapable of an ocean voyage."

The Cruise as Vacation at Sea

The cruise program typically comprises four main elements:

- Meals.
- Activities.
- Entertainment.
- Time on shore.

The balance of the various components will differ depending on the type of cruise. A warm-water cruise, for example, is likely to stress on-board activities and entertainment. An adventure cruise, on the other hand, is more likely to place the emphasis on time ashore. Even on a cruise where everyone shares a common interest—such as a theme cruise—the elements must be flexible enough to suit the needs and expectations of different kinds of passengers. Some passengers may expect to be served American-style meals; others may want to try ethnic cuisine. Some passengers want to spend their free time aboard ship playing backgammon; others may want to attend lectures. What follows is a typical vacation program for a contemporary, mass-market cruise.

Meals. Eating ranks as one of the most popular activities on most cruises. All cruise lines excel in the quality and quantity of their food. The cuisine can be international or feature ethnic dishes. Many of the foreign-owned lines offer a taste of their country of origin or registry. Norwegian Cruise Lines features such exotic specialties as reindeer pâté.

Illus. 6-5 *While some passengers are content to laze in the sun, others require more active pastimes.*
Source: Courtesy of Royal Caribbean Cruise Lines

Activities. Cruise directors schedule a full program of daytime activities while the ship is at sea. Exercise classes are popular with many passengers. On most of the larger liners, instructors are on hand to give lessons in golf, tennis, dancing, photography, painting, flower arranging, foreign languages, and even ukulele playing on Hawaiian cruises. Guest lecturers often give talks on the history and local culture of islands to be visited. There can also be swimming pool games and deck activities, a daily bingo session, as well as tournaments in shuffleboard, ping-pong, chess, backgammon, bridge, and other games.

Entertainment. After dinner, many passengers head to the main lounge for the nightly musical variety show. Cabaret singers and piano players perform in the more intimate lounges and bars on board. On many cruises, there is often a masquerade party and talent night for the ship's passengers. Most liners have at least one ballroom, where passengers can dance to the music of an orchestra. Discos and nightclubs have become standard features on many ships, as have casinos. First-run movies and classic favorites are shown in the ship's movie theater.

Shore Excursions. Shore excursions are an important part of almost every cruise. They can sometimes be the main attraction, especially on adventure/academic cruises. Passengers do not have to commit themselves to shore excursions when booking the cruise. They can be purchased individually or as a package from the shore excursion desk on board.

A cruise ship isn't always able to tie up to a pier when it reaches a port; the ship may be too big to use the normal docking facilities. In such cases, the ship rides at anchor in the harbor, and passengers are shipped ashore in small boats called *tenders* or *lighters*.

On three- and four-day cruises, the stay in port is limited to a few hours, giving passengers just enough time to do some sightseeing and shopping, and maybe take in some local entertainment. A few cruise lines have purchased islands or stretches of beach in the Caribbean for the exclusive use of their passengers during shore excursions.

On longer cruises, passengers can spend as long as two or three days at a destination. Occasionally the ship will move to another port, where the passengers will rejoin it after an escorted overland tour. A growing number of companies are now selling packages that combine a sea or river cruise with a land tour.

What Is/Is Not Included. One of the greatest attractions of a cruise is that it is essentially an all-inclusive vacation. In this respect, it has much in common with the tour package. Most major expenses are prepaid, so passengers don't have to carry large sums of money.

Included in the cruise price are:

- Ocean/river transportation.
- Shipboard accommodations.
- All meals.
- On-board entertainment and activities.
- Most services.
- Transfers from ship to shore when in port.

In addition, transportation to the port of embarkation can also be included.

Costs not included in the price are those that reflect personal choice:

- Shore excursions.
- Port taxes.
- Medical expenses.
- Laundry/valet, sauna, and other personal services.
- Expenditures in shops on board.
- Gambling chips in the casino.
- Beer, wine, and spirits.
- Tips.

Port taxes are taxes that every passenger has to pay on embarkation at any port during the cruise. They vary greatly, but are usually in the region of $15 to $20 per person at each port.

Tipping can be a cause of considerable confusion, since passengers are not always sure who or how much they should tip. Individual cruise lines usually issue recommendations for tipping hotel crew personnel and dining room personnel.

The Physical Layout of the Ship

Larger liners can have as many as ten decks extending from the top to the bottom of the ship. Passenger accommodations are usually concentrated in the lower decks, while the upper decks are reserved for public rooms, swimming pools, and activity areas. Meeting rooms are typically located away from the noisiest parts of the ship. Liners designed for warm-water cruising have larger areas of open sun deck on board than ships sailing to Alaska or Northern Europe. Some ships are fitted with all-weather sliding roofs, called *magrodomes*, which can be closed in bad weather.

Cabins, or staterooms as they are sometimes known, are either *outside cabins* or *inside cabins*. Outside cabins have portholes or windows and a view of the ocean; inside cabins have no access to natural light and face onto a central passageway. Today, most cruise lines design their vessels with the maximum possible number of outside cabins.

Most cabins are designed to accommodate two passengers, usually in twin beds but sometimes in a double. The beds can be fixed to the floor, convert to sofas, or recess into the wall. Regardless of the type of bed, all sleeping places in a cabin are referred to as *berths*.

Smaller cabins designed for singles or two economy-minded passengers have an upper and lower berth arrangement, with the second bed above the first. Larger cabins can accommodate up to four passengers and are suitable for families or young people who want to save money by sharing. The two extra passengers sleep in upper berths above the twin beds. The largest and most comfortable cabins are the suites and minisuites. They usually feature fixed double beds, separate dressing and sitting areas, and a bath as well as a shower.

Factors Affecting the Price of a Cruise

There are four major factors that determine the cruise price:

- Duration of cruise.
- Season.
- Cabin location and size.
- Ship profile.

Duration as a factor should be fairly obvious: a two-week cruise is likely to cost more than a seven-day cruise. Costs are usually figured out on a per diem or

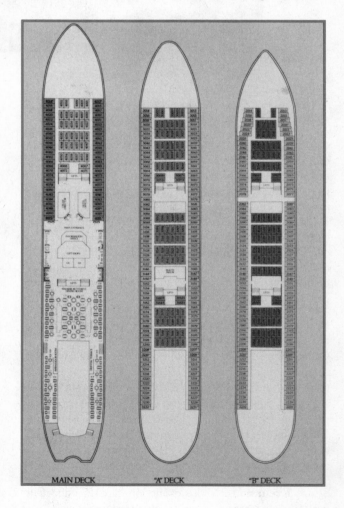

Illus. 6-6 *On large liners, passenger accomodations are usually concentrated in the lower decks. The cabins are either outside cabins or inside cabins.*

Source: *Royal Caribbean Cruise Line, Inc.*

daily rate basis. For example, the per diem for an $800, four-day cruise would be $200. Per diems make it easier to compare costs for different cabins or for different cruises.

Cruise prices can vary considerably depending on the time of year when the ship sails. Prices are highest during the peak or high season (winter in the Caribbean, summer in Alaska) and lowest during the off or low season.

The location of the cabin is the major factor influencing the cruise price. As a general rule, the higher above water, the more expensive a cabin will be, because higher cabins afford passengers a better view and are usually closer to public areas. And cabins located amidships are more expensive than cabins either forward or aft, because any side-to-side movement (roll) or up-and-down movement (pitch) is less pronounced amidships. Also, outside cabins are more expensive than inside cabins. In fact, an outside cabin on even the lowest deck invariably costs more than an inside cabin on the highest. As well as location, cabin size is also a cost determinant, as is the number of passengers in a cabin. In shared cabins, the third and fourth occupants usually travel at a reduced rate. At the other extreme, single occupants have to pay a single supplement. (It should be pointed out that even though there are many different cabin-price categories, all passengers are entitled to the same high level of service. A passenger traveling in the least-expensive inside cabin enjoys the same menu, the same entertainment, the same activities, and the same choice of shore excursions as does a passenger in a deluxe suite.)

The final factor affecting the price of the cruise is the ship profile, or type of ship. Some of the older vessels that have been converted from point-to-point service tend to command higher prices than do the newer cruise ships. This is true partly because the older ships are more spacious, with lower passenger densities. The space ratio for a ship can be calculated by comparing the *gross registered tonnage* (*GRT*) to the number of passengers carried. The GRT represents the amount of enclosed space on the ship.

Check Your Product Knowledge

1. What is the difference between the ship's crew and the hotel crew?
2. What are the four components of the cruise program?
3. What costs are usually not included in the price of a cruise?
4. List the four factors that affect the price of a cruise.

THE CHANNELS OF DISTRIBUTION

In the old days, tickets for point-to-point service were sold through direct sales outlets. The modern cruise passenger, however, almost never buys a ticket from a cruise line's sales office. Over 95 percent of all passengers book their cruises through travel agents. This makes the cruise industry more dependent on travel agents for distribution of its product than any other segment of the travel industry.

Selecting the Cruise

Selecting and selling a cruise is one of the quickest and least complicated of all travel agency transactions. It is also one of the most lucrative. Agency commissions on cruises are considerably higher than on other travel products. The travel agency gets a commission on every component of the cruise product—transportation, accommodations, meals, entertainment, and sightseeing—and all from a single supplier.

Probably the hardest task for the travel professional is matching the MNEs of different types of travelers to the different types of cruises. Few clients who come into a travel agency have a fixed idea of the specific ship they want to cruise on. Some may not even know what geographic area they want to visit. It is the travel agent's job to find the right ship for each potential passenger. The agent must first establish the MNEs of the client. Is he looking for a ship with lots of entertainment and opportunities to socialize? Does she prefer a quiet atmosphere, formal dining, and older passengers?

Once travel agents have some idea of client MNEs, they can start to narrow down the choice of possible ships and itineraries. There are a number of reference works to help them:

- The *Official Steamship Guide International* (*OSGI*): up-to-date listings of cruise schedules throughout the world, information on cruise lines and featured ports of call.
- The *OAG Worldwide Cruise and Shipline Guide*: much the same material as in *OSGI*, plus information on port taxes, staff/passenger ratios, and maps.
- *OHG Cruise Directory*: similar information as in *OSGI*, plus deck plans and ship profiles.
- *Ford's International Cruise Guide*: extensive coverage of individual cruise ships.
- *Ford's Freighter Travel Guide*: listing of freighter cruises, river cruises, and yacht charters.
- *Ford's Deck Plan Guide*: plans of over 130 ships.
- The *CLIA Cruise Manual*: profiles of ships and CLIA-member cruise lines, maps of ports, detailed descriptions of on-board cruise programs, and

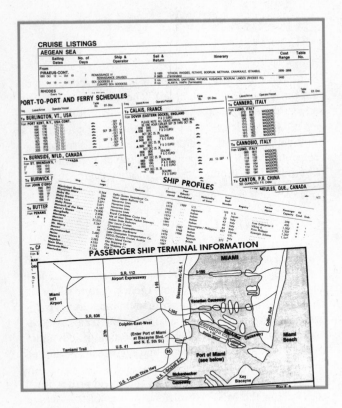

Illus. 6-7 *The* Official Steamship Guide International *provides listings of cruise schedules throughout the world.*

Source: *"Reprinted by special permission from the July–August 1991 issue of the OAG Cruise and Shipline Guide. Copyright © 1991, Official Airline Guides. All rights reserved."*

information on reservations procedures (published by CLIA).

- *Garth's Profile of Ships*: descriptions of about 200 vessels.

The agent will also show the client some cruise brochures to aid in the decision. Once a particular ship has been chosen, the next stage is to analyze deck plans and decide on cabin category and a specific cabin.

The Reservation Process

Many cruise reservations are still made manually—that is, the travel agent calls a toll-free number to reach the cruise company. Computer availability is, however, increasing. Several of the airline reservations systems used by travel agencies now have the capacity to offer cruise bookings (as well as cruise information). A number of cruise lines have set up links with Cruisematch, a reservations system owned by Royal Caribbean Cruise Lines.

Reservations for cruises are required well in advance, especially for longer cruises. They can be booked as far ahead as two years before sailing time. When the original reservation is made, the cruise line gives an option date by which a deposit must be made to confirm the reservation. Final payment is normally required between a month and two months before the cruise begins. Tickets are issued by the cruise line about 30 days before departure.

If a client should decide to cancel the reservation, he or she is usually charged a cancellation penalty (which gets progressively higher the closer to departure the client cancels). Details of the company's cancellation policy are spelled out in the contract that appears on the back of the cruise brochure. According to the contract, cruise lines guarantee to provide a full refund if a sailing is canceled. They reserve the right, however, to change the itinerary or substitute another ship.

Check Your Product Knowledge

1. By what distribution channel are cruises usually sold?
2. What is the normal procedure for paying for a cruise?

THE REGULATION AND PROMOTION OF CRUISES

The cruise industry is one of the least regulated sectors of the travel industry. While not totally free of federal and local government intervention, cruise lines are largely able to choose their own itineraries, vary their schedules, and set their own prices. The industry also benefits from government promotion.

Government Promotion and Regulation

The main way that the government serves as a promoter of the cruise industry is by building and maintaining ports, port facilities, and harbors. Just as airports are owned and operated by local governments, so too are seaports. Harbor and port authorities regulate the industry by charging port taxes.

The United States Coast Guard acts as harbor master and enforcer of government safety requirements. Construction plans for each new ship must be approved by the Coast Guard. Once in active service, all United States vessels are regularly checked to make sure that they meet current safety regulations. United States maritime safety standards are among the strictest in the world—a benefit in that American ships are exceptionally safe. At the same time, these standards also mean that United States ships are much more costly to build and operate than foreign ships.

All cruise ships that call at North American ports, regardless of country of registry, must not only meet United States safety requirements but also international safety standards, which are set by the Safety of Life at Sea (SOLAS) Convention.

Cruise ships picking up passengers at United States ports must put up a bond with the Federal Maritime Association. In the past, foreign flagships were restricted in the number of United States ports where they could call. Federal restrictions were greatly reduced in 1985 and any foreign vessel can now call at any number of United States ports during the course of a cruise, provided that the vessel also visits at least one foreign port.

One final federal regulatory agency is the United States Public Health Service. Agents regularly inspect the galleys and dining rooms of all ships calling at United States ports. They set standards of hygiene and overall sanitation.

Cruise Lines International Association

CLIA is a trade association of cruise lines that promotes cruises in North America. Since its founding in 1975, CLIA has devoted its efforts to promoting the cruise as a desirable vacation experience and to improving public relations. A recent CLIA program promoted February as National Cruise Vacation Month.

CLIA also functions as a regulatory body by setting rules and standards for travel agents who sell CLIA cruises. Agent training is a major CLIA priority. The association trains agents through the Agency Training Program (ATP) and a video training course. CLIA promotes agency cruise sales by encouraging vacationers to see member travel agents for cruise counseling.

Check Your Product Knowledge

1. In what ways do governments promote and regulate the cruise industry?
2. What is the role of CLIA?

CAREER OPPORTUNITIES

The cruise industry employs about 10,000 Americans. This makes it one of the smallest employers of United States citizens in the travel business. The problem is that most cruise ships are of foreign registry and they usually hire their crews overseas. The few exceptions are the positions of purser, social director, entertainer, lecturer, and, occasionally, medical officer.

There is, however, some hope for on-board employment with United States cruise lines. The number of United States flagships has increased significantly in recent years. Many of these vessels are in the 100-passenger market, cruising coastal waters and inland waterways. One of the larger companies is American Cruise Lines.

Employment prospects remain brightest for jobs ashore, especially in reservations and sales. Most foreign cruise lines maintain sales offices in the United States and employ United States citizens. These jobs may not sound as glamorous as the on-board positions, but they are an excellent way to gain entry into the cruise industry.

On Board

The two basic categories of employment on board a cruise ship are ship's crew and hotel crew or staff. Ship's crew members responsible for the mechanical operation of the ship are, of course, found on all types of vessels. Hotel crew members are specific to cruise ships and perform duties similar to those of a resort hotel staff.

Ship's Crew. The captain is the most important person on board. He or she is in charge of the whole ship and is responsible for its operation and for the safety of its passenger and crew. The captain is assisted by a staff of officers. First, second, and third officers direct the navigation of the ship and the maintenance of the deck and hull.

Engineers operate and maintain the engines and other mechanical equipment on board. The chief engineer supervises the engine department. Radio officers maintain contact with the shore and other ships through verbal communication and Morse code. They also receive and record weather information, maintain the ship's radio equipment, and arrange ship-to-shore telephone connections for passengers on board.

The purser is in charge of the ship's paperwork and handles monetary transactions. He or she assists the ship's passengers by, for example, exchanging traveler's checks, providing customs and immigration information, and selling shore excursions. On the larger cruise liners, there will also be a number of assistant pursers.

Able seamen are responsible for much of the deck equipment. They handle the ship's mooring lines when docking and departing and steer the ship according to officers' instructions. Ordinary seamen assist the able seamen and clean and maintain the ship's deck equipment and personnel quarters.

Hotel Crew. Staff members usually heavily outnumber ship's crew members on most cruise ships, especially on those that offer a wide array of services and activities.

A cruise ship will often have a hotel manager who is responsible for the smooth running of all hotel services

A Purser

I am a purser for a large cruise ship. My ship takes people on seven-day cruises of the Caribbean. It sails each Sunday from Miami and returns the following Saturday. I have many duties aboard ship, but my main job is to look after the passengers in much the same way that a hotel desk clerk helps hotel guests.

We are beginning a new cruise today so I will go to the airport and greet our cruise passengers. Our vans pick up the passengers and their belongings and drive them to the ship. On the ship, I will collect the passengers' return air tickets and lock the tickets in our office for safekeeping until the end of the cruise.

My fellow pursers and I will help the passengers find their cabins, check their valuables, and cash their traveler's checks. On the first day, passengers always have lots of questions and it is part of our job to answer them. Most people ask first about where and when they will be eating their meals and about where various shops and recreation facilities are located.

Including me, there are eight pursers on the cruise ship. Since we staff the purser's office 24 hours a day, we work different shifts. We also have different duties. While I work primarily with passengers, other pursers are in charge of the financial aspects of operating a cruise ship. They collect and count the revenues from the ship's shops and services. These include our shore excursions, casino, diving expeditions, hair salon, restaurants, and bars.

My boss is the chief purser. He supervises all of the pursers and several of the other cruise personnel. The chief purser is personally responsible for all of the ship's revenues and the passengers' valuables. He must also make sure that the ship and its passengers obey all laws and regulations in foreign ports.

My boss always says that to be a good purser you have to like people—and I do. Cruise passengers are on vacation, and they expect to be pampered. One of my main tasks is to make sure they enjoy themselves as much as possible. I must also be able to get along with my fellow crew members. I have to share a cabin with another person and I have to work closely with others for a week at a time.

A purser has to be able to react calmly and capably in the event of a crisis. A passenger may become seriously ill or have to leave the ship suddenly due to a personal emergency. I am the one who arranges for an ambulance or emergency transportation in those instances. Pursers must also enjoy being problem solvers. If passengers have complaints, they often come to me first, and it is my job to try to resolve the problems.

My job as a purser was not an easy one to get, nor are other cruise ship jobs. Hundreds of people apply for each position. The best way to prepare yourself for a purser's job is to learn a foreign language and some office skills such as typing, accounting, and computer operations. Many cruise lines will not hire a purser who cannot speak at least one foreign language. Most pursers have business training or backgrounds as travel agents or hotel desk clerks.

I started out as a reservations clerk at a resort hotel. Then I applied for jobs at small cruise lines that took people on lake and river cruises. My first shipboard job was as a cook on a Mississippi River paddleboat. Then I just kept applying to all of the Caribbean cruise lines until I finally landed this job. If you want a job on a cruise ship, you have to be very persistent.

Most people think a job like mine is very glamorous. For the most part, it is. I get to live on a beautiful ship and travel around the Caribbean from November to April, when the weather is very cold in the States. On the other hand, I have to be away from my family for five months at a time, and I am often too busy to really enjoy the ports we visit. Still, the pay is good, and the work is very enjoyable. I will probably look for a job on land in another three or four years. Meanwhile, I plan to keep on cruising.

on board. The cruise director arranges and supervises social and recreational activities for the passengers, functioning in much the same way as a tour escort on dry land. He or she will invariably be helped by a large staff of assistants.

The steward department has more employees than either the deck or engine departments on most cruise ships. Room (or cabin) stewards have the same duties as do hotel room cleaners. They clean cabins, change beds, and so on. Dining room stewards act as servers under the watchful eye of the captain of the dining room. Wine stewards serve wine at tables; night stewards provide room service; and deck stewards hand out deck chairs, serve drinks on deck, and otherwise see to the passengers' comfort. There is, of course, a large kitchen staff, including a number of chefs. Food and beverage managers arrange and cater private parties on board. Butchers and bakers will be present on all but the shortest cruises.

Depending on the size of the ship and the length of the cruise, many other service jobs must also be filled. These can include launderers, hairstylists, shop assistants, bartenders, athletic instructors, photographers, entertainers, lecturers, and librarians. Any ship that carries more than 12 passengers is required to have a doctor on board. The larger ships will have more than one, as well as a staff of nurses.

Ashore

A cruise line's general office ashore is divided into several departments:

- Sales and marketing.
- Individual reservations.
- Group reservations/sales.
- Fly/cruise (working with the airlines).
- Ticketing.
- Accounting.
- Management information.
- Computer/data processing.
- Systems analysis.

Entry-level positions ashore are primarily in reservations and telephone sales. The reservations and group sales departments of many cruise lines are almost identical to airline and tour operator facilities. Cruise lines also have professional, regionally based sales forces. Sales representatives target travel agencies, group and tour organizers, and other intermediaries. They do not sell directly to the public.

From entry-level positions in reservations and sales, employees can move to supervisory positions in the sales, group, or fly/cruise departments, or to the marketing department.

Summary

- The history of ships goes back at least 5,000 years. However, scheduled passenger service by ship was not introduced until the early nineteenth century.
- Mechanical improvements paved the way for the first superliners at the beginning of the twentieth century.
- The first half of the twentieth century was the great age for ocean liners. The comfort of passengers became an important consideration for rival shipping lines, which provided ever-more-luxurious accommodations.
- The advent of the jet age in 1958 signaled the decline of point-to-point passenger services.
- With the birth of the modern cruise industry in the early 1960s, the ship itself became the destination. Cruise lines, most of which are European owned and operated, began to offer a widening array of cruises.
- The availability of shorter cruises, special-interest cruises, fly/cruise packages, and land/cruise packages has broadened the industry's appeal, attracting younger passengers and more first-time clients.
- Large luxury liners serve the popular Caribbean, Mediterranean, and Mexican Riviera cruising areas. Other popular areas are Alaska, the Hawaiian Islands, the eastern United States, and Northern Europe. Smaller vessels cruise along inland waterways and to more exotic locations. Ferries provide point-to-point transportation over short distances.
- The cruise ship functions as a floating hotel, offering passengers a wealth of services, activities, and entertainment. The ratio of passengers to staff is often just 2:1.
- The price of a cruise is determined by duration, season, cabin location and size, and type of ship.
- The most desirable accommodations are outside cabins located high above the water in the midships section of the ship, where the view is at a maximum and motion of the ship is at a minimum.
- Almost all cruises are booked by travel agents.
- Federal governments regulate the cruise industry through certain health and safety requirements. Governments also promote cruising, as does the Cruise Lines International Association (CLIA).

Key Terms

steerage
liner
point-to-point
stabilizers
flag of convenience
embarkation

repositioning cruise
fly/cruise package
land/cruise package
tender
lighter
port tax
magrodome
outside cabin
inside cabin
berth
gross registered tonnage (GRT)

What Do You Think?

1. Bearing in mind the availability of worldwide air services, do you think that there is still a need for point-to-point liner service in the modern age?
2. Why is the cruise industry dominated by European companies?
3. Which do you think is more important to the cruise industry: the first-time passenger or the repeat client? Why?
4. More and more young people are taking cruises. On what type of cruises do you think that older people still make up the majority of passengers?
5. Why, do you think, are the vast majority of cruises booked through travel agents rather than directly?
6. What do you think will happen to the cruise industry in the future?

Dealing with Product

Somehow the message is not getting through. Despite the publicity and the promotion, fewer than 5 percent of all United States citizens have ever booked a cruise. Does that mean that more than 95 percent of all United States citizens are secretly afraid of becoming seasick? Or is it possible that most of us really don't understand the cruise product? What do you understand the cruise product to be? How does this product compare with other travel products? What measures can you think of for persuading more people to book cruises?

Dealing with People

A person's perception of a product—that is, the way a person thinks a product will be—is often quite different from reality. Such is the case in the cruise industry. Many travelers have an incorrect perception of a holiday at sea. Travel professionals often have to change clients' perceptions about cruises. They also need to avoid making wrong assumptions about clients' perceptions.

What follows is a series of two-part puzzles. First, can you guess how the following travelers perceive of a cruise? Second, what type of cruise would you recommend for these clients?

1. A high school teacher, his wife (a secretary), and their two children (ages seven and nine), who are planning a one-week spring vacation together.
2. A retired couple in their mid-sixties; they are inexperienced travelers who recently sold their vacation cabin at the lake.
3. A surgeon (age 45) and her husband, an accountant (age 46); they have no children.
4. Roommates, one of whom is 23 and a dental hygienist; the other is 22 and a registered nurse.
5. An outdoor enthusiast in his mid-thirties, who is a free-lance photographer and an avid hiker and cross-country skier.
6. A marketing researcher in her early thirties, recently promoted and recently divorced; she has traveled often, studied and worked overseas, and doesn't like crowds.

WORKSHEET 6-1   CRUISE MARKETING

You are a travel professional specializing in cruise products. Many people who have never experienced a modern cruise still have misconceptions about cruises. Tell how you would answer each of the following questions asked by in-experienced potential cruisers.

1. Isn't a cruise vacation expensive?

2. Are there different classes of service on cruise ships?

3. What's there to do on a cruise? I'd be bored sitting in a deck chair all day.

4. Don't mostly older people take cruises?

5. Would I need a tuxedo? Would my wife need an evening gown?

6. What does "different sittings" for meals mean?

7. What if I don't like the people I'm seated with for dinner?

8. What do I do about tipping?

9. I think I'd feel isolated out there in the middle of the ocean. Is there any communication with the rest of the world?

10. I'm afraid of getting seasick. Isn't this a common problem?

WORKSHEET 6-2   BROCHURE INFORMATION

Get brochures from two cruise lines and compare them.

Cruise line   _____   _____

Number of ships in line   _____   _____

Registry   _____   _____

Geographic areas offered   _____   _____

_____   _____

_____   _____

Special features   _____   _____

_____   _____

_____   _____

Deposit and payment schedule   _____   _____

_____   _____

_____   _____

Cancellation policy   _____   _____

_____   _____

_____   _____

Select one cruise from each brochure and compare them.

Cruise   _____   _____

Destination and duration   _____   _____

_____   _____

Accommodation you would choose _____   _____

Cost   _____   _____

Ports of call   _____   _____

_____   _____

Airfare tie-in (one example)   _____   _____

_____   _____

Special features   _____   _____

_____   _____

WORKSHEET 6-3   CHOOSING A CRUISE

You are a travel agent. A family consisting of two adults in their mid-forties, two children (ten and fourteen), and a grandmother in her late sixties wants to cruise the Caribbean for one week. They are not on a restrictive budget for this trip, but they do not want luxurious accommodations. They will be flying from and returning to Denver. Use newspapers, magazines, and brochures to narrow the possible cruises down to two. Then compare them on the following points.

Ship _____ _____

Cruise line _____ _____

Ship registry _____ _____

Passenger capacity _____ _____

Chosen accommodations _____ _____

_____ _____

_____ _____

Cost _____ _____

Transportation to and from port of
embarkation/disembarkation _____ _____

_____ _____

_____ _____

Cost of transportation _____ _____

Dates _____ _____

Itinerary _____ _____

_____ _____

_____ _____

Ports of call _____ _____

_____ _____

Activities _____ _____

_____ _____

_____ _____

Entertainment _____ _____

_____ _____

Medical services _____ _____

_____ _____

Facilities for children/teens _____ _____

_____ _____

Facilities for older people _____ _____

_____ _____

WORKSHEET 6-4   READING A DECK PLAN

Get a brochure from a cruise line. Choose one of the ships and study the deck plan. Then answer the following questions.

NAME OF SHIP AND CRUISE LINE

1. How many decks does the ship have?

2. What is the space ratio? (GRT ÷ number of passengers)

3. How many categories of cabins does the ship have?

4. Where are the most expensive cabins located? The least expensive?

5. What is the difference in accommodations between the most expensive and the least expensive cabins?

6. Where is the dining room(s)?

7. Where is the gift shop(s)?

8. How many lounges does the ship have?

9. Does the ship have a health and fitness center?

10. What other entertainment areas does the ship feature?

CHAPTER 7 THE HOSPITALITY INDUSTRY

"Whoe'er has traveled life's dull round,
Whate'er his various tour has been,
May sigh to think how oft he found
His warmest welcome at an inn."

—William Shenstone

Objectives

When you have completed this chapter, you should be able to:

■ Describe the role played by religion in the early history of the hospitality industry.
■ Give reasons for the growth of the hotel industry in the nineteenth century.
■ Distinguish between motels and motor hotels. Outline the development of resort hotels.
■ Describe the changes in hotel architecture in the last 25 years.
■ Classify hotels by form of ownership.

■ Explain what is meant by market segmentation.
■ Distinguish between transient and residential hotels.
■ Classify hotels by function, location, and scale.
■ Identify the factors that affect the price of a hotel room.
■ Describe the organizational structure of a hotel.
■ List the hotel reference books and specify the type of information that each contains.

Ever since the first lodging houses were built to accommodate travelers in ancient lands, people have been making a living by providing rooms for travelers. Today, of course, hotels offer far more than just a room for the night. Many hotels provide meeting rooms, restaurants, bars, and other facilities to attract business. Some cater to a particular segment of the travel market, such as the business traveler, the convention delegate, or the vacationer. Others offer basic, no-frills service to all guests.

Today in the United States, there are about 3 million rooms available in more than 44,000 hotels and motels. Lodging places range in size from inns with just a few rooms to huge hotels that can accommodate up to 4,000 guests. With more than 1.5 million workers, the lodging industry is one of the largest employers within the travel industry. The lodging industry is constantly evolving to meet the changing needs of travelers, making it an exciting and dynamic industry.

In this chapter, you'll learn how this giant industry developed, and how it is structured today. You'll also learn of the many decisions that go into the running of a successful hotel, motel, or resort, and of the many kinds of jobs offered by the industry.

A BRIEF HISTORY OF HOSPITALITY

As soon as people began to travel extensively by land and by water thousands of years ago, there was a demand for overnight resting spots. The earliest lodging places were probably built along trade and caravan routes in ancient Persia and elsewhere in the Near East. These simple structures—known as khans or caravansaries—provided shelter for traveling merchants and their animals.

Religion played an important role in the early history of hospitality. In addition to the merchants, there were large numbers of priests, pilgrims, and missionaries journeying to temples and other holy places throughout

163

the eastern Mediterranean region. Many of the first inns came into being because people wanted to open their homes to the religious travelers. These people believed that by so doing they would in some way ensure their own spiritual well-being.

The demand for lodging places increased significantly with the development of an extensive highway system throughout Europe during the Roman era. Roadside inns and taverns provided shelter for traveling merchants and scholars as well as for the growing number of travelers on military, political, and diplomatic missions. Accommodations in these *mansiones* were primitive: quite often there would be stables for the horses but no private rooms for the travelers themselves.

The most elegant inns of the period were developed by the Persians along caravan routes. These yams, as they were known, provided travelers with not only accommodations but also food and fresh horses. The explorer Marco Polo estimated that there were as many as 10,000 yams at the time of his journey to the Far East (1275–1292).

During the Middle Ages, hospitality was considered a Christian duty. Many monasteries and other religious institutions functioned as inns, offering free accommodations and food for pilgrims and other travelers. One of the largest and most famous lodging places of the period was founded in A.D.. 961 by Augustinian monks in the Great Saint Bernard Pass in the Swiss Alps.

An important turning point in the history of hospitality occurred in 1282, when a group of innkeepers in Florence, Italy, was incorporated as a guild and licensed to sell wine. This meant that hospitality was no longer offered as an act of charity. It had become a business venture. The concept spread, and by the early fourteenth century there were licensed inns throughout Italy.

From Stopping Place to Meeting Place

Few improvements were made in the quality of accommodations until the advent of long-distance stagecoach travel in the seventeenth century. Journeys by stagecoach over dirt roads were long and arduous. Passengers (most of whom were wealthy) came to expect a warm bed and a hearty meal on their overnight stops. English inns and taverns, in particular, gained a reputation for cleanliness and comfort and set the standard for accommodations in other parts of Europe.

A typical inn had a dining room in which food and drink were served, a number of private rooms with beds for individual travelers, a large communal room for stagecoach drivers and the staff of the inn, and stables for the horses, all arranged around a central courtyard. These inns were not only frequented by travelers; they became popular meeting places for local nobles, clergy, politicians, and other citizens.

Hotels, as such, first began to appear in France in the late 1700s. They can be distinguished from inns and taverns by their greater size and more luxurious accommodations. The Hotel de Henri IV, built in Nantes in 1788 with beds for 60 guests, was a particularly fine early example.

Early inns in North America were established in seaport towns rather than along stagecoach routes. The first inn was built in Jamestown on the Virginia coast in 1607. As the population moved inland, inns and taverns began to appear along rivers, canals, and post roads (routes over which mail was carried).

As in England, the New World inns provided travelers with a bed and food for themselves, and stables for their horses. The food was generally excellent and plentiful—meals of up to 15 courses were not uncommon. Accommodations, on the other hand, left much to be desired. There was little privacy and travelers were expected to share a bed if the inn was crowded. The concept of a reservation system was, as yet, unheard of.

American inns and taverns played an important role in community life as meeting places for local citizens. This was especially true during the Revolutionary War. Local residents would meet at the inns to plan strategy, and passing travelers would provide news of developments in other parts of the country.

The atmosphere in a typical American inn of the period was much more informal than in a European lodging place. Meals were served family style at a communal table, and guests from all walks of life mingled freely with one another. In Europe, by contrast, only the wealthy could afford to travel and stay in inns; once they had arrived, travelers kept to themselves for the most part.

The more democratic spirit of American inns was also reflected in the special status conferred on innkeepers. In Europe, innkeepers were regarded as servants. In colonial America, on the other hand, innkeeping was an honorable profession. An innkeeper was someone who could be entrusted with information and whose opinions were respected.

Early Hotels in the United States

The early nineteenth century was a period of transition for the hospitality industry in the United States. The new trend was to change from *inn* or *tavern* to *hotel*, a term (and concept) imported from France and considered more elegant. The 73-room City Hotel, which opened in New York City in 1794, was the first establishment specifically designed as a hotel. By 1820, there were more lodging places operating as hotels than as inns or taverns.

Thus, small roadside inns gradually gave way to larger, more elegant city hotels, which offered a much wider range of amenities. Boston's 170-room Tremont House, which opened in 1829, can be identified as the first modern first-class hotel. It was the largest building in the United States at the time. Among the innovative features it introduced were private single and double rooms with locks, free soap, French cuisine, room service, bellboys, and a staff of workers trained to provide polite service. Similar hotels soon appeared in other eastern cities, each city competing to build larger and more luxurious lodging places. All of these hotels became important social centers for local citizens.

The extension of the United States railroad system had an enormous impact on the hotel industry. New towns sprang up along tracks that spread westward to the Pacific coast. A hotel was usually one of the first buildings to be erected in a new town on a rail route. In the major centers of population, a few hotels were as elaborate as the grand hotels back east. Most, however, were small and less glamorous. They catered to the growing number of commercial travelers—in particular, the traveling salesmen.

With the invention of the elevator in 1853, hotels began to expand upward. A typical city hotel of the second half of the nineteenth century was five or six stories high and had as many as 200 guest rooms. Public rooms, such as dining and reading rooms, were now a feature of most hotels. Both men and women were welcome at all hotels, but it was not appropriate for the sexes to mingle in public areas. Women were provided with separate entrances and sitting rooms, and they dined apart from the men.

As cities grew and the volume of train travel increased, hotels in the major cities became still larger and more elaborate. San Francisco's Palace Hotel, built in 1875, was the epitome of grandeur. It had 800 rooms, a central marble courtyard, and a glass-domed roof. Other notable hotels of the period included the Brown Palace Hotel (1892) in Denver, the Netherlands Hotel (1894) in New York City (the first to have in-room telephones), and the Waldorf-Astoria (1896), also in New York City.

From Boom to Bust

At an opposite extreme to the luxury city hotels were these smaller hotels built close to railroad stations. These were inexpensive, but often lacking in standards of cleanliness, comfort, and service. Few commercial travelers at the beginning of the twentieth century could afford to stay in the luxury hotels, yet many found the railroad hotels unsatisfactory.

Ellsworth Statler, father of the modern commercial hotel industry, realized that there was a considerable market for moderate-priced hotels for the business traveler. He opened his first hotel—the Buffalo Statler—in 1908. Its 300 rooms were clean, comfortable, and, at $1.50 a night, affordable. Each had a private bath along with such

other innovative features as full-length mirrors, built-in closets, and in-room telephones and radios. The hotel was an immediate success, and Statler was encouraged to build more middle-class hotels in other parts of the country. In doing so, he originated the hotel-chain concept that has come to dominate the modern hotel industry. The Statler chain was later bought by Conrad Hilton, founder of one of the most famous hotel chains of all.

Hotel construction reached an all-time peak in the 1920s. Giant hotels were built, such as the 3,000-room Stevens Hotel (1927) in Chicago, while hundreds of smaller hotels opened in cities and towns across the United States. The boom, however, ended with the Depression, which had a devastating effect on all sectors of the travel industry—including the hotel business—in the 1930s. Because fewer people could afford to travel, there was a decline in the demand for accommodations. Between 1930 and 1935, almost 85 percent of all hotels in the United States went bankrupt.

Check Your Product Knowledge

1. In what ways did religion influence the growth of the hospitality industry?
2. How did early American inns differ from seventeenth-century English inns?
3. What effect did the building of the railroads in the United States have on the hotel business?

MODERN HOTELS AND MOTELS

The hotel industry rebounded during and immediately after World War II as the volume of travel increased. The postwar hospitality industry, however, has been markedly different from that of the prewar period. The automobile and the jet plane have radically affected the industry, changing travel patterns and leading to the development of different types of hotels. Motels, motor hotels, resort hotels, and convention hotels have evolved to cater to the varied needs of today's traveling public. At the same time, hotel chains have established themselves as the dominant force in the industry, both in the United States and abroad. We shall look at these important postwar developments in the sections that follow.

Motels and Motor Hotels

Motels evolved from the roadside tourist cabins and tourist courts that were first introduced in the early 1900s in response to the increase in automobile travel. *Tourist cabins* were usually built and operated by farm families who owned land adjacent to a main road. Most catered exclusively to traveling salesmen. They provided a bed for the night, a place to park a car, and little else in the way of services or amenities. But they were inexpensive and they saved the motorist the inconvenience of having to leave the main road to find a hotel in town.

Tourist courts differed from tourist cabins in that they were operated as full-time businesses rather than as sidelines for farmers. They usually consisted of between 10 and 20 detached cottages grouped around a central parking place. Services were still extremely limited, though most cottages did have private baths.

As the automobile began to replace the train as the primary means of travel in the United States, there was an increased demand for roadside accommodations. The first *motels* began to appear in the 1920s. They were usually one-story buildings, with an average of 25 units, or rooms, arranged lengthwise on either side of a central office. (The term *unit* is used throughout the hospitality industry to refer to a guest bedroom or suite.) Units opened onto the parking lot, so there was no need for the lobby that downtown hotels required.

Motels really came of age during the 1950s. Two main factors contributed to the boom in motel construction. One was the development of the interstate highway system, beginning in 1956, which encouraged more and more travelers to take to the roads on long-distance journeys. The other was the entry of motel chains into the market. Motels increased in size and, for the first time, added a number of services. Restaurants, swimming pools, and in-room televisions became standard features. Motels began to attract growing numbers of vacationers in addition to commercial travelers.

The next step in the development of the motel industry was the move away from highway locations into the downtown sections of larger cities. Many motels began to offer all the facilities that would be found in a downtown hotel and came to be known as *motor hotels* or *motor inns*. The only difference was that they still catered to the traveling motorist and continued to provide free parking for overnight guests. With the increase in air travel, motor hotels also began to move out to the airports.

An interesting reaction to the development of luxury motor hotels has been the recent rebirth of low-cost, no-frills motels. Chains such as Holiday Inns and Ramada Inns, which were originally conceived as providers of budget accommodations, have gradually raised prices as they have added more and more hotel services. Days Inns, Motel 6, and other budget operators have entered the market and returned to the original concept of the motel—offering clean, comfortable rooms with a minimum of service at low cost.

Resort Hotels

A *resort hotel* is one that people visit for relaxation, recreation, and/or entertainment. With the rise in mass tourism in the last 35 years, they have been established in great numbers at destinations throughout the world.

Resorts, as such, have existed since ancient times. Wealthy Romans used to escape from the cities during the hot summer months and spend the season at the shore, in the mountains, or at spa resorts. The idea of the resort hotel was born in eighteenth- and nineteenth-century Europe. Palatial hotels were built along the French Riviera, in the Swiss Alps, and at various mineral springs throughout the continent.

The resort hotel in the United States developed with the expansion of the railroads in the second half of the nineteenth century. Fashionable early resorts included the Homestead at Hot Springs, Virginia; the Greenbrier at White Sulphur Springs, West Virginia; and Grossinger's in the Catskill Mountains of New York. All catered exclusively to the rich and to the upper middle class. Families stayed for two or three months and returned to the same hotel year after year.

Some of these luxury resort hotels have survived, but today they are heavily outnumbered by resort hotels that cater to ordinary working people who stay from three days to two weeks. With increased leisure time and higher wages, most people now take at least one vacation away from home each year. The jet airplane has opened up areas of the world that were previously inaccessible to the vacationer. Resort hotel construction has boomed in tropical areas such as the Caribbean, Mexico, and Hawaii. Within the United States, resort hotels in Florida, California, and Colorado attract millions of vacationers each year. Some of these resorts are seasonal (skiers flock to Colorado hotels during the winter months), but many have developed into year-round operations.

Convention Hotels

A *convention hotel* is one that caters to large group gatherings. The rise of convention hotels has been one of the most recent developments in the hotel industry, and conventioneers now account for almost 20 percent of all hotel guests. Many downtown hotels saw occupancy levels drop during the 1950s and early 1960s as motels and motor hotels captured a larger segment of the market. In response, some hotels began to add facilities for conventions and other group gatherings as a means of survival. At first, conventions were scheduled for off-peak periods, but as the volume of convention business increased, they began to be scheduled year-round.

Large hotels that cater exclusively to convention groups began going up in the major cities in the late 1960s. All feature a wide variety of restaurants, banquet rooms, meeting rooms, and convention and exhibition halls. Some can accommodate up to 4,000 guests at a single convention. Resort hotels, motels, and airport hotels have also begun to offer convention facilities. Much of the business is generated by industrial conventions and trade shows, though conventions held by political, civic, fraternal, religious, and social organizations are also important sources of income.

The New Architecture

The arrival of the jet age led to the second major hotel-building phase of the twentieth century, lasting from 1958 to 1974. In the early part of this period, the hotel chains' major goals in planning new properties were economy, efficiency, and standardization of design. A Sheraton hotel in Miami, for example, might be almost identical to one nearly 3,000 miles away in Los Angeles, even in such minor details as the color of the drapes.

By the late 1960s, however, there was a reaction against this uniformity of design and a new hotel architecture was born. The breakthrough came in 1967 with the opening of the Hyatt Regency in Atlanta. John Portman, the hotel's architect, reintroduced the concept of the *atrium*—a roof-high central lobby courtyard. This style had been used in San Francisco's Palace Hotel and Denver's Brown Palace Hotel at the end of the nineteenth century. The opening of the Hyatt marked a return to the grandeur of the old luxury hotels. Portman's other innovations included scenic elevators, fountains, waterfalls, trees, huge sculptures, and bars and cafés in the atrium. The lobby was no longer just a place for registration and checkout; it also became the main eating, drinking, and meeting area. Even the guest rooms opened onto the central lobby, not onto dimly lit corridors as in earlier hotels.

The success of the Atlanta Hyatt Regency led to the building of similar atrium hotels in cities and resorts throughout the world during the 1970s and 1980s. Many are part of complexes that combine commercial, office, and hotel facilities with sporting and recreational facilities.

A related development has been the renovation of grand old hotels in downtown areas. Many have undergone total restoration, including Los Angeles' Biltmore, Philadelphia's Bellevue Stratford, and New York's Commodore. The new atrium hotels and the restored grand hotels function at the opposite end of the scale to the budget motels, offering excellence in architectural and interior design and the ultimate in services and amenities.

Country Inns

The small country inn is one type of lodging place that has not had to survive by offering increased services and facilities. In fact, many shun such modern conveniences as in-room televisions, radios, and telephones. Instead, they offer the attraction of old-world charm and coziness

Illus. 7-1 *The atruim—a large, spacious lobby— was first introduced at the end of the nineteenth century and has recently been reintroduced in some luxury hotels.*
Source: *Marriott Hotels and Resorts*

in a scenic or historic setting. Guests might expect to find working fireplaces in their rooms, handmade quilts on their beds, and antique furniture throughout the inn.

Many of the inns are direct descendants of the old inns and taverns that flourished along stagecoach routes 200 years ago. Some even occupy the same building. The smaller country inns, sometimes with as few as three or four rooms, are usually run by friendly couples who pride themselves on the comfort and cleanliness of their accommodations and the quality of the food that they serve.

The use of the name *inn* by some of the larger chain outfits (e.g., Holiday Inns, Ramada Inns) is a testament to the appeal of the inn. Motor inns, however, should not be confused with country inns. The chains use the name to suggest a feeling of warmth and friendliness, though their properties are quite different from the more intimate country inns. In the hospitality industry, the term *property* refers to a hotel, motel, or any other kind of lodging facility.

The Growth of Hotel Chains

As you have read, the first chain operation in the United States was started by Ellsworth Statler in the early 1900s. The success of Statler's hotels encouraged the formation of other chains, including Hilton Hotels, which opened its first property in Dallas in 1925. The Depression, which forced so many individually owned hotels out of business, proved to be a bonanza for the chains, since they were able to buy bankrupted properties at low prices.

Chains such as Hilton and Sheraton had established themselves before World War II. By the 1950s, they were being joined by scores of others. The introduction of the concept of franchising (described in detail later in this chapter) served as a tremendous stimulus to the growth of hotel and motel chains, and by the early 1970s there were almost 200 in operation. Hundreds of independent city hotels and mom-and-pop, or family-run, motels were forced into bankruptcy by their inability to meet rising costs and to compete with the chains. Today, over 50 percent of the rooms in United States hotels are provided by chain outfits.

Holiday Inn is the largest lodging chain in the world, with more than 360,000 units in about 1,900 properties. (Table 7-1 lists the 20 largest hotel/motel chains in the world.) Holiday Inn was launched in 1952 when en-

trepreneur Kemmons Wilson opened the first "Holiday Inn Hotel Court" on the outskirts of Memphis, Tennessee. Wilson had been dissatisfied with motel accommodations on a family vacation trip. He decided to build his own cabin in order to offer a full range of services at low to moderate prices.

Holiday Inn pioneered innovations that were revolutionary for the times but subsequently became standards for chain operations. These included a swimming pool and restaurant on the premises, air conditioning throughout, a television and telephone in every room, baby sitters on call, and free accommodations for children under 12 sharing a room with their parents. In 1965, the company installed the hotel industry's first nationwide computerized reservations system.

Over the years, the Holiday Inn hotel system has evolved from a chain of economy motor courts into a multibillion-dollar-a-year network of lodging places serving multiple markets. Holiday Inn is now a major presence in the United States resort and convention industry as well as in overseas markets.

The international growth of the big United States chains has been one of the major developments in the hospitality industry in the last 35 years. A few leading chains gained an early foothold on the overseas market—including Intercontinental in Latin America (1946), Hilton International in Puerto Rico (1949), and Sheraton

Rank	Name of Chain	Country	Number of Rooms	Number of Hotels/Motels
1	Holiday Corp.	USA	360,958	1,868
2	Sheraton Corp.	USA	135,000	465
3	Ramada Inc.	USA	130,932	769
4	Marriott Corp.	USA	118,000	450
5	Quality International	USA	112,810	978
6	Days Inns Of America Inc.	USA	104,625	775
7	Hilton Hotels Corp.	USA	95,862	271
8	Trusthouse Forte Pic	England	89,546	893
9	Accor	France	80,034	700
10	Club Mediterranee	France	61,860	249
11	Balkantourist	Bulgaria	56,250	386
12	Howard Johnson	USA	54,757	444
13	Motel 6	USA	51,572	452
14	Hyatt Hotels Corp.	USA	50,797	92
15	Raddison Hotel Corp.	USA	46,600	191
16	Ladbroke Group Pic	England	45,630	139
17	Saison Group	Japan	38,921	99
18	Econo Lodges of America	USA	37, 984	467
19	Super 8 Motels, Inc.	USA	35,991	574
20	Sol Hotels	Spain	35,994	140

Table 7-1 World's Largest Hotel/Motel Chains, 1988
Source: Hotels, formerly Hotels and Restaurants International

J. Willard Marriott, Sr.

In 1927, J. Willard Marriott borrowed $3,000 and opened an A&W root beer stand in Washington, D.C. The stand had nine stools and occupied half of a bakery shop. From that modest beginning, Marriott, the son of a poor Mormon sheepherder, built his business into the fifth largest service company in America with sales of more than $8 billion a year.

Marriott was born and raised in Utah. He began to learn about business at 14 when his father sent him on his own to San Francisco to sell a flock of sheep. Marriott graduated from Weber State College in Ogden, Utah, in 1926, and taught at the college for a year. While Marriott was attending college, two inventors named Allen and Wright developed a new root beer formula and opened their first stand in Salt Lake City. Marriott liked the new root beer and thought it would sell well in Washington, D.C., because of the city's hot, humid climate.

He purchased a franchise from A&W, packed up his belongings, and headed east with his bride, Alice. The root beer stand prospered until the weather turned cold and sales began to decline. Then Marriott cleverly put a barbecue machine in the window, changed the name of the stand to Hot Shoppe, and went into the business of selling hot food along with the root beer.

While Alice Marriott cooked chili and barbecued beef for hungry diners, J. Willard Marriott set about promoting his new restaurant with such gimmicks as coupons for free beverages. The Marriotts did so well that by 1932, they had opened six more Hot Shoppes. By then, the country was in the depths of the Great Depression and many fancier, high-priced restaurants went out of business because people could no longer afford the expensive meals. Marriott's Hot Shoppes survived because they were unpretentious family restaurants that offered good food at low prices.

Hot Shoppes were the foundation of Marriott's business empire. In 1937, he went into the business of supplying meals to airlines after he noticed that many people stopped by one of his Hot Shoppes to purchase meals to eat on board planes during flights. His restaurants and airline catering service grew steadily into the 1950s when he decided to branch out into hotels. He opened his first Marriott Motor Hotel on the outskirts of Washington in 1957.

By 1972, the Marriott Corporation owned or operated 20 hotels and nearly 1,000 restaurants including cafeterias, turnpike rest stops, and the Hot Shoppe, Big Boy, and Roy Rogers restaurant chains. Meanwhile, its airline food services had become the largest independently owned airline catering business in the world. Marriott also went into another very profitable food business, operating cafeterias and restaurants in schools, hospitals, and corporations.

Today, the Marriott Corporation operates more than 80,000 hotel rooms and serves nearly 5 million meals a day. As the business grew, Marriott involved more and more of his family members in it, including his three brothers. He turned over the day-to-day operations of the corporation to his son Bill Jr. in 1964, but remained chairman of the board until he died in 1985 at the age of 85. Bill Jr. currently serves as chief operating officer and chairman of the board. Marriott's other son, Richard, is vice chairman, and Alice Marriott has long served as a member of the board. Now a new generation of Marriotts is being groomed for corporate leadership. Two of Bill Jr.'s sons and a son-in-law work in Marriott hotels.

Marriott believed in treating his employees well. He began stock purchasing and profit-sharing programs for his employees in 1971. He also established incentive bonuses, management training, and career advancement programs to develop competent managers and promote company loyalty.

Marriott was a staunch Mormon and a political conservative all his life. He believed in the basic American values of family and hard work. Today, his name is carried on hotels, restaurants, and other businesses in 27 countries of the world.

Illus. 7-2 *From its early days in 1950s Memphis, Holiday Inn has grown into the largest lodging chain in the world.*
Source: Holiday Inns, Inc.

in Canada (1949)—but the greatest period of expansion came after the commercial debut of the jet airplane. Chains moved into the Caribbean and Europe and later into the Middle East, Africa, the Far East, and the Pacific. Holiday Inn, the leader, with properties in more than 50 countries outside the United States, is followed by Sheraton, Ramada, and Marriott. Other big names on the international scene include Quality International, Days Inn, and Hilton Hotel.

Not only have American chains expanded overseas, but more recently foreign chains have moved to the United States. Trusthouse Forte (United Kingdom), Meridien (France), Four Seasons (Canada), Regent International (Hong Kong), and Accor (France) are all well established in the United States. Total domestic and international hotel revenues are shown in Figure 7-1.

Overbuilding and Future Trends

By 1986, new properties were being built at a rate faster than any time since the late 1950s. In fact, many cities and destinations are now overbuilt with hotels. This means that there are more rooms than the market can fill. The current oversupply of rooms suggests that certain sectors of the hotel industry will experience difficult times in the near future.

The luxury segment of the market is a case in point. It has shown dramatic growth rates in recent years, largely because of the many chains that have upgraded their accommodations, added amenities, and moved into the luxury market. Room supply now exceeds demand,

however, and it is unlikely that this segment of the industry will be able to support much further expansion in the immediate future.

No hotel can afford to operate below **break-even point**, which is the point at which total revenues equal total operating costs. A break-even analysis determines the percentage of occupancy that a hotel must attain to cover expenses. The break-even point for United States hotels in recent years has averaged about 68 percent occupancy. Table 7-2 shows hotel occupancy rates in ten

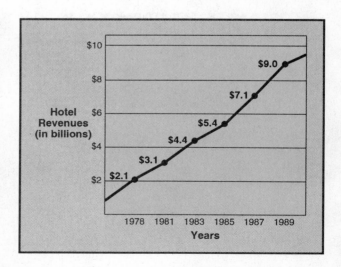

Figure 7-1 Total Domestic and International Hotel Revenues
Source: Louis Harris and Associates, Travel Weekly

major United States cities. When its costs increase, a hotel must either raise its room rates to break even or reach a higher occupancy level. In the current overbuilt market, it is difficult for hotels to raise rates and still remain competitive, so many have adopted aggressive marketing techniques to try to increase occupancy. The result has been a proliferation of incentive deals, such as weekend packages and special events. A similar development in the cruise industry was discussed in Chapter 6.

Hotel construction in the United States was beginning to slow down in the early 1990s. In the future, builders will most likely focus less on giant convention hotels and more on smaller properties aimed at specific markets. The outlook is brightest for economy-priced accommodations and for all-suite hotels (described later in this chapter). So far, economy and all-suite hotels have both shown strong growth without a resulting oversupply of rooms. There should also be fairly consistent growth for resort hotels and airport hotels. The trend toward chain operations will continue, and United States chains can be expected to expand overseas in greater numbers as new destinations are opened up. Holiday Inn and Marriott have already opened properties in Poland, and both Ramada and Sheraton are constructing hotels in the Soviet Union.

Check Your Product Knowledge

1. Why did motels become so popular during the 1950s?
2. What are the main differences between a resort hotel and a convention hotel?
3. List some of the architectural features that have been included in modern hotels.
4. What were some of the innovations introduced by Holiday Inn?

HOTEL OWNERSHIP

Until the twentieth century, almost all hotels were individually owned and operated. With the development of hotel and motel chains, however, a number of new forms of ownership have evolved, such as the lease, the joint venture, and, more importantly in recent years, the franchise and the management contract.

Individual Ownership

About 50 percent of all hotels in the United States operate as individual proprietorships. The majority of these, the family-owned establishments with fewer than 100 rooms, still make up the backbone of the hotel industry. They include mom-and-pop motels, small hotels, and country inns. The term "individually owned" also applies to individual properties owned by the large corporations that have been investing in the industry since the mid-1960s. These individual ownerships include giant city hotels and deluxe resort properties.

The chief benefits of individual ownership are that the owner is independent (with complete control of policies and operating procedures) and obtains full profit from the property. An obvious disadvantage is that the owner also assumes full risk.

Chain Ownership

Many chains with multiple properties own and operate a number of hotels directly. The chain owns the building and staffs it with its own employees. This form of ownership offers all the benefits of individual ownership. Expansion of the chain is limited, however, by the amount of capital available. Chains wishing to expand rapidly often do so by franchising and management contracts (explained later in this chapter) rather than by direct ownership.

	1984	1985	1986	1987	1988	1989
Atlanta	68.90%	66.60%	63.00%	63.20%	61.80%	63.00%
Boston	54.80	55.10	55.50	72.50	59.40	55.50
Chicago	57.36	57.60	57.30	60.60	55.40	52.80
Dallas	69.42	67.10	60.40	58.30	57.80	56.20
Los Angeles	68.68	70.80	69.00	74.40	70.20	70.60
Miami	68.50	78.70	80.80	80.40	81.00	79.80
New Orleans	60.70	53.60	60.20	66.80	62.00	66.60
New York	66.65	65.40	66.00	68.30	66.70	66.20
Philadelphia	52.29	52.50	51.40	64.90	65.00	60.90
San Francisco	68.19	66.60	62.00	63.70	63.10	67.90

Table 7-2 Hotel Occupancy Rates

Source: Pannel Kerr Forster, Business Travel News

Leases and Joint Ventures

An individual or a chain can operate a hotel without owning it by entering into a lease arrangement. Under a straight lease, a tenant pays a fixed monthly rent to a landlord for the complete use of a hotel. Profit-sharing leases, whereby the owner of the hotel participates in its profits, are more common.

A *joint venture* can be a partnership between two companies, two individuals, or a company and an individual. Joint ventures have been used in the development of motels, and, less frequently, in major hotel projects. Most are formed between an individual proprietor or developer who makes a large capital investment, and an established motel chain that contributes management and development know-how.

Franchises

Under a *franchise* system, a hotel owner contracts with an established chain to operate the property under the chain name. The owner of the hotel, or "franchisee," pays an initial development fee (from about $10,000 to $50,000 depending on the property) and a monthly franchise fee of about 3 percent to 6 percent of gross room sales. In addition, the franchisee agrees to abide by the management policies of the chain. In return, the chain, or "franchisor," provides assistance in staff selection and training, in marketing, sales, and advertising support, and in access to a central computer reservations system. Perhaps most importantly, the franchisor provides a recognizable image and the familiarity of the chain name.

Franchises are the most common form of hotel organization after individual ownership. Hotel and motel chains began to adopt the concept of franchising during the late 1950s and early 1960s as a way to expand without substantial capital investment. Kemmons Wilson of Holiday Inn fame was an early pioneer of franchising. In its first two years of operation, Holiday Inn had been able to build only four motels. Wilson realized that his chain could not grow fast enough if it relied on direct ownership of each property. Franchising presented itself as the most viable alternative, and within five years the company was operating 100 franchises. Many other chains were quick to enter the franchising field as well.

Management Contracts

Under the franchise system, an individual or a company owns and operates a hotel, with support from a chain. Under a *management contract* agreement, one company owns the property and another (the chain) operates it. The owner enjoys all the benefits of the franchise system without having to become involved in the operation of the hotel. The chain receives a managerial fee from the owner and has complete control of the operation of the property. Management contracts allow chains to expand with minimal or no capital investment; the owners, not the chain, are the investors.

The management contract concept was developed in the 1950s as a way for chains based in the United States to expand overseas. It enabled them to open hotels in countries where foreign ownership laws or political conditions prevented ownership by outside companies. Overseas hotel developers who wanted the managing and marketing expertise of United States chains began to invest in properties and to contract American hotel companies to operate them.

THE HOTEL/MOTEL/RESORT AS A PRODUCT

Thirty-five years ago, many hotels were built and operated with little concern about the different needs of specific groups of visitors. Today, there is a much greater awareness of the motivations, needs, and expectations (MNEs) of different kinds of travelers, including travelers with physical handicaps.

Through market research, hotels can define who their customers will be, anticipate their needs, and modify services accordingly. Properties are no longer built to serve a "general" traveler. Instead, they are aimed at specific groups—such as business travelers, convention groups, vacationers, weekenders, the affluent, the economy-minded, and so forth. The concept of developing different products for different groups of people is known as market segmentation.

Market segmentation has brought great changes to the hospitality industry, but one thing that it has not altered is the definition of the two basic types of properties. These are transient hotels and residential hotels.

The majority of hotels are *transient hotels*, catering to guests who stay for a limited time—for a night, a week, or a month, on business or for pleasure. Transient hotels can be commercial hotels, motels, motor hotels, convention hotels, inns, resort hotels, in fact any hotel that provides temporary accommodations for its guests.

Residential hotels can be defined as apartment houses that offer hotel services. They differ from transient hotels in that they cater to guests who reside on the premises *permanently*. Most residential hotels are located in the United States and most are luxury hotels, providing wealthy residents with suites, dining rooms, room service, and maid and valet service. Examples include the Pierre and the Sherry-Netherland in New York City. Some companies maintain suites in residential hotels for the use of executives who are in town on business overnight. At the lower end of the scale, there are a number of residential properties that function essentially as rooming houses for moderate- and lower-income city dwellers.

Few residential hotels cater exclusively to permanent residents; most supplement their income by offering a number of rooms to transient guests. At the same time, some transient hotels also have rooms for permanent residents.

Hotels are classified not only by type, but also by function (or level of service), location, and scale.

Function

The primary function of any lodging place is to provide clean, comfortable accommodations. At the most basic level, overnight guests expect to find a bed with fresh linen, a private bath or shower, and fresh towels and soap. A number of low-cost, no-frills chains (Motel 6, for example) offer nothing more than this basic service. Most of them operate highway motels that cater to transient guests who just want a bed for the night before resuming their journey the next morning. All motels offering basic services provide free parking facilities for their guests. Some also offer breakfast, though the vast majority do not have a restaurant on the premises.

Many of the smaller, individually owned properties in downtown areas offer similar basic services. As with the economy motels, their main attraction is their low cost. Guests neither need nor expect a high level of service. These guests can be commercial travelers, tourists on sightseeing trips, and people visiting friends or relatives in the area. Country inns generally provide basic services only, but their accommodations are usually more luxurious than those of the budget motels and small city hotels.

The majority of hotels in the United States offer considerably more than this basic level of service. Standard services include in-room telephones, radios, and color televisions (often with cable); parking facilities; coffee shops and/or dining rooms and cocktail lounges; room service; laundry, valet, bellstaff, and baggage service; and front-desk service (including cashiers, mail clerks, and information clerks). A service that was once considered a luxury can become a standard requirement as the MNEs of the traveling public change. For example, recreational facilities, such as exercise rooms, saunas, and pools, are now considered a standard feature by many of the major

Illus. 7-3 *Hotels are classified by the number and quality of the facilities they offer. Luxury resort and convention hotels (left) offer complex services and amenities not available in hotels providing standard service (right).*
Source: *(left) Hyatt Regency-Atlanta   (right) Holiday Inns, Inc.*

chains. Another feature that is becoming standard is the availability of special rooms, such as no-smoking rooms and rooms with accessibility for handicapped travelers. Motor hotels, airport hotels, and midsized city hotels all offer standard services, catering primarily to the business traveler but also to individuals and families traveling for pleasure. Holiday Inn is a good example of a chain operation providing standard services.

Moving up the scale, we come next to those hotels offering more complex services. These include properties catering to executive business travelers, convention groups, and the leisure/vacation market. Many business travelers may need and expect more amenities than can be provided in a standard-service hotel. They may require more spacious accommodations, with room to work and to hold meetings with clients. Some may need to use computers, fax machines, typewriters, dictation machines, telex and photocopying services, and to have at hand the services of a secretary, translator, or notary public. Business hotels operating at the upper end of the market must be able to provide all these services and sometimes more.

The widest range of services are provided by the enormous downtown convention hotels. Properties cannot schedule large-scale conventions and conferences unless they have numerous meeting, conference, and banquet rooms, at least one convention hall, exhibition space, and a wide range of audiovisual equipment. The Sheraton Centre New York, for example, has 30 meeting rooms ranging in capacity from 20 to 2,800, including a convention room that can hold 2,000, a banquet room seating 1,800, and 10,000 net square feet of exhibition space.

Convention hotels also cater to conventioneers' needs between and after meetings. Among the facilities and services that may be offered are the following:

■ Recreational facilities—swimming pools, gymnasiums, health centers, indoor games.
■ Shopping facilities.
■ Evening entertainment.
■ Medical services.
■ Banking services.
■ Transportation assistance—in-hotel car rental desks.

Guests staying in luxury resort hotels expect a similar array of services and amenities. This is especially true of resort hotels that function as self-contained units and must satisfy their guests' every need and desire. In many ways, such hotels resemble luxury cruise ships in level and complexity of service. Even more complex are those resort hotels that cater not only to vacationers but also to convention groups. These hotels are at the opposite end of the spectrum from the limited-service motels discussed at the beginning of this section.

Location

There is a close relationship between the location of a hotel and the type of accommodations and services it offers. Downtown areas of large cities—the commercial, financial, and cultural centers—attract more people for business and pleasure than do any other locations. It is only to be expected, therefore, that hotels exist here in the greatest number and greatest variety. They can range in size from small hotels with fewer than 50 units to giant convention hotels accommodating up to 4,000 guests; they can range in type from motor hotels to residential hotels; they can offer either basic, standard, or complex services according to the needs of the guests they serve. Location within the downtown area is an important factor in determining type of accommodations offered. Hotels in fashionable neighborhoods thrive as luxury hotels; hotels in marginal and slum districts cannot attract wealthy guests and often degenerate into rundown rooming houses.

A recent trend has been the development of hotels (motor hotels in particular) in suburban locations. There are two major reasons for this trend. One is economic—real estate prices in downtown areas have risen to a prohibitively high level. The other reason is practical—suburban hotels offer easy access to the new corporate headquarters and industrial parks that have been built in city suburbs. Suburban hotels provide not only standard services for transient guests, but also facilities such as restaurants, banquet rooms, and meeting rooms to attract local residents and business groups.

Many of the hotels in small and medium-sized cities and towns in the United States were built near railroad stations at a time when rail travel was at its peak. Now that most people travel by car or airplane, many of these small-city hotels are bypassed by all but a few business travelers, and occupancy levels have consequently dropped. The hotels make up for the loss in room revenue by promoting social functions for local residents. Much of their income is now generated by the restaurants, bars, and banquet rooms on the premises.

The development of hotels at or near airports is an excellent example of the hotel industry responding to the needs of the traveler. A few limited-service motor inns had been established at airports in the pre-jet age, but with the growth of the airline industry in the late 1950s, there was a much greater demand for airport accommodations. Almost all airports are located at some distance from the city center. It is often more convenient for passengers traveling by air to stay at a hotel/motel near the airport rather than downtown. Travelers with early-morning flights can avoid the morning rush-hour traffic if they check in at an airport hotel the night before. Travelers with connecting flights are saved the inconvenience of a trip in and out of the city. Airport hotels often provide free transportation to and from passenger terminals.

Business travelers generate much of the airport hotel business, but chain operations have begun to actively promote the use of their airport properties by convention guests, local residents, and even vacationers in recent years. To attract business, they have added conference rooms, meeting rooms, banquet rooms, and a full range of recreational facilities. Airport properties have evolved from being small, limited-service motor inns in the 1950s to 1,000-room luxury hotels providing complex services today.

Resort hotels are usually located at or near natural recreation areas, such as the shore, national parks, lakes, and ski slopes. Casino hotels are found in legalized gambling areas (Las Vegas and Atlantic City, for example). The area itself is the main attraction and offers its own recreational activities, though the hotel usually supplements these with swimming pools, tennis courts, and sometimes golf courses. The resort property must also provide restaurants, bars, entertainment, and convention services if it caters to the convention market.

Resort hotels that function as self-contained destinations rather than as bases for activities in natural recreational areas must necessarily offer a wider range of services. The hotel itself is the major attraction. Club Med resorts are probably the best example of self-contained vacation destinations. Each Club Med "village" offers sports and recreational facilities as well as food and accommodations.

Scale

The three basic price tiers in the hotel industry are budget/economy (e.g., Days Inn, Econo Lodge, and Motel 6), moderate/standard (e.g., Holiday Inn, Ramada Inn, and Howard Johnson), and deluxe/quality (e.g., Sheraton, Hilton, and Marriott). In general, the price category reflects the level of service: budget motels and hotels offer basic services, and standard and deluxe properties offer progressively more complex services.

A recent phenomenon has been the upscale movement of budget chains into the standard tier. Holiday Inn, for example, started out as a low-cost, limited-service chain, then segmented upward as it gained a greater share of the market. The primary reason for this upward trend has been the rise in per-room construction costs. Ten years ago, an average hotel room cost about $30,000 to build. Today, construction costs for that same room can be as high as $100,000. As a result, it makes economic sense to build for the upscale market in order to command higher room rates. Budget chains that have not segmented upward have survived by using less expensive modular-type construction and by limiting services to the bare essentials.

Another example of upscale movement is the more recent development of *all-suite* hotels by some of the big chains. Examples of all-suite hotels are Embassy Suites

Illus. 7-4 *All-suite hotels offer the extra space that many business travelers need.*
Source: Marriott Hotels and Resorts

and Residence Inns. All accommodations in such hotels include living room and kitchen facilities as well as a bedroom. There is no need for restaurants or meeting rooms on the premises, since guests can make their own meals and living rooms double as meeting rooms. The all-suite concept has proved popular with business guests who need the additional space for working and for meeting with clients and associates. All-suite hotels are expected to become one of the fastest-growing segments of the hotel industry.

Rating Systems

There are many different hotel classification systems worldwide, but no international standard that allows for country-to-country comparisons. Many countries use a rating system established by the national government. Properties can be rated by a star system, by a code system, or by name (e.g., economy, standard, first-class, deluxe). The variety of rating systems has obvious drawbacks: a property rated as "five-star" by one country may be little better than "standard" in the eyes of a visitor from another country.

There is no official rating system in the United States, though hotels are rated by automobile clubs, guidebooks, hotel associations, and hotel critics. *Mobil Travel Guide*'s star-rating system is the most widely used by hotel and motel reference books. It has the following ratings:

*   Good, better than average
* *   Very good
* * *   Excellent
* * * *   Outstanding—worth a special effort to reach
* * * * *   One of the best in the country

PART TWO   Transportation and Accommodations

OFFICIAL HOTEL GUIDE 1991
FRA
(MAP PG. 42)

● **Hotel Mercure Paris Vaugirard**   91 Rooms   B-4
69 Blvd Victor POST CODE: F-75015 PHONE: (1)45-33-74-63 CABLE: Hipari TELEX: 260844 F FAX: (1)48-28-22-11 MGR: J.C. Droal, G.M. **REPS:** UIL
First Class - Motor Hotel (1976) located across from Palais des Exhibitions on the Left Bank, 10 minutes from the Eiffel Tower - 5 km from Montparnasse Train Station and 15 km from Orly Int'l Airport - Soundproof rooms with climate control, private bath, phone, radio, color TV (movies) and minibar - Rooms for nonsmokers - Wheelchair accessibility - Restaurant and Bar - Meeting facilities to 150 - Car Rental - Renovations in 1988 - Government rated 4* - Formerly Holiday Inn-Porte de Versailles
RATES: EP SWB 690-1020 (138.83-205.23) D/TWB 770-1140 (154.93-229.38) EAP 180 (36.22) - PP-CP +54 (10.87) BB +72 (14.49) - SC & VAT incl COMM: R-08A CREDIT CARDS: AE AIR DC EC JCB MC VISA

● **Mercure Paris-Porte d'Orleans**   192 Rooms
13 Rue Francois Ory, Montrouge POST CODE: F-92120 PHONE: (1)46-57-11-26 TELEX: 202528 F FAX: (1)47-35-47-61 MGR: M. Fiston, G.M. **REPS:** RSN
Superior Tourist Class - Hotel (1977) located in South Paris, 3½ miles from city center or Montparnasse Train Station - 15 km from Orly Int'l Airport - Air-conditioned rooms with private bath, phone, radio, color TV and minibar - 6 Suites - Wheelchair accessibility - Room Service - Restaurant - Bar - Meeting facilities to 200 - Renovations in 1989 - Government rated 3*
RATES: EP SWB 450-750/480-780 (90.54-150.91/96.58-156.94) DWB 450-780/480-810 (90.54-156.94/96.58-162.98) Ste 600-900/650-950 (120.72-181.09/130.78-191.15) EAP 50 (10.06) - Max rates Jul 1-Dec 31 - SC & VAT incl COMM: R-08B CREDIT CARDS: AE DC EC MC VISA

● **Meridien Montparnasse Paris**   950 Rooms   C-4/34
19 Rue Commandant Mouchotte POST CODE: F-75014 PHONE: (1)43-20-15-51 TELEX: 200135 F FAX: (1)43-20-61-03 MGR: Michel Sabot, G.M. **REPS:** MER UIL
First Class - Multistory Convention-oriented Hotel (1974) located near St. Germain des Pres - 16 miles from Charles de Gaulle Airport - Soundproof, air-conditioned rooms with private bath, phone, radio, color cable TV and minibar - 33 Suites - Wheelchair accessibility - Restaurant - Coffee Shop - Piano Lounge - Lobby Bar - Convention facilities to 2000 - Guest Laundry - Babysitting Service - Shopping Mall - Renovations in 1989 - Government rated 3*
RATES: EP SWB 990-1200 (199.20-241.45) DWB 1100-1350 (221.33-271.63) - SC & VAT incl - Ste rates on request COMM: R-08B CREDIT CARDS: AE DC EC JCB MC VISA

● **le Meridien Paris Etoile**   1027 Rooms   B-2/54
81 Blvd Gouvion-Saint Cyr POST CODE: F-75017 PHONE: (1)40-68-34-34 TELEX: 290952 F FAX: (1)47-57-60-70 MGR: J. Pierre Waldbauer, G.M. **REPS:** LRI MER UIL
Superior First Class - Convention-oriented Hotel located at Porte Maillot, opposite the Convention Center and overlooking the Bois de Boulogne Park - 30 minutes from Charles de Gaulle Airport - Soundproof, air-conditioned rooms with private bath, phone, radio, color TV (videos) and minibar - Room Service - 3 Restaurants - Bar - Nightclub - Meeting facilities to 1600; audiovisual equipment available - Beauty Salon - Renovations in 1986 - Government rated 4*
RATES: EP S/DWB 1250-1850 (251.51-372.23) - SC & VAT incl COMM: R-10 CREDIT CARDS: AE BC DC EC MC VISA

● **Hotel Meurice**   184 Rooms   D-2/13
228 Rue de Rivoli POST CODE: F-75001 PHONE: (1)42-60-38-60 CABLE: Meurisotel Paris TELEX: 230673 F FAX: (1)49-27-98-06 MGR: Philippe Roche, G.M. **REPS:** CGA UIL
Deluxe - Elite, Palace Hotel (1815) facing the Tuileries Gardens, near Place Vendome and Rue de la Paix - 10 minutes from Orly Int'l Airport - Classical-style rooms with marble bath, hair dryer, bathrobes, phone, color TV and minibar; some with VCR - 30 Suites - Wheelchair accessibility - Room Service - Gourmet Restaurant - Cocktail Lounge - Bar - Meeting facilities to 600 - Shops and Services - Renovations in 1989 - Government rated 4*L
RATES: EP SWB 1950-2250 (392.35-452.72) D/TWB 2250-2650 (452.72-533.20) Ste 7500 (1509.05) EAP 350 (70.42) - PP-CP +120 (24.14) BB +180 (36.22) - SC & VAT incl COMM: R-20B CREDIT CARDS: AE DC VISA TRADE DISCOUNT: Inquire direct

● **Hotel Mont Royal**   105 Rooms   G-4
la Chapelle en Serval POST CODE: F-60520 PHONE: (1)45-57-85-25 FAX: (1)44-60-63-63 MGR: Jacques d'Hoir, Dir. **REPS:** RSN
New Castle-style Hotel (1990) situated in a 300-acre park, convenient to downtown Paris - 10 km from Chantilly and 15 km from Charles de Gaulle Airport - Rooms and suites with private bath, phone and color TV - Terrace Restaurant - Cocktail Bar - Piano Bar - Meeting facilities to 150 - Outdoor Swimming Pool - Sauna - 2 Tennis Courts - Squash Courts - Golf nearby
RATES: EP S/D/TWB 1100-1250 (221.33-251.51) - SC & VAT incl COMM: R-08 CREDIT CARDS: AE CB DC MC VISA

● **Mont-Thabor Hotel**   118 Rooms   D-3
4 Rue du Mont-Thabor POST CODE: F-75001 PHONE: (1)42-60-32-77 TELEX: 670596 F THABOR FAX: (1)40-20-09-60 MGR: Mr. Ishizuka, G.M.
Tourist Class - Older Hotel located near Tuileries Gardens - Rooms with private bath or shower, phone and minibar - 2 Restaurants - Bar - Elevator - Renovations in 1989 - Government rated 3*
RATES: EP SWB 437-677 (87.93-136.22) D/TWB 724-784 (145.67-157.75) - SC & VAT incl COMM: R-08D CREDIT CARDS: AE DC EC JCB MC VISA TRADE DISCOUNT: 8%

● **Montalembert Hotel**   60 Rooms   D-3
3 Rue Montalembert POST CODE: F-75007 PHONE: (1)45-48-68-11 CABLE: Hotemontal TELEX: 200132 F MONTAL FAX: (1)42-22-58-19 MGR: Jean Michel Desnos, G.M. **REPS:** ATH JDL
Moderate First Class - Hotel (1926) located on Left Bank near Pont Royal and the Louvre Museum in the publishing quarter - Traditional French-style rooms with phone, color TV and minibar; some with private bath or shower - 5 Suites - Air conditioning available - Cafe - Bar - Meeting Room to 40 - Renovations in 1990 - Government rated 4*

RATES: EP SWB 1350 (271.63) DWB 1550 (311.87) Ste 1800-2800 (362.1 563.38) - PP-CP +80 (16.10) - SC & VAT incl COMM: R-08A CREDIT CARDS: AE CB I MC VISA TRADE DISCOUNT: 25% (TA)

● **Napoleon Hotel**   102 Rooms   C
40 Av de Friedland POST CODE: F-75008 PHONE: (1)47-66-02-02 CABLE: Otenapol-Pa TELEX: 640609 F OTENAPO FAX: (1)47-66-82-33 MGR: J.M. Bollack, G.M. **REPS:** CDU l UIL
First Class - Mid-rise Hotel (1928) located near Etoile - Rooms with phone, radio, color and minibar; most with private bath or shower - 2 Suites - Wheelchair accessibility Restaurant and Bar - Meeting Room to 100 - Renovations in 1986 - Government rated
RATES: EP SWB 700-1250 (140.85-251.51) D/TWB 1150-1850 (231.39-372.23) ! 3750-6250 (754.53-905.43) EAP 350 (70.42) - PP-CP +60 (12.07) BB +85 (17.10 SC & VAT incl COMM: R-08B CREDIT CARDS: AE CB DC EC ENR MC VISA

● **New Roblin Hotel**   77 Rooms   D
6 Rue Chauveau-Lagarde POST CODE: F-75008 PHONE: (1)42-65-57-00 CABI Hotelroblin TELEX: 640154 F ROBLIN FAX: (1)42-65-19-49 MGR: Joseph Ghannam, G. **REPS:** JDL UIL
Moderate First Class - Traditional Hotel (1886) located in the Madeleine district, n shopping and the Opera - ½ mile from Saint Lazare Train Station and 16 miles fr airport - Rooms in period and modern styles, all with private bath, hair dryer, phone, color TV and minibar - 7 Suites - Restaurant and Bar - Lounges - Meeting Room to 4(Renovations in 1990
RATES: EP SWB 540-570/570-600 (108.65-114.69/114.69-120.72) DWB 64 670/670-700 (128.77-134.81/134.81-140.85) Ste 1200-1500/1500-1750 (241.4 301.81/301.81-352.11) EAP 130/150 (26.16/30.18) - PP-CP +50 (10.06) - N rates Sep-Feb - SC & VAT incl COMM: R-08D or E CREDIT CARDS: ACC AE AIR BC DC ENR JCB MC VISA TRADE DISCOUNT: 20%

● **Hotel Nikko de Paris**   779 Rooms   B-3/
61 Quai de Grenelle POST CODE: F-75015 PHONE: (1)40-58-20-00 CABLE: Niko TELEX: 260012 F FAX: (1)45-75-42-35 MGR: J.L. Ory, G.M. **REPS:** KEY LRI NHI l
Superior First Class - Towering Hotel (1976) located directly on the Seine, minutes from 1 Eiffel Tower and Champs-Elysees - Soundproof, air-conditioned rooms with private ba phone, radio, color TV and minibar - 11 Suites - 6 Executive Floors - Room Service - Fren Restaurant - Brasserie - Japanese Restaurant - Bar - Tea Lounge - Meeting facilities - Indc Swimming Pool - Sauna - Massage - Solarium - Shopping Center - Car Rental - Concierg Renovations in 1985 - Government rated 3*
RATES: EP SWB 1050-1580 (211.27-317.91) D/TWB 1240-1760 (249.50-354.12 SC & VAT incl - Ste rates on request COMM: R-7.5 CREDIT CARDS: AE BC DC EC MC VI

● **NORMANDY HOTEL**   D-3/5
128 Rooms   General Manager: Jean Francois Richomme

First Class	COMMISSION R-08D	PHONE (1)42 60 30 21
ADDRESS 7 Rue de l'Echelle (F-75001)	TELEX 213 015	TELEFAX (1)42 60 45 81
AFFILIATIONS — — —	RES/REPS * FEE KEY LRI SRS TBI UIL	CABLE — — —

Inviting Hotel (1877) located between the Louvre & Tuileries Gardens; a 5-minute walk to l'Opera & the best shopping areas — 12 km from Orly Airport — Rooms & suites in French Traditional styles, all with private bath, phone, cable TV & minibar — Attractive Restaurant & American Bar — Meetings for up to 70 — Renovations in 1981 — Gov't rated 4* **Rates: EP SWB 870-995 (175.05-200.20)** TWB 1220-1420 (245.47-285.71) — SC & VAT incl — Ste & group rates avail — Credit Cards: AE CB DC EC ENR JCB MC VISA — *Res: In USA 1(800)44-UTELL or 1(800)SRS-5848 — Apollo (SR 21538), Datas II, Pars (SH PARNO) Sabre (SR 13044), Sahara & SystemOne (PARNOR)

● **Novotel Bercy**   129 Rooms   G
85 Rue de Bercy POST CODE: F-75012 PHONE: (1)43-42-30-00 TELEX: 218332 F FA (1)43-45-30-60 MGR: Patrick Herain, G.M. **REPS:** RSN
Moderate First Class - Downtown Hotel (1987) located along the banks of the Seine, acro from the Paris-Bercy Omnisports Centre - 10 km from Orly Int'l Airport - Air-condition rooms with private bath, radio, color TV and minibar - 1 Suite - Wheelchair accessibility Grill Restaurant - Meeting facilities to 230 - Gardens - Government rated
RATES: EP SWB 580-600 (116.70-120.72) D/TWB 615-630 (123.74-126.76) - SC VAT incl - Ste rates on request COMM: R-08A CREDIT CARDS: ACC AE DC EC MC VI!

● **Novotel Paris les Halles**   271 Rooms   E-3/
Place Marguerite de Navarre POST CODE: F-75001 PHONE: (1)42-21-31-31 TELE 216389 F FAX: (1)40-26-05-79 MGR: Jacques Chenet, G.M. **REPS:** RSN
First Class - Six-story Hotel (1985) located in the renovated old Les Halles marketpla area, opposite the Church of St. Eustache and Forum Shopping Center - 12 km from O Int'l Airport - Rooms with climate control, bath, phone, color TV and minibar - 5 Suites Wheelchair accessibility - Restaurant and Bar - Meeting facilities to 150 - Renovations 1990 - Government rated 3*
RATES: EP SWB 725 (145.88) DWB 785 (157.95) Jr Ste 1050 (211.27) Ste 14((281.69) EAP 70 (14.08) - PP-BB +52 (10.46) - SC & VAT incl COMM: R-08B CRED CARDS: AE BC DC EC MC VISA TRADE DISCOUNT: 8% (TA)

Illus. 7-5 *The* Official Hotel Guide *ranks hotels according to a unique ten-level classification system.*

Source: "Reprinted with permission of Official Hotel Guide. Official Hotel Guide *is a trademark of Reed Publishing (Nederlands) B.V., used under license by Reed Travel Group."*

The Automobile Association of America (AAA) has a similar five-scale rating system, using diamonds instead of stars. *The Official Hotel Guide* uses a rating system with ten categories ranging from "moderate tourist class" to "superior deluxe." It is interesting to note that, in 1990, only eight hotels in the United States were awarded a five-star rating in the *Mobil Travel Guide*.

Factors Affecting the Price of a Room

Most hotels have a standard day rate for a room, which is known as the **rack rate**. Rack rates vary enormously, from under $20 a night in limited service budget motels to over $200 a night in luxury resort or convention hotels. A number of factors determine the price of a room.

Hotel Location. This is the single most important factor affecting the price of a room. A deluxe resort hotel overlooking a golden expanse of beach will clearly command higher room rates than a resort hotel on a major highway five miles from the same beach. Rooms in the hotel will be even more expensive if there are no other lodging places in the area. In cities, hotels that are convenient to commercial centers, sightseeing attractions, and fashionable shopping areas are more expensive than properties in more marginal urban locations.

Room Location. The location of a room within a hotel also has a direct bearing on price. This is particularly true of resort hotels, where rooms with the best view (usually those on the upper floors) are the most expensive. In most hotels, rooms located farthest from noisy public areas (e.g., restaurants, swimming pools, and discotheques) also tend to command higher prices.

Room Size and Fixtures. Some of the chains at the budget end of the market operate hotels with rooms of a single, standard size, but most hotels offer rooms of varied size. These may be single rooms (with one twin bed), twins (with two twin beds), doubles (with one large double bed), twin doubles (with two double beds), suites (with one or more bedrooms and a living room), and, at the top of the price scale, penthouse suites (with access to the roof, swimming pool, and tennis court). (Table 7-3 lists these and other commonly used hotel/motel terms and their definitions.) It should be noted that the number of people occupying a room does not necessarily affect the price—a single room can sometimes cost as much as a twin or double. Children under a certain age may be able to share their parents' room at no extra cost.

Fixtures are fairly standard in United States motels and hotels and usually include toilet, bath/shower, and air conditioning. Telephones, radios, and televisions are standard in all but the no-frills budget motels. In many parts of the world, however, such in-room fixtures are

Single	Room with one twin bed.
Twin	Room with two twin beds.
Double	Room with one large double bed.
Twin double	Room with two double beds.
Suite	Room with one or more bedrooms and a living room.
Penthouse suite	Suite with access to the roof, swimming pool, and tennis court.
Weekly rate	Discount rate charged for a stay of a week or more.
Rack rate	Standard day rate.
Weekend rate	Discount rate charged for weekend stay.
Run-of-the-house rate	Discount rate for block bookings.
Corporate rate	Discount rate for employees of large companies.
Continental breakfast	Light breakfast usually including coffee, juice, and a roll or pastry.
Full breakfast	Cooked breakfast often including eggs, bacon, toast, etc.
EP	European Plan. A hotel rate that includes the room only and no meals.
CP	Continental Plan. A hotel rate that includes continental breakfast.
MAP	Modified American Plan. A hotel rate that includes continental or full breakfast and dinner.
AP	American Plan. A hotel rate that includes continental or full breakfast, lunch, and dinner.
Family plan	Special family rate that allows children to share their parents' room at no additional charge.

Table 7-3 Hotel Terminology

considered a luxury and are only available in the more expensive rooms. Bathrooms, for example, can be located at the end of a corridor rather than in each room.

Length of Stay and Season. Some hotels, particularly in Europe, offer special weekly rates, whereby a guest can stay for seven days more cheaply than for four or five days at the rack rate. Weekend rates offered by commercial hotels in the United States are also lower than rack rates.

The time of year can have a significant bearing on the room rates offered by resort hotels. Summer rates are considerably lower in ski-resort areas, for example, than winter rates. The same is true for resort hotels in warm-weather destinations (such as the Caribbean, Mexico, and Florida). Winter is the high season and summer the low season.

Meals. Some hotels in the United States include meals in the room rate, though the practice is more common overseas, particularly in resort areas. Meals are, however, often included in the price of a package tour, both in the United States and overseas. Foreign hotels include different kinds of meal plans in their room rates:

- *European Plan* (*EP*): room only, no meals.
- *Continental Plan* (*CP*): continental breakfast (juice, coffee, roll or pastry)
- *Modified American Plan* (*MAP*): continental or full breakfast and dinner.
- *American Plan* (*AP*): continental or full breakfast, lunch, and dinner.

The AP room rate is clearly more expensive than the EP rate.

Special Features. The availability of special features, such as recreational facilities, in-room cable television, and 24-hour room service, also affects the price of a room. The high cost of building and maintaining swimming pools, tennis courts, health centers, golf courses, and other sports-related amenities has to be reflected in higher room rates. Use of these facilities may be "free," but the guest is paying for them in the price of the room.

If a hotel is of historical or architectural significance, room rates also tend to be higher. A guest can expect to pay more, for example, in a hotel boasting that "George Washington slept here."

Special Rates. People who stay in a hotel as part of a group can usually expect to pay less for their accommodations than guests who book individually. The rate charged for block bookings is known as the *run-of-the-house-rate*. Most hotels also offer a *corporate rate* for employees of large companies. The largest discount of all is given to overnight guests attending conventions and meetings in a hotel. Many chain operations have special

family rates—known as *family plan* rates—which allow children to share their parents' room at no additional charge.

Other Lodging Places

In discussing the hotel as product, we have largely concentrated on properties operated by United States chains. A number of other lodging places, found particularly in Europe, also deserve mention.

Youth hostels provide younger travelers with overnight lodgings at rock-bottom prices. Facilities are extremely basic—guests have to provide their own bedding, share a communal washroom, and prepare their own meals—yet youth hostels remain popular with students and other travelers on limited budgets. The idea has been slow to catch on in the United States. Of the 5,000 youth hostels worldwide, only about 225 are in this country.

Pensions are private homes that have been converted into guest houses. They offer meals and lodging in an informal family atmosphere. Found primarily in Europe and Latin America, they are usually less expensive than hotels of comparable quality.

Bed and breakfast accommodations are available throughout the British Isles, and they have been steadily gaining popularity in the United States and Canada as well. Bed and breakfast guests can expect a full breakfast, a comfortable room, and a shared bathroom.

Paradors in Spain and *posadas* in Portugal are castles and other historic buildings that have been converted into hotels by the government. They cater primarily to vacationers, offer full meal plans, and are reasonably priced. More luxurious castle accommodations are available in France (châteaus) and in Germany and Austria (schloss).

Resort condominiums, a comparatively recent addition to the industry's product line, offer an alternative to hotel accommodations in Florida, Hawaii, Colorado, and other popular vacation areas. Condominiums are individually owned residential units under common management within a multiunit project. Owners often use them for vacations and rent them out the rest of the year. Condominiums provide apartment-style accommodations, with kitchen facilities, and recreational amenities either on-site or nearby.

The concept of *time-sharing* was introduced first in Europe, then spread to the United States in the mid-1970s. It differs from the condominium concept in that an individual does not own a complete unit but shares ownership with several other people. Each owner buys a vacation segment (usually two weeks) for a guaranteed number of years. Segments are scheduled so that only one owner uses the property at a time. Some time-sharing companies allow clients to exchange segments with people who own time-sharing units in other resort areas.

Bed and Breakfast

A quaint Victorian cottage on Cape Cod. A colonial mansion in Virginia. A Mexican-style hacienda in Arizona. These are just a few examples of the wide variety of bed and breakfasts found in the United States. A bed and breakfast, or B&B, is a small, family-owned hotel or a private home whose owners rent out bedrooms and provide meals to travelers. There are about 15,000 bed and breakfasts in this country, with some in almost every state.

At B&Bs you won't find a vending machine down the hall from your room. You won't find an elevator. You might not even find a bath in your room. What you will find are attractive homes, some decorated with antiques and period furniture. You'll find cozy, comfortable bedrooms, perhaps with quilts and lace curtains. You'll also find friendly, courteous hosts who will give you breakfast and maybe even afternoon tea.

Some Americans familiar with bed and breakfasts may have first encountered them while traveling in Europe. B&Bs are very popular in many European countries, such as France, Great Britain, Italy, Spain, and the Scandinavian countries. For Americans, staying in a European bed and breakfast might be cheaper than a hotel, but more importantly, it allows them to experience firsthand the culture of the country they are visiting. Imagine the excitement of staying in a French château, a Spanish castle, or a 500-year-old English farmhouse. In the same way, foreign visitors to the United States can experience American culture at bed and breakfasts in this country.

There have always been bed and breakfasts in America, but until recently, they were usually known by other names, such as tourist homes or guest houses. These homes were identified by signs in the front yard reading, "Guests" or "Tourists." During the Great Depression, struggling families often rented their spare rooms to travelers passing by on their way to find work. The arrangement suited both the hosts, who needed the extra $2 a night a room would fetch, and many travelers who could not afford more expensive accommodations.

In resort areas, guest houses were and still are a popular alternative to hotels. Staying at a bed and breakfast or guest house might be the only way a family of modest means could afford to spend a week at the seashore or in the mountains. Price is not the only reason why people choose to stay at a B&B, however. Although the guest house may lack private baths in each room and a swimming pool, many people feel that the charm and family atmosphere of a bed and breakfast greatly outweigh the lack of amenities.

Many people mistakenly believe that bed and breakfasts are new to America. That is because, prior to the mid-1970s, there were no guidebooks to B&Bs in the United States. In 1975, one bed and breakfast operator, Betty R. Rundback of Greentown, Pennsylvania, began to search out and contact other American B&B owners. It was her idea to form an association and publish a booklet listing the names and addresses of associate members. That year, her Tourist House Association of America published a 16-page booklet listing about 40 B&Bs. By 1982, the association had more than 3,000 members.

Today, it is possible to walk into your local library or bookstore and find dozens of guidebooks to bed and breakfasts all over America as well as Europe. Travelers who want to stay at bed and breakfasts should obtain one of these guidebooks so they can know beforehand what kind of accommodations to expect. Some B&Bs will accept children and pets; others will not. Some take credit cards; others do not. Some require reservations far in advance, while others can accommodate guests without notice.

Facilities vary widely from one bed and breakfast to another. Some are small hotels with single and double rooms, televisions and private baths in each room, and a dining room serving three meals a day. Many, however, are private homes where the accommodations are simply a spare bedroom, a shared bath, and a television in the owner's living room.

Each bed and breakfast is unique. Regardless of the differences among them, however, there is a common thread throughout: they are operated by hosts who love to meet people and welcome them into their homes. What guests seem to remember most from their stay at a bed and breakfast is the personal service and warmth of the host family. In fact, many bed and breakfast owners have a large collection of thank-you notes from pleased guests.

Photo Source: Tony Freeman/Photoedit

Attracting Different Kinds of Customers

As noted earlier, a major development in the hospitality industry in the last 35 years has been the increasing segmentation of the hotel product. In today's highly competitive market, hotels compete to attract business from different groups of customers by offering more specialized services, extra amenities, and incentive rates.

Hotels are particularly keen to attract business travelers because they constitute the largest guest category in nonresort properties. Many hotels offer discounts and travel bonuses for frequent visitors. Marriott's "Honored Guest Awards" program, for example, offers room rate reductions, gift shop discounts, express reservations, and check-cashing privileges. Some major hotels designate executive floors for the exclusive use of business guests. Special features may include extra-luxurious rooms, libraries with business publications and international newspapers, private lounges for meeting and entertaining clients, and business centers with fax machines and secretarial, telex, and translation services.

A number of properties at the upper end of the market have introduced special features in response to the increasingly sophisticated needs of their guests. The idea of *concierge* service has been imported from Europe. A professional concierge (or "guest services person") handles travel arrangements, makes restaurant reservations, obtains theater tickets, arranges sightseeing tours, and handles other details to make the guest's stay more enjoyable. Valet parking and hotel-airport transportation are other services that many customers have come to expect. Responding to the physical fitness trend, quality United States hotels are installing health centers and exercise equipment, as well as offering special menus featuring more healthful foods.

A problem for hotels that cater primarily to the business traveler is how to fill their rooms on weekends. Many hotels promote special weekend packages for the vacation and leisure traveler, sometimes with tie-ins to local attractions and amusements. Theme weekends—for example, music weekends, western weekends, and mystery weekends (with the guests participating to solve a mystery)—are becoming increasingly popular. You read about a similar development in the cruise industry in the last chapter.

A large percentage of a hotel's guests are out-of-towners, but hotels are also developing facilities so that they can function as centers of activity for local residents. This is particularly true of hotels (and motels) in suburban and airport locations. Meeting rooms and banquet rooms are available for local business groups and for social functions; restaurants and entertainment features also attract local residents. In this way, hotels appeal to three distinct markets: guests traveling for business or pleasure; local businesspeople; and local residents.

The Organization of a Hotel

Small, individually owned properties without food and beverage and other services are able to operate with a small hotel staff, possibly with just the owners themselves and a maid or two to clean guest rooms. Most hotels, however, require a much more complex organizational structure that is comprised of six major departments.

Certain aspects of hotel organization are clearly visible to guests, such as the lobby, front desk, and uniformed attendants. These are often called the "front of the house." The "back of the house" consists of equally important, but less noticeable areas, such as the kitchen, storage areas, administration, engineering, and security.

Administration. Every hotel needs a manager, assistant managers, and a group of people to handle the business aspects of the hotel's operations. The people who work in the administration department include bookkeepers and other financial staff, and purchasing, sales, and marketing personnel. An important function of the administration department is to interview and select the hotel's employees.

Front Office. The front office is the most visible department in all hotels and motels. Employees are in direct contact with the public; they handle reservations, room assignments, mail, and baggage, and provide information about activities in the hotel and surrounding area. A well-organized front office is essential to the smooth running of any lodging place.

Housekeeping. Guest comfort is a top priority. Most hotels employ a large housekeeping (or rooms) department staff to ensure the cleanliness and neat appearance of guest rooms and public areas.

Food and Beverage. If hotels have restaurants, banquet rooms, and cocktail lounges, the preparation and serving of food and beverages will be a major part of the hotel's operations. More than half of the total hotel staff can be employed in this department.

Engineering. The engineering staff have little or no contact with guests, but they play an important role in the day-to-day running of the hotel. It is the engineering staff's responsibility to maintain and repair all mechanical and electrical equipment in the hotel.

Security. Few hotels felt the need to employ security staff until recent years, but for many large hotels (particularly in downtown areas) a security department is now essential. Security personnel work not only to protect hotel guests and their belongings, but also to protect hotel property.

Hotels that offer more complex services need additional departments. Luxury resort properties may employ people to organize and supervise recreational activities. Large city hotels often have a separate convention department to handle conferences and other group meetings. Additional staff will be required if the hotel has on-site stores, concessions, and garage facilities.

Check Your Product Knowledge

1. What are four ways of classifying hotels?
2. Give the three basic price tiers in the hotel industry, and provide examples of hotel chains in each tier.
3. What are the seven factors that affect the price of a room?
4. What kind of services do hotels offer to attract business customers?
5. Name the six major departments in a hotel.

THE CHANNELS OF DISTRIBUTION

As you know, the hospitality industry is an integral part of the travel industry. Hotels and motels depend on the travel industry to bring in their guests; as travel increases, the hospitality industry grows. With the growth of the airline industry, the hotel product has become more complex, as hotels tailor their services to meet the needs of business travelers, conventioneers, and vacationers. The hotel has evolved from the small wayside inn to the giant resort and convention hotel of today. In some cases, the lodging place is no longer just somewhere to stop en route to a destination, but the destination itself.

Methods of Making Reservations

Until recent times, there was no advanced reservations system; guests would simply arrive at a lodging place and hope that there was a room available for the night. Motels still rely on "walk-ins" for a large percentage of their business, but the majority of rooms at other properties are booked in advance.

Travelers can make reservations themselves or through a travel agency. There has been some friction between hotels and travel agencies in the past, chiefly over the question of commissions. Hotel–agency relations have improved in recent years, however, and most hotels now see travel agents as an important extension of their sales force. Figure 7-2 shows the methods that travel agents use to make hotel bookings.

As you learned in Chapter 3, the reservations process has become increasingly automated in the last 25

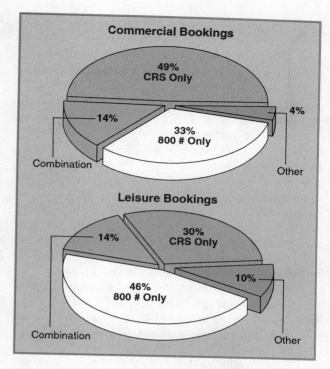

Figure 7-2 Methods Used by Travel Agents to Complete Hotel Bookings

Source: *Plog Research,* Hotel and Travel Index, Hotel Line

years, and almost all chains now have centralized computer reservations systems linking their properties worldwide. Using Holiday Inn's Holidex II system, for example, clients can make advance reservations at any Holiday Inn property in the world by calling toll-free a central reservations office.

Hotel reservations can also be made through the airline CRSs. Airlines that own hotels will obviously try to sell their own accommodations, but many of the large hotel chains also subscribe to the airline CRS systems. This reservation method is particularly convenient for clients making airline and hotel bookings at the same time.

Another alternative is to book accommodations through a hotel representative company. A number of chains appoint a single representative organization to handle reservations for all their properties.

A fourth method is to make reservations by direct contact (either by letter, telephone, fax, telex, or cable). Direct contact may be the only way to book rooms at many small, individually owned properties that are not linked to a reservations system, or that do not have a hotel representative. This is particularly true in the case of overseas properties.

Reservations can also be made through a tour operator or wholesaler if the hotel accommodation is bought as part of a tour package.

References

Several useful reference books are available for travel professionals and travelers. Many contain both objective information (such as factual descriptions of hotel facilities) as well as subjective comments (evaluations of individual properties in terms of service, atmosphere, etc.).

Hotel and Travel Index (*HTI*), published quarterly by Reed Travel Group, a division of Reed Publishing (USA), Inc., is the world's largest one-volume hotel directory. It lists over 45,000 properties worldwide, arranged alphabetically by country, city, and state. Although limited information is given for each property, *HTI* makes extensive use of advertising, which provides detailed information on over 10,000 hotels and motels. Other features of *HTI* include listings of hotel representatives and reservations systems, city information (including availability of rental cars and scheduled air service), and city and area maps with hotel and corporate headquarter locations noted. *The Hotel and Travel Index/ABC International Edition (HTI/ABC)* is similar to *HTI* but geared toward the international user.

The *Official Hotel Guide* (*OHG*), also published by Reed Travel Group, comprises three volumes. Volume I covers the United States (Alabama-Nebraska). Volume II covers the rest of the United States, the Caribbean, Mexico, and Central/South America. Volume III covers Europe, the Middle East/Africa, and the Asia/Pacific region. Properties are described in greater detail than in *HTI* and are rated according to the *OHG*'s own classification system. The guide makes liberal use of maps and contains descriptions of attractions in individual cities.

The quarterly *OAG Business Travel Planner Hotel and Motel Redbook* is available in North American, European, and Pacific–Asia editions. The North American edition has listings of properties in the United States and in resort areas (including Alaska, Canada, the Caribbean, Hawaii, and Mexico). The North American edition incorporates the *Mobil Travel Guide* ratings. The European edition is particularly strong on travel-related services (with listings of car rental companies, rail directory, and scheduled airline directory) and general travel information for visitors to Europe. The European guide has government ratings for hotels and incorporates the Automobile Association (UK) ratings for those nongovernment-rated countries. The Pacific–Asia edition provides extensive general travel information and hotel/motel listings for 50 countries in the Pacific–Asia area.

The *STAR SERVICE*, published by Reed Travel Group in Boston, is probably the most subjective reference guide. The *STAR SERVICE* is updated with quar-

Illus. 7-6 *The* Hotel and Travel Index *is the world's largest one-volume hotel directory.*
   Source: *Hotel Travel Index*

NASHVILLE, TN (CONT.)			AC 615
Hotels/City			
METRO MOTEL, 1404 Dickerson Rd.,37207, *Near Attractions*			⌂
$14-42	AX/CA/VI	45r	615/228-2531
MOTEL 6, 95 Wallace Rd.,37211, *I-24 Exit 56*			
$23-34	CC:ALL	126r	615/333-9933 ⓂMTL
MOTEL 6-NORTH, 311 W. Trinity Lane,37207, *I-24 Exit 87B*			
$28-34	CC:ALL	125r	615/227-9696 ⓂMTL
NASHVILLE MEDCENTER INN, 1909 Hayes St.,37203, *Near Downtown Area*			⌂
★ $44-68	ⓒⒹ	112r ■	615/329-1000 FAX321-4128 ⓂMED
Reps: TE			
OPRYLAND HOTEL, 2800 Opryland Dr.,37214, *At Convention Center*			⌂
★★★ $149-179	ⓒ	2011r ■	615/889-1000 FAX871-6942
Reps: KG			
PARK INN INTERNATIONAL-NASHVILLE, 2600 Music Valley Dr.,37214, *Near Attractions*			
★ $36-65	CC:ALL	200r ■	615/889-8235 FAX872-0019 ⓅPII
PARK PLAZA HOTEL-NASHVILLE, 920 Broadway,37203, *I-265 Exit 209B*			
★★ $59-75	CC:ALL	284r ■	615/244-0150 FAX244-0445 ⓅPPZ
Reps: UI			
PARK SUITES HOTEL-NASHVILLE, 10 Century Blvd.,37214, *4 Miles from Opryland* ⌂			
USA			
★★★ $94-149③	CC:ALL	ⓒⒹ 294s⑤ ■	615/871-0033 FAX883-9245 ⓅPAR

Hotels/Suburban			**NASHVILLE**
BRENTWOOD			
TRAVELERS REST INN, 107 Franklin Rd.,37027			⌂
★ $30-50	CC:ALL	36r ■	615/373-3033
FRANKLIN			
BEST WESTERN-GOOSECREEK INN, Peytonsville Rd. & I-65,37064			⌂
★ $27-51	CC:ALL ⓒⒹ	82r ■	615/794-7200 ⒷBW
BEST WESTERN-MAXWELL'S INN, Hwy. 96 & I-65,37064, *Exit 65*			
★★ $47up DWB©	CC:ALL ⓒⒹ	142r ■	615/790-0570 FAX790-0512 ⒷBW
HOLIDAY INN, Hwy. 96 & I-65,37064, *Saturn Complex 14 Mi S*			
★★★ $55-70	CC:ALL ⓒⒹ	99r ■	615/794-7591 FAX794-1042 ⒽHOL
GOODLETTSVILLE			
BUDGETEL INN-NASHVILLE N, 120 Cartwright Court,37072, *Near Shopping*			⌂
★ $35-45⑤	CC:ALL	102r ■	615/851-1891 FAX851-4513 ⒷBGT
DOWNTOWNER SUITES, 809 Wren Rd.,37072, *Near Shopping*			
★ $29-40	CC:MOST ⓒⒹ	48s	615/859-1771 FAX859-6404
KNIGHTS INN-NASHVILLE NORTH, 320 Long Hollow Pike,37072, *I-65*			
$35up	CC:ALL ⓒⒹ	118r ■	615/859-4988 ⓀKNI
MOTEL 6, 323 Cartwright St.,37072, *I-65 Exit 97*			
$23-36	CC:ALL	94r	615/859-9674 ⓂMTL
RED ROOF INN, 110 Northgate Dr.,37072, *I-65 Exit 97*			
★ $30-43	CC:ALL Ⓕ	109r ■	615/859-2537 FAX859-2567 ⓇRER

Illus. 7-7 *The North American Edition of the* OAG Travel Planner Hotel and Motel Redbook *lists properties in the United States and in resort areas.*

Source: *"Reprinted by special permission from the June–August 1991 issue of the* OAG Business Travel Planner—North American Edition. Copyright © 1991, Official Airline Guides. All rights reserved."*

terly revisions that can be inserted into a three-ring binder. It provides critical, detailed reviews of more than 10,000 hotels worldwide.

In addition to these standard reference guides, there are several consumer guides with subjective information about selected properties in different areas and countries. These include *Frommer's Dollar-Wise* and *$20-A-Day* guides, *Fielding's* series of travel guides, and *Fodor* guides. Hotels are listed and rated in guides such as *Michelin's Red Guide* series and the *Mobil Travel Guide* series.

Check Your Product Knowledge

1. What are the five ways that hotel reservations can be made?
2. What is the difference between objective information and subjective information in a reference book?
3. Name two multivolume hotel reference guides.

CAREER OPPORTUNITIES

The United States hotel industry employs over 1.5 million workers, considerably more than any other segment of the travel industry. The industry is expected to undergo stable growth in the 1990s, and the employment outlook should remain generally good for most hotel occupations. The positions discussed below exist in the larger hotels. In smaller properties, individual workers often perform multiple duties.

Front Office

The front office comprises two separate departments: the service department and the front desk. Service workers include doorkeepers, bellstaff (who show guests to their rooms, run errands, and sometimes perform room-service duties), baggage porters, and elevator operators. These are all entry-level positions. A superintendent of service is often appointed to supervise this department.

Front desk positions are clerical and include reservations clerks (who handle advance reservations), room clerks (who assign guests their rooms and handle registration procedures), rack clerks (who keep records of room assignments), mail clerks (who handle guests' mail and telegrams), and information clerks (who tell guests about local places of interest). With the increasing automation of the registration and reservations process, a hotel may need only one or two front desk clerks to perform all of these duties. The front office manager supervises all front office staff and operations; he or she may be helped by an assistant front office manager. Also part of the front office is the night auditor, whose job involves updating the guests' bills each night.

The security department is also sometimes considered to be part of the front office. A chief of security supervises a staff of house officers and patrol personnel. Staff members not only perform security duties but may also deal with guest queries.

Housekeeping/Rooms

Entry-level housekeeping positions include room cleaners, seamstresses, upholsterers, linen-room attendants, laundry workers, and valets. The position of executive housekeeper (in charge of all housekeeping operations) is essentially administrative, although in smaller hotels, executive housekeepers may perform cleaning and other duties themselves. In the largest properties, assistant housekeepers and floor housekeepers are sometimes appointed to ease the executive housekeeper's workload.

A Front Desk Manager

I am a front desk manager at a large resort hotel. My work is often demanding, but I enjoy the challenge. I supervise a staff of dozens of employees, and I must deal with such daily crises as overbooked rooms and missing luggage. I am the person guests come to with their complaints, questions, and comments. If I serve guests well, they will form a good impression of my hotel and they will come back again. Despite its demands, I love my work. I like supervising people and working as part of a team with the other managers in the hotel.

I didn't start out as a front desk manager, of course. My first hotel job was waiting tables in a hotel restaurant during summer vacations from college. After graduation, I took a job as a front desk clerk. When I started out in my first hotel job, my manager told me, "Do every task to the best of your ability because managers are always looking for ambitious, capable people to promote to better jobs." She turned out to be right because I have been promoted three times since then. Most hotels promote their managers from within.

Some hotel managers that I know started working in hotels right after high school. They took entry-level jobs and learned the business as they progressed up the management ladder. However, many hotels prefer to hire people who took hotel and restaurant management courses in college or who went to special schools to learn how to run a hotel. While in college, I took courses in accounting, hotel management, food and beverage control, business administration, and business finance. Many colleges in the United States offer courses in hotel and restaurant management.

Of course, after I started my first hotel job, I received a lot of on-the-job training. This was very important because some tasks you can learn only by actually performing them. I have to be able to do any of the jobs of the people I supervise—including cashiers, bell staff, reservations clerks, desk clerks, and telephone operators.

People sometimes ask me what special qualities a person needs to be a good front desk manager. I think that it is especially important that you like people and enjoy serving the public. In fact, sometimes I am as much a public relations expert as I am a front desk manager. Because I am one of the first employees that guests meet when they arrive here, I have to be friendly and helpful to them so they will carry away a good opinion of the hotel and its employees. That way, they will stay at the hotel again when they are in the area, and they will recommend the hotel to friends or colleagues.

Front desk managers must be patient, tactful, and skillful not only in dealing with guests but also in directing other employees. I want the employees under my supervision to enjoy their jobs and work well with each other because they reflect their feelings and attitudes when dealing with guests. It is also part of my job to coordinate front desk operations with those of other departments such as housekeeping and food services. If I were to check in guests to rooms that had not been cleaned or overbook reservations in the hotel's restaurants, I would annoy both the guests and my fellow hotel employees.

Front desk managers must be calm and capable in the face of emergencies. They must be able to make decisions and solve problems quickly. I have to deal with many different kinds of problems every day. Some are minor, such as when one of our magnetic keys fails to open a room door or the television in a room doesn't work. Others can be serious or very aggravating to guests. Just this morning, I had to deal with a family of six whose rooms had been accidentally booked to other travelers. Since my hotel was full, I had to find them accommodations at another hotel and arrange transportation for them.

There are several advantages to my job that you won't find in many other jobs. Among the advantages are that I get to meet people from all over the world, and I live in a comfortable hotel at a beautiful, sunny beach resort all year round. I eat in the hotel restaurant and can use its pool and other facilities whenever I am off-duty. Also, my pay is comparable to other kinds of management jobs.

One disadvantage to my job is that the front desk operates 24 hours a day, so I sometimes have to work a second or third shift. Since I live in the hotel, I am on call around the clock, seven days a week. For me, though, the advantages greatly outweigh the disadvantages. I plan to stay in this field for a long time to come.

Photo Source: Marriott Hotels and Resorts

Food and Beverage

This department involves the most complex organization. In the larger hotels, it can be subdivided into three separate departments: food and beverage, restaurant, and banquet. A food and beverage manager oversees the work of all three departments and supervises the purchasing of food and other food-service operations.

Entry-level positions include dishwashers, salad/sandwich makers and other kitchen helpers, dining room attendants, and servers. A chief steward is responsible for all the food served in the hotel and is in charge of general kitchen operations. He or she may be assisted by a pantry supervisor who trains and supervises kitchen helpers. An executive chef is in charge of the food preparation and supervises a team of cooks and chefs, which may include a roast chef, salad chef, fry cook, vegetable cook, short-order cook, pastry cook, and butcher.

Restaurant department personnel include restaurant managers, assistant managers, hostesses/maîtres d'hôtel, servers, and dining room attendants.

Hotels that schedule large-scale banquets usually employ a banquet staff, which may operate from a separate kitchen. A banquet manager oversees all banquet operations and also functions as part of the sales team. Many of the positions in this department are identical to those in the food and beverage and restaurant departments and include banquet chef, banquet servers, and banquet kitchen staff. Two positions unique to the department are those of decorator (responsible for the eye-catching appearance of the banquet table) and banquet housekeeper (responsible for setting up furniture, bars, and so on, in the banquet room).

Illus. 7-8 *The executive chef supervises a team of cooks and chefs who specialize in different aspects of food preparation.*
Source: *Marriott Hotels and Resorts*

Sales and Other Positions

Most of the larger properties employ a sales staff to market their product. A sales manager supervises a team of sales representatives who solicit business from travel agencies, tour operators, airlines, business firms, clubs, and social, political, and professional organizations. Group and convention sales are the major source of income; large convention hotels may appoint convention specialists (e.g., planners, consultants, and managers) to handle this lucrative market.

Mention should also be made of the accounts, engineering, and personnel departments. A controller, or chief accountant, heads a large staff of cashiers, night auditors, credit assistants, and payroll clerks, who are responsible for all the financial operations of the hotel. Assistant engineers, maintenance engineers, painters, carpenters, electricians, plumbers, and locksmiths work in the hotel under the supervision of a chief engineer. Personnel department staff, responsible for the hiring of employees, benefit programs, and training programs, include a personnel director, secretary, personnel assistants, interviewers, clerks, and typists.

Summary

- The hospitality industry is an integral part of the travel industry.
- Early lodging places developed along trade and travel routes.
- By the early nineteenth century, buildings were being designed specifically as hotels.
- The hotel industry grew tremendously with the extension of the railroad network throughout the United States.
- Luxury hotels developed in the major cities; smaller, less elaborate hotels along the railroad tracks.
- The first chain operations appeared in the early twentieth century.
- The automobile and the airline industry have had an enormous impact on the hospitality industry in modern times, leading to the development of motels, resort hotels, convention hotels, and airport hotels.
- Forms of hotel ownership include individual ownership, chain ownership, franchise, and management contract.
- Hotels can be classified by type, function, location, and scale.
- Hotel location, room location, room size, length/season of stay, and availability of special services and facilities are the main factors affecting the price of a room.
- Market segmentation has been a major development in the last 35 years.

- Hotels market their product to specific groups of customers, including business travelers, convention groups, vacationers, weekenders, and local residents.
- Hotels are organized into six main departments: administration, front office, housekeeping, food and beverage, engineering, and security.
- Hotel reservations can be made through central reservations offices, airline CRSs, hotel representative companies, or by direct contact.

Key Terms

tourist cabin
tourist court
motel
unit
motor hotel
motor inn
resort hotel
convention hotel
atrium
property
break-even point
"mom-and-pop" ownership
joint venture
franchise
management contract
transient hotel
residential hotel
all-suite
rack rate
European Plan (EP)
Continental Plan (CP)
Modified American Plan (MAP)
American Plan (AP)
run-of-the-house rate
corporate rate
family plan
youth hostel
pension
bed and breakfast
parador
posada
resort condominium
time-sharing
concierge

What Do You Think?

1. What effects might a sharp rise in airline fares have on the hospitality industry?
2. The hospitality industry has become increasingly specialized in recent years. Do you think there is po-

tential for further specialization? If so, in what areas?
3. What impact might the continued development of resort condominiums and time-sharing units have on the hospitality industry?
4. Why might a guest prefer to stay at a well-known chain hotel (for example, a Holiday Inn) rather than in a small, family-owned hotel in the same neighborhood?
5. What future do you see for the no-frills budget motels?
6. In recent years, hotels have been developing increasingly sophisticated services to attract different kinds of customers. What further services might they introduce to attract (a) business travelers, (b) convention groups, and (c) vacationers?

Dealing with Product

You have just accepted a promotion to become the director of sales for a brand-new 300-unit property located across the highway from the entrance to Yourtown International Airport. In fact, the grand opening of this new property is less than a week away.

Your first order of business is to design and implement a marketing plan. Your property includes a restaurant, a coffee shop, a cocktail lounge, an indoor swimming pool with a sauna and an exercise area, as well as ten function rooms that can be used for meetings and banquets. What types of travelers do you hope to have as guests? What can you do to keep the occupancy rate near 100 percent and the owners happy?

Dealing with People

In the airline industry, it is called "to bump"; in the hospitality industry, it is called "to walk." In other words, the traveler is denied either an airplane seat or a hotel room because of overbooking. Invariably, the traveler is less than thrilled to learn that his or her reservation is invalid.

Tonight is your night to learn all about irate travelers. It's 7:00 P.M., and you are the front desk manager at a 200-unit center-city hotel in Yourtown. You have a full house; there is no room at the inn tonight. Before you stands a weary traveler with a suitcase in one hand and a confirmation slip in the other hand. He has just been told that because he did not have a guaranteed reservation, the hotel canceled his reservation when he failed to check in by the 6:00 P.M. cutoff time. In fact, this weary traveler is the third person that you will have "walked" tonight.

What do you think about your hotel's policy of canceling reservations at 6:00 P.M.? What will you say and do to convert this very angry traveler into a repeat customer?

WORKSHEET 7-1   CHOOSING FACILITIES

You are a travel agent. Use the *Official Hotel Guide* or a similar publication to find appropriate hotels, motels, or resorts for the following customers. Narrow down the possibilities to two and describe them in the space provided. Include location, cost, facilities, services, proximity to tourist attractions, number of rooms, and so on.

1. A married couple from Ohio plan to visit friends living in Budapest, Hungary. Since their friends do not have room for guests in their apartment, the couple must stay at a hotel. The couple would prefer a moderately priced, older hotel in the center of the city.

2. A tired, overworked executive is looking forward to a two-week vacation. Since she travels a great deal for her job, the last thing she wants to do is spend her vacation traveling. A large resort sounds appealing. The executive imagines herself basking in the sun and being pampered by an attentive hotel staff.

3. A man from Seattle must travel to Hong Kong on business. He wants a suite in a Western-style hotel, preferably an American chain hotel. The hotel must provide a full array of business services, including a fax machine and a translator. The businessman would also like to be near the airport, if possible.

4. A family consisting of two adults and three children (ages 14, 11, and 7) plan to visit Boston and the surrounding area during the first week in July. They would like to stay in a motel in a northern suburb. The motel should be close to a subway station so they don't have to drive into the city. The children also want a motel with a swimming pool.

WORKSHEET 7-2   HOTEL MARKET SEGMENTATION

As you read in Chapter 7, today's hotels are built to meet the MNEs of different kinds of travelers. Find a newspaper or magazine ad for each type of hotel listed in the boxes below. Use information in the ads to complete each box.

Budget Motel

Name: _____

Location: _____

Price Range: _____

Market Segment: _____

Facilities/Services/Amenities:

_____

_____

_____

_____

_____

_____

Business/Convention Hotel

Name: _____

Location: _____

Price Range: _____

Market Segment: _____

Facilities/Services/Amenities:

_____

_____

_____

_____

_____

_____

_____

Resort

Name: _____

Location: _____

Price Range: _____

Market Segment: _____

Facilities/Services/Amenities:

_____

_____

_____

_____

_____

_____

Bed and Breakfast

Name: _____

Location: _____

Price Range: _____

Market Segment: _____

Facilities/Services/Amenities:

_____

_____

_____

_____

_____

_____

WORKSHEET 7-3   SELLING THE HOSPITALITY PRODUCT

You have read about the increasing segmentation of the hospitality industry. For each of the following groups, list facilities, services, or amenities that might attract the travelers to one hotel over another.

Traveling salespeople for struggling companies

Vacationing families with children

Affluent young singles

Handicapped businesspeople

College students on limited budgets touring the United States

Hotels that cater primarily to business travelers must make special efforts to attract weekend guests. For example, a hotel in New York City might offer a weekend package with reduced room rates and prearranged theater tickets and dinner in a well-known restaurant. What special weekend packages might the following facilities offer?

A medium-sized deluxe resort in the Louisiana countryside

A large moderate-priced hotel in Seattle

A small moderate-priced beachfront motel on Lake Michigan

A moderate-priced hotel near Chicago's O'Hare Airport

A large resort in Palm Springs, California

Name _____

WORKSHEET 7-4   EMPLOYMENT IN THE HOSPITALITY INDUSTRY

You are a personnel manager at a new hotel and conference center. You have job openings in all six of the hotel's main departments (administration, front office, housekeeping, food and beverage, engineering, and security). You have interviewed the applicants listed below and would like to offer each of them a job. What specific job would you offer each applicant? What are the opportunities for advancement?

A man with two years of college has worked summers on the bellstaff of a large city hotel. He has a friendly, attractive personality and enjoys dealing with people.

A college graduate, major in home economics, is very organized and has experience supervising other workers.

A vocational high school graduate has worked summers for a fast-food chain and wants eventually to be a chef.

A community college graduate has had business, advertising, and marketing courses. She is aggressive and motivated.

A former Marine, now a night watchman for a large office building, would like to have more contact with people.

A former travel agent who specialized in convention planning has a college degree in hotel administration and experience in public relations.

A skilled mechanic who has worked as an electrician and as a carpenter prefers not to work with the public.

A college graduate with a major in accounting has worked summers in the administration office of a large hotel chain.

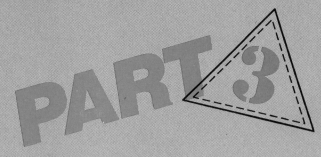

PART 3

TOURISM SYSTEMS AND SERVICES

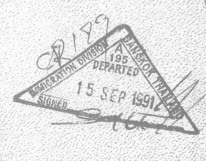

CHAPTER 8 DESTINATION DEVELOPMENT

"All travel has its advantages. If the traveler visits better countries, he may learn to improve his own; and if fortune carries him to worse, he may learn to enjoy his own."

—Samuel Johnson

Objectives

When you have completed this chapter, you should be able to:

- Determine what attracts travelers to different destinations.
- List and describe each of the five steps involved in the planning stage of destination development.
- Define carrying capacity.
- Evaluate the role of different levels of government in destination development.
- Describe the development of a major tourist destination.
- Identify the four stages of the product life cycle theory and apply them to a destination.

- Distinguish between the multiplier effect and revenue leakage.
- Discuss the social impacts of tourism.
- Define and give examples of the demonstration effect.
- Give reasons why local residents may resent tourists.
- Explain how tourism can help preserve a local culture.
- Identify the possible negative effects of destination development on a local environment.

In earlier chapters, you read about the different modes of transportation that travelers use to get to destinations throughout the world. In this chapter, we will focus on the destinations themselves and, in particular, on the subject of destination development.

Some destinations, of course, have existed for hundreds, even thousands, of years. They were not originally created as tourist destinations, but, over the years, they have become important centers of tourism. Obvious examples include cities such as London and Paris and natural attractions such as the Grand Canyon and Niagara Falls. Other destinations have been developed specifically to attract visitors. These include Caribbean resorts and theme parks such as Disneyland and Busch Gardens.

In this chapter, you'll learn about the complex planning involved in the development of a tourist destination. You'll also read about the role of government in developing and controlling destinations. Finally, you'll learn about the economic, social, cultural, and environmental impact that destination development can have on the people and resources of a region.

DESTINATIONS DEFINED

Every decision to travel is a response to one of two questions: Where do I want to go? Where do I have to be? Tourists and vacationers ask the first question. Business travelers and those who plan to visit friends or relatives ask the second. In both cases, the *destination* is a location that travelers choose to visit and where they spend time, no matter what their motivations, needs, and expectations (MNEs).

A destination can be as small as a single building or as large as an entire continent. A student might, for example, be inspired to spend an afternoon at the site of Thoreau's cabin in Concord, Massachusetts, after reading the book *Walden*. At the other extreme, a traveler with enough money and time might decide to visit Australia on a four-week tour.

No matter what the destination, adequate facilities and services must be available to satisfy the needs of visitors. To accommodate visitors to Mystic Seaport in Connecticut, for example, restaurants, shops, parking facilities, and places to stay overnight were added. Larger areas that are created as tourist destinations—such as resorts and theme parks—require a much greater degree of human intervention. In addition to hotels and restaurants, recreational, entertainment, and transportation facilities must be provided. Support services such as firefighters, police, and medical care are also needed. Even natural attractions that were not deliberately developed as tourist destinations need accommodations and other facilities in the area. Human intervention may also be necessary to make these locations accessible and to maintain them as attractive destinations.

What Attracts Travelers to Different Locations?

People choose a particular destination according to their motivations for travel. A vacationer who simply wants to lie in the sun for a week, for example, will probably choose a warm, seaside resort. Another traveler who wants to learn about Italian art might decide to visit museums in Rome, Florence, and Venice. We can identify nine motivators for travel that can influence a traveler's choice of destination (see Figure 8-1).

Recreation. People who travel for recreation might choose to relax on the beach at St. Thomas, go surfing in southern California, play golf at Hilton Head, South Carolina, or go skiing in Colorado. They are attracted to the destination because of the climate, the natural resources (beach or mountain), and the recreational facilities available. Recreational travel might also be for the purpose of shopping (for example, in Hong Kong), gambling (Las Vegas, Atlantic City), or socializing (dancing in a nightclub). And, of course, a vacationer might be attracted to a

Illus. 8-1 *Every tourist destination must provide adequate facilities and services for visitors. Here, a young visitor to Mystic Seaport takes part in a hands-on demonstration.*
Source: *Mary Anne Stets Photo, Mystic Seaport Museum, Inc.*

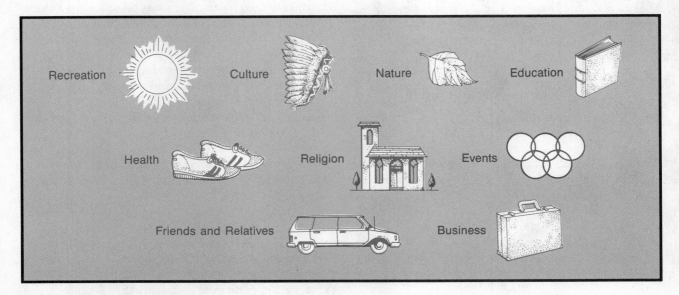

Figure 8-1 Motivators for Travel

destination because it offers the opportunity to engage in a wide range of activities. At a Club Med resort in the Caribbean, for example, vacationers can sunbathe, play tennis, water ski, socialize, shop, and amuse themselves in countless other ways.

Culture. Historic sites, museums, art galleries, and theaters are all examples of cultural attractions. People might travel to experience an earlier lifestyle (Colonial Williamsburg), to learn about European art and culture (the Louvre in Paris), or to enjoy live theater (London's West End). For many travelers, the local people themselves are a cultural attraction. Some cultural destinations can be exotic. They might include, for example, Eskimo encampments in Alaska, pre-Columbian sites in Central America, or the Polynesian Culture Center in Hawaii. The common denominator is that people travel to these destinations in order to enrich their cultural perspectives.

Nature. Many people travel to experience the great outdoors. They are attracted to natural wonders such as the Grand Canyon, Death Valley, and the White Mountains of New Hampshire. The desire to "get back to nature" often encourages vacationers to sacrifice the conveniences of hotel accommodations. They stay instead at campsites, lodges, and trailer parks.

Education. Some travelers choose a destination for its educational value. A student might, for example, stay with a family in Madrid in order to become fluent in Spanish, take a summer course at Oxford University, or go on a study tour with an expert guide.

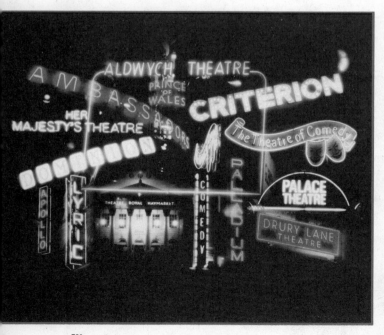

Illus. 8-2 *London's theater district.*
Source: ZEFA UK/H. Armstrong Roberts

Events. People sometimes plan a vacation around a special event. It can be a sporting event (for example, the Olympics, the Super Bowl, the Indianapolis 500, the Kentucky Derby), a celebration (New Orleans' Mardi Gras, the Carnival in Rio), a concert or play (the Tanglewood concerts in Massachusetts), or a parade (the Tournament of Roses parade in Pasadena, California). The event itself is the attraction rather than the city in which it is held. Most people who attend the Indianapolis 500, for example, do so because they want to watch a car race, not necessarily because they want to spend time in Indianapolis. If the race were held in Des Moines, they would go there instead.

Health. Many people are motivated by a desire to improve their health and physical fitness. Some travel great distances to visit a health spa or weight-loss camp for an extended stay. These latter destinations are popular not only because of the facilities available but also because they are usually in attractive locations, such as in the mountains or by the ocean.

Religion. Religion has been a prime motivator for travel for hundreds of years. Chaucer's fourteenth-century pilgrims in *The Canterbury Tales* were on their way to a religious shrine in southern England. Modern-day pilgrims travel to such religious sites as the Vatican, Lourdes, Jerusalem, and Mecca.

Friends and Relatives. Many people travel to a destination because they have friends or relatives who live there. As with event-oriented travel, the destination is of less importance than the motivation for traveling. (Vacationers may choose to visit friends or relatives in a destination that they also want to visit for other reasons—for recreation, a cultural experience, business, and so forth.)

Business. Business or professional travelers go to a destination to make sales calls, act as consultants, or attend conventions, conferences, seminars, or other types of meetings. They go to the destination simply because it is where they have to be. Meeting planners do, however, try to schedule meetings at appealing destinations so that those attending can combine business and pleasure. A conference, for example, might be held at a resort, with facilities for golf, tennis, swimming, and other recreational activities. Business travelers might also turn a business trip into a minivacation by tacking on a few nonwork days at the beginning or end of the trip. (For a more lengthy discussion of business travel, see Chapters 11 and 12.)

It should be clear that the categories outlined above are not mutually exclusive. A traveler doesn't necessarily visit a destination just because of its recreational attractions, nor solely because of its educational value. He or she may want to lie in the sun, learn how to windsurf, lose weight, participate in an educational seminar, and experience the local culture all at a single destination.

This traveler will be attracted to the destination that can best satisfy all of these motivations.

Other factors also affect the choice of destination. These include ease of access, price, and suitability of accommodations. However attractive a destination may seem, many people won't go there if it is hard to reach or if accommodations are priced beyond their budget. One final factor to consider is the attitude of the local people. Various surveys show that friendly people rank high on the list of what travelers consider important in a destination. Travelers are more likely to return to a destination where they are made to feel welcome than to one where they're not wanted.

Check Your Product Knowledge

1. How would you define the word *destination* as it is used in the travel industry?
2. What kinds of facilities are needed at almost all destinations?
3. List six motivations for travel that can influence a traveler's choice of destination.

DESTINATION DEVELOPMENT

Developing a destination for tourism means much more than looking at a lagoon and thinking it would be a good idea to put a hotel on the beach. Considerable research and planning must be done long before a shovelful of earth is turned or a building is designed.

Destination development begins with an idea and with the selection of a site. The idea can come from the government of a developing nation that sees tourism as a way to increase the flow of money into the country. Or the idea can come from an entrepreneur who sees the opportunity to make a profit, perhaps by converting an unspoiled island into a vacation resort.

Regardless of who has the idea for development, the next stage is planning. Tourism has a tremendous impact on the economy, environment, and social and cultural life of an area. This is particularly true in developing countries. With careful planning, the negative impact can be minimized and the positive impact maximized. Developers must take into account both the needs of the potential visitors and the effects that the development will have on the host community. Benefits must be weighed against costs.

The Planning Stage

Destination planning can be broken down into five main components: market analysis, site assessment, financial studies, environmental impact studies, and social impact studies (see Figure 8-2).

Market Analysis. By studying travel trends and travel preferences, market analysis can help determine the feasibility of a planned development. Unless it is shown that there is a market for the destination—that is, a sufficient number of potential visitors—there is little point in going ahead with the development. Market analysis can also suggest what type of development might be most successful. Surveys might reveal, for example, that travel for cultural reasons is on the increase. Or they might show that there is a trend toward seeking out more luxurious accommodations, or toward combining business trips with vacations. Such findings would influence the type of visitor facilities and amenities to be provided at the destination.

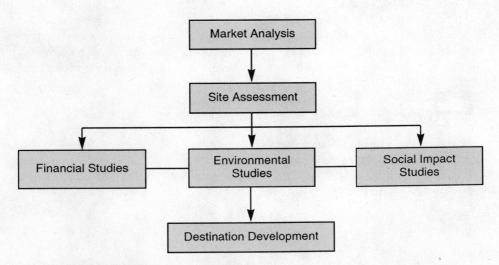

Figure 8-2 How a Destination Is Developed

CLUB MED

The antidote for civilization

Club Méditerranée, more commonly known as Club Med, promotes itself as "the Antidote for Civilization." The Club Med concept, played out in more than 100 vacation villages in 33 countries of the world, is simple. Club Med offers an all-inclusive vacation package in an exotic locale with an emphasis on recreation and relaxation. Guests are free to do anything and everything or nothing at all. This concept, coupled with an ever-broadening scope, has enabled Club Med to become the largest vacation-village operator in the world.

The Club Med of today is a far cry from its humble beginnings. In 1950, it was an austere nonprofit sports association with a "resort" in Majorca, Spain. There, guests prepared their own meals and stayed in army surplus tents. In 1954 Gilbert Trigano, who has since been credited with an "uncanny ability to see major trends before anyone else," joined the staff of Club Med. Though the company experienced some financial difficulties in the early sixties, by 1967 it was on its way to becoming the place to be for the young, the elegant, and the trendy.

All Club Med villages are set up along similar lines. Each is run by a group of *gentils organisateurs*, or GOs. Guests are known as GMs, for *gentils membres*. GOs are the most casual of social directors, acquainting GMs with the village and helping them to enjoy it fully. Entertainment includes plenty of opportunities for fun in the sun; nonstop sports activities; classes, races, and tournaments; special excursions; and nightlife. Meals and almost everything else are included in the package price. Only items like drinks at the bar are extra, and they are paid for not with money (guests lock their valuables in safety deposit boxes in their rooms) but with plastic pop-it beads that can be worn as campy jewels. The formula obviously works, because 50 percent of Club Med guests return.

Club Med's most astounding accomplishment, however, is not its initial success, but the company's continuing ability to adjust its focus to reflect changes in society. In the sixties and seventies, Club Med was a singles' par-

adise—its image was young, uninhibited, and unattached. In the late 1970s, however, Gilbert Trigano predicted the demise of "mindless sunbathing" and began to add features that would attract an older, married, more family- and career-oriented clientele. About 40 percent of today's Club Med guests are married couples, and more than 70 percent are between 25 and 44 years of age. Many guests participate in the wide variety of sports programs offered, including golf, horseback riding, tennis, and scuba diving.

Not that Trigano has excluded his original target market; the Buccaneer's Creek village in Martinique and Playa Blanca in Mexico still have a singles focus. Rather, he has broadened his market to include families. Families enjoy the Mini Clubs, where adults can engage in grown-up pursuits while their children participate in sports and creative activities all day. There are even Baby Clubs that allow new parents to enjoy athletic activities or just sit and read on the beach while their infants are cared for by a specially trained staff.

Computer workshops for both adults and children are available at six European Club Med villages. They enable novices to "get their feet wet" amid balmy breezes while more advanced computer users hone their skills. Club Med also welcomes corporate clients, hoping that companies will take over villages for conferences and offer Club Med vacations as sales incentives. Companies such as Xerox, Air France, Allstate Insurance, and Colgate Palmolive have done just this.

What does the future hold for Club Med? A profitable chunk of the vacation market, without a doubt. Besides opening Club Med villages on the French Riviera and in Ireland, Trigano has been working on a Club Med village on the island of San Salvador in the Bahamas. In 1990, Club Med entered the cruise business by launching its first sailing ship, *Club Med 1*. Its sister ship, *Club Med 2*, is scheduled to set sail at the end of 1992. Trigano is no doubt bursting with other ideas as well. His plans seem certain to capture the trends of the future.

Market analysis can help decision makers identify the socioeconomic and demographic characteristics of the tourists they want to target. These characteristics include income level, age, marital status, family size, and so on. A destination might be developed to cater specifically to upper-income people, or to senior citizens, or to young singles. Many destinations, of course, will try to appeal to several market segments.

Site Assessment. The assessment of the site involves two main questions: What do we have? What else do we need? Existing attractions might include a long, sandy beach; clear, blue water; and plenty of sunshine. Developers might conclude that they need a golf course and marina to attract more visitors.

The site assessment must note the availability of a local labor force. If the local population isn't large enough to supply the necessary labor, workers will have to be brought in from outside to build and staff hotels, restaurants, and other visitor facilities.

Assessment of the *infrastructure* will determine whether local roads, water supply, electricity, sewage systems, and related services are adequate to handle the influx of tourists. Questions that might be raised include: Do we need to build new roads or can we improve existing ones? Is there adequate drinking water? How do we dispose of garbage?

The assessment must also address superstructure needs. The term *superstructure* refers to all the buildings and other structures that are needed at the destination. The superstructure includes hotels, restaurants, convention centers, recreation facilities, shops, and other visitor amenities. In many developing regions, the superstructure has to be built from scratch.

Finally, the site assessment must study present and future transportation needs. The destination must be made accessible to major markets. New roads and railroads may have to be built. Airports and ports may have to be expanded.

Financial Studies. At an early stage in the planning process, developers must estimate the cost of the project. They must also determine where and how they are going to get the necessary capital. Financing can come from private investors, or, in the case of developing nations, from an international agency such as the United Nations Development Bank.

A good financial study must determine project costs at each stage of development. Also at each stage, the most favorable terms for borrowing capital must be arranged. Developers will, of course, want to make a profit. But they must also consider the likely economic impact of the development on the host community. The financial study might project, for example, the effect of the development on local property values and on local employment patterns. A successful development will be one that minimizes the negative economic impact and maximizes the positive.

Environmental Impact Studies. At some point in the planning process, decision makers must consider the physical effects that a sudden influx of visitors will have on the local environment. An environmental impact study might ask such questions as: How many visitors can our clean beaches handle while still remaining clean? How many high-rise hotels can we build before our destination loses its appeal? The term *carrying capacity* refers to the amount of tourism a destination can handle. A destination's carrying capacity is the maximum number of people that can use the site without causing an unacceptable deterioration in the physical environment and without an unacceptable decline in the quality of the visitors' experience.

Social Impact Studies. Equally important is a study of the likely impact of an influx of visitors on the residents of the host community. Local people might resent the presence of large numbers of affluent tourists. In developing countries, the introduction of foreign cultures with different social standards might compromise local customs and value systems. Social impact studies aim to minimize such negative impact and to create a healthy relationship between local residents and tourists. With careful planning, positive social effects on the host community can outweigh the negative effects of tourism.

Domestic Destination Development. Although many of the examples cited in this chapter involve destinations abroad, especially in underdeveloped countries, the development of a destination for domestic tourism will also have a major impact on the local people and on the local environment. Most of the problems created by the influx of visitors will be the same. For example, the development of a new ski resort in the mountains of Idaho would have far-reaching repercussions on the economy, sociology, and environment of the communities involved.

The Role of Government

Tourism can be an important source of revenue to a country, state, or city. As a result, governments at all levels are playing an active role in destination development. Public-sector tourist organizations are concerned mainly with promoting and regulating tourism. Sometimes, though, they also become involved in the planning stage of a destination.

World Tourism Organization. At the international level, the World Tourism Organization (WTO) represents all national and official tourist interests. Headquartered in Madrid, Spain, it acts as a consultative agency to the United Nations. The WTO's main objective is to promote tourism, not only as a source of revenue for tourist destinations, but also as a way to break down barriers between citizens of different nations. The organization views international tourism as a means of fostering peace, understanding, health, and prosperity throughout the world.

Another WTO objective is to facilitate people's access to education and culture through travel. It also aims to raise standards of living in developing countries by promoting tourism to these areas.

The WTO provides a forum for addressing problems that affect tourists everywhere, such as the problem of international terrorism. It also attempts to facilitate tourism worldwide by encouraging governments to ease restrictions on international travel.

One additional contribution of the WTO is in the area of research. It studies international tourism trends and devises standards, measurements, forecasts, and marketing strategies. This enables the organization to provide valuable information to tourism promotion agencies in individual countries.

National Tourism Organizations. National tourism organizations (NTOs) promote their countries as tourist destinations. There are more than 170 official NTOs throughout the world, more than 100 of which belong to the WTO. NTOs vary widely from country to country in their structure and organization. Some are independent government ministries. Others are government agencies or bureaus within larger departments. Still others are quasi-public tourism authorities. Most, however, have similar functions:

■ To promote inbound tourism through publicity and advertising campaigns.
■ To conduct research into tourism.
■ To draft tourism development plans (at both the national and regional level).
■ To regulate and/or license hotels, travel agencies, tour guides, interpreters, and so on.
■ To train hotel staff, tour guides, interpreters.
■ To operate resort facilities.

NTO goals and policies can range from simply attracting as many visitors as possible to protecting a nation's cultural heritage. Egypt's National Tourist Board, for example, vetoed a major resort proposed by a Saudi financier because of concerns over possible damage to the Pyramids.

In the United States, the National Tourism Policy Act of 1981 established the United States Travel and Tourism Administration (USTTA). This increased federal involvement in the promotion of inbound tourism. The USTTA promotes the entire United States as a destination. Individual regions, states, and cities are promoted by state and local agencies and by private tourist organizations.

Many NTOs have progressed beyond promotional and marketing activities to assume greater responsibility in the planning process. This is especially true in countries such as Mexico, Thailand, and South Korea, where planned destination areas are being developed. Governments develop these destinations in cooperation with domestic and foreign private industry. For example, Mexico's government helped to develop and fund the resort areas of Cancun and Huatulco.

Government involvement in tourism is most pronounced in Eastern European countries. Until recently, NTOs such as Intourist in the USSR and Cedok in Czechoslovakia had complete control over tourism in their respective countries. They even functioned as tour operators, selling travel arrangements to foreign visitors. Now, however, this is beginning to change. Although the NTOs remain dominant, private companies are allowed to compete with them and have begun to take a share of the tourism market.

State and Local Tourism Organizations. States and cities promote tourism for the same reasons that national governments do: to obtain tourist revenues and to encourage economic development. Tourism is among the largest retail industries in the United States. It is an important source of revenue in almost every state. Yet state tourism organizations (TOs) are a relatively recent phenomenon. Before 1950, only 15 states were actively involved in tourist development. Most of these were warm-weather states hoping to lure Frost Belt residents for winter vacations. Today, however, all states have an official agency responsible for travel promotion and development. State tourist offices develop and distribute promotional literature, entertain travel writers, and even try to lure film crews to their state in the hope that the resulting movie will generate favorable publicity. Following the lead of major cities, most states have also begun to promote themselves as convention sites.

Tourist promotion is just one aspect of the work performed by state and local TOs. Many are also involved in the long-range planning and day-to-day monitoring of existing tourist facilities. State and local TOs are now helping to form policies on land use, infrastructure needs, environmental impact, and attitudes toward tourists and tourism. TOs have graduated from simple "Visit scenic . . ." promotions to examining the long-term results of those visits.

The Need for Greater Government Involvement. The trend toward greater government involvement at all levels in tourism development is a positive one. In underdeveloped countries in particular, governments need to formulate policies to ensure that destination development suits the country, the area, and its residents. Developing nations cannot afford to rush headlong into destination development without considering the possible negative effects. If they do, they may be sacrificing their future in exchange for today's tourist dollars.

A DAY IN THE LIFE OF A
State Tourism Bureau Worker

What I like best about my job as a tourism training specialist is that there is always something different to do every day. I work for a state tourism bureau. My main assignment is to organize conferences and workshops for the travel and tourism industry. I am also involved in helping the colleges and universities in my state develop courses for people training for careers in the travel industry.

Yesterday, I conducted a workshop for several dozen employees of a city convention and visitors bureau to help them develop their communication skills so they can deal more effectively with the public. I had to give a short lecture, show a 20-minute film developed by my office, then lead the participants in role-playing exercises. In one such exercise, some of the participants pretend to be angry tourists whose hotel reservations have been canceled and others pretend to be hotel managers who try to find ways to help the travelers.

I give dozens of similar workshops each year to employees of hotels, restaurants, tourist attractions, and tour boats. My aim is to train tourism industry workers to be helpful and attentive to their customers so that visitors will form a good impression of our state and will want to come back. In addition to leading these workshops, it is my job to organize them, invite the participants, and solve any problems that may arise. One minor problem at yesterday's workshop, for example, was that there was no outlet to plug in the film projector, so I had to bring an extension cord.

I also serve on a committee sponsored by the state department of education to develop an eighth-grade career course. The course is intended to be an overview of the many different kinds of careers students can choose after they graduate from high school or college. My role is to make certain that travel and tourism careers are included in the course because tourism is the second largest industry in our state.

In addition to serving on several similar education committees, I send hundreds of information packets to high school and college guidance counselors throughout the state each year so they can advise students about travel careers. I have also developed a speakers' bureau so that high schools and colleges can invite people in the industry to come to their schools and talk to the students about travel and tourism careers.

Another part of my job is to field complaints form tourists and pass them on to the hotels, restaurants, and attractions that are the subjects of the complaints. Most complaints have to do with cancelled reservations, sold-out shows, long waits in line, and similar problems. As a state employee, I can't do anything about the complaints, but I try to impress on the restaurant, theater, or hotel how important it is to make guests feel wanted and appreciated. I try to convince them that it is worth their while to send a letter of apology.

I had to pass a very difficult civil service examination to qualify for this job. As part of the test, I had to give a mock marketing presentation for a panel of judges. Since the main part of my job involves giving presentations to groups of people, I had to show the examiners that I was able to do that. Fortunately, I have worked as a teacher, a travel agent, and an airline chief flight attendant, so I have had a lot of experience in talking to groups of people.

I was hired for a very specific job, but there are other jobs in state tourism bureaus that require less training and experience. For example, several people in my office answer calls on our state tourism hotline. These operators send out information packets, take complaints, and answer questions about such things as highway routes, attractions, ski conditions, and the weather. The main requirement for their job is the ability to be fast, accurate, and courteous. Hotline operators who can speak a foreign language are especially useful because more and more foreign visitors come to our state every year.

Like most state tourism offices, our office is small. We employ only about 30 people. The advantage is that we are friendlier and more like a family than a big, impersonal state office. The drawback is that because our office is so small, there is little room for advancement or promotion. Still, I enjoy my job so much that I can't imagine doing anything else.

Photo Source: Visual Education Corporation

With a carefully planned and well-managed program of tourism development, governments can reap positive benefits. These include not only economic benefits (such as tourism revenues and employment opportunities), but also intangible benefits. Among the intangible benefits may be an elevation of the country's image both at home and abroad, a widening of educational and cultural horizons, and a general improvement in the quality of life.

Before we move on to examine the positive and negative impacts of destination development, let's take a look at a specific example of development.

A Destination Developed: Walt Disney World

The development of Walt Disney World near Orlando in central Florida offers a textbook example of how to develop a destination for tourism.

The seeds for Disney World were planted almost 3,000 miles to the west, in California's Orange County.

Illus. 8-3 *Careful planning is responsible for much of the phenomenal success of Disney World.*
Source: *Hugh Rogers/ Monkmeyer Press Photo Service*

There, in the mid-1950s, Walt Disney built a 244-acre, family-oriented amusement park called Disneyland. Based on characters and events from Disney's popular movies, it offered everything from a ride in the Mad Hatter's giant teacups to a fairy-tale castle.

The only "mistake" Disney and his staff made was in underestimating just how popular Disneyland would become. Millions of people flocked there. They spent money, of course, inside the amusement park. But right outside the park, they gave their money for food, lodging, and recreation to independent businesses whose only reason for existence and success was their proximity to Disneyland. Every business in Anaheim, where the park is located, rode Disneyland's coattails to prosperity.

WED Enterprise, the corporation that developed the second Disney park, learned from the experience in Disneyland. Disney World, almost ten times as large as Disneyland, was planned as a self-contained resort. Hotels, restaurants, shops, and recreational facilities would all be located within the park, giving Disney total control over the Disney World environment. The Disney staff were no longer just entrepreneurs of an amusement park, but also hoteliers, restaurateurs, and real estate developers.

Florida offered a number of natural advantages as the site for Disney World. Its climate allowed year-round operation and construction. Its East Coast location meant that Disney World would not be competing with Disneyland. The Florida state government, aware of the potential revenue, passed statutes that gave Disney World virtual independence.

The development of Disney World took place in stages. The first stage entailed the building of the theme park (Main Street, U.S.A.; Fantasyland; Tomorrowland; Adventureland; Frontierland; and Liberty Square), three Disney hotels, and basic conservation projects. Subsequent stages added more hotels (not owned by Disney but paying rent for the privilege of their Disney World location), restaurants, shops, golf courses, swimming pools, and lakes. Later additions included the Walt Disney World Village and the Experimental Prototype Community of Tomorrow (EPCOT) Center. In 1989, the Disney-MGM Studios Park opened. The Disney complex continues to grow.

The Disney staff have had complete control over the whole project. Existing operations provided a source of capital for every phase of development. Planners and architects gained experience with each successive stage. Lessons they had learned in the development of the theme park, for example, were applied in planning and building EPCOT. The fact that they have had total control over the environment at Disney World has given them the opportunity to test solutions to urban planning problems.

The Disney World tourism complex has not been without its critics. Criticism has focused largely on what might be called the unreality of the venture, the fact that

Disney World is a fantasy world in which real city problems are not allowed to exist. While some of this commentary is valid, it also misses the point. Disney World is a corporate venture: its business is to make a profit, not to improve the world. It does exactly what it sets out to do, and does so very successfully.

The Life Cycle of Destinations

Disney World has been in operation for more than two decades. As yet, there is no indication of a decline in its popularity. Not all tourist destinations, however, are as fortunate as Disney World. Some, like rock bands and hairstyles, rise from obscurity to the height of popularity and then fall back into obscurity in a short space of time. Others go in and out of fashion cyclically. The Côte d'Azur in southern France, for example, has been through several phases of popularity and decline since its initial development as a health spa for the wealthy at the end of the nineteenth century.

To understand how destinations rise and fall in popularity, we can look at the *product life cycle* theory, a standard marketing concept (see Figure 8-3). The theory identifies four stages in the life cycle of a product:

1. Inception.
2. Growth.
3. Maturity.
4. Decline.

During the inception stage, the destination is discovered, usually by a few allocentric travelers who don't like to go where everyone else goes. The host community usually welcomes this first wave of tourists—as well as investors—and there is considerable personal contact between visitors and residents. As word spreads, this "unknown" spot increases in popularity and enters the growth stage. Hotels, restaurants, and other tourist-oriented facilities are built with local initiative, though typically without any well-thought-out plan. Toward the end of the growth stage, relations between tourists and residents tend to become more personal.

As advertising campaigns attract more and more visitors, the destination reaches the maturity stage. At this point, local residents begin to lose control over the development of tourism. Big hotels and restaurant chains move into the area, and facilities and services become standardized. A significant portion of the local population comes to depend on tourism for its living. Employment patterns and social standards are altered. By the end of the maturity stage, the local population has begun to resent the growing number of tourists and the loss of their own cultural identity.

The final stage—decline—is reached when the destination becomes oversaturated with tourists. When this occurs, the site has exceeded its carrying capacity, a term you will remember from the discussion of the planning stages of destination development. For the local population, the negative effects of tourism now outweigh the benefits. For the visitors, the destination's attractions have lost their appeal. Beaches have become overcrowded, the site is commercialized, and the natives are no longer friendly.

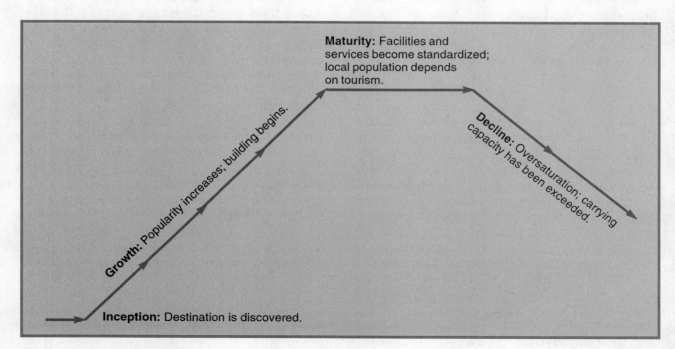

Figure 8-3 Life Cycle of a Destination

Illus. 8-4 *During the inception stage of a destination's life cycle, the destination is discovered and patronized by a small number of adventurous visitors.*
Source: *Colorado Department of Public Relations*

Carrying capacity can be measured in three different ways. If local residents are squeezed out of local activities, then a destination's *economic* carrying capacity has been reached. If the beaches become contaminated, or historical buildings become damaged, then *physical* carrying capacity has been exceeded. If local residents' tolerance of tourists has reached its limits, then the destination has surpassed its *social* carrying capacity.

Carrying capacity is based on two intangibles—the characteristics of the tourists and the characteristics of the destination and its population. It is therefore difficult to determine a destination's carrying capacity. The planning stage of a destination should, however, always include a reasonable estimate of carrying capacity. Keeping the carrying capacity in mind can help ensure that the destination remains in the maturity stage of its life cycle.

Not all destinations pass through every stage outlined here. A few never progress beyond the inception stage. This is especially true for remote destinations. Others go straight from discovery to maturity, bypassing the growth stage. The Fiji Islands and Guam offer good examples of this. And some, such as Disney World and the resort area of Cancun in Mexico, move directly to maturity without experiencing either of the two early stages.

Some destinations lose their appeal as tourist attractions before they ever reach their carrying capacity. This

can be the result of unpredictable factors. Political events, for example, have often changed tourists' minds on the desirability of a destination. Cuba was once a very popular vacation spot, especially for residents of the eastern United States. It was inexpensive, warm, and had magnificent ocean fishing and legalized gambling. When Fidel Castro overthrew the ruling government in 1959 and declared Cuba a communist country, American tourists stopped going to the island. Civil war has had similar effects on tourism in Lebanon (particularly Beirut) and Northern Ireland.

Unfavorable changes in currency rates can also discourage tourists from visiting a foreign country. (The reverse is also true, of course: Mexico became a very popular destination for people from the United States when the peso fell against the dollar.)

Another way in which a tourist destination can decline in popularity is through the loss of natural resources that made it attractive to begin with. A lake or river may run dry; a beach may be polluted by an oil spill. Finally, the growth of rival destinations can have a negative effect on existing destinations. Each new theme park, for example, draws travelers away from the others.

Sometimes an unpredictable factor can cause a destination to become more popular. When the television show "WKRP in Cincinnati" was on the air, for example, local hotel owners noticed a marked increase in tourism in Cincinnati, Ohio. The *Crocodile Dundee* movies had a similar impact on the number of people who visited Australia.

THE ECONOMIC IMPACT OF DESTINATION DEVELOPMENT

When a destination is developed for tourism, the influx of tourists has a tremendous impact on the local and national economy. Regardless of their reasons for traveling, all tourists spend money during their stay at a destination. Visitor expenditures provide income and profit for businesses as diverse as hotels, trailer parks, restaurants, gas stations, golf courses, grocery stores, and souvenir shops. Local, state, and national governments receive revenues from sales taxes, occupancy taxes, alcohol and gasoline taxes, and user fees for campgrounds, parks, ski slopes, highways, and other amenities. Perhaps most important of all, tourist dollars generate employment for local residents.

A few figures will show just how large a contribution tourism can make to the economy. In one recent year, United States residents and foreign visitors spent an estimated $579 billion on travel expenditures in the United States. In the same year, tourism generated more than 8 million jobs in the United States and about $68 billion in federal, state, and local taxes. Figures for other nations are not as high as those for the United States, but that is not to say that the economic impact of tourism is any smaller. In fact, in many developing countries it is considerably greater. Tourism can be virtually the only source of export income in countries that lack the agricultural and industrial resources needed to develop a more diversified economy.

Before we move on to consider the effect that destination development can have on a nation's balance of payments, we will first look at what happens to the money that enters a local economy from tourist expenditures.

Tourism Dollars and the Multiplier Effect

The flow of tourism dollars into a local economy is a complicated process. Let's look at an example to see how the money spent by a single tourist in a Caribbean resort is distributed.

Mary Hobbes spends $1,000 during her vacation at Montego Bay, Jamaica. We can break her expenditures down into $400 for a hotel room, $200 for restaurant meals, $125 for a rental car, $175 for recreation and entertainment, and $100 for souvenirs and miscellaneous items. These expenditures represent *direct spending*—that is, money that goes directly from the traveler into the economy. It would seem simple to deduce that the local economy has $1,000 more than it would have had if Ms. Hobbes had decided to vacation elsewhere. In fact, that $1,000 means considerably more to the economy because of what economists call the multiplier effect (see Figure 8-4).

Mary Hobbes' $1,000 does not stop working once it has reached the hotelier and the owners of the other tourist facilities. The money is respent several times, generating more income and further employment. The Montego Bay restaurants, for example, must buy food and beverages from local suppliers, who in turn must make purchases from local farmers. Part of Mary Hobbes' $1,000 will also go to pay wages to the employees who work in the hotel, the restaurants, and other tourist businesses. The workers in turn will pay rent, buy groceries, and so forth. These successive rounds of spending generated by the initial tourist expenditures are known as *indirect spending*—that is, money that is respent and generates more money and more employment.

The Tourism Multiplier. It can be seen that the total of all income is far greater than the initial $1,000 spent by Mary Hobbes. The actual amount by which the income will increase can be worked out using a formula called the *tourism multiplier.* Direct and indirect tourist expenditures not only have an effect on income. Multipliers can also be estimated for sales, output, employment, and payroll.

The Concept of Leakage. In the example of Mary Hobbes, we assumed that the whole of her $1,000 flowed into the Montego Bay economy. In reality, not all of that money will stay in the local economy. Many of the goods and services that are needed to satisfy tourist desires have to be imported. Mary Hobbes, for example, enjoys a glass of wine with her evening meal. Wine is not produced locally, so it has to be imported. Part of Mary Hobbes' $1,000 will leave the local economy for payment to overseas wine growers.

Money that flows out of the economy to purchase outside resources is known in economic terms as *leak-*

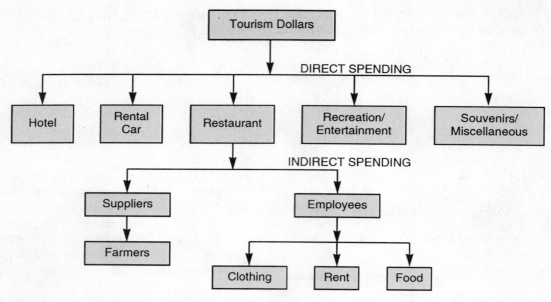

Figure 8-4 Tourism Dollars and the Multiplier Effect

age. The more imports that are necessary, the higher will be the leakage. And the less money that stays and is circulated within the local economy, the lower will be the tourism multiplier. Many of the resorts in the Caribbean have to import most goods for tourists. Consequently, they have a relatively low multiplier. Mary Hobbes' $1,000 may in fact only contribute $500 to the local economy. If, on the other hand, an area has sufficient resources to produce all the necessary goods and services, the full amount of tourist expenditures will remain in the area and the multiplier will be high. Clearly, the more developed the local economy, the higher the multiplier.

Tourism and the Balance of Payments

Countries develop tourist destinations in order to earn foreign currency and to reduce their balance of payments deficits. A country's balance of payments is the difference between payments for imports and receipts from exports (remember that tourism is an export industry). Unfortunately, many of the developing nations that have the most to gain from tourism are often the ones that suffer from the highest leakages. Foreign exchange receipts are substantially reduced because a large proportion of tourist expenditures and profits flow out of the country to foreign investors and foreign suppliers. As a result, tourism rarely eliminates large balance of payments deficits.

Where the Money Goes. You have already read that money can leak out of the economy to pay for imported goods and services. Our example showed how wine had

to be imported into Jamaica. Other destinations may have to import meat, vegetables, and even water to cater to tourist needs. Tourism can also create an increased demand for imported goods on the part of local residents. With the influx of affluent foreign tourists, residents of developing countries are exposed to new consumer goods. And with higher incomes as a result of tourism development, they can now afford to buy them.

Payment for imported consumer goods and services is just one of many ways in which tourist revenues can leak out of the economy. Raw materials may also have to be imported to meet increased demand, especially for utilities such as electricity and gas. Before a destination is developed for tourism, local raw materials may be sufficient to meet the resident population's needs. But with the influx of thousands of tourists, coal may have to be imported to generate the additional electricity required. Similarly, propane gas may have to be imported to fuel hotel and restaurant kitchens.

A significant proportion of tourist revenues may have to be used to pay for imported materials and equipment. If construction materials, for example, are not available in sufficient quantity in the host country, they will have to be purchased elsewhere. Countries with no domestic automobile industry will have to import cars and buses to satisfy tourist transportation needs. Even hotel equipment may have to be brought in from other countries—not just beds and bathroom fixtures, but also elevators and air conditioners.

Income earned by foreign investors is another factor that reduces a country's tourism revenues. The early stages of destination development require a massive investment of capital. Developing countries cannot afford to finance large-scale infrastructural and superstructural projects, so they are forced to seek financial assistance abroad. Without foreign investment, the destinations could not be developed for tourism. But the price the developing countries have to pay is high. They must spend years repaying loans and paying interest on the investments.

The emergence of multinational corporations has also affected the tourism revenues in host countries. International hotel and restaurant chains have opened properties in resort destinations throughout the world. Because they are foreign-owned, much of the revenue and profits from their ventures is transferred out of the host country. The payment of airfares to foreign-owned airlines is another way in which countries lose potential tourist revenues. (Few developing nations can afford to operate their own airlines.)

An example will illustrate how large amounts of money can leak out of the host economy. A couple from Iowa decide to vacation in the Bahamas. They make air and hotel reservations through a travel agency in Cedar Rapids, Iowa. They're booked on an American air carrier, they stay in a hotel that's part of an American chain, and they eat at an American-owned restaurant. They hire a Hertz rental car for a couple of days. The rest of the time they spend on the hotel beach drinking soft drinks bottled in the United States. The only money that remains in the host country is a few dollars for souvenirs and the wages paid to local employees.

Payments may also be due abroad for management fees. Many local hotels that are not part of a chain, for example, are managed by foreign corporations that are paid a fee for their services. If the local labor force is not big enough, foreign workers may have to be imported to fill jobs in hotels, restaurants, and other tourist-oriented businesses. Salaries may have to be paid to foreign entertainers who perform in the local nightclubs, to visiting sports pros who give golf and tennis lessons, and to other nonlocal employees. In all these ways, money is further drained from the host country's economy.

Necessary Leakage. One final expense is the cost of promoting the destination abroad. This can be viewed as "necessary leakage": it really can't be avoided if the destination is going to attract tourists. In the competitive Caribbean market, for example, each island resort has to advertise to convince potential customers that it is more appealing than all the other resorts. National tourist organizations promote their destinations by advertising in foreign media and by offering FAM trips to foreign travel agents and travel writers.

This discussion of leakage may make you wonder how any destination manages to make a profit from tourism. But many do, not only in developed nations (where leakages tend to be lower), but also in developing countries. As we have stressed earlier in this chapter, planning is the key to success. Developing countries can,

for example, minimize the loss of tourist revenues by implementing plans aimed at reducing imports of tourism-related items. They might do this by supporting local industries. Foreign control of the hospitality industry might be reduced by incentives offered to local hoteliers. The number of foreign employees in managerial and professional positions might be reduced if local residents are educated and trained in relevant disciplines.

All these measures will help to ensure that a greater percentage of tourist revenues stay in the host country. As a result, the economic benefits of destination development— employment, income, and tax revenue—will outweigh possible negative effects.

Check Your Product Knowledge

1. What is meant by the *multiplier effect*?
2. What is *leakage*, in the context of tourism?
3. List five ways in which tourist revenues can flow out of a country.

THE SOCIAL IMPACT OF TOURISM

The success of destination development is most commonly measured in economic terms. However, we should not overlook the social, cultural, and environmental implications of tourism.

It is now widely recognized that destination development brings about social change, with both positive and negative effects. The social effects of destination development tend to be less significant in developed countries. Less-developed nations are more likely to experience the negative social effects of tourism. When tourism replaces other economic activities, or when a destination is developed too rapidly or too intensively, the social impacts can be particularly damaging. Here again, intelligent planning is extremely important. With conservative scheduling, good management, and awareness of resident needs, the negative social impacts of destination development can be minimized.

Socioeconomic Impact

The economic impact of destination development can have social implications. The most obvious socioeconomic effects relate to population growth, changing employment patterns, an increased level of income, and rising property values. In the early stages of destination development, laborers must be hired to build new hotels and restaurants and to upgrade the local infrastructure.

Mount Rushmore National Memorial

The giant faces of George Washington, Thomas Jefferson, Theodore Roosevelt, and Abraham Lincoln gaze out over the Black Hills of South Dakota. They look serene, thoughtful, even kindly. A hint of sorrow shows in Lincoln's eyes. The faces appear to be endlessly watching for something.

Mount Rushmore Memorial commemorates four great American presidents. Located 25 miles southwest of Rapid City, South Dakota, the memorial consists of the heads of the presidents carved into the granite outcropping of the mountain. Each president represents ideals and events in the history of the United States: Washington symbolizes the nation's founding; Jefferson, its philosophy; Lincoln, its unity; and Roosevelt, its expansion.

The figures on Mount Rushmore, which rises 5,725 feet above sea level, are larger than any other sculpture in the world. The huge portraits can be seen from more than 60 miles away. Each head—from chin to forehead—is 60 feet high. If fully carved, each man would be 465 feet tall.

Doane Robinson, director of the South Dakota Historical Society, first conceived the idea of a gigantic mountain carving in 1923. He invited Gutzon Borglum, an American sculptor famous for his monumental works, to come to South Dakota and discuss the project. Borglum, who had had experience carving on mountainsides, was enthusiastic. After touring the area, he decided that Mount Rushmore would be the perfect site for the sculpture. It had a crown of even-grained granite that faced the sun for most of the day. Instead of featuring heroes of the Old West—which had been Robinson's original idea—Borglum suggested that the sculpture feature the four American presidents. It would be, as Borglum said, a "shrine to democracy."

Plans for the Mount Rushmore Memorial were approved by an act of Congress in 1925, and work began in 1927. It continued, with lapses, for the next 14 years. Since the Great Depression was in progress, most of the delays were due to funding problems. The final cost of the memorial was just under $1 million, a small sum by today's standards. About 80 percent of the money came from the federal government, with the rest coming from private donations—including the pennies of schoolchildren.

Besides designing the memorial, Borglum supervised its construction. Workers used dynamite to alter the mountain—granite debris can still be seen at the base. Models one-twelfth the size of the granite heads were lifted to the top of the mountain and used to guide measurements. Craftsmen on scaffolds cut out the eyes, noses, mouths, and other presidential features with compressed-air drills.

Borglum's original design called for the figures to be carved to the waist. For one reason and another, these plans—along with plans for an inscription, a stairway from the base of the mountain to the top, and a museum tunneled from behind the monument—gave way to the main project of carving the heads.

The head of Washington was the first to be completed. It was dedicated on July 4, 1930. The other heads were unveiled in 1937 and 1939. Borglum arranged a patriotic celebration for the unveiling of each sculpture. Military bands played, presidents gave speeches, and Air Force planes flew overhead.

The sculptor, however, was not able to arrange the formal dedication of the memorial. On March 6, 1941, Borglum died of a heart attack at the age of 74. His son Lincoln spent a few more months adding finishing touches—mainly to Washington's lapel—and the monument was declared completed. Because of the sculptor's death and because of the Japanese bombing of Pearl Harbor on December 7, 1941, plans for the dedication were interrupted. They were not resumed until half a century later. On July 4, 1991, Mount Rushmore was officially dedicated with an extravaganza Borglum would have loved.

Now more than 50 years old, the giant faces appear somewhat weathered. There's a crack across the bridge of Lincoln's nose, and another one through Roosevelt's forehead. Nevertheless, the sculptures should endure for centuries. In preparation for the Golden Anniversary celebration, geologists conducted a highly technical survey of the monument and found it to be structurally sound.

In designing Mount Rushmore, Borglum said, "I want to create a monument so inspiring that people from all over America will be drawn to come and look and go home better citizens." And, indeed, people from the United States and from all over the world—more than 2 million per year—have come to view the memorial. In the early 1990s, a $40 million fund-raising campaign was launched to upgrade facilities for a growing number of visitors. Perhaps as Washington, Jefferson, Roosevelt, and Lincoln gaze steadily ahead, they are watching to see how these visitors will carry out the nation's ideals.

Once the destination has opened to tourists, people will be needed to staff the tourist facilities. In developing countries, the local population is rarely large enough to provide the necessary labor force. Workers must therefore be brought in from outside. The migrant workers will require housing, perhaps new schools for their children, and other amenities.

A rapid influx of foreign workers can cause serious social problems. The new workers may find it difficult to fit into the community. The local residents may resent their presence and actively discriminate against the newcomers.

Another negative implication of destination development is the problem of what to do with construction workers when the development boom is over. Some of the migrant workers may stay on to work in the tourist facilities, but others will have to return home. People who worked steadily during the construction phase may be faced with unemployment. A similar problem arises in destinations where tourism is strictly seasonal. What happens to the local workers during the off-season? Some may return to traditional economic activities—such as farming or fishing—but this in turn can lead to other types of social strain.

Changing Employment Patterns. Many local residents may find their social status in the community altered when they obtain tourism-related employment. Again, there are both positive and negative effects.

Women may enter the job market for the first time when tourism development occurs. On the positive side, this may contribute to increased family income, greater self-esteem for the women, and expanded awareness of the outside world. But it can also disrupt the existing social structure particularly in countries where men have traditionally been the only wage earners. A husband may have difficulty dealing with the fact that his wife can earn more money working in a tourist hotel than he can earn from fishing or farming. Divorce rates may rise, as may incidents of juvenile delinquency. Women working in tourist-oriented jobs may decide to postpone marriage and childbearing.

Traditional relationships between the young and the old may change as young people enter the tourism employment marketplace. Established local industries, such as agriculture and fishing, may suffer as workers are drawn toward tourism. A farmer, for example, might decide that there's a better living to be made as a cook's assistant in a restaurant than by scratching out an existence from a rocky field. Or a young man whose father and grandfather both fished for a living may decide that instead of following the family tradition he'd rather wait tables, and earn more money, at a dockside tourist restaurant.

Increased Income. The increase in income that employment in tourism allows can have a radical effect on the lifestyles of local residents. They will be able to afford consumer goods, many of them imported, that were previously beyond their purchasing power. The change in lifestyle may also lead to demands for better housing and recreational facilities, as well as to changes in dress and eating habits. People who once worked the land or the sea for their living may readily come to appreciate the benefits of a steady paycheck. If tourists stop coming to the destination, however, local residents will have to either return to their traditional occupations—and spartan lifestyle—or leave the community. In either case, the social consequences can be serious.

Rising Property Values. Destination development can also affect local property values. If there is an increased demand for land for tourist facilities, property values can rise dramatically. Local buyers may be priced out of the market. Local renters may find that they have no place to live if low-priced rental properties are demolished to make way for luxury hotels. Small businesses may be forced to close if they can no longer afford to pay the increased rents.

Such effects can be particularly devastating in communities that have large numbers of fixed-income senior citizens or low-income families. When gambling was legalized in Atlantic City, for example, working-class residents were faced with the choice of paying high rents or moving out of the area.

The Demonstration Effect. It is only natural that local residents will want to imitate the consumption patterns of affluent tourists they've been exposed to. They will want to wear designer clothes and watches, listen to Sony Walkmans, watch color television, play golf, go skiing, and so forth. When local people try to adopt practices from tourists, what is known as the *demonstration effect* results. In some ways, the demonstration effect can have a positive influence. It encourages local people to work and save for the things they want. More commonly, though, it has an adverse effect. Local residents come to realize that, even with their increased income, they cannot afford to live like the tourists. The inevitable result is a feeling of envy or resentment toward affluent visitors.

Resentment tends to be most pronounced in those destinations where tourism is the community's main source of income. As you read earlier, tourists are typically welcomed in the early stages of development. But by late maturity, when all activities have become oriented to accommodating tourist demand, the limits of local tolerance have usually been reached. By this stage, the mere physical presence of large numbers of tourists may be a cause of resentment. Congestion may have become a problem and local residents are now tired of sharing overcrowded facilities and overtaxed services with visitors. They may see vacationers living in comfort and luxury while their basic needs go unmet. An extreme example of this clash between affluence and poverty occurred in the Ivory Coast. There, a resort hotel was using

150 gallons of water per room per day, while local villagers did not yet have running water in their homes.

Foreign ownership and employment is a further cause of resentment. This is especially true when foreign employees occupy managerial positions and earn high salaries, while the low-paid menial jobs are left to local residents. Additional anger may stem from the perception that tourists cause a decline in moral standards. The incidence of crime, gambling, and prostitution has been known to increase in areas that become tourist destinations.

Cultural Effects

An influx of tourists from other cultures can have profound effects on a local culture. One of the most common consequences of tourism is that the host community adopts the social and cultural values of the visiting tourists. Because most people who can afford to travel abroad are from the United States, Canada, and Western Europe, it is primarily Western values that are spread throughout the world. Critics argue that, as a result, many local cultures are in danger of disappearing as the world becomes westernized. Others contend that the adoption process works both ways. Local residents may adopt tourist values, but at the same time tourists also adopt the values of the countries that they visit. (This is known as *cross-adoption.*) American interest in foreign cuisine, for example, has in part resulted from American

tourists who enjoyed eating local foods while abroad.

There is also some disagreement about the effects that tourism development can have on traditional arts and crafts. Some people say that local artistic standards suffer when cheap reproductions of native crafts are mass-produced for tourist consumption. They also claim that commercialization has a negative effect on local religious and social customs. In some places, for example, ceremonial dances that were once performed for religious purposes are now staged to entertain tourists.

On the positive side, tourism has been credited with helping traditional arts and crafts to survive. There is ample evidence to support this claim. In the southwestern United States, for example, tourist exposure to native cultures has greatly increased the demand for Indian arts and crafts, such as pottery, jewelry, and weaves. Indians of the Southwest have resisted the temptation to turn out mass-produced imitations, so the quality of the products has remained high. A similar picture emerges in parts of Canada, where tourist demands for souvenirs have perpetuated the Eskimo craft of soapstone carving.

Tourism not only helps sustain native art forms but may also contribute to ethnic preservation. For example, the assimilation of the Cajun population of Louisiana into the general population began in the 1930s, and by the 1950s this group had almost lost its unique identity. But then Cajun Louisiana was developed as a tourist destination. Local residents began to take pride in their cultural origins. Tourists from all over the nation expressed

Illus. 8-5 *In the southwestern United States, tourism has helped Native American arts and crafts survive.*
Source: *Mimi Forsyth/Monkmeyer Press Photo Service*

their appreciation for the hot, spicy Cajun food and the distinctive Cajun music, and took an interest in the Creole language. In this way, tourism helped the Cajuns preserve their cultural heritage and retain a separate ethnic identity. (Incidentally, the Cajuns present a good example of the cross-adoption discussed earlier. Local residents adopt the values of visitors from other parts of North America, while the tourists adopt certain Cajun habits, as evidenced by the popularity of Cajun-style foods in restaurants throughout the United States.)

An influx of tourists from different cultures can, unfortunately, have less desirable consequences. The Pennsylvania Amish had lived in quiet obscurity for hundreds of years until they were "discovered" as a tourist attraction. The Amish people had no desire to make a profit from tourism. They just wanted to be left in peace. Others, however, had different ideas. They built motels, restaurants, golf courses, souvenir shops, and gas stations to cater to the growing bands of tourists. Today, the Amish are subjected to curious stares from busloads of visitors. They are photographed like freaks in a sideshow. Tourism has disrupted their way of life.

To end this discussion of the cultural effects of tourism on a positive note, the development of a destination can often pay cultural dividends to the residents of the host community. Entertainment and recreational facilities developed for incoming tourists—including cinemas and theaters, cultural centers, sports stadiums, golf courses, and ski slopes—may also be used by the local population. Local residents can enjoy cultural and sporting experiences that were previously unavailable. In the United States, events such as the Spoleto Music Festival in Charleston, South Carolina, the Telluride Film Festival in Colorado, and the Tanglewood Summer Concert series in Lenox, Massachusetts, not only provide a tremendous tourist attraction, but also enhance the cultural lives of the local population.

The Environmental Impact of Destination Development

One final aspect of destination development is the impact on the host environment. This is easier to assess than the cultural effects. Measurements can be taken of air, water, and soil quality. Traffic patterns can be charted. The local vegetation and wildlife can be studied and protected if necessary. Property values can be assessed.

In both developed and underdeveloped countries, the emphasis must be on a controlled rate of development to minimize harmful effects on the natural environment. Farsighted planning can reduce conflicts over land use that can arise between local residents and developers. If a destination is developed too rapidly, irreparable damage may be done. In developed countries, destination development can strain the existing infrastructure, causing

pollution and overcrowding. Even natural resources may be threatened. In certain national parks, for example, tourist traffic congestion and littering are constant problems. If the natural beauty of a site is ruined by commercialization and the local lake is teaming with tourists and soda cans, the residents will naturally resent the tourist intrusion. However attractive it seems to bring tourists to a destination, developers must always bear in mind the needs and feelings of the local people.

There are, however, some positive environmental impacts of destination development. In an underdeveloped area, destination development can upgrade an inadequate infrastructure. Development leads to improved water supplies, better sewage facilities, and better roads. In Africa, some wildlife species have been saved from extinction by conservation efforts. Governments realized that if they allowed native animals to die out, they would lose a natural resource that attracted thousands of tourists to their countries. Developers in other countries have enhanced the natural beauty of certain destinations by devoting part of their investment capital to conservation projects. As we have seen time and time again throughout this chapter, planning is the all-important factor in the development of a destination for tourism.

Check Your Product Knowledge

1. How do employment patterns change as a result of destination development?
2. What is the *demonstration effect*?
3. What are two positive effects of destination development on local culture? What are two negative effects?
4. How does the environmental impact of destination development differ between developed and underdeveloped countries?

CAREER OPPORTUNITIES

If you are thinking of a career in the tourism industry, you may not have considered the opportunities that are available in the field of destination development. As you learned in this chapter, destination development is a complex process that requires the creative energies of a wide range of experts. Most positions carry a great deal of responsibility and require a high level of education. Many workers in destination development careers work on a consulting basis.

Careers in destination development offer an area of tourism that entails more than scheduling, ticketing, and financing. While these careers may not bring the usual "perks" of the travel industry, they may ultimately be the careers most important to the future of tourism. Representative careers include planner, market researcher, architect, interior designer, landscape architect, anthropologist, and sociologist.

Planner

The first step in destination development is planning. A planner is responsible for examining each stage of development, taking into account data from market researchers, land-use specialists, architects, and others, and attempting to gauge the impact of that data.

The planner develops a master plan for the destination and analyzes the means to finance it. He or she must make sure that there is sufficient funding available at each stage of the plan.

Market Researcher

Market researchers help a developer decide if there is a market for the planned destination. They work for private developers and for tourist organizations. Most state tourist organizations, for example, have research staffs that help them spot market trends and aid in development planning.

Architect/Interior Designer/ Landscape Architect

Once it has been determined that there is a market for the destination, and once funding has been approved, architects, interior designers, and landscape architects can begin to submit blueprints for the development. In the case of a resort, for example, the architect will be responsible for the design of all the buildings in the complex. He or she may choose a common theme and try to blend the buildings into the natural environment. The interior designer designs the interior of individual buildings, choosing furnishings and other fixtures. The landscape architect is responsible for the design of the grounds around the hotels, restaurants, and other tourist facilities. He or she may add lawns, trees, and bushes to make the site more attractive, and design walkways and access roads.

The nature of the work means that architects, interior designers, and landscape architects must usually work together at each stage of development.

Sociologists and Anthropologists

Because the development of a tourist destination can have such tremendous social and cultural consequences, it is imperative that sociologists and anthropologists be consulted to assess this impact and, especially, to suggest ways in which negative outcomes can be minimized. Sociologists are especially helpful in assessing the effects of tourism on developed areas. Anthropologists, on the other hand, usually study tourism's impact on destinations in undeveloped areas.

While planning and research takes much of the guesswork out of development, sociology and anthropology, in a sense, put some back. Statistics might show, for example, that resort development in a Third World country is bringing economic prosperity to a local ethnic group. Sociologists and anthropologists, on the other hand, may show that the price paid in social conflict for that economic prosperity is too high to justify further development.

The earlier that social scientists are engaged in the planning process, the better the chances for successful destination development with little negative effect on the local population.

Summary

- A destination is a location that travelers choose to visit and where they spend time.
- People choose different destinations according to their motivations for travel. Motivators include recreation, culture, health, friends and relatives, and business.
- The five main steps in the planning stage of destination development are market analysis, site assessment, financial studies, environmental impact studies, and social impact studies.
- National, state, and local tourism organizations promote travel to individual countries and regions. They are also involved in the planning process.
- Destinations can rise and fall in popularity. The product life cycle theory identifies four stages of destination development: inception, growth, maturity, decline.
- Political changes, the loss of natural resources, and the growth of rival destinations can contribute to a destination's decline in popularity.
- Economic benefits of destination development include employment, income, and tax revenue.
- Tourist dollars are respent several times within a local community (the multiplier effect).
- Tourist dollars flow out of the local economy when imported goods and services are purchased (leakage).
- Destination development is an instrument for social change. It is the cause of population growth, changing employment patterns, and increased levels of income in the destination developed.
- The presence of affluent tourists can cause resentment on the part of the host community.

■ Destination development can serve to revitalize cultural traditions, but it can also put stresses on local culture.

■ Negative environmental effects of destination development can be minimized with careful planning.

Key Terms

destination
infrastructure
superstructure
carrying capacity
product life cycle
direct spending
indirect spending
tourism multiplier
leakage
demonstration effect
cross-adoption

What Do You Think?

1. Of the nine motivators for travel listed in this chapter, which do you think are likely to become more important? Which are likely to become less important? Why? Can you think of any other motivators that are likely to develop?

2. What destinations in your area would appeal to people who travel for culture? Education? Events? Health?

3. Market analysts study travel trends and travel preferences. What trends and preferences have emerged in the last two or three years? What trends do you think are likely to develop in the next few years?

4. If you were asked to plan a new tourist destination for your area, what sort of destination would you choose? How would you prepare local residents for this development?

5. What are the advantages of having multinational corporations develop tourist destinations in underdeveloped countries? What are the disadvantages?

Dealing with Product

Casino gambling is among the most controversial categories of tourism development. Those who favor casino gambling argue that it will generate millions of dollars in revenues, wages, and taxes. The opponents of casino gambling are equally convinced that the costs to society are far greater than the gains.

What is the casino gambling product? How might this product affect other travel and tourism products? What do you think the economic, social, and environmental impacts would be if Yourtown voted to approve casino gambling? Are you in favor of casino gambling or do you oppose it? Why?

Dealing with People

You are the Vice President of North American Operations for a multinational tourism development company with headquarters in Japan. Your firm has successfully developed resorts in Africa and Europe, and you are in charge of the first project in the United States.

Your company has been buying up farmland and forests for several months, and you are now ready to announce your plans to build a vast theme park and resort in Apple Valley. At tonight's open meeting of the local town council, you are going to present Phase One of your plan and explain to the community how tourism will help the economy. You will probably have a lot of hard questions to answer. The local paper has learned of your plans and today's headline charges: "FOREIGNERS BUY UP ALL OF APPLE VALLEY!!"

What can you tell the good citizens of Apple Valley? Are their worst fears justified? How will a huge theme park and resort affect this sleepy rural community? As director of this project, what steps can you take to ensure that you and your guests will be welcome?

Name _____

WORKSHEET 8-1   STATE TRAVEL ORGANIZATIONS

What does your state do to promote itself as a tourist destination? Obtain promotional material from your state travel organization and look through newspapers and magazines. For each of the motivations for travel listed below, briefly describe the attractions your state offers.

Recreation

_____

_____

_____

Culture

_____

_____

_____

Nature

_____

_____

_____

Education

_____

_____

_____

Health

_____

_____

_____

_____

Religion

_____

_____

_____

_____

Events

_____

_____

_____

Business

_____

_____

Can you think of any attractions in your state that are not promoted but should be?

_____

_____

_____

WORKSHEET 8-2   CREATING DESTINATIONS

What kinds of destinations not currently available do you think would be valuable to society or profitable to the travel industry? Create and describe one destination for each of the categories listed below. Locate your destination anywhere in the world. Explain your choices.

A museum

_____

_____

_____

_____

A shopping mall

_____

_____

_____

A theme park

_____

_____

_____

_____

A model culture or restoration

_____

_____

_____

A resort

_____

_____

_____

_____

A historical monument

_____

_____

_____

_____

Other

_____

_____

_____

Name _____

WORKSHEET 8-3   CARRYING CAPACITY

Carrying capacity refers to the amount of tourism a destination can handle without negative effects. In each of the situations described below, identify which of the three kinds of carrying capacity (economic, physical, or social) are being exceeded. Then suggest ways the problems can be alleviated.

1. The desert surrounding a small Arizona town has become a popular place to ride off-the-road vehicles and "dirt" motorcycles. The traffic is destroying plants and animals, disrupting breeding cycles, and scaring wildlife out of the area. Conservation groups and local residents are concerned about the irreparable damage being done, but businesspeople do not want to lose the income generated by the riders.

   _____

   _____

   _____

2. A beautiful lake in New Hampshire has been a summer vacation spot for more than 200 years. It formerly consisted of small individually owned cottages, but in the past decade several time-sharing condominiums and a large high-rise luxury hotel have been built. Chic boutiques and upscale interior design stores are driving the long-standing small businesses out of town. Business and residential rents and property taxes have skyrocketed. The new-growth concerns generally bring their own employees, so local employment has not risen. The locals bitterly resent what is happening.

   _____

   _____

   _____

3. A Texas port city on the Gulf of Mexico has become a popular tourist destination. Pleasure craft are crowding out the fishing boats that have traditionally used the public landing and harbor facilities. Waterfront property is so valuable for tourist-related purposes that some fish buyers and commercial marinas are selling. Fishermen, the businesses that support them (for example, marine supply, boat repair), and businesses that depend on them (fish processing, fish markets) are furious and getting desperate.

   _____

   _____

   _____

4. A small town on Puget Sound has become a favorite weekend and summer retreat for Seattle residents, who have bought second homes or rent property for the summer. From Friday night to Sunday night, the town is crowded and noisy. Year-round residents have to wait in line to get into restaurants and movies. New bars and a dance club have opened to entertain the big-city visitors. Drinking and drug use have increased among resident youths, and locals blame the influence of the visitors. Even some of the visitors are beginning to criticize the new honky-tonk atmosphere.

   _____

   _____

   _____

WORKSHEET 8-4   IMPACT OF DESTINATIONS

Describe the possible positive and negative socioeconomic, cultural, or environmental impacts on the local population of the following destination developments.

DEVELOPMENT	POSITIVE IMPACT	NEGATIVE IMPACT
1. A gambling casino on an Indian reservation in a state where gambling was recently legalized		
2. A convention center complex in the inner city of a major urban area in the United States		
3. A luxury hotel on the tropical island of Lombok, where fishing is the traditional way of life		
4. A wildlife preserve in Kenya		

"He that travels much knows much."
—Thomas Fuller

Objectives

When you have completed this chapter, you should be able to:

- Explain the difference between public and commercial recreation and leisure systems.
- Describe the national park system and list some of the facilities offered by national parks.
- Give examples of national forests, state parks, and local parks.
- Describe the nature and function of public museums, zoos, aquariums, fairs, and festivals.

- Give examples of public recreation facilities in other countries.
- List and describe the kinds of facilities provided by the commercial recreation sector.
- Explain how the travel industry packages and sells recreation.
- List career opportunities in public and commercial recreation and leisure systems.

Leisure is the time that people use to do the things they want to do rather than the things they have to do. For most people, leisure time includes evenings, weekends, and vacations. People need leisure time in order to add pleasure to their lives and to refresh their minds and bodies.

The activities that people pursue in their leisure time are referred to as their recreation. *Recreation* can take many forms. It can be active or passive; close to home or far away; exciting or relaxing; inexpensive or costly. Recreation often involves attractions or events. *Attractions* are either natural or constructed. Examples of natural attractions are the Grand Canyon, the seashore, lakes, and forests. Examples of constructed attractions are the Great Wall of China and the Eiffel Tower. *Events* range from one-time occurrences, such as a special rock concert or boxing match, to regularly scheduled occurrences, such as the Super Bowl or the Academy Awards.

Attractions and events are the magnets that draw people to participate in recreational activities. In general, the recreation business can be divided into two broad categories: one operated by the public sector, and the other provided by commercial organizations. Between them, they represent a major sector of the travel industry.

TYPES OF RECREATION SYSTEMS

You might spend your leisure time at home reading a book or working in your garden. On the other hand, you might go to a recreational facility or attend an event sponsored by public or commercial recreation systems.

Public Recreation Systems

The *public recreation system* refers to recreational opportunities operated by federal, state, and local governments or by nonprofit organizations. Parks, museums, zoos, fairs, and festivals are examples of facilities and events financed by the public sector. Some type of legislation sets up the facility and establishes guidelines for its use. Because they are funded by tax dollars, public recreational facilities are generally free or charge nominal entrance or user fees.

Public recreation facilities do not exist to make money. In fact, their primary purpose may not even be to provide recreation. Many public recreation facilities exist to preserve the natural and historical resources of the country. For example, the main function of most national parks is to preserve the beauty of a wilderness area. The provision of opportunities for hiking, horseback riding, and picnicking is a secondary benefit.

Commercial Recreation Systems

The *commercial recreational system* refers to privately owned small businesses or large corporations that create products, services, and facilities for recreational use. The commercial sector exists to make a profit. Entrepreneurs invest money in recreational outlets such as theme parks, shopping malls, casinos, and racetracks. To attract and retain paying customers, businesses must provide enjoyable recreational experiences and continually maintain or upgrade their facilities.

Public and commercial recreation and leisure systems are not divided into distinct segments. In some cases, they overlap. Both the public and private sectors, for example, provide golf courses. In other cases, they are interdependent. Private businesses operate the cabins, lodges, and other accommodations that enable people to visit national forests. These private businesses are known as *concessions*. And, in still other cases, the public and private sectors work together. In Hannibal, Missouri, the city government, nonprofit organizations, and private businesses teamed up to preserve and promote historic sites and attractions related to Mark Twain. Together, they provide a recreational experience that would not have been possible without such cooperation.

Recreation and the Travel Industry

Public and commercial recreation and leisure systems provide attractions that induce people to travel during their leisure time. The travel industry builds tour packages based on skiing, shopping, watching sports events, theatergoing, and many other recreational opportunities. Public and commercial systems provide additional recreational opportunities once travelers have reached their destinations. For example, people who travel to Las Vegas for gambling can also enjoy nightclub entertainment, take a tour of Hoover Dam, or play a game of tennis.

Public and commercial recreation and leisure systems generate millions of tourist dollars and employ thousands of people.

Check Your Product Knowledge

1. What is leisure? What is recreation?
2. What is the difference between public and commercial recreation?
3. What is the relationship between the travel industry and the recreation and leisure systems?

THE PUBLIC RECREATION AND LEISURE SYSTEM

The United States has a vast and growing array of public facilities that entertain and provide recreation for millions of people every year. These facilities offer a wide range of activities that cater to many interests and tastes. First among these facilities, in scope, is the national park system. Comprising parks, battlefields, monuments, historic sites, recreation areas, and seashores, the national park system totals almost 125,000 square miles—the size of Iowa and Oklahoma combined. The national forests add another 298,000 square miles to the recreational resources of the United States. State parks and forests add still more. National, state, and local museums are permanent showcases of art, science, history, and culture. Government-supported zoos and aquariums have introduced generations of visitors to the animals and sea creatures of the world. Public festivals and fairs occur seasonally to commemorate significant events and to exhibit agricultural or trade products, or arts and crafts.

National Parks

In 1872, Congress voted to make Yellowstone the country's first national park as a way of ensuring the preservation of the region's spectacular natural beauty for future generations. In subsequent years, other areas of publicly owned land were similarly converted into national parks: Yosemite and Sequoia in 1890; Mount Ranier in 1899; Crater Lake in 1902; Glacier in 1910; and in 1919, the first eastern park area, Acadia, on the coast of Maine. The concept of national parks widened to include not only the conservation of natural wonders but also the preservation

Illus. 9-1 *America's national park system occupies 125,000 square miles and offers a variety of recreational activities.*
Source: *Mimi Forsyth/Monkmeyer Press Photo Service*

of historic and cultural sites. By 1916, Congress had created 37 parks and monuments and placed them under the administration of the National Park Service, a new agency in the Department of the Interior.

Today, the National Park Service is responsible for administering more than 350 separate sites. The park system includes so many different kinds of parks that Congress and the National Park Service now classify them according to functions and purposes. The different kinds of national parks are listed and described in Table 9-1.

Park Facilities. The kinds of facilities offered in a national park vary widely depending on the location and nature of the park. Some large or remote parks, such as Yosemite, offer hotels, cabins, and campgrounds as well as service stations, general stores, gift shops, and restaurants. Sites located in or near cities or major highways may offer only a visitors center and gift shop, since food and accommodations are readily available nearby.

Visitors usually have to pay a small entry fee or camping fee at each park. Campsites at the largest and most popular parks have to be reserved. Some parks, such as Yosemite and Grand Canyon, are part of a computer reservations system that enables visitors to reserve accommodations or campsites through Ticketron, by phone, or by mail. In other cases, reservations must be made directly with the parks, usually by mail.

Depending on their location and climate, the national parks offer a wide variety of recreational possibilities, including hiking, swimming, boating, fishing, horseback riding, skiing, bicycling, and scuba diving.

National parks have paved roads, scenic overlooks, and, in some cases, shuttle bus service to take visitors from one site to another. One of the functions of the park service is *interpretation*. The term refers to the process of educating, informing, and even entertaining visitors through the use of marked trails, signs, demonstrations, lectures, pictures, and so on. The park service is committed to providing facilities for physically handicapped people. Several parks have ramps and paths for people in wheelchairs. Some have tactile exhibits, audio tapes, and Braille and large-type signs for visually impaired people, as well as captioned films and slides, sign-language interpreters, and written materials for the hearing impaired.

Modern Problems. In 1990, almost 260 million people visited the nation's parks. That figure compares with about 150 million in 1971. The number of visitors to na-

Type	Characteristics	Examples
National Parks	Usually cover a wide area, contain various types of natural resources and sufficient land or water to protect those resources.	Grand Canyon; Yellowstone; Everglades (Florida)
National Mounuments	Usually smaller parks intended to preserve a resource of national significance.	Statue of Liberty; Devils Tower (Wyoming)
National Preserves	Intended to protect swamps, forests, wetlands, and other undeveloped natural resources.	Glacier Bay (Alaska); Big Thicket (Texas)
National Seashores	Intended to protect fragile ecologies of shoreline areas and to provide recreational opportunities.	Cape Cod (Massachusetts); Indiana Dunes
National Rivers and Riverways	Parks that border free-flowing rivers.	Ozark National Scenic Riverways (Missouri)
National Historic Parks	Military parks, battlefields, monuments, and other historic sites.	Valley Forge (Pennsylvania)
National Memorials	Commemorative sites and less-significant historic sites.	Mount Rushmore (South Dakota)
National Parkways	Schenic areas along certain highways.	Blue Ridge Parkway (Virginia and North Carolina)
National Recreational Areas	Parks surrounding reservoirs at federally built dams.	Cuyahoga Valley (Ohio)

Table 9-1 United States National Parks

tional parks is expected to grow, reaching an estimated 450-500 million people by the year 2010 (see Figure 9-1). Since the 1970s, park managers, naturalists, environmentalists, and legislators have been seriously addressing the problems of pollution, vandalism, and environmental stress that such heavy use has caused. Should the parks be preserved primarily as wilderness sanctuaries or, in response to demands for new recreational uses, should they be allowed to become public playgrounds? In an attempt to balance the two objectives, the park service is experimenting with programs to restrict the number of visitors, to encourage off-peak seasonal use, and to promote patronage of some of the lesser-known parks, such as Voyagers National Park in Minnesota and Channel Islands National Park in California.

National Forests

When Europeans first arrived in North America, the continent's forests seemed inexhaustible. But by the late 1800s, many forests had been destroyed, and others had been purchased by lumber and mining companies, railroads, and land speculators, who chopped down trees by the thousands.

To save precious forestlands, the United States government established the first national forests, Shoshone and Teton, in 1891, 19 years after Yellowstone was designated the first national park. The Forest Service, part of the Department of Agriculture, is charged with preserving the nation's forests, as well as grasslands and wilderness areas. The largest and the greatest number of national forests are in the West—in Oregon, California, Washington, Utah, Montana, Idaho, and Colorado. These states were settled later than the eastern half of the United States, and thousands of acres of virgin forests were still publicly owned when the government started to set aside areas of land as national forests.

In addition to conserving woodlands, national forests provide a great many recreational opportunities. Visitors to national forests can swim, boat, fish, hunt, hike, ride horses, climb mountains, picnic, and sightsee. Many of the national forests in the West, the Northwest, and northern New England have ski trails and lodges. The Forest Service estimates that 263 million people visited the nation's 155 national forests in 1990. As with the national parks, some national forests are overused, causing the forest service to restrict the number of daily visitors.

Travelers will find a wide range of accommodations in national forests. Most have a hotel, lodge, or cabins, and campers can usually find campsites with toilets and running water. Forest service policy has always been to allot campsites on a first-come, first-served basis rather than to permit campers to reserve sites. Very few national forests have stores or restaurants, so visitors must travel to the nearest town for these facilities.

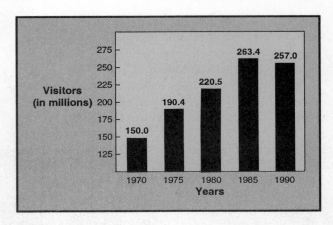

Figure 9-1 Number of Visitors to United States National Parks
Source: National Park Service

State and Local Parks

National parks and forests are not the only places in the United States where you can enjoy nature and outdoor recreation. Each state has its own network of state parks and forests, offering many of the same facilities as sites administered by the federal government. Almost every city has one or more public parks. Municipal swimming pools, tennis courts, and golf courses are common in urban and suburban areas.

State Parks. More than 4,500 state parks have been created for the same reasons as national parks—to conserve wilderness areas, preserve historic sites, and provide recreation and enjoyment. For example, a leisure traveler can enjoy miles of sandy beaches at Island Beach State Park on the New Jersey shore, explore old Indian campsites in Missouri's Cuivre River State Park, or visit Charles A. Lindbergh's boyhood home in Little Falls, Minnesota. New York State boasts the largest single state park in the country, Adirondack State Park, totaling more than 2 million acres. Nearly every state park offers camping, picnicking, and hiking facilities, and many also feature cabins or lodges.

Most states have a bureau of state parks, a state forestry board, and a fish and game commission to regulate hunting and fishing on state-owned lands. In addition, a state historical society may oversee the state's historical sites. Some popular state parks suffer from overcrowding and sometimes need to restrict daily visitors or campers.

Local Parks. To city dwellers hemmed in by concrete and steel, the open space and greenery of city parks offer a welcome relief. City parks have picnic areas and paths for walking, jogging, and bicycling. Many parks are equipped with tennis courts, basketball courts, and other sports facilities.

Some city parks have become tourist attractions in themselves. While Central Park in New York City is probably this country's most famous urban park, Fairmount Park in Philadelphia is the largest. Covering more than 4,000 acres, it includes a zoo, a theater, and an outdoor amphitheater. San Francisco's Golden Gate Park also attracts many tourists each year.

Museums

Museums are storehouses and display centers for objects considered worthy of preservation because of their artistic, historic, or scientific value. Almost anything, from prehistoric people to antique cars to television sets, can be the subject of a museum exhibit. Visiting museums is an important part of many travelers' itineraries.

Until the seventeenth and eighteenth centuries, the pleasures of collecting and displaying works of art and curiosities of nature were reserved for the upper classes. As education spread to the middle classes, the concept of public museums took root and grew rapidly. The first museum in North America, a natural history museum, opened in Charleston, South Carolina, in 1773.

At present, there are about 12,000 museums in the United States and Canada. Many are owned and operated by governments—federal, state, and local—and are largely financed by tax revenues. Others are owned by nonprofit associations. These museums may be supported by admission fees, private donations, government grants, and corporate contributions. Some museums, such as the Peabody Museum of Archaeology and Ethnology in Salem, Massachusetts, and the Fogg Art Museum at Harvard, are supported and operated by universities.

Illus. 9-2 *Almost any object with artistic, historic, or scientific value can be found in a museum.*
Source: © Elizabeth Chews/The Image Works

Of the many different types of museums, art museums and historical museums are the most popular. Table 9-2 contains a list and brief description of the major types of museums.

Type	Characteristics	Examples
Historical Museums	Collections or buildings of historical interest.	Buffalo Bill Historical Center (Wyoming)
Art Museums	Collections of paintings, sculpture, or other art.	National Gallery of Art (Washington, D.C.)
Science and Technology Museums	Illustrate principles, uses, and history of science.	Museum of Science and Industry (Illinois)
Natural History Museums	Show animals, fish, and primitive people in their natural habitats.	National Museum of Natural History (Washington, D.C.)
Encyclopedic or General Museums	Exhibit a wide range of objects.	Milwaukee Public Museum
Special-Interest Museums	Focus on a single subject.	The Baseball Hall of Fame (New York)
Children's Museums	Specialize in exhibits that explain how things work.	Nashville Children's Museum

Table 9-2 United States Museums

Today's museums are centers of learning and culture and places for recreation and entertainment. An art museum, for example, may offer courses and lectures in painting and art appreciation, provide trained guides to lecture on the artists whose works are represented and the art works that are on display, and rent tape players and cassettes to visitors. It might also hold film festivals, concerts, or any number of similar events to educate and entertain its patrons.

Zoos and Aquariums

The word *zoo* is short for zoological garden or park. A zoo is a place set aside to study and display wild animals. Aquariums are special zoos for fish and aquatic mammals, such as dolphins and seals. In effect, zoos and aquariums are special kinds of museums that collect and exhibit living creatures rather than inanimate artworks or artifacts. The various types of zoos and aquariums are shown in Table 9-3.

In many respects, zoos perform functions similar to museums and parks. They entertain and educate visitors and take care of the wildlife in their charge. Zoos also serve as centers for scientific research in all areas of zoology and biology, and many zoos are involved in efforts to rescue endangered species through carefully controlled breeding programs.

Like the earliest museums, the first zoos were set up by monarchs and nobles for their own amusement but were, in time, opened to the public. Other public zoos were founded by government agencies or associations of scientists and animal lovers.

Illus. 9-3 *Travelers can go to a zoo to observe the behavior of wild and exotic animals.*
Source: *Ron Garrison/San Diego Zoo*

Aquariums may seem like modern inventions, but they are not. The Sumerians built the first known aquariums 4,500 years ago, and the ancient Chinese bred ornamental goldfish in artificial ponds.

The first public aquariums were established in the 1850s in London and in New York City. These aquariums were constructed as long halls with exhibition tanks

Type	Characteristics	Examples
Municipal Zoos	Animals are maintained for public display, mostly in large natural enclosures.	Bronx Zoo (New York)
Wild Animal Parks	Animals roam freely in natural settings.	San Diego Wild Animal Park
Children's Zoos	Allow youngsters to see and touch various animals.	Philadelphia Children's Zoo
Inland Aquariums	Exhibit freshwater fish and animals.	John G. Shedd Aquarium (Chicago)
Oceanariums	Maintain sharks, whales, dolphins, and other marine life in saltwater tanks.	Sea World (Florida and California)

Table 9-3 United States Zoos and Aquariums

built into the walls. In 1938, Marineland, near St. Augustine, Florida, opened an outdoor aquarium featuring large tanks, ramps, and viewing windows. Visitors were able to observe large-size aquatic animals, such as sharks and porpoises, from above and below the waterline. Marineland proved so popular that many other aquariums around the country adopted the same basic design. Aquariums that specialize in saltwater animals are called *oceanariums*. Many oceanariums feature shows by trained seals and dolphins, along with other exhibits and educational programs.

Fairs and Festivals

Although closely identified with agriculture and commerce, fairs have also been a form of recreation since the Middle Ages. People enjoy strolling from exhibit to exhibit—comparing products, admiring handicrafts, or finding out about the latest technological innovation. To attract larger crowds, many fairs offer food and entertainment. World's fairs began when various industries wanted to display their products on an international scale.

The earliest festivals were usually gatherings for religious purposes, but people have found many other reasons to hold festivals. Recognizing the enormous economic benefits that festivals can bring to an area, both public and private sectors develop and promote them. Sometimes parades are part of a festival, or a parade can be the main event. The principal types of fairs and festivals are listed and described in Table 9-4.

Public Recreation and Leisure Systems Abroad

Every nation and continent has its own culture, history, climate, and natural resources, all of which determine the attractions that can be offered to leisure travelers. Nations with great natural beauty and pleasant climates emphasize sports and recreational opportunities. The islands of the Caribbean, for example, attract vacationers with sun, sandy beaches, and tropical waters. Countries with long histories, such as Greece, concentrate on preserving, displaying, and promoting the structures and artifacts of their national heritage.

The attitudes and values of a nation also play an important role in the kinds of attractions and facilities it develops or promotes. For example, Mexico and the nations of South America that were once European colonies have museums and archaeological sites that highlight the glories of their precolonial periods. And the conservation of wildlife and natural resources has become a priority in most parts of the world, so national parks and nature reserves can be found in many countries.

Type	Characteristics	Examples
Agricultural Fairs	Feature livestock and agricultural products, along with carnival midways and rides.	Iowa State Fair
Trade Fairs	Companies display latest developments or products in a particular industry.	Auto Show; Computer Fair
Historic Fairs	Recreate food and entertainment of great fairs of medieval and Renaissance Europe.	Renaissance Fairs
World's Fairs	Feature nation-by-nation exhibits of industry and culture.	1992 World's Fair in Seville, Spain
Festivals	Seasonal celebrations, cultural events, or commemorations.	Mardi Gras (New Orleans); Winter Carnival (St. Paul, Minnesota)
Parades	Marching bands, floats, and celebrities.	Rose Bowl (Pasadena, California); Mummers' Parade (Philadelphia)

Table 9-4 Fairs and Festivals

National Parks Around the World. The United States originated the national park concept, and the idea has since spread to more than 130 countries. In fact, the United States National Park Service has been very active in providing assistance to virtually every country with a national park system. Today, there are approximately 3,500 national parks or similarly protected areas established throughout the world.

The largest national park areas are located in North America (the United States and Canada) and Africa. Parks vary widely in the accommodations they offer travelers, and many are open only during certain seasons of the year. In Asia, for example, the parks may close during the summer monsoon season.

The national parks of Africa serve primarily as large game reserves. Two of the best known wildlife sanctuaries are Kruger National Park in the Transvaal, South Africa, and Nairobi National Park in Kenya. Even though most countries in Asia are densely populated, there are many national parks and wildlife sanctuaries. Perhaps the most famous is Fuji-Hakone-Izu National Park in Japan, where Mount Fuji is located.

Zoos Around the World. Zoos vary widely in the size and quality of their settings. Some zoos still follow the nineteenth-century model of small, square cages housing bored, lethargic animals. Other zoos have made an effort to create natural, open settings that are more pleasant for animals and onlookers alike. England's Regent's Park Zoo, which opened in 1931, was one of the first to use the concept of open surroundings and concealed bar-

riers to display its animals. The Basel Zoo in Switzerland pioneered efforts to make zoo habitats more like the natural surroundings of each species.

Some zoos are noted for the number and kinds of animals they contain. The Taronga Zoo, located just across the harbor from Sydney, Australia, has a collection of more than 5,000 animals and birds. The Stanley Park Zoo in Vancouver, British Columbia, is noted for its collection of polar bears and for an exceptional aquarium that displays some 9,000 freshwater and saltwater marine animals. On the outskirts of Tokyo, the Tama Zoological Park features an insect pavilion.

Museums Around the World. The history, resources, and culture of a region or a nation largely determine the kinds of museums that are developed there. Thus, nations such as Egypt and Israel have museums that feature treasures of antiquity. The Museum of Egyptian Antiquities in Cairo contains treasures from the tomb of King Tutankhamen, and the Israel Museum in Jerusalem displays the Dead Sea Scrolls.

Visitors on a tour of Europe can expect to spend a great deal of time in art and history museums, such as the National Gallery in London, the Louvre in Paris, and the Uffizi Gallery in Florence. The nations of Europe have even turned hundreds of castles and churches into museums.

The countries of Africa, Asia, and Latin America abound with anthropological and archaeological museums that celebrate their precolonial cultures and heritage. At the National Museum of Anthropology in Mexico City, visitors can view a vast collection of the art and artifacts of pre-Columbian Indians.

The museums of newer nations settled by northern Europeans, such as the United States and Australia, are more likely to emphasize art, science, natural history, and colonial history. The Australian Museum in Sydney, for example, focuses on the exotic animal and plant life of Australia and on the history and culture of the continent's aborigines.

Illus. 9-4 *Because many animals in Africa are threatened with extinction, the African government has established wildlife sanctuaries to protect the animals from poachers and to provide a natural habitat.*
Source: *Milt and Joan Mann*

Check Your Product Knowledge

1. For what reasons did the United States government begin creating national parks?
2. What is the major problem confronting national and state parks and forests?
3. List the three main functions of museums.
4. How do zoos and aquariums differ from other kinds of museums?
5. How do the attitudes and values of a nation's citizens influence the kinds of attractions it provides?

I.M. Pei

I.M. Pei is probably the most famous architect in the world, after Frank Lloyd Wright. Pei's graceful buildings dominate the skylines of cities throughout the world. Millions of people visit his museums, concert halls, hotels, shopping centers, and office buildings each year in cities as far removed as Dallas, Texas; Paris, France; and Beijing, China. His buildings are easily recognized by their geometric solutions and precise detail and execution.

I.M. (Ieoh Ming) Pei was born in Canton, China, in 1917. His father, a well-to-do banker, moved his family to Shanghai a few years later. As Pei grew up in Shanghai, he watched the city undergo a tremendous building boom. Inspired by watching the Shanghai builders, Pei decided to become a builder and architect. He came to the United States in 1935 and studied architecture at the Massachusetts Institute of Technology and Harvard University.

Pei was prevented from returning to China by World War II and the Chinese Communist revolution. He went to work for a major New York City developer where he was soon collaborating in the design of buildings such as the Mile High Center in Denver, the Roosevelt Field Shopping Center on Long Island, and the Kips Bay Apartments in Manhattan.

In 1954, Pei became a naturalized United States citizen. The following year he formed his own architectural firm, I.M. Pei & Associates, which later changed its name to I.M. Pei & Partners and in 1989 became Pei Cobb Freed & Partners. Pei has specialized not only in designing individual buildings but in urban development, the renewal of whole neighborhoods and areas within cities. He has designed low- and moderate-income housing projects, such as the Society Hill Towers in Philadelphia and the Erieview Plaza in Cleveland, Ohio.

It is his public buildings, however, that have made Pei famous. In 1964, while still relatively unknown, he was chosen to design the John F. Kennedy Memorial Library at Harvard University. His monumental design so pleased architectural critics that, a few years later, he was hired to design an addition to the National Gallery of Art in Washington, D.C. One problem that faced Pei with that project was how to connect the new building with the old one across a wide Washington street. Pei solved the problem by building an underground arcade and restaurant between the buildings. The restaurant was capped by a small street-level pyramid in the courtyard of the National Gallery.

Echoes of that earlier design are evident in Pei's controversial design for the renovation of the Louvre, the French National Museum, in Paris. Pei placed a modern, 71-foot-high glass pyramid in the center courtyard of the Louvre. The pyramid, surrounded by smaller pyramids, is the main entrance to an underground complex of offices, shops, restaurants, exhibition halls, parking garages, and storage areas below the museum.

While that phase of the renovation was under construction, Pei was criticized for his pyramid design. Critics felt that he was defacing the classic lines of the nineteenth-century Louvre with a gaudy, ultramodern addition. Once it was finished, however, Parisians loved it and the criticism died down. The pyramid's 600 floodlights light up the dark Louvre courtyard at night and brighten the whole center of Paris.

Pei has designed and built buildings in so many cities that it is hard to travel anywhere and not see one of his creations. In fact, in some cities, it is not necessary even to leave the airport. The pentagonal control towers now in use at many American airports are his design, as is the TWA Domestic Terminal (Formerly the National Airlines Terminal) at John F. Kennedy Airport in New York City.

Among his most famous buildings are the Morton H. Meyerson Symphony Center in Dallas, Texas, the Fragrant Hill Hotel in Beijing, China, The Bank of China Tower in Hong Kong, and the National Center for atmospheric Research in Boulder, Colorado. Recently, Pei was hired to design the Rock 'n' Roll Hall of Fame in Cleveland, Ohio.

Pei is often described as a pleasant, honest man who is a perfectionist when it comes to designing and constructing buildings. Through his work, he has left his own unique stamp on the world.

COMMERCIAL RECREATION

The commercial sector provides something for everyone. Theme parks, model cultures, restorations, special museums, and industrial tours educate as well as entertain. Millions of sports fans travel to large metropolitan areas to cheer their favorite professional teams. For those who prefer to be more active, the commercial sector offers ski resorts, white-water rafting, golf resorts, and many other recreational sports. Visitors can also enjoy recreational shopping in enormous megamalls. While at their destinations, travelers can view live entertainment in the form of concerts, opera, dance, and theater. Gambling casinos and racetracks are other attractions provided by the commercial sector.

Theme Parks

In 1955, Walt Disney opened Disneyland near Anaheim, California. Based on themes and characters from Disney movies, the park was designed to be an exciting environment for family entertainment. As the nation's first major theme park, Disneyland was an immediate success. It has inspired the development of many other theme parks across the country. In 1989, the top 40 theme parks en-

tertained 122 million visitors. Table 9-5 shows the top ten theme parks in the United States.

The Themes. Most tourist attractions have their roots in the natural or historical environment in which they are located. The theme park is an exception. By establishing a theme and then having all exhibits, rides, shops, and restaurants relate to it, the theme park creates its own environment. The visitor enters Disney's Fantasyland, for instance, through Sleeping Beauty's castle; meets Captain Hook, Cinderella, and Peter Pan on the streets; takes an aerial journey in Dumbo the Flying Elephant. Everything is familiar, comfortable, but exciting.

Themes derived from history, animal life, and cartoons have been particularly popular for theme parks. Some parks carry out a strong central theme. Busch Gardens—The Dark Continent (Tampa, Florida) revolves around an African theme. The three Sea World parks (Orlando; San Diego; and Aurora, Ohio) are devoted to marine life. Other parks can have a variety of themes. Rivertown, Wild Animal Safari, Oktoberfest, and Coney Island are theme areas at Kings Island in Cincinnati.

Characteristics of Theme Parks. Before the family automobile became commonplace, amusement parks were built at the end of a streetcar line. Their customers came primarily from the immediate community. They hopped

Rank	Park and Location	Estimated Attendance (in millions)
1	Walt Disney World's Magic Kingdom, EPCOT Center, Disney-MGM Studios Theme Park, Lake Buena Vista, Florida	28.5
2	Disneyland, Anaheim, California	12.9
3	Knott's Berry Farm, Buena Park, California	5.0
4	Universal Studios Hollywood, Universal City, California	4.6
5	Sea World of Florida, Orlando	3.8
6	Sea World of California, San Diego	3.2
7	King's Island, Kings Island, Ohio	3.2
8	Six Flags Magic Mountain, Valencia, California	3.1
9	Cedar Point, Sandusky, Ohio	3.1
10	Busch Gardens The Dark Continent, Tampa, Florida	3.0

Table 9-5 Top Ten United States Amusement/Theme Parks, 1990
Source: Amusement Business

on the streetcar, stayed a few hours at the park, and then took the streetcar home again. Today's theme parks, however, are located on the outskirts of major urban areas, cover vast tracts of land, and offer a wide range of recreational activities and events: roller coaster rides, theatrical performances, exhibits, tours, movies, and celebrity appearances, all of which can be entertaining and educational. People drive or fly for miles to get to these parks; they tend to stay longer and spend more money.

By advertising in newspapers and magazines and on national television, theme parks attempt to draw tourists from all over the country. Because a visit to a theme park is now likely to be part of a vacation trip—or the destination itself—hotels, restaurants, and other entertainment facilities have sprung up around theme parks to service the needs of travelers. The appearance of Disneyland, for instance, was followed by the construction of 7,000 hotel/motel rooms, a convention center, and an American League baseball park in Anaheim, California.

Theme parks are large-scale enterprises employing thousands of people and requiring millions of dollars in operating funds. Sophisticated computer technology is used to operate many of the rides and other attractions. Every detail is carefully managed. Grounds and restrooms are immaculate, and employees wear informal but spotlessly clean uniforms. At Disneyland, even the brass rails on the merry-go-round receive a daily polishing.

Variations on a Theme. In recent years, variations of the major theme parks have developed. Mini-theme parks, such as Sesame Place in Langhorne, Pennsylvania, are smaller entertainment facilities, primarily geared toward young children. At theme restaurants, such as Show-Biz Pizza Place, patrons play electronic games and watch animated shows while waiting for their food.

The most significant variation, however, is the participatory theme park. Rather than being passively strapped into a ride or seated in a theater, visitors actively participate in events such as grass skiing, Grand Prix racing on a miniature track, and kamikaze sliding into a pool that makes its own waves. At the Vernon Valley Action Park in McAfee, New Jersey—the largest action park in the United States—patrons drive military-style tanks around a pen and shoot tennis balls at other tanks. Participatory areas are now being added to the established theme parks.

Amusement Parks, Carnivals, and Circuses

In past generations, circuses, carnivals, and amusement parks were great places to spend a Saturday afternoon. In recent years, these old standbys have been overshadowed by theme parks, television spectaculars, and other more

Illus. 9-5 *Theme parks create their own environment, where visitors can enjoy exciting rides and exhibits.*
Source: Conklin/Monkmeyer Press Photo Service

trendy forms of entertainment. But circuses, carnivals, and amusement parks are still around and popular with young people and families.

Amusement Parks. Coney Island was established in the 1880s on six miles of beach in New York City. It became the model for the gaudy amusement parks of the twentieth century. In addition to the midway with its rides, freak shows, cotton candy, and penny arcade, traditional amusement parks had tables and benches for family picnics. Those with waterfront locations offered a beach for swimming.

Amusement parks typically charged a low admission fee, but for every ride or event there was an additional fee. (Theme park developers have reversed this concept, charging a high fee at the gate that includes all the rides and events inside.)

Because of the overwhelming popularity of theme parks, the number of amusement parks has decreased considerably over the years. Some of the most popular amusement parks, such as Elitch's Gardens and Lakeside Park in Denver and the Boardwalks in Santa Cruz, California, offer clean, modern, and safe facilities.

Carnivals. A carnival is a traveling amusement park. In the late 1890s, newly developed technology allowed entire midways—rides, refreshment and souvenir stands, and shows—to be transported from city to city. Today's carnivals are not as elaborate as earlier carnivals. They usually travel from small town to small town, setting up their rides in the parking lot of a shopping mall.

Colonial Williamsburg

Colonial Williamsburg is one of the most popular tourist destinations in the United States. It attracts more than 1 million visitors a year from every state in the union and from nearly every country in the world. What is Colonial Williamsburg and why is it so popular? In effect, it is a large, open-air history museum exhibiting colonial life in America.

Williamsburg was the capital of colonial Virginia from 1699 to 1780. During that period, it became a large, bustling town with many public buildings, shops, taverns, homes, and lodging houses. After 1780, when the capital of Virginia was moved to Richmond, Williamsburg became a quiet county seat and market town.

Williamsburg's history made it ideal for restoration and conversion into a historical museum. Because it remained a small town throughout the nineteenth century, dozens of its eighteenth-century buildings remained intact. In addition, as the eighteenth-century capital of Virginia, Williamsburg was the scene of several historic events.

Despite these factors, Williamsburg might well have been forgotten had it not been for the Rev. Dr. W. A. R. Goodwin, the rector of Williamsburg's Bruton Parish Church. Goodwin was struck by the many fine examples of eighteenth-century architecture still visible in the town as well as by its historical significance.

Goodwin dreamed of restoring Williamsburg to its eighteenth-century magnificence. In 1926, he approached John D. Rockefeller, Jr., the oil magnate. Rockefeller loved the idea, and over the next 30 years he devoted a considerable portion of his vast personal fortune as well as much of his time and energy to restoring Williamsburg as it had been in the eighteenth century.

Rockefeller hired a group of preservationists who set to work looking for deeds, letters, maps, and any other documents that could tell them what the town looked like and what life was like 150 years earlier. In the meantime, Rockefeller purchased the existing eighteenth-century buildings as well as the newer homes, shops, and other buildings from their owners. He then tore down the newer buildings and mapped out a 173-acre historic area to be restored.

The Colonial Williamsburg Foundation, established by Rockefeller, was able to salvage and restore 88 original buildings. The foundation also rebuilt 50 buildings that had been destroyed. These included the Governor's Palace, the Capitol, and the Public Hospital. The hospital had been the first American institution established for the care of the mentally ill.

Visitors to Williamsburg can observe dozens of specially trained employees, dressed in colonial garb, as they demonstrate colonial crafts, such as blacksmithing, candle-making, weaving, barrel-making, and printing. Other costumed employees act as jailers and storekeepers. Tourists can eat in restored taverns and buy reproductions of colonial-era goods in many shops.

Special events at Williamsburg vary according to the season. In the winter, Williamsburg stages an authentic colonial Christmas. In the summer, visitors can watch a costumed militia and fife and drum corps parade on the Williamsburg Commons.

Visitors to Williamsburg can also visit other nearby attractions. The Colonial Williamsburg Foundation operates an archaeological site, Wolstenholme Towne; a seventeenth-century English settlement; and Carter's Grove, an eighteenth-century plantation. Jamestown, site of the first permanent English settlement in North America, and Busch Gardens, a large amusement and theme park, are only a few miles away.

Travelers can choose from more than 9,000 hotel and motel rooms in the Williamsburg area. Colonial Williamsburg operates four hotels—the Williamsburg Inn, the Governor's Palace, the Motor House, and the Williamsburg Lodge. Visitors can also stay in a restored home or tavern right in the historic area.

Colonial Williamsburg is much more than just another tourist attraction. It is an important means of preserving our national heritage for future generations.

Circuses. With daring and skilled performers, trained animal acts, and clowns, circuses offer audiences a wonderful spectacle. In the golden age of the circus, about ten major circuses traveled the country, and the arrival of the circus was the major event of the summer. Today, Ringling Brothers and Barnum & Bailey Circus is the only major circus. But a number of small local circuses still delight children across the land.

Model Cultures and Restorations

In a *model culture* or restoration, visitors learn about the material culture (houses, vehicles, artifacts) and performing arts of a historical age or a different nation. Buildings have been constructed or restored so that they resemble an actual town, village, or fort. Costumed employees serve as guides and demonstrate the arts, crafts, and daily practices of the time or culture. Old Sturbridge, a reconstructed colonial village in Massachusetts, stages an authentic, old-fashioned Thanksgiving celebration every year.

Along with colonial towns and pioneer villages, towns of the Old West are popular restoration projects in the United States. One of these is Old Tucson, a replica of Tucson in the 1860s. With a saloon, jail, blacksmith shop, and general store, Old Tucson was originally built as a movie and television set, and visitors can still see western movies being filmed there. They can also watch a gunfight or take a ride in a stagecoach.

A well-known example of a model culture is the Polynesian Cultural Center. Located 40 miles north of Honolulu, it is one of Hawaii's most visited attractions. The center recreates the thatched-hut villages of Samoans, Tahitians, Fijians, Tongans, and other Pacific Island people who originally populated the Hawaiian Islands. The Church of Jesus Christ of Latter-day Saints (Mormons) built the village in 1963 in order to preserve the Polynesian culture, provide employment for Pacific Island students attending the Honolulu campus of Brigham Young University, and provide financial aid to BYU-Hawaii.

Museums

The commercial sector also operates museums. Most of these are small and devoted to one type of collection, such as dolls or automobiles.

Nostalgia for the golden age of the railroad has led to the creation of numerous railroad museums across the country. Railroad museums display passenger and freight locomotives, coaches, boxcars, cabooses, and other railroad paraphernalia. Trolleys are featured as well. Many of these museums also offer excursions on the old-time railroads. Indiana alone has six operating steam and electric railroads.

Sometimes a museum is the result of one person's special interest or collection. The Liberace Museum in Las Vegas, for example, exhibits the famous showman's jewelry collection, outlandish wardrobe, classic autos, and pianos.

Spectator Sports

Armed with peanuts, hot dogs, and soft drinks, more than 50 million professional baseball fans get out to the ballpark each year and root for their favorite team. Americans are avid sports spectators. They take delight in analyzing the skills of the players and second-guessing the coaches. Besides, spectator sports offer a wonderful way to vent emotions.

Along with baseball, the major spectator sports in the United States are basketball, football, hockey, boxing, tennis, golf, and racing (car, thoroughbred, harness, and greyhound). The most popular spectator sport in the United States is pari-mutuel racing at the track, which draws nearly 100 million people each year (see Table 9-6). The Olympic Games, featuring athletes from around the world, are the largest single spectator event.

Except for the Green Bay Packers, all professional sports teams are privately owned. To the owners, professional sports is a serious business in which they do everything possible to produce a winning team and keep the fans in the stands. In recent years, owners have applied a number of promotional devices to boost fan interest and attendance.

Spectator sports bring profits to the community as well as to the owners. As with other recreational events, people attending sporting events spend money for concessions, transportation, and parking. Many patronize local stores and restaurants before and after the event. Fans attending from out of town spend money on hotel accommodations and entertainment attractions. Amateur sporting events also bring profits. By hosting the 1980

Activity	Annual Attendance (in millions)
Pari-mutuel racing	96.4
Major league baseball	53.8
College football	35.6
College basketball	32.5
Professional football	17.0
Professional basketball	14.1
Professional hockey	12.4

Table 9-6 United States Spectator Sports Attendance

Source: Statistical Abstract of the United States, 1990

Winter Olympics, Lake Placid, New York, reestablished itself as a major winter resort. The 1996 Summer Olympics in Atlanta, Georgia, should have a major economic impact on that city.

Because of the economic impact of spectator sports, cities vie with each other to host major events such as the Super Bowl or National Collegiate Athletic Association (NCAA) championship games. They also compete to become the permanent home of a major-league franchise. To be a winner in this competition, a city must be able to offer a first-class facility—basketball arena, hockey rink, football stadium, or racetrack. In recent years, many cities have built gigantic sports facilities in hopes of attracting more business to the area. Enormously expensive to build and maintain, these facilities are designed to serve many purposes. The football field at Aloha Stadium in Honolulu converts to a baseball diamond. The parking lot at Texas Stadium, where the Dallas Cowboys play, is also used for a drive-in movie theater. When a facility has several uses, more events can be held, and more operating revenue is generated for the facility.

The travel industry, of course, also profits from spectator sports. For some time, the travel industry has been building package tours around major sporting events such as the World Series, Kentucky Derby, and Indianapolis 500. But now a new phenomenon is occurring. When the home team goes on the road, the fans—rather than staying at home and watching the games on television—are going on the road, too. They're traveling to watch regular-season games—not just championship games. And, for the most avid sports fans who can't wait until the baseball season opens, there are package tours to Florida that enable them to watch their team in spring training.

Recreational Sports

While millions of Americans are sitting at spectator events, millions of other Americans are actively participating in recreational sports—both indoors and outdoors. The greatly increased interest in active sports reflects the American public's increased consciousness of the importance of physical fitness.

Americans' interest in traditional recreational sports such as bicycling, swimming, and hiking remains high. At the same time, the popularity of newer sports such as jogging, exercise walking, racquetball, and white-water rafting continues to grow. There has also been a renewed interest in roller skating, thanks, in large part, to the development of Rollerblades. For the more adventurous, such recreational sports as hang gliding, parasailing, and bungy jumping are gaining in popularity. In bungy jumping, a long rubber cord, or bungy rope, is attached to a person. Then the person leaps off a high bridge, and the rope acts like a huge rubber band, causing the jumper to bounce up before hitting the water.

Illus. 9-6 *The popularity of recreational sports continues to grow along with Americans' passion for physical fitness.*
Source: *Ernest H. Rogers/Photoedit*

The types of sports in which people participate often depend on where they live. Skiing and scuba diving, for example, can only be done in certain parts of the country. On the other hand, tennis courts and golf courses exist nearly everywhere. Bowling is the number-one recreational sport in the United States because of the accessibility of bowling alleys in almost every neighborhood.

The area of recreational sports illustrates how the public and commercial sectors can overlap. For instance, almost every city park provides tennis courts. Privately owned businesses also operate tennis courts. The difference is that private tennis clubs—for a fee—offer more amenities, such as a clubhouse, reserved court time, saunas, locker rooms, and refreshments.

Facilities. As mentioned earlier, national and state parks and forests provide facilities for many recreational sports. Recreational sports, however, have been classified in the commercial sector because of the potential for private enterprise to make a profit in this area. Sporting goods stores provide all sorts of equipment—running shoes, cross-country skis, guns, racquets. Some businesses, called *outfitters*, provide services, such as fishing and hunting guides or white-water rafting equipment, while others stage events for recreational enthusiasts. Each year, the Boston Marathon generates thousands of dollars of revenue for the city in travel services, hotel accommodations, and food.

The commercial sector also profits from providing and operating facilities for recreational sports—skating rinks, marinas, fishing resorts, fitness centers. Tennis players who are very serious about improving their game can now spend their vacation at privately operated tennis camps.

Some types of facilities, such as ski resorts, require more financial investment and are riskier to operate than others. If the weather is too warm and there is not enough snow, ski resorts lose money. Operating costs are high. During the summer months, expensive ski-lift equipment sits idle. To generate off-season income, many ski resorts have developed year-round programs, offering scenic chair lifts and convention sites for the summer months. By clustering their facilities, resorts at Vail and Aspen, Colorado, are able to provide more nightlife, restaurants, and shopping in one area. This strategy tends to draw more patrons than does the isolated resort.

The travel industry, of course, is primarily interested in those recreational sports, like skiing, that require most people to journey some distance from home. But the travel industry also likes to advertise recreational sports as features that round out the attractiveness of a particular destination.

Recreational Vehicles. One type of recreational facility that has grown tremendously is the private campground. Kampgrounds of America (KOA), this country's largest privately owned campground franchise, had seven facilities in 1964. By the early 1990s, the number had risen to more than 650.

This growth does not mean that more people are pitching tents and building bonfires. It is related to the rise in popularity of the recreational vehicle (RV) for travel. Campgrounds cater to these homes on wheels by providing them with a parking spot, electricity, running water, and sewer access. Some campgrounds have even installed swimming pools, golf courses, kennels, restaurants, and cocktail lounges.

The recreational vehicle represents a new way of traveling that has contributed to the tourism boom. However, because they take their beds and kitchens with them, RV owners do not make much use of hotels/motels and restaurants. Convention and entertainment centers seek to capitalize on RV traffic by establishing nearby campsites.

The RV industry is currently promoting RV rentals. The industry hopes to install RV rentals in the channels of distribution used for other travel products. Thus, like a car rental, travelers could rent an RV at an airport or as part of a fly/drive package arranged through a travel agency. Some computer reservations systems have already begun to list RV rental companies among their subscribers.

Recreational Shopping

Visitors to the Statue of Liberty usually purchase a souvenir to remind them of their trip (and to prove to friends back home that they were really in New York City). Travelers to the Old Southwest might buy Navaho blankets and jewelry because similar merchandise is not available back home.

Shopping has long been a by-product of traveling. Recently, however, shopping itself has become a reason for traveling. The development of three types of facilities—the megamall, the waterfront shopping complex, and the factory outlet center—has greatly increased recreational shopping. These facilities, which provide stimulating shopping environments, are promoted as tourist attractions. Chartered buses and planes bring thousands of tourists to them each year.

Megamalls. *Megamalls* are gigantic indoor shopping and entertainment complexes—a shopper's paradise. Under one roof, shoppers can find department stores, hundreds of shops, restaurants, theaters, banks, health clubs, and art galleries. Sculptures, fountains, and tropical gardens add to the luxurious atmosphere. The largest shopping mall in the world is being built in Bloomington, Minnesota. When construction is completed in the late 1990s, the megamall will cover 78 acres and will have its own indoor amusement park, miniature golf course, and nightclubs.

By attracting out-of-town visitors, megamalls have

helped to restore vitality to the downtown areas of several big cities. Downtown St. Louis, for example, was deserted until developers converted an old train station into a shopping mall, hotel, and restaurant complex. Now the center city is alive. With enclosed malls, northern cities can attract visitors year-round, instead of only in the warm summer months.

Waterfront Marketplaces. With names such as Riverwalk and Harborplace, waterfront marketplaces are shopping and entertainment complexes built along a river or bay. The architecture of the complex gives visitors a pleasant view of the waterfront. Usually a waterfront marketplace is part of an effort to restore the historic section of a city and thus becomes the scene of civic events and festivals. The success of waterfront marketplaces in Boston, New York City, and Baltimore has stimulated similar developments in other cities.

Factory Outlet Centers. A factory outlet center comprises several stores that sell name-brand merchandise at cut-rate prices. Discounts can be as high as 50 percent. Whereas megamalls and waterfront developments have been an economic boon to large cities, factory outlet centers have revitalized once-dying small towns. Not many years ago, the retail shops along the main street in Boaz, Alabama, were empty. Then, a shopping center for factory outlet stores was opened nearby. Busloads of bargain hunters now pour into Boaz every weekend. Their zest for shopping has spilled over, so that stores on the main street have reopened for business.

Another area that has become a prime location for factory outlet centers is along the border between the United States and Canada. The Niagara Factory Outlet Mall in Niagara Falls, New York, is a popular destination for Canadian shoppers looking for good buys. Prices for many items in the outlet stores are much lower than those found in Canada. Another large factory outlet center in Niagara Falls is scheduled to open in 1992.

Celebrity and Industrial Tours

Recognizing the American public's fascination with the lives of famous people, the commercial recreation sector has been quick to turn the homes of celebrities into tourist attractions. For example, in Beverly Hills, California, visitors can buy a map that directs them to the homes of movie stars. When Jimmy Carter was president, tour buses regularly drove through his hometown of Plains, Georgia. Graceland in Memphis, Tennessee, has become a shrine to thousands of devoted Elvis Presley fans who journey there each year.

Factories, processing plants, and breweries around the country have also become popular tourist attractions. People enjoy seeing how various products, from breakfast food to jet planes, are made. In addition to providing a guided tour through the plant, a company might explain its product through an exhibit or a movie.

Since companies generally do not charge an admission fee, industrial tours are nonprofit ventures for the commercial sector. However, companies do gain enormous public relations benefits for their products.

Live Entertainment

Despite the popularity of television and movies, many people enjoy the sense of involvement they get from live entertainment. While the theater, ballet, opera, and symphony orchestra can be public or private enterprises, rock concerts and nightclub shows are almost always commercial ventures. In 1990, Paul McCartney performed at four of the ten top-grossing concerts, gaining revenues of approximately $13 million.

The audiences for live entertainment tend to be specialized. That is, people go to events they understand. If you're unfamiliar with ballet, you probably won't appreciate the skill of the dancers. Likewise, a rock concert can be ear-shattering clatter if you're not a fan of the performers and their music.

Sometimes, live entertainment is the main attraction for a vacation trip. For instance, people travel to Nashville just to hear country and western music at the Grand Ol' Opry. Opryland USA—Nashville's theme park—and other area attractions are spin-offs of the Grand Ol' Opry. A theater tour to see Broadway plays is another example of live entertainment as the main attraction for a trip. Most often, however, live entertainment adds to the recreational activities available at a particular destination and increases the likelihood that tourists will visit that destination.

In the past, only a few cities—notably New York, Boston, Chicago, and Los Angeles—offered top-quality live entertainment. Now, however, opportunities to attend excellent performances are available throughout the country. In 1990, there were 88 symphony orchestras in the United States with annual operating incomes of more than $1 million. About 50 grand opera companies exist in this country. Regional theaters, such as the Playhouse Square Center in Cleveland and the Tyrone Guthrie in Minneapolis, provide outstanding productions. Regional ballet and modern dance associations flourish in many states. In addition to professional-level live entertainment, countless colleges and community groups offer concerts and plays for recreational pleasure.

Sometimes, people attend a concert or a play just to see the concert hall or theater. New York City's Carnegie Hall and the JFK Center for Performing Arts in Washington, D.C., for instance, have become famous arenas for live entertainment.

Gambling and Gaming

Do Americans spend more money on gambling or on movie tickets? If you answered gambling, you're correct. Americans spend billions of dollars on gambling every year. Gambling (also known as gaming) has been a leisure-time activity for centuries. In the United States today, gambling continues to be a popular—but controversial—form of recreation. No state has legalized all forms of gambling, and only a few states have any form of legalized gambling. More states, however, are looking into gambling as a way of raising revenue.

There are four types of gambling: casino gambling, pari-mutuel wagering, lotteries, and the activities of non-profit organizations (mainly bingo and raffles). Since lotteries, bingo, and raffles are geared toward the residents of a particular area, the travel industry is primarily interested in casino gambling and pari-mutuel wagering.

Casino Gambling. Casino gambling consists of playing slot machines or table games such as roulette, craps (dice), blackjack (twenty-one), baccarat, and poker. Casinos are either free-standing operations or part of a large hotel-entertainment complex. They are privately owned by independent businesspeople or by corporations. For instance, the Tropicana in Las Vegas is a casino hotel operated by the Ramada Corporation.

Only four states—Nevada, New Jersey, Colorado and South Dakota—allow regular casino gambling. As you learned in Chapter 6, two states—Iowa and Illinois—have recently begun to allow casino gambling on riverboats. The major casino concentrations are in Las Vegas, Reno-Sparks, and Lake Tahoe (Nevada), and Atlantic City (New Jersey). The more than 200 casinos in Nevada make gambling the basis for the state's most important industry—tourism. Colorado has permitted gambling in Cripple Creek and Central City, two old Rocky Mountain Mining towns. South Dakota just recently began to allow limited gambling in Deadwood, an old gold-rush town. The state plans to use the gambling profits to restore the town's many historic buildings in the hope of bringing more tourists to the area.

Travel for the purpose of casino gambling has increased. In 1970, casino revenues were only $6 million, as compared with more than $8 billion in 1990. The slot machines bring in more money than all the table games together. A new innovation in gambling occurred when the first cashless casino opened in Australia recently. The casino's slot machines take debit cards, which are similar to credit cards, rather than quarters, dimes, and nickels. This system is expected to come to the United States as well and further increase the haul of the one-armed bandits.

Atlantic City, where casino gambling has been legal since 1978, is trying to challenge Las Vegas as the casino capital of the United States. Located in a densely populated area, Atlantic City draws 70 percent of its business from people who live within a 300-mile radius. Las Vegas, on the other hand, depends on tourists from all over the country.

Pari-Mutuel Betting. *Pari-mutuel betting* occurs at dog races, horse races, and jai alai tournaments. People bet on the first-, second-, and third-place finishers, and winners share the total amount bet minus a percentage for the management. Florida has the largest number of pari-mutuel activities.

More people attend thoroughbred horse racing than any other racing event. There are over 100 thoroughbred tracks in the United States, many of them located in New York and California.

Harness racing, in which the jockey rides behind the horse in a small, two-wheeled cart, is especially popular around Chicago and in Delaware, upstate New York, and Michigan.

Quarter-horse racing, popular in the West and Northwest, usually takes place at state and county fairs. As the name implies, the quarter horses run a quarter of a mile on the track.

In dog races, greyhounds chase a mechanical hare around the track. Well-attended dog tracks are in Revere, Massachusetts; St. Petersburg, Florida; and West Memphis, Arkansas.

Commercial Recreation and Leisure Abroad

Outside the United States, travelers can find an abundance of recreational opportunities sponsored by privately owned businesses. Most of these exist in Canada and the countries of Europe, which have well-established tourist routes and the economic resources to develop and support commercial attractions. Even more recreational opportunities will become available as new destinations in South America, the Orient, and Australia are developed. Only a glimpse of the possibilities for commercial recreation abroad can be given here. Table 9-7 lists some of the highlights.

Check Your Product Knowledge

1. What are the characteristics of theme parks?
2. What important service do model cultures and restorations provide?
3. What is the difference between a spectator sport and a recreational sport?
4. As it relates to the travel industry, how has the importance of shopping changed?
5. What are four types of gambling?
6. Why are the attractions of Europe more familiar to Americans than are those of Asia and South America?

Type	Examples
Amusement/Theme Parks	■ Tivoli Gardens, Copenhagen, features outdoor cafes, flower gardens, midway, and specialty shops. ■ Tokyo Disneyland, Japan. ■ Euro Disneyland, France.
Restorations	■ Fort Louisbourg, Canada, reconstructed eighteenth-century French fort.
Sports	■ Wimbledon tennis tournament, London. ■ 1992 Olympics—France and Spain. ■ Paris Air Show.
Shopping	■ Indian Craft Market, Mexico City. ■ Cloth Alley, Hong Kong. ■ Edmonton Mall, Canada, giant shopping-entertainment complex with over 800 shops.
Industrial Tours	■ Perfume factories in France. ■ Diamond cutting in Amsterdam. ■ Cheese-making in Switzerland.
Casino Gambling	■ Casinos of Monte Carlo, Monaco; Estoril, Portugal; Caribbean.
Live Entertainment	■ Classical music—symphony orchestras, opera—Berlin, London, Milan, Paris, Vienna. ■ Theater in London, Stratford-upon-Avon. ■ Nightclubs—Folies Bergere in Paris, native gaucho music in Buenos Aires, Kabuki theater in Japan.

Table 9-7 Commercial Recreation and Leisure Abroad

RECREATION AS PRODUCT

To the travel industry, recreation is a product—something that must be created, packaged, and sold in the same way as other products.

The Package Tour

To make travel more appealing, convenient, and less expensive, the travel industry groups its products into packages. For example, transportation and accommodations products are often packaged together. The package tour is discussed in detail in Chapter 10.

Some travel packages are built around specific recreational attractions. In addition to entrance to the attraction, the package generally includes transportation and accommodations. Extra features, such as meals or free baggage handling, can be included to make the package more enticing. Recreational package tours, which can be put together by hotels, airlines, travel agencies, wholesale operators, or the attraction itself, are becoming increasingly popular. There is an infinite variety of packages, depending on the options selected, the length of stay, the quality of accommodations, and the number of persons participating. Here are a few examples based on commercial recreation.

■ *Gambling junkets.* Bargains for gamblers are available in package tours to casinos. Typical packages include bus or airfare, accommodations, a supply of poker chips, tickets to nightclub shows, and a discount coupon book. Big-spending gamblers might be offered an all-expenses-paid trip, known as a *junket*, to a casino hotel in the Caribbean.
■ *Theme park vacations.* Walt Disney World Travel Agency has a variety of package tours to Disney World. These include transfers between airport, hotel, and Disney World; accommodations; admission to Disney World; and additional sightseeing.

- *Adventure tours.* Many companies now offer guided rafting tours in the United States. A typical package might include a two-day white-water expedition, with all the necessary gear, an experienced guide, transportation to and from the river, one night's accommodations at the company campground, breakfast, and box lunches for two days.

- *History and art tours.* Sometimes a tour package is planned around a number of related attractions. Someone interested in English history and architecture might take a 15-day motorcoach tour of the castles of Great Britain, including accommodations; most meals; visits to castles and great houses in England, Scotland, and Wales; and the services of a professional guide.

Channels of Distribution

Traditionally, the public sector of the recreation and leisure system has been a passive participant in the promotion and sale of the travel product. As the interest in travel and tourism grows, however, so does the awareness in the public sector of the need to promote and compete. Many museums, zoos, aquariums, and other sites have established marketing and public relations departments that advertise, offering group discounts, annual memberships, and cooperative tie-ins. Admission and entrance fees are often included in tour packages. Kentucky was the first state to acknowledge the importance of the retail travel agency as a generator of visitors and the first to pay commission to agencies for bookings in its state park system. More public-sector sites are now considering the uses of mass distribution systems like Ticketron in order to sell their products.

With the growth in travel and tourism have come problems of overcrowding and congestion. To keep the crowds within bounds, public facilities are going to have to use some sort of automated reservations systems. The days of first-come, first-served may soon be a thing of the past in our most popular parks and monuments.

The situation is also changing in the private sector, which consists of hundreds of large companies and thousands of mom-and-pop operations. In the past, few of the latter were willing to pay a commission to a travel agency or offer a discounted price to a tour operator. This, too, is changing as travel and tourism continues to grow and the number of visitors increases each year. The theme park, a comparatively new product, has had a tremendous impact on the methods of marketing and promoting commercial recreation and leisure systems.

Each year, more and more travelers and tourists make long trips to visit and enjoy new recreation and leisure systems. As more public- and private-sector systems realize that their visitors are just as likely to come from across the nation—or from across the ocean—as from across town, these systems will develop methods to place their products in the channels of distribution.

Check Your Product Knowledge

1. What does a tour package based on a recreational attraction generally include?
2. Why are public-sector recreation facilities taking a greater interest in promoting their products?
3. Why is the first-come, first-served system in our national parks likely to change?
4. What effect is the growth in tourism likely to have on mom-and-pop recreation operations?

CAREER OPPORTUNITIES

Public and commercial recreation and leisure systems offer interesting career opportunities. Many of these relate to managing a recreational facility, such as a golf resort or nightclub. Others involve helping people enjoy their leisure time.

Compared with other components of the travel industry, public and commercial recreation systems employ more part-time and temporary workers. These workers are needed to handle crowds during peak seasons or one-time events. The public sector also makes use of volunteer workers to help with fund-raising or routine clerical work or to serve as guides. Part-time work or volunteer work in the public sector can be an excellent introduction to a full-time career in recreation.

Parks and Forests

National and state parks and forests employ many different kinds of specialists such as botanists, ecologists, and wildlife biologists. However, the worker you are probably most familiar with is the park ranger.

Some park rangers work primarily with people, enforcing federal and state laws, issuing permits, providing information, and giving tours. Others work alone, patrolling isolated wilderness areas and keeping an eye on park or forest conditions. Many park rangers are directly involved in environmental management, such as fighting fires and planning recreational facilities.

Park rangers need to be strong and healthy because they work out-of-doors in all kinds of weather. Job candidates are usually required to have a college degree, but high school graduates can sometimes become rangers. Candidates usually must pass a civil service test to enter the park service. Eventually, park rangers can work their way up to supervisory and administrative jobs.

A DAY IN THE LIFE OF A
National Park Student Intern

I just spent the summer working as a student intern at Yosemite National Park. It was a wonderful experience. I got to work outdoors all day, make new friends, and meet people from all over the world who came to visit the park.

I was hired last spring and spent two weekends in May being trained for the job. The main part of my job was to be an "interpreter." An interpreter at a park does not work with languages but instead "interprets" the sights and sounds of the park for visitors. I gave many talks to groups of visitors about the park's history, wildlife, plantlife, and geology. Some summer interns work in the visitors center answering questions about park attractions, giving directions, and taking reservations. Other interns do clerical work in the park offices. A few interns even dress up in pioneer costumes and give presentations about early settlers at the park's pioneer history center.

My job really began in mid-June. At that time, my 16 fellow interns and I received another week's training. During the training session, National Park Service (NPS) trainers took us around the park so we could become familiar with all of its attractions and facilities. After the training period, we were assigned to a specific area of the park and given roommates for the summer.

I was assigned to a part of the park called the High Country, a large area of Alpine meadows and woodland trails. Those of us assigned to the High Country lived in tent cabins. These are large tent-sided wooden platforms containing a wood stove for heat and cooking, cold running water, and electricity. Bath and toilet facilities were in a separate building.

Most days we woke up early and reported for work by 8 A.M. Some of us worked repairing trails, picnic areas, and other facilities or taking people hiking in the Sierra Nevadas. My favorite assignment was to lead groups of children on junior ranger hikes. Usually I would teach the children how to spot animals and animal signs, such as tracks and nests. I liked to show the children how the animals survive by adapting to their environment.

At night the interns took turns leading the campfire talks. I enjoyed that activity because it reminded me of nights around the campfire when I went to summer camp as a youngster. I've taken geology courses in college, so I sometimes gave presentations about the special geology of Yosemite National Park and the surrounding mountains.

I applied for the summer internship at my college through the Student Conservation Association (SCA). The SCA is a government and donor-supported organization that recruits interns on high school and college campuses. The interns work for several federal government programs such as the National Park Service, the Fish and Wildlife Service, and the Bureau of Land Management, which manages the national forests. Other internships and seasonal jobs are available through various colleges and universities, at individual parks, and through the national office of the National Park Service.

The National Park Service tries to choose interns who have had some part-time work experience and who are studying in a related field. The NPS also looks for students who have had some experience in public speaking—such as student teaching—because so many summer jobs involve giving talks and presentations to park visitors.

Summer internships at the national parks pay very little. Usually the intern gets a uniform allowance, a small salary, and if needed, a travel allowance to get to the park and back home again. Despite the fact that interns don't make a lot of money, being a summer intern is a very popular job. Not only is it a fun job, but interns also gain valuable work experience.

Interns learn how to manage natural resources and work with tourists. In addition, being a summer intern at a national park is a great way to get your foot in the door if you are aiming for a career in conservation management or tourism.

I made several good friends and had a lot of fun working as an intern at Yosemite. During our off-duty hours, we were able to hike, rock-climb, canoe, ride horses, swim, and camp throughout the park. All in all, working for the National Park Service was the best summer vacation I ever had.

Photo Source: National Park Service, Deleware Water Gap National Recreation Area

Museums

To fulfill their functions as collectors, educators, and entertainers, museums employ specialists in many different fields. A new and high-growth career is that of curator.

Museum curators are highly educated experts who locate, acquire, and display the works of art and artifacts that museums exhibit. They are also responsible for protecting, preserving, and repairing museum collections and for supervising assistants and technical experts.

Other people who work in museums include conservators, experts concerned with the preservation of objects on display; taxidermists, who prepare animal specimens for exhibit; and designers, who plan and prepare the display cases and exhibits where objects are shown. Finally, there is the museum director, an administrator who oversees the entire operation.

Zoos

Zoos require several types of highly educated administrators. Zoo directors generally hold a doctorate in some branch of zoology. They supervise the staff, manage the budget, establish priorities, and serve as the link between the government and the zoo board. Animal curators, who must have a master's degree in zoology, decide on the best location for the animals, study their behavior, and encourage breeding. Zoo veterinarians must have earned a Doctor of Veterinary Medicine degree, which requires six years of post-college schooling. To keep the animals healthy, veterinarians monitor their diets, watch for parasites, and run routine tests.

Zoos also require a great many animal caretakers. These workers feed, exercise, and clean up after the animals. Candidates for a caretaking job usually need only a high school diploma, but they may have to pass a civil service test to work at a publicly owned zoo.

Theme Parks

Theme parks provide thousands of job opportunities. Disney World is the single largest employer in Florida. The theme park employs about 32,000 people. Disney World also offers a college internship program in which students work at the park and receive classroom instruction.

Seasonal workers at theme parks are usually high school or college students who learn their responsibilities on the job. They can be food-service workers, game attendants, souvenir and gift store clerks, guides, maintenance and sanitation workers, ride operators, or security personnel. These unskilled positions offer a behind-the-scenes view of the inner workings of a theme park. In fact, many theme parks do not hire anyone for a professional staff position who has not at some time worked as a seasonal employee or an intern.

A variety of managerial or executive positions are available at a theme park—food-service manager, ride superintendent, entertainment director, director of group sales, operations manager. People with degrees in a food services, business management, liberal arts, merchandising, and other areas can expect to find positions to match their training.

Since theme parks are constantly adding new features to attract visitors, creative people who can design show productions, exhibits, rides, festivals, and other attractions are needed. Also, with an increased interest in providing participatory recreation, theme parks are seeking people skilled in recreational programming. Many participatory facilities are designed to accommodate physically handicapped people and offer an excellent resource for recreational therapists.

Stadiums

The growing number of stadiums and the growing number of events held in stadiums mean employment opportunities for many people. Racetracks, arenas, and theaters provide similar opportunities.

Stadiums have a regular staff of office and maintenance personnel. One of the most important positions is that of groundskeeper. Groundskeepers mow the grass or maintain the artificial turf, plow and smooth baseball diamonds, and convert the playing field from one sport to another.

For stadium events, platoons of workers are brought in—ushers, security guards, concession workers, ticket takers, parking-lot attendants. Many people are needed to sweep up after an event. Generally, part-time stadium workers are employed through an agency under contract to provide services to the stadium.

Overseeing all activities and personnel is the stadium manager. Realizing the necessity of keeping the stadium filled with events, the stadium manager also promotes the stadium's use and negotiates contracts with organizations that rent it. Candidates for this position must generally have a degree in business administration or public relations and experience in managing a small athletic field or assisting in the management of a large stadium.

Resorts

Ski resorts and tennis camps hire instructors to help guests improve their skills. Other resorts offering recreational sports facilities might provide tennis pros and golf pros. In addition to demonstrating skill in a certain sport, these instructors need to know about equipment, physical fitness, and safety. A college degree is not necessary, but the instructor should have a record of varsity or professional experience. In fact, a well-known instructor lends prestige to a resort.

Hunting and fishing lodges employ guides to go on expeditions with guests. Guides must be expert hunters or fishers. They must know the wildlife of the area, be familiar with the territory, and know conservation laws. Besides pointing out the best place to catch a trout or shoot a deer, guides prepare campsites and help clean, skin, or preserve the animals.

Resorts also hire fitness instructors, recreation workers, and lifeguards to make their guests' stay safer and more enjoyable. Since resorts usually operate on a seasonal basis, the jobs of these workers are also seasonal. Instructors, guides, and recreation workers need to find alternate employment for the off-season.

Casinos

Many employees are needed in order for a casino to operate smoothly. A single game of craps, for instance, requires a crew of four. Besides knowing their game extremely well, dealers must be able to handle bets and payoffs efficiently and keep the game moving. Dealers must also be courteous and pleasant toward the gamblers.

Like other business managers, casino operators worry about making profits. But, since casinos have very high operating expenses, the worries of casino operators are even greater. If the volume of gamblers is low or if too many high rollers hit hot streaks, the casino's profit margin may suffer.

Summary

- Recreation refers to the activities that people pursue in their leisure time.
- Recreational facilities and services are provided by public and commercial recreation and leisure systems.
- The public sector refers to government-funded and government-operated facilities—primarily national and state parks and forests, zoos and aquariums, museums, and fairs and festivals. These are not intended to make a profit, but to preserve the country's natural and historic heritage.
- The commercial sector refers to recreational facilities operated by private businesses. Theme parks, stadiums, resorts, shopping malls, theaters, and casinos are generally part of the commercial sector. The purpose of these recreational facilities is to make money for their owners.
- The public and commercial sectors often overlap and are interdependent.

- National and state parks and forests provide recreational areas for millions of Americans. Both systems face problems from overcrowding and pollution.
- Museums serve as repositories for valued objects, centers of learning and culture, and places for recreation and entertainment. Museums reflect the culture, history, and resources of the nations where they are located.
- Zoos and aquariums are museums that display live animals and marine life and provide education and entertainment for visitors.
- The theme park—for example, Disneyland—is the outstanding example of a commercial venture in recreation.
- Model cultures and restorations demonstrate how people of another time or culture lived.
- Spectator sports are an example of a passive form of recreation. Recreational sports are an active form. Both provide the commercial sector with millions of dollars in profits.
- Megamalls, waterfront shopping complexes, and factory outlet centers have turned shopping into a major tourist attraction.
- The travel industry is primarily interested in recreational opportunities that entice people to travel or that make a particular destination more appealing. The industry builds tour packages around recreational attractions and advertises them in the media.
- The public and commercial recreation and leisure systems provide interesting career opportunities, particularly in management. This component of the travel industry also requires thousands of part-time and temporary employees.

Key Terms

leisure
recreation
attraction
event
public recreation system
commercial recreation system
concession
interpretation
oceanarium
model culture
outfitter
megamall
pari-mutuel betting
junket

What Do You Think?

1. Should America's national parks be preserved primarily as wilderness sanctuaries or be further developed as public playgrounds? Give reasons for your answer.
2. With so many of Africa's people starving, should time and money be spent on trying to save the continent's wildlife? Why or why not?
3. Should gambling be legalized throughout the United States? Explain your point of view.
4. How does the economy of a country influence the development of commercial recreation?
5. Do you think that Americans depend too much on commercial recreation to fill their leisure time? Explain your answer.

Dealing with Product

You have just inherited a private golf course and campground next to Shady Acres State Park and the Big Bear State Wildlife Preserve. A quick look through the financial records shows clearly that your property has a seasonality problem. Business is booming in the late spring, the summer, and the early autumn. However, there has been no business whatsoever from late fall to early spring, and no wonder—who wants to play golf in the snow or camp out when it's 5 degrees below zero?

What can you do? Is it best to shut down the park each Labor Day and reopen the following Memorial Day? Is there any way to turn those snowstorms into money-making attractions and events? What about creating some cross-country ski trails? Would a skimobile course be a good method of making money each winter? What other ideas can you think of?

Dealing with People

You have just been appointed the Director of Parks and Recreation in Yourtown. Unfortunately, the city newspaper does not share your enthusiasm for recreation and leisure. In fact, in today's editorial, the newspaper has charged that public parks and recreation programs are a waste of the taxpayers' money and a luxury that Yourtown can no longer afford. The editorial urges the city council to cut your budget by two-thirds and to spend the money on the school system and on expanding the police and fire departments. The mayor has just ordered you to prepare a speech defending your department, to be delivered next Monday at the city council meeting. What will you say?

WORKSHEET 9-1   YOURTOWN RECREATION FACILITIES

List the recreational facilities and services found in Yourtown. Indicate which are public and which are commercial. If there is an entrance charge, note it.

Parks and Forests

_____

_____

_____

Zoos and Aquariums

_____

_____

_____

Theme Parks, Amusement Parks

_____

_____

_____

Celebrity Attractions

_____

_____

_____

Spectator Sports

_____

_____

_____

Model Cultures and Historical Restorations

_____

_____

_____

Recreational Shopping

_____

_____

_____

Museums

_____

_____

_____

Fairs and Festivals

_____

_____

_____

Historic Sites

_____

_____

_____

Industrial Tours

_____

_____

_____

Recreational Sports

_____

_____

_____

Live Entertainment

_____

_____

_____

Gambling

_____

_____

_____

WORKSHEET 9-2   NATIONAL PARK SERVICE

The National Park Service administers hundreds of separate sites. For each of the kinds of national parks below, locate the ones closest to Yourtown or Yourstate. Describe the facilities offered. If two or more are equally close, choose the one you prefer.

National Park

_____

_____

_____

National Preserve

_____

_____

_____

National Lakeshore

_____

_____

_____

National Historical Park

_____

_____

_____

National Recreational Area

_____

_____

_____

National Cemetery

_____

_____

_____

National Monument

_____

_____

_____

National Seashore

_____

_____

_____

National River or Riverway

_____

_____

_____

National Memorial

_____

_____

_____

National Parkway

_____

_____

_____

Performing Arts Center

_____

_____

_____

Name _____

WORKSHEET 9-3 RECREATION AND LEISURE ABROAD

Governments and private enterprises throughout the world provide opportunities for recreation and leisure. The chart below lists just a few examples. Use travel guides and encyclopedias to help you locate and describe each attraction.

LEGOLAND PARK

Location: _____

Description: _____

_____

_____

_____

LA SCALA

Location: _____

Description: _____

_____

_____

_____

SERENGETI PLAIN

Location: _____

Description: _____

_____

_____

_____

THE GINZA

Location: _____

Description: _____

_____

_____

_____

THE HERMITAGE

Location: _____

Description: _____

_____

_____

_____

GREAT BARRIER REEF NATIONAL PARK

Location: _____

Description: _____

_____

_____

_____

UPPER CANADA VILLAGE

Location: _____

Description: _____

_____

_____

_____

CARNEVALE

Location: _____

Description: _____

_____

_____

_____

WORKSHEET 9-4   RECREATIONAL VEHICLES

You have read something about how the popularity of recreational vehicles has affected the travel industry. Read some recent newspaper and travel magazine articles to get more specific information.

Statistics (for example, number of RVs owned by individuals, cost of an average RV, number of RVs rented yearly)

Attractions (for example, freedom of travel)

Drawbacks (for example, awkward to drive and park in cities)

Travel components that have benefited (for example, campgrounds)

Travel components that have suffered (for example, motels, restaurants)

Modifications that have been made in travel components (for example, campgrounds provide electricity, water, sewer access; RV rentals)

Outlook for the future (for example, more or fewer, cheaper or more expensive)

Factors that determine the future (for example, price of gas, condition of highways)

CHAPTER 10 TOURS AND CHARTERS

"Traveling is almost like talking with men of other centuries."
—René Descartes

Objectives

When you have completed this chapter, you should be able to:

- Describe the development of the package tour.
- List the components of a package tour.
- Discuss the role of the tour operator.
- Summarize the benefits of package travel.
- Distinguish between independent, hosted, and escorted tours.
- Classify tours according to destination and purpose.
- Explain why age is an important factor in defining the traveler.

- Describe the work of a tour manager.
- Explain how tours are regulated.
- Show how a package tour is put together.
- Give reasons for the popularity of charter travel.
- Distinguish between private and public charters.
- Diagram the distribution channels of the tour industry.
- List the career opportunities in the package tour industry.

It's one thing to decide to go on a tour, but quite another to organize the trip. Many people don't have the time or the inclination to plan a tour for themselves. They prefer to have somebody else make the decisions and the arrangements. For this reason, among others, the tour package came into being. Tour packages offer travelers prearranged transportation, accommodations, meals, and other vacation preparations—all at a predetermined price. They take some of the aggravation out of travel and usually provide significant cost savings as well.

Americans are turning on to package tours in a big way. Today, the package tour industry is one of the fastest-growing segments of the travel industry. In this chapter, you'll learn about the many different kinds of tours, discover some reasons for their popularity, and read about the career opportunities that the package tour industry presents.

A BRIEF HISTORY OF THE PACKAGE TOUR

As you have learned, the concept of travel is an ancient one. But package travel, comprising combined arrange-

ments for transportation, accommodations, sightseeing, and other features, is a comparatively recent development. We can trace its origins to the grand tour. This extended journey through continental Europe was traditionally undertaken by the sons (and later the daughters) of the British aristocracy during the seventeenth and eighteenth centuries.

The primary purpose of the grand tour was to educate. Indeed, no education was considered complete without it. While he was abroad, the young nobleman was expected to enrich his knowledge of the classical past, acquire antiques and works of art, learn foreign languages, and develop socially desirable skills and manners. France and Italy—the cities of Paris, Rome, and Naples in particular—were the main destinations. Some itineraries also included stays in Germany, Holland, Austria, and Switzerland.

Travel through Europe by stagecoach or riverboat was dangerous and arduous, and the grand tour could last as long as three years. (By contrast, a comparable modern tour of Europe takes about three weeks.) There were no travel agencies, tour operators, or tour escorts in those days. The individual traveler might carry letters of introduction to aristocratic European families, who would provide him with lodging and entertainment. But for the most part, he was on his own.

The development of railroads and hotels in the nineteenth century encouraged increasing numbers of middle-class travelers to embark on tours of Europe. With this middle-class "invasion" came a change in the motivation for foreign travel. The emphasis moved away from education and culture toward recreation and pleasure. It was the beginning of mass tourism.

The Pioneer of the Package Tour

Thomas Cook, a Baptist missionary from England, was the innovator of the organized package tour. In 1841, he chartered a train to carry 570 people to a temperance meeting. This first tour featured a number of components that were to become standard for later package tours. It included transportation (a 40-mile round-trip rail journey); meals (a picnic lunch and afternoon tea); entertainment (a band playing hymns); an event (the temperance meeting); and the services of a tour escort (Cook himself).

The success of this and subsequent excursions encouraged Cook to form the world's first travel agency and to branch out into overseas travel. In 1856, Cook led the first conducted grand tour of Europe. By the late 1860s, his agency was offering Nile cruises, rail trips to India, and guided tours of the United States. Other firsts for Cook included the introduction of travel brochures, passenger itineraries, and vouchers to speed payment for the services of suppliers.

The Evolution of Tour Formats

While personally conducted group tours were an important service offered by early travel agencies, the bulk of their business was in handling travel and hotel arrangements for people making independent trips. An American planning a grand tour of Europe, for example, would consult a travel agent to arrange his or her personalized itinerary. The travel agent would then organize the traveler's steamship passage across the Atlantic, rail travel within Europe, accommodations, and sightseeing. Such custom-made tours—known either as *Foreign Independent Tours* (*FITs*) or *Domestic Independent Tours* (*DITs*)—were the norm for the vast majority of vacation travelers right up until the early 1960s.

The breakthrough for the prearranged package tour came with the arrival of the jet age in 1958. Transatlantic crossing time was cut to seven hours (from 18 hours by propeller aircraft or four days by ocean liner). Time savings, together with increased prosperity and low airfares, brought overseas travel within reach of ordinary working Americans, who had only two or three weeks of annual vacation. International travel was no longer exclusively

for the wealthy few.

Tour operators developed a variety of packages to cater to the new class of travelers. The packages offered bargain prices, convenience, and reliability. Taking advantage of charters, reduced excursion fares, and all-inclusive tour packages, the number of Americans visiting Europe rose from under 700,000 in 1958 to almost 7 million in 1989.

Not only have package tours become more accessible in the jet age; they have also become more flexible in terms of length. In the days when overseas travel entailed a journey by steamship, tours were necessarily longer, commonly lasting two or three months. A few tour operators offer lengthy packages: Globus-Gateway, for example, offers a 38-day "Super European." But most have scaled down the itineraries of multicountry European tours to around 22 days. As a result, tours are less leisurely than they used to be, and less time is spent at each destination. Shorter tours, featuring only two or three destinations, have also been developed.

Check Your Product Knowledge

1. What was the grand tour?
2. What role did Thomas Cook play in the history of tourism?
3. What effect did the jet airplane have on the package tour?

THE MODERN TOUR

A *package tour* is a combination of several travel components provided by different suppliers, which are sold to the consumer as a single product at a single price. The package tour typically comprises two or more of the following components:

- One or more forms of transportation (including fly/drive, fly/cruise, motorcoach tour, and rail tour packages).
- Accommodations.
- Meals.
- Attractions and events (including sightseeing and admission to natural and commercial attractions, entertainment, recreation, and a variety of special events).
- Extras (including transfers and baggage handling, tips and taxes, the services of a professional tour manager and tour guides, travel bags, and discount coupons for restaurants and shops).

Package tours vary in complexity from the two-component package (for example, air transportation and limited sightseeing, or hotel accommodations and rental car) to the multicomponent, all-inclusive package. With the popular *all-inclusive package*, the traveler pays one price that covers just about all trip expenses, including transportation, accommodations, meals, sightseeing, and so on. When a tour involves air travel to the destination or point of departure, the components are usually separated into air arrangements and land arrangements. Land arrangements include surface transportation while on the tour, accommodations, meals, sightseeing, and other activities. Some tour companies quote an all-inclusive price for both air and land arrangements. Others quote air and land rates separately. When the rates are given separately, clients can opt to buy just the land package and make their own arrangements to get to the starting point of the tour.

The Role of the Tour Operator

A *tour operator* or *tour wholesaler* contracts with hotels, transportation companies, and other suppliers to create a tour package to sell to the consumer. By buying hotel bednights, airline seats, and admission tickets in bulk, the tour operator can get lower rates than those that would be offered to an individual traveler. The savings are passed on to the consumer (after allowance for business overheads, profit, and any commission to the seller).

The terms *tour operator* and *tour wholesaler* are often used interchangeably, although *operator* refers more specifically to a company that sells packages directly to the consumer, while a *wholesaler* sells the package through a retail travel agency. For the purposes of this discussion, we will use the general term *tour operator* throughout.

There are four different kinds of tour operators. The first is the independent tour operator. This can be an individual or a multinational corporation. American Express is an example of the latter. The second category is the travel agency that functions as a tour operator. The agency packages tours that it sells to its clients or that it wholesales to other travel agencies. In-house tour operators make up the third category. These are owned and operated by air carriers (United Airlines and Qantas, for example). The fourth category consists of travel clubs and incentive travel companies, which do not sell their products to the public.

All tour operators take risks when they put together a package tour. They must make block reservations far in advance, with no guarantee that their tours will sell in the competitive market. (In reality, many will not.) Suppliers are willing to reserve their product for the tour operator if they are given a deposit. However, the percentage of the deposit that will be refunded decreases progressively as the departure time gets closer.

Illus. 10-1 *Package tours vary in complexity from the two-component package to the multi-component, all-inclusive package.*
Source: *Sara G. Matthews*

The Popularity of Tours

The package tour industry is one of the fastest-growing sectors of the travel industry. The number of tour operators in business in the United States rose from 588 in 1978 to more than 2,000 in 1989. Package tours represent an important share of domestic tourism and an even more significant portion of overseas tourism. Why have package tours become so popular? The main reason is that they offer a variety of practical benefits that independent travel cannot provide.

Known Costs. Because all package tours are prepaid, the client can fairly accurately calculate the total cost of the tour in advance. This is especially true of an all-inclusive package. Accommodations, meals, sightseeing, entertainment, transfers, and taxes will all have been prepaid before departure. The only additional expense, therefore, would be for personal items such as souvenirs, gifts, and drinks.

Bargain Prices. The single greatest attraction of the package tour is its relatively low cost. Because they buy in bulk from suppliers, tour operators can offer packages at a considerably lower rate than the sum of the individual components bought separately. Just as an institutional-sized can of beans costs less per ounce than a single-serving can, so a block reservation of hotel rooms costs less per room than a single room reservation. Tour operators who provide a guaranteed high volume of bookings to a hotel chain can pay as little as 50 percent of the standard rack rate. Even after the markup and standard (10 percent) travel agent commission, the room is still less expensive than it would cost an individual. Volume discounts allow similar savings on other components of the package.

Guaranteed Arrangements. When travelers buy a package, they are also buying peace of mind. Independent travelers may have to cope with unpleasant surprises en route, such as being bumped off a flight or finding that a hotel has no record of their reservation. A package tour takes the anxiety out of traveling, because all arrangements have been made in advance by the tour operator. In addition, group reservations are invariably honored because suppliers rely heavily on the business generated by tour operators.

Guaranteed Entrance. It is often easier to get into a special event as a member of a tour than as an individual. This is true because tour operators make block ticket purchases to assure entrance to tour participants. For example, it's almost impossible to attend the Oberammergau Passion Play, staged every ten years in Germany, unless you are part of a tour. There are even some countries that will permit access to certain places only to visitors who are part of a tour group.

Tried-and-True Sightseeing. Tour operators have the experience to know which attractions are worth a special trip. They know which local nightspots offer the best entertainment, and which restaurants can be recommended. Unlike the individual traveler, the tour member doesn't have to worry about winding up in a second-rate museum or a restaurant with inedible food.

Time Savings. On a package tour, the traveler doesn't have to spend time looking for accommodations, arranging transfers, or getting tickets for a show. Group travel can also lead to time savings at theaters and other attractions. Tour participants often don't have to wait in line; they can enter and exit more easily than individuals.

Check Your Product Knowledge

1. What are the typical components of a package tour?
2. What is meant by the term *land arrangements*?
3. What are the benefits of package tours over independent travel?
4. Why are tour operators able to offer reduced prices for tour components?

TOURS, TOURS, TOURS

The common image of a package tour is of a group of senior citizens traveling through Europe aboard a motorcoach under the watchful eye of a uniformed tour escort. Such tours do indeed exist, but recent years have seen a rapid growth in the number and types of tours to virtually every corner of the world.

Wholesalers have developed tours to fulfill the needs of an increasingly sophisticated travel public. They cater both to the mass market and to specific segments of the market. There are tours tailored to attract young singles, families, middle-aged couples, senior citizens, and handicapped people. Some tours are designed for people who prefer to relax on their vacation, while others cater to those who want to find adventure or learn as they travel. There are one-day sightseeing tours, weekend escape packages, two-week special-interest tours, and one-month cultural packages. A sample eight-day package tour is shown in Figure 10-1. People can sign up for all-inclusive tours or for independent tours, for leisurely tours or fast-paced tours, for budget tours or deluxe tours. These tours are not limited to tourists. Travelers visiting friends and relatives (VFR), for example, can purchase a package for the bargain price and then use only part of it, such as the airfare and the car. In such cases, the tour is called a "throwaway."

The Tauck Family

When Arthur Tauck was 18, he was fired from his job as a bank teller in New Jersey. He had accidently dropped 60 rolls of dimes, breaking the rolls and scattering 3,000 coins. His employer told him not to come back unless he could find a better way to handle rolls of coins. Tauck did just that, inventing an aluminum coin tray that most American banks still use today.

The invention of the coin tray changed Arthur Tauck's life in a completely unforeseen way. First, he was rehired by the bank and started selling the trays to other banks on his lunch hour. Next, Tauck abandoned his bank job to begin peddling the trays full time to banks throughout New York and New England. While traveling from bank to bank during the early 1920s, Tauck noticed that very few people, except other salesmen, went traveling among the scenic wonders of rural New England. He also noticed that for the few tourists who did venture out into the hinderlands, there were no guides or guidebooks to tell them where to stay or what to see.

This gave Tauck an idea. In 1925, he advertised his next selling trip in a local New Jersey newspaper, inviting people to go along with him on a tour of New England. He would act as a tour guide, pointing out local attractions and arranging for stays in the best hotels. Those who signed up would pay one fee. Tauck would take care of all of their hotel and meal expenses. All they would have to do when it came time to pay a bill, he told them, is "merely sign Arthur Tauck's name to the check rather than their own."

Six people signed up for that first tour and went off sightseeing with Tauck in his 1924 Studebaker. Tauck had tried the tour on a whim and had not planned to continue it. However, friends of the original six tourists soon wrote requesting similar excursions, and Tauck Tours was born. Tauck's new business grew steadily, and Tauck was able to purchase a fleet of tour coaches to take travelers on tours of the northeastern United States.

The Great Depression of the 1930s nearly destroyed Tauck Tours. Times were hard and most people had no money for vacations or sightseeing trips. Then, in 1933, the Chicago World's Fair opened for business. One of Tauck's brothers suggested that Tauck use his tour coaches to transport people to the fair. Soon, Tauck was dispatching eight or nine buses a day from New York to Chicago for the fair. The fair saved Tauck's tour business, and by the late 1930s the business had expanded to include tours up and down the East Coast.

In 1941, the company showed a healthy profit for the first time. Tauck decided to invest the surplus in a national advertising campaign. He placed full-page ads in five major travel newspapers. Unfortunately, the ads ran on December 7—the same day that Japan bombed Pearl Harbor and plunged the United States into World War II. Tauck received only eight inquiries as a result of the ads.

The government forced Tauck to suspend his tour business during the war years, and he went back to selling coin trays. He resumed the tour business in 1947, offering tours of Williamsburg, the Carolinas, New Orleans, Niagara Falls, and the Gaspé Peninsula in Quebec. Even in the 1940s, conditions were so primitive in Gaspé that Tauck's tour directors had to hire teams of oxen to pull the motorcoaches uphill on Gaspé's muddy dirt roads.

Tauck really enjoyed running a tour company. He was an outgoing, friendly man who liked people and preferred to lead the tours himself when he could. Tauck's son, Arthur, Jr., grew up in the business. He started leading his own tours in 1950 while he was still in college. In 1958, Tauck, Sr., retired and Tauck, Jr., became president of the company.

Tauck, Jr., brought his own innovations to the tour business. In the 1960s, he realized that people would soon be doing a great deal of traveling by air. He launched a new series of tours that combined air travel and coach tours of the western United States. He also developed coach tours to many of the nation's national parks. In the 1970s, Tauck Tours introduced helicopter tours of the Canadian Rockies. In a matter of minutes, helicopters whisked sightseers to glaciers, waterfalls, and Alpine meadows that had taken days to reach on foot. Also in the 1970s, Tauck, Jr., started offering steamboat excursions on the Mississippi River.

Tauck Tours continued to expand throughout the 1980s. In 1992, it offered 50 tours of Canada, Alaska, Hawaii, and other parts of North America. The company also had 11 European tours and 2 tours of Australia and New Zealand.

The younger Tauck's five children also grew up in the business. Three are now executives in the company. "We all started in the mailroom," said Tauck's daughter Robin. As children, they often visited the company's headquarters in Westport, Connecticut, and grew up knowing its employees. Robin Tauck says that her father often took his family on vacations that later became company tours. "Now I see my brother taking his son to Australia. The next generation is also beginning to grow up in the business," she said.

Photot Source: Judith Pszenica

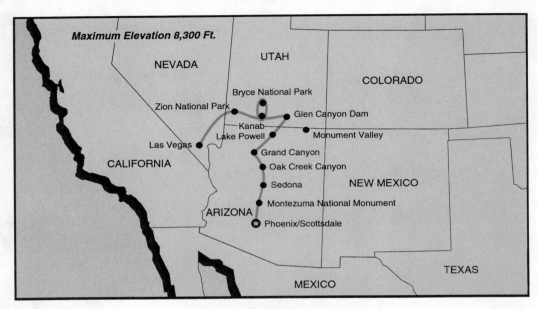

EIGHT-DAY CANYONLANDS TOUR:

Day 1 Depart: Phoenix/Scottsdale   *Day 5* Glen Canyon Raft Trip
Day 2 Montezuma/Sedona/Oak Creek Canyon   *Day 6* Bryce National Park/Kanab
Day 3 Grand Canyon/Navajo Lands   *Day 7* Zion National Park/Las Vegas
Day 4 Lake Powell/Rainbow Bridge;   *Day 8* Las Vegas; tour ends
         option: Monument Valley

Figure 10-1 Sample Package Tour
Source: Tauck Tours

All tours can be categorized by the package format, by destination, or by purpose.

Basic Package Formats

Deciding to go on a package tour is just the beginning. The traveler then has to decide what kind of package he or she wants. The tour package is a product that comes in many different formats.

Independent. The independent package tour is the least structured of all formats. It offers participants the benefits of package savings but allows them the flexibility and freedom of traveling alone. An independent package features a minimum of components. Typically, it includes hotel accommodations plus one other land arrangement (for example, round-trip transfers, use of a rental car, a daily continental breakfast, or a half-day sightseeing tour).

When booking an independent tour, participants can choose their departure and return dates. They can also choose from a variety of different-priced hotels, and extend their stay by adding a fixed extra-night rate for each additional night. A fly/drive package is a good example of an independent tour. Popular destinations for independent tours include resort areas (for example, Hawaii and Cancún).

Independent tours should not be confused with Foreign Independent Tours (FITs) and Domestic Independent Tours (DITs), which are custom-made for clients by travel agencies. FITs and DITs have become less common in recent years because they are much more expensive than package tours and far more time-consuming for the travel agent.

Hosted. On a *hosted tour*, a host is on hand at the hotel to arrange optional excursions, answer questions, and help people plan their free time. The host is not an escort and does not accompany the group on sightseeing tours or on overland journeys. If the tour visits more than one destination, a different host will be available at each hotel on the itinerary.

Hosted tours are ideal for vacationers who wish to strike a balance between organized events and free time. Aside from scheduled sightseeing and entertainment features, participants are free to arrange their time as they please. As in an independent tour, they have the freedom to choose their departure date, level of accommodations, and length of stay.

Escorted. The escorted tour is the most structured of all formats. It offers participants accommodations at a number of destinations, meals, point-to-point transportation, and a full program of organized activities. A professional tour manager or escort accompanies the group for the duration of the tour. In recent years, there has been a rise in the number of escorted tours, due in part to an increase in the number of tours to Eastern European countries. On these tours, participants need a bilingual escort to ease the language-barrier problem.

Escorted tours appeal to travelers who want their entire vacations to be planned in advance. For this privilege, they sacrifice the flexibility and independence that travelers on other tours enjoy. Participants travel as a group throughout, and have limited free time to branch out on their own. They must begin and end the tour according to schedule and stay in hotels selected by the tour operator.

Special Tour Formats. In addition to the three basic tour types, there are a number of packages that are not available to the general public.

- *Incentive tours* are offered by companies as a reward to employees for achieving a sales goal or similar corporate objective.
- *Convention tours* are packaged for sale to members of an association or group attending gatherings such as conventions, conferences, exhibitions, or trade shows.
- *Special-interest group tours* are arranged for clubs, societies, and organizations whose members share a common interest (for example, photography, bird-watching, opera).

All three special tour formats are developed jointly by the tour operator, travel agent, and company, association, or club. Tours designed primarily for the business and professional traveler are discussed in greater detail in Chapter 12.

Incoming Tours. An *incoming tour* is one that originates in a foreign country and has the United States as its destination. The product is essentially the same as an outgoing tour with the itinerary reversed (for example, Rome—New York—Rome instead of New York—Rome—New York). Foreign visitors are of great importance to the United States (as they are to other nations). They generate jobs, income, and tax revenues.

Tours Defined by Destination

Many tours are aimed at providing travelers with the general flavor of particular destinations. This is especially true of escorted tours that cover several countries in a short space of time. The grand tour of Europe, which sometimes visits as many as nine countries in 17 days, is a prime example. Spending a maximum of three days in any one country, tourists can only catch a glimpse of the major highlights.

An *area tour* allows for more time in each country, although there is little opportunity for an in-depth appreciation of any destination. A 15-day tour of Scandinavia, for example, might entail four nights in Denmark, five in Sweden, and five in Norway, with two nights in each capital. Other popular destinations for area tours include Alpine Europe and the British Isles.

Single-country tours are more focused and enable the traveler to see and do much more than is possible on an area tour. England, France, Italy, Germany, Spain, Israel, Japan, New Zealand, and countless other countries all lend themselves to this kind of tour. Some single-country tours concentrate on a particular area to give the visitor a more in-depth view. There are, for example, eight- and ten-day tours of Shakespeare country, of the French château country, and of the Canadian Rockies.

Tours to one or two cities are the most focused of all packages. These are usually independent or hosted. *Two-city tours* are ideal for travelers who do not want to be tied to a single destination. Equal time is usually spent in each city, with transportation between the two included in the price of the package. The two cities can be in the same country (for example, Rome and Florence, Montreal and Quebec), or in different countries (for example, London and Paris, Bangkok and Hong Kong). The two-country combination allows the tourist to experience more than one culture.

Travelers who really want to get to know their destination might choose a *single-city tour*. This can be a four-day sightseeing tour, or a more extended visit focusing on the unique attractions of a particular destination (for example, theater in London or New York, shopping in Hong Kong, art museums in Paris, or opera in Milan).

Tours Defined by Purpose

While the destination itself can be the strongest selling point of many tours, others are popular because they focus on a specific type of activity. The activity can be as strenuous as white-water rafting or as relaxing as lying on a beach. Tour operators have developed packages to satisfy a multitude of motivations, needs, and expectations (MNEs).

Relaxation. Many people want nothing more from a vacation than the chance to relax, with plenty of sun, a sandy beach, good food, and perhaps some nightly entertainment. Such stay-put resort vacations are available in many parts of the world (for example, the Caribbean, Hawaii, Mexico, and the Mediterranean). The vacations may be combined with some sports and recreation (as in a Club Med package), shopping, or limited sightseeing, but the main purpose is relaxation.

Scenic. Tours for people who want to enjoy spectacular scenery while they are away from home exist in great variety. Most involve a fair amount of traveling, either by motorcoach (New England fall foliage packages, tours throughout Europe), train (trans-Canada packages, national parks of the American West), or ship (Alaska's Inside Passage, Rhine River cruises). They are almost always escorted trips.

Illus. 10-2 *A single-country tour, such as a ten-day journey through France's Loire Valley, enables travelers to get acquainted with a country.*
Source: Milt and Joan Mann

Learning. Every tour provides a learning experience, but here we refer specifically to those tours taken by people traveling because of their interest in culture, history, science, or education. Some tour operators package this product under the generic term *intelligent travel*. Cultural tours come in various formats. Typically, they involve a structured program of visits to museums and art galleries, or attendance at theater productions, music festivals, and so on. Individual travelers can also arrange to stay with host families, thereby gaining a greater understanding and appreciation of the cultures they experience. Historical tours can entail participation in an archaeological dig or study of ancient civilizations. Members of a scientific tour might take part in a geological expedition or study the botany of a particular region. Historical and scientific tours usually feature guest lecturers and other subject experts. The distinction between historical or scientific tours and educational tours is often hazy, but the latter generally focus more on study in the classroom than on study in the field. All educational tours allow participants to achieve personal enrichment from their travels. As an additional bonus, some offer the opportunity to earn college credits.

Religious and Ethnic. The pilgrimage has been an important reason for travel since ancient times. Tour operators continue to develop packages to holy sites for members of different religions (for example, Catholics to Rome, Jews to Israel, and Muslims to Mecca). Ethnic travel is a related category, covering Americans who visit the country from which their parents, grandparents, or earlier ancestors came. Recent examples of ethnic travel include black Americans going to West Africa, especially The Gambia, and Italian Americans visiting Italy.

Adventure. Travelers seeking adventure on vacation form a rapidly growing segment of the market. Tour operators such as Mountain Travel, Sobek's International Explorers Society, and Society Expeditions Cruises offer a staggering array of escorted packages to exotic destinations.

Here's a small sampling of adventure tours offered:

- Mountaineering in the Himalayas.
- Camel expeditions in the Sahara.
- Dogsledding in the Northwest Territories.
- Trekking in Nepal.
- African safaris.
- Horseback riding in the Canadian Rockies.
- Hot-air ballooning over Kenyan game preserves.
- Amazon jungle expeditions.
- River rafting in Alaska.

The selection is likely to grow larger as travelers continue to seek something new and exciting.

Ecotourism. The ecology movement has not gone unnoticed by the tour industry. *Ecotourism*, or nature tourism, is one of the fastest growing travel fields. Tours that take the vacationer to discover and observe unusual ecological systems and endangered wildlife species in their natural habitat are becoming quite popular. Tourists are flocking to such diverse areas as the lush Amazon rain forests, the Annapurna Mountain Range of Nepal, and the Antarctic peninsula. Nature tourists can view the harp seals in Canada, the white heron colonies in New Zealand, and the hawksbill sea turtles on Antigua. These tours provide an interesting insight into the world of nature and the environment.

Sports and Recreation. The sports and recreation market has been strong since the early days of the package tour and has become more diversified in recent years. For those who want an active vacation, there are golf, tennis, and ski packages, as well as organized biking and walking tours. Recreational travel also includes visits to theme parks (for example, Disney World) and gambling packages (Las Vegas, Atlantic City). The recreational activity can be the sole purpose for the trip, or it can be combined with other features, such as sightseeing, relaxation, or study.

Spectator sports packages feature a special sporting event as the main attraction. Examples include the Olympics, World Series, Super Bowl, Kentucky Derby, Indianapolis 500, and Masters Golf Tournament. (Similar tours are also designed around other types of special events, including New Orleans' Mardi Gras, Munich's Oktoberfest, and the Cannes Film Festival).

Special Interest. This is a travel product with great potential for future development. Tour operators have packaged a wealth of different tours for groups sharing common interests. These include chocolate lovers' tours of Switzerland, bird-watching tours of China, and, in the United States, garden tours of Southern mansions. Some enthusiasts travel with a preformed group, club, or organization. Others buy a special-interest package as individuals.

Weekend. Statistics show that Americans are taking shorter and more frequent vacations, instead of a single, extended, annual vacation. Cut-price weekend packages, in particular, are becoming increasingly popular. These can be family packages (with free accommodations for children); second honeymoon packages; recreational, educational, or special-interest packages; or theme weekends (for example, a murder mystery package). The common denominator is the concept of a "quick fix" or escape from the daily routine.

Special Needs. Wheelchair-bound travelers clearly have needs different from those of more mobile travelers. Access to hotels and public buildings is limited to those fitted with ramps, wide doorways, and other features that reduce architectural obstacles. Physically disabled people require specially equipped guest rooms and hydraulic lifts to help them on and off vehicles. Special arrangements must also be made for developmentally handicapped people and for those whose hearing or sight is impaired. Tour operators have only recently begun to tailor packages for this potentially large market. Those catering exclusively to handicapped people include Flying Wheels Tours, Evergreen Travel, and New Horizons.

Defining the Traveler

Tour operators develop packages by determining where people want to go (destination) and what they want to do when they get there (purpose). In addition, tours must be designed to fit the MNEs of different kinds of travelers. We can identify a number of basic MNEs. These include:

- *Security.* Many people do not feel confident about traveling alone—especially overseas, where the language and customs may be unfamiliar. An escorted tour, with an experienced tour manager at the helm, offers these travelers the security that an independent tour lacks.
- *Companionship.* Some people are perfectly happy traveling on their own; for others, participation in a group tour fulfills their need for companionship while away from home. They may simply want to share experiences with others on the tour or they may hope to form long-lasting friendships.
- *Status.* Being first on the block to visit China or some other exotic destination can be an important motivation for travel.
- *Romance.* "Love Boat" cruises, Club Med singles' packages, and honeymoon packages fulfill a desire for romance while on vacation.

The Traveler's Age. While some tours are designed for people of all ages, others are tailored to attract specific age categories. These categories include:

- The student market.
- The youth market.
- The family market.
- The middle-aged/mature market.
- The senior citizen market.

Each market has its own particular MNEs. Economy is likely to be a major consideration for students on a limited budget. Young people typically demand action, adventure, and entertainment, with free time to go off on their own. Families are attracted to packages designed with children's interests in mind, such as visits to amusement parks and zoos. Middle-aged travelers tend to have more money than other groups and can afford the luxury of traveling in style. If they are experienced travelers, they may be keen to explore new and exotic locations. Finally, senior citizens traditionally favor worry-free tours conducted at a leisurely pace and with plenty of scheduled activities.

Flexibility and Pacing. Every tour must be flexible enough to suit the divergent tastes of the different participants. On a general-interest tour of the capitals of Europe, for example, it would be unwise to schedule three consecutive nights at the opera. Opera lovers might be delighted, but others would want more diversified entertainment. Meals have to be varied, too. Some group members might want to experience exotic local cuisine at every stop. Others would flinch in horror at the thought of a plate of frog legs and would prefer more familiar food.

Balance is the key word here. To keep everyone happy, the package must offer a variety of entertainment and a choice of meals. It must also achieve a balance between scheduled activities and free time. Not all travelers want their every waking hour filled with organized activities. Many appreciate an occasional quiet night at a

Tours for the Handicapped

Peter would love to travel, but he dreads the hassle of maneuvering his wheelchair through narrow doorways and worries about how he will get up and down steps in unfamiliar places. Grace, who is blind, enjoys guided tours of museums and historic sites, but she becomes frustrated because many tour guides do not understand her special needs. When Carol travels, she needs to stay in hotels that have visible fire alarm and telephone systems, but few facilities of this type are available for the deaf.

According to the Society for the Advancement of Travel for the Handicapped (SATH), approximately 40 million physically and mentally disabled Americans would travel if obstacles were removed from their path. Added to that number are family members and friends who might accompany the disabled on their travels. Altogether this represents an enormous, and largely untapped, market for travel services and products.

Evergreen Travel, located in the state of Washington, is a good example of one of several small companies meeting the needs of handicapped travelers. Company founder and tour operator Betty J. Hoffman has provided travel services for wheelchair-disabled and sight-impaired clients since the early 1960s.

A retail travel agent and a wholesale packager of tours for the handicapped, Mrs. Hoffman provides packaged and customized vacation tours to almost anywhere in the world. With Evergreen Wings on Wheels Tours, mobility-impaired and wheelchair-disabled clients have visited South America, the South Pacific, and the Far East; tours have gone around the world twice. With Evergreen White Cane Tours, blind and sight-impaired clients have visited the Caribbean, Europe, and North America. The company also arranges adventure, business, and convention travel for its clients.

Mrs. Hoffman has been an industry pioneer in travel for the handicapped. Her company operated the first tour for the blind to Europe in 1966 and printed the first travel brochure in braille. In 1990 it led the first group of wheelchair disabled on a tour of the Soviet Union. Nothing daunts this company in its efforts to help the handicapped experience the wonders of the world. It has carried clients up the Great Wall of China and constructed ramps that allowed wheelchair travelers to ride elephants in India. The company even arranges for quadriplegics to obtain scuba-diving certification.

While Evergreen provides complete travel services for the disabled, other companies are more specialized. Some specialize in a particular type of disability or a particular type of vacation experience. Flying Wheels Travel in Owatonna, Minnesota, arranges group and independent tours and cruises for wheelchair disabled. The Guided Tour Inc. in Melrose Park, Pennsylvania, serves the developmentally disabled. Another specialized travel company for the disabled is Unique Reservations in Indian Rocks Beach, Florida. The company takes kidney dialysis patients on cruises all over the world.

As might be expected, arranging and conducting tours for the handicapped presents some challenges. For one thing, it usually takes longer to make arrangements. All accommodations and attractions must be thoroughly checked ahead of time for accessibility and safety. Even though hotels, motels, and restaurants say they are handicap accessible, they must still be inspected in person. And, although the number of accessible hotel rooms and cruise cabins is growing, available accommodations are still limited. This further complicates planning.

Arrangements must also be made for properly trained and compassionate escorts to assist the handicapped on the tour. Some companies employ attendants to accompany the tour group. Evergreen, for example, trains and furnishes one sighted guide for every three blind or sight-impaired clients. Or companies may require that clients provide their own traveling companions. Concerns about insurance liability or industrial injury are a major part of working with the handicapped.

Scheduling arrivals and departures can be challenging, too. By necessity, a handicapped tour group moves at a slower pace than a nonhandicapped group. The disabled cannot whip in and out of tourist attractions the way many nondisabled groups do. Evergreen has turned this characteristic of handicapped travel into a positive feature by promoting the "leisurely" nature of its tours.

Companies specializing in travel for the handicapped need to arrange for, or invest in, special equipment or devices. Motorcoaches need to be equipped with electric lifts, wheelchair tiedowns, and—ideally—on-board wheel-in restroom facilities. For clients who wish to travel independently, Evergreen provides cars and vans with hand controls and other special features.

Because of the special arrangements that must be made, companies may be required to charge more for handicapped tours. Despite the challenges of planning travel for the handicapped, the results can be most gratifying. Accessing the market will become easier as the government continues to mandate handicapped accessibility in public facilities and accommodations and as the travel industry itself discovers this important group of potential travelers.

Photot Source: Jack Hoffman, Evergreen Travel Service, Inc.

hotel, as well as free time for relaxation, sightseeing at leisure, and so forth.

The pace of a tour is another consideration. Many tours stop at a different destination virtually every night. This may look appealing in the brochure, but, in reality, a succession of long days on the road can be exhausting, especially for older travelers. Again, balance is essential. A good tour operator will try to schedule a day without travel after a particularly long journey (or after a tiring initial flight).

Price. A tour is a product, just like a television set or any other commodity. Not everyone can afford the deluxe color television with wide screen and stereophonic sound. Similarly, the deluxe, all-inclusive tour package is beyond many people's budgets. Tour operators must offer a range of products at a range of prices to appeal to different markets. American Express, for example, has European tour packages in four price categories—freelance, value, select, and priceless. Itineraries can be similar in each category, but the number of features included and level of accommodations vary.

are put together by a tour operator and sold through travel agents to the clients. Our feature tour was created, let's say, by European Horizons, a Boston-based tour operator, and marketed to travel agents throughout the United States. The 27 tour participants come from cities all over the country and from a variety of backgrounds.

Not every tour, however, is the brainchild of a tour operator. Some tours are the idea of a member of an organization or club. For example, a high school Spanish teacher might want to put together a summer study trip to Spain. In this case, he or she is known as a *tour organizer*. The organizer may have little expertise in travel and will most likely cooperate with a local travel agency, tour operator, and possibly an airline representative.

To return to our feature package, an integral part of the escorted tour is the work of the *tour manager* (also known as the tour conductor or tour escort). Our tour

---

Check Your Product Knowledge

1. What is the difference between a hosted tour and an escorted tour?
2. What is an area tour? Give examples of possible area tour destinations.
3. List six different types of tours that focus on a specific activity and explain the purpose of each.
4. Why are flexibility and pacing important on any tour?

THE INGREDIENTS OF A TOUR

To illustrate the many ingredients of a package tour, we have created a fictitious tour. It is an escorted 12-day European package with overnight stops in five countries (England, the Netherlands, Germany, Switzerland, and France) and daytime passage through one other (Belgium). The tour is tailored to the general-interest traveler, with extensive sightseeing and some entertainment features. A detailed itinerary is given in Figure 10-2.

The Human Element

Tours do not magically materialize out of thin air. Someone has to have the original idea for the tour and package the product so that it is attractive enough to sell to the consumer. As you read earlier in this chapter, most tours

Illus. 10-3 *Ecotours that take vacationers to observe unusual ecological systems and endangered wildlife are becoming popular.*
Source: *Anna Zuckerman/Photoedit*

LONDON, PARIS, AND EUROPEAN HIGHLIGHTS

- First-class hotels throughout—all rooms with private bath or shower.
- Continental breakfast daily.
- Dinners included in Amsterdam, Frankfurt, Lucerne, and Paris.
- Round-trip airport transfers, including baggage handling.

- Touring by luxury, air-conditioned motor-coach.
- Rhine River cruise.
- London theater reservations.
- Local entertainment.
- Sightseeing in all major cities, including admission charges and guide fees.
- Experienced tour manager.

Day 1 DEPART USA. Overnight transatlantic flight.

Day 2 LONDON. Arrival in the British capital, with welcome from our tour manager who sees us settled in our London hotel. Balance of day free to relax—or perhaps to start exploring. Evening cocktail party gives us a chance to get acquainted.

Day 3 LONDON. Morning sightseeing with a professional London guide. See Buckingham Palace, Big Ben, and the Houses of Parliament before our visit to the eleventh-century Westminster Abbey. Free afternoon for independent activities or join an optional excursion to the Tower of London. Tonight, we have reserved seats to a London show.

Day 4 LONDON–AMSTERDAM. Morning drive to Dover on the South Coast. By hovercraft to Calais. Motorcoach through Belgium, then on to Amsterdam, arriving in time for a Dutch dinner party at the hotel.

Day 5 AMSTERDAM–COLOGNE. Morning sightseeing features a visit to a diamond factory and a look at Rembrandt's masterpieces in the Rijksmuseum. After lunch, we head for the German Rhineland and overnight in the cathedral city of Cologne.

Day 6 COLOGNE–FRANKFURT. After a leisurely breakfast, we board an excursion steamer and cruise the romantic Rhine—past castles, terraced vineyards, and medieval towns. Then by motorcoach to Frankfurt, for dinner, complimentary beer, and entertainment provided by a local German band.

Day 7 FRANKFURT–HEIDELBERG–LUCERNE. Morning stop in Heidelberg, for sightseeing in

Germany's oldest university town and tour of the castle. Then on through the Black Forest, past the thundering Rhine Falls, and into Switzerland. After the eventful day, a quiet night at our Lucerne hotel at the foot of the Swiss Alps.

Day 8 LUCERNE. Our morning sightseeing takes us around the city walls, over a fourteenth-century wooden bridge, and to the famous Lion Monument. This afternoon, perhaps shop for watches or cuckoo clocks, cruise the lake by paddle steamer, or take an optional cable car ride up Mt. Pilatus for stunning Alpine views. Tonight's Swiss folklore party features fondue dinner, unlimited wine, and yodeling and alpenhorn blowing.

Day 9 LUCERNE–PARIS. Today's drive takes us into France and through the world-renowned vineyards of Burgundy. A photo stop at the Palace of Fontainebleau and then on to Paris.

Day 10 PARIS. Morning sightseeing takes in the French capital's famous landmarks: the Eiffel Tower, Arc de Triomphe, Opera, and more. A special visit to the magnificent Notre Dame Cathedral. Balance of the day at leisure, perhaps to visit the Louvre, cruise on the Seine, or enjoy some shopping. For tonight, why not treat yourself to a gourmet dinner, followed by a lively cabaret show?

Day 11 PARIS. A morning tour to Versailles, then a chance to relax before our gala farewell party at the hotel.

Day 12 RETURN TO USA. Jet back home, arriving the same day.

Figure 10-2 Sample European Tour Itinerary

manager is Mary DeVries. Mary works for European Horizons and it is her responsibility to oversee the group for the duration of the tour and to make sure that everything runs smoothly. Her work begins long before the departure day.

Mary has been involved with the preparation of the package from an early date. She has even negotiated contracts with suppliers at a couple of destinations. Before departure, she will have familiarized herself with the itinerary. She will know about interesting sights en route, and will have thought about lunch stops for each of the days the group is on the road. Mary will take with her copies of all contracts and correspondence with the various suppliers, just in case there is a problem with hotel bookings or dinner reservations.

The next stage is the tour itself. Mary will greet the tour members as they arrive at the hotel in London, allocate rooms, and briefly describe the scheduled itinerary. She will also discuss the itinerary with the driver to get a fairly exact idea of traveling times and suitable rest stops. In preparation for the next night, she might call the theater to confirm reservations for the show, and possibly the hotel in Amsterdam where the group will stay on Day 4. A tour manager must always be thinking ahead.

On Day 3, Mary will get everyone on the bus for the morning's sightseeing. She will not, however, lead the guided tour of London's landmarks (although she will be on the bus). This will be the job of a professional *tour guide*, who has an in-depth knowledge of the city's attractions. There will be a different tour guide in each city. That night, Mary will accompany the group to the theater.

The first real traveling begins on Day 4 with the trip to Amsterdam. Mary must make sure that all the baggage gets loaded onto the bus (and onto the hovercraft). Since this is a day with a lot of traveling, she will try to break up the day with rest stops (and, of course, lunch). When they finally arrive at the hotel, Mary will go inside to register while the group waits on the bus.

And that, in outline, is the nature of the tour manager's job. The other days will follow in a similar manner. In reality, the tour manager will be expected to do a lot more. He or she will answer a constant barrage of questions, give advice on how best to spend free time, deal with complaints, take care of medical problems or other emergencies, and deal with any visa or other documentation problems. In short, the tour manager needs to have a limitless supply of patience, energy, and good humor.

Transportation

All tours include at least one form of transportation, and many combine several different modes. Our feature tour, for example, entails travel by air (not included in the package price), motorcoach, hovercraft, cruise ship, and airport-hotel transfers in London and Paris. If tour members opt for the Mt. Pilatus excursion on Day 8, they will also experience travel by cable car.

Many other combinations are possible, including transportation by rail, rental car, bicycle, barge, gondola, and even by camel or pack mule. All add variety to the tour experience and can be a strong selling point for the package.

Meal Plans

The number of meals included in the package is a major factor in determining the overall price of a tour. If maximum economy is uppermost in the tour operator's mind, a limited number of meals will be provided—probably just a daily continental breakfast, consisting of juice, rolls, and tea or coffee. A more substantial full breakfast (eggs, meat, toast, juice, hot beverage) is traditionally served in England and Ireland.

If the operator provides no meals at all, the package is known as a European Plan. At the opposite end of the scale, an American Plan includes three full meals a day. A Modified American Plan involves two meals a day (usually breakfast and dinner). Other combinations are also possible—our feature tour includes a daily continental breakfast, dinner on only four nights, and no lunches.

Deluxe tours tend to offer diners greater choice at each meal. *À la carte* means that you can choose from the complete menu, regardless of price. *Table d'hôte*, on the other hand, limits you to a set three-course meal at a fixed price. A *dine-around plan* gives you the option of eating at any of a variety of restaurants. Tour members are issued vouchers and coupons that they can use at participating restaurants.

While there are obvious advantages to buying an American Plan package (prepayment, guaranteed reservations), it is not without drawbacks. You may grow tired of the hotel meals—especially if the menu is limited—and wish you could eat in a local restaurant once in a while. You are, of course, free to do so, but there are no refunds for missed meals.

Accommodations

Our tour group of 27 consists of eight couples, a family of four, a family of three, and four single people. Almost all tours are based on *double occupancy*, that is, two persons sharing a room. Accommodations for the eight couples are straightforward enough—each couple will occupy either a twin with bath (TWB) or a double with bath (DWB). The former has two twin beds; the latter, one double bed.

The family of four can either reserve two separate rooms, or might be able to share the same room (a *quad*). Similarly, the family of three might share a *triple* room. Quads and triples are not necessarily larger than twins and doubles. A common practice is for hotels to add cots or rollaway beds to a regular room to make a triple or a quad. Under this arrangement, children are sometimes allowed to stay for free. Most tour operators offer a slight price reduction for triple or quad occupants.

Single people, on the other hand, have to pay extra if they want a room to themselves. A *single supplement* can sometimes add as much as 50 percent to the package price. A hotel may have a few smaller rooms for individual guests, with one twin bed and bath or shower (SWB), but most singles have to use a regular double room. Some tour operators get around the single supplement by matching singles and allowing them to share a room. Not everyone wants to share a room with a stranger, however. Many singles prefer to pay the supplement for the privilege of privacy. On our tour, two singles have decided to share a room, while the other two have opted for separate rooms.

The Itinerary

Our tour would be considered relatively fast-paced because participants will stop at several cities in a short space of time. The configuration is:

2 1 1 1 2 3   (10 nights spent in 6 cities)

A more leisurely paced tour might have three nights at each destination.

Even though the tour includes a lot of cities, there are only three full days of traveling (Days 4, 6, and 9). Time and distance on the road per day is an important consideration, and few tour operators schedule more than ten hours or 350 miles of travel in any one day. Even fewer have consecutive days of almost nonstop traveling.

Our tour also achieves a fairly good balance between scheduled activities and free time. Although there is no single day when tour participants are free from dawn to dusk, Days 2, 3, 8, 10, and 11 offer free afternoons, while Days 5, 7, and 9 have quiet evenings. Days 4 and 6 are the only two filled with scheduled activities.

Another consideration in selecting the itinerary is the location of the hotel. A central location is preferable, especially on a tour such as ours with overnight stays in major cities. Participants do not want to be inconvenienced by traveling long distances into the city center when they have free time for their own activities.

Check Your Product Knowledge

1. What is the difference between a tour manager and a tour guide?
2. Define each of the following: (a) European Plan, (b) American Plan, (c) Modified American Plan.
3. Give three considerations involved in planning an itinerary.

SELF-REGULATION AND ETHICS

The Interstate Commerce Commission's control of the tour industry effectively ended with the deregulation of the bus industry in 1982. Federal regulation may be a thing of the past, but it has been replaced by regulation from within. Two trade associations—the United States Tour Operators Association (USTOA) and the National Tour Association (NTA)—set standards for the tour industry.

USTOA's 39 members include some of the biggest names in tour packaging—American Express, Globus-Gateway, Maupintour, Olson-Travelworld, and Tauck Tours. The association has strict eligibility requirements. Member operators must:

- Have been in business for at least three years.
- Handle a certain volume of business.
- Carry at least $1 million in liability insurance.
- Post an indemnity bond for consumer protection.

In addition, members are pledged to the highest ethical standards in working with the consumer and retailers, as described in the USTOA publication, *Ethics in U.S. Tour Operations: Standards for Integrity*.

The NTA is the largest group travel industry association in North America. Its members include 575 tour operators who package and sell tours in the United States, Canada, and Mexico and over 2,000 suppliers (including hotels, airlines, bus and sightseeing companies, restaurants, and attractions). In addition, about 750 public-sector organizations (local, state, and provincial tourism agencies, convention and visitors bureaus, chambers of commerce, and so on) are members of the NTA.

Since deregulation, the NTA has functioned as a consumer advocate for the quality of group tours. Like the USTOA, the association demands high standards from its members. They are required to adhere to a strict code of ethics and to carry at least $1 million in professional liability, errors, and omissions insurance.

Recent years have seen an increased emphasis on education in the tour industry. The NTA's Certified Tour Professional (CTP) program rewards individuals who successfully complete requirements in academic study and service to the industry. To be eligible to participate, candidates must have been employed full-time in the tour industry for at least two years.

The International Air Transport Association

IATA plays a primary role in the regulation of tours outside the United States. It requires that:

1. The tour include air transportation on the flights of an IATA member (although the airfare can be quoted separately).
2. Accommodations be included for the duration of the tour.
3. At least one additional feature be included (for example, sightseeing, entertainment, transfers).
4. The tour price be not less than 20 percent of the airfare (if departure is from the United States).
5. The tour brochure meet IATA standards.

Although these requirements are specifically for overseas tours, many domestic tour operators choose to follow the same guidelines.

Once a tour has been approved, it is registered with an identifying number (*IT number*). American Express's "French Impressions" tour, for example, might appear in the brochure with the IT number IT1AF1AE549. Here's a translation of that number:

IT: Inclusive Tour.
1: 1991 (the year the tour was approved).
AF: Air France, the carrier.
1: Area 1 (the Western Hemisphere)— the area in which the tour will be sold.
AE549: The identifying number chosen by the tour operator (American Express).

The Performance Bond

As discussed earlier, the tour operator is a speculator and risk taker. Individual suppliers—hotels, motorcoach companies, and sightseeing companies—will insist on a deposit from the tour operator before reserving the product. But the client and travel agent need protection in case the tour operator goes into default or out of business. A performance bond offers such protection. It is a special type of insurance policy that guarantees payment to all parties owed any money—the clients, their travel agents, and all of the suppliers—in the event that the operator experiences financial difficulties. The tour operator pays a premium and is said to post a bond. Performance bonds are sometimes worth millions of dollars.

Statement of Conditions

All tour operators are required to include in their brochures a statement of terms and conditions. This appears at the back of the tour brochure, usually in fine print. Typically, it includes information on the following:

- What is and is not included in the package.
- Reservations procedures.
- Deposit and payment schedule.

- Travel and health documents required (passports, visas, vaccinations).
- Cancellation and refund policy.
- Status of fares, rates, and itinerary (all may be subject to change).
- The tour operator's limited responsibility and liability.

In this age of lawsuits, it is essential that the travel agent make sure that the client understands the statement of conditions.

Check Your Product Knowledge

1. Which two trade associations regulate the tour industry?
2. What is an IT number?
3. List the items that would appear in a tour brochure's statement of conditions.

THE TOUR AS PRODUCT

A package tour, like any other complex product, is the end result of the work of many different people. Putting together the tour product involves a close working relationship between the following groups:

- Suppliers (hotels, restaurants, airlines, cruise ships, bus companies, sightseeing companies, attractions, resorts, and so on).
- Public-sector organizations (state and local tourism agencies, convention bureaus, and so on).
- Tour operators.
- Travel agents.

The suppliers are the producers of the various components of the tour product. Their primary aim is to sell their product to the consumer at a profit. Suppliers usually sell to intermediaries rather than to the consumer. What direct contact there is between the sales representatives for the suppliers and the prospective tour client is seldom one-on-one, but through group presentations, public speaking, and the occasional travel trade show open to the public.

The sales offices for the suppliers are often organized and structured in much the same way as airline sales offices—that is, by city, district, region, and nation. Locally owned or franchised suppliers, however, seldom have the need for a nationwide sales force.

Public-sector organizations (PSOs) promote group travel to a destination such as a city or entire state. They include state departments of tourism, local and municipal

NEW YORK THE BIG APPLE

Illus. 10-4 *Public-sector organization, such as the New York Convention and Visitors Bureau, promote their destinations to tour operators.*
Source: *NY Convention and Visitors Bureau*

tourism councils, and convention and visitors bureaus, all of which market their destinations to tour operators. Popular marketing approaches include direct mailing and the development of catchy slogans (New York's "Visit the Big Apple" and "I Love New York" are good examples). The NTA's annual fall convention and spring Tour and Travel Exchange provide PSO representatives with a forum where they can market their destinations to tour operators.

National tourist offices (NTOs) exist to promote tourism to an entire country. In the United States, the federal government takes a low-key approach to the promotion of incoming tours through the United States Travel and Tourism Administration (USTTA), a branch of the United States Department of Commerce. The governments of some other countries play a much more active role in the promotion of tourism.

Tour operators consolidate the services of suppliers into a marketable tour package that is sold either directly or indirectly to the consumer. In the United States, tour operators are private business firms. Since deregulation,

it has become relatively easy for tour operators to enter the market. The industry is characterized by low initial capital requirements, fast cash flow, and the potential for high return on equity invested. In the nations of Eastern Europe where, until recently, there was little or no free enterprise, the tour business is undergoing change. In the past, a single, state-controlled tourist board functioned as tour operator/travel agent, as in the USSR (Intourist), Czechoslovakia (Cedok), and Poland (Orbis), or there were a handful of state-controlled tour operators, as in Hungary and Yugoslavia. This is changing as the different countries introduce free market economies and encourage free enterprise.

Travel agents are the final link in the chain, handling the actual sale of the tour package to the consumer. They represent the outlet for the suppliers' and tour operators' products, and are compensated for their services with a commission (usually 10 percent). The client is not required to pay a fee for the services of the travel agent.

Packaging the Components

The work involved in producing the package can be divided into four main stages:

- Operations.
- Costing.
- Brochure production.
- Promotions.

Operations. The operations stage begins with planning. Market research enables the tour operator to determine which tours will sell. (Tours may also be created in response to an offer from a supplier who wants to attract group business, or in response to a suggestion from a representative of an organization.) Once the tour destination, approximate dates, and length of tour have been determined, the next stage is to negotiate with the suppliers of transportation and ground services. This ties in with developing a detailed itinerary for the tour.

Costing. An accurate costing of the various components of the package is a vital stage in the development of the tour. The package must be offered to the consumer at an attractive price. That price must allow markup to cover promotional costs, business overheads, commissions, and profit. Costs can be fixed or variable. Fixed costs are those that must be paid regardless of the number of tour participants. If a tour operator books hotel rooms or bus seats in blocks, the cost will be the same whether 15 or 25 people take the tour. Such are the risks of block booking. Variable costs are those charged on the basis of the number of people on the tour. If hotel rooms are not block booked, for example, the tour operator pays the supplier only for the rooms that are used.

Tour operators can vary the cost of a package by

omitting or including various features. An all-inclusive tour will cost more than one that features accommodations and transportation only. A tour operator can economize by limiting the number of meals included in the package (and by offering table d'hôte rather than à la carte), by choosing first-class rather than deluxe hotels, and by scheduling more free time and fewer organized activities.

Brochure Production. The next stage of development is the production of a brochure for distribution to travel agents and potential clients. The brochure will typically contain general information on the tour operator and its product, listings of all available tours (featuring what is included, detailed daily itineraries, prices, maps, and so on), and a statement of conditions. Many of the larger tour operators produce their own brochures. Smaller companies often customize "shells" produced by airlines, hotels, and tourist offerings. Shells are brochures that contain full-color photos and possibly a short generic text. The tour operator then fills in details of its own tours. Shell brochures offer considerable savings in time and expense for the tour operator.

Promotions. The final stage is the promotion of the tour. Media advertising has long been recognized as an effective means of promotion and includes advertisements to travel industry professionals (in trade publications such as the NTA's monthly *Courier*, *Travel Weekly*, and *The Travel Agent*) and to potential consumers. Trade advertisements tend to be more informative, while consumer advertisements stress the glamour of particular tours. Tour operators also use direct mailing and group sales presentations to retailers considered to be good prospects for selling their tours. The familiarization (FAM) tour, offered to travel agents either at a discount or for free, is another promotional technique that has proved successful in generating interest in tours.

References

A number of publications listing both domestic and overseas tours are available to the trade. The *Consolidated Tour Manual* (CTM) catalogs tours to destinations in the United States and in Canada, Mexico, the Caribbean, and Central and South America. It is published in four editions: All Year, Winter, Spring/Summer/Fall, and Winter Sports. Tour operators pay a fee to be included in the *CTM*.

The *Official Sightseeing Sales and Tour Guide* is published annually by Gray Line Corporation. The Gray Line guide lists net rates for sightseeing, transfers, limousine rental, and even shore excursions. Though it focuses on destinations in the United States, Canada, Mexico, and the Caribbean, it also includes many other international destinations.

The *Official Tour Directory* is published twice a year by Thomas Publishing. It covers tours to destinations in the United States and around the world. It also provides an alphabetical listing of tour operators with their addresses and phone numbers.

Check Your Product Knowledge

1. Which four groups of people must work together to produce a package tour?
2. What is the role of the tour operator in the production of the tour package?
3. What are the four main stages in the development of a tour package?

CHARTERS

A *charter* is a travel arrangement in which transportation equipment is leased or rented at a net price. The company (or individual) that charters the airplane, bus, ship, or train is the charterer. Tour operators handle the bulk of the charter business, but travel agents, individuals, and groups can also act as charterers.

Charters present a number of advantages and disadvantages, both for the charterer and the traveler. First, the advantages:

- The greatest attraction for the traveler is the charter price. If the charter is fully occupied or sold out, per-passenger cost can be as low as 40 percent of the regular fare.
- The operator can make a higher per-passenger profit when the charter is fully occupied or sold out.
- Charters can offer greater convenience than scheduled transportation. A charter from Omaha to Hawaii, for example, could fly direct without stopping. Passengers on a scheduled flight might have to change planes at least once.
- Charters give a group or an organization a sense of exclusiveness. Group members will refer to the charter vehicle as "our plane" or "our bus."
- Charters can often be customized to meet the MNEs of the passengers.

And now the disadvantages:

- Pricing is based on an expectation of near-capacity. If the chartered vehicle is only partially occupied, the cost per seat can be high.
- The operator can lose money if the number of seats sold doesn't cover costs.

Illus. 10-5 *A charter trip that is booked full means that the price for each seat is cheaper for every tour-goer.*
Source: © D. Wells/The Image Works

■ Charter flights have a worse on-time performance record than do scheduled flights. Because the charter flight coming into an airport is usually scheduled to take off again on another charter as soon as it's serviced (back-to-back scheduling), the chances for delay are comparatively high. Charters are also subject to cancellation.

■ A charter ticket is nontransferable. If a traveler misses his or her charter flight to Las Vegas because of a flat tire en route to the airport, no other carrier will honor the ticket.

■ Charter operators can consolidate two or more charters into one viable departure if the charters are not selling well. This can cause last-minute changes in departure times, airports, and even itineraries.

■ Charterers might add a last-minute surcharge. An increase in fuel costs, for example, might lead to a sudden fare hike. (Charterers are legally allowed to increase fares by as much as 10 percent up to ten days before departure.)

The charter operator, just like a tour operator, is a speculator and risk taker. When arranging a charter with a carrier, the operator must sign a contract and pay a deposit. The deposit is passed on to the sales intermediaries and/or passengers, as is the case with a tour.

Chartering Different Modes of Transportation

Most people think of charters as involving a plane or a bus. However, it is also possible to charter a train or a ship. An entire train might be chartered for a whistle-stop political campaign, or to carry a circus group. Such charters, however, are the exception. More commonly, groups or individuals charter a single railroad car and hook it up to a scheduled train. Vessels that are available for charter tend to be small (such as windjammers, riverboats, and yachts), although it is possible to charter an entire liner.

It is less complicated to charter a school bus than a cruise ship or a DC-10. But, regardless of size and price, all charters require some sort of contractual agreement.

Many charter flights take place on board scheduled carriers, while others are provided by all-charter airlines (known as supplemental carriers), which usually do not have scheduled services. United Airlines is an example of a scheduled carrier that offers charters (for professional football teams, among others). When scheduled airlines dedicate a portion of their fleet to charter service, the plane configuration changes. Almost all charter flights are economy only, with no first-class section. Supplemental carriers in the United States include American Trans Air, Key Airlines, and Evergreen.

The deregulation in the United States of the airlines and motorcoach industry has had a significant effect on the charter market. Scheduled airlines can now compete in price and access with the supplemental carriers. They can also offer equally attractive packages with fewer restrictions and less risk. Several supplemental carriers in the United States chose to become scheduled carriers after deregulation. Deregulation of the motorcoach industry has made it easier for bus companies to obtain a tour broker's license. This, in turn, has led to a great increase in the number of charter companies.

Different Types of Charter

Charters can be either private or public. *Private charters* are not for sale to the general public. Some private charters, known as *single-entity charters*, are paid for in full by a single source. For example, the Denver Broncos football team charters a 727 from United Airlines to fly the team and staff to a game in Miami. Or IBM charters a Northwest 767 and flies 250 of its top salespeople and their spouses to Barbados for an incentive tour/holiday. As a rule, the passengers do not pay for their own tickets: these are provided, along with any accommodations, by the company that arranges the charter.

Other private charters are available for sale to an organization, such as a club or association. These are called *affinity charters*, indicating some sort of voluntary membership or affinity to an organization. An affinity charter can be sold to the membership through direct mailing or publications, and each passenger reimburses the sponsoring organization for the tour. For example, a college alumni association charters an American Airlines 727 for a trip to Bermuda. The charter is promoted and sold by direct mail and in the alumni newsletter. Those who decide to take the tour send their money to the alumni association.

As the name suggests, *public charters* are open for sale to the general public either through a travel agency or by a tour or charter operator. There are no restrictions in terms of membership in an organization. The public charter may include transportation only (either one-way or round-trip) or be part of a package (known as a charter tour).

Pricing

Charterers determine the price of a charter by dividing the total price quoted by the carrier (plus any markup) by the number of seats, berths, or cabins. Most private charters are not marked up, since they require no commissions to sales intermediaries.

As an example, a school charters a 40-seat bus for a trip to the circus. The bus company charges $200 for the bus. If all seats are sold, the price per passenger will be $5 ($200 ÷ 40). Similarly, a seat on a 250-seat 767 that has been chartered for $50,000 will cost each passenger $200 ($50,000 ÷ 250).

Important Charter Terms and Concepts

You will understand the concept of chartering better if you become familiar with the terms used in the charter business. Some of these are outlined below.

- Charters are priced by the carrier as *wet* or *dry*. Wet means fuel is included; dry means no fuel is included.
- When the carrier provides the crew, this cost is included in the quote.
- If the driver of a motorcoach has to wait for three hours while the group tours an attraction or attends a show, an hourly *wait charge* will be figured into the price.
- Most charters base their price on cost per mile and/or cost per hour. A one-way charter can, therefore, cost as much as a round-trip charter because the operator has to get the vehicle home (unless the operator practices *back-to-back scheduling*, whereby the vehicle will return with a full load).
- When planning multiple charters, operators try to establish a *pattern*. They might organize, for example, one flight per week, May 15–August 31, New York City–Rome, or one flight per week, May 15–August 31, Chicago–Rome. Patterns make *consolidation* much easier: if the May 30 departures from New York City and Chicago are both undersold, the operator can stop the Chicago flight in New York City and proceed to Rome with all passengers in a single plane.
- Consolidation can also mean consolidating dates. A Friday departure and a Sunday departure, for example, can be consolidated into a single Saturday departure.

References

Charters are never listed in the *Official Airline Guide* (*OAG*) or other travel schedules. The best source of charter information is *JAX FAX Travel Marketing Magazine*, a monthly directory of air tours published by the Jet Air Transportation Exchange. Other sources include charter operators' programs and brochures.

Check Your Product Knowledge

1. List three advantages and three disadvantages of traveling by charter flight.
2. What is the difference between a scheduled carrier and a supplemental carrier?
3. How are charters priced?
4. What is meant by back-to-back scheduling?

THE CHANNELS OF DISTRIBUTION

All products, including the tour package, must be moved from producer to consumer. The tour industry has its own distribution system, with wide variations, combinations, and interactions. We can identify four main channels of distribution—one direct and three indirect.

With the one-stage/direct sale system, the individual or group traveler can buy the tour product directly from the producer or supplier of tour services. This cuts out all sales intermediaries. An example would be a client who buys an air tour through an airline reservations center. Some hotels and sightseeing attractions also package tours for direct sale to the consumer.

The two-stage distribution system involves the intervention of a single sales intermediary. Usually the intermediary will be a tour operator who packages the various supplier services into a single tour product. Some travel agents also buy directly from the suppliers, as do incentive travel companies, travel clubs, convention planners, and corporate travel offices.

The three-stage system involves the intervention of a second sales intermediary between the tour operator and the consumer. The additional intermediary is usually a retail travel agent who is paid a commission for handling the tour operator's product.

The four-stage system is the most complex of all, involving three intermediaries. The additional intermediary is normally a specialty channeler, whose role it is to intervene between the consumer and the travel agent. An organization planning a convention for its members, for example, might first consult a convention planner for advice on transportation and accommodations. The convention planner might then make the necessary arrangements with a travel agent, who in turn will contact a tour operator.

The Tour Organizer

Tours that are promoted and sold to a specific group or within a local market often entail the participation of a tour organizer. He or she may either be a member of the group (for example, the president of a garden club who leads a tour to the Chelsea Flower Show in London), or a media celebrity who shares an interest with the group (for example, a sportscaster who leads a tour to the Super Bowl).

The tour organizer will be compensated with a free trip if there are enough people on the tour (15 is usually the minimum). The tour organizer may also receive a certain amount of money for each tour participant. The tour operator will either add a pro rata surcharge to each fully paid package or build the cost of the organizer's free trip into each package.

Local and Nationwide Tours

The terms *local tour* and *nationwide tour* refer to the marketplace in which the tour is promoted, not to the destination. An example of a local tour is a high school spring trip to Washington, D.C.; such a tour would be marketed only to local high school students. Local tours are often joint efforts, involving a tour organizer, local travel agency, tour operator, and transportation representative. Sign-up parties with promotional film shows might be held to attract potential buyers.

Nationwide tours, on the other hand, are promoted and sold from coast to coast. You can buy the same American Express, Tauck, or other big-name tour in any of the 37,000 travel agencies throughout the United States.

Check Your Product Knowledge

1. Describe how the tour product gets from producer to consumer in a three-stage distribution system. Give an example.
2. What is the difference between a local tour and a nationwide tour?

CAREER OPPORTUNITIES

The rapidly expanding tour industry offers a wide variety of career opportunities at entry-level positions with good prospects for advancement. Many people are attracted to the tour operator field by the promise of unlimited free travel to glamorous destinations throughout the world. In reality, only a few employees (such as tour managers) get to travel extensively. For the rest, the work entails year-round office work, with only limited opportunity for travel at discount prices.

Careers are available in four main areas:

- The tour operator office.
- Tour management.
- Tour sales and promotion.
- Entrepreneurship.

The Tour Operator as Employer

A tour operator's office employs a number of clerical workers and supervisory staff. Some positions are described below.

Reservationist. The primary duty of the reservationist is to handle incoming calls from travel agents who are interested in booking the operator's tours. Reservationists also handle bookings made through the computer. Reservations can be confirmed over the phone or in writing. The reservationist must be familiar with all the components of each tour.

Operations Clerk. This position requires little or no personal contact with the travel agent or general public. Operations clerks process information from the reservationists to prepare passenger lists, rooming lists, and updates on the status of tour availability. Other duties can include typing confirmations and mailing them to travel agents, and preparing passenger tour documents.

Reservation Supervisor. A reservationist can advance to the position of reservation supervisor and be placed in charge of all reservation staff and procedures. He or she will be responsible for the interviewing, hiring, and training of all new reservationists. Group bookings and major accounts will usually be handled by the supervisor rather than by a less-experienced reservationist.

Operations Supervisor. This is another supervisory position, entailing responsibility for all operational staff and procedures.

Other positions within the tour operator office include group coordinator, who handles special-interest groups booked by travel agencies; accountant; and costing specialist.

Tour Management

As outlined in an earlier section, the tour manager or director is responsible for the day-to-day, even minute-by-minute, operation of the escorted tour. It is a pivotal position: the reputation of a tour operator can hinge on how successfully the tour manager performs his or her job.

Tour managers must have strong skills in negotiating, finance, accounting, and planning, as well as a limitless supply of patience and energy. Knowledge of a foreign language (or several foreign languages) is essential for a tour manager who hopes to conduct tours overseas. Opportunities for managers of European tours are extremely limited, since tour operators usually like to employ native Europeans.

Certification through the NTA program is an excellent qualification for a tour manager, as is membership in the International Association of Tour Managers (IATM).

It should be noted that tour management is not only a career field in itself, but also an entry-level step toward management of an entire tour operator company. In addition to professional tour managers who work full-time, there are also opportunities for part-time tour managers. Part-time positions are also available as tour guide (working at local sites and attractions) and tour organizer. These positions are often held by people with full-time jobs (for example, teachers) or by retirees or special-interest enthusiasts. Students can sometimes be employed as tour guides if they have an in-depth knowledge of a certain destination or subject.

Tour Sales and Promotion

The sales representative is the most visible employee in this department. The position entails personal calls on travel agents and group presentations to promote the company's tours. Other positions within the promotional department include publicist and writer. In addition, graphics specialists are employed to design and lay out brochures and other promotional material.

Entrepreneurship

Since deregulation, a flood of new tour operators, transportation companies, and charter operators have entered the market. Those who aspire to own and operate their own businesses might consider the following:

- Motorcoach and sightseeing companies.
- Small tour operator companies.
- Charter operators.
- Incoming or reception operators.
- Freelance tour management.

Most people need experience working in the tour industry before they go into business for themselves.

Summary

- The tour has evolved from the grand tour, through custom-made tours, to the package tour.
- The package tour is a combination of two or more travel components put together by a tour operator and sold to the consumer as a single product at a single price.
- Package tours have become increasingly popular because they offer travelers worry-free vacations, with the benefits of known costs, bargain prices, and guaranteed arrangements.
- Tours can be categorized by format, destination, and purpose.
- Independent, hosted, and escorted are the three basic package tour formats.
- Tour operators develop packages to fit the MNEs of different kinds of travelers.
- The need for flexibility, pacing, and different price ranges are important considerations in developing tours.
- A tour manager accompanies a group for the duration of an escorted tour, making sure that all the ingredients come together as planned.

A Tour Manager

If you have ever taken a tour, you probably already have a good idea of what a tour manager does. I am the person who shepherds the tour group from place to place and makes sure all aspects of the tour run smoothly. I take care of hotel reservations, arrange for meals and transportation, obtain tickets for local attractions, and so on. This allows the members of the group to simply relax and enjoy their vacation.

The first day of the tour, I greet the members of my tour group, make sure they have all of their luggage, and brief them on the schedule for the day. Then we set off to our first destination. Most of the members of my tour groups are retired people and we usually travel by bus. When we arrive at our hotel, I check in for my group and get everyone room assignments. Later, at dinner, I will tell everyone about the next day's schedule.

A lot of people have misconceptions about what tour managers do. Some people think I'm some kind of drill sergeant who bosses people around and tries to fill every minute of their day with organized activities. Nothing could be further form the truth. My job is to take care of the paperwork and headaches involved in traveling so people can concentrate on doing the fun things they want to do.

It is true that I do organize group activities because the group expects it and because it is cheaper for people to visit local attractions at a group rate. However, the members of my tour always have the option of joining in the activity, doing something else, or simply relaxing. In addition, on my tours, I always leave plenty of free time in my activities schedule for people to go off and do things on their own.

Some people think tour managers are experts on the history of the tour area. This is not necessarily true. Many tour managers lead tours of the same routes over and over again and do become experts on the local area. In some cases, however, the tour company provides a sightseeing guide, in addition to the tour manager, to inform the tour members about the history of the area. Sightseeing guides specialize in one specific region, museum, park, or building.

My main job is to act as the liaison between my tour group and the hotels, restaurants, and attractions that my group will visit. I make all the reservations, pay the bills and tips, and stand ready to solve any and all problems that may arise during the course of a tour. I must always be resourceful and calm in the face of a crisis because no tour ever goes completely smoothly. On a recent tour, our bus broke down. I had to arrange for another bus to pick us up, and then I had to keep the tour members occupied while we waited.

My job requires tact, organizational skills, and leadership ability. Knowledge of a foreign language is a major advantage, even in America, because so many foreign tourists have started visiting our country in recent years. Some tour managers lead tour groups on wilderness and adventure tours. They may lead tourists on hikes through the foothills of the Himalayas, on whitewater rafting trips down the Colorado River, or on horseback tours of the Sierra Nevada Mountains. These guides need strength and stamina as well as all the other attributes of a good tour manager. Some tour managers specialize in archaeology, art history, fine dining, or wine appreciation. These managers need special training in those fields.

When my tour company hired me, it put me through an intensive training course. Then it sent me out in the field with an experienced tour manager. That's how I learned my job. Being a tour manager is not a high-paying job, but it gives me the opportunity to travel and stay at nice resorts for free. Many tour managers work only part-time with long gaps between tours. Some are freelance tour managers who keep busy by working for several tour operators instead of just one company.

I like being a tour manager because I like people and I like to travel. I think the nicest thing about my job is that I start out with a group of strangers and I help them become a group of friends who are sharing the fun and adventure of a trip together. When that happens, I know I have done my job well.

Photo Source: Judith Pszenica

- Since deregulation, the USTOA and NTA have set financial and ethical standards for the industry.
- All overseas tours are required to conform to IATA regulations.
- The production of the tour product entails a close working relationship between suppliers, public-sector organizations, tour operators, and travel agents.
- Operations, costing, brochure production, and promotions are the four main stages in the preparation of a tour package.
- Charters, either private or public, offer travelers the advantage of considerable savings on transportation costs.
- The tour product is channeled from producer to consumer by one of four distribution systems.
- Tours can also be categorized as local tours or nationwide tours, depending on the area in which the tour is promoted.

Key Terms

Foreign Independent Tour (FIT)
Domestic Independent Tour (DIT)
package tour
all-inclusive package
tour operator
tour wholesaler
hosted tour
incentive tour
convention tour
special-interest group tour
incoming tour
area tour
single-country tour
two-city tour
single-city tour
ecotourism
tour organizer
tour manager
tour guide
à la carte
table d'hôte
dine-around plan
double occupancy
quad
triple
single supplement
IT number
charter
private charter
single-entity charter
affinity charter
public charter
local tour
nationwide tour

What Do You Think?

1. What effects might a reintroduction of federal regulation have on the tour industry as a whole?
2. Despite the considerable savings that package travel allows, why, in your opinion, do many travelers still prefer to travel independently?
3. What special arrangements could tour operators make for hearing-impaired travelers and sight-impaired travelers?
4. Why do you think some travel agents make it their policy not to handle charters?
5. Do you think that hotels are justified in charging a single supplement for travelers who room alone? Explain your answer.

Dealing with Product

Marketing specialists believe that the secret to successful marketing is finding the right product at the right time for the right person at the right price. Romantics will tell you that "Somewhere, somehow, there is something or someone for everyone."

Try your skills as a "romantic marketing specialist." What type of package tours would you recommend for the following clients:

- A garden club.
- High school seniors.
- An amateur theater club.
- A family of five (three children ages 8, 5, and 2).
- A neighborhood senior citizens center.
- Honeymooners.
- Race-car fans.
- Stamp collectors.
- A middle-aged widow with no dependent children.
- Two 25-year-old secretaries who are single.

Dealing with People

You are the vice president of a large retail travel agency. Your board of directors has decided to develop a special tour department and to begin promoting a series of escorted tours for the coming summer season.

Your job is to take charge of the hiring and training of the tour managers. Your first order of business is to write a job description for the tour manager. What qualifications should a candidate have? Are education and experience important? Does "personality" enter the picture? What do you expect each manager to be able to do? Can you train a candidate with lots of enthusiasm but no previous experience?

Name _____

WORKSHEET 10-1   CHOOSING TOURS

You are a travel agent. Use the *Consolidated Tour Manual* or a similar publication to pick tours for the customers listed below. Describe cost, air and land travel arrangements, accommodations, meals, sample itinerary, and additional components.

1. A middle-aged couple wants a leisurely paced escorted tour of Europe. They want first-class accommodations, and price is not of great concern.

    _____

    _____

    _____

    _____

2. A single woman wants a hosted scenic tour of the Canadian Rockies that is moderately priced.

    _____

    _____

    _____

    _____

3. Two amateur archaeologists want to participate in a dig on the Yucatán Peninsula. They need an inexpensive tour.

    _____

    _____

    _____

4. A young woman wants to relax in the Caribbean for two weeks. She also wants to do some sightseeing and shopping. She wants nice, but not deluxe, accommodations.

    _____

    _____

    _____

    _____

    _____

5. A group of hearing-impaired travelers wants an escorted historical tour of South America

    _____

    _____

    _____

    _____

    _____

6. A family consisting of two adults and two teenagers wants a low-budget adventure tour in Alaska.

    _____

    _____

    _____

WORKSHEET 10-2   INBOUND TOURISM

You are a receptive tour operator. Your job is to package and promote tours for Japanese visitors to the United States.

A major part of your job is to negotiate contracts with suppliers of transportation, hospitality, and tourism. In addition to basic services, you expect your suppliers to furnish special services and amenities for your Japanese customers. What could each of the following tour components do to help your tour groups feel welcome in this country? (For example, hotels along the tour route might agree to make Japanese newspapers available for guests to read.)

Airlines _____   Stores_____

_____   _____

Hotels/Motels _____   Tourist Attractions _____

_____   _____

Restaurants _____

_____

What could you do to promote your tour package to Japanese consumers? (For example, you might hire an ad agency to create ads for Japanese television.) Create a slogan for your ad campaign.

_____   _____

_____   _____

_____   _____

_____   _____

In addition to packaging and promoting outstanding tour products, you could also lobby the U.S. government to promote inbound tourism. What specific things might the government do to encourage more foreigners to visit the United States? (For example, the government could make customs and immigration procedures easier.)

_____   _____

_____   _____

_____   _____

WORKSHEET 10-3   TERMS AND CONDITIONS

Get brochures for two tours that are currently available. Compare the terms and conditions.

Tours
_____   _____
_____   _____
_____   _____
_____   _____

What is and is not included
_____   _____
_____   _____
_____   _____

Reservations procedure
_____   _____
_____   _____
_____   _____

Deposit and payment schedule
_____   _____
_____   _____
_____   _____

Travel and health documents required
_____   _____
_____   _____
_____   _____

Cancellation and refund policy
_____   _____
_____   _____
_____   _____

Status of fares, rates, and itinerary
_____   _____
_____   _____
_____   _____

Tour operator's limited responsibility and
liability
_____   _____
_____   _____
_____   _____

WORKSHEET 10-4   Ecotours

One of the hottest travel trends in the 1990s is ecotourism. Ecotours take travelers to various areas of the world to observe wildlife or to explore nature. Ecotourists might hike through the rain forests of Indonesia, trek across the ice of Antarctica, or cruise down the Amazon River. In addition to enjoying a great adventure, ecotourists gain appreciation and concern for the environment.

Select an ecotour currently being advertised. Find out as much information about the tour as you can. Then complete the items below.

Name of tour

Name of ecotour operator or company

Tour destination

Tour price

Description of tour

Educational element (What makes this trip different from other trips to the area?)

Qualifications of person leading the trip

Company history (How long has it been in business? How long has it been offering ecotours?)

Environmental impact (Does the company seem genuinely concerned about the environment? Is it possible the tour could actually damage the environment?)

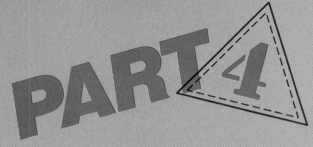

PART 4

BUSINESS AND PROFESSIONAL TRAVEL

CHAPTER 11 THE BUSINESS OF BUSINESS TRAVEL

"Business is like riding a bicycle. Either you keep moving or you fall down."
—*John David Wright*

Objectives

When you have completed this chapter, you should be able to:

- List reasons for business travel.
- Explain the main differences between business travel and vacation travel.
- Describe the motivations, needs, and expectations (MNEs) of business travelers.
- Tell how airlines compete for the business of the business traveler through business-class service, frequent-flier programs, discounts, and rebates.

- Describe the efforts of car rental chains and railroads to meet the needs of the business traveler.
- List the special services and facilities that the hotel industry offers business travelers.
- Describe the work of the business travel department (BTD) and corporate travel agency.
- Discuss careers related to business travel.

Flight 086 from Chicago to Washington, D.C., is nearly full. Occupying seat 6A, near the window, is Jill Rosendahl. Jill works for a company that produces training materials for Fortune 500 companies. Part of Jill's job is to interview clients to find out what information and skills they want their sales representatives to learn. On this trip, Jill plans to meet with the marketing staff of a software company.

Sitting in seat 6C, on the aisle, is John Wu. John is a field engineer for a laboratory equipment manufacturer. He travels 80 percent of the time, helping customers install equipment and troubleshooting when problems develop.

Across the aisle from John, in seat 6D, is Maria Rodriguez. Maria is a microbiologist for the Illinois State Department of Health. While in Washington, she'll attend the annual meeting of the American Society of Microbiology. When she returns to work, she'll report to her colleagues on what she learned at the meeting.

Frank Delgado has seat 6F. Just a few months ago, Frank started his own small-tool manufacturing company. At present, Frank employs ten people. He's going to the Washington area to visit manufacturing plants that might be able to use his company's tools in their production process.

What do these four people have in common? You probably recognize that they are all business travelers. Unlike tourists who travel for fun and pleasure, business travelers must travel to do their job. Travel is part of their job description.

Business travelers may work for a private company, a government agency, a nonprofit organization, or they may be self-employed. They travel to buy and sell goods and services, visit branch offices, attend company meetings, or seek new business opportunities. They may also travel to attend conferences and seminars related to their jobs, although sometimes this type of travel is referred to as professional, rather than business, travel.

TRAVEL FOR BUSINESS

People who live in Missouri may wear jeans manufactured in California. Their television sets may have been put together in Tennessee, and their cars may have come off the assembly line in Detroit. Americans can purchase products from all over the United States because businesspeople negotiated agreements with each other. And, in most instances, those businesspeople had to travel in order to accomplish this.

A Brief History of Business Travel

Travel for the purpose of exchanging goods and services has been going on for centuries. In early times, farmers traveled to local markets where they could trade their vegetables, grain, and eggs for a piece of cloth or pottery. A famous business traveler of the thirteenth century was Marco Polo of Venice. He traveled to China and brought back silk, tea, and other exotic products. When Europeans desired a constant supply of these products, trade routes between Europe and the Far East developed. Inns sprang up along the major routes to provide food and lodging for the merchant caravans.

During the Middle Ages, trade fairs, especially those of England, stimulated business travel. Merchants and craftspeople from all over the country brought their wares to villages and towns such as Winchester, Abington, and Smithfield. Even then, village officials recognized the economic benefits of travelers coming to the community. In order for a village to host a fair, the king had to grant permission, and there was much competition among villages for this privilege.

Travel for the purpose of developing new business opportunities has also been going on for some time. Early explorers, who searched for precious metals and new lands, were actually business travelers because they were interested in enriching themselves and in expanding the trade and economy of the country that sponsored their voyage. In the seventeenth century, for example, Henry Hudson was commissioned by the Dutch East India Company to find a northwest waterway to the Far East. Although Hudson didn't find the Northwest Passage, his explorations helped develop the fur-trading business in North America.

In the nineteenth century, people began to travel to international trade expositions where they could display new products. The first of these was the Great Exhibition of 1851 held at the Crystal Palace in London. Inventors and entrepreneurs from the United States and Europe displayed new products, such as reapers and dental instruments. When visitors to the exposition became interested in obtaining these products, businesses were encouraged to manufacture and distribute them on a wide scale.

Following World War II, major corporations expanded their facilities throughout the United States and the world. They did this to be closer to local markets or to take advantage of more advantageous tax rates or a cheaper labor force. The need for on-site visits provided another stimulus for business travel. At the same time, worldwide trade markets expanded. Today, Americans can purchase jeans manufactured in Mexico, television sets made in Japan, and cars assembled in Germany. Likewise, many products made in the United States fill the shelves of stores in other countries.

Business Travel and the Travel Industry

Business travel has grown dramatically in recent years. In 1989, approximately 34 million Americans took a total of almost 170 million business trips (see Figure 11-1). This number is constantly increasing and includes

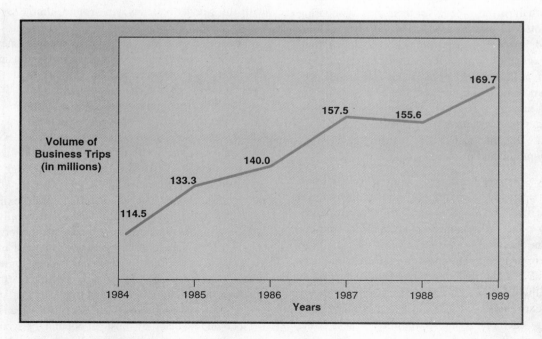

Figure 11-1 The Growth of Business Travel
Source: United States Travel Data Center

Category	Women Business Travelers	Men Business Travelers
Age		
18–34	37%	42%
35–44	29	27
45 or Older	34	31
Education		
Some College or Less	63	59
College Graduate or More	37	41
Household Income		
Less than $40,000	58	50
$40,000–$49,999	15	17
$50,000 or More	27	33
Occupation		
Professional or Managerial	21	24
Lower Level Technical or Managerial	31	30
Clerical or Sales	18	11
Self-Employed	27	30

Table 11-1 Demographics of Women and Men Business Travelers
Source: United States Travel Data Center

a growing number of women. Today, more than one-third of business travelers are women. Table 11-1 compares the demographics of women and men business travelers.

The travel industry supplies products and services that make business travel possible. Travel agencies help travelers with the arrangements for their trips by securing airline tickets and making hotel reservations. Airlines and railroads provide transportation to the destination. Car rental agencies furnish local transportation while travelers are at their destination. Hotels and motels provide accommodations and, in many instances, are the site for business meetings. To relax between appointments or in the evening, business travelers can shop, attend a concert, go to a ballgame, or take part in many other events provided by public and private recreational systems.

The Business-Travel Bonanza. To the travel industry, business travelers are a gold mine. American firms spend $115 billion a year on business travel. Business travelers fill more than half of all nonresort hotel rooms and domestic airline flights.

There is much competition within the travel industry to win a share of the business-travel revenue. Airlines compete with other airlines, car rental agencies compete with other car rental agencies, and hotels compete with other hotels—each one trying to woo the business of the business traveler with the best products and services at the best price.

Characteristics of Business Travel. Business travel has other features that make it attractive to the travel industry. Unlike vacation travel—which tends to be heaviest during the summer months and then tapers off during the winter months—business travel is not seasonal. It occurs with the same frequency year-round, thus providing a steady source of income.

Business travelers also tend to spend money more freely than other travelers. Money spent on business-related travel and entertainment is often tax deductible because it is viewed as a cost of doing business.

Business travel also tends to be inelastic, or inflexible. When a meeting is scheduled out of town or an emergency arises in an out-of-town plant, businesspeople must be there. They can't wait for bargains. Unlike vacation travelers, business travelers often book flights at the last minute and consequently are ineligible for advance-purchase discounts. This characteristic of inflexibility is attractive to the travel industry because it usually translates into higher revenues from business travelers.

If there's an economic recession, the cost of travel goes up and vacation travelers tend to stay home. Business travelers, on the other hand, continue to travel at whatever the going rate happens to be. In fact, a recession might even encourage business travel because businesspeople feel that they must get out and try even harder to develop their accounts.

Another reason why the travel industry likes business travel is that it can generate revenue for vacation travel. If business travelers are favorably impressed with a destination, they may return to it for a vacation—this time bringing their families along.

For travel agencies, business travel can require less work than vacation travel. Many business travelers visit the same destinations over and over. Thus, once the account has been established, arrangements usually become straightforward and routine. However, many business travelers are notorious for last-minute changes in their itineraries. This results in extra work under pressure for the travel agent.

Check Your Product Knowledge

1. What is the main difference between a vacation traveler and a business traveler?
2. What are some reasons for business travel?
3. Why does the travel industry actively seek the business of business travelers?
4. Explain how business travel tends to be inelastic and what this means to the travel industry

THE FREQUENT BUSINESS TRAVELER

At age 30—and with degrees in engineering and computer science—John Wu fits the profile of the frequent business traveler. The majority of frequent business travelers are:

- Male.
- Between the ages of 25 and 44.
- College-educated.
- Working in a professional, technical, or managerial occupation.
- Upwardly mobile, earning an annual salary of $40,000 or more.

Most areas of the travel industry define frequent business travelers as people who take ten or more trips per year, with each trip lasting—on the average—four nights. Because of the potential for repeat business, the travel industry is most interested in satisfying the motivations, needs, and expectations (MNEs) of the frequent business traveler.

Motivations, Needs, and Expectations

Frequent business travelers must accomplish a task while they're away from the home office. They have definite needs—and expectations—for getting their work done. Hotels, airlines, car rental agencies, and travel agencies attempt to design products and services to meet these needs.

Business travelers are on tight schedules. They must be at appointments on time. When meetings run longer than expected or the meeting time is changed at the last minute, they must be able to adjust airline and hotel reservations immediately. For business travelers, time is money and they don't want to waste it through delays, such as waiting in a long line to check out of a hotel, or through mistakes, such as luggage lost by an airline. Nor do business travelers want to waste time waiting for flights or for transportation to a hotel. Quick, reliable service is a priority for most travelers, but especially for business travelers.

Business travelers often want to do paperwork or plan their strategy while traveling to a business appointment. Being seated next to a screaming toddler on an airplane would certainly disrupt a traveler's thought processes. Business travelers also look for prompt, efficient and courteous service from hotel employees. They want to know that they can check in and out quickly, and will be assigned to a room that offers the comforts and conveniences that they need. No one wants to hold a business meeting in a room next to a group of high school students celebrating their team's victory in the state basketball tournament. Business travelers need quiet to think and relax. Often this means separating them from the mass of travelers.

When traveling abroad, business travelers may have additional needs. They appreciate ease in making international telephone calls to their office or home. If they're not fluent in the language of the country, they may require translation services in order to conduct business.

As you can see, frequent business travelers value efficiency, speed, and comfort. They demand respect and recognition. To achieve these expectations, they are often willing to pay higher airfares, pay more for better accommodations, and pay for larger rental cars.

Women Travelers

In the early 1970s, when women began traveling for business in large numbers, the travel industry wasn't quite sure how to treat them. Some travel industry employees couldn't get used to seeing a woman traveling by herself. If a woman was standing behind a man in a hotel check-in line, the desk clerk often assumed that they were together.

Women business travelers have the same MNEs as men business travelers. When surveyed about their needs and wants, women and men give the same responses. Convenience of schedule is the number one factor in choosing an airline, and convenience of location is the number one factor in choosing a hotel.

Women also want the same respect and high quality of service that the travel industry offers to men. Travelers like Jill Rosendahl don't want to be called "honey" or "dear" by hotel maids. They don't want to be ogled by desk clerks and bellstaff or treated rudely by airline flight attendants. And, when they dine alone in restaurants, they don't want to be seated in a dark corner by the kitchen. Although attitudes toward women traveling alone have improved greatly, airlines and hotels still need to train employees to treat women travelers with more courtesy.

The Cost Factor

With business travel, the company, and not the traveler, usually foots the bill. Although expense may not seem to be as much of a concern for the business traveler as it is for the vacation traveler, business travelers cannot be wildly extravagant. After convenience, the cost of a ticket or of a room ranks high in the business traveler's choice of an airline or a hotel.

The circumstances of the business traveler also determine how much money is spent. The expectations of a corporate executive with an unlimited expense account will be different from those of a struggling entrepreneur like Frank Delgado. A government employee, such as Maria Rodriguez, may be traveling on a per diem allowance. (A *per diem* ["by the day"] allowance refers to the amount of money a business traveler is permitted to spend each day for expenses.)

With changing federal tax laws and competition in the airline industry shrinking because of mergers and bankruptcies, travel costs are expected to increase even more. As a result, many companies are making concerted efforts to control their travel expenditures. For example, employees may be asked to take a less convenient flight—a night flight or a flight requiring a stopover—in order to get a lower airfare. Many companies also try to save money by negotiating discounts directly with hotels (or airlines and car rental agencies). In such cases, employees can stay only in certain hotels.

Another way companies attempt to control costs is through travel policies. Many of this country's largest companies have written travel policies. Such policies specify who may fly first class and who must fly coach (usually determined by position in the company or by the distance or duration of the flight), at what type of hotel employees can stay, and what size rental car they can obtain.

Check Your Product Knowledge

1. What qualities do business travelers need—and expect—from travel products and services?
2. What are the MNEs of women business travelers?
3. Why might business travelers spend different amounts of money for travel products and services?
4. What is the purpose of a company travel policy?

TRANSPORTATION SYSTEMS AND BUSINESS TRAVELERS

When making arrangements for a business trip, travelers can choose to fly, drive, or take a train to their destination. The average distance of a business trip is 1,200 miles. Driving to the destination might be less expensive in terms of travel costs, but more expensive in terms of time lost for conducting business. Consequently, business travelers are more likely to choose air transportation, and they generally choose the airline with the most convenient flight schedule.

There are situations, however, where taking a train is the best choice. This is particularly true for trips between major cities located in densely populated areas, such as Washington, Philadelphia, New York City, and Boston in the northeastern United States, and parts of Western Europe and Japan.

Once at their destination, travelers need transportation from the airport to their hotel. They may also need transportation to meeting sites or for making scattered sales calls. For local transportation, travelers can choose among taxis, limousines, subways, buses, or rental cars. Since rental cars and taxis provide on-demand transportation (that is, transportation whenever the traveler needs it), business travelers are more likely to choose these means of travel. On-demand transportation is generally more expensive than buses or rapid transit, but for the time-conscious business traveler, the flexibility is well worth the extra cost.

Airline Service

When John Wu arrived at Chicago's O'Hare International Airport, a manager of special services was there to help him and other frequent business travelers make their connecting flights. If there had been time, John could have relaxed for a while in a VIP lounge.

As you know, after deregulation of the airlines, competition for passengers became very intense. Whereas airlines have tried to attract vacation travelers primarily through discounts, they have tried to attract business travelers primarily through special services. A wide array of products and services now caters to the needs of the business traveler.

Business-Class Service. Some airlines have *business-class* sections on their planes, especially those used for international flights. Business class falls between coach class and first class in terms of price and amenities. It aims to satisfy the business traveler's need for comfort, quiet, and special attention. Passengers receive complimentary drinks and headsets, better meal options, and increased service. Since business travelers generally prefer to keep their briefcases and suitcases with them, there is more room for carry-on luggage. The seats are larger and farther apart so that there is more legroom. TWA even has extra wide seats specifically designed for the frequent business traveler. Called "Business Loungers," these seats also feature extra padding and automatic footrests.

Canadian Airlines International has gone a step further with a fleet of all-business-class planes. Linen and crystal are used for meal service aboard flights. The airline provides an exclusive reservation line and departure lounge for business travelers. In the United States, Air One and Air Atlanta also experimented with the all-business-class plane, with mixed results.

For the ultimate in speed, comfort, and prestige—and for $3,200 each way—the international business traveler can fly from New York to London or Paris on the supersonic Concorde. Although not exclusively for business travelers, the Concorde is first class all the way. Passengers sip champagne from crystal goblets and savor gourmet meals served on bone china. Flying at twice the speed of sound, the executive traveler can cross the Atlantic in less than four hours.

Many airlines are now providing amenities even after the flight is over. The most notable service is free transfers between local airports or from the airport to downtown. For example, Japan Air Lines offers free minibus transfers between LaGuardia Airport and Kennedy Airport in New York City, and British Airways provides limousine service into New York City or London after a Concorde flight.

Frequent-Flier Programs. Pioneered by American Airlines, *frequent-flier programs* were originally designed to pull travelers away from the multitude of low-fare carriers that sprang up after deregulation. The strategy was to encourage brand loyalty by awarding bonuses to faithful travelers. Developers believed that if travelers had to choose among airlines for a particular flight, they would choose the airline with which they had already accumulated mileage points.

Since 1981, frequent-flier programs have become very popular. Every major airline has its own program, with millions of travelers participating. John Wu belongs to Mileage Plus, the frequent-flier program of United Airlines. Every time he flies on United, he earns mileage points. When his account reaches 10,000 miles, he can cash in for a free upgrade from economy class to first class on his next flight. (A *free upgrade* means that the customer does not pay the difference in going from a lower class of service or product to a higher class of service or product.) Or John can let his miles accumulate to the 100,000-mile level. Then he's entitled to two airline tickets to Europe.

Most frequent-flier programs have tie-ins with hotels, car rental chains, other airlines, and even cruise lines. Sample tie-ins are shown in Table 11-2. John, for example, can also earn mileage points in Mileage Plus by flying on Air France, staying in a Hyatt Hotel, or renting a car from Hertz. Companies participating in a tie-in program benefit from increased patronage—thus they pay the airline to participate in its club.

A question that arises with the frequent-flier program is: Who should be able to keep the business traveler's bonus points? Some companies feel that since they pay for their employees' tickets, the coupons should be turned in to them. Companies can then reduce travel costs by redeeming the coupons for free business travel for other employees. Other companies regard frequent-flier points as dividends for having to travel and allow employees to keep these benefits for their personal use.

Keeping track of mileage points can become quite confusing, especially if the traveler belongs to more than one program. Books, newsletters, and computer software are available to help travelers with record keeping and to inform them about changes in the programs. A company's business travel department or travel agency may keep track of a traveler's mileage points.

Although frequent-flier programs have been very successful, there have been some problems. One problem has been overcrowding on flights to popular vacation destinations, such as Hawaii, when travelers are using their bonus vouchers or coupons. On any given flight, it's entirely possible that not one passenger in first class has paid for his or her ticket! Awarding free seats to frequent fliers, of course, prevents the airlines from selling those seats to cash-paying customers and making a profit on them. Attempts on the part of airlines to raise mileage requirements for popular destinations have angered club members, who feel that this is the equivalent of changing the rules in the middle of the game.

Another problem has been with coupon brokers. These people buy bonus points from frequent fliers. They redeem the points and then turn around and sell the awards to the public at a discount. For example, John has earned enough points for two coach tickets to Europe, airfare that might ordinarily cost about $1,200. John could sell his points to a coupon broker for $500. The broker could then obtain the tickets and sell them to a couple from Des Moines for $750. Everyone—except the airline—would make money on this deal.

Although coupon brokering is legal, airlines have been battling this practice on the grounds that it deprives them of ticket sales (the couple should have bought the tickets from the airline for $1,200). In addition to lawsuits, airlines have been formulating new rules to curb abuses, such as the requirement that bonus tickets be transferred only to persons with the same last name.

Because of the problems, some airlines would like to do away with frequent-flier programs altogether, but nobody wants to be the first to do so. Certainly the programs have been very effective marketing tools and it seems likely that the airlines will continue to use them.

Frequent Traveler Program

If you fly 100,000 miles on Continental Airlines the company will give you two round-trip, first-class tickets to Hawaii or two round-trip, business-class tickets to Europe. The Sheraton Hotel chain awards points for every dollar you spend at one of their hotels, which you can redeem for discounts on gifts and travel expenses. If you rent a car from General Rent-A-Car, you can earn credits toward free car rentals, free mileage, or the use of more luxurious cars.

These are all examples of frequent-traveler programs. Airlines, hotels, and other suppliers use frequent-traveler programs to attract, keep, and reward loyal customers. The idea is simple: the more you use the same companies for your travel needs, the more free travel and other discounts you receive in return.

Most of the major airlines began frequent-flier programs in the early 1980s after the airlines were deregulated and began to compete more aggressively for customers. Since then, the frequent-flier programs have mushroomed into multimillion-dollar giveaways. An estimated 22 million travelers are enrolled in frequent-traveler programs and several hundred thousand people take free trips each year.

The frequent-flier programs have been a particular boon to business travelers who must fly thousands of miles each year on company business. In some cases, the corporations allow their employees to keep the frequent-flier bonuses for their own personal use. Many companies, however, require that their employees turn their free mileage over to the company travel department so other employees can use it for business trips. In this way, the company can save on travel costs.

The airlines have the oldest and most extensive frequent-traveler programs, but other travel suppliers also have similar plans. Several hotel chains have "frequent-stayer" clubs or plans that allow guests to earn points toward free rooms, discounted meals, and other perks. Some chains offer "recognition" to frequent guests in the form of extra services. These services can include express check-in and checkout, newsletters, gift certificates, and exclusive weekend packages. One hotel goes so far as to embroider the names of frequent guests on hotel robes.

Many car rental agencies and some cruise lines also offer special programs to repeat customers. A typical car rental program offers a free weekend day with a minimum two-day rental. Most cruise lines work in conjunction with airlines. For example, a flier who has logged 80,000 miles on USAir can buy a three-day cruise on a Carnival ship and get a second three-day cruise for free. Other cruise lines offer discount rates to frequent fliers.

Commonly, frequent-traveler plans are tied into one another. If you are a member of American Airlines AAdvantage frequent-flier club, you can use your accumulated miles to receive discounts on certain foreign airlines, such as Qantas and British Airways. Other options are to rent a car at Avis, stay at a Hilton hotel, or take a cruise on a Royal Viking ship, all at discounted rates.

Travel agents have long been ambivalent about frequent-flier clubs. Many do not like the programs because they do not receive commissions on free flights. Other travel agents accept the clubs because a free flight often generates commissions from hotel bookings and car rentals. Travel suppliers have had mixed results with their frequent-traveler programs. Many hotel chains have tried, then dropped, their point systems in favor of recognition programs, and some car rental agencies have had only modest success with their programs.

For many airlines, the frequent-flier clubs may be too successful. An airline has to spend just as much to honor a free ticket as one that had been paid for, but free flights generate no income for the company. By the late 1980s, the airlines began to realize that they had given away a lot of free miles that had not yet been used. By 1989, according to one analysis, frequent fliers had accumulated $750 million worth of unclaimed free travel.

Fearing a run on free tickets, the airlines began to look for cheaper ways to entice customers to cash in their free miles. Some held auctions at which customers could bid accumulated miles for such prizes as golden retriever puppies and round-the-world trips. Others issued glossy catalogs in which they offered discounts on the purchase of cars, jewelry, furs, and vacation homes. The auctions and discount purchase programs were only moderately successful. Most frequent fliers, the airlines have found, still want free travel more than anything else as a reward for their loyalty.

Photo Source: Sara G. Matthews

Airline	Domestic Connection	Foreign Connection	Car Rental	Hotel	Cruise Line
America West	None	Air France Singapore Airlines Virgin Atlantic	Budget Thrifty	Doubletree Compri Marriott Red Lion	Cunard
American	None	British Airways Singapore Airlines Qantas Cathay Pacific	Ansa Avis Hertz	Inter-Contintental Sheraton Wyndham Hilton Resorts Marriott	Royal Viking Norwegian Cruise Line
Delta	None	KLM Air Canada Swissair Air New Zealand Japan Airline Singapore Airlines	National Alamo Avis	Marriott Prefereed Trusthouse Forte Hyatt Hilton	None
United	Aloha	Air France Lufthansa Alitalia Swissair British Airways Iberia Sabena KLM	Hertz Alamo Dollar	Hilton Westin Kempsinki Hyatt Sheraton	Royal Viking
USAir	Hawaiian Airlines Northwest (international flights only) TWA (international flights only)	British Airways Finnair Lufthansa Philippine Airlines Swissair Air France KLM Alitalia Air New Zealand Sabena	Hertz National	Omni Westin Stouffer Radisson Marriott Hyatt Hilton	Carnival

Table 11-2 Sample Frequent-Flier Tie-Ins

Besides encouraging product loyalty, club memberships provide airlines with convenient databases. Instead of paying for expensive advertising time on national television, airlines can market their products and services through direct mailings to frequent fliers—the group most likely to purchase them anyway.

Airport Comforts. Airlines provide private lounges where their frequent fliers can relax or work between flights or before an appointment. Airports, too, provide special facilities geared toward business travelers.

At many airports, travelers can take advantage of full-service business centers. The Tele-Trip Company, for example, operates business centers in airports at 19 destinations. These centers provide foreign money exchange, postal, and notary public services. Business travelers can also use the photocopying and fax machines. And travelers who find themselves short of cash can obtain emergency funds.

Most major airports have conference rooms that they rent to corporations. Executives from all over the country can fly in, attend a meeting, and fly out again without ever having to leave the airport.

Corporate Discounts. American consumers are accustomed to seeing advertisements proclaiming 10 percent off the price of a refrigerator or 25 percent off the price of a sweater. Discounting—selling merchandise at less

Illus. 11-1 *Travelers can take advantage of the full-service business centers found at many airports.*
Source: Tele-Trip Company

than the published price—is a standard practice in American marketing.

Airlines, too, offer discounts directly to corporations in order to gain their business. By designating an airline as its preferred carrier and promising a certain volume of travelers, the corporation gets dollars off each airfare it purchases.

Airlines offer various types of discounts. A systemwide discount, offered by major carriers with extensive routes, applies to any combination of cities to which the company's employees normally travel. A city-pair discount is offered where there is intense airline competition between two points, such as Chicago to New York City. A group discount—different from a discount offered to groups for a one-time trip—may be given when a corporation has many employees consistently traveling to the same place. For example, a California movie studio periodically sends production-crew members from Los Angeles to San Francisco for filming. These employees fly at a discounted rate each time they make the trip.

Although discounting is commonplace—and legal—in American marketing, the airlines don't advertise the fact that they give corporate discounts. Deals are made behind closed doors and are not discussed publicly. Airlines don't want the specifics of a particular deal revealed, for fear that they would have to make the same deal with every other corporation.

Airlines don't particularly like giving discounts. For one thing, there is no assurance that corporations will remain loyal, so time and effort spent in negotiations may be wasted. Airlines also worry about fighting discounting wars with other airlines, which could drain them financially. Revenues lost to discounting must be recovered either through higher costs to vacation travelers or through reduced services. But these solutions can backfire on an airline if they turn customers away.

Corporate Rebates. Another popular sales tool in the American marketplace is the *rebate*. Whereas a discount is money off the listed price, a rebate is cash back after the purchase has been made. For example, in a typical rebate offer, a consumer purchases three packages of light bulbs and sends proof of purchase to the manufacturer. The manufacturer then sends the consumer a check for $1. Offers of cash rebates are commonly used in advertising for new cars and appliances.

Airlines, too, offer rebates. After a corporation, for instance, has purchased products and services totaling $25,000, the airline might give the corporation a rebate of 4 percent.

At present, it is illegal for United States carriers to give rebates on international airfares. However, the law is not strictly enforced. On the one hand, the government wants to appear to be in harmony with the regulations of foreign governments. On the other hand, the government wants to keep fares lower for American consumers.

Car Rental Service

To compete for the business of the business traveler, car rental chains employ tactics similar to those of the airlines. These tactics include corporate discounts and rebates, club memberships with tie-ins to frequent-flier and frequent-stay programs, and special incentives.

Illus. 11-2 *Car rental companies offer many special services to attract frequent business travelers.*
Source: Hertz Corporation

To get a standard discount, corporations contract to do a certain amount of business (say $10,000 a year) with the car rental agency. Each time an employee rents a car from that agency for business travel, the corporation may get from 10 percent to 30 percent off the regular price. The type of car—luxury or economy—and whether or not there are mileage restrictions are specified in the type of discount.

At present, the major car rental chains—such as Hertz, Avis, and National Car Rental—have fairly well saturated the corporate market. They are now competing with second-tier rental companies for small-business customers. By requiring lower dollar-volume and offering attractive incentives, lesser-known companies—such as Alamo Rent-A-Car, Dollar Rent-A-Car, and Payless Rent-A-Car System—are doing well against the industry giants.

Because of the tie-in with United Airline's Mileage Plus, John Wu usually rents from Hertz. As a member of Hertz #1 Club, John is entitled to speedy rental procedures at airports. By calling ahead and reserving a car, John can bypass the rental counter and go directly to the rental lot. When returning the car, all he has to do is leave it in the lot—his company is billed by mail. Avis Express and Budget Rapid Action provide similar services for the business traveler in a hurry.

In response to business travelers' needs, many agencies now offer mobile telephones in some cars. (There is a per-minute charge for each call made.) With a mobile phone, a person riding in a car can make calls to and receive calls from almost any regular telephone in the world. This is ideal for businesspeople who must be in constant communication with their home office or with clients. Even when trapped in a traffic jam, they can conduct business via phone.

Car rental agencies are constantly introducing other incentives as well. These include computerized driving directions, 24-hour emergency road service, and destination travel guides.

Rail Service

To go from Washington, D.C., to New York City by air costs about $140 and takes approximately two hours. This includes the cost of a taxi and the time it takes to drive from the airport to downtown. (The actual flight time is usually about one hour.) To go from Washington, D.C., to New York City by rail costs $79 and takes slightly less than three hours. The traveler goes from city center to city center without having to deal with traffic.

For certain trips, taking the train is easier and less costly than taking the plane. This is particularly true where the distance between major cities is not great. In the United States, trips between cities in the Northeast Corridor (New York City to Washington, D.C.; New

Illus. 11-3 *Some business travelers have found that, for certain trips, taking a train is easier and cheaper than flying.*
Source: *Amtrak Photo*

York City to Boston; Washington, D.C., to Philadelphia) lend themselves well to train travel. Los Angeles to San Diego or Milwaukee to Chicago are other examples of convenient train trips. In Europe, where many major cities are only 250 to 350 miles apart, travel by train is the rule rather than the exception.

Domestic Rail Service. Amtrak's Metroliner Service between New York City and Washington, D.C., is designed for the business traveler. There are frequent arrivals and departures. Travelers can make reservations by telephone any hour of the day or night. They can pick up their tickets at a special express window shortly before their train leaves.

Once on board, passengers have room to relax. Club cars with tables allow business travelers to spread out their paperwork. Using Railfone®, business travelers can communicate with clients from coast to coast. Complimentary continental breakfasts and free hors d'oeuvres are additional amenities designed to lure business travelers away from airlines.

The Metroliner is developing a reputation for speed and efficiency. Since there is a high demand for this service, the price of a ticket is not discounted.

Foreign Rail Service. In Europe, the International Inter City trains are designed for business travel. These modern, clean, and comfortable trains even provide stenographic and photocopying services for their business passengers. American travelers who travel frequently in Europe can purchase various types of passes that allow unlimited travel for a specific time. Some passes, such as the France Vacancespass, are good for one country only, while others, such as the famous Eurailpass, are good for many countries.

In Japan, a nation with short distances between cities, train service has developed to a high level. Japan, in fact, has some of the fastest, safest, and most punctual trains in the world. A business traveler who needs to get from Tokyo to Osaka (a distance of about 200 miles) in a hurry can take the Shinkansen, a train that travels 256 miles per hour. Japanese National Railways (JNR) also boasts the world's most tightly scheduled train service. American travelers to Japan can purchase rail passes through Japan Air Lines.

HOSPITALITY SERVICES AND BUSINESS TRAVELERS

The hospitality industry provides two types of facilities geared to the needs of business travelers—hotels/motels and conference centers. Convention centers, a third type of facility, are usually built with public funds. The hospitality industry, however, strongly promotes the construction of convention centers. Convention centers and conference centers will be described in more detail in Chapter 12.

Hotels and Motels

At 6:00 A.M., John Wu hears a knock on the door of his hotel room. As he had expected, it's the executive-floor concierge with his morning wake-up call. When John opens the door, the concierge greets him with a cheery "Good morning" and hands him a cup of coffee and the morning newspaper.

At a roadside motel, a wake-up call might be a phone call from the desk clerk to a guest's room. At a hotel catering to frequent business travelers, however, services are provided with much more style and flair. Although convenience of location is the main reason for selecting a certain hotel, business travelers look for other

features as well. Increased competition among hotels for the business of the business traveler has brought about a host of special facilities, amenities, and services.

Business-Class Accommodations. In response to the business traveler's demand to be separated from tourists, hotels primarily for business travelers have been developed. These hotels, which include the luxurious all-suite hotels and the more practical budget hotels, offer a more sedate, serious atmosphere.

An all-suite hotel is a hotel in which each unit consists of two main rooms—a living room and a bedroom—along with a bathroom. The living room may feature a kitchen area with refrigerator and microwave oven, so that guests may prepare meals or snacks if they wish. All-suite hotels allow business travelers more space and more comfort than regular hotels. Most importantly, though, the living room of the suite provides business travelers with a suitably professional and private place to meet with clients.

Hotel consultants say that all-suite hotels are now the fastest-growing segment of the hospitality industry. In 1991, there were an estimated 96,000 suite units, and that number is expected to continue to grow. Embassy Suites and Residence Inns are among the better-known all-suite hotels.

Budget hotels provide accommodations for business travelers on a tight budget. Middle-level managers, limited-expense-account travelers, and travelers paying their own expenses would be typical guests. A room at a budget hotel generally costs less than $60 per night, which is 20 to 50 percent lower than a suite in an all-suite hotel. There are no bellstaff, ballrooms, or fancy restaurants. Budget hotels do try to provide some amenities, however, such as remote-control television and hair dryers.

Budget hotels have also been a fast-growing segment of the hospitality industry. Days Inn of America Inc., one of the best known of the budget hotels, has 540 franchises. Another established chain is Red Roof Inns.

Other major hotels may scatter suites among their regular hotel rooms, or they may offer executive floors for business travelers. Executive floors are usually the top floors of the hotel. For further privacy, guests may enter the hotel through a separate entrance and ride a separate elevator to their floor. There may also be a special hotel desk to serve business travelers.

The rooms in the executive section generally cost from 5 to 25 percent more than the price of a regular double room. The room decor is more elegant, and there are more amenities, such as bathrobes, hair dryers, and coffee makers.

A popular feature of the executive floor is the common living room, where business travelers can relax after a long day of meetings. There, travelers can find snacks, a wet bar, and books and magazines provided by the hotel. The hotel may also employ a concierge, whose job

A Hotel Concierge

As a hotel concierge, my job is to solve problems for the guests in my hotel. I sit at a desk in the lobby where guests can come to ask for information, complain, or seek help. Usually their most pressing problem is where to find a good restaurant or how to get tickets for a theater performance. Sometimes their needs are more difficult to meet, but I take great pride in trying my best to solve every problem.

To many Americans, a concierge is a doorkeeper at a European hotel or apartment house. *Concierge* is French for "guardian" or "doorkeeper." It can also mean a janitor or building superintendent. In fact, however, at European hotels, a concierge is more like a private secretary for guests, especially business and professional travelers. The concierge makes the arrangements and performs tasks that a private secretary might perform, such as making restaurant reservations, booking airplane flights, reserving rental cars, and hiring limousines.

Concierges are very common in European hotels, and they are gaining popularity in American hotels as well. In some American hotels, the concierge is called the assistant manager for guest relations. Some American hotels consider having a concierge an unaffordable luxury. Others have learned that concierges are very useful because they free the front desk staff to concentrate on making reservations, renting rooms, and preparing bills. In addition, concierges generate much goodwill for the hotel, thus ensuring return visits.

I am a member of Les Clefs d'Or, which means the Golden Keys. this is an international association of concierges. We have about 4,000 members worldwide. Many concierges wear the concierge's symbol of crossed gold keys on their lapels. Many years ago, the crossed keys meant that the concierge was the person in charge of the hotel's keys. Now, of course, we don't literally keep the keys, but I like to think we are the key to making sure our guests have a pleasant stay.

Concierges are sometimes asked to do very difficult, if not impossible, tasks. One of my colleagues was once asked to stock a guest's private zoo with 20 pairs of animals, another arranged a facelift for a client, and still another colleague once organized the purchase of a town house for a guest. More often, however, the problems we solve are less difficult. We find lost luggage and passports, make reservations for guests at nearby restaurants or at hotels in other cities, arrange for baby-sitters, and help foreign guests with language problems.

As a concierge, I must be very resourceful and discreet. Concierges have to know a lot of people because we have to be able to tap many different sources to obtain hard-to-get items like tickets for sold-out shows and sporting events. In addition, concierges enjoy the confidence of their clients, even up to the point of helping them out of embarrassing situations. Our clients count on us to keep our mouths shut about their business and we do.

At the best hotels, the concierge is a high-level employee, sometimes even a member of management rather than of the service staff. Some concierges at large hotels head their own staffs of five or six assistant concierges. Concierges usually have to work their way up to their position by serving in lower-level service jobs such as a desk clerk. It usually takes several years on the job for a person to acquire the training and experience necessary to be a first-class concierge.

I was promoted to concierge at my hotel after graduating from a university school in hotel and restaurant management and working at the front desk for five years. Some people learn to be concierges at the International Concierge Institute in Paris, a training school for concierges. In addition to my formal training, I also know how to speak French and Spanish as well as English. Knowing at least one foreign language is a must for concierges. Some o the best concierges know several languages.

I love my job because it is so interesting and challenging. I enjoy helping people and I especially enjoy being confronted with a difficult problem that takes all my ingenuity to solve. That is when I function at my best. I think being a concierge is the perfect job for me.

it is to pamper business travelers. He or she may find missing luggage, arrange sightseeing tours, sew broken zippers, send flowers, call a taxi, and much more.

Business Facilities. Most hotels that cater to business travelers set aside an area where they can work. This area typically contains typewriters, photocopying machines, fax machines, personal computers, and other business equipment. It might also include a business library, with reference books too heavy for a traveler's suitcase, as well as business journals and newspapers. If necessary, the hotel will find secretaries to help prepare documents for presentation at a meeting or to take care of correspondence.

Some hotels, such as the Waldorf Astoria in New York City, offer a full-service business center. In addition to supplying office space and equipment, this center has a receptionist, secretary, and notary public. Translating service is also available.

Other Facilities. Hotels might feature other facilities that appeal to business travelers. Among these are health and fitness facilities—possibly including an exercise room, jogging trails, swimming pool, tennis and racquetball courts, and a fully equipped spa—where guests can unwind from the stress of working and traveling or continue their usual exercise regimen. For guests who prefer to exercise in private, the hotel may furnish in-room aerobics on a closed-circuit television channel.

For guests who prefer to eat in their rooms rather than dine alone in a restaurant, hotel room service is available. The quality of room service in most hotels is improving, as management sees another source of profit. Guests can now order gourmet meals late at night. The meals will be prepared quickly and served elegantly.

Illus. 11-4 *Hotels seek to attract fitness-conscious business travelers by offering a pool and exercise facilities.*
Source: Marriott Hotels and Resorts

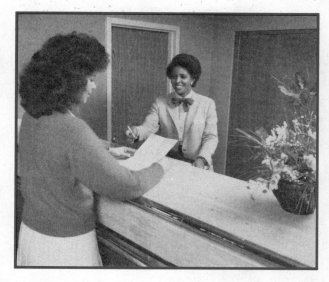

Illus. 11-5 *More and more hotels are now making special provisions to attract women business travelers.*
Source: Marriott Hotels and Resorts

Facilities for Women. Jill Rosendahl appreciates the full-length mirrors, skirt hangers, women's magazines, cut flowers, and other amenities that hotels provide in order to please their women guests.

The advent of women business travelers has improved hotel service in two important ways: there is now more attention to details and better security. These improvements have benefitted men travelers as well as women travelers. For example, hotels installed better lighting in their bathrooms so that women could see to put on their makeup. However, men also need good lighting when they're shaving. Men also appreciate the free toiletries, such as shampoo, and the free use of hair dryers.

Improvements in security decrease the chances that hotel guests—men or women—will be robbed or attacked. Largely because of women business travelers, many hotels now provide adequate lighting in halls and parking ramps, keyless or deadbolt locks and viewers on guest-room doors, and closed-circuit surveillance in elevators and hallways. On request, hotels will also provide security escorts to and from parking ramps.

Frequent-Stay Programs. Similar to the airlines' frequent-flier programs, *frequent-stay programs* are offered by many hotels. To encourage repeat business, these programs offer incentives, such as room discounts, complimentary cocktails, and express check-in and checkout. After staying a certain number of nights, guests are entitled to bonuses, such as free travel, free rental cars, or free accommodations. Some hotel chains even award United States savings bonds. Table 11-3 shows samples of the benefits offered by some frequent-stay programs.

Hotel Chain	Benefits
Holiday Inns	Discounted membership events; travel and merchandise awards; travel bags; staff incentive program.
Hyatt	Check-in by phone; video checkout system; priority reservations; upgrades; newsletter; gifts; reception; concierge service; priority restaurant seating; gift certificates to friends; travel, food, and beverage awards; airline and car rental upgrades.
Marriott	Video checkout system; free travel; bonus points when flying Continental, Northwest, TWA, and USAir, or when renting Hertz; complimentary newspaper; turndown service; check cashing; guaranteed reservations; free upgrades when space allows; show tickets; dining discounts; sports bags.
Sheraton	Guests' club with special weekends; points can be supplemented with cash for travel awards and can be transferred for mileage credits in the American or Pan Am programs; awards can be used for cash for travel with most air carriers, cruise lines, rail lines, or Sheraton hotels; merchandise catalogs.

Table 11-3 Sample Frequent-Stay Benefits

Because of the tie-ins with United Airlines and Hertz, John Wu frequently stays at a Hyatt Hotel. As a member of the Hyatt Gold Passport program, John is automatically entitled to speedy check-in and checkout. He also earns bonus points that can be redeemed for food and beverage awards at Hyatt hotels and for travel awards. After a certain number of stays, he receives a free upgrade to a more deluxe room.

John also patronizes Marriott Hotels, where he can earn bonus points for a variety of free travel awards. Since he is always in a hurry, John appreciates the Marriott's in-room video checkout system. When he presses a code on a box near the television, his bill appears on the screen. He can quickly review it and authorize it for checkout. On his way out of the hotel, he can pick up a printed copy at the desk or have it mailed to his office.

Conference Centers

When Jill Rosendahl's company underwent a reorganization, the management needed to explain the new structure to the employees and help them establish new working relationships. Rather than trying to do this in an office setting—where there are all sorts of distractions—the management decided to conduct a two-day retreat at a conference center.

A conference center is a special facility to enhance various types of corporate learning. A company might rent space at a conference center in order to have sales meetings, brainstorm new directions, or train employees on new procedures. The center is like a resort, with sleeping accommodations, dining rooms, and recreational opportunities. But there are also excellent facilities and equipment for meetings. Often located in a rural area, such as the woods or the mountains, a conference center provides a quiet setting in which employees can concentrate and gain a fresh outlook.

Convention Centers

Every year, millions of Americans like Maria Rodriguez travel for the purpose of attending conventions, conferences, seminars, and workshops. In the early 1990s, annual revenues from meetings and conventions in the United States totaled approximately $40 billion. Because of the economic benefits that conventions bring to a community, cities compete with each other to attract them. Cities with a convention center—a huge facility providing exhibition areas and a variety of meeting spaces—have an edge in the competition. Consequently, almost every city with a population of 50,000 or more has already built a convention center or is building one. Examples of major convention centers include the Las Vegas Convention Center and the Washington Convention Center in Washington, D.C.

Check Your Product Knowledge

1. What are three types of hotel accommodations designed to meet the needs of the business traveler?
2. How do hotels meet the business traveler's need to get work done?
3. What changes have hotels made to accommodate women business travelers?
4. How do travelers become members of frequent-stay programs? What are the benefits of belonging?

THE CHANNELS OF DISTRIBUTION

In the days before airline deregulation, making arrangements for a business trip was fairly easy. There were only two or three airlines flying between major city pairs. Each one offered about the same services and charged about the same fares. Most business travelers made their own arrangements or had their secretaries make them.

Since deregulation, however, making travel arrangements has become more complicated. With the influx of new airlines, innumerable products have flooded the marketplace, and prices of products and services are constantly changing. Following airline deregulation came deregulation of the channels of distribution. This meant that businesses other than travel agencies could sell airline tickets—further complicating the marketplace. Figure 11-2 shows the methods that are used to arrange business travel.

At present, business travelers depend on two main channels of distribution to help them through the travel maze. They use the services of either a business travel department or a corporate travel agency. Travel managers from both these channels of distribution may choose to belong to the National Business Travel Association (NBTA), a professional organization that seeks to educate and inform both its members and the greater business community.

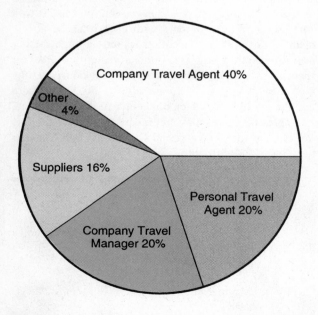

Figure 11-2 Methods Used to Arrange Business Travel
Source: Louis Harris Survey, Business Travel News

Business Travel Department

A *business travel department* (*BTD*) is a separate department within a corporation that handles the travel arrangements of the corporation's employees. In some cases, the BTD staff work with a selected commercial travel agency. In other cases, the staff are organized to function like a commercial travel agency. They may have their own supply of air tickets, schedules, and tariffs as well as direct access to a sponsoring airline through a computer reservations system. They look up flights, call airlines, make reservations, and issue tickets. BTD staff also make hotel/motel reservations and arrange for car rentals and other services.

Companies that have their own BTDs have a large volume of travel, which they feel they can handle more efficiently themselves. Some also feel that they can negotiate better discounts and rebates by dealing directly with the airlines.

BTDs can also provide travelers with detailed information about their destinations. For example, an executive planning a trip to Nigeria can ask the BTD to do research and provide information on the culture and business practices of that country. Travel agencies cannot be expected to conduct thorough political and economic research on every country in the world. BTDs, on the other hand, can gather detailed information on the countries with which their company deals.

BTDs can have other functions as well. In some companies, they handle personnel relocation and plans for meetings and conventions. If the company has a fleet of cars, the BTD will often be in charge of scheduling and maintenance. If the company operates corporate aircraft, the BTD will coordinate scheduling with the corporate flight department.

More and more companies are installing satellite ticket printers (STPs). As you learned in Chapter 3, a satellite ticket printer is a machine that prints tickets. At the end of 1989, STPs were being used in approximately 3,840 locations, mainly remote areas. For example, the BTD of a company in Hanover, New Hampshire, calls its ticketing agency in Boston and says it needs some airline tickets by the next day. Since even an express delivery service might not be able to get the tickets to Hanover by the next day, the travel agency sends the necessary information over the wire and the company's STP prints the tickets.

Corporate Travel Agency

Aisle seat; low-calorie meals; compact car. These are some of the details in John Wu's computerized client profile. John's travel agent keeps this information on file so that she can make arrangements for John's trips quickly and accurately. This is just one of the ways the agency seeks to please its corporate clients.

John Bacon

No one has yet invented a substitute for business travel and John Bacon, air travel and materials manager for Tenneco, Inc., is confident no one ever will.

"Technology like teleconferencing is fine," he said in an interview, "but when you're talking about a multi-million-dollar deal, things just don't get done over a tele-conference screen. Sooner or later, you're going to want to shake hands face to face with the guy or gal you've just handed that kind of money to."

Bacon, a Louisiana native, started out with a Tenneco subsidiary, Tennessee Gas Pipeline, 25 years ago. He worked first as a dispatcher and later in the aviation department. Over the years, he progressed up the corporate ladder to his current position as manager of travel services for Tenneco.

As a travel manager, his duties involve scheduling travel for all Tenneco employees, overseeing the scheduling and maintenance of the company's corporate aircraft, setting corporate travel policy and procedures, and negotiating rates and services with airlines, hotels, and other travel suppliers. Tenneco's travel department arranges about 1,000 trips a year for some 8,000 travelers.

When Bacon started out, the idea of a corporate travel department was still relatively new. Today these travel departments perform a very necessary service for many corporations, keeping business travel costs as low as possible. Bacon has witnessed two major innovations that he says have revolutionized business travel and spurred the growth of corporate travel departments—airline deregulation and automation.

When Congress was considering airline deregulation in the late 1970s, Bacon was serving on the board of directors of the National Passenger Traffic Association (NPTA), the professional organization for corporate travel managers. He and his colleagues lobbied hard for deregulation at congressional hearings. They believed that deregulation would spur competition and lower airfares for business travelers.

Throughout the 1980s, Bacon went on to become treasurer, president, and chairman of the board of the NPTA, which recently changed its name to the National Business Travel Association (NBTA). The organization's primary purpose is to educate and assist its members in carrying out their jobs as corporate travel managers.

Another important function of the NBTA, according to Bacon, is to enable members to "network with one another." For example, if a travel manager needs to arrange for an employee's trip to an unfamiliar city, he or she can call a counterpart in that city to get directions to the employee's meeting place and to find out where the best hotels and restaurants are located.

Bacon believes that automation has been nearly as important, if not more important, than deregulation in helping corporate travel managers save money. In the early days, corporate travel departments had to depend on airlines and travel agents to seek out the lowest fares and rates. Now, well-equipped departments have their own computerized reservations systems and hotel reservations systems.

One of the continuing problems of business travel is that it is often spur of the moment. A company executive may not know until the week before or even the day before that he or she has to take a long-distance trip. Thus business travelers often cannot take advantage of discount rates that other airline passengers can get by making reservations weeks or months in advance. But, Bacon says, computerized reservations systems do help corporate travel departments to plan ahead as much as possible and to seen out the lowest fares and rates even at the last minute.

Bacon believes that automation will continue to cause business travel and travel in general to change dramatically. "It won't be long before you'll make airline reservations on a piece of plastic, like a credit card. Then, when you check in at the gate, you'll run your card through a reader and walk through a turnstile to board the plane. There'll be no people," he said.

Bacon believes that, if anything, business travel will greatly increase in years to come. The opening of the Soviet Union and Eastern Europe to Western markets, the forging of the European Community into one big market in 1992, and the expansion of business in Japan, Korea, and the Far East will all have American business executives traveling more than ever.

"It's just human nature to be curious, to want to see your counterpart face to face, to cultivate acquaintances and seek out new customers," he said. "Travel is still a major tool to enhance business opportunities, no matter what kind of business you have."

Travel agencies are still the primary channel of distribution for corporations. However, there is a great deal of competition. Travel agencies face competition from other channels of distribution, mainly the business travel departments. As you have learned, BTDs can negotiate discounts and rebates with suppliers. To stay competitive, some travel agents feel compelled to offer their corporate clients similar rebates. The rebates come out of the commissions that travel agencies receive from their suppliers.

A great deal of competition exists among travel agencies themselves as they bid against each other for corporate contracts. According to one industry consultant, there were 32,500 travel agencies in 1988. These agencies had a combined total of $42 billion in air sales. Of that total, 19 percent, or $8 billion in air sales, was generated by just 25 agencies. This shows that a handful of agencies is handling a disproportionate share of the travel business. These 25 agencies are the *mega-agencies*—travel agency chains such as Carlson Travel Network and American Express. Mega-agencies bring millions of dollars of business to suppliers, and can often receive greater-than-average commissions. As a result, they are willing and able to provide rebates and other services demanded by major corporate buyers. Smaller agencies could not offer the same rebates and stay in business.

Travel Management Services. Because of deregulation, travel agencies are no longer just providing basic ticketing and reservations services. To win commercial accounts, travel agencies must offer complete *travel management services*. No longer can they expect to gain a company's business by mailing out a simple brochure. Now they must present a well-prepared proposal in which they demonstrate an understanding of the client's needs and show how the client will save time and money. Among the travel management services that clients expect from a corporate travel agency are:

- Help in developing and monitoring a travel policy.
- Quarterly and monthly travel management reports.
- Delivery of tickets to the corporate office or to a dropbox at the airport.
- A WATS (Wide-Area Telecommunications Service) line so that employees can change arrangements easily while traveling.
- Extended office hours.
- A frequent-flier monitoring program.
- Group-meeting planning.
- Up-to-date information on changes in the travel industry.

Of course, to provide these services an agency must be fully automated—especially because business travelers tend to make frequent itinerary changes at the last minute. Computer software has been developed to help

travel agencies audit a corporation's total travel budget. Some functions of the software include tracking employees' travel and entertainment spending, and reviewing trips to ensure that they meet travel policy requirements.

It's becoming more commonplace for corporations to deal directly with suppliers, particularly with the airlines. Industry analysts believe, however, that the majority of corporations will continue to rely on the expert services of travel agencies to help them sort out a complicated market. Although suppliers may wish to reduce their dependency on travel agencies, they realize that travel agencies can provide a much wider distribution network.

Government Accounts. Another result of deregulation has been that the federal government and many state governments have turned to commercial travel agencies to make travel arrangements for their employees. The federal government has been doing business with travel agencies since 1982.

Federal and state government accounts have opened up a whole new market for travel agencies. In 1990, the government travel market was estimated to be $15 billion. There is even a professional organization for agents who specialize in government travel—the Society of Travel Agents in Government (STAG).

Travel agents have discovered a great deal of difference between working with the federal government and working with state governments. The federal government is easier to work with because there is a centralized authority—the Government Services Administration (GSA). The GSA imposes uniform rules, regulations, and requisites on contracting travel agents. State governments

Illus. 11-6 *In order to compete in the highly competitive business travel market, a corporate travel agency must offer complete travel management services.*
Source: © David R. Frazier Photolibrary

are generally more difficult to work with because there is no centralized authority, and procedures vary from state to state and from department to department within a state.

Check Your Product Knowledge

1. Give three reasons why a corporation would establish its own business travel department.
2. What advantages does a mega-agency have over a small travel agency?
3. How have travel agencies that handle corporate accounts changed since deregulation? Why have these changes occurred?
4. List the eight travel management services that are designed to meet the needs of the business traveler.
5. What new market has opened up to travel agencies in recent years?

Illus. 11-7 *Mega-agencies often focus on corporate travel, thus providing intense competition for smaller agencies.*
Source: *Sara G. Matthews*

CAREER OPPORTUNITIES

As a future travel professional, you may want to choose a career related to serving the needs of the business traveler. Two challenging and rewarding careers are those of corporate travel manager and commercial travel agent. Perhaps the primary quality required for each of these careers is flexibility. You must be able to adapt to changes that occur in the traveler's itinerary and in available products and services. These changes occur weekly, daily, and sometimes even by the minute!

Corporate Travel Manager

Corporate travel managers establish and monitor a company's travel budget and travel policy. They may serve as a liaison between the company and an outside travel agency, or they may manage a company's in-house travel department. As a liaison, they have responsibility for choosing the agency that will handle the company's account.

Managers of a BTD are responsible for the travel arrangements for executives, salespeople, and other employees authorized to travel. Depending on the size of the company, they may make these arrangements themselves or supervise a staff. If the company is very large, a corporate travel manager may also supervise the travel of other divisions of the company.

Another responsibility of the BTD manager is to find new and innovative ways to provide business travel services that will benefit the company and its employees. The BTD manager arranges corporate discounts with suppliers and must therefore possess excellent negotiating skills.

As business travel increases and as companies seek to control business travel costs, more and more companies will employ corporate travel managers. In fact, many current positions were created by persons who at one time worked in the purchasing or accounting departments of their company. They saw a need for travel to be handled as a separate function and convinced company executives to let them set up a program.

Because of the need to prepare financial reports, corporate travel managers should have a business background in marketing and accounting. They should also be thoroughly familiar with computer reservations systems. Many corporate travel managers have experience as reservationists with an airline or as travel counselors with a travel agency.

At present, about 70 percent of corporate travel managers are women. Corporate travel managers can advance by assuming the same position in a larger company.

Commercial Travel Agent

Commercial travel agents work for agencies specializing in making travel arrangements for corporations. Besides being able to look up schedules and rates, make reservations, and write tickets, commercial travel agents must be well acquainted with products and services geared to the business traveler. They must be able to relate information such as:

■ Special business services and amenities offered by hotels.

- How to qualify for lower airfare.
- The most convenient hotel.
- The best way from the airport to downtown.
- Changes in frequent-flier programs.

Agents keep up-to-date files on their business clients. These files state the client's travel preferences so that arrangements can be made quickly and accurately.

Commercial travel agents with more experience may become involved in writing and presenting proposals to gain corporate accounts and in managing corporate accounts. They need strong negotiating skills for these tasks. They may also be asked to analyze the profitability of accounts. For example, although some accounts may offer high volume, they may not be profitable for the agency to handle because of low-yield tickets and delays in payment.

College-level training is becoming increasingly important for travel agents. Courses in computers, business administration, and accounting are essential for agents working on commercial accounts. If business travelers will be going abroad, agents must know about foreign fares and transportation. They must also know about the culture and customs of an area and about the international health and visa requirements. Of course, personal travel experience is invaluable.

Commercial travel agents can advance by becoming agency managers or directors. They can even go into business for themselves. As with hotels, there are more opportunities for advancement in an agency with many branch offices. Because of agency mergers and competition, the employment outlook for commercial travel agents is uncertain.

Summary

- Business trips are taken for the purpose of buying and selling goods and services, developing business opportunities, visiting branch offices, and attending business-related meetings.
- Business travelers provide the travel industry with a great deal of income. The travel industry appreciates business travel because it tends to be non-seasonal and inelastic.
- The various components of the travel industry compete with each other for the business of the business traveler. They especially attempt to meet the needs and expectations of the frequent business traveler.
- Business travelers expect speed, efficiency, and comfort from travel products and services. They are willing to pay higher prices to have their needs met, but cost is still a factor in selecting an airline or a hotel.

- The number of women business travelers is increasing. In general, women business travelers have the same motivations, needs, and expectations as do men business travelers.
- Airlines attempt to meet business travelers' needs through frequent flights to major destinations, business-class service, and special airport lounges. Airlines reward frequent fliers with bonus points, which they can redeem for free travel and other prizes. Airlines and corporations also negotiate discounts and rebates on airfares.
- Car rental chains compete for the business of the business traveler by offering discounts, special privileges for club members (such as speedy rental procedures), and other incentives (such as free upgrades and phones).
- In areas of dense population and where the distance between major cities is not great, rail service is often a less costly and more efficient means of transportation for the business traveler.
- Hotels help business travelers relax and get work done by providing all-business-class accommodations and office space. Hotels also offer frequent-stay programs to encourage repeat business.
- Business travel departments and corporate travel agencies help business travelers make arrangements for their trips. To win corporate accounts, travel agencies must propose a program of travel management and offer a wide array of services.

Key Terms

per diem
business class
frequent-flier program
free upgrade
rebate
frequent-stay program
business travel department (BTD)
mega-agency
travel management services

What Do You Think?

1. List as many differences as you can between vacation travelers and business travelers.
2. Should frequent-flier awards be taxed like interest on a savings account? Why or why not?
3. What can airlines do to prevent abuses in their frequent-flier programs?
4. Should airlines and other suppliers of travel products offer corporate discounts and rebates? Explain your point of view.

5. Will automation, such as the satellite ticket printer, replace travel agents? Why or why not?
6. Do business travelers spend too much money on travel? Explain your point of view.
7. What factors are likely to stimulate or reduce the amount of business travel in the future?

Dealing with Product

You are the manager of a medium-sized travel agency, the fourth largest of the 12 retail travel agencies located in Yourtown. The largest employer in Yourtown is the Ajax Widget Manufacturing Company, which has three separate plants plus a large warehouse facility near the airport. You have just learned that Ajax intends to consolidate all of its company travel activity into a single business travel department (BTD) and to award all of its business to a single travel agency through competitive bids. At present, Ajax uses four travel agencies, including yours. It is common knowledge that Ajax generates more than $5 million of corporate travel per year.

Do you want to be the low bid for this commercial account? Exactly what would you guarantee to do for Ajax in your proposal? What does Ajax expect you to do? How might this commercial account affect your organization?

Dealing with People

By now, you have become proficient in recognizing that every traveler has a special set of MNEs. Although we seldom think of a business as a "person," most companies also have a set of MNEs when it comes to a corporate travel policy.

You are the manager of a large business travel department. At today's departmental meeting, the treasurer is recommending a new company travel policy on frequent-traveler awards. The present policy allows employees to keep their bonus points, free flights, and other prizes. The treasurer insists that since the company paid for the travel, the company is entitled to all frequent-traveler awards. These "freebies" are company property, and the company will save money by using the free trips and travel services for future company travel.

"No way!" says the vice president of sales. She manages a sales force with 30 sales representatives in the field. These salespeople are on the road and away from home for days, even weeks at a time. They live in an often-hectic world of flight delays and cancellations, rescheduled appointments, and high pressure. She insists that the sales force should be allowed to keep all free trips and bonuses that they have earned. Furthermore, she believes that taking away these "freebies" would cause a severe employee morale problem.

You are expected to share your wisdom at today's meeting. What will you say to the treasurer and to the vice president of sales? What will you recommend to the president?

WORKSHEET 11-1   MEETING THE MNEs OF BUSINESS TRAVELERS

Contact an airline, a hotel, a car rental agency, and a travel agency in Yourtown. Find out what services and amenities each one offers to meet the MNEs of business travelers. Use the boxes below to record your findings.

AIRLINE _____	Yes	No
Business-class section		
Airport lounge		
Free transfers		
Frequent-flier program		
Other:		

HOTEL _____	Yes	No
Business-class area		
Office facilities		
Recreational facilities		
Frequent-stay program		
Other:		

CAR RENTAL AGENCY _____	Yes	No
Express Service		
Mobile phones		
Tie-ins		
Emergency road service		
Other:		

TRAVEL AGENCY _____	Yes	No
Client profiles		
Ticket delivery		
Frequent-flier monitoring		
WATS line		
Other:		

WORKSHEET 11-2   ARRANGING BUSINESS TRAVEL

You work in the business travel department of a large New York City corporation. What kind of travel and accommodations arrangements will you make for the company employees listed below? Describe the kind of transportation, accommodations, and services you will arrange (in general terms, not specific flights, names, and so on).

1. A vice president of research and development will tour facilities in Europe, stopping in Munich, Vienna, Budapest, Warsaw, and Berlin. He does not speak a foreign language. He would like to be able to work while traveling from city to city. He would also like to do a little sightseeing.

2. A computer technician will be spending a week in Cincinnati to help set up satellite facilities. He needs to get to and from several locations by himself at various times of the day and night.

3. A member of the board of directors is meeting with an important potential client in Washington, D.C. The board member has been confined to a wheelchair since being injured in a car accident several years ago. He will spend two nights in Washington and would like to be able to take the potential client to dinner at one of the city's finest restaurants.

4. A company lawyer is spending three days in Tokyo and two days in Osaka, Japan, for intensive contract negotiations. She will need space to meet with clients and will need to have papers typed and copied. She will have to be in touch with the main office and have access to a fax machine.

5. The 20-member marketing staff is hosting a four-day sales conference for the 500 company salespeople.

6. The executive vice president for corporate affairs will be traveling to Philadelphia to give the keynote address at the annual meeting of the chamber of commerce. Immediately after her speech, she must travel to Detroit for another meeting. After an overnight stay in Detroit, she must be in Chicago early the next morning.

WORKSHEET 11-3   WOMEN BUSINESS TRAVELERS

The number of women traveling for business is steadily increasing. Consequently, the hospitality industry is increasingly concerned with appealing to this market. A woman business traveler would probably appreciate the convenience of a hair dryer in her hotel room, for instance, so that she would not have to pack one. You work in the public relations department of a large, nationwide hotel chain. You are planning a promotional letter to be sent to members of the National Society of Women Executives. What features, facilities, or services could your chain offer particularly to attract women business travelers?

Which of these features would also attract men business travelers?

Besides direct mailings to professional women's organizations, how can your chain promote itself to women business travelers?

WORKSHEET 11-4   STATE GOVERNMENT BUSINESS TRAVEL

Contact the appropriate government office to determine the travel policy for state officials and employees in Yourstate. What are the regulations or guidelines for the following.

Official cars and limousines

Air transportation

Surface transportation

Car rental

Hotel/motel accommodations

Attendance at conferences or special meetings

Expense accounts for travel

Per diem allowances for travel

Frequent-flier benefits

CHAPTER 12

MEETINGS, CONVENTIONS, AND INCENTIVE TRAVEL

"There are dancing rooms and dining rooms, listening rooms and talking rooms . . . big rooms, small rooms, banquet rooms, ballrooms . . . pink rooms, red rooms, blue rooms, bedrooms . . . fun rooms, sun rooms . . . old rooms, new rooms—altogether six hundred and two rooms."

—Advertisement for St. Regis Hotel, New York

Objectives

When you have completed this chapter, you should be able to:

- Explain why the number of meetings held every year has grown dramatically in recent decades.
- Identify the six major types of locations where meetings are held.
- Distinguish between conference centers and convention centers.
- List the different kinds of meetings.
- Name the different categories of associations that hold meetings.
- Determine the needs of the association market.

- Identify the six types of corporate meetings.
- Outline the characteristics of the corporate market.
- Describe the role of the meeting planner.
- Explain the difference between pure incentives and sales incentives.
- Distinguish between trade shows and exhibitions.
- List characteristics of international trade shows.
- Identify the channels by which the meetings product is distributed to the consumer.

Meetings, conventions, and incentive travel have become an important source of income for travel industry suppliers. In the past 35 years, the meetings and conventions business has grown from comparative insignificance into a multibillion-dollar-a-year industry. Today, it is estimated that more than a million meetings are held every year in the United States alone, generating almost $40 billion worth of goods and services. In addition, thousands of corporations have introduced incentive travel programs, spending millions of dollars a year on these programs.

THE WHERE, WHAT, AND WHY OF MEETINGS

Until the late 1950s, most meetings were regional. Ford Motor Company might, for example, hold a meeting in Chicago for midwestern Ford dealers, a meeting in New York for northeastern dealers, another meeting in Los Angeles for dealers in the West, and so on. National meetings were rare because long-distance travel was im-

practical. A few airlines offered limited transcontinental services in the early 1950s, but most long-distance travel was still by rail or by road. Business executives could rarely afford the time to travel to meetings on the other side of the country.

The Growth of Meetings

The breakthrough for the meetings business came with advances in the transportation industry. As you have read so often in this book, the advent of the jet age brought major changes. When American Airlines introduced nonstop passenger jet service between New York and Los Angeles, coast-to-coast crossing time was cut to five hours. Jet planes made travel to meetings faster, more convenient, and, in many cases, less expensive. With the extension of domestic jet routes, many destinations became accessible for national meetings. International meetings became possible with the introduction of daily flights to overseas destinations. In recent years, lower fares resulting from airline deregulation have acted as a

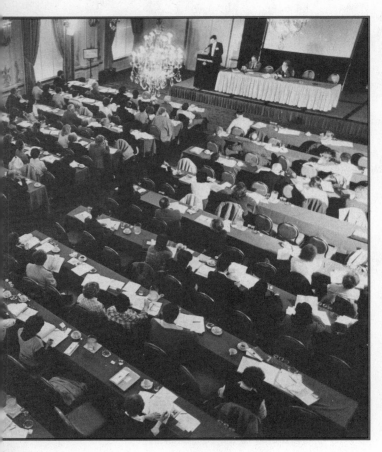

Illus. 12-1 *Meetings provide an important source of revenues to the travel industry*
Source: © Nina Winter/The Image Works

further stimulus to the growth of the meetings business.

Improvements in ground transportation services have also contributed to the expansion of the meetings market. State-of-the-art motorcoaches transport delegates and businesspeople to local meetings in luxury. Car rental fleets have been expanded to accommodate even the largest of meetings crowds.

One final factor in the growth of the meetings market has been the increased use of automation in the travel industry. Computer reservations systems have made it possible to coordinate meetings of as many as 10,000 or more delegates.

Not only has the volume of the meetings business grown; so, too, has the number of destinations with facilities to handle large meetings. Hub cities—those cities at the center of an air carrier's route structure—have presented themselves as ideal meeting sites. They include midsized cities such as Nashville, Memphis, Denver, Phoenix, Cincinnati, and Charlotte. The 1970s and 1980s were a boom period for the construction of convention centers in cities throughout the United States. Resort locations have also become increasingly attractive as sites for meetings.

The increased demand for meetings expertise has created a new field of services, including meeting planning and destination management. We will look at these developments in the sections to come. You will also read about the different kinds of meetings and about the two basic segments of the meetings market.

Locations for Meetings

Off-site meetings—those that do not take place on the premises of the sponsoring company—can be held at any of six main types of location:

- Hotels.
- Resorts.
- Conference centers.
- Convention centers.
- Civic centers.
- Cruise ships.

Hotels. Today, meetings generate about 20 percent of total hotel revenues. Some individual properties derive as much as 40 percent of their income from meetings and conventions. Thirty-five years ago, however, few hotels actively solicited meetings business. In fact, many were reluctant to open their doors to convention groups, preferring to rely on individual business travelers and vacationers. What meeting rooms there were in hotels were usually small and designed for weddings, balls, and other social functions.

By the mid-1960s, hoteliers had begun to realize that the growing meetings business could provide a valuable source of income, particularly during off-peak periods. Giant showcase hotels, such as the Hyatt Regency, built in downtown Atlanta in 1967, were specifically designed to cater to the meetings market. They were equipped with spacious assembly rooms and exhibition areas and a full range of audiovisual aids. Convention hotels were also built at airports and in suburban locations. By the 1980s, almost all new commercial hotels featured meetings facilities.

Resorts. Resorts have become increasingly popular as sites for meetings. A resort's secluded, scenic location is a prime attraction for meeting planners, as is the availability of on-site recreational facilities. The history of resorts as sites for meetings mirrors that of hotels. In the early days, resort owners had little interest in attracting group business. Convention-goers were regarded as second-class citizens, inferior to the wealthy upper classes who constituted the bulk of the resort clientele.

However, changing social values in the post-World War II period forced resorts to review their policy. Fashionable resorts such as the del Coronado near San Diego and the Arizona Biltmore in Phoenix changed with the times and added extensive conference facilities. Meetings now account for a large percentage of business at both the del Coronado and the Arizona Biltmore. While many older resorts have been converted to accommodate the growing meetings market, some new resorts have also been built as year-round convention sites.

Conference Centers. Conference centers cater almost exclusively to meetings, especially corporate meetings. For this reason, many meeting planners regard conference centers as ideal meeting locations. The emphasis is on a working environment with few outside distractions. Conference rooms are specifically designed for meetings (whereas in many hotels, conference space often has to double as a banquet room and/or ballroom). Guest rooms have work areas with ample lighting so that delegates can work at night. A professional meetings staff is on hand to cater to the needs of delegates and planners.

To provide delegates with some relief from work, some conference centers have added resort-type amenities. Centers such as the Scottsdale Conference Resort in Arizona and Arrowwood in Westchester, New York, have a health club and golf course. These conference centers are not much different from resorts with meetings facilities.

Convention Centers. Hotels, resorts, and conference centers can rarely accommodate groups of more than 1,000 people. Larger meetings and exhibitions are held in convention centers. In addition to being larger than other facilities, convention centers differ from conference centers in other ways. For example, they are always located in cities and they do not have guest rooms on the premises. They are also usually built with public funds.

Before 1960, there were only a few sites capable of hosting large national conventions and trade shows. They included the National Guard Armory in Washington, D.C., and Madison Square Garden and the Coliseum in New York City. The first convention centers with extensive exhibit areas all on one level were opened in 1960. Detroit's Cobo Hall, with 400,000 square feet of exhibition space, was the largest at the time. Since then, convention centers have been built in cities all over the country, and more are on the way.

New York's Jacob Javits Convention Center, which opened in 1986, is one of the largest, with 720,000 square feet of exhibition space. Such huge centers cost a lot to build—a staggering $487 million for the Javits Center—but they can provide a valuable boost to a city's economy. In its first six months of operation, the Javits Center generated over $500 million in revenue for New York City, largely in convention dollars spent in hotels, restaurants, and retail stores. Table 12-1 shows how much the average convention delegate spent on specific items in recent years.

Illus. 12-2 *New York's Jacob Javits Convention Center is one of the largest convention facilities in the nation.*
Source: *NY Convention and Visitors Bureau*

Civic Centers. Civic centers serve a function similar to that of convention centers. They are used for large regional and national conventions, exhibitions, and trade shows. They are usually located in downtown central business districts. Meetings are not necessarily their primary source of income, though. Cultural and sporting events are also held at civic centers.

Category	1988	1989	1990
Hotel Room and Incidentals	$264.56	$275.51	$298.38
Hotel Restaurants	56.87	59.22	64.14
Other Restaurants	59.08	61.53	66.63
Hospitality Suites	26.86	27.97	30.29
Entertainment	25.95	27.02	29.27
Retail Stores	42.44	44.20	47.87
Local Transportation	22.39	23.32	25.25
Other	20.50	21.35	23.12
TOTAL	$518.65	$540.12	$584.95

Table 12-1 What the Average Convention Delegate Spends per Stay
Source: *International Association of Convention and Visitor Bureaus*

Alicia Vargas

Alicia Vargas sells a product she really believes in—her hometown of San Antonio, Texas. She serves as the director of marketing for convention sales and services for the San Antonio Convention and Visitors Bureau. Her job involves enticing groups and organizations from all over the nation and the world to hold their meetings and conventions in San Antonio.

"Because I'm a native, I have a strong emotional connection to the product that I sell," she said. "It's a part of me because it's my home. I always feel as though I am offering people an invitation to come to my home as my guests."

Vargas received all of her training for her role as a convention marketer on the job. Born in San Antonio in 1947, her first job after high school was as a secretary in the city's tax collection office and later the city attorney's office. When San Antonio hosted HemisFair, the 1968 world's fair, Vargas wanted very much to be a part of it. She took a job at the newly opened Hilton Hotel as a secretary in the hotel sales office. Then, in 1973, she went to work for the San Antonio Convention and Sales Bureau, where she has remained ever since.

Vargas started out as a secretary for the bureau's sales staff, and later became a convention coordinator. As a coordinator, her job was to assist visiting groups in planning and carrying out their conventions and meetings in San Antonio. After five years as a convention coordinator, she was promoted to the convention bureau's sales staff, where her job was to invite various groups to hold their meetings in San Antonio.

"I was assigned to the area of religious organizations, which was an area that had never been tapped before. I was very proud of the way I developed that area," she said. During that period, Vargas succeeded in bringing the Southern Baptist Association to San Antonio. That convention numbered 35,000 people. She also landed the American Lutheran Church Youth Gathering, a convention of 16,000 high school and college-age delegates.

"That to me was one of the most exciting things I have ever done," she said. "When I walked into that arena full of young adults, I was overwhelmed to think that I had brought them to San Antonio. It was wonderful to see them experience the city for the first time and to see them get back on their airplanes carrying huge longhorns and Mexican piñatas home for souvenirs."

Vargas was promoted to director of the convention sales and service staff in 1985. She supervises a staff of 29 full-time employees and 34 part-time workers. The sales staff recruits conventions, and the service staff works with convention planners to organize their hotel accommodations, meetings, and activities. In 1993, the convention bureau will host the largest convention ever to be held in San Antonio—the Shriners International Convention, with 45,000 participants.

The San Antonio Convention and Visitors Bureau can capitalize on a number of local attractions, including the Alamo. But the heart and soul of San Antonio is the riverwalk, a meandering sunken walkway along the banks of the San Antonio River. The riverwalk is lined with restaurants and shops where visitors can browse and eat and enjoy the view.

Ever since HemisFair, San Antonio has been gradually building up its convention and tourism industry. Its large convention center, built in 1968, was first used for HemisFair exhibits. Since then, many large hotels have been built in the city—and San Antonio's convention business has tripled from 400 conventions a year in 1977 to 1,200 conventions a year in 1991. During the same 1977–1991 time period, the convention bureau estimates that revenue from visitors and conventioneers has increased from $29 million to more than $375 million.

"Because I've been here since it first started to grow, one of the most rewarding things for me is to see how much the city has changed, to see the progress the city has made," Vargas said. "And I get a lot of satisfaction from seeing visitors enjoying the city to the fullest. I want to help them in any way I can."

As someone who had learned her profession completely on the job, Vargas says she is glad to see that so many schools and colleges are now offering formal training for people interested in travel and hospitality careers. She advises people who want to go into convention marketing to get experience in the service area first before going into sales. By doing so, they will better understand the product they are selling.

Cruise Ships. Meeting planners looking for more exotic locations began to use cruise ships for offshore meetings in the late 1960s. Foreign-owned cruise ships were popular until 1976 because they offered tax advantages over American ships. In 1976, however, the federal government changed the tax laws and took away the advantage previously enjoyed by foreign vessels. American cruise and yacht companies were quick to step into the market, and several now have vessels fully equipped to handle small and medium-sized meetings. Cruise ships are also used for incentive travel programs (discussed later in this chapter).

Kinds of Meetings

So far in this chapter, we have used the general term *meetings* to refer to all types of gatherings. There are, however, several different classifications used in the meetings field. The classification used depends on the number of participants, the kinds of discussions and presentations involved, the amount of audience participation, and whether the meeting is formal or informal.

One type of meeting is called a *convention*. Conventions typically involve a general group session held in a large auditorium, followed by committee meetings in small breakout rooms. (The term *breakout* is used when a large group "breaks out" into several smaller groups.) Most conventions are held regularly (usually annually) and meet for a minimum of three days. Trade and technical conventions are often held in conjunction with exhibitions. Attendance varies from 100 participants to 30,000 or more.

Conferences are similar to conventions, but they usually deal with specific problems or developments rather than with matters of a general nature. The American Medical Association, for example, might call a conference to discuss a breakthrough in the treatment of a particular disease. Conferences involve much member participation. Attendance varies, though it is rarely as high as at conventions. *Congresses* are similar to conferences. The term is commonly used in Europe to describe international gatherings.

A *forum* involves back-and-forth discussion on a particular issue. It is usually led by panelists or presenters. Audience participation is expected and encouraged. A *symposium* is similar to a forum, though it tends to be more formal and involves less audience participation. *Lectures* are even more formal. An individual expert addresses the audience, usually from a raised platform. The presentation is sometimes followed by a question-and-answer period. Attendance at forums, symposiums, and lectures varies greatly.

Seminars are informal meetings involving face-to-face discussion. Participants share their knowledge and experiences in a particular field under the supervision of a discussion leader. *Workshops* are small group sessions (usually a maximum of 35 participants) held for a period of intense study or training. The emphasis is on exchanging ideas and demonstrating skills and techniques. *Clinics* offer drills and instruction in specific skills for small groups. An airline reservations agent, for example, might attend a clinic to learn how to operate a computer reservations system. Many people attend clinics when they want to learn a sport, such as golf or tennis. Both clinics and workshops can last for several days.

The *panel* format calls for two or more speakers and a moderator. Panelists present their viewpoints on a particular subject. The meeting is then open for discussion among the speakers and with the audience.

Exhibitions are used for the display of goods and services by vendors. They are staged as part of a convention or conference. The term *exposition* is used in Europe to describe this same kind of presentation.

Trade shows (or *trade fairs*) feature freestanding vendor displays. Unlike exhibitions, they are not held as part of a convention. Trade shows are typically the largest type of meeting. Attendance at a major show lasting several days can top 500,000.

Teleconferencing is a way of holding a meeting from several different locations simultaneously. Participants use advanced communications technology that enables them to see and hear participants at other locations. Teleconferencing is a way of bringing people together without the time and expense of long-distance travel. Several hotel chains, convention centers, and conference centers have introduced teleconferencing facilities in response to the growing demand for this means of communication.

The Need for Meetings

Why has the number of meetings held every year grown so dramatically in recent decades? The simplest explanation is that technology has made the world we live in a much more complicated place than it was 35 years ago. As a result, there is a much greater need for communication in the business world. Companies must keep up-to-date with the latest technological advances if they are to remain competitive. Salespeople must be aware of new products coming onto the market. Technicians, scientists, and members of the medical profession need to learn about new discoveries and techniques in their respective fields on a regular basis. Employees must be trained to operate sophisticated new machinery.

Face-to-face meetings have proved to be the most effective way of sharing information and knowledge. In addition, they present a valuable opportunity to exchange viewpoints, resolve problems, and discuss matters of mutual concern.

Illus. 12-3 *Advanced communications technology permits teleconferencing, whereby companies hold meetings at several locations simultaneously.*
Source: Photo courtesy of Satellite Business Systems Communications

Check Your Product Knowledge

1. What have been the major factors in the growth of the meetings business in the last 35 years?
2. List the kinds of locations used for off-site meetings.
3. What is the difference between a conference center and a convention center?
4. List six types of meetings that involve a high degree of audience/member participation.

THE MARKETPLACE

The previous section outlined the types of meetings and the various locations at which meetings are held. In this section, you will read about the different kinds of groups and organizations that hold off-site meetings. The meetings market can be divided into two basic segments: the association market and the corporate market. Each market has different characteristics and different motivations, needs, and expectations (MNEs).

The Association Market

The association market is the better known and more visible segment of the meetings field. There are associations for almost every subject and interest. Of the 80,000 asso-

ciations in the United States, about one-third are national or international. The remainder are regional, statewide, or local associations. Most associations in the United States hold an annual convention; many have several meetings a year. In addition to holding conventions, associations also sponsor thousands of educational seminars and workshops.

The association market can be divided into the following main types:

Trade Associations. Almost every trade has at least one national association, as well as several at the regional and state level. Within a single trade, there may be separate associations for manufacturers, wholesalers and distributors, and retailers. Trade conventions at the national level tend to be large gatherings: the National Restaurant Association's annual meeting in Chicago, for example, attracts more than 100,000 delegates over a five-day period. Trade conventions are often held in conjunction with exhibits.

Professional Associations. Members of professional associations are individuals, companies, or corporations with similar business needs. Examples include the American Medical Association, the American Bar Association, the American Bankers Association, and the American Institute of Architects. All hold annual national conventions and conferences as well as regional meetings throughout the year. They use exhibits less frequently than do trade associations.

Scientific and Technical Associations. Organizations in this group are another lucrative source of meetings business. Representative associations include the American Institute of Physics and the Society of Petroleum Engineers. In addition to holding regularly scheduled conventions, such organizations often call special meetings when the need arises to discuss new developments. Meetings tend to be highly technical and often require sophisticated presentation equipment. Social events are typically kept to a minimum so that delegates are not distracted from the business at hand.

Educational Associations. National and state teacher associations are the best known of the educational organizations, though this group also includes professional educators in a wide variety of other fields. In the travel industry, for example, the Society of Travel and Tourism Educators and the Council on Hotel, Restaurant and Institutional Education are prominent associations. Educational meetings are often held in the summer months when schools are closed. This makes them particularly attractive to downtown hotels, because in many cities this is the period when hotel occupancy levels are at their lowest. Educational conventions tend to be longer than most other kinds, commonly involving a full five-day meeting program.

Veterans and Military Associations. Veterans groups such as the American Legion and Veterans of Foreign Wars hold annual reunions for former members of the armed forces. Conventions at the national level attract large numbers of attendees and are primarily social in purpose. Military organizations such as the Air Force Association have conventions for active service personnel.

Fraternal Associations. There are probably more fraternal associations in the United States than any other type of association. They can be divided into three main categories:

- Student fraternities and sororities.
- Groups whose members have a common interest or purpose, such as assisting the needy.
- Special-interest associations.

All hold regular conventions. National conventions of the second category—which includes the Elks, Loyal Order of Moose, and Rotary International—are particularly large gatherings. The emphasis is on social events, recreation, and entertainment rather than on technical, business, or professional matters. Examples of organizations in the third category include the Philately Society, the American Contract Bridge League, and the Sports Car Club of America.

Ethnic and Religious Associations. Ethnic organizations are similar in general philosophy and purpose to the second category of fraternal associations. They place a similar emphasis on comradeship and include such or-

ganizations as the Order of the Sons of Italy and the National Association for the Advancement of Colored People (NAACP). Religious conventions are held both for those people whose vocation is religion (such as priests and ministers) and for laypersons. The U.S. Catholic Conference is an example of the former.

Charitable Associations. These include such organizations as the American Red Cross and the National Multiple Sclerosis Society. They exist to raise money for charitable causes.

Political Associations and Labor Unions. The most visible political conventions are those held by the Democratic Party and Republican Party every four years to nominate a candidate for the presidency. Many other political meetings are held at state and local levels. Labor unions such as the AFL-CIO are similarly represented at both national and local levels. National meetings are usually held in large convention centers and attract thousands of delegates.

Characteristics of the Association Market. We have touched on some of these characteristics in the description of the different types of associations. The main characteristics can be summarized as follows:

- Large number of participants (especially at national conventions).
- Voluntary attendance—participants often pay for their own travel and accommodations.
- Tourist attraction or resort often chosen as destination.
- Different destination each year.
- Meetings held on regular cycle (usually annually or semiannually).
- Annual meetings planned two to five years in advance.
- Three- to five-day average duration (less for smaller meetings and seminars).
- Major conventions often include exhibitions.

The MNEs of the Association Market. Destination is a key motivator in attracting participants to an association meeting. Since attendance is voluntary, the organizers must choose a destination that is appealing to the maximum number of potential attendees. Delegates often like to combine a business trip with a vacation, so the destination selected must have adequate recreational facilities and access to sightseeing and entertainment attractions. Spouses are more likely to attend if there is something for them to do while their husbands or wives are in a meeting. For these reasons, resorts are popular venues for association meetings. Some destinations are selected because they relate to the particular interests of the association. The Sports Car Club of America, for example, might hold a convention near an auto racing track.

Delegates who regularly attend annual conventions do not want to go back to the same destination over and over. As a result, associations usually change their meeting place each year. There is little point, however, in choosing an exotic, faraway location if delegates can't afford to get there (remember that most association members have to pay their own travel expenses). Ease of access is an important consideration in selecting a site, especially for regional meetings. The destination chosen will often be the one that is closest to the greatest number of members.

Association decision makers rate availability of suitable meeting rooms as the number one factor in the choice of a particular meeting site. Depending on the size and scope of the meeting, there may be a need for a large general auditorium as well as space for workshops and committee meetings. The availability of exhibit space, meeting support services, and audiovisual equipment may also be crucial. Another very important consideration is the experience and efficiency of the convention center management.

Almost all national conventions need overnight accommodations. Hotels must be within the delegates' budgets. Ideally, an association tries to book all attendees in a single property. This isn't always possible if the convention is large. In such cases, a number of hotels in close proximity often cooperate to accommodate all the association members. The quality of guest rooms (and suites, if necessary) is clearly an important factor in the selection of a hotel. Other considerations might be the quality of food service and the efficiency of check-in and checkout procedures.

The Corporate Market

The corporate market is the most rapidly growing segment of the conventions market. As communication becomes ever more essential in the modern business world, the need for meetings as vehicles for educational exchanges grows more and more important. The corporate market generates a greater volume of meetings business than does the association market, yet corporate meetings are less visible to the public. This is true because companies generally have no need to publicize off-site meetings. The delegates are required to attend.

The corporate market in the United States is made up of millions of businesses and corporations. Meetings are held at all levels of business and industry and can be divided into six main types:

Sales Meetings. Sales meetings are the best known kind of company meeting. Held at both the regional and national level, they can be used either as morale builders or to introduce new products, new company policy, or suggested sales techniques. Locations for sales meetings vary considerably. Some are conducted at hotels with access to a company's manufacturing plant (so salespeople can see the product in the production stage). Others are held in major market areas (so salespeople can make customer contacts between meetings). Average attendance is 60 people for regional meetings and 175 people for national meetings.

Dealer Meetings. These are meetings between a company's sales staff and dealers and distributors who represent the retail sales outlets. Similar to sales meetings, they are held to encourage sales performance. Dealer meetings are commonly used for introducing new products and for launching new sales and advertising campaigns. Attendance can vary from under 20 to several thousand, depending on the size of the corporation and the number of retail outlets maintained.

Technical Meetings. These meetings are held frequently to update engineers and other technical personnel on the latest technological developments and innovations. The seminar and workshop formats are widely used for technical meetings.

Executive/Management Meetings. This category includes both executive conferences and management development seminars. The former vary greatly in attendance; the latter are usually small. As the most prestigious company personnel, executives expect the finest in accommodations and service. Deluxe hotels and conference centers, especially those in isolated resort locations, are suitable venues.

Training Meetings. Training meetings form the largest and fastest-growing segment of the corporate meetings market. They are conducted for all levels of personnel, even for top executives. Attendance at workshops and clinics is usually under 50 and can be as low as ten. Isolated resorts with a minimum of outside distractions are popular locations, particularly off-season. For shorter training sessions, a location convenient to the company workplace is usually chosen.

Public Meetings. Public meetings are those that are open to nonemployees. Stockholder meetings are the most common type. They rarely last longer than a day and therefore require no overnight accommodations.

Characteristics of the Corporate Market. The corporate market is different from the association market in a number of respects. Its main characteristics include the following:

- Smaller number of participants per meeting.
- Mandatory attendance—travel and accommodation expenses paid for by corporation.
- Destination sometimes keyed to location of company office or factory.

Illus. 12-4 *Stockholder meetings are the most common type of public corporate meetings.*
Source: © *Harriet Gans/The Image Works*

- Same destination possible year after year.
- Meetings held as need arises.
- Significantly shorter planning/booking period—less than one year in advance.
- Slightly shorter average duration—usually about three days.
- Less use of exhibits.

The MNEs of the Corporate Market. The selection of an attractive destination is not as important for the corporate market as it is for the association market. Attendance at corporate meetings is mandatory—the choice of destination therefore has no effect on the number of people attending. Corporate meeting planners do not have to "sell" the destination. Nor do they have to vary the meeting site to attract participants. In fact, many companies use the same hotel year after year (especially for training meetings). A hotel with a proven service record is usually guaranteed repeat business. This is a fundamental difference between the corporate and association markets.

Location is an important factor in destination selection. Sites close to the company facility are usually chosen. The more distant and inaccessible the location, the more it will cost the company in travel expenses. Time spent traveling also means time away from the job for company employees, who must be paid while they are attending the meeting.

The emphasis at corporate meetings is on work, with considerably less time for leisure and social activities than at association meetings. Privacy and a distraction-free environment are consequently of more importance in site selection than the availability of recreational facilities and ease of access to entertainment, sightseeing, and shopping attractions.

Corporate decision makers have similar needs to association decision makers when it comes to selecting a particular hotel or other venue for the meeting. They look for properties with adequate meeting space, enough guest rooms, and quality service. Because corporate meetings tend to have fewer participants, they can often be held in small and medium-sized hotels. Not all corporate meetings require overnight accommodations: many last for a day or less.

Check Your Product Knowledge

1. What are the nine main types of associations that hold regular meetings?
2. List six ways in which association meetings differ from corporate meetings.
3. What is the difference between a sales meeting and a dealer meeting?
4. In what ways are the MNEs of the corporate and the association markets similar? How do they differ?

THE ROLE OF THE MEETING PLANNER

The meetings market has become larger, more sophisticated, and more specialized. As a result, a new career area has developed. Today, there is a need for professional decision makers who are responsible for all stages of meetings preparation and presentation. Until recently, meeting planning was one of several functions performed by association and corporate executives. Now, it has emerged as a profession in its own right.

The Meeting Planner Defined

In the United States, there are approximately 100,000 people who are involved in meeting planning. We can identify three main categories of meeting planners:

- Association executives.
- Corporate meeting planners.
- Independent meeting planners and consultants.

A DAY IN THE LIFE OF
A Meeting Planner

I'm a full-time meeting planner for a large corporation. I do just what my title implies: I plan, schedule, and supervise all the elements of the meetings the corporation holds. My goal is simple—to run a successful meeting—but my job is not. Coordinating travel, accommodations, food, and sometimes even entertainment takes a lot of doing. A good meeting planner needs to be aggressive in making deals with hotels, but sensitive in communicating needs. He or she has to be detail-oriented, yet creative. The best way to show how important these qualities are is to go through the steps I usually follow in planning a large meeting.

The first step is to choose where the meeting will take place. I have to consider a number of factors, including the nature of the event (What is its purpose?); the makeup of the attendees (Will spouses attend?); the geographical location of the site (Is it easy to get to?); and so on. I have to investigate a number of things about a hotel, from banquet facilities to the kind of lighting available in meeting rooms. Most of all, I have to try to find out the quality of service a place gives. Attendees will remember how they were treated long after they've forgotten what they had for dinner each night.

I always visit and inspect a possible site personally, even if I've booked meetings there before. Mostly, I'm concerned about the meeting facilities. Meeting rooms come in all types. I remember one time when I visited a prospective site that used accordion-type flexible partitions to divide a large room into two smaller rooms. I had been told that the rooms were soundproof, but in fact they let in plenty of noise. I could just imagine a serious discussion meeting being punctuated by bursts of laughter from a sales presentation next door.

Lighting is another important but easily overlooked aspect of a meeting setting. Early in my career, I booked a meeting in a room with several of those wagon-wheel-type fixtures that have bare bulbs hanging from them. A lot of the people complained about the glare. After that, I paid special attention to lighting.

Once I decide on a site, I sit down with the hotel's convention service manager. I provide the service manager with as many details of the program as I can; the more he or she knows, the better. Then I make my requests for accommodations, meals, meeting rooms, equipment, and so on, and get every guarantee in writing. I'm always wary of people who say things like, "Don't worry, we'll take care of everything." I need written confirmation. At the same time, I try to get every concession I can—like complimentary morning coffee and newspapers for attendees—from the hotel. Little touches like that score points with people.

During the preparation phase, I use lots of checklists. They help me keep track of which things are done and which need to be done. I also negotiate with airlines, car rental firms, and other services to ensure that attendees will get to the meeting and back comfortably.

A couple of days before the meeting, I fly to the site. Once there, I make sure everything is set up. The night before the meeting opens, I check all the equipment and run through any slides in the actual rooms where they'll be used, even if I've been assured that everything was checked "back at the office." One time, a worker had jostled a slide carousel while packing it, dislodging some slides. He put them all back, but some were upside down and out of order. My preliminary run-through saved the speaker an embarrassing moment.

During the meeting, I always assume that Murphy's Law will operate: Everything that can go wrong will go wrong. I'm on hand to figure out how to prevent disaster when emergencies arise. The hotel helps me there, too. I've returned to some hotels partly on the basis of their ability to replace a dead microphone quickly or change a meeting room at the last minute.

But even when the last attendee has gone home, my job isn't done. After the meeting, I get together with hotel representatives for a postmeeting critique. At these face-to-face meetings, I often gain valuable insights into how attendees and meeting planners can make meetings run more smoothly. After a good meeting, I have a feeling of accomplishment. I know that I've planned well, that the company's business needs have been met, and that people's personal and social needs have been met, too.

Association Executives. These meeting planners are full-time professional administrators employed by the various associations. They are responsible for the planning, coordination, execution, and promotion of annual conventions and smaller association meetings. Association executives are the key decision makers in the selection of meeting sites. About 20,000 are members of the American Society of Association Executives (ASAE).

An association executive represents a single association. Many smaller associations, however, cannot afford to employ a full-time meeting planner. Such associations can use the services of a multiple association management organization, which functions as a meeting planner for several associations.

Corporate Meeting Planners. Corporate meeting planning is a comparatively new and rapidly growing field. In the recent past, the job of planning meetings and conferences was often the responsibility of the director of sales or vice president of marketing. Today, however, most large corporations and businesses have a full-time meeting planner and staff who coordinate all meetings arrangements. They may also appoint a company training executive to organize group training sessions. (If a company does not have a meetings department, corporate group travel and meetings arrangements are often arranged through the in-house business travel department.)

A number of organizations have been formed to facilitate the exchange of ideas between meeting planners and to provide continuing education programs. Meeting Planners International (MPI), founded in 1972, is the most prominent of these. Its 9,000 members are responsible for planning hundreds of thousands of meetings each year. MPI members include corporate meeting planners, association executives, and independent consultants, as well as travel and meeting service suppliers.

The Association of Conference and Events Directors-International (ACED-I), founded in 1980, is an organization of colleges, universities, and associations. It arranges conferences and other meetings on university campuses.

Independent Meeting Planners. Associations and corporations that do not have in-house meetings departments often hire independent consultants on a freelance basis. The number of individuals and companies offering this service is growing rapidly. The Association of Independent Meeting Planners (AIMP) promotes education and communication among planners in this field.

The Meeting Planner's Responsibilities

Regardless of whether meeting planners work for associations, corporations, or independent consultancies, their primary objective is to run a successful meeting. Fundamental responsibilities of the meeting planner include:

- Establishing meeting objectives.
- Selecting the meeting site.
- Scheduling meetings and meeting rooms.
- Negotiating rates with suppliers.
- Budgeting and controlling expenses.
- Making air and ground transportation arrangements.
- Planning audiovisual and technical details.

It is clear from this list—which could easily be extended—that meeting planners are more than just travel and accommodations organizers. They are involved from the earliest planning stages to the final execution of the meeting. The success of the meeting depends heavily on how well they perform their tasks.

Experienced meeting planners may receive the Certified Meeting Professional (CMP) designation from the Convention Liaison Council. Certification is awarded to meeting planners who have reached standards of proficiency as measured by experience and examination.

The MNEs of Meeting Planners

The meeting planner must keep his or her employer's needs in mind when selecting destinations, choosing hotels, making travel arrangements, and so on. When negotiating with suppliers, the meeting planner must ensure that the sponsoring organization is getting the best possible deal and the best value for its money. Strong negotiating skills are a prime requirement for the meeting planner.

Top priorities in selecting sites for meetings are the quality of service and the availability of meeting room facilities. Meeting planners must ensure that meeting areas are large enough, suitable for both general sessions and breakout meetings, well lighted, soundproof, and so on. The needs for each meeting that a planner organizes will be different. Other important priorities are the site's accessibility, the quality of guest rooms, room rates, and the quality of food service. The availability of recreational facilities and geographic location are usually of lesser importance.

The Meeting Planner and the Hotel Staff

Meeting planning involves a high degree of cooperation between the meeting planner and the hotel staff. The convention service manager is usually the meeting planner's contact person in the hotel. The relationship between the two is important to the success of the meeting.

Both must have the needs of the meeting participants in mind. The meeting planner wants to secure the best possible services at the lowest possible rates. The convention service manager wants to satisfy the guests so that they will return for subsequent meetings, but he or she must also ensure that the hotel makes a profit.

Meeting planners who use the same hotel time and time again can often negotiate favorable rates and secure other privileges. They may, for example, negotiate for free function rooms. For an especially large or important meeting, the hotels may agree to host a cocktail party for delegates or offer complimentary coffee and breakfast. Using the same hotel over and over again is not always a good idea, however. Meeting planners may find that the hotel's services deteriorate over time, or that other hotels can offer better services at better prices.

Check Your Product Knowledge

1. What are the three different types of meeting planners?
2. What is the function of Meeting Planners International? Who are its members?
3. List six important responsibilities of a meeting planner.

INCENTIVE TRAVEL PROGRAMS

Incentive travel programs have become an important segment of the corporate travel market (they are not used in the association market). Major corporations began to use travel as an incentive in the 1950s. Incentive travel programs have since been introduced by thousands of small and medium-sized companies.

Incentive Travel Defined

There is some disagreement within the industry as to how incentive travel should be defined. Purists maintain that the term should be used only to describe incentive trips that are strictly for pleasure. Others include those trips that combine business and pleasure. It is, however, universally accepted that incentive travel is used as a motivational reward for top company producers and achievers.

James E. Jones, former president of MPI, defines incentive travel as "the application of travel as a motivational award for the accomplishment of a business objective." The objective is most commonly a sales target. A company sets a specific quota for its sales staff. Salespeople who meet the quota qualify for the trip. The theory is that the increase in sales more than covers the cost

of the trips awarded. Companies run incentive travel programs not only to reward sales performance, but also to achieve new sales goals and to improve morale and reduce employee turnover. Whatever the reasons for incentive travel programs, all involve travel as a motivational tool.

Salespeople, dealers, and distributors are the most popular targets for incentive programs. In recent years, travel has also been used to motivate other types of employees, such as engineers, production personnel, and management. It is anticipated that these will be the prime growth areas for incentive programs in the future.

Incentive travel has proved effective in most business environments. It has been used extensively by food and insurance companies and by automotive, pharmaceutical, and appliance manufacturers (see Table 12-2).

Type of Company	Expenditure (in thousands)
Food	$733,021
Insurance	$615,012
Tires/Batteries/Accessories	$436,072
Pharmaceuticals	$428,950
Auto/Boat/Air	$381,336
Durable Goods—Wholesale	$243,388
Nondurable Goods—Wholesale	$221,136
Books	$216,098
Housewares	$168,069
Office Equipment	$146,815

Table 12-2   Top Ten Users of Incentive Travel in 1990
Source: Business & Incentives

Characteristics of Incentive Travel Programs

Incentive travel programs can be categorized as either pure incentives or sales incentives.

Pure incentives, as the name implies, are strictly for pleasure. No business meetings or sales calls are scheduled during the vacation. Having reached the required performance objective, the employee is rewarded with the prize of a luxury vacation for a job well done. Destination is the key motivator. Workers are more likely to increase production if the reward is a trip to a glamorous location. It might be a big city, a foreign capital, a resort, or a natural attraction. The most popular destinations for incentive trips in a recent year are shown in Figure 12-1. The incentive might also be a cruise. Pure incentives represent about one-third of incentive travel programs.

Destination	Percent of Response
Florida	43.7%
California	38.9%
Las Vegas	28.9%
The Caribbean	23.1%
Hawaii	22.1%
New York State	22.1%
Arizona	19.8%
Europe	17.0%
Cruise	13.2%
Canada	10.9%

Figure 12-1   Top Ten Incentive Travel Destinations in 1990

Source: Business & Incentives

Sales incentives are combination vacation and business trips that usually include mandatory meetings. As such, the incentive trip is used as a vehicle for meetings. The amount of time spent on business-related activities varies, depending on the objectives of the sponsoring company. There may be a single visit to a company factory or a series of meetings in which participants are introduced to new product lines, shown new sales techniques, and so on. In general, more time is allotted to pleasure than to business. An attractive destination is still the most important factor, but the availability of suitable meeting facilities must also be considered. Sales incentives represent two-thirds of incentive travel programs.

Regardless of whether the trip is a pure incentive or a sales incentive, it is always of the highest quality. Winners expect a better class of service than do most other travel clients—accommodations are deluxe and all-inclusive. Employees are often accompanied by their spouses, whose vacation expenses are also paid for by the company.

Incentive travel programs typically last about five days; few are longer than a week. Weekend incentive trips are growing in popularity. Almost all programs involve group rather than individual trips. Incentive programs have been organized for groups as large as 10,000, but between 50 and 100 is a more common size. The greatest growth in recent years has been in the small-group market, with an average of ten participants per trip.

Incentive Travel Planners

Large corporations and businesses that sponsor incentive travel programs sometimes have their own in-house incentive planners. These company employees rarely spend all of their time on incentive travel. They can also be involved in meeting planning, trade shows, public relations, and advertising. Incentive travel planning is often the responsibility of the corporate meeting planner.

There are a small number of incentive travel companies in the United States that do nothing but arrange incentive travel programs. Large, full-service incentive houses include E.F. MacDonald and Maritz Travel. They negotiate with suppliers and create an attractive package in much the same way that a tour operator does. Incentive companies are usually both wholesalers and retailers. Incentive planning typically involves more promotion than does meeting planning. Professional planners are not just involved with the travel aspect of the incentive program, but also with setting the objectives of the program.

Not all companies can afford to use the larger incentive organizations. They may turn instead to a travel agency that specializes in incentive travel. Incentive travel planning is similar to group travel planning although it typically means more work, and the agency is involved in the marketing of the incentive program. Like incentive travel companies, travel agencies may also work with the sponsoring company to set objectives for the program.

The Society of Incentive Travel Executives (SITE), with a membership of 2,000, is the major organization for incentive travel planners. SITE holds numerous trade shows and seminars throughout the year.

Check Your Product Knowledge

1. What types of organizations use incentive travel programs?
2. What is the difference between a pure incentive and a sales incentive?
3. What are the three different types of incentive travel planners?

TRADE SHOWS AND EXHIBITIONS

Trade shows and exhibitions are another important segment of the meetings market. A trade show (or trade fair) is an event with free-standing vendor displays that is not connected to a convention. An exhibition, on the other hand, is always staged as part of a convention. In 1990, about 11,000 trade shows were held in the United States and Canada.

National Trade Shows, Inc.

How does a person get into the business of putting on travel trade shows? Bill Gardiner, Sr., did it almost by accident. He was working in the advertising department of a large New Jersey newspaper when a group of travel advertisers asked his paper to sponsor a travel trade show. After running a small annual trade show for the paper for a few years, Gardiner branched out on his own and started National Trade Shows, Inc. Today, NTS stages nearly 70 mini travel trade shows around the United States each year. The company is still a family-owned business run by Bill, Sr., and his son, Bill, Jr., in New Jersey.

The Gardiners' mini-shows are very different from a typical travel trade show. A typical show takes place in a large exhibition hall and lasts one or more days. It involves 100 or more exhibitors and attracts thousands of people. Such shows usually feature elaborate displays, tons of literature, and plenty of wining, dining, and entertainment.

Bill Gardiner, Jr., calls these kinds of trade shows "pipe and drape" shows after the materials used to construct the exhibition booths. The Gardiners' mini-shows are much less elaborate. Each is just three hours long and takes place in a hotel ballroom. Each show is limited to a maximum of 30 exhibitors and 110 local travel agents. According to Bill, Jr., the mini-shows are actually more efficient than the large trade shows because they cut out the "browsers" who attend the large shows but don't intend to buy anything.

The exhibitors who participate in the NTS shows include hundreds of hotel chains, resorts, airlines, tour operators, rental car operators, cruise lines, and several government tourist bureaus. The British Tourist Authority, Club Med, Peter Pan Tours, and Alamo Rent-A-Car are among NTS's distinguished list of clients.

The format of the shows is simple. During the first hour, the travel agents visit tables placed around the edge of the ballroom, which are staffed by the exhibitors. The second hour is reserved for a sit-down dinner for the suppliers and agents. Many of the suppliers then spend the third hour speaking informally and handing out door prizes such as free trips, airline tickets, travel bags, and champagne.

National Trade Shows, Inc., recruits its exhibitors by sending out mailers announcing the schedules for upcoming mini-shows several times a year. Once the suppliers sign up for a specific mini-show or week of shows, they provide NTS with lists of travel agents to invite to the shows. The agents who are invited to participate in each show are limited to two people per agency. Usually they are the owners or managers of the agency.

According to Bill Gardiner, Sr., the mini-shows serve several purposes. They enable the suppliers to reach 100 travel agents in just three hours. It would take each supplier several weeks to visit the same agents by traveling from office to office. In addition, by limiting the numbers of participants, the suppliers and agents have the time and opportunity to really get to know one another.

The NTS mini-shows are grouped geographically. For example, the Gardiners might stage a week of shows in Florida and another week in Arizona and California. Suppliers pay several hundred dollars to participate in one show and more than $2,000 to participate in a week-long series of shows. Most suppliers sign up for a week's worth of shows. Chartered buses take the suppliers from one show to another during the week.

Despite the high fees, there is usually a waiting list of suppliers and agents who want to participate in each show or week of shows. Bill, Sr., believes that the NTS shows are so successful because they tap a market that the large shows don't reach and that the suppliers can't cover as efficiently any other way. "These shows aren't cheap, yet the same suppliers keep coming back year after year so we must be doing something right."

Trade Shows

For many years, trade shows were used solely to advertise products. Nothing was sold at the show. Since the 1950s, however, they have also been used to market and sell products. Today, a significant percentage of purchases in industry, trades, and professions are prompted by visits to trade shows. Vendors rent enclosures called *booths* to display a wide variety of products—from computer hardware to boats—and often demonstrate their products to potential buyers. Some trade shows, such as auto shows and home and garden shows, are open to the general public. Many more are by invitation only. American companies may participate in both international and domestic trade shows.

International Trade Shows. Modern international trade shows came into being after World War II, when efforts were made to rebuild Europe. Since then, Germany has remained the leading host country for international trade shows.

International trade shows provide the ideal means for companies to test overseas markets. Representatives have the opportunity to meet potential buyers and distributors from all over the world. Buyers come to the seller in one central location, so there is no need to spend time and money on individual sales calls. Even allowing for transportation costs, international trade shows have proved to be the most cost-effective way to enter world markets.

International trade shows differ from trade shows in the United States in several ways. First and foremost,

they are more heavily sales-oriented. People go to trade shows to do business, not to attend meetings. Attendance is considerably larger at international shows. The Hannover Fair in Germany regularly attracts up to 500,000 attendees over an eight-day period. Many thousands of people also attend the annual Photokina Camera and Optics Trade Show in Cologne, Germany. Individual exhibits are more elaborate than at United States trade shows. A company may have as many as 1,000 employees working a single exhibit. Major exhibitors' booths (or *stands* as they are called in Europe) include several meeting rooms as well as display space. One final difference is the international flavor of overseas shows. Interpreters are on hand to assist visitors from all over the world.

The United States government often helps American companies exhibit their products in overseas trade fairs through the offices of the Department of Commerce and the Department of Agriculture. Financial assistance is available for small and medium-sized businesses that hope to penetrate overseas markets. The government also encourages foreign visitors to attend trade shows in the United States.

Domestic Trade Shows. Trade shows in the United States grew up as an extension of conferences that featured trade booths. These shows generally put more emphasis on attending meetings and are not as sales-oriented as international trade shows. They are also less formal and are attended by smaller numbers of participants. Even so, domestic trade shows can be an important source of business for hotels in the host city. The largest

Illus. 12-5 *The Dallas Infomart is the world's largest permanent trade show of computers and computer-related products.*
Source: Courtesy Infomart

shows are held in the giant convention centers—such as the Jacob Javits Center in New York, McCormick Place in Chicago, and the Las Vegas Convention Center. A number of convention hotels have exhibit space for smaller trade shows.

Trade shows generate more than $20 billion in expenditures in North America. There are shows for every conceivable trade, industry, and profession. The Henry Davis Trade Show and the International Travel Industry Expo are examples of shows for the travel industry. At these shows, travel industry suppliers set up booths to showcase their products and services, and travel agents visit the booths to gather information and make contacts.

The Trade Show Bureau is an organization that conducts research into the trade show industry and disseminates information to those involved in trade show planning.

Exhibitions

The number of exhibitions held every year has increased with the growth of the meetings business as a whole. As mentioned earlier, they differ from trade shows in that they are tied to a convention. They are used more frequently in the association market, particularly by trade,

technical, scientific, and professional associations.

Exhibits are important for associations both as a way to attract attendance and as a revenue producer. By allowing exhibitors to promote their wares within the convention, associations make money to offset the expense of staging the meeting. Exhibitors pay for the amount of space they rent to display their products.

Vendor displays and booths vary from simple to elaborate, though they are rarely as elaborate as at trade shows. A vendor will sometimes sponsor a "hospitality suite," offering free food and beverages to delegates. Exhibitors may also agree to sponsor coffee breaks and meals during the course of the convention in exchange for recognition and, possibly, the right to display their products in the coffee area.

Attendance at the exhibition necessarily depends on the number of people attending the convention. Exhibitions are not open to the general public. The duration of the exhibition is also tied to the length of the meeting, though most are at least three days long.

The International Exhibitors Association (IEA) is the major organization within the exhibitions field.

Illus. 12-6 *Exhibits are used frequently in the association market as a way to attract attendance and as a revenue producer.*
Source: National Restaurant Association

Check Your Product Knowledge

1. What is the difference between a trade show and an exhibition?
2. What are four ways in which international trade shows differ from domestic trade shows?
3. What types of organizations commonly hold exhibitions?

THE CHANNELS OF DISTRIBUTION

We have established that associations and corporations are the two major types of organizations that hold meetings. They are the *buyers* of group travel, group accommodations, and meetings services. The *sellers* are the hotels, resorts, conference/convention/civic centers, and cruise ships that host meetings. The airlines and ground transportation companies that transport participants to the meetings are also sellers. As you have read in earlier chapters, the buyer does not always purchase travel products and services directly from the seller. The same is true for the meetings business. The seller uses intermediaries as distribution channels to facilitate the sale of services to the buyer. Intermediaries in the meetings field include tour operators, travel agencies, meeting planners, and incentive travel companies.

In this section, you will also read about other companies that intervene between the supplier and the consumer. These include site destination selection companies, destination management companies, convention services and facilities companies, and convention and visitors bureaus.

Tour Operators

In many ways, the business and convention product is similar to the product that the vacationer buys as a holiday tour package. The product includes transportation, accommodations, activities, and/or events. In Chapter 10, you read that it is more convenient (and cheaper) for a vacationer to buy a package of travel products from a single source than to buy each component from individual suppliers. The same is true for the person attending a meeting.

Tour operators are experienced in group travel arrangements. Some tour operators arrange packages for meetings and conventions, especially for the association market. Here's an example. The Omaha chapter of Kiwanis International (a fraternal association) plans to attend the association's annual convention in Washington, D.C. A representative of the chapter contacts a local tour operator to make the arrangements. The tour operator makes the necessary flight reservations, arranges transfers, and books rooms for delegates in a hotel (or hotels) close to the Washington Convention Center. The tour operator may also make car rental reservations for members of the group, schedule group activities (such as sightseeing and entertainment), and so on. Because the tour operator buys in bulk from suppliers, the package will be less expensive than if each Omaha Kiwani made his or her own arrangements.

Tour operators don't only sell directly to the consumer. Some also place a deposit on an allotment of rooms for a large, popular trade show and package the rooms for resale through retail travel agencies and business travel departments. In this way, the tour operator who works in the meetings business is also a risk taker.

Travel Agencies

Travel agencies that have an ongoing relationship with a corporation or company often make travel arrangements for meetings. They are also becoming increasingly involved with incentive travel programs. The companies that they work with are often small or medium-sized firms that do not employ a full-time, in-house meeting planner. The meetings and incentive programs that the travel agencies service typically have less than 100 participants.

The work involved in making arrangements for meetings and incentives is more complex than that for group travel. An agency will usually assign this work to its convention department or incentives department. In addition, the agency may staff a service booth at the convention site to handle reconfirmations, complaints, and so on.

Meeting Planning Companies/ Incentive Travel Companies

These are the firms or individual consultants that provide full-service planning for businesses and associations for a fee. They are involved not only with travel and accommodations arrangements but also with the promotion and marketing of the meeting or incentive program. Meeting planning companies and incentive travel companies usually don't use travel agencies or tour operators: they deal directly with carriers, hotels, and other suppliers.

Airlines, Hotels, and Car Rental Companies

An airline is often designated as the "official carrier" for a particular meeting or convention. Northwest Airlines, for example, served as the official carrier for the American Home Economics Association's 1991 annual convention in Minneapolis. The airline assisted in the promotion and marketing effort and offered a discount for participants. Similarly, a hotel may be appointed as the "official hotel," or a car rental company as the "official car rental agency." This practice is more common in the association market than in the corporate market.

The official carrier may set up a temporary department in its reservations center. Or it may staff an existing group or convention desk with sales representatives to assist with check-in and arrival. Major carriers have staffs that work full-time on meetings arrangements. American Airlines, for example, has a large staff of professional meeting specialists. They help clients select an appropriate meeting site, secure discounted fares, arrange hotel accommodations, and coordinate car rentals and ground transportation. They may also provide assistance with audiovisual equipment and recommendations for multimedia presentations.

Site Destination Selection Companies

These companies suggest possible meeting sites based on corporate or association needs. Meeting planners and incentive travel planners may consult a *site destination selection company* several years before a meeting or incentive program is scheduled. Destination companies conduct familiarization tours to give planners the opportunity to inspect and sample hotels and meeting facilities at potential sites. White Glove is one of the larger companies in the field. In the late 1980s, they offered a five-day FAM tour of Atlanta for corporate and association meeting planners and a seven-day tour of Thailand for corporate incentive travel planners. For a nominal registration fee, participants received round-trip air transportation, lodging, planned meal functions, ground arrangements, and special activities.

Destination Management Companies

Destination management companies (DMCs) provide on-the-scene meetings assistance for corporations and associations at a particular location. If, for example, a Miami-based company is planning a meeting in New York City, it might hire a DMC in New York to handle all the details. The DMC will be able to arrange for ground transportation, deal with restaurants, line up local speakers, and perform numerous other useful services.

Convention Services and Facilities Companies

This group comprises a wide variety of independent companies that provide support materials that are not available at the convention site. They include companies that design and install stages, booths, and modular exhibit systems; audiovisual specialists; sound and light specialists; employment agencies for temporary personnel; talent agencies that provide actors and entertainers for industrial shows; and security companies.

Convention and Visitors Bureaus

A few years ago, there were only about 300 *convention and visitors bureaus (CVBs)* in the United States. Today, there are an estimated 900 CVBs throughout the country. A CVB may be a department within a city's chamber of commerce, a department within a municipal government, or a completely independent organization. CVBs have two main functions: to promote travel to the city that they represent (either for pleasure, business, or meetings); and to assist in servicing conventions and trade shows that are held in the city. Their job is to sell the whole city: not just convention centers and other meetings sites, but also hotels, restaurants, local retail outlets, transportation companies, and other suppliers. A CVB is a nonprofit organization funded by its members—suppliers who profit from conventions held in the city. The International Association of Convention and Visitors Bureaus (IACVB) represents major CVBs around the world. You will read more about convention and visitors bureaus in Chapter 14.

Check Your Product Knowledge

1. Name four intermediaries in the meetings business between supplier and consumer.
2. What role do tour operators play in the distribution of the meetings product?
3. What are (a) site destination selection companies and (b) destination management companies?

CAREER OPPORTUNITIES

The tremendous growth of the meetings business in recent decades has stimulated a demand for specialists in several fields. Meetings-related careers fall into three main categories:

- Planning jobs with the organizations that hold meetings and within the travel industry.
- Convention-service jobs at the various locations that host meetings (hotels, resorts, convention centers, and so on).
- Entrepreneurial jobs with companies that work independently in the meetings field.

Meeting/Incentive Planners

In an earlier section of this chapter, you read about the nature of the work of those who arrange, manage, and promote meeting activities. The largest employers of meeting planners are the associations and corporations that hold regular conventions and other meetings. These jobs are within the private sector, but you should also be aware of possible openings with government agencies. The Department of Agriculture and the Department of Commerce, as well as a number of United Nations affiliates, hold frequent meetings and employ people to plan these meetings.

Many of the corporations and businesses that hold meetings also sponsor incentive travel programs. Several of these companies employ in-house incentive planners to coordinate their programs.

Meeting planning and incentive travel planning have become important sources of income for retail travel agencies. Many agencies have separate departments for meetings and/or incentives. A number of major airlines also employ full-time meetings staffs.

Meeting planning is rarely an entry-level position. People typically come into the business from the hospitality industry, where they may have gained experience in dealing with meetings and meeting planners. Competition for jobs with associations and corporations is growing tougher. It is often easier to get into a meetings department if you have worked for the organization as an administrative assistant or as another member of the support staff. Similarly, travel agencies and airlines also promote from within.

Meeting planners may rise to heads of their departments in corporations and associations, or they may be promoted to marketing and public relations positions within their organizations. For some, the job of meeting planner with an association, corporation, travel agency, or airline is a stepping stone to a career as an independent meeting planner.

Convention Service Managers

Convention service managers work in hotels, resorts, conference centers, convention/civic centers, and on cruise ships—that is, at the locations that host meetings. They work on the scene with meeting planners, coordinating all aspects of the meeting.

Almost all hotels involved in the meetings business employ convention service managers. As with meeting planners, promotion is usually from within. An individual is typically promoted to convention service manager after experience in some other hotel department. A background in sales and in food and beverage management is useful.

Convention managers with experience in hotels sometimes advance to positions with conference/convention/civic centers. Convention center management is a particularly responsible job, involving extremely complex logistics. Management positions at convention centers include transportation director, security director, public relations director, and events coordinator. The largest convention centers—such as the Jacob Javits Center in New York or the Las Vegas Convention Center—may employ as many as 1,000 people. In addition to management positions, there are hundreds of blue-collar jobs, such as equipment mover, electrician, plumber, carpenter, security guard, and so on.

Entrepreneurs

This group includes all those people who own their own business or work independently in the meetings field. Convention services and facilities companies are the largest category. They provide a wide variety of meetings support materials to associations and corporations. Other areas of interest for those considering an entrepreneurial role in the meetings business include trade show management, site destination selection, and destination management.

One final category is independent meeting/incentive consultancy. This includes both freelance meeting planners (hired by associations and organizations) and incentive travel companies (hired by corporations only).

Summary

- Advances in the transportation industry—the advent of the jet age, in particular—have spurred the growth of the meetings market.
- Off-site meetings are held in hotels, resorts, conference centers, convention centers, civic centers, and on cruise ships.
- Meetings classifications include the convention, conference, forum, seminar, workshop, exhibition, and trade show.
- Technological advances have resulted in a greater need for meetings.
- The association market and the corporate market are the two major segments of the meetings market.
- Associations that hold regular meetings include trade, professional, scientific, educational, and fraternal organizations.
- Sales meetings, dealer meetings, technical meetings, executive meetings, training meetings, and public meetings are held by corporations and businesses.
- Association meetings differ from corporate meetings in that they are held on a regular cycle, at a different destination each year, and attract a larger number of participants (who attend voluntarily).
- With the increased demand for meetings expertise, meeting planning has emerged as a profession in its own right.
- Meeting planners work for associations, corporations, travel agencies, and as independent consultants.
- Incentive travel programs are used as motivational tools for employees by corporations and businesses.
- Trade shows differ from exhibitions in that they are not staged as part of a convention.
- Tour operators package convention travel for sale to associations and corporations, either directly or through retail travel agencies.
- Site destination selection companies, destination management companies, and convention services and facilities companies provide support services for meeting planners.
- Convention and visitors bureaus promote and service conventions for a particular destination.

Key Terms

off-site meeting
convention
breakout
conference
congress
forum

symposium
lecture
seminar
workshop
clinic
panel
exhibition
trade show
trade fair
teleconferencing
pure incentive
sales incentive
booth
stand
site destination selection company
destination management company (DMC)
convention and visitors bureau (CVB)

What Do You Think?

1. The number of meetings held every year has grown tremendously in recent decades. What factors might cause a slowdown or halt in the growth of the meetings business?
2. Which segment of the market do you think is more important to the meetings business: the association market or the corporate market? Explain your point of view.
3. What problems might a travel agency face in trying to enter the meetings and incentives business?
4. Meetings are currently held at hotels, resorts, conference/convention/civic centers, and on cruise ships. What other locations might conceivably be developed as meetings sites in the future?
5. Why, do you think, are international trade shows more heavily sales-oriented than domestic trade shows?
6. Why might an individual choose to work as an independent meeting planner rather than as an association executive or as a corporate meeting planner?
7. What site features might you stress to attract meetings business if you were employed as convention service manager (a) at a downtown hotel, (b) at an airport hotel, (c) at a resort, and (d) on a cruise ship?

Dealing with Product

You are the meeting planner for a corporation that has a dozen regional sales offices located around the country. It is Monday morning and the vice president of sales expects you to present a plan for the annual sales meeting during this afternoon's departmental meeting. You have nearly completed the rough draft when the vice president of human resources phones.

It seems that she has just finished reading an article on teleconferencing, which describes how delegates gather in front of wall-sized television screens capable of two-way communication. She argues that teleconferencing could save the company thousands of dollars. It would cut down on the costs of transportation, lodging, meals, and time away from work. Furthermore, she feels that teleconferencing would cut down on the fatigue often associated with business travel.

What will you tell the attendees at today's departmental meeting about the two types of meeting—the traditional sales meeting and teleconferencing? Do you think the former will become obsolete as a result of the latter?

Dealing with People

You are the owner and manager of a 100-unit hotel and resort located on a lake in the mountains of a southeastern state. Your hotel is a popular vacation destination, but your business is seasonal. The summer and early fall are your busiest months. You have decided to actively seek convention and meetings business in order to "fill the house" throughout the year.

Imagine that you are going to prepare sales presentations for the following decision makers. What do you think that their MNEs will be and what can you offer to fulfill them?

1. The executive director of a scientific research association.
2. The president of a trade union local.
3. The vice president of marketing for a computer software manufacturing company.
4. The social director of the branch of Parents Without Partners in Yourtown.
5. The president of a chapter of the American Society of Travel Agents.

WORKSHEET 12-1   MEETINGS, MEETINGS, MEETINGS

You are an independent meeting planner. You have been asked to help plan the following meetings. First identify the type of association or corporate meeting involved (religious association, corporate training, etc.) and the format (convention, seminar, clinic, etc.) the meeting is likely to follow. Then suggest an appropriate location for the meeting.

1. The International Booksellers Association will hold a book fair in Frankfurt, Germany. Thousands of publishers and book dealers from around the world will attend.

   _____

   _____

2. Infosystems, Inc., a consulting firm, has been hired to improve interpersonal communication within the Parck Corporation. Part of the process will be to bring executives and middle management together for face-to-face dialogue.

   _____

   _____

3. Compton, Inc., a meat-packing plant, will hold a one-day meeting of its stockholders.

   _____

   _____

4. The American Society of Microbiology will conduct a three-day meeting to discuss ways to prevent groundwater pollution. About 250 microbiologists from around the country will attend.

   _____

   _____

5. About 30,000 Shriners and their wives are expected to attend the organization's national meeting. The week-long event includes general assemblies, special-interest-group meetings, banquets, a tour of the city, and a parade.

   _____

   _____

6. Royal Viking Line wants to familiarize midwestern travel agents with its cruise products. Knowing what a cruise is like may stimulate the agents to sell more cruises to their customers.

   _____

   _____

7. At a meeting of the chamber of commerce, the president of a department store chain, a newspaper publisher, a vice president of a public utility, and a demographer will discuss diversity in the work force in the year 2000. After their presentation, members of the audience will be invited to ask questions.

   _____

   _____

8. The state teachers' federation will hold its annual two-day meeting. Well-known educators will address the teachers on current trends in education. There will be an opportunity to attend small-group sessions on a variety of topics related to education and to view the latest materials produced by textbook publishers. Approximately 4,000 teachers are expected to participate.

   _____

   _____

9. Levy Laboratories, a manufacturer of medical equipment, has developed a new sterilizer for surgical instruments. During a two-day meeting of its regional sales force, the company wants to acquaint sales representatives with the new product.

   _____

   _____

10. A state association of builders and contractors will hold its annual home show.

    _____

    _____

WORKSHEET 12-2   MAKING A CONVENTION WORK

Imagine that a three-day regional convention for 100 industrial engineers will be held in Yourtown. What will the following people do before and during the convention to ensure that all goes well?

Meeting planner _____

_____

_____

_____

_____

Hotel convention service manager _____

_____

_____

_____

_____

Hotel staff _____

_____

_____

_____

_____

Caterer and staff _____

_____

_____

_____

_____

Security director and staff _____

_____

_____

_____

_____

_____

Audiovisual specialist_____

_____

_____

_____

_____

Air and ground transportation suppliers

_____

_____

_____

_____

Entrepreneurs _____

_____

_____

_____

_____

Others _____

_____

_____

_____

_____

WORKSHEET 12-3   MULTIPLIER EFFECT AND LEAKAGES

You learned about the concepts of the multiplier effect and leakage in Chapter 8. Think about how these concepts would apply to a large meeting or convention held in Yourtown.

Use the expenditures of one attendee or a group of attendees to demonstrate how tourist dollars are spent and respent.

Describe how part of the tourist income might flow out of Yourtown's economy to purchase goods or services from elsewhere.

WORKSHEET 12-4   CONVENTION AND VISITORS BUREAU

Locate the convention and visitors bureau closest to Yourtown and obtain information and promotional materials from it. What facilities does the city offer for the following?

Small to medium-sized meetings _____

_____

_____

_____

_____

Conventions _____

_____

_____

_____

_____

Exhibitions and trade shows _____

_____

_____

_____

_____

Visitors in general _____

_____

_____

_____

_____

How large a convention or meeting could the city accommodate?

_____

_____

_____

_____

_____

Are any improvements or expansions planned? If so, what?

_____

_____

_____

_____

_____

Read the Yourtown newspapers. List the conventions, conferences, trade shows, or exhibitions that will be held in Yourtown in the next six months

_____

_____

_____

_____

_____

Will any of them be open to the public?

_____

_____

_____

_____

_____

PART 5

THE TRAVEL AND TOURISM MARKETPLACE

CHAPTER 13 TRAVEL AND TOURISM DISTRIBUTORS

"If you be a traveler, have always two bags very full, that is one of patience and another of money."

—John Florio

Objectives

When you have completed this chapter, you should be able to:

- Explain how the travel agency is similar to, and different from, a traditional retail store.
- Discuss how travel agencies are compensated.
- Describe the relationship between the travel agency, customer, and supplier.
- List several types of travel agencies.
- Explain how airline deregulation, the competitive market decision, and automation have affected United States travel agencies.

- Describe the trend toward consolidation of travel agencies.
- List the steps involved in opening a retail travel agency.
- Describe how a travel agency functions.
- Identify other travel and tourism distributors.
- Name the main professional associations for travel agents.
- Explain how to become a professional travel agent.

Tim Ayers, a self-employed management consultant, is also his own travel agent. He recently planned the itinerary and made all the arrangements for a trip to Ireland for himself, his wife, and another couple. Tim checked out books on Ireland from the public library and read about places to visit. Months before their departure, he wrote letters to bed and breakfast establishments requesting accommodations. To purchase round-trip air tickets from New York City to Dublin, he drove from his home in the suburbs to a downtown airline ticket office. Tim then drove to another airline office to purchase tickets for a connecting flight from his hometown to New York City. And by dialing a special toll-free phone number, he was able to reserve a rental car for ground transportation while in Ireland.

Tim is an exceptional traveler. Most travelers have neither the time nor the know-how to make their own travel arrangements. They're also not interested in sorting through complicated schedules and fares. And they don't want to worry about everything connecting smoothly. Instead, travelers depend on travel and tourism distributors—travel agencies, business travel departments (BTDs), scheduled airline ticket offices

(SATOs), and travel clubs—to take care of all the arrangements.

THE TRAVEL AGENCY AS INTERMEDIARY

In all channels of distribution, as you know, there is usually an intermediary, or link, between the supplier and customer. One type of intermediary is the retail store. Hardware stores, supermarkets, clothing shops, drugstores, and many other retail stores provide a convenient place for consumers to purchase a variety of products. Retail stores are also convenient for the suppliers. Without them, suppliers would have to set up their own outlets or send sales representatives all over the country.

The travel agency also functions as a retail store, providing suppliers with a link to the public. In this case, the suppliers consist of airlines, cruise ship lines, bus companies, railroads, hotels and motels, car rental agencies, and wholesale tour operators. The customers include vacation and leisure travelers, business travelers, and travelers visiting friends and relatives (VFR).

Of all the travel intermediaries, the travel agency is the most important. Retail travel agencies reserve more airline seats, cruise reservations, hotel accommodations, and package tours than does any other intermediary. Figure 13-1 illustrates supplier dependence on the travel agency.

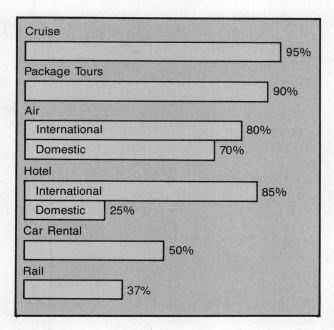

Figure 13-1 Percent of Travel Product Sold by United States Travel Agencies
Source: Travel Industry World Yearbook

Compensation

Like other retail stores, travel agencies are in business to make money. However, the way travel agencies earn their money, or compensation, differs from that of most other retail outlets.

Most retailers buy goods for a certain price from a supplier and then sell these goods, for a higher price, to the customer. The owner of a hardware store, for example, buys nuts and bolts, tools, wood, and other merchandise from a manufacturer or a wholesale dealer. Because the owner buys these products in bulk, he gets them for a reduced rate. Before selling them to the public, he marks up the price of each item. The customer pays for the item at its retail price, and the difference between the wholesale price and the retail price, which is called the markup, is the owner's compensation.

In travel agencies, the supplier—not the customer—compensates the agency in the form of commissions and overrides. The supplier compensates the agency for the time and money it spends on promoting and selling the supplier's products. Customers pay no more for travel

products at a travel agency than they would pay if they went to the supplier directly. In fact, travel agents can often save clients money by comparing different products to determine the best value. Furthermore, travel agents offer free counseling on destinations, routing, transportation, accommodations, and sightseeing.

Figure 13-2 shows the sources of travel agency revenue. As you can see, almost 60 percent of travel agency compensation comes from the sale of airline products and services. The airlines have a tremendous influence on travel agencies. Because of this, much of the information in this chapter focuses on the relationship between the airlines and travel agencies.

Commissions. A commission is a percentage of the total sale price paid to an agency. If an airline ticket costs $100 and the airline has agreed to pay a commission of 10 percent, then the agency—or agent—receives a commission of $10 ($100 x .10 = $10). At 10 percent commission, $1 million in sales will gross $100,000 in commissions, from which operating expenses and taxes must be paid. Since the profit margin in the travel industry can be quite low, managers and owners must watch finances carefully.

The standard commission paid by most transportation components is presently 10 percent. (Commission on the sale of tour packages, however, runs from 11 percent to 22 percent.) Since deregulation, the rate of commission has been negotiable between airlines and travel agencies. In 1990, total commissions from airline ticket sales were $5 billion.

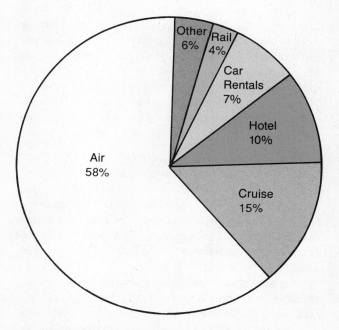

Figure 13-2 Sources of Travel Agency Revenue
Source: Louis Harris and Associates

Overrides. Suppliers also compensate travel agencies through overrides. As you learned in Chapter 3, an override is a bonus or extra commission for doing volume business. For example, a cruise line might pay a travel agency a commission of 10 percent on the sale of every cruise package. However, if the agency sells $10,000 worth of cruises, then the cruise line agrees to pay an additional 1 percent—a total of 11 percent—for every cruise sold after that.

Some suppliers offer overrides on a graduated scale up to 15 percent. The scale may increase as follows:

Sales	Override
$10,000–14,999	1 percent
$15,000–24,999	2 percent
$25,000–34,999	3 percent
$35,000–44,999	4 percent
$45,000 and over	5 percent

Suppliers might also make overrides retroactive once an agency has reached a certain total. In the case of an agency that has reached a sales total of $45,000, the supplier might pay a 15 percent commission for all previous sales.

Rebates. As a means of attracting and maintaining customers, some travel agencies share a portion of their commissions and overrides with their clients. This takes the form of rebates, or money back on the price of a ticket. Rebates for air tickets are commonly given to corporations. In fact, some corporations demand a certain percentage of an agency's commissions before they will contract to do business with the agency.

Rebating is a legal practice for domestic air travel. However, under the terms of the 1958 Federal Aviation Act and bilateral agreements, it is illegal for international air travel. The United States government, in the spirit of free competition, has followed a "no-see" policy and has turned a blind eye on rebating for international air travel. This puts professional travel agents in an uncomfortable position. They don't want to break the law, but they feel pressure to do so in order to remain competitive.

Service Charges. To cover their expenses, some travel agencies charge customers for certain services. This situation has been brought about largely because of airline deregulation. With the onslaught of low airfares, travel agencies are earning less in commissions. (A commission of 10 percent on a ticket costing $75 yields less revenue than a commission of 10 percent on a ticket costing $100.)

Services that some agencies now charge for include preparing a lengthy and involved itinerary, making a noncommissionable hotel reservation, obtaining visas, sending telegrams, and making long-distance telephone calls. Because it is time-consuming to undo arrangements, agencies may also charge for trip cancellations. A consulting fee may be charged if a travel agent spends an hour talking to a customer about a trip and the customer doesn't book. Fees may be waived in certain circumstances. For instance, clients booking a round-the-world cruise would probably not be charged for long-distance telephone calls made in connection with their excursion.

Agencies that do charge service fees should clearly state this fact to customers. Many people feel that charging fees violates the service nature of the travel agency industry, and the practice is currently under debate.

Relationships

Travel agencies have relationships both with suppliers and with clients. They have agreements, written or implied, to sell the products of their suppliers. They are expected to represent suppliers honorably and faithfully and to avoid dishonest practices. At the same time, agencies depend on suppliers to deliver products and services as promised. Once a trip has started, travel agents have no control over supplier error, although clients tend to blame the agents when things go wrong. Agencies need to select carefully the suppliers with whom they'll do business.

Travel agencies also act on behalf of their clients. Agents have an obligation to provide competent travel planning for clients who are spending money on travel products which, unlike most other consumer goods, cannot be returned if the buyer is not pleased. Clients expect travel agents to represent suppliers' products truthfully.

Illus. 13-1 *A travel agent performs three roles with a client: clerk, sales representative, and travel counselor.*

Commercial

A commercial travel agency specializes in the business travel requirements of firms or corporations. Because destinations are determined by the nature of the business, agents do less counseling with business travelers. The emphasis is on making arrangements quickly and efficiently. Commercial travel agencies benefit from consistent year-round business, free from the seasonal or economic fluctuations of vacation and leisure travel. Some commercial agencies may branch into leisure travel for their business clients.

Vacation and Leisure

The vacation and leisure agency generally has a more relaxed atmosphere, and agents do more counseling with clients. This type of agency may sell nationally advertised tours—such as Caravan and Globus-Gateway—or organize its own tours. Vacation and leisure agencies also design foreign and domestic tours for individual clients. Called Foreign Independent Tours (FITs) or Domestic Independent Tours (DITs), these arrangements cost more, but they meet the traveler's personal expectations better. Vacation and leisure agencies may also assist VFR travelers, although travelers driving to familiar locations usually don't require the services of a travel agency.

All-Cruise

Some agencies, with names like "Ship Shop," specialize in vacation cruises. Since only 5 percent of the traveling public has ever taken a cruise, a tremendous potential for business exists in this area. Also, since cruises represent a complete vacation package (transportation, accommodations, meals, sightseeing), commissions are calculated on the full amount of sale, and the compensation can be quite high. Through workshops and mailings, the National Association of Cruise Only Agents (NACOA) helps agencies increase their cruise identity.

Specialty

While conducting a general retail business, some agencies may have a branch or division that concentrates on one form of travel or on services to a special group of travelers. These agencies are usually located in metropolitan areas, where there is greater market segmentation. Agencies also tend to specialize when there are many agencies competing in one location. Some specialty agencies reflect the talents and interests of the owner and staff. The following list describes a few specialty agencies.

Government. From 1953 to 1981, travelers on official business for the federal government had to make their arrangements through a scheduled airline ticket office or directly through an airline. In 1982, as part of a movement away from monopolies, the Civil Aeronautics Board (CAB) decided to allow federal travelers to use the services of travel agencies. This decision opened up a lucrative market for travel agencies.

Adventure. Adventure travel is a fast-growing segment of the travel market. Agencies specializing in this area package trips to exotic and difficult-to-reach destinations. Such trips often include much physical activity. Examples are rafting on Chile's Bío-Bío River, camping on Easter Island, and cross-country skiing in the Arctic.

Senior Citizen. Many people say that their dream for retirement is to travel more. Agencies concentrating on senior citizen travel help make those dreams come true. Providing escorted tours for senior citizens is another fast-growing segment of the travel market. In planning such tours, agencies recognize that senior citizens may have special needs. For example, travelers whose sense of hearing is diminishing appreciate a guide who speaks clearly and loudly. For travelers who tend to tire easily, there should be no long walks or flights of stairs necessary for viewing attractions.

Singles. People who aren't married—or people who are married to someone who doesn't like to travel—can take advantage of tours and cruises arranged exclusively for singles. Some agencies provide matching services to help singles find travel companions. Singleworld, one of the best-known companies in this specialty area, sells its tours through travel agencies.

Ethnic. Ethnic travel agencies exist in cities with large ethnic communities. They arrange individual or group travel to the parent countries of these communities—most notably Greece, Italy, Poland, Israel, and Japan. In Minnesota, which has a sizable population of Scandinavian heritage, a travel agency in Minneapolis charters flights to Norway, Sweden, and Denmark. In San Francisco's Chinatown, a travel agency specializes in trips to China.

Handicapped. At present, only about a dozen travel companies offer tours specially designed for physically disabled people. The companies that do exist have organized trips in the United States and abroad for quadriplegics, for blind and deaf people, and for people suffering from emphysema, muscular dystrophy, and multiple sclerosis. Patients on dialysis have also been taken on trips. Other types of travel agencies are willing to adapt travel plans to the needs and abilities of physically handicapped people if they are told specifically what is needed.

Illus. 13-2 *An ethnic travel agency is located in a large city within an ethnic community and arranges group or individual tours to the native countries of such communities.*
Source: *Tom Vano/San Francisco Convention and Visitors Bureau*

Check Your Product Knowledge

1. Name four types of travel agencies.
2. What is the difference between a general travel agency and other types of travel agencies?
3. What factors might induce an agency to offer travel products for a select group of people?

THE GROWTH OF THE TRAVEL AGENCY

In 1841, Thomas Cook arranged for a railroad company to transport 570 British working-class people to a temperance convention. He thus became the first travel agent. As you learned in Chapter 1, the agency of Thomas Cook and Son dominated the early travel industry. Cook conducted tours to Europe and later to the United States. His agency represented various transportation companies, including several steamship lines.

The idea of organized travel assistance spread to the United States. By the end of the nineteenth century, numerous agencies were in operation. These included the

American Express Company, an offshoot of the famous Wells Fargo Company. Travel agencies at this time sold mainly steamship tickets and grand tours to the wealthy.

Where there were no agencies, suppliers found other ways to sell their products. Steamship companies sent agents on horseback to small towns across the United States. These agents sold steamship tickets to people who wanted to bring their relatives from Europe to this country. In the 1920s, railroad companies compensated hotel porters for getting train tickets for hotel guests. Early airlines also sold tickets through hotel porters, giving them a 5 percent commission.

Airlines soon realized that travel agencies offered a more efficient way of distributing airplane tickets. In particular, they saw the potential of travel agencies for selling pleasure travel on the popular DC-3s. At the beginning of World War II, about 1,000 agencies existed in the United States. With increased public acceptance of air transportation following the war, commercial airlines continued to grow and so did the number of travel agencies.

The Effects of Jet Travel

In the history of the travel industry, 1958 is considered to be the dawn of the modern age of travel. The flight of the first transatlantic passenger jet ushered in an era of pleasure travel for millions of people. Between 1960 and 1980, the number of passengers on United States scheduled carriers increased 378 percent, from 62 million to 297 million. The growth of travel has been matched by the growth in the number of travel agencies. In 1958, there were fewer than 3,000 agencies. Today, there are more than 37,000. Figure 13-3 illustrates the growth in the number of travel agencies and in the volume of airline sales from 1979 to 1989.

In 1958, before most people had taken their first jet flight (or any airplane flight, for that matter), travel agencies were quite different from the majority of travel agencies today. The travel agency of the 1950s was usually a part-time business, with a staff of one or two people. It may have been located in a back office of the local bus depot or in a cafe. Office furnishings were bare, and there were no computer terminals blinking information. Selling bus tickets and railroad tickets was often the main business. If a customer wanted to travel to a faraway place, the agent wrote letters to make reservations.

The Post-Deregulation Travel Agency

Of the more than 37,000 travel agencies in the United States today, about one-half are located in attractive offices in metropolitan areas. Two-thirds take in revenues totaling less than $2 million yearly. The majority of agencies are owned by women, and more women than men work in agencies.

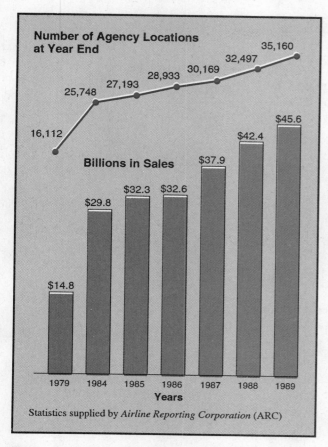

Number of Agency Locations at Year End

35,160
32,497
30,169
28,933
27,193
25,748
16,112

Billions in Sales

$45.6
$42.4
$37.9
$32.6
$32.3
$29.8
$14.8

1979 1984 1985 1986 1987 1988 1989
Years

Statistics supplied by *Airline Reporting Corporation* (ARC)

Figure 13-3 United States Travel Agent's Airline Sales
Source: Travel Industry World Yearbook, 1900 *produced by Child and Waters, Inc., New York*

In the late 1950s, travel agencies were concerned mainly with pleasure travel, but today business travel accounts for a large percentage of a general agency's bookings. In fact, today's travel agency offers an array of products that were not dreamed of 35 years ago. Travelers are more sophisticated, too, and demand more services. In contrast to the simple, quiet atmosphere of an agency in 1958, the environment in today's agency is likely to be fast-paced and hectic. Agents receive and send information instantaneously, using sophisticated technology. The work is complex and intense, made even more so by airline deregulation and competitive marketing.

Deregulation. As you know, the Airline Deregulation Act of 1978 led to an increase in the number of airlines. This, in turn, resulted in a multitude of new routes, schedules, and airfares—all of which were constantly changing. For flights from Detroit to Los Angeles, 100 price alternatives might be available—depending on the airline, day, and various restrictions. As airlines scrambled for passengers, price wars broke out. A highly competitive climate developed, with offers of rebates and discounts.

Deregulation, then, had an immediate effect on travel agencies. Prior to deregulation, routes and airfares

followed an orderly, predictable pattern. Agents could practically memorize the information they needed. Following deregulation, the system became confusing and difficult to handle. And, as mentioned earlier, lower airfares and negotiable commissions decreased revenue for travel agencies. Many agencies have been pressured into dealing in volume sales (selling large quantities of product at reduced prices) to counteract low revenues.

Most travel agents, however, believe that deregulation has made travel agents even more important. Customers are baffled by complex airfares and routes and need travel agents to help them through the maze. Suppliers, too, depend on travel agencies to sort things out for the customer. As you can see in Figure 13-4, the total dollar volume of travel agency bookings has increased dramatically since 1978.

Competitive Marketing Decision. From the mid-1940s until the early 1980s, travel agencies—by agreement with the airlines—possessed the exclusive right to sell airline tickets. Nobody else, except the airlines themselves, could sell tickets. Then, in 1984, the Civil Aeronautics Board abolished this exclusivity, stating that the practice stifled genuine competition.

Referred to as the *competitive marketing decision*, the CAB's ruling opened up new distribution channels. For example, business travel departments, hotels, department stores, and even grocery stores may now sell airline tickets. The effects of competitive marketing aren't yet clear. However, automated ticketing machines (ATMs)—like automated bank tellers—are already dispensing tickets at major airports and may soon be installed in supermarkets and shopping centers. An increasing number of travelers have begun to shop for tickets at home using personal computers (PCs) and home shopping television programs.

The new intermediaries may have features, such as convenience and low cost, that will appeal to suppliers and customers. To remain competitive, travel agencies must use aggressive and innovative marketing skills. They must also provide services not available from the competition. For instance, agencies might provide lawn maintenance or pet accommodations for travelers who book trips through them! Of course, travel agencies should promote the service they can perform best, and that is personalized travel counseling.

Automation. To keep up with the rapid changes in airfares and schedules and to increase sales volume, computer reservations systems have become a necessity for almost all travel agencies. Automation also simplifies accounting and facilitates information gathering for managerial purposes.

More than 95 percent of the nation's travel agencies are now automated. For automation to be cost-efficient, an agency should generate $1 million annually in airfare sales, of which $100,000 should be with the airline installing the equipment.

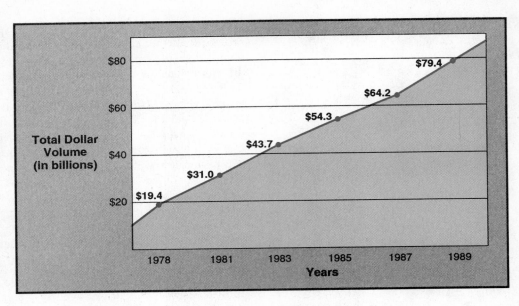

Figure 13-4 Total Dollar Volume of Travel Agency Bookings
Source: Louis Harris and Associates, Travel Weekly

The Consolidation of Agencies

Another way of categorizing travel agencies is by the amount of business they do annually. The breakdown might be as follows:

- Small—$2 million or less.
- Midsized—$3 million to $24 million.
- Large—$25 million to $49 million.
- Very large—$50 million and over.

The travel agency industry is overwhelmingly composed of small businesses (see Figure 13-5). However, a handful of very large agencies, or mega-agencies, do a disproportionate share of the business. In 1988, mega-agencies made up less than 1 percent of the total number of agencies, but they had 19 percent of total air sales. Mega-agencies became large and continue to grow by taking over midsized and large agencies or by squeezing them out of business.

Mega-Agencies. Mega-agencies, such as the American Automobile Association (AAA), Liberty Travel, The Carlson Group, Thomas Cook Travel USA, American Express, and Rosenbluth Travel, are primarily interested in multimillion-dollar corporate accounts. With offices in many cities (and perhaps several offices in a single city), mega-agencies represent the supermarkets and giant discount houses of travel. Because they are so large, they can purchase travel products in bulk. The more volume they do, the easier it is to offer rebates, which cost-conscious corporations earnestly seek. Mega-agencies can offer many services, such as monitoring fre-

quent-flier programs and compiling lists of travel and entertainment expenses, which may be beyond the capability of smaller agencies.

Consortiums. To compete against mega-agencies, some independent travel agencies have banded together into consortiums. A *consortium* is a group formed to achieve a goal that is beyond the resources of any one member. Travel agencies pay a fee to become members of a consortium. Membership rules may also specify that an agency must have a certain gross income or a certain degree of automation. Not all independent agencies are able to join a consortium. A comparison of several consortiums is shown in Table 13-1.

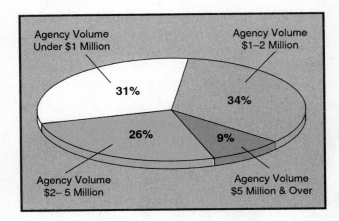

Figure 13-5 Profiling United States Travel Agencies: Breakdown by Volume
Source: Lodging Hospitality

American Express Company

American Express Company, in business over 140 years, has grown and changed with the times. It started out in the express cargo business and later moved on to a variety of travel-related services. Today, it is becoming well known for its international financial operations.

The original company was founded in 1850. It resulted from the merging of three firms involved in the express transport of goods, valuables, and money between the East Coast and the Midwest. By the mid-1860s, it had 900 offices in ten states. It also had a major competitor called the Merchants Union Express Company. After several years of cutthroat competition, the two rivals merged to become the American Merchants Union Express Company, renamed the American Express Company in 1873.

The travel arm of American Express (often referred to as AmEx) was brought into being after James Fargo, the son of the original president, took over the company. During James Fargo's 33 years of leadership, the American Express Money Order was introduced (1882), as was the American Express Traveler's Cheque (1891). The traveler's check was designed to replace the more cumbersome traveler's letter of credit that was then in use. AmEx opened its first European office in Paris in 1895.

In 1918, the United States government nationalized the express industry. American Express compensated for the resulting loss of business by focusing more heavily on its travel and banking operations.

Today, AmEx is known in four major business areas: travel, insurance, banking, and investment. Travel-related services still account for a large portion of company profits. American Express traveler's checks are still the most popular ones among travelers. For one thing, they are internationally recognized and accepted. Also, AmEx provides several special services. For example, travelers can get emergency refunds 24 hours a day and can obtain checks in many foreign currencies. Traveler's checks are profitable for AmEx, too. Most buyers purchase traveler's checks well in advance of the time they will actually use them. The money they spend on their traveler's checks amounts to an interest-free loan from the customers to AmEx. (In addition, travelers pay a 1 percent fee for purchasing checks, though much of that amount goes to the issuing agent.) AmEx puts the cash it receives into high-yield investments. Related services for travelers include travel agencies, tour packages, and motel and car rental reservations services.

AmEx was not the first company to introduce the credit card (Diners Club did so in 1950), but the AmEx "green card," introduced in 1958, was the best-known card for a number of years. (Since then, a "gold" and "platinum" card have been issued.) After bank cards such as MasterCard and Visa were introduced, AmEx faced heavy competition. However, clever marketing has brought many into the AmEx fold. First, there was the "Don't leave home without it" campaign, which warned travelers of the dire consequences of forgetting their American Express card (or not having one at all). In the mid-seventies and early eighties, the "Do you know me?" campaign thrived. It spotlighted high achievers (such as designer Bill Blass and writer Stephen King) whose names were better known than their faces. Their AmEx card gave them instant recognition. More recently, there has been the "Interesting Lives" campaign, designed to attract women to the card. These 30-second commercials show women in various roles making use of their American Express card. This, too, has been a huge success.

Although AmEx now makes as much money from its banking and investment activities as from its travel services division, many people still think of it as a premier travel service supplier. AmEx seems to like it that way. Executives don't plan anytime soon to phase out the division that made the American Express Company famous and continues to be a money-maker today.

Organization	Number of Members	Locations
Carlson Travel Network (Ask Mr. Foster)	1,000 locations (approx. 500 locations are wholly owned by Carlson; others are associates)	Primarily United States; owns a Canadian subsidiary and is expanding worldwide
GEM	1,125 companies; 1,375 locations (includes 70 cruise-only)	United States
GIANTS	900 companies; 1,815 locations	United States and Canada
Hickory	80 companies; 600 locations	Worldwide
MAST (Midwest Agents Selling Travel)	107 companies; 124 locations	Midwest United States
Travelsavers	Approx. 1,400 companies; 1,900 locations	All states in United States
Travel Trust International	114 companies; 2,000 locations	International
Uniglobe	Approx. 775 companies; 800 locations	United States and Canada (plans to expand into other countries)

Table 13-1 Comparison of Several Consortiums

Source: Reprinted from ASTA Agency Management, *published by Pace Communications, Inc. For the American Society of Travel Agents.*

Consortiums exist for both leisure and business travel, and they may be regional or nationwide. Woodside Travel Management Corp., one of the best-known consortiums, specializes in commercial travel. In 1988, Woodside comprised 85 agencies, with 1,500 locations worldwide. Its revenues from air sales were $6 billion. Other consortiums are Hickory Travel Systems, Associated Travel Network, and Travel Trust International.

Independent agencies benefit greatly from the bargaining power of consortiums. Consortiums are able to obtain bulk discounts for their members that would be unavailable to individual agencies. They also provide a forum for information exchange.

Consortiums do have some problems, however. With the help of a consortium, some independent agencies become so successful that they become mega-agencies themselves. If an agency—especially a strong one—leaves the consortium, the entire organization is weakened. Consortiums also tend to raid each other's ranks for members.

A variation of the travel consortium is the *cooperative*. In a cooperative, independent agencies band together temporarily to achieve a goal. Usually they have a joint interest in promoting a product or an event.

Franchises. To combat mega-agencies and consortiums, an independent agency might join a nationwide franchise, such as Ask Mr. Foster Travel, Empress Travel,

and Uniglobe. An agency that is part of a franchise retains its individual ownership. And, in contrast to the agencies in a consortium, a franchise agency adopts a company name and image. Franchises deal mainly with leisure and vacation travel.

To join a franchise, an agency pays an initial fee and an annual percentage of its gross earnings. In return, it receives bulk buying power, advertising support, training programs in business development, and brand-name recognition. Agencies may convert to franchises, or they may start out in business as franchises.

Small Agencies. Small agencies are the corner grocery store or the modest boutique of the travel industry. They may employ only four or five people and have little automation.

Whereas midsized and large agencies are in danger of being gobbled up, small agencies have a strong chance of surviving if they find the right market. For example, they might specialize in organizing FITs, or in arranging travel for small commercial firms (such as law offices) or for senior citizens. Cutting costs by reducing automation or office size will also help the small agency survive. Locating in a small town or city may be a key to success, too.

Small agencies have the advantage of being able to offer personalized service. They can offer more thorough trip counseling. When clients return from a trip, small agencies are more likely to call them up and ask how things went. Agents might write letters expressing regret if a trip is cancelled or if something goes awry. Says one small-agency employee, "If you make yourself valuable enough on a personal level, customers will not be looking around for discounts."

Check Your Product Knowledge

1. What has been the most important influence on the growth of travel agencies?
2. What effect did airline deregulation have on travel agencies?
3. What was the competitive marketing decision?
4. What new channels of distribution challenge the travel agency?
5. Why has automation become necessary for the majority of travel agencies?
6. What has been the effect of the mega-agency on the travel agency industry?

OPENING A TRAVEL AGENCY

Suppose you want to enter the retail travel business. Assuming you don't want to purchase a franchise or an existing agency, how would you go about opening your own full-service travel agency? How would you get airlines, cruise lines, and other suppliers to furnish you with tickets and pay you a commission?

Conference Appointments

Compared with other retail businesses, the travel agency industry is still highly accessible to entrepreneurs. Of the more than 37,000 travel agencies in the United States, more than half were started after 1980. Many people become owners of travel agencies as a second career after retirement or as a career change in midlife.

To open officially, a travel agency must be appointed, or approved, by industry conferences. In this context, a conference is not a meeting but a regulatory body that formulates standards for acceptance, reviews and appoints new agencies, and disciplines existing agencies when necessary. The four major conferences are:

- Airline Reporting Corporation (ARC)—for selling domestic air tickets.
- International Air Transport Association (IATA)—for selling international air tickets. (The International Airline Travel Agency Network, or IATAN, is a subsidiary of IATA. It serves as a link between United States retail travel agencies and IATA.)

- Cruise Lines International Association (CLIA)—for selling cruises.
- National Railroad Passenger Corporation (Amtrak)—for selling domestic rail tickets.

The membership of each conference consists of companies that sell transportation. IATA, for example, consists of 200 airlines from 116 countries. The companies, of course, want the people selling their products to be competent and honest, and the *conference-appointment system* is a way of assuring this. An agency that receives a conference appointment has the right to sell the products of all the conference's members and to receive commissions from them.

ARC Requirements

Each conference maintains requirements, or standards, that an agency must meet in order to be approved. While an agency needs the approval of all conferences, it should concentrate on meeting the Airline Reporting Corporation requirements first, because the sale of domestic air tickets forms a major part of an agency's business. By satisfying the ARC, the agency is likely to satisfy the other conferences.

The *Industry Agent's Handbook*, which is published by the ARC, details rules and regulations for setting up a travel agency, as well as many other procedures for selling air transportation. These requirements are modified from time to time. In the spring of 1987, for example, the ARC responded to a lawsuit filed by the Association of Retail Travel Agents (ARTA). It agreed to allow agents increased participation in formulating and enforcing the rules that govern their agencies. The new intermediaries created by the competitive marketing decision do not have to go through a formal accreditation process.

Open for Business. To receive ARC approval, the agency must be open for business and actively selling airline tickets. You might wonder how the agency can sell tickets before it's even been approved. While waiting for approval, it can obtain tickets from the airlines on a cash basis. When the appointment has been received, the agency can apply to receive commissions retroactively.

Experience. The agency must be under the direction of a qualified manager. The manager must have had at least two years' experience in promoting and selling travel products and services, as well as one year's experience in issuing tickets. If the owner doesn't possess this experience, he or she must hire someone who does.

Location. The agency must be accessible to the public and clearly identified as a travel agency. The sign must be visible from the street. The ARC does not allow agencies to be located in a hotel room, club, apartment, or

Illus. 13-3 *A travel agency should be located in a highly visible downtown store or in a shopping mall.*
Source: *Sara G. Matthews*

private home. A downtown store with a good display area that can be seen by pedestrians or people in cars provides an ideal location, as does a store in a high-traffic suburban mall. A low-rental upstairs office is acceptable if the agency is doing primarily business or charter travel.

Finances. The agency must have received a minimum bond of $20,000. Bonding, which is a form of insurance, indicates that the agency has a good credit rating and assures that the financial interests of the airlines and public will be protected. In addition, the agency must have a cash reserve—from $20,000 to $25,000—that it can use for paying salaries and operating expenses during the first year it's open. Since it may take almost two years before the agency receives accreditation and can begin to make a profit, most experts suggest an even larger cash reserve.

Promotion. The agency must be actively involved in the promotion of travel. It must advertise its products and services in newspaper, television, or radio ads, or through brochures, flyers, or direct-mail letters. Seeking a broad base of clients is important because an appointed agency is not allowed to do more than 20 percent of its business through a single client.

Procedure for ARC Appointment

The first step in obtaining accreditation is to submit an official application to the ARC. Along with the application, the owner must send various documents to prove that the agency meets the ARC requirements. These documents include the manager's résumé, financial statements, samples of promotional materials, and photos of the agency's interior and exterior.

After the application has been received, the ARC will send an official to inspect the agency. The inspector will interview personnel to verify that the information in the application is correct and will check to see that proper procedures are being followed for issuing tickets. The inspector will also check to see that there is a fireproof safe for storing ticket stock and that there are secure locks on all agency doors. Since ticket stock represents an airline's inventory, having blank tickets stolen could lead to financial loss for the airline.

Following the on-site investigation, the inspector forwards a report to the ARC. The applicant can expect to be notified within 90 days whether or not the agency has been accredited. If the agency has been approved, it will receive the ARC Passenger Sales Agency Agreement. This is a standard contract specifying the business relationship between the airlines and their appointed agents.

The agency will also receive an identification number, an agency ticketing plate, ticketing plates from the individual airlines, and a supply of generic ticket stock known as **standard ticket stock**. Rather than having each airline print its own tickets, the ARC decided several years ago that standard ticket stock would be less confusing for agencies to store. Using the ticketing plates, the agent imprints the name of the agency and the airline each time a ticket is issued. With tickets and validating plates, the agency is now officially open and ready to do business. No additional licensing is required by the federal government. However, some states require state licensing of travel agencies.

Check Your Product Knowledge

1. What are the four major conferences?
2. Why must an agency receive conference appointments?
3. What are the main requirements for receiving accreditation by the ARC?
4. List the procedures for obtaining ARC approval.

HOW A TRAVEL AGENCY FUNCTIONS

When customers enter most retail stores, they expect to see the merchandise on display. Before purchasing an item, customers want to look it over and find out something about it. They'll try on a new suit or coat to see how it looks and fits. They'll ask the salesperson to demonstrate how to operate a washing machine or a microwave oven. And they would never buy a car without first taking it for a test drive. If, after purchase, the product turns out to be defective or otherwise unsuitable, customers can return it to the store or receive some sort of adjustment to their account.

What's for Sale

The products sold by a retail travel agency seem quite different. Although some are tangible, most are intangible.

The Travel Product. Travel agencies sell products such as a ride on an airplane, a stay in a hotel room, a view of the mountains, or a cruise on a ship. None of these products can be displayed in the retail agency. Nor can they be inspected or tried out before they're purchased. Once customers buy these products, they have them for only a short time. If travel products prove unsatisfactory, they can't be returned—although suppliers and agencies might compensate dissatisfied customers in some way.

Why would anyone buy a product that can't be seen or touched and that doesn't come with a warranty? In selling travel products, the industry doesn't emphasize the technical features of aircraft or the dimensions of a hotel room. Instead, the industry promotes the psychological benefits of its products.

Travel agents sell dreams to vacation and leisure travelers. A travel ad might show a beautifully tanned young couple dancing in a moonlit tropical garden. The ad suggests that by purchasing certain travel products travelers will experience glamour, romance, relaxation, pleasure, and excitement. The vacation, long after it is over, will continue to exist as a wonderful memory.

To business and professional travelers, travel agents sell time, convenience, and prestige. A travel ad might show a flight attendant serving a gourmet meal to a distinguished-looking executive, or a chauffeur putting a business traveler's luggage into a limousine. Such ads tell travelers how important they are. By purchasing certain travel products, they will receive the efficient, prompt service they require.

Related Products. To make a major purchase more enjoyable, customers often buy accessories or optional items. Travel agencies sell products that make trips safer, easier, and more pleasant. These products include traveler's checks, passport photos, luggage, sportswear, and travel books.

A related product that has become a significant source of revenue for agencies is travel insurance. Different types of insurance are available, and they may be sold separately or in a package.

■ Flight insurance.
■ Accident/health insurance.
■ Baggage and personal possession insurance.

Illus. 13-4 *Travel agents sell dreams of glamour and excitement to vacation and leisure travelers.*

■ Trip cancellation or interruption insurance.
■ Bad weather insurance.

Even though travel insurance seems to emphasize what can go wrong on a trip, it is usually offered to clients as a means of adding to their peace of mind.

A new product that is being combined with travel insurance is travel assistance. Travel assistance not only covers the costs of emergencies during travel but also provides personal counseling or aid. For example, a husband and wife were traveling in Mexico. The husband, who had a history of heart trouble, became seriously ill. By calling the 24-hour assistance hotline, the wife received directions to the nearest hospital. The assistance/insurance company also paid the required, on-the-spot hospital admission costs and all hospital and doctor bills. In addition, it consulted with the man's doctors in the United States regarding his treatment.

The Staff

In a retail travel agency, as in other retail stores, the number of employees and their responsibilities depend on the size of the agency. Employing many people, a mega-agency might be organized like a corporation, with separate departments for sales, personnel, accounting, public relations, and word processing. A small agency, on the other hand, may simply have an owner/manager, one or more travel agents, and one or more outside sales representatives.

Manager. By assigning duties and work schedules, the manager directs the work of the other employees. He or she trains new employees or trains current employees in new procedures. The manager is responsible for developing new products, improving agency efficiency, and overseeing financial transactions. He or she must also plan for the future of the agency.

Travel Agents. As mentioned earlier, travel agents can also function as clerks, sales representatives, and counselors, and there are appropriate times for each role. As clerks, travel agents use automated systems to secure airline tickets, lease cars, and reserve hotel rooms for customers. As sales representatives, travel agents interest customers in various destinations and types of travel. And, as counselors, travel agents help clients verbalize their dreams, which are usually only partly formed when they come into the agency. The majority of clients need advice on the trip arrangements best suited to their values and lifestyles.

Outside Sales Representatives. A travel agency frequently has agreements with people known as outside sales representatives. Outside sales representatives attempt to arouse people's interest in traveling. They might show slides or movies at a meeting of a social or

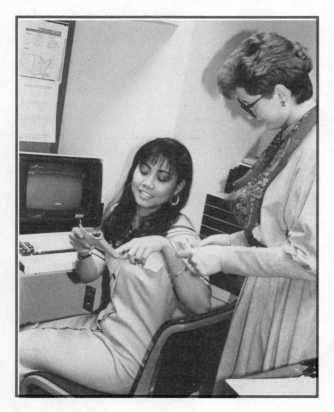

Illus. 13-5 *An important part of a travel agency manager's work is to train new employees in procedures and the use of equipment.*
Source: American Society of Travel Agents

special-interest group, or they might arrange meetings with business managers. Wherever they are—in the produce section of the supermarket or on the telephone with their friends—outside sales representatives seek to direct business toward the agency with which they've contracted.

Many outside sales representatives work on commission. If people they introduce to the agency actually make a booking, then the representatives get from 25 to 50 percent of the commission—depending on how much work they've done for the sale. For example, if the commission on the sale of an airline ticket is $20, the representative might get $5. Some representatives become involved in writing tickets.

Outside sales representatives are frequently homemakers, retirees, or other people wanting to work part-time. Aggressive representatives who work full-time, however, can develop a large clientele, called a following, who are often more loyal to them than to an agency.

Money Matters

Travel agencies handle large sums of money. As trustee of both the customer's payments and the supplier's funds, agencies must keep accurate records of money received and disbursed.

Sending Payment to the Airlines. How do agencies pay the airlines for the sale of tickets? Does each agency send each airline a payment—say twice a month? That's the way it used to be done, and the amount of record keeping, reporting, and auditing was staggering for both the agencies and the airlines.

In the mid-1960s, at the same time it introduced standard ticket stock, the Air Traffic Conference, which was later replaced by the Airline Reporting Corporation, instituted a much more efficient system. Under this system, known as the *Area Settlement Plan* (*ASP*), the ARC contracts with a commercial bank in Louisville, Kentucky, that serves as a clearinghouse.

Each week, the travel agency's bookkeeping staff prepares an **air report**, which is an accounting of the agency's weekly sales of airline tickets. Then the agency sends the report and ticket copies to the bank in Louisville. The bank calculates the amount of money the agency owes the airlines and requests a draft for that amount from the agency's bank. When the bank has received drafts from all the agencies, it sends a payment for the full amount owed to each airline. Rather than receiving more than 37,000 checks each week, each airline receives one payment from the bank. Nonaccredited intermediaries can use standard ticket stock and remit through the Area Settlement Plan.

Sending Payment to Other Suppliers. Since most agencies generally sell fewer products for cruise lines, railroad companies, tour operators, and other suppliers, they issue checks directly to them. Before doing so, they must be sure that the client has paid in full. Agencies deduct their commission before sending payment to the suppliers. A cover letter explains what the check is for and how payment was calculated.

The client is given the appropriate tickets and vouchers by the agent. *Vouchers* are coupons and documents that can be exchanged for travel products, for example hotel accommodations or sightseeing tours.

Check Your Product Knowledge

1. What is the difference between the products sold by retail travel agencies and those sold by other retail stores?
2. What are some related products sold by travel agencies?
3. Name staff positions held by employees in a typical small agency.
4. What is the function of an outside sales representative?
5. What is the Area Settlement Plan?

OTHER TRAVEL AND TOURISM DISTRIBUTORS

Instead of using travel agencies, some travelers go to other established intermediaries to obtain travel products and to receive help with trip arrangements. These channels of distribution include business travel departments, scheduled airline ticket offices, and travel clubs.

Business Travel Department

Some business travelers are able to use the services of their company's business travel department. As you learned in Chapter 11, some companies employ their own staff to make travel arrangements for the company's employees. Since BTDs are not open to the public, and since the BTD employees are paid by the company, BTDs are not accredited by the ARC. Nor do they receive commissions on the sale of airline tickets. Instead, BTDs operate as freelancers. They negotiate with the airlines for the right to sell their products and to receive discounts and rebates.

A variation of the BTD is the inplant agency. An inplant agency is a retail travel agency located on the premises of a corporation and doing business primarily with that corporation. Since the ARC does not recognize inplant agencies as full-service agencies, they receive

much lower commissions from the airlines—usually from 3 percent to 5 percent. The classification of inplant agencies is currently a subject of hot debate in the travel agency industry.

Another variation is the outplant agency. An outplant agency is an accredited, full-service travel agency located near a corporation's premises. The corporation has its own BTD to handle most travel arrangements, but it depends on the outplant agency to issue tickets. The outplant agency splits airline commissions with the BTD.

Scheduled Airline Ticket Office

Scheduled airline ticket offices are transportation bureaus jointly run by the airlines. They service official government travel at civilian and military facilities. Since SATOs are run by the carriers, no commission is paid.

As mentioned earlier, since 1982 the CAB has allowed government travelers to book through retail travel agencies. In other words, SATOs are now in competition with travel agencies. To make up for a decline in business, SATOs have recently entered the leisure field by selling package tours. Travel agencies view this as direct competition from the airlines.

Travel Club

As you know, travel products are extremely perishable. A seat on Delta Airlines' 2:00 P.M. flight from Denver to Phoenix on March 23, 1993, exists only for that moment. If it isn't sold, the airline receives absolutely no income from it. Because of the perishability of travel products, travel suppliers, like other retail suppliers, also rely on marketing techniques such as clearance sales.

The travel club is the travel industry's version of a clearance sale. Travel clubs specialize in the sale of unsold travel products to vacation and leisure travelers. These products are usually cruises and international airfares to Europe. To take advantage of bargain prices (anywhere from 20 percent to 60 percent off), travelers must belong to the club. They join by paying a nominal annual fee—usually around $50.

There are two main types of travel club. One type requires a membership fee and deals almost exclusively with last-minute bookings. The other type is more like a tour operator. It publishes a catalog of tours that is distributed to all members. Ports of Call is one such club. Some travel clubs even operate their own aircraft and offer private charter packages that range from weekend gambling junkets to trips around the world.

Here's how travel clubs generally work. At some time before the departure date, suppliers discount unsold inventory. To avoid offending travelers who have paid the full price, suppliers advertise their clearance sales only through travel clubs. Club members find out the latest information on departures by calling a secret hotline. They must keep all information they hear confidential. If members wish to purchase a sale item, they can use a credit-card number to complete the transaction over the telephone. The travel club then receives the commission for the sale.

While travelers can save substantially through membership in a travel club, their selection may be quite limited and may not meet their personal MNEs. Members must also have very flexible schedules in order to leave for a trip on short notice.

At the present time, there are about ten travel clubs operating nationwide. Ports of Call, centered in Denver, has 70,000 members. The club even operates its own terminal at Denver's Stapleton International Airport.

To promote membership, some travel clubs offer their members additional bargains, such as discounts on car rentals and rebates on tour and hotel bookings. Some clubs have frequent-traveler plans. After purchasing $3,000 in air travel, for instance, a member might be entitled to a free week aboard a cruise ship.

Check Your Product Knowledge

1. How is a business travel department different from a commercial travel agency?
2. What is SATO?
3. What is the purpose of travel clubs?

ASSOCIATIONS

Not too long ago, several hundred people in ten states became the victims of a telemarketing travel scam. These people each paid $200 for a travel certificate that, they were led to believe, could be applied toward discount travel. But when they tried to buy round-trip airfare to Hawaii for $29.95, they discovered their certificates were worthless.

Protecting the public from fraud such as this is one of the purposes of the American Society of Travel Agents (ASTA). Founded in 1931, ASTA's other main goals are to:

■ Promote and advance the interests of the travel agency industry.
■ Provide a public forum where travel agents can speak out on issues that concern them.

With 21,000 members in 129 countries, ASTA is the world's largest professional association of travel agents

and agencies. ASTA's membership also includes airline, steamship, railroad, and bus companies, as well as car rental firms, hotels, government tourist offices, and other travel-related organizations.

ASTA provides many services to its members. These include publishing a newsletter and magazine and sponsoring workshops and seminars. Through these methods, ASTA keeps members informed on current happenings in the industry and helps them develop new skills.

Another professional association for travel agents is the Association of Retail Travel Agents. With about 3,500 members, ARTA is smaller than ASTA. Unlike ASTA, ARTA does not allow travel industry suppliers to be members. ARTA's purposes are similar to ASTA's, although ARTA emphasizes improving the working relationship between the airlines and the agents. ARTA was founded in 1963.

Check Your Product Knowledge

1. Name two professional associations for travel agents.
2. What are the main purposes of professional associations?

BECOMING A TRAVEL AGENT

Do you enjoy helping other people? Are you able to solve problems? Can you work under pressure? Do you pay close attention to details? If you can answer "yes" to these questions, you possess qualities necessary for becoming a travel agent.

The position of professional travel agent is currently a high-growth career. Because of the expansion of the travel industry, ASTA has predicted that several thousand additional agents will be needed each year for the next several years. The Bureau of Labor Statistics (BLS) forecasts a 54 percent increase in the number of agents by the year 2000.

Only a few states require travel agents to be licensed, and the federal government doesn't require licensing at all. However, all travel agencies expect their agents to possess a certain body of knowledge and skills and to have completed some specialized training.

General Knowledge and Skills

When hiring new agents, managers try to determine the applicant's knowledge and skills in certain general areas. Foremost among these is a knowledge of geography. Travel agents must know where in the world they're

A DAY IN THE LIFE OF
A Travel Agent

In my work as a travel agent, service is top priority. I do a lot of different tasks, but they're all aimed at serving the customer well. Primarily, I'm a counselor and information provider. I answer the many questions travelers have. People who are making their first trip abroad, for example, often rely on me to advise them about obtaining passports, getting required immunizations, and figuring out exchange rates. I have to have the latest information to serve my customers well. I'm also an intermediary—between clients and airlines, clients and hotels, clients and resorts. The most detailed part of my job comes as I arrange for flights or room reservations or make out itineraries—double-checking facts is important to ensure a smooth trip.

I'm also, at times, a "friend in need." I remember one incident a few years ago, when a honeymoon couple lost their voucher for their prepaid accommodations. The hotel in Puerto Rico refused to let them depart unless they paid or came up with the voucher. The couple was frantic by the time they called me. I got on the telephone with the manager and convinced her to locate the copy of the voucher that had been mailed to the hotel and have the couple sign that. A very relieved couple left the island that day. Efforts like this are part of good service.

The most crucial skill for a travel agent, however, is the ability to size up a client quickly and to translate that client's ideas into tangible plans. If clients don't really know what they want, I ask a few leading questions to get started. Different kinds of people have different needs. Suppose a retirement-aged couple walks into my office. I discover through conversation that they want to relax in a warm climate and that they like to be waited on. Money is not an issue. I suggest a cruise on one of the lines that specializes in slow-paced, luxurious trips. They've never been on a cruise before, but they love the idea.

Perhaps a young engaged couple comes in, looking to plan a honeymoon. They want some seclusion, but also the possibility of evening entertainment. They're very athletic, and they want to be able to enjoy the out-

doors during the trip. And their budget is limited. My suggestion? A hotel in Bermuda that has separate beach-front cottages. The island has plenty of nightlife and lots of opportunities for activity—swimming, hiking, tennis, and so on. And the total cost is very reasonable.

The next clients to walk in may be a couple with young children. They want a place the whole family can enjoy. My suggestions to them include Colonial Williamsburg, Virginia, with nearby Busch Gardens, a fantastic theme park; Disneyland or Walt Disney World; and some of the "club" package vacations that provide activities for both adults and children. Their needs are totally different from those of another typical client—the business traveler, who wants the right flight at the right time and a hotel that is convenient to business contacts. To serve each of these clients well, I have to discover and translate their unique needs.

Other skills are important, too. Travel agents need good math skills, typing ability, a good command of English, a knowledge of geography, and an awareness of what's going on in the world. (I don't want to send someone to an island that is about to experience an armed revolution!) In addition, I need to be able to locate information about schedules and prices quickly—and to be able to react fast in an emergency such as an airline strike or a resort shutdown.

Like any job, being a travel agent has its disadvantages. I deal with the public all the time, and some people can be demanding and difficult to please. Business is affected by the season—with overtime one month and layoffs the next—and by the economy. On the other hand, my job allows me to take free or inexpensive trips and since I love to travel, that's very important. The flip side of putting up with demanding people is being able to serve appreciative ones well. I encourage clients to come back and tell me how things went. It's satisfying to know I did a good job, and I get to relive their trips with them, too. It's a way of traveling without leaving my desk, while learning how best to serve my future clients.

341

sending their clients. They must be able to locate destinations on a map. Agents must know about the climate, culture, and attractions of an area so that they can answer clients' questions about what to wear, how to act, and what to see.

A knowledge of arithmetic is important, since travel agents are constantly computing fares, preparing invoices, reading timetables, and exchanging currency. For agents who wish to advance to a managerial position, a knowledge of accounting will be most useful.

Travel agents must demonstrate good communication skills and sales techniques. They must be able to converse pleasantly with their clients, encouraging them to express their MNEs so that appropriate travel products can be suggested. A pleasant telephone manner is important, too, because many clients shop by phone to locate bargains.

Since most travel agents must produce their own letters, itineraries, reservation requests, and invoices, the ability to type well is important. And of course, since almost all agencies are now automated, computer skills are essential for the modern travel agent.

Education and Training

In the past, people who wanted to be travel agents started out doing clerical work for an agency. They learned the job by "looking over the shoulder" of an experienced agent. Agencies were even willing to let high school students type invoices, answer phones, and file documents.

The situation, however, has changed in today's travel agency. Computer reservations systems have eliminated much of the simpler clerical work. Because of the complexity of the modern agency, managers are very reluctant to allow an inexperienced individual to work on an account. And with their low profit margins, most agencies can't afford to lose accounts because of a trainee's errors. Then, too, managers find little time to train a completely inexperienced person.

Consequently, to break into the industry as a travel agent, a person now must have some specialized schooling or experience. People who have worked as airline reservationists, for example, are in great demand by travel agencies. Applicants who can transfer skills learned in other businesses would also be acceptable— especially if they have a network of business contacts to whom the agency could sell products. Outside sales representatives frequently learn enough about an agency's operations to break in as travel agents. Extensive domestic and foreign travel experience is also valuable for the prospective travel agent.

Specialized Schooling. Throughout the country, courses in travel agency operation and the travel industry are offered in various kinds of schools and colleges. These include vocational schools, private business schools, pro-

prietary schools, community colleges, adult education centers, and universities. In addition, many of the mega-agencies and franchises have established their own schools. In this way, they can tailor training to match the procedures followed in their particular organization, and they can recruit new agents from among the best students.

Advanced Training. Experienced travel agents can take an advanced course offered by the Institute of Certified Travel Agents (ICTA). Successful completion of the course leads to the prestigious title of Certified Travel Counselor (CTC). ASTA offers a variety of educational programs designed to help travel agents learn new skills and procedures. Membership in ASTA or ARTA signifies that an agent has professional status.

CAREER OPPORTUNITIES

The career path for travel agents depends on the size of the agency where they work. In a small or midsized agency, a person might start out as an agent, advance to an agent specializing in a certain type of travel or destination, and then advance to manager. Many managers go on to become owners of agencies. In a large or mega-agency, there are more levels of management and thus more opportunities for advancement.

People with training and experience as travel agents can work in places other than a retail travel agency. They might become the owner of a travel club, or they might work for a business travel department, automobile club, or government tourism office. Travel agency experience would also be beneficial preparation for work with an airline, cruise line, or other transportation company.

Summary

- The travel agency is the main intermediary in the travel industry's channels of distribution. In many respects, the travel agency is like a retail store, linking suppliers to the public.
- The airlines have had the most influence on the growth and development of agencies.
- Travel agencies are compensated through commissions and overrides. To attract and maintain customers, agencies grant rebates.
- In addition to making arrangements for trips and selling travel products, agents provide information about destinations. Counseling clients as to the products best suited to their motivations, needs, and expectations is the service that distinguishes the travel agency from other intermediaries.
- Different types of travel agencies exist to meet the needs of various segments of the travel market. These segments include general, commercial, vacation and leisure, all-cruise, and specialty.

■ More than 37,000 travel agencies currently exist in the United States, and the number is growing. The majority of agencies are operated as small businesses.

■ Airline deregulation and the competitive marketing decision have made the travel agency industry more complex. Automation has become a necessity for sorting out a multitude of fares and schedules.

■ There is a trend toward combining smaller, independent agencies into larger, more powerful agencies—mega-agencies. Consortiums, cooperatives, and franchises have developed in response to this trend.

■ To be able to sell suppliers' products and obtain commissions, an agency must receive conference appointments. Accreditation by the Airline Reporting Corporation is the most important. The ARC has specific requirements regarding the location, finances, and management of an agency.

■ Most of the products sold by travel agencies can't be seen or touched, tested before purchase, or brought back. Agencies sell experiences, which yield psychological benefits. As in other retail stores, employees are needed to sell the products.

■ Agencies send payment to the airlines following the Area Settlement Plan.

■ The business travel department, scheduled airline ticket office, and travel club are other distributors of travel products.

■ The American Society of Travel Agents and the Association of Retail Travel Agents promote the travel industry and uphold the professional standards of their members.

■ To become a travel agent, a person needs some specialized schooling or work experience that relates to the travel industry. Job openings for agents are expected to remain ample through the 1990s.

Key Terms

competitive marketing decision
consortium
cooperative
conference-appointment system
standard ticket stock
Area Settlement Plan
air report
voucher

What Do You Think?

1. What are the advantages and disadvantages of negotiable rates of commission for travel agencies?

2. Why do you think rebating is legal for domestic air travel, but not for international air travel?

3. Do you think that travel agents should charge service charges? If so, what kinds of services do you think they should charge for? What effects might increased service charges have?

4. If you were to open a travel agency, what type would you choose? Why?

5. In what ways has airline deregulation harmed the travel agency industry? In what ways has it helped it?

6. Do you think that the travel agency will lose its dominance as the main intermediary? Why or why not?

7. Travel clubs sell travel products at clearance-sale prices. What other ways can you think of for selling unsold tickets?

8. In what ways have the education and training requirements of travel agents changed in the past few years?

Dealing with Product

You are a travel counselor employed by a medium-sized travel agency in Yourtown. Your clients, Mr. and Mrs. West, are inexperienced travelers. In fact, Mrs. West has never flown before. Nevertheless, these recently retired senior citizens have long dreamed of a trip to Europe, and now you have an opportunity to help make their dreams come true.

As a travel professional, you know that there are literally hundreds of seemingly similar products available. How would you decide which products would best suit Mr. and Mrs. West's MNEs? Which of the travel insurance products would you recommend, and why?

Dealing with People

You are an outside sales representative employed by a medium-sized travel agency in Yourtown. One of your most productive accounts is Beta Industries, located in the new airport industrial park. Much to your dismay, Mr. Black, the manager of Beta's travel department, tells you he has just read an article in the local newspapers about consolidators.

Consolidators are travel intermediaries, not unlike brokers, who buy large quantities of airline tickets for as little as half price directly from certain airlines, and then distribute these tickets through travel agents. The travel agents that use the so-called consolidator can often earn 25 to 35 percent commissions as opposed to the traditional 10 percent rate.

Mr. Black insists that you use a consolidator for all of his company travel, and he expects you to give his company a 15 percent rebate on all airline tickets. Mr. Black wants an answer by the end of the week. What will you tell your boss at the agency? What do you think you and your boss can do for Mr. Black?

WORKSHEET 13-1   SPECIALIZED TRAVEL AGENCY

You want to open a travel agency that specializes in serving physically and mentally handicapped people.

What special facilities and services will you require of your transportation suppliers?

What special facilities and services will you require of your accommodations suppliers?

What knowledge, abilities, or qualities will you require of your tour operators?

How will you locate suppliers who are appropriately equipped or are willing to become so?

How will the motivations, needs, and expectations of handicapped travelers differ from those of nonhandicapped travelers? How will they be similar?

How will you find customers?

How might the employees you hire affect your business?

Will you expect special compensation? If so, from whom?

WORKSHEET 13-2   OWNING A TRAVEL AGENCY

You are interested in having your own business. You see the following ad in the travel section of Yourtown newspaper and decide to contact the seller for more information. As someone who knows about operating a travel agency, what questions do you need to ask? Write them in the space below.

FOR SALE
TRAVEL AGENCY

Present volume approximately 2 million. Strong growth upside. Good suburban office and staff. Cash with some terms to qualified buyer. Respond to:

45 Main St.
Yourtown, USA 04082
555-2626

WORKSHEET 13-3   YOURTOWN TRAVEL AGENCIES

Select six of the travel agencies located in Yourtown or in the closest town or city that supports a large number of agencies. Briefly describe each. Include whether it is ARC accredited or awaiting accreditation; its size; whether it is independent and/or a member of a consortium, cooperative, or franchise; the type of product it sells (for example, general, commercial, vacation and leisure, all-cruise, specialty); whether it is computerized and, if so, which system it uses; and any special services it offers or special marketing methods it employs.

1.

2.

3.

4.

5.

6.

Do you think there are travel needs in Yourtown that are not being met by existing travel agencies? If you do, what are they and how would you meet them?

WORKSHEET 13-4   CONFERENCE APPOINTMENTS

You have learned about the standards a travel agency must meet to receive ARC approval. You have also learned about the procedure for receiving ARC accreditation. Choose one of the other major conferences: International Air Transport Association, Cruise Lines International Association, or National Railroad Passenger Corporation. Research the conference's requirements and procedure for accreditation. (See Appendix B for conference addresses.) Write your findings in the spaces below.

Name of Conference _____

Requirements for Appointment _____

Procedure for Appointment _____

CHAPTER 14 PROMOTION AND SALES

"In the modern world of business, it is useless to be a creative, original thinker unless you can also sell what you create. Management cannot be expected to recognize a good idea unless it is presented to them by a good salesman."

—David MacKenzie Ogilvy

Objectives

When you have completed this chapter, you should be able to:

- Distinguish between marketing and sales.
- Explain the difference between product-oriented marketing and consumer-oriented marketing.
- Identify the types of advertising used in travel and tourism promotion.
- List the advantages of print media advertising.
- Explain the difference between intrusive advertising and directional advertising.

- Identify the major sales-promotion techniques.
- Show how public relations differs from advertising.
- Describe the role of the government in the promotion of travel and tourism.
- Give examples of public-sector promotional campaigns.
- Distinguish between outside sales and inside sales.
- Explain how travel agents sell.

Imagine a tropical island paradise with miles of white-sand beaches, secluded bays, and crystal-clear waters. With such outstanding natural resources, it would be no surprise if the island were developed as a vacation resort. This might involve improving the infrastructure by constructing an airport to handle flights from overseas and by upgrading port facilities so that cruise ships could dock at the island. Development would also require an expansion of the superstructure, including the building of hotels, restaurants, and other tourist amenities to cater to foreign visitors. Golf courses, tennis courts, and a conference center might be added to increase the appeal of the destination.

You might think that our imaginary resort now has all the necessary ingredients to prosper as a tourist destination. Yet one vital ingredient is missing: a promotional campaign to encourage people to visit the destination. After all, few travelers will go to a place unless they know something about it. The same is true for every kind of travel product or service. Whether we are talking about a flight, a rail journey, a car rental service, a cruise, a hotel room, or a tour package, all depend for their profitability on effective promotion.

In this chapter, you will learn about the various types of promotion that are used to communicate the benefits of travel products to potential consumers. Special emphasis will be placed on the use of advertising as a promotional tool. Then you will read about the different organizations that promote travel and tourism, within both the public sector and the private sector.

An effective promotional campaign creates a demand for a product or service. Once the demand has been created, the product must be sold to the consumer. The latter part of this chapter focuses on travel and tourism sales, with specific reference to the ways suppliers sell and the ways travel agents sell.

TRAVEL AND TOURISM MARKETING

Before we look at promotion and sales in detail, we must first place them within the broader context of marketing.

The American Marketing Association defines marketing as: "the performance of business activities directed toward . . . the flow of goods and services from producer to consumer or user." Many people confuse marketing with sales; they believe that marketing and sales are one and the same. In fact, the sales function is the culmination of the marketing process, but it is only one aspect of that process. Other elements of marketing include market research, product development, pricing, distribution, and promotion. In short, *marketing* is the sum of all the activities that bring buyer and seller together.

Marketing Strategies

Until the 1950s, almost all marketing was product-oriented. A product-oriented marketing strategy would typically begin with the question, "What do we want to sell?" The marketing process involved developing a product and hoping that customers would buy it. Modern marketing, on the other hand, approaches the process from the consumer's viewpoint. A consumer-oriented marketing strategy asks the question, "What do our customers want to buy?" The marketing process is one of determining what customers want or need and then developing a product to meet those needs.

Travel and tourism marketing is heavily oriented toward the consumer. Suppliers and other tourist organizations identify potential customers, or markets, by conducting *market research*. Market research involves gathering and analyzing information about present and potential clients in an attempt to predict what they will want to buy. More specifically, market research involves:

- Surveying clients through questionnaires and personal interviews.
- Reviewing past bookings.
- Analyzing census bureau studies and information from sources such as the United States Travel Data Center.
- Predicting social and economic trends.

Information obtained from market research allows suppliers to divide the market into different segments (market segmentation). Products can then be developed to match the motivations, needs, and expectations (MNEs) of each target market. TWA, for example, introduced its Ambassador Class service on domestic flights to cater to the MNEs of the business traveler. TWA's market research had shown that business travelers were dissatisfied with the existing two-class service. Business travelers complained that seating in coach class was too cramped, while first class was too expensive. The new Ambassador Class gave passengers room to work and a number of first-class perks at a cost only a little above coach fare.

The Four Ps

Once the target market has been identified by market research, the travel supplier develops a marketing strategy to satisfy the needs of this market. As you learned in Chapter 1, the various elements involved in the marketing process are often referred to as the four Ps. These are:

- Product.
- Price.
- Place.
- Promotion.

Product. The product stage involves selection and development of the right range of products and services. Suppliers of transportation, such as airlines, railroads, and motorcoach companies, must decide which routes to serve and what level of service to offer. Suppliers of accommodations, such as hotels, motels, and resorts, must decide where to locate their properties and what type of guest amenities to provide. Cruise lines and tour operators must select destinations and itineraries and decide on the right mix of travel components for their cruise or tour packages. Travel agencies must choose whether to sell a wide range of travel products or to specialize in just a few. All these decisions will be affected by the MNEs of the markets that the travel companies have chosen to serve.

Price. Pricing follows logically from product selection. When developing a pricing policy, suppliers must bear in mind not only the MNEs of the target market but also the prices charged by competitors. Suppliers can choose to sell their product at, below, or above the market price.

The *market price* is established by supply and demand and is often an average price. Many travel products are *parity products*—that is, one company's product is very similar to that of another. When companies offer parity products, the competitive forces of the market help establish a market price. A company charging below-market prices bases its pricing policy on no-frills service. A company selling above the market price emphasizes premium service. Some companies use more than one pricing strategy to appeal to different market segments. Choice Hotels International, for example, markets one product for economy-minded guests (Comfort Inns), one for midprice guests (Quality Inns), and one for those who are prepared to pay for luxury (Clarion Hotels). The company also markets several products for guests on a tight budget (Sleep Inns, Rodeway Inns, Econo Lodges, and Friendship Inns).

Place. Place, the third of the four Ps, refers to the channels used to distribute the product from producer to consumer. Suppliers may sell directly to the client or through one or more intermediaries (travel agents, tour operators, and so on). Most car rental firms, for example, use direct distribution. Cruise lines, on the other hand, usually distribute their product through travel agencies. The distribution channel chosen will be the one that gets the product to the target market most effectively.

PROFILE
Michael Eisner

When Michael Eisner took over as chairman of the Walt Disney Company in 1984, he told its board of directors that he felt like a kid turned loose in a toy store. "I don't know which toy to take home because they're all fabulous and they all work and I'm so excited I can't sleep at night."

Eisner and Disney turned out to be a perfect match. When Walt Disney died in 1966, his legendary movie, animation, and theme park empire began to go into a slow decline. Company executives were afraid to branch out into new ventures or to change the company image that Disney had established. The Disney Company continued to turn out children's movies and animated features, but children were deserting it by the millions for action-packed thrillers like *Star Wars* and *Raiders of the Lost Ark*.

While the Disney Company declined, Eisner was busy establishing his credentials as a major creative programming talent in television and the movies. He was born in 1942 into an affluent New York City family. He attended the prestigious Lawrenceville Preparatory School in New Jersey, then attended Denison University in Ohio. Eisner graduated with a degree in English literature and theater in 1964 and went to work as a clerk at the National Broadcasting Company (NBC).

Within a few months Eisner jumped ship and went to the American Broadcasting Company (ABC), where he was put in charge of specials and later Saturday morning children's programming. His experience in children's programming came in very handy when he became head of the Disney operation.

In 1976, Eisner was named president of Paramount Pictures. Applying what he had learned in television, Eisner helped turn the financially ailing company into the top-ranking movie studio in Hollywood. Eisner seemed to have a genius for choosing movie projects that would become big hits with the public. His formula was simple: produce low-cost hit movies and steer clear of big-budget pictures and high-priced stars. Among his most spectacular successes at Paramount were *Beverly Hills Cop, Flashdance, Airplane,* and *Raiders of the Lost Ark*. Eisner also produced two very popular TV series, "Cheers" and "Family Ties," and the syndicated entertainment news show, "Entertainment Tonight."

In 1983, the troubled Walt Disney Company fought off corporate raiders who had intended to break up the com-

pany and sell its assets. Walt Disney's nephew, Roy Disney, then persuaded the company's board of directors to hire Eisner to try to revive it. Frank Wells, former vice president of Warner Brothers, joined Eisner at the Disney Company. Wells became president and chief operating officer. Everyone expected Eisner to take at least two or three years to turn the company around, but he surprised everyone by doing it in a matter of months.

Eisner has been a whirlwind at Disney. Under his direction, the Disney Company and its adult film production company, Touchstone Pictures, have produced one blockbuster hit after another. These films include *Three Men and a Baby*; *Who Framed Roger Rabbit?*; *Honey, I Shrunk the Kids*; *Dick Tracy,* and *Pretty Woman*. The Disney Channel, the company's pay TV network, has grown from a few hundred thousand to nearly 4 million subscribers. In the early 1990s, the Disney Channel's profits were more than $5 million. The company's TV feature, "The Golden Girls," and cartoon shows, "Duck Tales" and "The Adventures of the Gummi Bears," have attracted millions of viewers.

Eisner has also transformed Disney's aging theme parks at Disneyland in Anaheim, California, and Disney World in Orlando, Florida. He has built $500 million worth of new attractions, including the Disney-MGM theme park, and a number of hotels, at Orlando. A new park, Tokyo Disneyland, is operating in Japan, and Euro Disneyland is under construction and scheduled to open near Paris in 1992. Revenues have skyrocketed under Eisner's aggressive leadership, and in 1990, Disney Company profits approached $824 million.

Eisner takes great pride in being the idea man at the Disney Company. He likes to think up new projects and hire competent executives to develop them. The amiable, six-foot, three-inch tall Eisner became well-known to television watchers during the late 1980s when he served as host for the Disney Sunday Movie.

Eisner, an unabashed family man and father of three, has remained true to Walt Disney's ideal of producing top-quality family entertainment. At the same time, he has managed to wrench the Disney Company from its 1950s time warp and bring it squarely into the 1990s.

Photo Source: The Walt Disney Company

351

Promotion. Promotion is the final stage in the marketing process before the sale of the product. Promotional techniques are used to attract attention, create interest in the product, and prepare prospective clients for the selling message. Promotional activities used to create a demand for travel and tourism products and services can be divided into three main categories:

- Advertising.
- Sales support/sales promotion.
- Public relations.

Promoters of travel and tourism seldom employ just one technique to reach prospective clients, but rather a combination of all three. Determining the right promotional mix is a crucial part of developing an effective marketing strategy.

Check Your Product Knowledge

1. What is marketing?
2. What is the difference between product-oriented marketing and consumer-oriented marketing?
3. What are the four Ps of marketing?

ADVERTISING

Advertising is the best known, most visible, and most widely used of the three promotional techniques. It can be defined as the use of paid media space or media time to present a product in such a way as to attract consumers. The three main functions of advertising are to inform, to remind, and to persuade. If the advertising message effectively performs these functions, it will develop

leads that can be followed up with sales. The bridge between advertising and sales is typically provided by a call to action at the end of the message, such as "See your travel agent for details," "Mail this coupon for a free brochure," or "Call our toll-free number for further information."

The major advertising media can be classified as:

- Print (newspapers, magazines).
- Broadcast (television, radio).
- Direct mail (letters, brochures).
- Out-of-home (billboards, transit signs).

In addition to these four, we can also include two minor categories: directory advertising and specialty advertising.

Travel organizations spend a great deal of money to advertise their products. Table 14-1 shows how advertising expenditures have increased in recent years. Most travel organizations use a combination of two or more media to get their message to the public. The choice of media depends to a large extent on the advertiser's budget and on the target market that the advertiser is trying to reach. If the target market is wide (as in the case of a hotel chain promoting all its properties), the advertiser will typically choose media such as network television and national magazines. The message will reach millions of viewers and readers, although only a small percentage of them are likely to be potential customers. This is known as the *shotgun approach*. If the target market is narrow (as in the case of a tour operator promoting a theme package), the promoter will tend to advertise in special-interest magazines and by direct mail. The message will reach far fewer people, but a greater percentage are likely to be interested in the product. This is known as the *rifle approach*.

	Dollar Amount (in thousands)			
Categories	1985	1986	1987	1988
Airlines	$654,883	$719,876	$697,327	$706,228
Cruise Lines	126,424	127,384	134,335	167,353
Domestic Destinations	80,966	100,791	101,562	130,091
Foreign Destinations	64,787	79,623	80,201	99,510
Grand Total	$927,060	$1,027,674	$1,013,425	$1,103,182
Annual Percent Change	+9	+11	−1	+9

Table 14-1   Trends in Advertising Expenditures in the United States
Source: Ogilvy & Mather

Print Media

Newspapers and magazines are the major print media for advertising. Together, they account for almost half of all travel and tourism advertising expenditures.

Newspapers. In considering newspapers as an advertising medium, we must distinguish between mass-circulation dailies and local weeklies. The former serve wide metropolitan areas and include such publications as *The New York Times*, *USA Today*, and the *Los Angeles Times* (each with a daily circulation in excess of 1 million). The major advertisers in the dailies tend to be national and international travel organizations, such as airlines and car rental firms, which have broad target markets. Smaller travel companies do, however, advertise in the Sunday travel sections that are a feature of most large city newspapers.

Local weekly newspapers have a much smaller circulation, sometimes as low as 5,000. They are used as an advertising medium by local travel firms that serve a small geographic market. A suburban travel agency, for example, will reach its target market more effectively, and more economically, if it advertises in a local weekly paper rather than a mass-circulation daily.

Both types of newspaper have distinct advantages and disadvantages compared with other advertising media. First, the advantages:

- Frequency of publication.
- Wide readership. About 85 percent of the United States population look at a newspaper every day.
- Comprehensive coverage of selected geographic markets.
- Relatively low cost, especially for local weeklies. (Note: the greater the circulation, the higher the advertising rates.)
- Short lead time. Advertisements can be placed in most newspapers as late as one day before publication. This allows for flexibility in making changes to ads that run for several days.
- Ease and speed of response. Newspaper ads often have coupons that readers can mail in for further information.

And now for the disadvantages:

- Waste circulation. Newspapers reach a broad cross-section of the population. Many of the people who see the ad will have no interest in the travel product advertised.
- Low print quality, especially for color reproduction.
- Short life. Most people discard a newspaper soon after they have read it.

Illus. 14-1 *Almost half of all travel and tourism advertising expenditure goes into newspaper and magazine ads.*
Source: Sara G. Matthews

Magazines. The type of magazine that can be used most effectively by travel and tourism promoters is the specialty magazine. There are literally thousands of these magazines in circulation, appealing to special interests as diverse as motorcycling and stamp collecting. The travel advertiser has a good idea of each magazine's readership, and can target specific markets. A tour operator promoting garden tours, for example, would clearly

Illus. 14-2 *Different magazines have different readerships, making it easy for travel advertisers to target specific markets.*
Source: Sara G. Matthews

reach more potential clients by advertising in *Flower and Garden* than in *Sports Illustrated*. Consumer travel magazines like *Travel and Leisure*, *Condé Nast Traveler*, and *Travel/Holiday* are particularly useful for travel advertisers because their readers are predisposed to travel. Within the travel trade, there are professional magazines such as *Travel Weekly*, *The Travel Agent*, and *ASTA Agency Management*.

General-circulation magazines, such as *Reader's Digest*, *Time*, and *Newsweek*, tend to attract the same travel advertisers as do the daily newspapers, namely, the major organizations. United States and foreign destinations also advertise heavily in the national magazines. Some publications have regional editions that allow advertisers to target geographic markets at lower rates.

One final magazine category is the city or state magazine, which is a popular advertising medium for local travel organizations.

The advantages of magazine advertising include:

■ Good selectivity of target markets according to interests. (This is less true for the general-circulation magazines, though they have the added advantage of wide readership.)

■ Excellent print quality and color reproduction.

■ Long life. People tend to save magazines far longer than they save newspapers. Magazines kept in libraries, waiting rooms, and other public areas reach a large number of secondary readers.

■ Prestige. Advertisers benefit by association with well-known magazines. Readers might think, "If XYZ Travel Company is advertising in *Time* magazine, it must be a reputable outfit."

The disadvantages are:

■ Long lead time. Many magazines require ads as much as three months before publication date. This makes it very difficult to make last-minute changes to advertising copy.

■ Infrequency of publication. Weekly magazines appear 52 times a year, monthlies only 12 times a year. (Compare this with daily newspapers at almost 365 days a year.)

■ High production costs, particularly for color ads.

Broadcast Media

Television and radio are the major broadcast media. Of the two, television is more widely used by travel and tourism advertisers. Both media rely heavily on repetition to get the message to the consumer, which means that the same ad may be aired several times a day.

Television. Television can be divided into the categories network, local, and cable. Network advertising is accessible largely to the high-budget travel organizations: airlines, hotel chains, cruise lines, car rental companies, Amtrak, and destinations. Local television, on the other hand, is suited to firms serving a small geographic area. Cable television offers advertisers the best opportunity to target markets by interest (sports channels, entertainment channels, and so on). Not all cable channels, however, accept advertising.

Some of the advantages of television as an advertising medium are:

■ Large audiences. Prime-time programs on network television are watched by millions of viewers.

■ Strong audiovisual image. No other medium can match television for its ability to show the product in moving format. This powerful visual element makes television a natural for destination advertising.

■ Viewer identification with product. This is especially true if celebrities are used to advertise the product.

And on the negative side:

■ Very high costs for media time and production. A 30-second commercial on network prime time can cost hundreds of thousands of dollars.

■ Time restrictions. Commercials must fit a standard time length, called a *spot*, that usually lasts 15, 30, or 60 seconds.

■ Short life. Once a commercial is seen, it is soon forgotten. This is the reason why so many are repeated over and over again.

■ Waste coverage, especially on network television.

■ Long lead time. Advertising spots usually have to be booked at least three months in advance.

■ Difficulty of response. Viewers are less likely to respond to a phone number at the end of the message than to mail in coupons or return envelopes.

TWA's Travel Channel offers excellent potential for travel and tourism advertisers. It is a 24-hour cable channel devoted entirely to travel. Suppliers and destinations using the Travel Channel as an advertising medium can avoid some of the disadvantages associated with network and local television. People who watch the Travel Channel form a highly targeted market: the mere fact that they have tuned in is an indication that they are interested in travel products. In addition, advertising costs are relatively low and time slots are longer.

Radio. Some radio programs are aired nationally, but the majority reach a fairly small geographic market. Nevertheless, many major travel and tourism companies, especially airlines and hotels, use local radio for advertising. An airline such as USAir, for example, might use a local radio station in Buffalo, New York, to advertise its flights to destinations served from that city. The various categories of radio stations—all news, classical music, hard rock, country and western, and so on—make it possible to segment the market both demographically (according to age, income, education, occupation) and by special interest.

The advantages of radio advertising are:

- Good selectivity of target markets based on geography, demography, and special interest (except for nationwide, general-interest broadcasts).
- Low cost.
- Short lead time. Radio is much more flexible than other media. It is much easier to change a radio ad at short notice than it is to alter printed copy or visual messages.
- Personal touch. The sound of the human voice makes radio a more intimate medium.

The disadvantages:

- Lack of visual appeal.
- Time restrictions.
- Waste coverage on general-interest or nationwide broadcasts.
- Difficulty of response.
- Inability to hold the listener's attention. For many people, radio is only a background medium—they may not even hear the commercials.

Direct Mail

The most widely used form of direct mail advertising is the sales letter sent to past and prospective clients. The letter may be mailed alone or combined with travel catalogs, brochures, fliers, and other materials. Travel agencies, tour operators, and cruise lines are the major travel organizations that advertise by direct mail. The three major sources of direct mail lists are mailing list brokers, local directories, and records of past customers.

Newsletters also fall within the category of direct mail. They are used not only as promotional tools but also as information services to members of travel clubs, frequent fliers, frequent stayers, regular clients of travel agencies, and other good travel prospects.

The main advantages of direct mail are:

- Excellent selectivity of target markets. Once a mailing list has been compiled, direct mail pieces can be sent out just to those who are likely customers. There is little waste circulation. No other medium can reach identifiable market segments as effectively.
- Personal touch. Direct mail can be addressed to individual prospects by name.

- Flexible production. There are few restrictions on space or format—direct mail packages can be as large or small as the advertiser desires.
- Lack of competition. Newspaper or magazine ads may run ten or more to a page. Television and radio may air five commercials in a row. The direct mail ad stands alone with no other messages competing for attention.
- Ease of response, via coupons, prestamped reply cards, and so on.

There are, of course, disadvantages:

- Some waste coverage. Not everyone will read or even open the packet.
- Poor image. Many people are wary of offers they receive in the mail. If the offer sounds too good to be true, they might think there is a catch.
- High expenses per potential reader. Postage is expensive, as is the cost of obtaining mailing lists, preparing the message, and so on.
- Difficulty of obtaining and maintaining accurate mailing lists.

Out-of-Home Media

Outdoor advertising takes two main forms: billboards and transit signs. Billboards are usually placed along highways and at points of high pedestrian traffic (for example, at airports, railway stations, and bus terminals). Transit signs are displayed on the sides of buses, streetcars, and taxis. Out-of-home advertising is usually used to supplement advertising in print and broadcast media.

The advantages of outdoor signs are:

- Good selectivity of geographic markets. The best signs are typically placed close to the tourist attraction advertised—for example, "Holiday Inn: 3 miles at Exit 24," or "Visit Busch Gardens—next exit."
- Eye-catching appeal, due to physical size and good color reproduction.
- Relatively low cost.
- Repetitive value. Travelers see the same sign day after day.

On the negative side:

- Very high waste coverage. Many people will not consciously take in the message. Even if they do, only a few will be potential customers.
- Length of message restriction. It's no use putting a long message on a sign that people will see for only a few seconds.
- Difficulty of changing copy.
- Restriction on use, due to highway signing laws.

Illus. 14-3 *Billboards are a highly visible form of advertising.*

Directional Advertising

Almost every form of advertising you have read about so far can be classified as *intrusive advertising*. This type of advertising forces itself on the reader's, viewer's, or listener's attention with a persuasive message. *Directional advertising*, on the other hand, is informational rather than persuasive, emphasizing where to buy a product, not what to buy. A key difference is that potential customers seek out directional advertising, whereas intrusive advertising seeks out customers.

The yellow pages in the phone book are the best example of directional advertising. Companies pay an annual fee to be listed, and they may also buy ad space. There are, in addition, other private local telephone directories, city directories, chamber of commerce directories, and various business directories. Two forms of advertising you read about earlier have some of the characteristics of directional advertising: travel sections in newspapers and TWA's Travel Channel.

Specialty Advertising

Giveaway items bearing a company name are a popular, though minor, form of advertising. Virtually anything can be given away to advertise a travel organization. Some examples are pens, calendars, T-shirts, hats, key rings, and shoehorns.

Co-Op Advertising

Many ads, particularly in the print media, are jointly sponsored by two or more mutually interested compa-

nies. This is known as *co-op advertising* (or cooperative advertising). In one of its most common uses, tour operators or other suppliers provide the ad copy to which a travel agency adds its name (for example, American Airlines and Liberty Travel). Suppliers also cooperate with other suppliers in co-op advertising and with government tourist offices. Air France, for example, cosponsors ads with the French Government Tourist Office for vacation packages to France. Qantas Airlines and the Australian Tourist Commission advertise jointly to promote their country as a tourist destination. There are hundreds of other examples.

Check Your Product Knowledge

1. What are the three main functions of advertising?
2. What are the four main classifications of advertising media?
3. List the main advantages of newspaper advertising over other types of advertising media.
4. What advantages does television offer as an advertising medium?
5. Explain the difference between intrusive advertising and directional advertising.

OTHER TYPES OF PROMOTION

Advertising can do only so much. The two other types of promotion—sales support/sales promotion and public relations—fill some of the gaps created by the limitations of advertising.

Sales Support/Sales Promotion

Sales support is an extension of the advertising effort. Ads are limited by space or time in the amount of information they can convey, so they must be supplemented by more detailed sources of information. Sales support materials such as brochures, booklets, slides, films, guides, and maps provide this additional information. While advertising creates the initial demand for a product or service, sales support can help turn this demand into bookings. It is one step further along the road to sales. Suppliers sometimes mail sales support materials directly to prospective clients, but they are more commonly distributed through travel agencies and other retail intermediaries. Sales support functions as a vital channel of communications between the supplier and the sales distributor. If agents have specific information in an attractive format to present to the client, they are more likely to be able to sell the supplier's product.

Brochures. Brochures are issued by almost every type of travel and tourism organization, and by tour operators, cruise lines, and government tourist offices in particular. They may be as simple as a small leaflet promoting a single tourist attraction, or as elaborate as a 200-page, full-color travel catalog featuring a complete program of tours to a number of destinations. Most of the major tour operators put out lengthy catalogs twice a year (summer and winter editions), with detailed descriptions of itineraries, schedules, accommodations, and prices.

Travel Videos. These take the brochure one step further and show the product in a moving format. Clients are particularly receptive to the video message, since they can actually see the destinations that they are thinking about visiting. Videos are produced by government tourist offices and some suppliers and are distributed to travel agencies. Consumers can also rent travel videos—just like movies—at many video rental stores or borrow them from some libraries.

Point-of-Purchase Materials. This type of sales support includes posters, sales literature racks, and cardboard stands for floor and counter display. Suppliers place the display materials in their sales offices and/or in travel agencies. These materials serve mainly to reinforce the advertising message at the point of purchase.

Promotional Activities. Sales promotional activities are one-time events used to stimulate consumer interest. They may be targeted at prospective clients (to encourage them to buy the product promoted) or at travel agents and tour operators (to motivate them to sell the product). Sales promotion directed at the consumer includes:

- Special offers, such as promotional airfares and hotel rates, free gifts with purchase, and free trips offered as prizes in contests.
- Travel fairs and exhibitions. These are particularly effective promotional events, because they allow suppliers to reach a large number of potential travelers in a single location. Sales literature is distributed at the event.
- Travel nights. Staged by travel agencies and sometimes cosponsored by suppliers, travel nights are often used to promote tours and cruises. Prizes may be awarded to further stimulate consumer interest.

Popular promotional activities targeted at travel intermediaries are:

- Familiarization, or FAM, trips. As you learned in Chapter 1, suppliers offer FAM trips to travel agents and tour operators so that they can experience a product firsthand. These inspection/information tours are usually offered free or at minimum cost. They are used by airlines (to promote new routes, new destinations, and new aircraft), by hotels (to promote new properties), and by government tourist offices (to promote cities, regions, or whole countries as tourist destinations). The theory behind the FAM trip is that "you cannot sell what you haven't seen."
- Sales contests. These are sponsored by suppliers to reward travel agents who sell a certain number of airline tickets, hotel rooms, cruises, and so on.
- Travel trade shows, travel marts, and travel seminars. Held for members of the trade, these gatherings offer an excellent opportunity for government tourist offices and suppliers to meet face-to-face with travel agents and other distributors. They are particularly effective forums for promoting new products and services.

Public Relations

Public relations, or PR, the third of the main promotional techniques, is used to reinforce advertising and sales support activities. It can be defined as the use of planned communications efforts to create a positive image for a company and its products. Unlike the other forms of promotion, it is not directed at prospective clients or travel intermediaries, but rather at journalists, editors, travel writers, and other media representatives. Travel companies target these individuals because they are in a position to influence public opinion.

Typical public relations activities include press releases, press conferences, guest appearances on radio and television, and FAM trips for travel writers.

A *press release*, the most commonly used PR tool, is a document prepared by a travel or tourism organization and mailed out to newspapers, magazines, and television and radio stations. The release might announce an inaugural flight; the opening of a hotel, travel agency, or government tourist office; the introduction of a new product or service; or any other newsworthy event.

A *press conference* is used to publicize travel-related events. Instead of sending out a press release, the company holding the press conference sends out invitations to reporters from the print and broadcast media. Those attending the press conference are issued a press kit with background information on the company and its new product or service. If the press conference achieves its goal, the event will receive favorable coverage in the news media.

Guest appearances on radio and television talk shows give travel company representatives an excellent opportunity to promote their products at no cost. All-expense-paid FAM trips for travel writers can be a very effective way to receive publicity. They can backfire, of course, especially if things go wrong (maybe a missed flight connection or a bad choice of hotel).

Public relations has much in common with advertising in that it aims to promote a product, a service, or a destination. There are, however, important differences between the two:

- Public relations involves the securing of *free* media space or time. No payment is made for the print or broadcast of press releases. For this reason, public relations is sometimes referred to as "free advertising."
- Because it is written or printed by a third party, public relations tends to have more credibility than advertising. People are often skeptical of the advertising message, but they are inclined to believe what they see, hear, or read in the media.
- On the negative side, promoters have far less control over public relations than advertising. A press release, for example, may be edited or not even used at all. In addition, public relations is hard to evaluate because of the difficulty in measuring its cost effectiveness.

Check Your Product Knowledge

1. Name three types of sales support materials.
2. List five sales promotional activities.
3. What are the main promotional tools used by public relations firms?
4. How does public relations differ from advertising?

THE PROMOTERS

Several references have already been made in this chapter to the various organizations that promote travel and tourism. In this section, we will look more closely at the promoters and give examples of some memorable promotional campaigns.

Travel and tourism organizations fall into two main categories:

- Public-sector organizations (government tourist offices).
- Private-sector organizations (airlines, railroads, and other transportation suppliers; hotels and other accommodations suppliers; attractions; tour operators; travel agencies).

In addition to the two main categories, we can identify another category that is neither public nor private. It comprises quasi-governmental agencies such as convention and visitors bureaus (CVBs) and regional tourism organizations.

Government tourist offices and private-sector suppliers differ in many ways, but there is one fundamental difference: government tourist offices promote but they do not sell; suppliers do both. The Italian Government Travel Office, for example, promotes travel to Italy, but the organizations that sell the travel arrangements are the airlines, railroads, tour operators, and so on. There are a few exceptions, namely some Eastern European government tourist offices that both promote *and* sell travel products.

Public-Sector Promoters

Public-sector tourism organizations can be divided into national tourist offices (NTOs) and state tourist offices (STOs).

National Tourist Offices. National tourist offices represent the highest level of government involvement in travel and tourism promotion. Many nations around the world have an NTO, though the NTOs vary considerably in their roles in promoting inbound tourism. Some NTOs are autonomous ministries within the government, such as the Bermuda Department of Tourism. These tend to play a major promotional role. Others are agencies within ministerial departments and play a lesser role. The United States Travel and Tourism Administration (USTTA), an agency within the Department of Commerce, is an example of the latter category.

The United States federal government has traditionally left the job of tourism production to the private sector. As a result, funding of the USTTA is relatively low compared to funding in many other nations. The

Outside Sales Representative

If you walked into the travel agency where I work and saw me sitting at a desk, you would think that I am a travel agent employed by the agency. Actually, I am self-employed. As an outside sales representative, I use the travel agency's office space, literature, and equipment, but I find and serve my own clients and the income I make depends solely on the amount of business I generate for myself.

Some outside sales representatives (or commissioned sales agents as we're also called) work full time and some work part time. I used to work as a salaried travel agent for a big agency. I became an outside sales representative at the same agency after I had my first child and I needed to have more flexible work hours. For a while I worked only part time, but as my list of clients grew, I found I had to work full time to take care of all of them.

I do all of the same things that a regular travel agent does. I plan vacation packages; book airline and hotel reservations; provide advice, literature, and information; and so on. In addition, I spend most of each day on the telephone with clients or doing paperwork, just like a salaried agent. The major difference is that I get no salary or benefits from the agency where I conduct my business. I work strictly on commission, and I share the commission with the agency in exchange for being able to use its facilities.

Because I work on commission, I feel that I have to work harder than a salaried travel agent. After all, I am selling exactly the same thing as every other travel agent. My livelihood depends on providing my clients with an extra measure of personal service that they don't get from a regular agent. I will deliver tickets and itineraries, and I will spend hours on the phone trying to find just the right resort or airline flight for a client. If there's any kind of problem, I will do everything I can to solve it.

Another difference between me and a salaried travel agent is that I cannot serve customers who walk into my agency off the street. I have to have my own clientele, but if I left this agency and went to another one, I could take my clients with me. I find my clients through my

family, friends, and business contacts. Many of my clients recommend me to their family and friends as well. I also find clients by passing out my cards at church suppers, bar and bat mitzvahs, business dinners, and PTA meetings. I even found a client once while sitting in my dentist's chair having my teeth cleaned!

I usually receive about 50 or 60 percent of the commission that my agency collects for booking a trip. That's because I do virtually all the work. Some outside sales representatives are homemakers, ministers, or retirees who drum up business among their friends and acquaintances. They bring their agencies business but don't do the planning and booking. In that case, they normally receive a small percentage of the commission, perhaps 10 or 20 percent, as a finder's fee.

You need the same attributes to be an outside sales representative as you do to be a travel agent. You have to like people, be skillful in matching clients to the right vacation destinations, be knowledgeable of geography and world events, and of course be able to operate the agency's computers.

Some travel agencies won't use outside sales representatives, others are made up of a manager and a group of commissioned sales agents only, and some are a mix of salaried and commissioned agents. My agency is a mix. The owners like my work because I bring in business that they wouldn't get otherwise. Many of my clients are from out of the area and even out of state. They book trips through my agency instead of a local agency only because they want to do business with me.

I like the flexibility of being an outside sales representative. I can come and go as I please and make my own hours. One part I don't like about it is that things sometimes go wrong that are out of my control. If a plane was late or the food was lousy, the clients sometimes come back and complain to me. I tend to take these complaints personally because my clients nearly always become my friends. On the other hand, I often receive postcards and thank-you notes from clients who had a wonderful time on their vacation. That makes it all worthwhile.

Photo Source: © Earl Dotter

Some travel agencies, especially large agencies and those that specialize in commercial travel, maintain professional outside sales representatives. They perform tasks similar to those performed by sales reps employed by airlines, hotels, and car rental companies. In many medium-sized and smaller agencies, the owner and/or manager assumes responsibility for outside sales. Among smaller agencies, outside sales work is also done by part-time employees.

CAREER OPPORTUNITIES

Marketing career opportunities are available within both the public and private sectors. Public-sector positions are related exclusively to promotion (with the exception of convention sales careers at the semipublic CVBs). Private-sector careers include both promotion and sales.

The Public Sector

There are openings in the public/semipublic sector at federal (NTOs), state (STOs), and local (CVBs) levels.

National Tourist Offices. The highest level that you can work at within the area of public-sector travel promotion is the United States Travel and Tourism Administration. Openings are, however, extremely limited, because the USTTA has a staff of fewer than 100. About one-half of these employees work in USTTA offices abroad. The work involves marketing, research, and public relations. Employees can rise to the position of director or deputy director in the overseas offices. (Note: some of the USTTA staff are political appointees—you may lose your job when the administration changes.)

Americans are also hired by some of the foreign NTOs.

State Tourist Offices. Career opportunities at the state level are considerably brighter. Every state has an STO, employing an average of 32 workers per office. The top position is state travel director, which is a political appointment. Other STO job titles include assistant to the director, public relations officer, advertising officer, and travel researcher.

Convention and Visitors Bureaus. CVBs are not always part of the local government, but it is more appropriate to consider them here than under the private sector. The number of CVBs in operation has increased dramatically within recent years, and CVBs offer excellent opportunities in destination-promotion careers. CVBs are headed by an executive director and staffed by up to 60 employees. Convention sales is a key area, involving considerable contact with corporate and association meetings planners. A convention sales manager directs the sales effort. Entry-level positions are available in a variety of administrative and marketing areas.

The Private Sector

Most of the larger suppliers have their own promotional and sales departments. Airlines, cruise lines, car rental companies, and hotels are the major employees. Amtrak also has a large marketing staff.

Careers are available in advertising, public relations, market research, and sales. The sales force is divided between those who work in the office and those who make sales calls outside the office.

Advertising/Public Relations Agencies. A few advertising and public relations agencies specialize in travel promotion, working both for travel suppliers and government tourist offices. Ad agency employees must have strong creative skills and may rise to the position of art director or senior media planner. Public relations professionals write press releases, handle press inquiries, and arrange interviews and press conferences.

Travel Writing and Travel Photography. Travel writers and photographers are employed by the travel trade press (*The Travel Agent*, *Travel Weekly*, and others) and by the consumer press. The latter category includes travel publications such as *Travel & Leisure*, general-interest magazines that feature occasional travel articles, and the major newspapers that have weekly travel sections. Travel writers and photographers are employed both full-time and as freelancers. Competition is intense, especially for travel photographers.

Summary

- Marketing is the sum of all the activities designed to bring buyers and consumers together. It involves market research, product development, pricing, distribution, promotion, and sales.
- Products are developed to satisfy the needs of different markets.
- Advertising, the promotional tool used most widely in the travel industry, is the use of paid media space or time to attract customers.
- Newspaper and magazine advertising accounts for almost half of travel advertising expenditures. Other advertising media used include television, radio, direct mail, and billboards. Each has specific advantages and disadvantages.
- Co-op advertising is the sponsoring of advertisements by two or more companies.
- Sales support, an extension of the advertising effort, features brochures, travel videos, and point-of-purchase displays.
- Sales promotional activities are targeted at prospective clients and travel intermediaries. They include

special offers, travel shows, FAM trips, and sales contests.

- Public relations activities, targeted at the media, are staged to create a positive image for a company and its products. Press releases and press conferences are popular PR activities.
- Within the public sector, travel and tourism is promoted by national and state travel offices. These offices promote destinations, but they do not sell travel products.
- Within the private sector, travel and tourism is promoted and sold by airlines, by hotels and other suppliers, and by tour operators and travel agents.
- The majority of supplier sales representatives sell to travel intermediaries, not to the general public.
- Outside sales reps work outside the employer's office. Inside sales reps make sales by telephone and personal contact with prospective clients in the office.
- Travel agents sell products on behalf of the suppliers to individual clients, groups, and corporations.

Key Terms

marketing
market research
market price
parity product
advertising
shotgun approach
rifle approach
spot
intrusive advertising
directional advertising
co-op advertising
press release
press conference
outside sales
inside sales
cold call

What Do You Think?

1. Do you think the United States Travel and Tourism Administration should play a more active role in the promotion of travel and tourism? Explain your viewpoint.

2. Why do you think that travel organizations as a whole advertise most heavily in newspapers?
3. Do you think that travel suppliers could sell their products without spending so heavily on advertising? Explain your viewpoint.
4. What type of publicity might have negative effects on a tourist product or service?
5. Do you think it is important to have a catchy slogan at the heart of an advertising campaign? Think up an original slogan for (a) the United States; (b) the state where you live; and (c) the town where you live.

Dealing with Product

You have been appointed the sales and marketing manager of Yourtown's new convention and visitors bureau (CVB). The product that you have to promote is the sum of all the attractions and events that Yourtown has to offer, plus all the travel and tourism services that bring hosts and guests together.

The mayor and city council have promised you a generous budget and their enthusiastic support. However, before the funding can begin, they will need to see a thorough and well-written marketing plan from you.

Design a master marketing plan for Yourtown. What does Yourtown have to offer? What are the various MNEs of the clientele you hope to attract? What methods will you use in order to promote your product?

Dealing with People

"He's a born salesman." "She's a born saleswoman." How many times have you heard such comments? Do you believe some people are born to be successful salespeople, or do you believe that almost anybody can be taught to be a sales pro? Here's your chance to express your beliefs.

Imagine that you have just become the owner of a wholesale tour operation. You plan to offer a dozen different Caribbean tour programs, and you have determined that your initial market will consist of Yourtown plus the entire state. What type of sales force do you think you will need? What qualifications would you look for in your salespeople? How important will high school or college transcripts and character references be? Will you be looking for a particular type of personality? If so, what type, and why?

WORKSHEET 14-1   TRAVEL ADVERTISING

The chart below lists various organizations that promote travel and tourism. Find an ad (print, broadcast, direct mail, out-of-home, or directory) sponsored by each promoter. In the appropriate box on the chart, list the promotional slogan or theme used in the ad. Identify the product or service being advertised.

AIRLINES	**ATTRACTIONS**
RAILROADS	**TRAVEL AGENCIES**
MOTORCOACH COMPANIES	**STATE TOURIST OFFICES**
CAR RENTAL COMPANIES	**HOTELS/MOTELS**
CRUISE LINES	**OTHER**

WORKSHEET 14-2   PROMOTING THE TRAVEL PRODUCT

Tell how you would promote each of the following travel products. Choose one advertising technique, one sales support/sales promotion technique, and one public relations technique. Write your suggestions in the chart below. Be as specific as possible.

Product	Advertising	Support/Promotion	Public Relations
1. A tour of Washington, D.C., for grandparents and their grandchildren			
2. A bus tour of Scandinavian countries, hosted by a local radio personality			
3. A 14-day Alaskan cruise			
4. The opening of a new vacation resort in Mexico			
5. A wilderness camping trip for physically disabled adults			
6. New air service to Eastern Europe and the Soviet Union			
7. A university alumni tour to China			
8. A budget motel near the interstate			
9. Travel insurance			
10. Vacation travel arranged by a small neighborhood travel agency			

WORKSHEET 14-3   SELLING TRAVEL PRODUCTS

Study the following conversation between a travel agent and a potential client. Note how the travel agent performs each of the five sales tasks: (1) qualifies the customer, (2) identifies the customer's needs, (3) recommends a product, (4) overcomes objections, and (5) closes the sale. On the lines provided, write the number of the task which is being performed by the travel agent.

Client: Do you sell cruises?

Travel Agent: We certainly do. We offer Caribbean cruises, Mediterranean cruises, and cruises to Alaska and Mexico. Now that Eastern Europe has lifted its ban on American travel, we can even offer cruises to Albania and Yugoslavia.   _____

Client: Well, I like to go someplace warm in the winter. I need to rest and unwind. I've gone to Florida the last three years, but I'm getting tired of going there.

Travel Agent: It sounds like you're ready for something new and exciting.   _____

Client: Yeah, that's what I've been thinking.

Travel Agent: How long do you want to be gone?   _____

Client: Well, I've never been on a cruise before. I don't know if I'd like it.

Travel Agent: Does a week sound about right?   _____

Client: Yeah, but it has to be in January. That's when I get my vacation.

Travel Agent: Oh, that's no problem. There are cruises leaving all the time. Now, where do you think you'd like to sail?   _____

Client: Gee, I don't know.

Travel Agent: Well, tell me. What did you enjoy seeing and doing while you were in Florida?   _____

Client: Well, you know, I'm a real baseball fan. I like watching the pros in spring training.

Travel Agent: It sounds like you might enjoy a theme cruise designed for baseball fans. You'd even get to mingle with sports celebrities.   _____

Client: No kidding! I'd love to meet some baseball players. But there's just one thing. I'd be going by myself. Wouldn't I feel out of place on a cruise?

Travel Agent: Not at all. It's really easy to meet people on a cruise—especially a theme cruise. You'll have a lot to talk about with other baseball fans. But if you like, I could arrange a double occupancy cabin for you. That way you'd be sure to meet someone.   _____

Client: Oh, no, that's okay. I'd rather stay by myself. Nothing too fancy either.

Travel Agent: Would you prefer an outside cabin or an inside cabin?   _____

Client: I'd want one with a porthole.

Travel Agent: Okay. Now how does this sound? Royal American has a seven-day theme cruise to Mexico called "Great Sports Legends." It departs from Los Angeles on January 15. Players from the Oakland A's and California Angels will be on board. I can book you in a single-occupancy outside cabin on B Deck for $1,495.   _____

Client: That sounds great. I'm not sure about the price, though.

Travel Agent: A cruise package is a great deal. Remember, the cost includes your transportation, meals, accommodations, and entertainment. And it's all right there on the ship. You don't have to wear yourself out finding a place to stay or eat.   _____

Client: Yeah, I never thought of that.

Travel Agent: These cruises fill up fast. I can book you today if you like.

Client: Well, okay. Do you take credit cards?

Travel Agent: We sure do.   _____

Name _____

WORKSHEET 14-4   SELLING TRAVEL

You are a travel agent. How would you handle the following situations?

1. A retired couple was planning to pay a deposit on an expensive tour of the Middle East, but a recent outburst of terrorism has caused them to reconsider. What will you do?

    _____
    _____
    _____
    _____
    _____
    _____
    _____
    _____
    _____

2. A young couple has consulted with you repeatedly over the last three weeks. You have spent a lot of time trying to define their motivations, needs, and expectations and to select a perfect travel package. Tomorrow is the last day they can qualify for the reduced airfare you arranged for them. They are still going back and forth in their decision. How do you close the deal?

    _____
    _____
    _____
    _____
    _____
    _____
    _____
    _____
    _____

3. You are trying to book a tour for a special-interest club with a membership of more than 100. You have had a fair response but are still three people short of the minimum number needed for the tour. How do you sign up three or more additional club members?

    _____
    _____
    _____
    _____
    _____
    _____
    _____
    _____
    _____

4. A family of six purchased airlines tickets from you for a cross-country flight. Today there was a terrible accident involving the airline they are booked on. The family refuses to fly on that carrier and is considering cancelling the trip. What do you do?

    _____
    _____
    _____
    _____
    _____
    _____
    _____

CHAPTER 15 THE FUTURE AND YOU

"The way to find the limits of the possible is by going beyond them to the impossible."
—*Arthur C. Clarke*

Objectives

When you have completed this chapter, you should be able to:

■ Explain why the travel and tourism industry will continue to grow.

■ Give reasons why the academic community and governments are recognizing the importance of travel and tourism.

■ Discuss the future of deregulation.

■ Indicate technological advances that will affect the future of travel and tourism.

■ List different kinds of automated channels of distribution.

■ List situations and events that may curtail or discourage travel and tourism.

■ Cite demographic changes that are likely to have an impact on the travel industry.

■ Explain why increased education will be important for future travel professionals.

"Without a passport, you're stuck in travelers' limbo. You can't go anywhere." That's the way one travel journalist described the importance of a passport. As you know, this official government document identifies its owner as a citizen of a particular country. Without it, most other countries won't let you in.

By providing basic information about the travel and tourism industry, this book has been your passport into a career as a travel professional. The previous chapters have introduced you to the past and present operations of the components of the travel industry—air transportation, maritime transportation, ground transportation, the hospitality industry, and the tourism industry. You have learned about the nature of travel products and services and the motivations, needs, and expectations (MNEs) of travelers, and how the channels of distribution bring them together. You have also read about the many career opportunities available in travel and tourism.

Yet another area to explore before you continue on your journey as a travel professional is the future of travel and tourism. Since you'll be directly involved, you'll certainly want to have some idea of the directions in which the industry is headed. Although no one can predict the future with certainty, this chapter suggests the trends, issues, and developments that are likely to be important for travel and tourism in the next decade.

CONTINUED GROWTH OF TRAVEL AND TOURISM

As you know by now, the travel and tourism industry has grown tremendously in the last few years. Can this growth be expected to continue? Current indications are that travel by all three types of travelers will continue to increase in the years ahead.

Vacation and Leisure Travel

The conditions that gave momentum to the growth of vacation and leisure travel are expected to continue:

■ *Increased discretionary income.* As long as economic growth remains steady and people feel positive about the future, they're willing to spend their money for discretionary products.

■ *Leisure time.* The number of retirees increases every year as the nation's population ages. These

373

retirees have plenty of leisure time, and more and more of them have the inclination and resources to travel.

■ *Higher educational levels and the desire for non-material experiences.* With more education, people are more aware of and interested in all the things there are to do and see in the world.

In addition, more travel promotion and the creation of new travel products will stimulate interest in travel.

Vacation and leisure travelers will continue to be cost-conscious. Low-cost group travel will characterize pleasure travel in the 1990s. In fact, some analysts predict that the demand for charter flights will be 50 percent higher than that for scheduled flights. American travelers have become accustomed to low prices for air travel, and they will demand that such price incentives continue. The travel industry will need to follow the pattern of other competitive industries by regularly selling merchandise at a discount.

Because of its culture and history, Europe will always be a traditional destination for outbound American travelers. However, as American travelers become more experienced, they will also become more adventurous and will look for more variety. With the removal of barriers to trade and tourism in the 1990s, the popular destinations will probably include China, the Soviet Union, and the countries of Eastern Europe. Already, the Pacific Rim region—Hong Kong, Thailand, Singapore, and Japan—has shown a tremendous growth in tourism, and this trend is likely to continue. Improved infrastructures and control of costs will make mass travel to these areas possible.

Of course, Americans will not be the only people to travel. Analysts predict that worldwide tourism will grow at an annual rate of 7 to 14 percent over the next 20 years. Increased industrialization will also provide citizens of developing countries with the time and money to travel, and the United States should be ready to receive many more visitors. In the future, the number of tourists coming to the United States from Japan is expected to exceed the number of tourists from Western Europe.

Business and Professional Travel

Business travel will continue to grow as domestic and international business continue to expand. The competitive climate and the increase in acquisitions and mergers make travel an integral part of business.

Offices, plant locations, and sources of supply are being decentralized and internationalized. For example, International Business Machines (IBM), with its corporate headquarters near New York City, has hundreds of other locations in the United States and facilities in many foreign countries. The need for managers and executives

from different areas to meet or work together on a regular basis increases the need for travel.

Corporations aren't likely to curtail travel spending drastically, but they will be looking for better value. The trend toward administrative control over travel arrangements will continue. Some industry observers foresee a change in the relationship between the airlines and business travel departments that would allow BTDs to collect commissions and thus become a profit-making department for businesses.

Professional travel will increase, too, as people recognize the need to communicate more with others in their profession and to keep their skills and knowledge up-to-date. The travel industry will develop new marketing techniques to meet the needs of professional travelers.

Visiting Friends and Relatives Travel

The United States began as a nation of immigrants, and Americans continue to migrate. To find or maintain employment or to change their lifestyles, people move from the country to the city, from the city to the country, from city to city, or from Frostbelt to Sunbelt. The members of today's families are likely to be scattered in many parts of the country. Most people have friends who have moved to different areas. As the population of the United States continues to grow and the proportion of retired people increases, there will be more people visiting

Illus. 15-1 *Visiting friends and relatives is the number one reason for travel.*

friends and relatives. Visiting friends and relatives (VFR) is already the main reason for travel.

Consider the case of Ruth and Ed Soto. Ed recently retired from his teaching position at a midwestern university. Because they wanted to live in a warm, dry climate, he and Ruth moved to Arizona. They can now play golf year-round and make new friends who have similar lifestyles and interests. Ruth and Ed also spend much time traveling. They've been to Hawaii and Mexico, and they also make periodic visits to their children. One married daughter lives in Texas and another lives in Colorado. After graduating from college, their son moved to Boston, where he works for a law firm. Whenever they visit their children, Ruth and Ed also try to see friends who live in the area. Every summer, they attend a reunion of Ed's World War II combat battalion. The Sotos appreciate having the time to travel so that they can keep in personal contact with family and friends.

Check Your Product Knowledge

1. What changes can be expected in the area of vacation and leisure travel in the next decade?
2. What characteristics of modern business make travel a necessity?
3. Why is VFR travel likely to increase?

INCREASED RECOGNITION

Until recently, the travel industry was more or less ignored by the academic community, by government, and by other industries. However, with the growing realization of the power of travel and tourism to employ millions of people, to improve international relations, and to help balance foreign trade, the travel industry is gaining new respect. Airlines, cruise lines, hotels, and other travel components are also beginning to see their interrelationship and project themselves as a single industry.

Academic Community

People who work in the travel industry need practical job skills. They also must know how to negotiate deals in the profit-motivated commercial sector. This type of orientation has not fit the philosophy of United States colleges and universities.

Undergraduate programs at United States institutions of higher education have traditionally presented students with a general curriculum. The objective was to acquaint students with many areas of knowledge so that they would become well-rounded individuals. Students took courses in art, literature, history, and science. The

development of intellectual skills received the most emphasis.

In part because of pressure from businesses, this situation is changing. Schools are beginning to focus more on practical skills that will have a direct application in the working world. In the area of travel, programs are being introduced to prepare students for careers in the travel and tourism industry. At the present time, there are well over 200 programs at the college or university level for training travel professionals. Students can now go to college and major in:

■ Lodging, tourism, and restaurant management.
■ Tourism and travel administration.
■ Transportation, travel, and tourism.
■ Hospitality management.
■ Travel agency management.

Government

Governments around the world are recognizing the benefits of tourism—especially inbound tourism—to their countries' economies. To promote tourism and to assure that it's well planned, countries such as Canada, New Zealand, Australia, France, and Indonesia have created tourism ministries. This means that the minister of tourism may be as important in these governments as the minister of transportation or the minister of education. Tourism ministries are generously funded in many foreign countries.

In the United States, the most recent formal recognition of the importance of international travel and tourism came with the enactment of the National Tourism Policy Act in 1981. This legislation, which established the United States Travel and Tourism Administration (USTTA), has 12 broad goals. These goals include:

■ Increasing the United States share of international tourism.
■ Expanding United States export earnings through trade in tourism.
■ Promoting international understanding, peace, and goodwill.

Nonetheless, the efforts of the United States government in the area of travel and tourism have not equaled those of foreign countries. The USTTA, which is the only federal agency dealing with tourism, is buried within the Department of Commerce and is seriously underfunded. In fact, on at least two occasions in the 1980s, the Reagan Administration attempted to dismantle the USTTA by budget starvation. Only the efforts of the Congress and travel industry affiliations rescued it.

Why is the federal government reluctant to promote tourism? The ambivalent attitude derives from policy-

Ernest Boger

What Ernest P. Boger likes most about teaching hospitality management at Bethune-Cookman College is the practicality of it. He knows that his students will go out into the world equipped not just with academic theory but with very real skills that they can use to become successful managers in the travel and hospitality industries.

Boger is director of the hospitality management program at Bethune-Cookman, a small liberal arts college in Daytona Beach, Florida. He has more than 20 years experience both in working in the hospitality industry and in teaching hotel and restaurant management at the college level. He has managed luxury apartment buildings and hotels in Texas and Jamaica and has taught hospitality management at the University of South Carolina and the University of the West Indies in Nassau, Bahamas.

Like many veteran hospitality and travel professionals, Boger fell into the industry almost by accident. He started working part-time washing dishes and waiting tables in a restaurant while working his way through college. In 1965, Boger became the first black student to graduate from the University of South Florida, where he earned a degree in psychology. He was then drafted to serve in the United States Army during the Vietnam War. He was stationed in Dallas, Texas, where he took a part-time job with a property management company managing an apartment complex.

After his Army service, Boger continued working for property management companies while earning a master's degree in business. In 1973, he was hired to set up and direct a hospitality and travel program at Wiley College in Marshall, Texas. Later Boger went on to manage a small inn in Kingston, Jamaica. Eventually, his experience in both the business and academic world led him into teaching where, he says, he is very happy to stay.

"Like virtually everyone else of my generation, my career path was not one where I chose to study hospitality management at the college level, but today to succeed in the hospitality industry, students must take a formal course of study at a college or university," he said.

Boger says that when his students read biographies of industry giants like Marriott or Hilton, he always tells them, "That's very interesting from a historic perspective, but keep in mind that their path to the top is not yours. Your way to the top is what you are doing here now."

Today more than 200 American colleges and universities offer programs in hospitality management. Boger wants to make certain that his students can compete successfully with the graduates of those programs for high-level jobs in the travel industry. Bethune-Cookman has about 125 hospitality management students a year who take courses in such subjects as food production principles, convention management, personnel management, and marketing of hospitality services.

Like most schools that offer hospitality studies, Bethune-Cookman's education is not all classroom training. The students operate a small hotel in Daytona Beach, the St. Regis, which has 15 rooms and a 95-seat restaurant. The college is also building a new facility that will have 25 rooms as well as classroom and office space.

Boger says that many of his students are recruited form hospitality magnet high schools. These are schools that offer courses in business management and hotel and restaurant training as well as the standard high school curriculum. Students from magnet schools come to college having already had both classroom instruction and on-the-job training in various aspects of the travel and hospitality industries.

When his students graduate form Bethune-Cookman, Boger wants them to be well-versed in management, marketing, and business skills. He also wants them to have developed a sensitivity to other cultures and customs and to have adopted what he calls "the hospitality attitude"—the customer is always right. By the time they graduate, Boger's students have had at least two summer internships at a major hotel or restaurant.

Boger says that his main goal is to equip his students so that they can have a wide choice of careers and so that they can move comfortably from one aspect of the business to any other. "I don't want them to feel that they are locked into food and beverages, travel, or hotels. I want them to know all of those areas so that they can go from a restaurant to a hotel or from a hotel to a travel agency. That's the education philosophy I've evolved over the years."

Boger believes that the hospitality and travel industries will continue to grow and so will the demand for well-trained managers. He says that every year his graduates get more offers of jobs from industry recruiters than they are able to accept, and he expects that trend to continue into the next century. Boger's own position as program director at Bethune-Cookman is endowed by the Walt Disney Company, an indication of the travel industry's growing interest in hospitality education.

Photo Source: Cookman College

Illus. 15-2 *Governments around the world are recognizing the importance of tourism to their country's economy. This travel poster advertises the island of Madeira.*

makers who are uncertain about the government's proper role in relation to the travel and tourism industry. In the spirit of United States capitalism, these people believe that government should not intervene in private enterprise. If the government were to promote tourism, they say, travel companies and their stockholders would gain an unfair advantage. Government involvement in travel would also establish a precedent for the government to subsidize other industries.

This attitude has started to change with the Bush Administration. Many policymakers believe that travel and tourism, among the leading retail industries in the United States, has a tremendous potential to benefit the public interest. Furthermore, maintaining a favorable trade balance in tourism is a federal concern and not something that can be left to the states or to private industry. These policymakers would like the federal government to promote inbound tourism by funding advertising in foreign countries, by removing visa requirements and other barriers to international tourism, and by supporting the construction of tourist facilities.

The relationship between the government and the travel and tourism industry will be an interesting area to watch in the coming years. In the future, a national tourism policy may become an important part of the nation's economic policy.

Continued Deregulation

More than a decade has passed since the Airline Deregulation Act was enacted, but the effects of deregulation are still being debated. Each time there is a midair collision or an airline goes bankrupt, a certain segment of the population cries out for *reregulation*. And, indeed, there are signs that deregulation may not be achieving what was intended. Three areas, in particular, concern both advocates and opponents of deregulation:

- The level of service and safety in the airline industry—in an attempt to cut costs, airlines may be tempted to reduce service or take shortcuts that compromise safety.
- The trend toward concentration—just a few large carriers could end up controlling all the business.
- The inequitable spread of savings among travelers—airlines may be tempted to charge higher fares on routes where they have less competition and use the profits to subsidize discounted fares on intensely competitive routes.

For the immediate future, airline deregulation, which has achieved lower airfares and improved operating efficiency, will continue. However, if abuses caused by the pressure of competition become too great and steps aren't taken to correct them, there will probably be a swing back toward government regulation.

On a related note, governments abroad are beginning to deregulate airlines and other travel components. (Actually, the word *privatize* would be more accurate than *deregulate*, because foreign governments not only regulate but also own travel enterprises. The term *privatize* means to transfer control or ownership of an industry from public to private hands.) In 1987, for example, the British government sold British Airways to private investors. Operating the airline had become a severe drain on the public treasury.

Check Your Product Knowledge

1. Why is the travel and tourism industry gaining new respect?
2. In what ways are many foreign governments demonstrating their awareness of the importance of travel and tourism?
3. What is the National Tourism Policy Act? How successful has it been?
4. What circumstances might lead to reregulation of airlines in this country?

ADVANCED TECHNOLOGY

When travelers return from a vacation, one of the first questions they are asked is, "Well, how was the weather on your trip?" The weather has a major influence on how much people enjoy their travels. If it rains for nine out of ten days of a vacation, travelers are sure to be glum.

In the future, meteorologists may be able to predict precisely what the weather will be like weeks—even months—ahead. Travelers would be able to plan their vacations according to weather forecasts. Travel suppliers might offer discounts on the use of products and services during periods when bad weather was expected.

Developments in technology take place every day, and many new developments—not yet dreamed of—will occur in the future. Travel planning according to weather forecasts provides one example of how technological advances could affect the travel and tourism industry. Some developments will make travel more pleasant, efficient, and comfortable. Others may have a harmful effect on the industry. Three areas that are bound to feel the impact of technology are transportation, the hospitality industry, and the channels of distribution.

Transportation

In late 1986, test pilots Jeana Yeager and Dick Rutan guided their *Voyager* aircraft around the world nonstop without refueling. This historic flight was possible because the *Voyager* was constructed of a new, composite material—plastic reinforced with graphite fibers—that made the aircraft ultralight, but strong.

Research scientists are currently rearranging molecules to create new materials. These materials—known as superstuff—include nonbrittle and heat-resistant ceramics that conduct electricity without losing energy (*superconductors*), extremely strong plastics that can replace steel, and advanced cements that will not crumble. When this technology is applied to the manufacture and operation of airplanes, ships, and trains, it will help get travelers to their destinations more quickly and economically.

Aircraft. Present-day jets, which are voracious consumers of fuel, will gradually be taken out of service. The latest models of the Boeing 747 (the 747-400) and McDonnell Douglas DC-10 (the MD-11) are far more fuel efficient than the earlier models. In addition, the new models are equipped with state-of-the-art technology called *electronic flight information systems* (*EFISs*). EFIS is sometimes referred to as "the glass cockpit" because the dials and gauges found in the older planes have been replaced with a large video screen, similar to a television. Aircraft equipped with EFISs require only two pilots instead of three.

The big aviation news, however, may be the return of propellers. By the late-1990s, airliners powered by new-technology prop-fan engines may be transporting passengers. These planes will be constructed of lightweight, advanced composite materials and new aluminum-lithium alloys. While capable of flying as fast as present-day jets, the new planes will use from 30 to 50 percent less fuel. The cockpit will look like an electronic office, with computers monitoring all systems.

Innovations can also be expected in passenger areas. The interior of the passenger cabin will be designed so that seating configuration can be quickly changed—for example, from economy to first-class sleeperettes. Rather than craning their necks to see a movie screen at the front of the cabin, passengers are already able to view movies on individual seatback video screens on some planes.

Another expected development is the *hypersonic* transport (HST). Possibly fueled by hydrogen, the HST will cruise at a speed of 4,000 miles per hour—six times the speed of sound. (By way of comparison, the *supersonic* Concorde flies at a mere 1,550 miles per hour.) The HST will be able to fly from New York to London in less than an hour—a trip that now takes about seven hours by conventional jet. This incredible plane will fly at an altitude of 120,000 feet and carry 200 passengers.

Trains. Trains will also become faster and more fuel-efficient—which should encourage more people to return to rail transportation. The French National Railroad's TGV trains already travel at 186 miles per hour and, at 65 percent occupancy, use four times less energy than private automobiles carrying the same number of people. Amtrak has plans to expand the electrification of its Northeast Corridor route.

Scientists are working to develop magnetically levitated trains—trains that don't touch the track but are propelled along a cushion of air. Made possible by advances in superconducting electromagnets, these trains will race along at 300 miles per hour—twice as fast as Japan's bullet trains.

Hospitality Industry

Advances in the field of communications—state-of-the-art interactive computers and television screens—are certain to affect the hospitality industry. While still in the introductory stages, these developments may eventually bring additional revenue to hotels and motels from business and professional travelers.

One of these communications developments—teleconferencing—is already being used throughout the United States. As you learned in Chapter 12, teleconferencing enables people at different locations to meet together via satellite-transmitted audio and video signals. It is particularly useful for introducing a product or piece of

A DAY IN THE LIFE OF
A Family Hotel Operator

You could say that I was quite literally born into my job. I own a hotel with 35 rooms in the beach town of Cape May, New Jersey. My grandfather bought the hotel in the 1940s, and when he retired 20 years later, my parents took over the business. I've lived in my parents' hotel all my life and began working here when I was about eight or nine.

My first jobs were to turn on the lights at night and put out the silverware in the dining room for lunch and dinner. Later I did all sorts of jobs around the hotel—cleaning rooms, cooking, waiting tables, fixing toilets, patching the roof, manning the front desk. By the time I went to Widener University School of Hotel and Restaurant Management, I was already able to perform every job in my family's hotel.

After I graduated, I went to work for a large hotel chain as an assistant desk manager. It just wasn't the same as working for my own family, though. I soon quit and returned to Cape May to help my father manage our hotel. A couple of years later I met my wife. She had taken a summer job waitressing in our dining room. Today she is our bookkeeper and office manager.

My parents retired five years ago and turned the entire hotel over to me and my wife. Now, we have two sons who are beginning to learn the business. Of course, I hope that when they grow up they will want to continue running the hotel.

During the summer tourist season, my day usually starts in the dining room and kitchen. I supervise the kitchen staff and help the waitresses serve breakfast to our guests. Then I may hold a management meeting with my supervisory staff or spend a couple of hours in the office doing paperwork. In the afternoon, I visit the housekeeping and maintenance staff and check in with the front office to make sure everything is running smoothly. In the evenings, I again help out in the kitchen and dining room. I also spend a lot of time mingling with the guests, getting to know them and listening to their comments and complaints.

During the winter, I plan for the next season, order supplies, and oversee maintenance and repairs. I also attend trade shows and conventions to drum up business for my hotel among travel agents and tour operators.

Sometimes I make recruiting trips to colleges that offer hotel and restaurant degrees to find new employees. Because ours is a seasonal business, we have to hire a new staff each year. Some years, many employees from the year before come back; in other years, most of our employees are new people.

Running a small family hotel like ours is very different from working for a large hotel chain. When you work for a chain, you are just a wage earner. When you run a family hotel, you are the owner of your own business. Chains employ large staffs. You may do only one job or learn only one part of the business. You can take a day off and someone else will be there to do your work. At a small family-owned hotel, you must be able to do every job because if someone takes a day off, there's no one else to step in. You have to roll up your sleeves and pitch in.

Running a family-owned hotel can be very difficult, but it also has special rewards. One of the great pleasures of running my hotel is that I have made a great many friends over the years. Some guests come back year after year. As a child, I played with the children of our guests. Now their children play with mine. I always look forward to a new tourist season because it means I will be able to renew many old friendships.

I am a member of the Society of Family Hoteliers, which is a new group formed a couple of years ago to promote the running of hotels as family businesses. Our group now has more than 100 members. It is a part of the American Hotel and Motel Association, but it is open only to hoteliers who have another family member in the business. Most of our members run small hotels and resorts, but a few own large chains of hotels. The purpose of the group is to try to help members deal with problems that are common to family-owned businesses, such as promoting family members, estate planning, and interesting the next generation in hotel careers.

I love owning my own hotel because I like being my own boss. I really like working with the people—the employees and guests—who come to the hotel each year. Sometimes when the chef calls in sick or a toilet is overflowing, I might wish I were in another line of work, but not really. I love it even then.

equipment not easily moved, for announcing mergers or other major events, or for performing highly technical presentations. By using teleconferencing, massive meetings, such as stockholders' meetings, can be arranged on short notice.

Teleconferencing allows businesses to reduce the time and expense allotted for long-distance travel. Although the cost of a teleconference depends on many factors—the number of participants, the number of locations, the length of the meeting, and the time of day—it is usually much lower than the cost of travel. The average cost per person for a teleconference runs from about $25 to $50, while the average cost per person for a face-to-face business meeting is about $500.

Of course, the significance of this has not been lost on the hospitality industry (or, for that matter, on the airlines). If the use of teleconferencing becomes widespread, hotels, motels, and restaurants could lose substantial amounts of revenue. To meet this challenge, Holiday Inn, Hilton, Marriott, and InterContinental hotels have established their own teleconferencing divisions. By arranging meetings and providing the necessary equipment and technical assistance, these hotels are promoting themselves as sites for teleconferences.

Channels of Distribution

As discussed in Chapter 13, the channels of distribution are expanding. Many of the new intermediaries will be machines.

Personal Computers. Using a personal computer and the appropriate software or a modem, people have already begun to shop for travel products without leaving their homes. Monitors display computerized information about the availability of airline seats, hotel rooms, and other products. A person who is planning a trip to Cincinnati, for example, might get a listing of the available hotels and their prices. Along with this information might come a full-color picture of the exterior of each hotel and pictures of the interior of various rooms. There might even be pictures showing the view from the hotel's windows. The home shopper can then book a room by calling a toll-free number.

Video Kiosks. *Video kiosks* are being installed in high-traffic locations, such as shopping malls. Customized for the travel industry, these viewing booths contain a video catalog that displays a number of travel packages. A computerized voice explains the various packages and answers basic questions. For more complicated questions, the customer can use the kiosk phone to call the firm that manages the kiosk. Customers confirm their choice of a travel package by using a major credit card. Tickets and documents are mailed within 24 hours. New units may eventually be able to issue all documents on

the spot. Although video kiosks have appeared in only a few places, industry observers predict that thousands will become available in the near future.

Automatic Ticketing Machines. To help fill half-empty planes, airlines are likely to install automatic ticketing machines not only in airports, but also in convenience stores, shopping malls, and other high-traffic areas. These machines dispense low-cost tickets for simple point-to-point travel. Because of the perishability of their product (in this case, seats on a particular flight), airlines are anxious to establish additional outlets for selling tickets. Ticketing machines provide a way of reaching new markets.

In a move to attract the business of more college students, Southwest Airlines installed ticketing machines in several 7-Eleven stores in Texas. The machines sell cheap tickets to and from college towns in the area. Since college students frequently travel between home and school, the airline hopes to get them in the habit of flying back and forth, rather than taking the bus or driving a car.

Service Versus Self-Service. Now the question is, will travelers prefer doing business with machines, or will they want to deal with human beings? If people can secure reservations through computers, the travel agent's role as a clerk or a ticketing agent may become obsolete.

On the one hand, Americans have become accustomed to waiting on themselves. What is happening in the travel industry has already occurred in other retail industries. For example, Americans patronize self-service

Illus. 15-3 *To help fill half-empty planes, airlines are installing automated ticketing machines in airports and other high-traffic areas.*

gas stations, fast-food restaurants, convenience food stores, and one-hour photo finishing shops. Their only time for shopping may be during their lunch hour or on their way home from work. They want to get in and out of stores in a hurry, and even where salespeople are available to give advice, busy shoppers may not want to take time to listen to it.

On the other hand, the purchase of travel products and services often represents a major investment. Many industry observers believe that the majority of people in the leisure market want personal service—not high-technology equipment. Feeling unsure about their plans, they want to talk to a human being about their vacation. Human contact is especially important in an industry dealing with intangible products. Furthermore, while a machine may be able to generate a ticket, it can't describe what the driving conditions are like in Ireland or help the customer obtain a passport.

Electronic channels of distribution represent a trend to which travel professionals must adapt. Many are already doing this by promoting their services as travel consultants. In fact, it may become common practice for travel agents to charge fees for their professional services, much as doctors and lawyers do. Other travel agents are finding ways to incorporate the new technology into their businesses. For example, an agency might use video kiosks to market some products. In this way, it could expand without having to establish a full-service branch at every location.

Finally, in the travel industry of the future, the amount of human contact may be the standard for measuring the worth of a travel product. In other words, the more luxurious the product, the more service the traveler will receive from the hotel staff, airline personnel, and other travel professionals.

Check Your Product Knowledge

1. What developments are expected in the design and manufacture of aircraft?
2. How will advances in communications affect the hospitality industry?
3. Name three electronic channels of distribution. What advantages do they have over traditional channels, such as travel agencies?

WORLD PROBLEMS

Although the future of the travel industry appears bright, certain conditions and events may occur that would discourage or curtail travel and tourism. In fact, a few pessimistic observers believe that congested and unsafe airways, labor strikes, terrorist hijackings and bombings, and overcrowded and polluted destinations may return travel to its original meaning of *travail*—that is, dangerous and hard work.

Overcrowding and Pollution

A couple recently returned from a trip to Yellowstone National Park with their children. Both adults had visited the park before, as children, and were surprised at the changes in Yellowstone. They recalled that 25 years ago tourists were allowed to park their cars close to the geysers and hot springs. They could throw coins for good luck into Morning Glory Pool. And, from the safety of their cars, they could feed candy and ice-cream cones to bears along the road.

Today, however, Yellowstone operates under a strict management program. Automobile traffic has been diverted away from the geysers and hot springs. Visitors must now walk along a boardwalk—sometimes for over half a mile—to view many of the attractions. There are many more park rangers. Besides teaching tourists about the wonders of Yellowstone, the rangers manage and protect its resources. For instance, the park service now confines bears to the back country, where they will not serve as entertainment for tourists.

Such regulatory measures became necessary because overcrowding—and accompanying abuses—were threatening to destroy the natural beauty of Yellowstone. Several of the geysers, for example, were plugged up by garbage. Coins and litter had discolored Morning Glory Pool.

Yellowstone illustrates the danger that overcrowding and pollution present to many popular attractions and destinations, both natural and constructed. If this is allowed to continue, the attraction begins to lose its appeal and visitors stay away.

An important task for the tourism industry in the years ahead will be the careful management of attractions. Requiring reservations, limiting the number of visitors, or charging user fees will be some of the management techniques employed. A few countries—believing that the environmental and social damage caused by tourism is not worth the economic benefits—may even develop antitourist policies or restrict the number of visitors allowed.

Availability of Oil

Oil is the lifeblood of the travel and tourism industry. Without it, there would be no travel. An increase in oil prices means an increase in the cost of travel products; and if travel products become too expensive, consumers won't purchase them.

Consequently, the availability and price of petroleum are ever-present concerns to the industry. When Syrian and Egyptian forces invaded Israel in 1973, disrupting oil shipments in the Persian Gulf, a worldwide energy crisis was set off. This seriously curtailed airline and automobile travel. Again in 1979, when Iranian terrorists seized the American embassy in Tehran, the United States cut off oil imports, and another petroleum crisis resulted.

Oil prices dropped sharply in the early 1980s and then remained stable for several years. But as tensions in the Middle East increased, uncertainty returned and oil prices began to edge up again. The Persian Gulf, an essential transit point, was mined, and the passage of tankers through it was interrupted a number of times. In the summer of 1990, Iraq invaded Kuwait, cutting off a major oil supplier. This act, and the ensuing Persian Gulf War in early 1991, sent oil prices soaring once again.

When an energy crisis occurs, the travel and tourism industry can expect the following developments:

- An increase in package tours and organized tour groups (as opposed to independent travel).
- An increase in travel closer to home.
- A decrease in the number of trips, but an increased length of stay.

Political Instability

June 1985 was to have been the beginning of the season for global tourism. Instead, it became the beginning of the season for global terrorism:

- At Athens Airport, terrorists hijacked a TWA aircraft carrying 145 passengers.
- At Frankfurt airport, a terrorist bomb exploded, killing 3 people and injuring 42.
- At Narita airport in Tokyo, a terrorist bomb exploded as luggage was being removed from a Canadian Pacific aircraft.
- Terrorists hijacked the Italian cruise ship *Achille Lauro*, with many Americans aboard.
- Terrorists gunned down travelers at Vienna and Rome airports.

According to one report, there were over 800 international terrorist incidents in 1985. Because of continued unrest in the Mediterranean region, 1986 was a disastrous summer for European travel. Millions of Americans decided to stay home or go elsewhere, rather than risk being victims of terrorist attacks. The Persian Gulf War in the early 1990s had a similar effect on travel.

Terrorism, as well as open warfare in many countries, has become a major deterrent to travel and tourism. Although a traveler's chances of being hijacked are one in a million, many people are still afraid to travel. To deal with the threat, international airports are taking measures to improve security. Books such as *Everything You Need to Know Before You're Hijacked* (by Douglas McKinnon, former chair of the Civil Aeronautics Board) advise travelers on how to minimize the risk of being victimized by terrorists. Even so, terrorism remains an insidious problem that is extremely difficult to control.

Fluctuating Currency Rates

Another important factor in travel and tourism is fluctuating currency rates. The value of currency has the power to shift travel patterns—sometimes even making or breaking destinations. When the exchange rate is favorable at a destination, travelers will go there. But, when their money buys less at a destination, travelers tend to stay away.

In recent years, the value of the United States dollar has been weak in Japan and most of the countries of Western Europe. Indeed, in the summer of 1991, travelers to Europe were probably more concerned about the value of the dollar than they were about terrorism. At a restaurant in Vienna, for example, travelers paid the equivalent of $63 for dinner for two. A room at a moderately priced hotel in London cost $233, and a gallon of gas in Paris topped $4.

Even if the dollar remains weak against many foreign currencies, Americans will continue to travel abroad. They'll compensate for having less buying power by cutting the length of their trips, settling for

Illus. 15-4 *Fluctuating currency rates have an impact on whether or not people travel to certain destinations.*
Source: John Neubauer/Photoedit

lower-cost accommodations, taking package tours with guaranteed prices, and seeking the lowest possible airfares. They'll also switch to destinations where the dollar will buy more—possibly Yugoslavia, Greece, Brazil, Australia, and China.

While a devalued United States dollar makes outbound travel to certain destinations less appealing, it also has the effect of pulling in more visitors from abroad. Since they're able to buy more United States dollars with their currency, travel to the United States becomes a bargain for many foreign visitors. Bringing in more foreign exchange and discouraging the export of dollars help to reduce the federal trade deficit. A long-term pattern of growth in inbound tourism can be expected.

Disease and Poverty

Travelers avoid going to areas where they might become seriously ill. If, for example, an outbreak of typhoid occurs at a destination, the tourist business there will certainly drop off.

Tourists also stay away from areas where poverty is widespread. They want to be able to enjoy themselves. Seeing people who live in shacks on top of garbage dumps is too distressing for most tourists. This is the reason why some resorts in the Caribbean and other places are built in secluded areas, away from the disease and poverty of a nation.

Africa is an example of a destination that suffers from a poor image. Only about 2 percent of Americans traveling abroad visit the "Dark Continent." Years of television viewing—especially news coverage of drought, famine, and civil war in Ethiopia—have reinforced Americans' concept of Africa as a land of disease, poverty, and strife. While it's certainly true that parts of Africa have these problems, the continent contains 53 different countries, with a wide variety of cultures, traditions, people, scenery, and wildlife.

Check Your Product Knowledge

1. What are some of the factors that discourage or curtail travel and tourism?
2. What can be done about overcrowding and pollution of tourist attractions?
3. Why is fuel efficiency an important concern in the design of new aircraft?
4. Why did travel to Europe drop off dramatically in the summer of 1986?
5. How does the devalued dollar affect travel and tourism?

CHANGING DEMOGRAPHICS

You'll recall that demographics is statistical information that describes a group of people: how many are male and how many are female, what their ages are, what their occupations are, where they live, how many are married, what religions they belong to, and so on. From these facts, researchers draw conclusions about people's lifestyles. The statistics can also be used to determine any changes in the population. For the travel and tourism industry, certain demographic changes are significant in planning and promoting products and services.

Age

The United States is growing older. Fewer babies are being born, and the number of teenagers and young adults is decreasing. People aged 25 to 44 comprise the largest group of Americans, with the number of people aged 65 or older growing as well. Figure 15-1 shows the changing age distribution of the population.

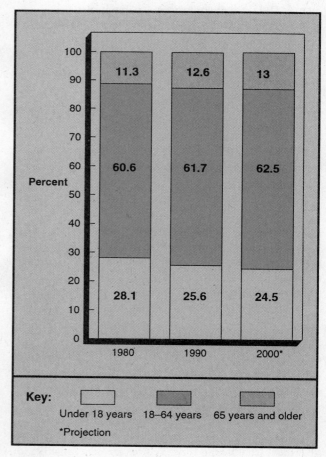

Figure 15-1 United States Resident Population—Age Distribution

Source: U.S. Bureau of the Census

Age 25 to 44. In 1990, about one-third of the population of the United States was between the ages of 25 and 44. These people offer excellent prospects for travel. For one thing, they're an affluent group and tend to spend the most money. Most of these people grew up in families that took vacation trips, and they tend to think of travel as a necessary part of life—even as a birthright—rather than as a luxury. Furthermore, they're well educated and appreciate the benefits of travel. From this group come the middle managers who form a large part of business travel.

Despite their favorable attitude toward travel, it's sometimes more difficult to sell discretionary pleasure travel to people in the 25–44 age group. This is true because they have so many other things to pay for: homes, furnishings, automobiles, and other tangible products. Perhaps the approach to take is to emphasize the practical, long-lasting values of travel products. Also, the industry might make the point to the parents in this age group that many tourist attractions are educational for children.

Age 65 and Older. In 1985, people aged 65 and older—senior citizens—outnumbered teenagers for the first time. In 1900, they comprised 4 percent of the population; by the year 2000, they will form about 13 percent of the population. Clearly, Americans are living longer, and this is important information for the travel industry.

Besides being a growing market segment, senior citizens make good travel prospects because they have the time to travel. Retired from their jobs, they can take long vacations (ten or more nights and at least 100 miles away from home). They're also free to travel any time of the year. Many senior citizens belong to the group of "snowbirds" who migrate from the North to the South during the winter months.

The majority of senior citizens also have the means to travel. The amount of money required for routine expenses (such as mortgage payments, food and clothing for the family, and school tuition) has decreased, leaving them with more discretionary income. Furthermore, many senior citizens today have had the benefit of better financial planning for their retirement.

In promoting travel to seniors, the travel industry needs to keep several factors in mind. Although they have the money to travel, many seniors are reluctant to do so because of their value system. Having grown up in the Depression era, they may tend to look on travel as an extravagance. When they do travel, they may favor budget accommodations.

The travel industry also needs to be more aware that many seniors lack a traveling partner, and this may prevent them from taking trips. Seniors are also sensitive to security and safety while traveling. Of course, any products that the industry promotes should be appropriate for the needs and interests of older travelers.

Illus. 15-5 *Senior citizens make good travel prospects because most of them have the time and the means to travel.*
Source: Mimi Forsyth/Monkmeyer Press Photo Service

Finding the best way to advertise to the senior citizen market can be a challenge. The message needs to be delivered without making seniors feel like old fogeys. The Tennessee Office of Tourism, for instance, created an upbeat and lively advertising campaign using "The Senior Class" as its theme.

Work

Changes in the workplace—particularly in work schedules—have a direct impact on vacation and leisure travel. Some employers today are experimenting with the four-day work week, job sharing, flex time, and two vacations per year.

Three-Day Weekends. A current trend in pleasure travel—and one which is likely to grow—is the three-day weekend, or "mini" vacation. Rather than taking the traditional two-week vacation, many families and individuals are taking several weekend vacations during the year. According to some surveys, these shorter vacations have surpassed longer vacations in popularity.

Several factors account for this shift in vacation scheduling. Because the modern workplace tends to be fast-paced and hectic, workers feel the need to escape from the pressure. But with two wage earners in a family, it's often difficult to coordinate extended vacation time. It's easier to get away from work for a few days. Shorter, more frequent vacations provide a healthy release throughout the year. For single parents who work, short vacations have two advantages: it's easier to arrange for the care of children at home or to take them along on vacation. Workers in the United States have an average of 17 vacation days and holidays per year, but they have 104 weekend days. This represents a tremendous potential for pleasure travel, and the travel and tourism industry is now developing products—such as "getaway" weekends at hotels—to take advantage of this market.

The trend toward shorter vacations has been a boon to state tourism, as travelers look for attractions close to home to visit. In the future—especially with more advanced transportation systems—it may become commonplace for people living in all parts of the United States to travel to such places as Las Vegas, Honolulu, Mexico City, and London for the weekend.

The travel and tourism industry will increasingly need to come up with fresh ideas for weekend excursions. For example, a travel agency in Baltimore recently organized a tour to a small, midwestern town for an old-fashioned Fourth of July weekend. The tour, which sold out almost immediately, featured a parade down Main Street, a picnic and band concert in the town park, and fireworks.

Increased Leisure Time? While it's generally believed that people have more leisure time today, recent studies indicate that this may not really be the case. For most Americans, two weeks of vacation a year is still the norm. Manufacturing industries have maintained the same work hours for the past 20 years. In some companies, workers have agreed to work longer hours without taking additional pay. The executive work week is longer, too, with managers expected to place high priority on their jobs. In view of these findings, it will become even more important for the travel industry to develop the concept of weekend travel.

Other Trends

Demographic information suggests other trends that will be important for the travel and tourism industry to follow:

- By the year 2000, approximately 67 million women will be in the labor force. Many of them will be in executive positions, a job level requiring business travel.
- The Hispanic and Asian population is growing rapidly, forming a good source of labor in the Southwest and on the West Coast.
- The proportion of adults completing additional years of school is increasing. Education not only stimulates people to travel but also makes them more sophisticated and demanding consumers of travel products.
- The number of professional, technical, and managerial workers is growing. People in these occupations tend to travel more.
- Later marriages, fewer children, and more single-parent households will cause shifts in recreational activities, times, and locations.

Check Your Product Knowledge

1. How can the travel industry use demographic information?
2. Why is the travel industry particularly interested in people aged 25 to 44 and in senior citizens?
3. Why has weekend travel become popular?

INCREASED EDUCATION AND PROFESSIONALISM

Doctors, lawyers, and teachers are commonly recognized as professionals. What makes them professional? A professional is someone who has mastered a specific body of knowledge and possesses certain skills not readily available to those outside the profession. After completing an approved curriculum at an accredited institution, these people are licensed by the state to practice their profession. They may be required to demonstrate knowledge of their field by passing difficult examinations. To maintain their status, they must keep up-to-date on the latest developments in their field and constantly refine their skills. Professionals are also expected to maintain high ethical standards. Years of experience add to their professional stature.

Throughout this book, the term *travel professional* has been used to describe your career in the travel and tourism industry. While most workers in the industry don't need to be licensed, the concept of professionalism is still important. The increasing competition and complexity of the industry, as well as the sophisticated demands of tomorrow's traveler, mean that travel and tourism employees will need to be better educated. Education will also be important for adapting to an industry that is constantly changing. To inspire the confidence of the public, the travel and tourism industry will need to develop a more professional image among its employees.

Traditional and Continuing Education

Opportunities for industry-related education for the travel professional are expanding. Colleges and universities, trade schools, professional associations, and the industry itself now provide courses of study that help prepare men and women for the field. Experienced professionals can update their knowledge and skills in seminars and workshops, as well as through coursework.

College and Trade School Curricula. As mentioned earlier, more two-year and four-year colleges are offering degree programs specifically related to travel and tourism. General programs in business administration, computer science, and accounting would also be useful in many areas of the travel and tourism industry. In addition, private business schools, vocational schools, community education classes, and travel agencies offer coursework for the travel professional.

More and more, travel companies are looking for entry-level employees with academic and vocational training. It's no longer practical in this fast-paced, complex industry to train people from the ground up. Furthermore, the industry's vulnerability to consumer liability makes travel managers hesitant to hire workers who have had no exposure to travel and tourism. By showing students what the industry is like, colleges and trade schools tend to weed out students who are looking only for glamour—thus providing travel companies with employees who are more likely to remain with the job. Students also demonstrate their commitment to the industry by completing a course of study.

Other Coursework. Various components of the travel and tourism industry provide training programs. These courses are designed both for people already in the industry and for those hoping to enter the field.

The airlines, in particular, are noted for their training programs. The airlines and computer reservations system (CRS) vendors offer computer training programs for travel agencies who subscribe to their systems. Airlines also offer courses in advanced ticketing procedures, interpreting fare schedules and tariffs, and developing sales skills.

A number of professional associations related to travel and tourism have education divisions that offer coursework—complete with textbooks and other learning materials. The Educational Institute of the American Hotel & Motel Association (AHMA), for instance, offers a full range of hotel, motel, and food-service management courses. Students receive a certificate for each course or combination of courses they complete. These certificates are recognized throughout the hospitality industry and indicate the recipient's commitment to professionalism.

Illus. 15-6 *Travel professionals can expand their knowledge and skills in seminars in workshops.*
Source: *National Business Travel Association*

Organizations devoted exclusively to travel and tourism education also exist. The Council on Hotel, Restaurant and Institutional Education (CHRIE), the Travel and Tourism Research Association (TTRA), and the Society of Travel and Tourism Educators (STTE) publish newsletters, hold education conferences, and foster improved teaching methods.

Seminars and Workshops. Attending seminars and workshops is another way to learn about the travel and tourism industry. Seminars and workshops generally focus on current issues and trends of interest to the profession. They also provide opportunities for professionals from different areas to meet each other and share ideas.

Professional associations and industry associations and organizations sponsor seminars and workshops, many of which are designed to acquaint travel professionals with various travel products. One of the best known is Cruisefest, sponsored by the American Society of Travel Agents (ASTA) and the Cruise Lines International Association (CLIA). This three-day seminar, held once a year, provides travel agents and agency owners and managers with information on packaging and selling cruise travel.

Certification Programs

When most people hear or see the initials "CPA," they immediately translate them into certified public accountant. These initials after an accountant's name mean that

What can travel agents do when they are unable to collect their commissions from hotels, car rental firms, or other travel suppliers? If their agencies are members of the American Society of Travel Agents (ASTA), they can turn the matter over the organization's litigation department. The department, in turn, will contact the suppliers and urge them to pay. If necessary, the department will start court proceedings.

ASTA is the largest travel trade association in the world, with 21,000 members in 129 countries. Its primary purpose is to enhance the professionalism and profitability of its members. It also seeks to promote travel by identifying and meeting the needs of the traveling public.

ASTA was founded in 1931 as the American Steamship and Tourist Agents' Association. Originally the association was intended only for retail travel agencies, but its members now include suppliers as well. About one-third of its membership consists of transportation companies, hotels, and government tourist offices. Travel schools also belong to ASTA.

Domestically, ASTA is divided into 18 areas. Each area is further divided into chapters; there are presently 32 chapters in the United States. Internationally, ASTA is divided into 14 areas, with 39 chapters. International, regional, and chapter meetings provide members with an opportunity to network and exchange information. ASTA headquarters—with a staff of about 80 people—is located in Alexandria, Virginia. Another small office is located in San Diego.

ASTA provides many services to its members and to the traveling public. ASTA's government affairs department lobbies federal, state, and local legislators on issues important to travel agencies. For example, working together with other travel industry groups, ASTA has played an important role in enacting legislation that allows travel agencies to bid on government contracts. It has been successful in getting the government to lift visa requirements for citizens of certain countries—a measure that is very important for the flow of tourism.

For a number of years, ASTA has worked on legislation to protect passengers holding tickets on a bankrupt airline. Other current issues include preventing banks from owning travel agencies and preventing Congress from imposing new or increased taxes on travelers or travel companies. Since most ASTA travel agencies are small businesses, the organization seeks to influence legislation benefiting small business owners.

ASTA's consumer affairs department acts like a sort of "better business bureau." It solves problems between the traveling public and travel suppliers, alerts the public to financially unsound or disreputable travel companies, and checks into questions of member misconduct. ASTA members found in violation of the organization's code of ethics are expelled. The consumer affairs department also seeks to educate the public on the characteristics of travel scams.

ASTA sponsors one of the industry's outstanding educational programs. Every year the education department conducts about 40 seminars around the country on topics such as sales and marketing, finance, automation, legal issues, and personnel. The Travel Management Academy—a five-day course given four times a year—is the organization's best and most important educational program. Another program is Cruisefest, which takes travel agents aboard various ships and acquaints them with the cruise industry.

Along with the education department, the meetings and conferences department plans ASTA's World Travel Congress. Many travel professionals consider this to be the premier industry event of the year. In 1990 the World Travel Congress was held in Hamburg, Germany, and attracted more than 6,000 participants.

ASTA keeps its members informed of fast-breaking industry news through *ASTA Notes*, published bimonthly. *ASTA Stat*, a monthly newsletter, contains statistical information of interest to travel agents, such as surveys on salaries and benefits.

Other ASTA publications include *ASTA Agency Management Magazine*, a membership directory, and a travel agent manual. All ASTA publications are available to members free or at a reduced rate. In addition, members receive discounts on travel and health insurance, seminars and meetings, and office supplies and equipment.

this person has achieved the highest standards of the accounting profession. The public has confidence that this person is competent, knowledgeable, and skillful. The names of travel professionals may also be followed by initials, such as CTC, CTP, or CHA. Although they may not yet be as familiar to the public as CPA, these initials also signify that the travel professional has achieved the highest distinction in his or her segment of the industry.

In place of government licensing or academic accreditation of travel professionals, various travel-related institutes and professional associations have set standards of knowledge and skill for travel professionals. Travel professionals achieve these standards by completing a certification program. Certification programs not only recognize excellence in the profession, they also motivate workers in the travel and tourism industry to pursue advanced education, thus increasing their own professionalism and that of the industry.

Each component of the travel and tourism industry has its own certification program. Although the specifics of each program differ, they do share some general characteristics. To apply for certification, candidates must be actively employed in the industry. In many cases, candidates must also qualify by having worked in the industry for a certain number of years and by passing an entrance examination. Some programs require that the candidate be at a certain level of employment. To fulfill certification requirements, candidates must complete a number of educational courses and participate in leadership roles in their professional association. They may be required to pass a written examination or write a research paper.

Perhaps the best-known certification program in the United States travel industry is that offered by the Institute of Certified Travel Agents (ICTA). As you learned in Chapter 13, ICTA awards the title of Certified Travel Counselor (CTC) to travel agents who complete its CTC Travel Management Program. (The Canadian Institute of Travel Counsellors conducts a similar program.) To qualify for certification, candidates must complete a series of courses on topics such as marketing, personnel management, and business management. They must then pass four 3-hour examinations and write a research paper. Candidates are allowed three years to complete the certification program. Since 1964 when the institute was formed, more than 13,700 travel professionals have earned the right to place the initials "CTC" after their names.

Other certification programs include the following:

■ The National Tour Association awards the designation Certified Tour Professional (CTP) to tour operators, suppliers of tour components, and other persons employed in group travel. To remain certi-

fied, CTPs must continue to earn education credits.

■ National Business Travel Association offers a certification program leading to the Certified Corporate Travel Executive (CCTE). One of the newer programs, the CCTE is for retail travel agents dealing with business travel or for managers of business travel departments. Candidates must earn a total of 100 points in the areas of education, industry experience, and professional activities (a written thesis is required).

■ The Hotel Sales & Marketing Association International administers the Certified Hotel Sales Executive (CHSE) program. Professionals who have worked in the hospitality industry as sales or marketing director, convention service manager, account executive, or hotel manager qualify for this program.

■ The American Hotel & Motel Association offers several certification programs. The most advanced and prestigious is that of Certified Hotel Administrator (CHA). To apply, a candidate must be a general manager or corporate executive in the hospitality industry, with at least three years of experience in that position.

Check Your Product Knowledge

1. What is a professional?
2. Why is increased professionalism important to the travel and tourism industry?
3. Where can travel professionals find appropriate educational opportunities?
4. What is the purpose of certification programs?
5. What are some general requirements for being certified as a professional by the travel industry?

CONCLUSION

As the world changes, so will the travel and tourism industry. Technological, social, and geopolitical changes will make the travel market and travel consumer of the future different from what they are today.

As the world becomes smaller through advances in transportation and communications, travel professionals will have an excellent opportunity to help people get to know their world neighbors. As travel and tourism increases, the industry will become even more intertwined with the economic health of nations. Nations will be less likely to engage in conflict if it means risking economic benefits. Thus, the travel and tourism industry can play an important part in establishing political stability in traveled regions.

To be successful as a travel professional, you will need to be open to change and flexible in dealing with it. You will also need the knowledge and skills to manage change. The travel and tourism industry itself can be the finest of schools for learning about yourself and others. If you enjoy change and growth, you will find travel and tourism a rewarding career.

Summary

- Travel by all three types of travelers—the vacation and leisure traveler, the business and professional traveler, and the traveler visiting friends and relatives—is likely to increase in the years ahead.
- Colleges and universities are recognizing travel and tourism as a professional career field by creating programs of study.
- Governments around the world are recognizing the importance of travel and tourism by creating tourism ministries and establishing tourism policies. The United States government, however, has not shown the same degree of commitment to the promotion of international travel and tourism.
- Airline deregulation, which has been a major influence in the travel industry for the last decade, is likely to continue.
- Technological advances, primarily in the areas of material science and communications, will have a significant impact on the travel and tourism industry. The industry must be able to adapt to these changes.
- Pollution, overcrowding, disease, poverty, political instability, fluctuating currency rates, and changing oil prices are some of the conditions and events that can have a negative impact on travel and tourism. The industry must be prepared to deal with these situations.
- Changes in the way Americans are living and working will affect the future of travel and tourism. Because people are living longer and retiring earlier, the senior citizen market will become increasingly important. Another major trend is weekend vacations.
- As travel and tourism becomes more complex, workers in the industry will need more education. Colleges, trade schools, professional associations, and the industry itself are providing a wealth of learning resources. Certification programs recognize the achievements of travel professionals in the various components of the industry.

Key Terms

reregulation
privatize
superconductor
electronic flight information system (EFIS)
hypersonic
supersonic
video kiosk
travel professional

What Do You Think?

1. What trends and developments do you predict for the travel industry?
2. What, in your opinion, is the proper relationship between the government and the travel industry?
3. Is deregulation working? Explain your point of view.
4. How will teleconferencing affect the need for business travel?
5. If you were asked to write a national tourism policy, what would you include in it?

Dealing with Product

Cottage industry is a term used to describe work that takes place in the home rather than in a factory or an office building. Traditional cottage industries have included knitting and weaving or light manufacturing, often involving piecework.

Many futurists predict that our society may soon have an "electronic cottage industry." They forecast that automation will make the traditional office obsolete; that personal computers, interactive telecommunications, and similar systems will enable tomorrow's clerical and administrative employees to work in their own homes. Obviously, there would be benefits for both the employer and the employee in this electronic evolution, but are there also risks to be considered?

What do you think would happen in Yourtown? How would this new type of cottage industry affect the travel and tourism industry? How many travel and tourism products would be replaced and how many would be changed? Finally, how would such a major change in the marketplace affect the channels of distribution for travel products?

Dealing with People

This chapter has focused on the process of change in the

travel industry. Some of those changes are already happening; others are expected to occur. Many of the changes are the results of new technologies, new products, and new markets. However, one of the most significant changes has taken place in an area as old as business itself—that is, the change in relations between management and labor.

New working conditions have been introduced, partly as a result of deregulation, unrestricted competition, and a volatile marketplace. Labor has been forced to change its stand in three key areas: pay scales, part-time employment, and concessions known as "give backs." The change in pay scales has created the "two-tiered" system in which newly hired employees earn less money for doing the same job as more senior employees. Part-time workers seldom earn the same benefit packages as do their full-time counterparts. And "give backs" are concessions of previous labor–management agreements. All of these steps are taken in the search for greater productivity.

You are the vice president for human resources at a large resort with a work force of 600 persons. Your employees are members of an international union. For the third consecutive year, the resort has lost money. Quite frankly, business is bad and not expected to improve in the near future. The general manager has formed a crisis management team, and you have been instructed to develop a personnel plan that will cut costs without damaging the level of service. The union representatives will attend today's meeting, as will the management team. What will you propose? What will you tell your teammates and the union representatives? Is your proposal really fair or just expedient?

WORKSHEET 15-1   TRAVEL INDUSTRY PAST AND FUTURE

Choose an aspect of the travel and tourism industry that you might like to work in.

How has that part of the industry changed in the last ten years?

How do you think it will be different ten years from now?

Are there any ways you prefer the industry as it was in the past compared with what it may be in the future? If so, explain. If not, why not?

WORKSHEET 15-2   EDUCATION

Contact two-year and four-year colleges and universities in or near Yourtown. Find out if they offer degree programs related to travel and tourism. Choose one program and describe it below.

Name of college or university

Title of degree program

Course requirements

Other requirements

Industry jobs related to program

Placement services available

Contact a vocational school, business school, or travel school. Find out what courses they offer related to travel and tourism. Choose one school and describe its coursework below.

Name of school

Courses offered

Industry jobs related to coursework

Name _____

WORKSHEET 15-3   CERTIFICATION

Select a certification program that interests you and find out its specific requirements.

Certificate

Program offered by

Employment requirements/level of employment

Entrance exam

Educational/course requirements

Experience/leadership requirements

Written exam(s)

Professional activities

Requirements to remain certified

Other

WORKSHEET 15-4   THE FUTURE OF TRAVEL

Below are several trends that are expected to be important for the travel and tourism industry. For each one, suggest what the United States travel industry should do in response to the trend.

Increasing civil rights for physically and mentally disabled Americans

Evolving European economic unity

An increasing number of single-parent families in the United States

An increased demand for energy conservation and environmental safeguards

Continued tension in the Middle East

An increase in the number of Americans age 65 or older

Continued advances in technology

An increase in the number of foreign travelers to the United States

APPENDIX A COMMONLY USED ABBREVIATIONS

AAA	American Automobile Association	CMP	Certified Meeting Professional
ABA	American Bus Association	COD	Channel of Distribution
ACED-I	Association of Conference and Events Directors-International	CP	Continental Plan
ADS	Agency DataSystems	CPU	Central Processing Unit
AHMA	American Hotel and Motel Association	CRS	Computer Reservations System
AIMP	Association of Independent Meeting Planners	CTC	Certified Travel Counselor
		CTM	Consolidated Tour Manual
AP	American Plan	CTP	Certified Tour Professional
ARC	Airlines Reporting Corporation	CVB	Convention and Visitors Bureau
ARTA	Association of Retail Travel Agents	DIT	Domestic Independent Tour
ASAE	American Society of Association Executives	DMC	Destination Management Company
ASP	Area Settlement Plan	DOT	Department of Transportation
ASTA	American Society of Travel Agents	EFIS	Electronic Flight Information System
ATA	Air Transport Association	EP	European Plan
ATM	Automated Ticketing Machine	ETDN	Electronic Ticket Delivery Network
ATP	Agency Training Program	FAA	Federal Aviation Administration
ATPCO	Airline Tariff Publishing Company	FBO	Fixed-Base Operator
BTD	Business Travel Department	FCU	Fare Construction Unit
CAB	Civil Aeronautics Board	FIT	Foreign Independent Tour
CCTE	Certified Corporate Travel Executive	GRT	Gross Registered Tonnage
CHA	Certified Hotel Administrator	GSA	Government Services Administration
CHRIE	Council on Hotel, Restaurant and Institutional Education	HTI	Hotel Travel Index
		IACVB	International Association of Convention and Visitors Bureaus
CHSE	Certified Hotel Sales Executive	IAMAT	International Association for Medical Assistance to Travelers
CLIA	Cruise Lines International Association		

IATA	International Air Transport Association		PSO	Public Sector Organization
IATAN	International Airline Travel Agency Network		RAA	Regional Airlines Association
IATM	International Association of Tour Managers		RV	Recreational Vehicle
ICAO	International Civil Aviation Organization		SABRE	Semi-Automated Business Research Environment
ICC	Interstate Commerce Commission		SATH	Society for the Advancement of Travel for the Handicapped
ICTA	Institute of Certified Travel Agents		SATO, Inc.	Scheduled Airline Ticket Office, Inc.
IEA	International Exhibitors Association		SITA	Societe Internationale de Telecommunications Aeronautique
MAP	Modified American Plan		SITE	Society of Incentive Travel Executives
MNEs	Motivations, Needs, and Expectations		STO	State Tourist Office
MPI	Meeting Planners International		STP	Satellite Ticket Printer
NACOA	National Association of Cruise Only Agents		STTE	Society of Travel and Tourism Educators
NBTA	National Business Travel Association		TO	Tourism Organization; Tourist Office
NTA	National Tour Association		TTRA	Travel and Tourism Research Association
NTO	National Tourist Office		UBOA	United Bus Owners of America
OAG	Official Airline Guide		USTOA	United States Tour Operators Association
OHG	Official Hotel Guide		USTTA	United States Travel and Tourism Administration
PATA	Pacific Asia Travel Association		VFR	Visiting Friends and Relatives
PC	Personal Computer		WATA	World Association of Travel Agents
PNR	Passenger Name Record		WTO	World Tourism Organization

Air Transport Association of America
1709 New York Avenue NW
Washington, DC 20006-5206

Airline Reporting Corporation
1709 New York Avenue NW
Washington, DC 20006

Airport Ground Transportation Association
901 Scenic Drive
Knoxville, TN 37919

Airport Operators Council International
1220 19th Street NW, Suite 200
Washington, DC 20036

American Association for Leisure and Recreation
1900 Association Drive
Reston, VA 22091

American Association of Airport Executives
4212 King Street
Alexandria, VA 22302

American Association of Retired Persons
1409 K Street NW
Washington, DC 20049

American Automobile Association
8111 Gatehouse Road
Falls Church, VA 22407

American Bed and Breakfast Association
1407 Huguenot Road
Midlothian, VA 23113-2644

American Bus Association
1015 15th Street NW, Suite 250
Washington, DC 20005

American Buyers of Meeting and Incentive Travel
Old Route 17, Box D
Harris, NY 12742

American Car Rental Association
927 15th Street NW, Suite 1000
Washington, DC 20005

American Hotel and Motel Association
1201 New York Avenue NW
Washington, DC 20005-3931

American Park and Recreation Society
1800 Silas Deane Highway #1
Rocky Hill, CT 06067

American Public Transit Association
1201 New York Avenue NW
Washington, DC 20005-3931

American Recreation Coalition
1331 Pennsylvania Avenue NW, Suite 726
Washington, DC 20004

American Sightseeing International
211 East 43rd Street, Suite 1001
New York, NY 10017-4707

American Society of Association Executives
1575 Eye Street NW
Washington, DC 20005-1168

American Society of Travel Agents
1101 King Street, Suite 200
Alexandria, VA 22314

Association of Corporate Travel Executives
P.O. Box 5394
Parsippany, NJ 07054-5394

Association of European Airlines
Avenue Louise 350, Bts 4
1050 Brussels, Belgium

Association of Group Travel Executives
424 Madison Avenue, Suite 707
New York, NY 10017

Association of Retail Travel Agents
1745 Jefferson Davis Highway, Suite 300
Arlington, VA 22202-3402

Association of Travel Marketing Executives
P.O. Box 43563
Washington, DC 20010

Caribbean Hotel Association
18 Marseilles Street, Suite 1-A
Santurce, PR 00907

Caribbean Tourism Association
20 East 46th Street
New York, NY 10017

Confederation of Latin American Tourist Organizations
Viamonte 640, Piso 8
1053 Buenos Aires, Argentina

Convention Liaison Council
1575 Eye Street NW, Suite 1200
Washington, DC 20005

Council on Hotel, Restaurant and Institutional Education
1200 17th Street NW, 7th Floor
Washington DC 20036-3097

Cruise Lines International Association
500 Fifth Avenue, Suite 1407
New York, NY 10110

Department of Transportation
400 Seventh Street SW
Washington, DC 20590

European Travel Commission
630 Fifth Avenue
New York, NY 10111

Evergreen Travel Service, Inc.
4114 198th Street SW
Lynnwood, WA 98036-6742

Federal Aviation Administration
800 Independence Avenue SW
Washington, DC 20591

Flying Wheels Tours
143 Bridge Street
Owatonna, MN 55060

Gray Line Sightseeing Association
350 Fifth Avenue, Suite 1409
New York, NY 10018

Greater Independent Association of National Travel Services
915 Broadway Avenue
New York, NY 10010

The Guided Tour, Inc.
613 West Cheltenham Avenue, Suite 200
Melrose Park, PA 19126-2414

Hotel Sales and Marketing Association International
1300 L Street NW, Suite 800
Washington, DC 20005

Institute of Certified Travel Agents
P.O. Box 82-56
148 Linden Street
Wellesley, MA 02181-7900

International Air Transport Association
IATA Building, 2000 Peel Street
Montreal, Quebec H3A 2R4
Canada

International Airline Passengers Association
4341 Lindburg Drive
Dallas, TX 75244

International Association of Amusement Parks and Attractions
4230 King Street
Alexandria, VA 22302

International Association of Conference Centers
900 South Highway Drive
Fenton, MO 63026

International Association of Convention and Visitors Bureaus
P.O. Box 758
Champaign, IL 61824-0758

International Association of Fairs and Expositions
Box 985
Springfield, MO 65801

International Association of Tour Managers
(North American Region)
1646 Chapel Street
New Haven, CT 06511

International Civil Aviation Organization
International Aviation Square
1000 Sherbrooke Street W
Montreal, Quebec H3A 2R2
Canada

International Exhibitors Association
5501 Backlick Road, Suite 200
Springfield, VA 22151

Meeting Planners International
Infomart
1950 Stemmons Freeway
Dallas, TX 75207

National Air Carrier Association
1730 M Street NW, Suite 806
Washington, DC 20036

National Air Transportation Association
4226 King Street
Alexandria, VA 22302

National Association of Business Travel Agents
3255 Wilshire Boulevard, Suite 1514
Los Angeles, CA 90010

National Association of Exposition Managers
719 Indiana Avenue, Suite 300
Indianapolis, IN 46202

National Association of Passenger Vessel Owners
1511 K Street NW, Suite 715
Washington, DC 20005

National Association of Railway Passengers
326 Massachusetts Avenue NE, Suite 603
Washington, DC 20002

National Business Travel Association
1650 King Street, Suite 301
Alexandria, VA 22314-2747

National Campground Owners Association
11307 Sunset Hills Road, Suite B-7
Reston, VA 22090

National Caves Association
P.O. Box 106, Route 9
McMinnville, TN 37110-8629

National Park Service
U.S. Department of the Interior
P.O. Box 37127
Washington, DC 20013-7127

National Railroad Passenger Corporation (Amtrak)
60 Massachusetts Avenue NE
Washington, DC 20002

National Recreation and Park Association
3101 Park Center Drive, 12th Floor
Alexandria, VA 22302

National Restaurant Association
1200 17th Street NW
Washington, DC 20036-3097

National Tour Association
P.O. Box 3071
546 East Main Street
Lexington, KY 40596-3071

Pacific Asia Travel Association
1 Montgomery Street, Telesis Tower
Suite 1750
San Francisco, CA 94104

Professional Guides Association of America
2416 South Eads Street
Arlington, VA 22202

Recreation Vehicle Industry Association
1896 Preston White Drive
Reston, VA 22090

Regional Airline Association
1101 Connecticut Avenue NW, Suite 700
Washington, DC 20036

Society for the Advancement of Travel for the Handicapped
26 Court Street
Brooklyn, NY 11242

Society of American Travel Writers
1155 Connecticut Avenue NW, Suite 500
Washington, DC 20036

Society of Corporate Meeting Professionals
2600 Garden Road, Suite 208
Monterey, CA 93940

Society of Incentive Travel Executives
21 West 38th Street, 10th Floor
New York, NY 10018

Society of Travel Agents in Government
6935 Wisconsin Avenue, Suite 200
Bethesda, MD 20815

Society of Travel and Tourism Educators
19364 Woodcrest
Harper Woods, MI 48255

Trade Show Bureau
1660 Lincoln Street, Suite 2080
Denver, CO 80264

Travel and Tourism Government Affairs Council
1133 21st Street NW
Washington, DC 20036

Travel and Tourism Research Association
P.O. Box 58066
Salt Lake City, UT 84158-0066

Travel Industry Association of America
Two Lafayette Centre
1133 21st Street NW
Washington, DC 20036

United Bus Owners of America
1300 L Street NW, Suite 1050
Washington, DC 20005

United States Forest Service
P.O. Box 16090
14th Street and Independence Avenue
Washington, DC 20090

United States Tour Operators Association
211 East 51st Street, Suite 12B
New York, NY 10022

United States Travel and Tourism Administration
U.S. Department of Commerce
14th Street and Constitution Avenue NW
Washington, DC 20230

United States Travel Data Center
Two Lafayette Centre
1133 21st Street NW
Washington, DC 20036

World Tourism Organization
Calle Capitan Haya 42
E-28020 Madrid, Spain

BOOKS

Ames, Margaret. *The Travel Agency of DC—A Job Simulation.* Cincinnati, OH: South-Western Publishing Co., 1991.

Ames, Margaret. *The Travel Agency of San Diego.* Cincinnati, OH: South-Western Publishing Co., 1986.

Astroff, Milton T. and Abbey, James R. *Convention Sales and Services,* 2nd ed. Cranbury, NJ: Waterbury Press, 1988.

Bryant, Carl L., Reynolds, Ike, and Poole, Terese. *Travel Selling Skills.* Cincinnati, OH: South-Western Publishing Co., 1992.

Brymer, Robert A. *Introduction to Hotel and Restaurant Management,* 5th ed. Dubuque, IA: Kendall-Hunt, 1987.

Burke, James and Resnick, Barry. *Marketing and Selling the Travel Product.* Cincinnati, OH: South-Western Publishing Co., 1991.

Capwell, Gerald K., Lee, Wendy, and Resnick, Barry P. *SABRER Reservations: Basic and Advanced Training.* Cincinnati, OH: South-Western Publishing Co., 1989.

Coltman, Michael M. *Introduction to Travel and Tourism: An International Approach.* New York: Van Nostrand Reinhold, 1989.

Convention Management and Service. East Lansing, MI: The Educational Institute of the American Hotel and Motel Association, 1986.

Coyle, John J., Bardi, Edward J., and Cavinato, Joseph L. *Transportation,* 3rd ed. St. Paul: West Publishing Co., 1989.

Davidoff, Philip and Davidoff, Doris. *Sales and Marketing for Travel and Tourism.* Elmsford, NY: National Publishers of the Black Hills, 1983.

Deland, Antoinette. *Fielding's Worldwide Cruises,* 5th ed. New York: Wm. Morrow, 1990.

Ferguson, Stewart A. and Howell, David W. *Northstar One: United States Destination Geography Using the Microcomputer.* Cincinnati, OH: South-Western Publishing Co., 1989.

Fuson, Robert. *Fundamental Place-Name Geography,* 6th ed. Dubuque, IA: Wm. C. Brown Co., 1988.

Gee, Chuck Y., Choy, Dexter, J.L., and Makens, James C. *The Travel Industry,* 2nd ed. New York: Van Nostrand Reinhold, 1988.

Gray, William S. and Liguori, Salvatore C. *Hotel and Motel Management and Operations,* 2nd ed. Englewood Cliffs, NJ: Prentice-Hall, 1990.

Gregory, Aryear. *The Travel Agent—Dealer in Dreams,* 3rd ed. Elmsford, NY: National Publishers of the Black Hills, 1989.

Gunn, Clare A. *Tourism Planning,* 2nd ed. New York: Crane Russiak, 1988.

Howell, David W. *Discovering Destinations: Geography for Travel and Tourism,* 2nd ed. Elmsford, NY: National Publishers of the Black Hills, 1987.

Howell, David W. *Principles and Methods of Scheduling Reservations,* 2nd ed. Elmsford, NY: National Publishers of the Black Hills, 1987.

Hudman, Lloyd E. and Hawkins, Donald E. *Tourism in Contemporary Society: An Introductory Text.* Englewood Cliffs, NJ: Prentice-Hall, 1989.

Jedrziewski, David R. *The Complete Guide for the Meeting Planner.* Cincinnati, OH: South-Western Publishing Co., 1991.

Johnson, H. Webster and Faria, Anthony J. *Creative Selling,* 4th ed. Cincinnati, OH: South-Western Publishing Co., 1987.

McIntosh, Robert W. and Goeldner, Charles R. *Tourism: Principles, Practices, Philosophies,* 6th ed. New York: John Wiley and Sons, 1990.

Mancini, Marc. *Conducting Tours: A Practical Guide.* Cincinnati, OH: South-Western Publishing Co., 1990.

Mancini, Marc. *Selling Destinations: Geography for the Travel Professional.* Cincinnati, OH: South-Western Publishing Co., 1992.

Mill, Robert Christie. *Tourism: The International Business.* Englewood Cliffs, NJ: Prentice-Hall, 1990.

Notturno, Francis and Russ, Frederick. *Effective Selling,* 8th ed. Cincinnati, OH: South-Western Publishing Co., 1990.

Nykiel, Ronald A. *Marketing in the Hospitality Industry,* 2nd ed. New York: Van Nostrand Reinhold, 1988.

Nylen, David W. *Advertising: Planning, Implementation, and Control,* 3rd ed. Cincinnati, OH: South-Western Publishing Co., 1986.

Powers, Thomas E. *Introduction to Management in the Hospitality Industry,* 3rd ed. New York: John Wiley and Sons, 1988.

Reilly, Robert T. *Travel and Tourism Marketing Techniques.* Albany, NY: Merton House/DELMAR, 1988.

Rubin, Karen. *Flying High in Travel: A Complete Guide to Careers in the Travel Industry.* New York: John Wiley and Sons, 1986.

Sebo, Roberta. *The Traveler's World: Destination Geography.* Cincinnati, OH: South-Western Publishing Co., 1991.

Smith, Valene L. ed. *Hosts and Guests: The Anthropology of Tourism,* rev. ed. Philadelphia: University of Pennsylvania Press, 1989.

Starr, Nona. *Travel Career Development,* 4th ed. Wellesley, MA: Institute of Certified Travel Agents, 1990.

Tourism's Top Twenty: Fast Facts on Travel and Tourism. Boulder, CO: University of Colorado, 1987.

Travel Industry World Yearbook: The Big Picture. New York: Childs and Waters, Inc., 1990.

Wagner, Paula E. *Communicating with SABRE<R>.* Cincinnati, OH: South-Western Publishing Co., 1988.

Weissinger, Suzanne S. *Hotel/Motel Operations: An Overview.* Cincinnati, OH: South-Western Publishing Co., 1989.

Wells, Alexander T. *Air Transportation: A Management Perspective,* 2nd ed. Belmont, CA: Wadsworth Publishing Co., 1989.

Zedlitz, Robert H. *Getting a Job in the Travel Industry.* Cincinnati, OH: South-Western Publishing Co., 1990.

PERIODICALS

Advertising Age, Crain Communications Inc., 220 East 42nd Street, New York, NY 10017-5806.

Adweek, ASM Communications, 49 East 21st Street, New York, NY 10010.

Airline Executive, Communication Channels Inc., 6255 Barfield Road, Atlanta, GA 30328-4369.

Airport Pocket Guide, A M Data Services, Inc., 67 South Bedford Street, Suite 400W, Burlington, MA 01803.

Amusement Business, Box 24970, 49 Music Square West, Nashville, TN 37202.

Annals of Tourism Research, Pergamon Press (Journals Division), Maxwell House, Fairview Park, Elmsford, NY 10523.

Association Meetings, Laux Co., Inc., 63 Great Road, Maynard, MA 01754.

ASTA Agency Management, American Society of Travel Agents, Yankee Publications, 666 Fifth Avenue, New York, NY 10103.

ASTA Notes, American Society of Travel Agents, 1101 King Street, Alexandria, VA 22314.

Auto Rental News, Bobit Publishing Company, 2512 Artesia Boulevard, Redondo Beach, CA 90278.

Automation News, Grant Publications, 450 Park Avenue, No. 2702, New York, NY 10022-2605.

Aviation Week and Space Technology, McGraw-Hill, 1221 Avenue of the Americas, New York, NY 10020.

Business Flyer, Holcon, Box 276, Newton Center, MA 02159.

Business Travel News, CMP Publications Inc., 600 Community Drive, Manhasset, NY 11030.

Business Travel Review, National Business Travel Association, 1650 King Street, Suite 301, Alexandria, VA 22314-2747.

Business Traveler's Airport Hotel Directory, National Association of Business Travel Agents, 3255 Wilshire Boulevard, Suite 1514, Los Angeles, CA 90010.

Business Traveler's Newsletter, Runzheimer International, Runzheimer Park, Rochester, WI 53167.

Bus Ride, Friendship Publications Inc., Box 1472, Spokane, WA 99210-1472.

Commuter Air Communications Channels Inc., 6255 Barfield Road, Atlanta, GA 30328-4369.

Condé Nast Traveler, Condé Nast Publications, 360 Madison Avenue, New York, NY 10017.

Consumer Reports Travel Letter, Consumers Union of the United States, Inc., 256 Washington Street, Mount Vernon, NY 10553-1017.

Cornell Hotel and Restaurant Quarterly, Cornell University, School of Hotel Administration, Ithaca, NY 14853.

Corporate and Incentive Travel, Coastal Communications Corporation, 488 Madison Avenue, New York, NY 10022.

Corporate Travel, Gralla Publications, 1515 Broadway, New York, NY 10036.

Courier: Official Magazine of the National Tour Association, National Tour Association, P.O. Box 3071, 546 East Main Street, Lexington, KY 40596-3071.

Cruise Digest, Box 886, FDR Station, New York, NY 10150-0886.

Cruise Travel, World Publishing Company, 990 Grove Street, Evanston, IL 60201.

Entree, Entree Travel, 1470 East Valley Road, Suite W, Santa Barbara, CA 93108.

Family Motor Coaching, Family Motor Coach Association, 8291 Clough Pike, Cincinnati, OH 45224.

Flying, D C 1, Inc., 1633 Broadway, New York, NY 10009.

Go Greyhound, Greyhound Corporation, Greyhound Tower, Phoenix, AZ 85077.

Hotel and Motel Management, Edgell Communications, 7500 Old Oak Boulevard, Cleveland, OH 44130.

Hotels, Cahners Publishing Company, 1350 East Touhy Avenue, Des Plaines, IL 60017-5080.

ICTA News, Institute of Certified Travel Agents, P.O. Box 82-56, 148 Linden Street, Wellesley, MA 02181.

Incentive, Bill Communications Inc., 633 Third Avenue, New York, NY 10017.

Introduction to Successful Cruise Selling, CLIA, 500 Fifth Avenue, Suite 1407, New York, NY 10110.

Jax Fax Travel Marketing, Jet Airtransport Exchange, 280 Tokeneke Road, Darien, CT 06820.

Lodging, American Hotel and Motel Association, 1201 New York Avenue NW, Suite 600, Washington, DC 20005-3917.

Lodging Hospitality, Penton Publishing, 1100 Superior Avenue, Cleveland, OH 44114.

Marketing News, American Marketing Association, 250 South Wacker Drive, Suite 200, Chicago, IL 60606.

Mass Transit, PTN Publishing Corporation, 210 Crossways Park Drive, Woodbury, NY 11797.

Meeting News, Gralla Publications, 1515 Broadway, New York, NY 10036.

Meeting Planners Guidebook, M P G Productions, 6 Morton Court, Suite C, Mill Valley, CA 94941.

Meetings and Conventions, Reed Travel Group, 500 Plaza Drive, Secaucus, NJ 07096.

Meetings and Incentive Travel, Maclean-Hunter Ltd., Maclean-Hunter Building, 777 Bay Street, Toronto, Ontario, M5W 1A7, Canada.

National Geographic, National Geographic Society, 17th and M Streets NW, Washington, DC 20036.

OAG Frequent Flyer, Official Airline Guides, Inc., Dun and Bradstreet, 888 Seventh Avenue, New York, NY 10016.

OAG Pocket Flight Guides, Official Airline Guides, Inc., 2000 Clearwater Drive, Oak Brook, IL 60521.

Passenger Transport, American Public Transportation Association, 1201 New York Avenue NW, Washington, DC 20005.

Premium Incentive Business, Gralla Publications, 1515 Broadway, New York, NY 10036.

Progressive Railroading, Murphy-Richter Publishing Company, 2 North Riverside Plaza, Room 2115, Chicago, IL 60606.

Public Relations News, 127 East 80th Street, New York, NY 10021.

Recreation Executive Report, Leisure Industry-Recreation News, Box 43563, Washington, DC 20010.

Resort and Hotel Management, Source Communications, Inc., Del Mar, CA 92014.

RV Business, 29901 Agoura Road, Agoura, CA 91301.

Sales and Marketing Management, Bill Communications Inc., 633 Third Avenue, New York, NY 10017.

Specialty Advertising Business, Specialty Advertising Association International, Walnut Hill Lane, Irving, TX 75038.

Successful Meetings, Bill Communications Inc., 633 Third Avenue, New York, NY 10017.
Tradeshow Week, 12333 West Olympic Boulevard, Suite 236, Los Angeles, CA 90064-9956.

Trailer Life, T L Enterprises, Inc., 29901 Agoura Road, Agoura, CA 91301.

Training, International Association of Conference Centers, Lakewood Publications, Inc., 900 South Highway Drive, Fenton, MO 63026.

Travel Age East, OAG Publications Inc., 888 Seventh Avenue, New York, NY 10106.

Travel Age Mid-America, Official Airline Guides, Inc., 320 North Michigan Avenue, Suite 601, Chicago, IL 60601-5901.

Travel Age West, OAG Publications Inc., 100 Grant Avenue, San Francisco, CA 94108.

The Travel Agent, American Traveler, Inc., 825 Seventh Avenue, New York, NY 10019.

Travel and Leisure, American Express Publishing Company, 1120 Avenue of the Americas, New York, NY 10036.

Travel-Holiday, Reader's Digest Association, Inc., Pleasantville, NY 10570.

Travel Trade, Travel Trade Publishing Company, 6 East 46th Street, New York, NY 10017.

Travel Weekly, Reed Travel Group, 500 Plaza Drive, Secaucus, NJ 07096.

INDUSTRIAL SOURCES

Airlines

ABC Air Travel Atlas, Reed Travel Group, Reed International Place, Church Street, Dunstable, Bedfordshire LU 4HB, England.

ABC Executive Flight Planner, Reed Travel Group, Reed International Place, Church Street, Dunstable, Bedfordshire LU 4HB, England.

The Air Charter Guide, 55B Reservoir Street, Cambridge, MA 02138.

ATPCO Passenger Tariff set, Airline Tariff Publishing Company, Washington-Dulles International Airport, P.O. Box 17415, Washington, DC 20041.

IATA Ticketing Handbook—International Air Tariffs, International Air Transport Association, 2000 Peel Street, Montreal, Quebec, H3A 2R4, Canada.

The Industry Agents Handbook, Airline Reporting Corporation, 1709 New York Avenue NW, Washington, DC 20006.

Official Airline Guide—North American Edition and Official Airline Guide—Worldwide Edition, Official Airline Guides Inc., 2000 Clearwater Drive, Oak Brook, IL 60521.

Cruises

ABC Passenger Shipping Guide, Reed Travel Group, Reed International Place, Church Street, Dunstable, Bedfordshire LU 4HB, England.

CLIA Cruise Manual, CLIA, 500 Fifth Avenue, New York, NY 10010.

Ford's Deck Plan Guide, Ford's Travel Guides, 19448 Londelius Street, Northridge, CA 91324.

Ford's Freighter Travel Guide, Ford's Travel Guides, 19448 Londelius Street, Northridge, CA 91324.

Ford's International Cruise Guide, Ford's Travel Guides, 19448 Londelius Street, Northridge, CA 91324.

Garth's Profile of Ships, Cruising with Garth, P.O. Box 34697, Omaha, NE 68134.

Official Steamship Guide International, Transportation Guides Inc., 111 Cherry Street, New Canaan, CT 06840.

Surface Travel

ABC Rail Guide, ABC Star Service, Reed Travel Group, Reed International Place, Church Street, Dunstable, Bedfordshire LU 4HB, England.

American Sightseeing International Worldwide Tour Planning Manual, American Sightseeing International, 211 East 43rd Street, New York, NY 10017.

Amtrak Sales Guide, Amtrak, 60 Massachusetts Avenue NE, Washington, DC 20002.

Consolidated Tour Manual, 11510 Northeast Second Avenue, Miami, FL 33161.

Gray Line Sightseeing Sales and Tour Guide, Gray Line Worldwide, 13760 Noel Road, Dallas, TX 75240.

Official Railway Guide—North American Edition, Thompson Transport Press, 424 West 33rd Street, New York, NY 10001.

Official Tour Directory, Thomas Publishing Company, 5 Penn Plaza, New York, NY 10001.

Russell's Official National Motorcoach Guide, Russell's Guides Inc., 834 Third Avenue SE, Box 278, Cedar Rapids, IA 52403.

Thomas Cook European Timetable and *Thomas Cook Overseas Timetable,* Thomas Cook Ltd., P.O. Box 36, Peterborough PE3 6SB, England.

Worldwide Travel Planner, Wineberg Publications, 7842 North Lincoln Avenue, Skokie, IL 60077.

Hotels/Motels, Meetings, and Conventions

ABC Star Service, Reed Travel Group, Reed International Place, Church Street, Dunstable, Bedfordshire LU 4HB, England.

Directory of Conventions, Successful Meetings, Directory Department, 633 Third Avenue, New York, NY 10017.

Hotel and Travel Index, Reed Travel Group, 500 Plaza Drive, Secaucus, NJ 07096.

International Youth Hostels Handbook, A H Y, Inc., Box 37613, Washington, DC 20013-7613.

OAG Travel Planners Hotel and Motel Redbook—European, North American, and Pacific Asia editions, Official Airline Guides Inc., 2000 Clearwater Drive, Oak Brook, IL 60521.

Official Hotel Guide, Reed Travel Group, 500 Plaza Drive, Secaucus, NJ 07096.

Official Meeting Facilities Guide, Reed Travel Group, 500 Plaza Drive, Secaucus, NJ 07096.

Star Service, Reed Travel Group, 131 Clarendon Street, Boston, MA 02116.

APPENDIX D OCCUPATIONAL TITLES IN TRAVEL AND TOURISM

Airline baggage and freight handler

Airline instrument technician

Airline mechanic

Airline meteorologist

Airline pilot

Airline reservations agent

Airline ticket agent

Airplane safety inspector

Airport manager

Airport operations agent

Association executive

Baggage porter

Business travel agent

Bus mechanic

Bus sales representative

Bus ticket agent

Bus tour representative

Cabin steward

Captain

Car maintenance/service worker

Car reservations agent

Chef

Civil engineer

Concession vendor

Concierge

Conductor

Convention planner

Cook

Cruise director

Cruise line reservations agent

Cruise office salesperson

Cruise operational officer

Destination developer

Dining room steward

Engineer

Environmentalist

Exposition manager

Fitness instructor

Fixed-base operator

Fleet service clerk

Flight attendant

Flight engineer

Food and beverage manager

Forest ranger

Freight airport agent

Front desk manager

Golf course supervisor

Graphic artist

Groom

Historic-site supervisor

Hotel bellstaff

Hotel cashier

Hotel controller

Hotel desk clerk

Hotel director of catering

Hotel director of personnel

Hotel engineer

Hotel executive housekeeper

Hotel houseworker

Hotel information clerk

Hotel manager

Hotel valet

Hunting and fishing guide

Inbound tour operator

Incentive tour planner

Landscape architect

Layout artist

Lifeguard

Limousine driver

Local transit driver

Marina worker

Market analyst

Meeting planner

Museum curator

Museum director

Museum worker

Outbound tour operator

Outside sales representative

Package tour dealer

Passenger service agent

Pastry chef and baker

Photographer

Publications representative

Purser

Railroad reservations clerk

Receptive operator

Restaurant host and hostess

Restaurant manager

Restaurant steward

Sales representative

Sociologist

Stadium manager

Stadium worker

State tourism department worker

Surveyor

Taxi driver

Theme park worker

Ticket taker

Tour creator

Tour distributor

Tour escort

Tour guide

Tour manager

Tour operator

Tour operator reservationist

Tour organizer

Translator

Transportation engineer

Travel agency manager

Travel agency owner

Travel agency receptionist

Travel agent

Travel club director

Travel journalist

Sales agent

Server

Ship engineer

Ship purser

Social director at a resort

State tourism department clerk

Subway driver

Subway operator

Wholesale tour packager

Wildlife manager

Zoo administrator

Zoo caretaker

Zoologist

GLOSSARY

advertising The use of paid media space or time to promote a product.

affinity charter A private charter for members of an organization who are bound together by a common interest.

airport limousine A privately operated bus, van, or extended car that provides passenger service between airports and city centers.

air report An accounting of a travel agency's weekly sales of airline tickets.

à la carte A meal choice from a complete menu, regardless of price.

all-inclusive package A vacation package in which the traveler pays one price that covers almost all trip expenses, including transportation, accommodations, meals, sightseeing, and so on.

allocentric personality According to Stanley Plog, a type of personality that seeks adventure, variety, and excitement.

all-suite A type of hotel that offers units that include a living room and kitchen as well as a bedroom.

American Plan (AP) A hotel rate that includes the room plus continental or full breakfast, lunch, and dinner.

Area Settlement Plan A system whereby a specific bank handles all the transactions involved in the sale of airline tickets by travel agents.

area tour A tour that spends a limited amount of time in several countries.

association executive A full-time professional administrator who is employed by an association and is responsible for planning and promoting annual conventions and association meetings.

atrium An architectural feature consisting of a roof-high central lobby courtyard.

attraction A natural or constructed feature that attracts tourists.

automated ticketing machine (ATM) A self-service machine that provides customers with flight information, reservations, tickets, and boarding passes.

back office system A computer system used for behind-the-scenes business operations.

bed and breakfast Lodging that provides a room, full breakfast, and a shared bathroom.

berth A sleeping place within a cabin.

bias The preferential display on a CRS of host carrier flight schedules.

booth The display space rented by a vendor at an exhibition.

break-even point The point at which total revenues equal total operating units.

breakout A term used to describe small-group meetings that are held as part of a general convention.

BritRail pass A pass used for train travel in Great Britain.

business class An airplane seating section designed to satisfy the needs of the business traveler.

business travel department (BTD) The department in a corporation that handles travel arrangements for the corporation's employees.

cargo terminal One or more separate buildings at an airport where mail or freight is processed.

carrying capacity The amount of tourism a destination can handle.

charter 1) To hire an airplane, bus, or ship for group travel, usually at lower rates than regularly scheduled transportation. 2) The purchase of the use of transportation equipment at a net price.

charter airline See *supplemental airline*.

charter tour A tour taken by a club, organization, or other preformed group.

circle trip A type of round-trip journey in which the return journey differs from the outbound journey in terms of routing or class of service.

city package tour A tour that is similar to an independent package tour, but visits only one city.

clinic A small group session of drills and instructions in specific skills.

code sharing An agreement between a major airline and a small regional airline, under which the small airline flies under the larger company's code.

cohost An airline that does not own its own CRS but that shares a data base with a host vendor.

cold call A personal sales visit to a prospective client, made without any advance warning.

commercial recreation system Recreational products, services, and facilities created and operated by privately owned small businesses or large corporations.

commission The percentage of a selling price paid to a retailer by a supplier.

common carrier A privately owned air carrier offering public transportation of passengers, cargo, and mail.

compact An average-size car.

competitive marketing decision The decision by the Civil Aeronautics Board to open up the travel industry to new channels of distribution.

computer reservations system (CRS) A computer system that provides information on schedules, seat availability, and fares and permits travel agents to make reservations and print itineraries and tickets.

concession A private business that operates at a public recreation facility.

concierge A hotel employee who handles restaurant and tour reservations, travel arrangements, and other details for hotel guests.

conference A large meeting convened to deal with a specific problem or development.

conference-appointment system A system whereby four regulatory bodies formulate standards for acceptance of new travel agencies and discipline existing agencies.

configuration An airplane seating arrangement.

congress An international gathering, similar to a conference.

consortium A group of independent firms that band together to pool their financial and company resources.

consulate A branch office of an embassy that is located in a major city other than the capital.

Continental Plan (CP) A hotel rate that includes the room plus a continental breakfast.

control tower A tower from which air traffic controllers direct planes in the air and on the ground.

convention A meeting involving a general group session followed by committee meetings in breakout rooms.

convention and visitors bureau (CVB) An organization that promotes travel to the city it represents and assists in servicing conventions and trade shows held in the city.

convention hotel A hotel that caters to large group gatherings.

convention tour A tour for members of an association or group attending such events as conventions, trade shows, or conferences.

co-op advertising Advertising that promotes and is sponsored by two or more companies.

cooperative A group of independent travel agencies formed temporarily out of a joint interest in promoting a product or event.

corporate rate A reduced room rate that hotels offer employees of large companies.

couchette A sleeping bunk in a second-class train compartment.

cross-adoption A process by which local residents adopt tourist values and tourist adopt values of the countries that they visit.

customs The government regulation of goods that enter and leave a country.

deluxe A large luxury car usually equipped with many amenities.

demographics Statistics and facts, such as age, sex, marital status, occupation, and income, that describe a human population.

demonstration effect The tendency of local people to adopt practices and consumption patterns of tourists visiting their region.

departure tax A tax that visitors to a country must pay when they leave that country.

deregulation Removal of government control over the operation of an industry.

destination A location that travelers choose to visit and where they spend time.

destination management company (DMC) A company that provides on-the-scene meetings assistance for corporations and associations.

dine-around plan A plan that permits tourists to dine at a variety of restaurants using vouchers and coupons.

directional advertising Advertising in directories and other sources that customers seek out.

direct spending Money that goes directly from a tourist into the economy of the destination.

discretionary travel Travel undertaken voluntarily or by choice.

documentation Government-issued papers used to identify travelers.

Domestic Independent Tour (DIT) A custom-made tour of a part of the United States planned exclusively for a client by a travel agent.

double occupancy Hotel accommodations for two people who share a room.

drop-off charge A fee charged for dropping a rental car at a different location from where it was picked up.

duty A tax paid on items purchased abroad.

duty-free A term used to describe overseas purchases that are exempt from taxes.

ecotourism A type of tourism in which vacationers travel to unusual places to observe ecological systems and endangered wildlife species in their natural habitat.

electronic flight information system (EFIS) State-of-the-art technology in the cockpit of newer aircraft; it replaces the dials and gauges found in older planes.

electronic ticket delivery network (ETDN) A ticket printer that is similar to an STP but owned by an outside vendor rather than a travel agency.

embarkation The boarding of passengers onto a ship, plane, train, etc.

embassy The official residence of an ambassador representing his or her country in a foreign capital.

escorted tour An organized tour led by a professional tour manager.

Eurailpass A pass that allows unlimited train travel throughout certain European countries.

European Plan (EP) A hotel rate that includes the room only and no meals.

event An occurrence that attracts tourists.

exhibition A display of goods and services staged as part of a convention or conference.

family plan A hotel rate that allows children to share their parents' room at no extra cost.

FAM trip A familiarization trip for travel professionals to inspect hotels and restaurants, sample attractions, and experience local culture.

fare construction The process of computing international airfares.

fixed-base operator (FBO) A company that rents space at an airport and that provides a particular service.

flag carrier A national airline representing an individual nation.

flag of convenience A flag flown by a ship of one country that is registered under the flag of another nation.

fly/cruise package A vacation package that includes the air transportation to the port of embarkation and the cruise itself.

fly/drive package A vacation package that includes air transportation and rental car use.

foreign flag A United States term for any carrier registered in a nation other than the United States.

Foreign Independent Tour (FIT) An international tour planned exclusively for a client by a travel agent.

forum A meeting involving discussion on a specific issue, usually led by panelists and involving audience participation.

franchise A contract between a company owner and an established chain under which the owner pays a fee to operate the company under the chain name.

free enterprise system A system that permits competition among privately owned businesses with a minimum of government interference.

free upgrade A switch to a higher class of service or product, for which no charge is made.

frequent-flier program A program that awards travelers free travel, discounts, and upgrades for flying a certain number of miles on a single airline.

frequent-stay program A program that awards discounts and other incentives to customers who use a particular hotel chain frequently.

gateway airport An airport that services international flights.

gross registered tonnage (GRT) A number representing the amount of enclosed space on a ship.

hangar A place where airplanes are stored and repaired.

hosted tour A tour whose members are assisted by a host who arranges optional excursions and answers questions.

host vendor An airline or other organization that owns and operates a computer reservations system.

hub-and-spoke route A flight pattern whereby a major airport is the center point, or hub, for arrivals from and departures to smaller airports that surround it. The smaller airports are considered the rim; the connecting flights the spokes.

hypersonic A term used to describe transportation that can travel at five or more times the speed of sound.

inbound tourism Vacation and leisure travel to the United States from overseas.

incentive tour A tour offered by companies to employees as a reward for achieving a corporate goal.

incoming tour A tour that originates in a foreign country and has the United States as its destination.

independent package tour A tour that visits several cities or places of interest on regular scheduled buses.

indirect spending Money that is spent initially by a tourist and then respent within the destination.

industry A group of businesses or corporations that provide a product or service for profit.

infrastructure The basic facilities of a site, such as local roads, sewage system, electricity, and water supply.

inside cabin A ship's cabin that has no access to natural light and faces a central passageway.

inside sales Sales efforts conducted within the employer's office.

intangible A term used to describe a product that is experienced rather than seen or touched, such as an airplane flight, a family reunion, or an ocean vista.

interface To work together. Used to describe computer reservations systems that can transmit information to and receive information from each other.

interline connection A flight during which the passenger changes both airplanes and airlines.

interlining The use of one standard type of airline ticket that is recognized and honored by all scheduled airlines.

intermediary A person or company that acts as a link between the producer of a product or service and the consumer of that product or service.

intermodal package A vacation package that includes more than one form of transportation.

intermodal tour A motorcoach tour that ties in with other forms of transportation, such as airline service or cruise line transportation.

International Certificate of Vaccination A certificate that lists the immunizations that a traveler has received.

interpretation The process of educating visitors to national parks and other recreation facilities through the use of marked trails, signs, etc.

intrusive advertising Advertising that forces itself upon the consumer's attention with a persuasive message.

itinerary A planned route for a trip.

IT number A registration number that is assigned to a tour package.

joint venture A business partnership between two companies, two individuals, or a company and an individual.

junket An all-expenses-paid trip.

land/cruise package A vacation package that includes a cruise and hotel accommodations at or near the port of embarkation.

leakage The amount of income that flows out of a local economy to purchase outside resources needed to generate that income.

lecture A formal presentation in which an expert addresses the audience from a platform.

leisure The time people use to engage in pleasurable and relaxing activities.

lighter See *tender*.

light-rail transit Trolley car.

limousine A privately owned and operated chauffeur-driven car, often hired for special occasions or for business purposes.

linear route A flight pattern in which an airplane flies to its destination in one direction, turns around, and repeats the flight in the opposite direction.

liner An oceangoing passenger vessel that runs over a fixed route and on a fixed schedule.

loading apron A parking area at an airport terminal where the airplane is refueled, loaded, and boarded.

local tour A tour that is marketed to a local group or organization.

loss/damage waiver (LDW) An option offered by car rental firms that relieves clients of their liability for an initial amount of damage to a rental car; it also provides coverage for loss of the use of the rental car should an accident occur.

magrodome A sliding roof on a cruise ship that is used to cover a deck area in bad weather.

management contract An agreement under which one company owns a property and pays a management fee to a chain to operate the property.

manifest A passenger list.

maritime A term used to describe any type of transportation that crosses water, such as ocean cruise liners, river ferries, and harbor cruises.

marketing The promotional activities that bring buyers and sellers together.

market price The average price consumers are willing to pay for a product based on supply and demand.

market research The gathering and analyzing of information about products and consumers.

market segmentation The concept of dividing a market into different parts.

mart Marketplace.

mass transit The movement of people in large metropolitan areas, usually via buses, subways, and taxicabs.

mega-agency A large travel agency with branch offices in many cities, primarily interested in multimillion-dollar corporate accounts.

megamall A vast indoor shopping and entertainment complex consisting of hundreds of shops and restaurants.

midcentric personality According to Stanley Plog, a type of personality who enjoys the experience of traveling but who tends to travel to familiar destinations.

mileage cap A car rental plan that allows clients a certain number of free miles each day and charges an extra fee for each additional mile driven.

model culture A facility in which the houses, artifacts, and way of life of another age or nation are displayed.

Modified American Plan (MAP) A hotel rate that includes the room plus continental breakfast or full breakfast and dinner.

monorail An elevated urban transit system that runs on one rail.

motel A type of accommodation, usually built near the highway and catering to motorists.

motorcoach A bus that provides transportation between cities.

motor hotel A hotel catering primarily to motorists, and usually located in a downtown area or near an airport. Also known as motor inn.

motor inn See *motor hotel*.

nationalize To bring an industry under the control of the federal government.

nationwide tour A tour that is promoted and sold to people throughout the nation.

new-entrant carrier Any one of the airlines that came into business after the deregulation of the airlines.

nondiscretionary travel Travel undertaken out of necessity, such as business or professional travel.

no-show A person who makes a reservation but fails to use it.

oceanarium A type of aquarium that features saltwater animals.

off-site meeting A meeting held at a location other than the sponsoring company's premises.

on-demand public transportation Those transportation services, such as taxicabs and limousines, that don't have regular schedules; passengers arrange individually for service.

one-way trip A journey that begins in one city and ends in another.

on-line connection A flight during which the passenger changes airplanes but remains on the same airline.

open-jaw trip An air journey interrupted by surface travel, or a flight that has a return destination other than the originating city.

outfitter A business that provides services or equipment at a recreational facility.

outside cabin A ship's cabin that has a porthole or window and a view of the ocean.

outside sales Sales efforts that involve personal calls by the sales staff on prospective accounts.

overbook To sell more seats or rooms than are available.

override A financial incentive paid by a supplier to a retailer to encourage high volume sales.

package A combination of various travel components, which are sold as a single product.

package tour A combination of several travel components provided by different suppliers, which are sold to the consumer as a single product at a single price.

panel A meeting in which at least two speakers give their viewpoints on a particular subject, followed by discussion among the speakers and the audience.

parador A Spanish castle or historic building that has been converted into a hotel.

pari-mutuel betting Betting on the first three places of horse or dog races and jai alai tournaments.

parity product A product that is similar to other products offered by other producers.

passenger name record (PNR) A record of a passenger's travel arrangements that is stored in a CRS.

passport A document, issued by a government, that enables people to enter a foreign country and to return to their own country.

pension A private home that has been converted into a guest house, found mainly in Europe and Latin America.

per diem A term meaning "by the day" used to indicate the amount of money budgeted each day for travel expenses.

personal accident insurance (PAI) Insurance offered by car rental firms that provides coverage in the case of bodily injury to the client.

point-to-point Transporting passengers from one destination to another.

port tax Tax paid by passengers on embarkation at any port during a cruise.

posada A Portuguese castle or historic building that has been converted into a hotel.

press conference A conference for the media that is organized by a public relations company to promote that company's client.

press release A document prepared by a public relations company for the media to promote that company's client.

pressurization Artificial increase of air pressure in a jet cabin so that the air pressure is almost equivalent to the air pressure at ground level.

primary research Market research in which product suppliers study consumers' responses to surveys, questionnaires, and interviews.

private charter A charter that is not for sale to the general public.

privatize To transfer control or ownership of an industry from public to private hands.

product life cycle A standard marketing concept that identifies four stages in the life cycle of a product.

proof of citizenship A document, such as an expired passport, birth certificate, or voter registration card, that can be used in lieu of a current passport by travelers entering certain countries.

property In the hospitality industry, any lodging facility, such as a hotel or motel.

psychocentric personality According to Stanley Plog, a type of personality whose thoughts tend to be focused on himself or herself and who tends not to venture far from home.

psychographics Marketing information based on people's opinions, attitudes, and interests.

public charter A charter that is open for sale to the general public, either through a travel agency or by a tour or charter operator.

public recreation system Recreational facilities and events operated by federal, state, or local governments or by nonprofit organizations.

public transportation Organized passenger service available to the general public within a small geographic area.

pure incentive An incentive travel program designed strictly for pleasure.

quad A hotel room that is shared by four people.

rack rate The standard day rate for a hotel room.

rail/sail package A vacation package that includes both train fare and cruise ticket.

rebate Cash returned to a purchaser after a purchase has been made.

receptive operator A travel professional who specializes in arranging tours for visitors from other countries.

recreation The activities that people pursue in their leisure time

repositioning cruise A cruise organized to transfer a ship from one cruising area to another between seasons.

reregulation The reintroduction of government controls over an industry that has been deregulated.

residential hotel A hotel that caters to guests who are permanent residents.

resort condominium An individually owned residential unit that is under common agreement and is located in a vacation spot.

resort hotel A hotel located in a place where people go to spend a vacation.

rifle approach In advertising, the use of small circulation media to produce a high percentage of leads.

round trip A journey that begins in one city, goes to another city, and ends in the originating city.

run-of-the-house rate A reduced room rate that hotels offer for block bookings.

runway A strip of land on which airplanes land and from which they take off.

sales incentive An incentive travel program that combines a vacation with scheduled business meetings.

satellite ticket printer (STP) A machine that allows travel agents to deliver tickets electronically to a client's premises.

scheduled airline An airline that offers regular flights that are scheduled to depart and arrive at certain times.

secondary research Market research based on information that has been collected and processed.

seminar An informal meeting in which participants hold discussions under the supervision of a leader.

shotgun approach In advertising, the use of large circulation media to produce a small percentage of leads.

single-city tour An in-depth tour of an individual city that offers travelers the opportunity to experience that city's culture.

single-country tour A tour of a single country that gives travelers an in-depth view of that country.

single-entity charter A private charter that is paid for in full by a single source.

single supplement Hotel accommodations for a single person in a private room.

site destination selection company A company that investigates and suggests potential meeting sites to suit corporate or association needs.

special-interest group tour A tour for clubs, societies, and organizations whose members share a common interest.

specialty channeler An intermediary, such as an incentive travel company, a meeting/convention planner, or a travel club, that organizes specific kinds of tour packages.

spot A standard length of time used for airing commercials on television and radio.

stabilizer A feature on a ship that minimizes the effects of the ship's side-to-side roll.

stand European term for an exhibitor's booth.

standard A full-size car.

standard ticket stock Airline ticket blanks that are recognized and used throughout the country.

steerage The lowest class of accommodation on board a passenger ship.

stopover An interruption to a trip lasting 12 or more hours.

subcompact A very small car.

subway A rail transportation system that provides local rapid-transit passenger service either wholly or partially underground.

superconductor A substance capable of conducting electricity without losing energy.

supersonic A term used to describe transportation that can travel at between one and five times the speed of sound.

superstructure All the buildings and structures, such as hotels, restaurants, shops, and convention centers, that are built at a tourist destination.

supplemental airline An airline that offers charter flights and other nonscheduled flights. Also called charter airline.

surface transportation Any type of transportation system that runs on the ground; includes buses, rental cars, trains, and taxis.

symposium A formal meeting arranged to discuss a specific issue.

table d'hôte A set three-course meal at a fixed price.

tangible A term used to describe a product that can be seen and touched.

tariff A schedule of fares charged by transportation companies.

taxiway A lane where airplanes travel from the apron to the runway or from the runway to the hangar.

teleconferencing A way of holding a meeting from several locations simultaneously using advanced communications technology that enables participants to see and hear each other.

teleshopping Using a personal computer to obtain flight information and make reservations.

teleticketing The issuing of airline tickets by a machine linked to an airline computer reservations system.

tender A small boat that carries cruise passengers between ship and shore. Also known as lighter.

TGV A French train that travels at high speeds (*train à grande vitesse*).

time-sharing Shared ownership of a single condominium unit that each owner can use each year for a specified period of time.

tour guide The leader of a guided tour who possesses in-depth knowledge of an area's attractions.

tourism multiplier A formula used to determine the total income generated from money spent by tourists.

tourist cabin An early form of roadside motel that catered to traveling salesmen.

tourist card A card obtained from a foreign country's embassy or through a travel agency or airline that can be used instead of a passport in some countries.

tourist court An early form of roadside motel that consisted of a group of detached cottages located around a central parking area.

tour manager A person who supervises an escorted tour to oversee the group and to make sure that everything runs smoothly.

tour operator A company that contracts with hotels, transportation companies, and other suppliers to create a tour package and then sells that package directly to the consumer.

tour organizer A person who may have little travel expertise and who works with a travel agency and tour operator to organize a specialized tour.

tour wholesaler A company that contracts with hotels, transportation companies, and other suppliers to create a tour package and then sells that package to the consumer through a retail travel agency.

trade fair See *trade show*.

trade show A meeting that features freestanding vendor displays and booths. Also known as trade fair.

train/drive package A package that includes train transportation as well as automobile transportation.

transfer Any change in transportation in the course of a journey.

transient hotel A hotel that caters to guests who stay for a limited time.

travel management services Services offered by a corporate travel agency to help a client control and monitor its business travel costs.

travel professional A person who has received the specialized training needed to work in the travel industry of today.

trip A journey of at least 25 miles from home, excluding commuting to or from work.

triple A hotel room that is shared by three people.

trolley A streetcar that runs on electricity.

two-city tour A tour of two cities, either in the same country or in different countries.

unit In the hospitality industry, a guest bedroom or suite.

unlimited mileage A car rental plan that allows clients to drive a rental car as far as they want for a flat fee within the allotted rental period.

urban bus A bus that operates over short distances within a city.

vertical marketing The promotion of products or services by several different channels of distribution owned by a single company.

voucher A coupon or document that can be exchanged for a travel product.

video kiosk A booth in which travel consumers can watch promotional videos.

video marketing The use of cable television to promote and sell products and services.

visa A stamp or endorsement issued by a foreign government that is placed in a traveler's passport specifying the conditions for entering the country.

wagon-lit A train coach containing a private sleeping compartment for one or two persons.

wait list A numbering system listing passengers hoping to get a seat on a booked flight.

workshop A small group session of intense study or training that emphasizes an exchange of ideas or demonstration of skills.

youth hostel A facility that offers basic overnight lodging at rock-bottom prices for younger travelers.